Israel's Moment

Israel's Moment is a major new account of how a Jewish state came to be forged in the shadow of World War II and the Holocaust and the onset of the Cold War. Drawing on new research in government, public and private archives, Jeffrey Herf exposes the political realities that underpinned support for and opposition to Zionist aspirations in Palestine. In an unprecedented international account, he explores the role of the United States, the Arab States, the Palestine Arabs, the Zionists, and key European governments from Britain and France to the Soviet Union, Czechoslovakia and Poland. His findings reveal a spectrum of support and opposition that stood in sharp contrast to the political coordinates that emerged during the Cold War, shedding new light on how and why the state of Israel was established in 1948 and challenging conventional associations of left and right, imperialism and anti-imperialism, and racism and anti-racism.

Jeffrey Herf is a Distinguished University Professor of Modern European history at the University of Maryland. He is the author of *Undeclared Wars with Israel: East Germany and the West German Far Left, 1967–1989* (2016). He is a member of the American Historical Association and the German Studies Association.

Israel's Moment

*International Support for and Opposition
to Establishing the Jewish State, 1945–1949*

Jeffrey Herf

University of Maryland, College Park

CAMBRIDGE
UNIVERSITY PRESS

CAMBRIDGE
UNIVERSITY PRESS

University Printing House, Cambridge CB2 8BS, United Kingdom

One Liberty Plaza, 20th Floor, New York, NY 10006, USA

477 Williamstown Road, Port Melbourne, VIC 3207, Australia

314–321, 3rd Floor, Plot 3, Splendor Forum, Jasola District Centre, New Delhi – 110025, India

103 Penang Road, #05–06/07, Visioncrest Commercial, Singapore 238467

Cambridge University Press is part of the University of Cambridge.

It furthers the University's mission by disseminating knowledge in the pursuit of education, learning, and research at the highest international levels of excellence.

www.cambridge.org
Information on this title: www.cambridge.org/9781316517963
DOI: 10.1017/9781009049221

First published 2022

Printed in the United Kingdom by TJ Books Limited, Padstow Cornwall

A catalogue record for this publication is available from the British Library.

ISBN 978-1-316-51796-3 Hardback

For Sonya

Contents

Figures

Maps

Preface

During the years in which the establishment of the state of Israel took place, the political vocabulary of imperialism and anti-imperialism, racism and antiracism, and left and right differed greatly from what it came to mean after the Soviet purges of 1949–53, and the shift of the international radical left to anti-Zionism during and after the Six Day War of 1967. In the two years of what I am calling "Israel's Moment" the "imperialism" against which liberals fought was Britain's attempt to preserve its influence in the Middle East while the "anti-imperialism" was that of Zionists who sought to form a Jewish state in what was then Palestine under the British Mandate. The "antiracists" were Zionists who fought against antisemitism and the "racists" were leaders of the Arab Higher Committee who celebrated the supposed racial homogeneity of Arab societies.

It will come as a surprise to many readers that liberals and leftists in the late 1940s rallied to the Zionist cause, while those government officials who helped to launch the Western Cold War saw a Jewish state in Palestine as a benefit for the Soviet Union, a danger both to the policy of the containment of communism and to Western access to Arab oil. That surprise will be pleasant or unpleasant, depending on the reader's views. Israel's Moment was a unique and fleeting period when the anti-Nazi passions of the "united nations" that fought in World War II persisted into the very different, at times reversed, currents of the first years of the Cold War. The foundation of the state of Israel was most importantly the result of the efforts of the Jews themselves. Yet it was made possible by the contingent, short-lived, and unexpected agreement between an American president and the leaders of the Soviet bloc just as the international anti-Hitler coalition split apart into the reversed fronts of the Cold War. The simultaneity of past and present in those crucial months and years marked the international history of the establishment of the state of Israel. The following work seeks to offer a fresh perspective on a fascinating and oft-told tale.

Acknowledgments

Scholarship requires large amounts of uninterrupted time. A reduced teaching load made possible by the Distinguished University Professor program at the University of Maryland, College Park gave me many needed hours. A research fund, also from the university, supported travel in summer 2019 to France's Archives Nationales in Pierrefitte-sur-Seine and the Centre des Archives Diplomatiques de la Courneuve, both near Paris. The diplomacy and good judgment of Philip Soergel, our current chair, and the respect for academic norms of my colleagues have fostered an environment in the History Department at the University of Maryland, College Park that is conducive to important historical research and fine teaching.

As has been the case for many years, my research in the invaluable National Archives of the United States, conveniently also located in College Park, benefited greatly from the staff of its reading room. David Langbart again offered helpful advice regarding the State Department files; Eric van Slander did as well regarding the military and intelligence files; Amanda Weimar assisted my Freedom of Information Act requests for Department of Justice files; David Fort did likewise for my FOIA requests for CIA, State Department, and military intelligence files. The archivists at the Library of Congress Manuscript Division facilitated my work in the papers of Robert Jackson and Emanuel Celler, and in the records of the Assemblée Nationale, the French Parliament. The reference librarians working in the Newspaper and Current Periodical Room facilitated access to American and French newspapers. Special thanks are due to Gary Johnson who, in the days before the library was completely closed due to the coronavirus pandemic, sent me scans of important United Nations records. Ted Jackson, manuscript archivist at the Georgetown University Booth Family Center for Special Collections, and its helpful staff assisted my research in the papers of Robert F. Wagner. The same was the case with archivists at Columbia University's Rare Book and Manuscript Library for work on the papers of Telford Taylor. Thanks are due as well to the archivists of the Center for Jewish History in New York, where I examined the Jewish and Zionist press in Paris. My thanks as well to Louise Fischer in the State Documents Department of the Israel State Archives for providing a copy of a map of the 1949 armistice lines. For assistance with photos, maps, and documents from the United Nations archives in New York, thanks are due to Natalie Melville, and Brenda L. Fong at the Photo Library; to Maricela Martinez at the Dag Hammarskjöld Library; and to Stephan Haufek and Aleksandr Gelfand at the UN Archives Unit.

Professor Frederic Bozo of the Sorbonne University in Paris helped me contact archivists at the Centre des Archives Diplomatiques, and they in turn facilitated my work in those files. Thanks are due to Caroline Piketty and Violaine Challeat-Fonck at the Archives Nationales for their helpful replies to my emails and on-site assistance. Anouk Brodier efficiently and quickly checked several files for me in Pierrefitte. The interlibrary loan desk of McKeldin Library at the University of Maryland delivered books I needed from libraries around the United States and in Europe. Eric Lindquist, McKeldin's librarian for History, American Studies, Classics, and Religion, has generously responded to my many requests for additions to our library that I think are important for its modern European collections. I extend my thanks to Izabella Tabarovsky of the Kennan Institute at the Woodrow Wilson International Center for Scholars in Washington, DC for the invitation to present work in progress dealing with George Kennan's performance as head of the State Department's Policy Planning Staff.

As a historian whose work has focused on Germany in the twentieth century, I had much to learn in writing *Israel's Moment*. I have learned much from fellow scholars. My intellectual debts to the publications of many scholars are in the footnotes, but particular thanks are due to Ronald and Allis Radosh, whose work on Truman and the establishment of the state of Israel was one starting point of this work. David Greenberg offered helpful comments on the American press. Anson Rabinbach shared views about the shift from World War II to the Cold War. The importance of William Roger Louis's published work on the British Empire and his comments in a paper from this work in progress is evident in the following pages. Thanks are due to Shlomo Slonim for his original scholarship on the American arms embargo. The same is true of Benny Morris's very important scholarship on the Arab-Zionist conflict and the Arab-Israeli war of 1948. Tuvia Friling and Anita Shapira, both in their published work and in conversations that began at the Yitzak Rabin Center in Tel Aviv in the spring of 2000, contributed a great deal to my understanding of the Zionist response to the Holocaust, both in pre-state Palestine and in the new state of Israel, as well as of Ben-Gurion's views.

Thanks are due also to many other colleagues and good friends in Germany and in Israel.

Comments and questions in response to lectures about the work in progress were most helpful. Thanks are due to colleagues at the Kennan Institute at the Woodrow Wilson Center in Washington, DC, and at the Leibniz Institute for Jewish History and Culture – Simon Dubnow in Leipzig, Germany. Thanks are due to journal editor Mark Kramer, and to anonymous reviewers of my article "The US State Department's Opposition to Zionist Aspirations during the Early Cold War: George F. Kennan and George C. Marshall in 1947–1948," *Journal of Cold War Studies* 23, no. 4 (Fall 2021): 1–28.

At Cambridge University Press, thanks are due to the careful and informed comments of three anonymous reviewers, and again to my fine editor, Michael Watson, for his support and good judgment from start to finish; to content manager Ruth Boyes; editorial assistant Emily Plater, and Mary Starkey, the book's excellent copy-editor.

My greatest debt is to my wife, Sonya Michel. She read the manuscript with the eye of the fine editor and fine historian that she is. Her edits, suggestions, probing questions, and valuable insights enhanced the book a great deal. Historians know the value of understatement. Suffice it to say, she is a very great blessing. The book is dedicated to her, with much love.

A Note on Style

In the 1940s the common spelling of the city on the French Mediterranean coast was "Marseilles"; in recent decades the French have dropped the final "s" and spelled it "Marseille." When quoting directly from French documents, I have kept the final s, but when referring to it in my own prose I use the standard contemporary spelling, Marseille. I use the abbreviation MFA (Ministry of Foreign Affairs) to refer to the Ministre des Affaires Étrangères or MAE in France. The ministry is also referred to as the Quai d'Orsay. After the establishment of the state of Israel, Moshe Shertok Hebraized his name to Moshe Sharett; as he appears in all the documents of 1945–9 as Moshe Shertok, I have decided to keep that name. In notes, "Washington" refers to Washington, DC, not the state of Washington. Before the establishment of the state of Israel, the area governed by the British Mandate from 1919 to 1948 was called "Palestine." The files of the State Department for 1945–9 are listed as "the Palestine Files." The use of the term "Palestine" in those years did not imply an anti-Zionist perspective. The term for the Jewish community in pre-state Palestine from the 1920s to 1948 is the "Yishuv." I have left the grammar and spelling in the original documents of the 1940s intact. For example, "Negev" is left as "Negeb." I have refrained from inserting definite articles in texts of telegraphic and telex diplomatic except when essential for clarifying meaning for the contemporary reader. Capitalization in some footnotes to diplomatic cables was in the original texts.

1   Introduction

"Israel's Moment" comprised the two years from May 1947 to May 1949 when both the Soviet Union and the Soviet-bloc states of Eastern Europe as well as the president of the United States supported the establishment of a Jewish state in Palestine. That rare agreement took place in the interregnum between the end of World War II and the Holocaust, and the first months of the Cold War. In these years anti-Nazism, antifascism, and anticommunism existed in an uneasy simultaneity. The foundation of the state of Israel was a highly contingent event that was facilitated by the short-lived and, as we shall see, tenuous agreement between the Soviet Union and the United States.

The present study draws on existing scholarship and on a close reading of various primary sources to reach four core conclusions: First, although the favorable decisions of President Harry Truman were a necessary precondition for the establishment of the state of Israel, the United States government from 1945 to 1949 was far less supportive of or important for that outcome than were the Soviet Union and the Soviet-bloc states, particularly in the years of Israel's Moment, which ran from May 1947 to the end of the Arab-Israeli war in early 1949. Second, though there were some moderate conservatives in the United States and France who supported the Zionist cause, the core of the Zionist passion in the United States and Europe, in addition first of all to the enthusiastic support of Jewish organizations and leaders, came over-whelmingly from American liberals and left-liberals, French socialists and, between 1947 and 1949, from communists in France and in the Soviet bloc, especially in Czechoslovakia. For these two years Stalin viewed the establishment of a Jewish state in Palestine as a possible instrument to eliminate or certainly reduce British and American presence and power in the Middle East. Yet, as records of United Nations debates indicate, support for the Zionist project in the Soviet Union and in Eastern Europe during these years also drew on the powerful memories and the antifascist passions of World War II on the Eastern Front and the Holocaust. Emotions and power politics were both motivating factors.

Third, while historians have documented the well-known active opposition to Zionist aspirations on the part of the British Labour government and the Division of Near Eastern and African Affairs in the State Department, a close reading of the American files reveals a hitherto underexamined depth and intensity of opposition not only among the State Department's Arabists but among leading officials in that department, in the Pentagon, and the Central Intelligence Agency. The belief that the establishment of a Jewish state in Palestine would undermine American national security interests remained a consensus of those officials when the issue hung in the balance. During the four decades of the Cold War, outside Israel, the limits of American support, the extent of American opposition, and the degree of support from left-of-center politicians and the press in the West, and from the Soviet Union and Soviet-bloc states, faded from public view. The American alliance with Israel that emerged only decades later was projected backward onto a romanticized – or demonized – view of early American support, as if President Truman's sympathies overcame the reservations of American diplomats and military leaders. The Soviet Union as well, after turning against Israel in late 1949, treated the short era of Soviet Zionism as anathema. The actual international history of the establishment of the Jewish state did not fit at all well into the communist and anticommunist binaries of the Cold War. This work offers a fresh look at the realities of the four years from the Holocaust to the Cold War during which the Zionists won their struggle to create a Jewish state in Palestine.

Fourth, the passions of two eras – World War II and the Holocaust, and the Cold War, one just past and another just beginning – shaped Israel's Moment. The controversies during this period reflected the lingering passions of the former and the new-found zeal of the latter. This work recalls and reveals political coordinates on the left–right spectrum that stand in stark contrast to those that have emerged in subsequent decades. In the years in which Israel was established, its supporters saw it as part of a broad movement against imperialism and racism, while its opponents outside the Arab world viewed the Zionist project as a hindrance to the British Empire and then to American power in the Middle East.

This history of the ideas and passions that motivated support and opposition to Zionist aspirations focuses primarily on events in the United States, but also those in France. It follows debates at the United Nations in New York, policy decisions and discussions in the State Department and Pentagon in Washington, DC, assessments of the US Central Intelligence Agency, and decisions made in France's Ministry of Interior and its Ministry of Foreign Relations. It is also a history of

American and French dissenters from an anti-Zionist consensus in the American national security institutions – those who saw a Jewish state in Palestine as both the logical outcome of the anti-Nazi passions of World War II and a state that would serve as a bulwark against, rather than a vehicle for, Soviet expansion in the Middle East.

It was in spring 1947, when Britain asked the United Nations to address "the problem of Palestine," that the issue of whether or not there would be a Jewish state in Palestine first became an issue engaging many powers in international history. From the time of the Balfour Declaration in 1917 to that spring, it had primarily involved Britain, the Jews and the Arabs of Palestine, and other Arab states. While others, including the United States, had expressed views on the matter, it was not until the years after World War II, and especially after the involvement of the United Nations, that many other states exerted an impact on the outcome of events. The "international" history examined in the following pages focuses on only a few of the many states expressing views on the matter. The United States, the Soviet Union, Great Britain, France, Czechoslovakia, Poland, the Arab Higher Committee, and the Arab League loom largest because they, more than others, were at the center of this chapter of international history.

Support in the United States and Europe for the establishment of a Jewish state in Palestine was one aspect of the general shift to the left that was evident in the immediate aftermath of World War II and the Holocaust. There were conservative figures such as Winston Churchill, Senator Robert Taft, and a number of French Christian Democrats who looked favorably on the Zionist project. Yet Zionism's most emphatic support came from those infused with the liberal and leftist anti-Nazi passions of World War II and from Jewish survivors of the Holocaust and their fellow Jews. They included liberals and noncommunist leftists in the United States, socialists in France, and the governments of the Soviet Union and the communist regimes in Eastern Europe, especially Poland and Czechoslovakia. In the United States, Zionism's strongest advocates evoked the moods of Franklin Roosevelt's anti-Nazism and the alliance of the first "United Nations," that is, the alliance of nations united to defeat Nazi Germany during World War II. These liberals denounced the American and United Nations Organization decision to embargo arms shipments to both Israel and the Arab states as a form of "appeasement" that benefited the Arabs who, they pointed out, already had the advantages of statehood. In their view, support for the establishment of a Jewish state in Palestine, far from being an example of Western imperialism, was instead a product of the continuing antifascist passions of World War II that persisted up to 1949.

This history of the debate about the Zionist project offers added perspective on a familiar theme, that of acknowledgment of the Holocaust in the immediate postwar years. There was no German government in these years, but the history of the memory and forgetting of the crimes of the Nazi era resonate in this work.[1] Historians of Germany have examined judicial and political reckoning as well as the inclination to silence and amnesty that accompanied the displacement of the imperatives of the Nuremberg war crimes trials with those of rebuilding West Germany as an anticommunist bulwark.[2] Historians of postwar Europe have drawn attention to a European-wide "Vichy syndrome," which downplayed or apologized for the actions of non-German collaborators with the Nazis while exaggerating the extent of national resistance.[3] That syndrome was also evident in the discourse of anticolonialism that took the form of apologia and denials about the realities of collaboration with the Nazis by some Arab leaders who played central roles in opposing the UN Partition Resolution of 1947 and then launching the war of 1947–8.

This work connects the scholarship on memory and politics in postwar Europe with the international history of Zionism/Israel debates of 1945–9. It offers a history of support and opposition to the Zionist project which brings the perspectives and questions that emerged from that historiography to bear on the question of why there was support in 1947 to establish a Jewish state in Palestine and why, once established, it received outside

---

[1] See the discussion of these issues in Jeffrey Herf, *Divided Memory: The Nazi Past in the Two Germanys* (Cambridge, MA: Harvard University Press, 1997); Jeffrey Herf, *Nazi Propaganda for the Arab World* (New Haven: Yale University Press, 2009); Jeffrey Herf, *Undeclared Wars with Israel: East Germany and the West German Far Left, 1967–1989* (New York: Cambridge University Press, 2016); and Mary Fulbrook, *Reckonings: Legacies of Nazi Persecution and the Quest for Justice* (New York: Oxford University Press, 2018).

[2] On the Nuremberg trials see, recently, Francine Hirsch, *Soviet Judgment at Nuremberg: A New History of the International Military Tribunal after World War II* (New York and Oxford: Oxford University Press, 2020); and Kim Christian Priemel, *The Betrayal: The Nuremberg Trials and German Divergence* (Oxford: Oxford University Press, 2016).

[3] On narratives of national resistance in postwar Europe that obscured the extent of collaboration see Tony Judt, *Postwar: A History of Europe since 1945* (New York: Penguin, 2006); Pieter Lagrou, *The Legacy of Nazi Occupation: Patriotic Memory and National Recovery in Western Europe, 1945–1965* (Cambridge and New York: Cambridge University Press, 2007). On France and the "Vichy syndrome" see Henry Rousso, *The Vichy Syndrome: History and Memory in France since 1944* (Cambridge, MA: Harvard University Press, 1991). Also see Istvan Deak, Jan Gross, and Tony Judt, eds., *The Politics of Retribution in Europe: World War II and Its Aftermath* (Princeton: Princeton University Press, 2000); and Jan Werner Muller, *Memory and Power in Postwar Europe: Studies in the Presence of the Past* (New York and Cambridge: Cambridge University Press, 2002). However, on the existence of memory of the Holocaust in France see Francois Azouvi, *Le mythe du grand silence: Auschwitz, les français, la memoire* (Paris: Fayard, 2012); and Laura Jockusch, *Collect and Record! Jewish Holocaust Documentation in Early Postwar Europe* (New York: Oxford University Press, 2015).

support that helped it win its war for independence in 1948. On the whole, those who remembered the Holocaust and extolled the ideas of wartime anti-Nazism supported the Zionist project, while those who forgot or were uncomfortable with them, and wanted to turn the page quickly to the fight against communism, did not.

The East European dimensions of World War II, though a common-place among historians, remain on the margins of American memory.[4] Most of the refugees seeking to come to Palestine after the war came from Central and Eastern Europe. The most passionate supporters of the Zionist project were those who remembered World War II on its Eastern Front and the Holocaust. For Zionists in Palestine, and for American liberal and left-leaning supporters of the Zionist project, the fresh memory of World War II, the Holocaust, Nazi Germany's war on the Eastern Front, and the alliance of "the United Nations," the coalition that included the Soviet Union as well as the United States and its West European allies, loomed large. With the emergence of the Cold War, a forgetting or even reinterpretation of the realities of the anti-Hitler coalition took place both in Moscow and Washington. In both capitals the memory of *that* United Nations and *that* alliance became an embarrassment at best and evidence of communist sympathies or imperialist deviations at worst. In the Britain- and America-centric version of World War II, the history of the war on the Eastern Front and the Holocaust played a diminished role. In Europe the immediate postwar years witnessed leniency toward those accused of collaborating with Nazi Germany. Zionism's liberal and left-leaning supporters in the United States criticized the refusal of the governments of Britain, France, and the United States to indict Haj Amin al-Husseini, the former Grand Mufti of Jerusalem, for war crimes. Husseini had collab-orated with the Nazis, especially in the fields of propaganda. These governments also refused to publish the evidence in their files of his collaboration. This work draws attention to the arguments and evidence of the critics of the leniency shown toward Husseini. They viewed that official reluctance in Washington, London, and Paris and the opposition to the Zionist project as related aspects of

---

[4] See the now-standard overview Gerhard Weinberg, *A World at Arms: A Global History of World War II* (New York: Cambridge University Press, 2005); as well as Omer Bartov, *The Eastern Front, 1941–45: German Troops and the Barbarization of Warfare* (New York: Oxford University Press, 1985); Horst Boog et al., *Germany and the Second World War*, vol. 4: *The Attack on the Soviet Union* (New York and Oxford: Oxford University Press, 1998); Richard Evans, *The Third Reich at War* (New York: Penguin, 2009); Christina Morina, *Legacies of Stalingrad* (New York: Cambridge University Press, 2011); and Richard Overy, *Why the Allies Won* (New York: W. W. Norton, 1995).

the above-mentioned shift from the passions of World War II to those of the early Cold War.[5]

The documents of the US State Department's "Palestine File" and those of the Pentagon on "The Problem of Palestine" from those years are notable for how little the events of World War II, especially the Nazi race war of extermination on the Eastern Front, and the Holocaust, seem to have influenced policy. In these files the press of ongoing events crowds out the very recent cataclysm. The absence was particularly striking since the secretary of state in the crucial two years was George C. Marshall, who had been chief of the Joint Chiefs during the war, and George F. Kennan, the conceptual architect of the policy of the containment of communism who served as the first Director of the State Department's Policy Planning Staff, had worked in the US Embassy in wartime Moscow. All the members of the Joint Chiefs of Staff and leaders of the postwar US armed forces had served in the military in some capacity in World War II. Yet their postwar memoranda and policy statements about the Zionist project contain scant reflection on the impact of the war and the Holocaust on events in the postwar Middle East.

That was unfortunate because American and Soviet support for the Zionist project at the UN in November 1947 turned out to be the last political expression of what remained of the anti-Nazi coalition that had won World War II. The controversy about the establishment of the Jewish state in Palestine has not occupied a large place in the historiography of the early years of the Cold War.[6] It should. The following pages draw attention to the simultaneity between Israel's foundation and the beginnings of the Cold War. Recent historians of Western decision making in the early Cold War have underestimated the extent of antagonism to the Zionist project, overestimated pangs of guilt among Western policy makers, and overlooked the passions of antifascism, anti-Nazism, and anticolonialism among Zionism's most determined advocates.[7]

Though historians have documented aspects of the short but important era of Soviet and Soviet bloc support for the Zionist project, its existence

---

[5] On the consequences of the failure to indict Husseini see Matthias Küntzel, *Nazis und der Nahe Osten: Wie der Islamische Antisemitismus Entstand* (Berlin and Leipzig: Hentrich & Hentrich, 2019).

[6] The paucity of attention is evident in the otherwise valuable first volume of the *Cambridge History of the Cold War*. See Melvyn P. Leffler and Odd Arne Westad, eds., *The Cambridge History of the Cold War*, vol. 1: *Origins, 1945–1962* (Cambridge and New York: Cambridge University Press, 2010).

[7] For example, Odd Arne Westad writes, "Israel was first and foremost expiation for the Holocaust – an easy way of atoning to Jews for not having done enough to save them from Hitler's policy of extermination": *The Global Cold War: Third World Interventions and the Making of Our Times* (Cambridge and New York: Cambridge University Press, 2007), 127.

and its significance remain too little known, both in the scholarship and even more among a general readership.[8] Instead, what looms larger in both are the results of forty years of antagonism to the state of Israel on the part of the USSR and its satellites. From 1949 until the Gorbachev era, Stalin and his successors made "Zionism" into a term of abuse. Soviet diplomats waged political warfare against Israel at the United Nations, and the Warsaw Pact countries armed and trained Israel's Arab enemies.[9] For four decades, with a modest reduction in the Gorbachev years, the Soviet Union claimed that the state of Israel was a tool of "US imperialism" and that Zionism was a form of racism.

Yet in 1947–8 the Czech, Polish, Ukrainian, and Soviet communist representatives at the United Nations were far more emphatic than the United States in support of Zionist aspirations. They opposed American, and of course British, efforts to postpone the establishment of the Jewish state and, once founded, to deprive it of territory it had been promised in the famous UN Partition Resolution 181 of November 29, 1947.[10] Moreover, and very importantly, when the United States imposed an embargo on arms deliveries to the Jews and the Arabs, and then sought and gained United Nations support for that embargo in spring 1948, communist Czechoslovakia was the only government anywhere willing to violate the embargo. It did so by selling weapons first to the Jewish Agency, the political representative of the Jewish population in Mandate Palestine, and then to the new state Israel after it was established on May 14, 1948. These efforts by the Soviet bloc states in the UN deepened State Department and Pentagon suspicions of the Zionist project and the new state of Israel.

This study draws attention to the contingent meanings of famous oppositions such as "left and right," progressive and reactionary, imperialism and anti-imperialism, fascism and antifascism, racism and antiracism in the late 1940s in connection with the Zionist project. Their meanings changed – in some cases were even reversed – in the "anticosmopolitan purges" carried out in the Soviet bloc from 1949 to 1953, and then again

---

[8] See Laurent Rucker, *Stalin, Israël et les Juifs* (Paris: Presses Universitaires de France, 2001); and his "Moscow's Surprise: The Soviet-Israeli Alliance of 1947–1949," Working Paper #46 (July 15, 2005), Woodrow Wilson International Center for Scholars. On the role of Czechoslovakia see Arnold Krammer, *The Forgotten Friendship: Israel and the Soviet Bloc, 1947–53* (Urbana: University of Illinois Press, 1974).

[9] On the East German chapter see Herf, *Undeclared Wars with Israel*. On Soviet policy toward Israel see Robert Wistrich, "The Soviet War against Zion," in *A Lethal Obsession: Anti-Semitism from Antiquity to the Global Jihad* (New York: Random House, 2010); and Yaacov Ro'i, *Soviet Decision Making in Practice: The USSR and Israel, 1947–1954* (New Brunswick, NJ, and London: Transaction Books, 1980).

[10] The resolution, passed by a two-thirds majority in the UN General Assembly, called for the partition of the former British Mandate in Palestine into an Arab and a Jewish state.

after the leftist attack on Israel and Zionism beginning in the 1960s and continuing for many decades.[11] From the 1960s the association of Zionism with imperialism became conventional wisdom, first in global politics, then in leftist academic discourse. The coupling of those terms with one another was foreign to supporters of the Zionist project in the late 1940s because in those years those who would be labeled "imperialists" in London and Washington opposed that project, while "anti-imperialists" supported it. Moreover, those officials in the United States and Europe who opposed Zionist aspirations did so, on the whole, to fight communism in the Middle East and preserve access to Arab oil, not to defend human rights or oppose racism. The establishment opponents were convinced that the Jewish state would undermine both past British and French colonial positions and new American efforts to expand economic and military influence. In 1947–8, other than in the Arab states and the Arab Higher Committee in Palestine, the principal opponents of the Zionist project came from the British Foreign Office, the US State Department, and the Pentagon – the very institutions and persons whom the communists castigated as imperialists.

The extent and intensity of opposition to the Zionist project in the entire top leadership of both the State Department and the Pentagon compose an important theme in the following pages. While historians have examined the antagonism to Zionism among State Department "Arabists," this work demonstrates the degree to which opposition to the Zionist project extended well beyond them and became a constitutive aspect of American foreign policy at the dawn of the Cold War. It was shared by Secretary of State Marshall; the under secretary of state, Robert Lovett; the head of the Department's Near East Division, Loy Henderson; the secretary of defense, James Forrestal; members of the Joint Chiefs of Staff; and Admiral Roscoe Hillenkoetter, the first director of the Central Intelligence Agency; as well as Kennan and his Policy Planning Staff in the State Department.

As the first director of the Policy Planning Staff, Kennan played an important role, the key conceptual role, in connecting opposition to the Zionist project with the policy and strategy of the containment of communism. He did so in important memoranda of January and February 1948 in

---

[11] In that sense, this work contributes to what historians call "the history of concepts," *Begriffsgeschichte*. On *Begriffsgeschichte* see Melvin Richter, *The History of Political and Social Concepts: A Critical Introduction* (New York: Oxford University Press, 1995); and Reinhard Koselleck, *The Practice of Conceptual History: Timing History, Spacing Concepts* (Stanford: Stanford University Press, 2002). On key concepts in the Cold War see Anson Rabinbach, *Begriffe aus dem Kalten Krieg: Totalitarismus, Antifaschismus, Genozoid* (Göttingen: Wallstein Verlag, 2009).

which he echoed but also elaborated on the conviction that establishing a Jewish state in Palestine would severely undermine American national security interests in the emerging Cold War in the Middle East and around the world. Kennan was among those who argued that the American alliance with its closest ally, Great Britain, required broad agreement with British policy in Palestine. Kennan articulated this consensus, but he did not create it. The view that the Zionist project opened a dangerous opportunity for Soviet expansion in the Middle East became widespread among diplomats, military officials, and intelligence analysts in Washington and London. Those associating Zionism with Soviet expansion generally did so with scant acknowledgment that the association of Jews with communism had been central for Nazi Germany's attack on "Jewish Bolshevism" and had become common in the vocabulary of antisemitic abuse.

The American policy makers who established the postwar Atlantic Alliance initiated the policy of containment of communism and launched the Marshall Plan of economic assistance to postwar Europe saw far and clearly when they examined totalitarianism in its communist form. Marshall, Lovett, and Kennan understood that containment in Western Europe would fail without support from left-of-center democratic parties. While they found common cause with the British Labour Party, French and Italian Socialists and West German Social Democrats, they did not do so when it came to the Zionist movement and then the new state of Israel, which were both predominantly on the democratic left. There were voices in American politics who did argue that the Jewish state in Palestine would be a significant asset to the Western democracies, comparable in its political outlook to the left-of-center democratic parties that the USA supported in Western Europe. But officials in the State Department did not see a center-left state of Israel as a comparable bulwark. American liberals criticized the State Department policy as a moral failing and a strategic blunder.

Historians have amply demonstrated that in these crucial years American policy toward Palestine and Israel operated on two tracks. The first came from the White House. It was apparent in President Truman's decision to support the UN Partition Resolution of November 29, 1947 and become the first country to recognize the new state of Israel on May 14, 1948. Truman's decisions to reject the unanimous advice of the diplomatic and military leadership of his administration have received much attention from historians.[12] As important as

---

[12] See Peter L. Hahn, *Caught in the Middle East: U.S. Policy toward the Arab-Israeli Conflict, 1945–1961* (Chapel Hill and London: University of North Carolina Press, 2004); Allis and Ronald Radosh, *A Safe Haven: Harry S. Truman and the Founding of Israel* (New York: HarperCollins, 2009).

those decisions were, the opponents of his policies regarding the Zionist project succeeded in limiting the extent of support the United States offered to the Zionist project and the infant state of Israel. The impact of this limitation is an important theme of the following pages.

Track two, supported by the State Department and the Pentagon, included an attempt to replace the Partition Plan with a trusteeship proposal in spring 1948, support for the Bernadotte Plan of summer and fall 1948, and, crucially, an embargo on arms to the Arab states and Israel, which caused more difficulties for Israel than for the Arab states. The embargo persisted even after the invasion on May 15, 1948 of the new state of Israel, primarily by Egypt, Iraq, Lebanon, Syria, and Transjordan, with the participation of Saudi Arabia and Yemen. In accord with the views of the Departments of State, Defense, and the CIA, the arms embargo remained in place throughout the Arab-Israeli war of 1948.[13] This work gives to track two, the successful effort of American national security leaders to prevent more robust support for the Zionist project when its outcome hung in the balance, the overdue attention it deserves.

In April 1948, angered over the State Department's efforts to undermine his own efforts regarding Israel, Truman began to bring control over Middle East policy back into the White House. Yet, though the State Department lost some battles, it did not completely cede influence in this area, in part because Truman himself was the author of a doctrine that came to bear his name and that launched Western policy of containment of communism in the Cold War.[14] While the State Department, Pentagon, and CIA failed to prevent Truman from supporting the Partition Plan and recognizing the new state of Israel, they did succeed in keeping the American connection to Israel cool and distanced, and in preventing military assistance from arriving when the Jews needed it the most.

American military support for Israel began to some extent in the Kennedy and Johnson administrations but reached significant dimensions

[13] Track one did have an ally in the State Department: Truman's appointee, James McDonald, the first US ambassador to Israel; but his support for the Zionist project was an exception. See Norman J. W. Goda, Barbara McDonald Stewart, Severin Hochberg, and Richard Breitman, eds., *To the Gates of Jerusalem: The Diaries and Papers of James G. McDonald, 1945–1947* (Bloomington: Indiana University Press/ United States Holocaust Memorial Museum, 2015); and Norman J. W. Goda, Richard Breitman, Barbara McDonald Stewart, and Severin Hochberg, eds., *Envoy to the Promised Land: The Diaries and Papers of James G. McDonald, 1948–1951* (Bloomington: Indiana University Press, 2017).

[14] On control of the policy see John Lewis Gaddis, *George F. Kennan: An American Life* (New York: Penguin, 2012), 308.

only after the Six Day War of 1967. The tendency to project that deeper post-1967 US-Israel connection back into the early decades obscures the realities of track two in Israel's crucial formative years. During the war of 1947–8 the offshoot of Jewish Agency's Haganah, the Mossad Le'Aliyah Bet, sought to bring immigrants and arms to Palestine and then Israel. At the behest of the State Department and the Pentagon the United States did what it could to prevent both from a timely arrival. In May 1949 the Israeli prime minister, David Ben-Gurion, told Ambassador McDonald that if the Jews had been dependent on the United States for survival in the 1947–8 war they would have been exterminated. The following pages indicate why Ben-Gurion had reached that grim assessment.

In the United States, critics in politics and the press of the State Department and Pentagon policy took a very different view of the connections between World War II and the Holocaust and the Arab-Zionist conflict than did the architects of the policy of containment. Of the many members of Congress who supported Zionist aspirations, Senator Robert Wagner and Congressman Emanuel Celler were central to the effort. Wagner was the co-sponsor of the Social Security Act, and an act carrying his name created the National Labor Relations Board. A major supporter of the Roosevelt-era New Deal, his was a leading pro-Zionist voice in the United States Senate. In the House of Representatives Celler, a Democrat from Brooklyn and a leader in the reform of American immigration law, initiated important congressional resolutions on Israel, conveyed his views in writing to Secretary Marshall, and engaged in substantive exchanges with Under Secretary of State Robert Lovett, who oversaw Palestine policy. Both Wagner and Celler argued that a Jewish state in Palestine would enhance, not undermine, American national security interests in the Middle East. Sumner Welles, the under secretary of state in the Roosevelt administration from 1937 to 1943, emerged as a minority voice from within the American diplomatic establishment who expressed support for the Zionist project.[15]

Among journalists, Freda Kirchwey, editor of the liberal-to-left-liberal magazine *The Nation*, was a strong supporter of Zionist goals. She played a key role in publishing material about the Nazi collaboration of Haj Amin al-Husseini and other members of the Arab Higher Committee when they sought recognition as representatives of the Palestine Arabs at the United

---

[15] See Sumner Welles, *We Need Not Fail* (Boston: Houghton-Mifflin, 1948); William Roger Louis, "Postmortem Appraisal of the United Nations Game: Sumner Welles and the Zionists," in *The British Empire in the Middle East, 1945–1951: Arab Nationalism, the United States, and Postwar Imperialism* (New York and Oxford: Oxford University Press, 1984), 487–493; Benjamin Welles, *Sumner Welles: FDR's Global Strategist: A Biography* (New York: St. Martin's Press, 1997).

Nations. The left-leaning journalist I. F. Stone, in the pages of *The Nation* and in the daily left-leaning paper *PM*, reported on the Jewish refugees seeking to get to Palestine from Europe, excoriated British policy, and denounced the impact of the oil industry on American policy and what he called the "red smear" efforts of the British Foreign Office and the State Department to associate Zionism with the communists.[16] The journalists Edgar Ansel Mowrer and Alexander Uhl, in the pages of the *New York Post*, published material on Husseini's Nazi collaboration and sought, unsuccessfully, to convince the chief US prosecutor at the Nuremberg trial, Robert Jackson, to indict him for war crimes in the International Military Tribunal in Nuremberg. Henry Wallace, Roosevelt's vice president from 1940 to 1944 and editor-in-chief of *The New Republic* during the Arab-Israeli war, also criticized British and American policy on similar grounds.

The American Zionist Emergency Council (AZEC) was the US representative to the Jewish Agency in Palestine. Hence its principals had the opportunity to meet with high-ranking officials in the State Department. Speaking for AZEC, Benjamin Akzin, Benzion Netanyahu, Joseph Schechtman, Rabbi Abba Silver, and Rabbi Stephen Wise wrote memoranda offering the outlines of an alternative Palestine policy. In 1945 and 1946 they urged that the United States indict Husseini for war crimes and bring him to trial. They regarded the Zionist project as an extension of the moral and political purposes for which World War II had been fought, and as a continuation of a struggle against racism and antisemitism in the Arab states and in the Arab Higher Committee. They described the Zionist project as a defense of otherness and difference that stood in opposition to Arab advocates of racial homogeneity. They argued that a Jewish state in Palestine would be a firm ally of the United States and the Western democracies and thus supportive of US national security interests. The State Department officials listened, but adopted none of their suggestions.

The records of the public political battles about the Arab-Zionist conflict at the newly established United Nations are important and revealing. What was called "the "problem of Palestine" loomed large. It was discussed frequently in the Security Council, and in five separate meetings of the General Assembly between May 1947 and May 1949. The UN records present the interventions of Warren Austin (1877–1962), the US ambassador to the UN. They also offer compelling

---

[16] On Stone's writing on Zionism in those years see Susie Linfield, *The Lion's Den: Zionism and the Left from Hannah Arendt to Noam Chomsky* (New Haven: Yale University Press, 2019).

evidence that at all of those five meetings of the General Assembly, at its associated committees, and in the more numerous sessions of the Security Council, the Jewish Agency prior to May 14, 1948 and the state of Israel thereafter received their strongest support from representatives of the communist states in Europe – Czechoslovakia, Poland, the Ukrainian SSR – and most importantly from the Soviet Union. Their advocacy was apparent in the famous interventions of Soviet UN ambassador Andrei Gromyko as well as in the less well-known statements of the Polish representatives, including Oskar Lange, and in particular Alfred Fiderkiewicz, who, as he made the case for the Partition Resolution, revealed that as a survivor of Auschwitz he had personally witnessed the murder of Jews. As the Israel representatives, Moshe Shertok (later Sharett) and Aubrey (later Abba) Eban, made their case, they repeatedly found that it was representatives from the Soviet bloc, countries where most of the Holocaust had taken place, who were the Zionists' strongest supporters – far stronger, more emphatic, and more passionate than the American representatives. Indeed, during the 1947–8 debates at the UN they were the only members, aside from Moshe Shertok, who spoke at length about the mass murder of the Jews of Europe.

France, and Paris in particular, was the headquarters of Zionist politics in Western Europe. The memory of the Holocaust among Jews and in the political circles was vivid, a memory that took political expression in support for establishment of the Jewish state in Palestine.[17] Sympathy for Zionist aspirations extended beyond the organizations of French Jewry. It was voiced as well by Jews and non-Jews among Gaullists, Socialists, Communists, and veterans of the French Resistance.[18] In the coalition governments of France's Fourth Republic, a policy difference emerged between the predominantly pro-Arab Foreign Ministry and Zionist supporters in the Ministry of the Interior. In 1945 and 1946, when Georges Bidault (1899–1983) served as the French foreign minister, the beginnings of that debate concerned what to do with the Grand Mufti of Jerusalem, Haj Amin al-Husseini, whom French soldiers

---

[17] See David Lazar, *Opinion française et la naissance de l'état d'Israël, 1945–1949* (Paris: Calmann-Levy, 1972).

[18] For example, Alfred Coste Floret, a Gaullist veteran of the French Resistance; Florimond Bonté, a member of the Central Committee of the French Communist Party; Jean-Paul Sartre, the author in 1946 of *Anti-Semite and Jew*; and leaders of French Jewish organizations, such as Marc Jarblum. On French government and public debates see two important works by Frédérique Schillo: *La France et la création de l'état d'Israël, 18 février 1947–11 mai 1949* (Paris: Éditions Artcom, 1997) and *La Politique française à l'égard d'Israël, 1946–1949* (Paris: André Versaille Éditeur, 2012); and Tsilla Hershco, *Entre Paris et Jerusalem: la France, le sionisme et la creation de l'état d'Israël, 1945–1949* (Paris: Honoré Champion Éditeur, 2003).

captured in the French occupation zone in Germany in May 1945. The history of Husseini in these years is familiar. The history of the decisions not to bring him to trial to face accusations regarding his collaboration with the Nazis, and instead to facilitate his return to the Middle East, is less so. It was an important chapter in the broader history of shifting alliances from those of World War II to those of the Cold War. This work offers the first English-language account of the French government's decisions to resist calls to indict him for war crimes based on the files of the French Foreign Ministry. French files on Husseini document an example of the above-mentioned decisions to displace judicial reckoning for the crimes of the Nazi era with efforts to gain allies in the early period of the Cold War, and of a variation of the "Vichy syndrome" applied to a collaborator from the Arab world. His "escape" into friendly Arab hands in June 1946 contributed to a unique feature of Arab politics after World War II, namely the ability of a personality such as "the Mufti" to return to political life without abandoning the radical antise-mitism that he articulated when he collaborated with the Nazi regime in sending Arab-language propaganda to the Middle East.[19]

The support for Zionist aspirations in the French Ministry of Interior (the counterpart to the US Department of Justice) was an important chapter of *Israel's Moment*. Three socialists, Adrien Tixier, Édouard Depreux, and then Jules Moch, served as minister of interior during the crucial period from 1946 to 1949. They did so as members of the coalition governments led by socialists Paul Ramadier and then Robert Schuman of the Christian Democratic Popular Republican Movement (MRP). Georges Bidault, also of the MRP, served as foreign minister in these coalitions during the crucial period of 1947–8.[20] The files of the French Interior Ministry document their efforts to support the Zionist project, primarily in facilitating Jewish

---

[19] On Husseini's return to the Middle East and the distinctive feature of Arab politics toward Nazism see Küntzel, *Nazis und der Nahe Osten*. On Husseini in Nazi Germany see Herf, *Nazi Propaganda for the Arab World*; Richard Breitman and Norman J. W. Goda, "Nazis and the Middle East," in *Hitler's Shadow: Nazi War Criminals, U.S. Intelligence and the Cold War* (Washington, DC and College Park, MD: US National Archives and Records, 2010); and Martin Cüppers, *Walther Rauff – in deutschen Diensten: Vom Naziverbrecher zum BND-Spion* (Darmstadt: Wissenschaftliche Buchgesellschaft, 2013). On the role of ex-Nazis in Egypt see Ulrike Becker, "Die deutsche Militärberatergruppe in Ägypten 1951–1958," in Martin Cüppers, Jürgen Matthäus, and Andrej Angrick, eds., *Naziverbrechen: Täter, Taten, Bewältigungsversuche* (Darmstadt: Wissenschaftliche Buchgesellschaft, 2014), 319–334.

[20] On the sequence and political character of the government coalitions of the Fourth Republic see William I. Hitchcock, *The Struggle for Europe: The Turbulent History of a Divided Continent, 1945 to the Present* (New York: Anchor Books, 2004), 76–77; Paul-Marie de la Gorce, *Naissance de la France moderne: l'après guerre, 1944–1952* (Paris: Bernard Grasset, 1978); and Jean Pierre Rioux, *The Fourth Republic, 1944–1958* (New York: Cambridge University Press, 1987).

emigration from Europe to Palestine. They were in a position to do so because the Interior Ministry's control over borders, passports, seaports, and the police enabled them to assist what the British called "illegal Jewish immigration" to Palestine. To the great irritation of the British Foreign Office the French socialist ministers facilitated the Mossad Le'Aliyah Bet's efforts to foster "clandestine" emigration despite the British naval blockade.[21] Depreux and Moch believed, in contrast to the American policy makers, that the political orientation of the Zionist mainstream was similar to the democratic leftist anticommunism which the French socialists had adopted for themselves and had demonstrated in May 1947, when the socialist prime minister Paul Ramadier expelled the French communists from the government coalition. The history of the practical assistance that the French socialist ministers of interior offered to Zionist aspirations is an important but little-known chapter in the history of the foundation of the state of Israel. The French Foreign Office under Bidault and prime minister Robert Schuman, focused on retaining close ties to Britain, cultivating support in the Arab world, and responding to the concerns of the Catholic Church, voted in favor of the UN Partition Plan only after intense internal debate. As in the United States, leftist and liberal opinion, and the broader legacy of the French Resistance, was far more sympathetic to the Zionists in the crucial years.

Communist Czechoslovakia was the one government anywhere that was willing and able to sell heavy weapons to the Jews of the Yishuv, the Hebrew name for the Jewish community in Palestine, and then to the new state of Israel.[22] It appears in the following pages primarily through concerned reports of American diplomats and military attachés who were observing the flow of tanks, planes, artillery, and trucks that the Czech government sold to the Jewish Agency before May 14, 1948 and to the new state of Israel thereafter. The Czech-Israeli connection reinforced the view in American policy-making circles that the new state of Israel did indeed have a suspicious connection to the Soviet bloc. Israel turned to the Czechs because the United States delivered not weapons but an embargo on weapons, and no other Western government, including France, stepped into the breach. Nevertheless, the suspicions in Washington lingered. In a tragically ironic turn of events, at the Slansky trial in 1952 the significant

---

[21] On Britain's irritation see Arieh Kochavi, *Post-Holocaust Politics: Britain, the United States and Jewish Refugees, 1945–1948* (Chapel Hill: University of North Carolina Press, 2001).

[22] On Czechoslovakia and Israel see Uri Bialer, "The Czech-Israeli Arms Deal Revisited," *Journal of Strategic Studies* 8, no. 3 (1985): 307–315; Krammer, *The Forgotten Friendship*; Jiri Valena and Leni Friedman Valena, "The Birth of Israel: Prague's Crucial Role," *Middle East Quarterly* 25 (Winter 2019): 1–14; and Martin Wein, *A History of Czechs and Jews: A Slavic Jerusalem* (London: Routledge, 2015).

assistance provided by certain Czech communists who sent weapons to the Yishuv and to Israel was turned against them and used as evidence that they had participated in an American–Zionist conspiracy against the communist regime. This led to their convictions and executions.[23]

An excellent historiography already presents the basic political history of the key events related to the foundation of the state of Israel. The reader will see that this work draws on the previous works by Uri Bialer, Michael J. Cohen, Peter J. Hahn, J. C. Hurewitz, Arieh Kochavi, Benny Morris, Allis and Ronald Radosh, Yaacov Ro'i, Anita Shapira, and Shlomi Slonim.[24] *Israel's Moment* explores in greater detail the intellectual and ideological texture of arguments in the debate, the interactions of war and politics at the United Nations, and the transition from World War II to the Cold War. It also inserts these events into the early history of the Cold War more than has been the case in some recent assessments of the origins and early years of that conflict.[25] Scholarship of recent decades on France by Frédérique Schillo, as well as Tsilla Hershco, has documented and interpreted the role of the French government. Also, in French, Laurent Rucker has examined Stalin's policy.[26] William Roger Louis's work on British decolonization encompassed valuable work on British strategy and opposition to the Zionist initiative.[27]

---

[23] On the Slansky trial see, for example, Karel Kaplan, *Report on the Murder of the General Secretary* (Columbus: Ohio State University Press, 1990); Meir Kotic, *The Prague Trial: The First Anti-Zionist Show Trial in the Communist Bloc* (New York: Herzl Press, 1987); and Herf, *Divided Memory*.

[24] Uri Bialer, *Between East and West: Israel's Foreign Policy Orientation, 1948–1956* (New York and Cambridge: Cambridge University Press, 1990); and his *Israeli Foreign Policy: A People Shall Not Dwell Alone* (Bloomington: Indiana University Press, 2020); Hahn, *Caught in the Middle East*; J. C. Hurewitz, *The Struggle for Palestine* (New York: W. W. Norton, 1950; repr. Greenwood Press, 1968); Kochavi, *Post-Holocaust Politics*; Louis, *The British Empire in the Middle East, 1945–1951*; Benny Morris, *1948: The First Arab-Israeli War* (New Haven: Yale University Press, 2008); Radosh and Radosh, *A Safe Haven*; Ro'i, *Soviet Decision Making in Practice*; Anita Shapira, *Land and Power: The Zionist Resort to Force, 1881–1948* (Stanford: Stanford University Press, 1999); Shlomo Slonim, "The 1948 American Embargo on Arms to Palestine," *Political Science Quarterly* 94, no. 3 (1979): 495–514. On the embargo also see Amitzur Ilan, *The Origins of the Arab-Israeli Arms Race: Arms, Embargo, Military Power and Decision in the 1948 Palestine War* (New York: New York University Press, 1996).

[25] Odd Arne Westad, "The Cold War and the International History of the Twentieth Century"; Melvyn P. Leffler, "The Emergence of American Grand Strategy, 1945–1962"; and Mark Bradley, "Decolonization, the Global South and the Cold War, 1919–1962," all in Leffler and Westad, eds., *The Cambridge History of the Cold War*, vol. 1: *Origins, 1945–1962*, 1–19, 67–89, and 464–485 respectively.

[26] Schillo, *La France et la création de l'état d'Israël*; Schillo, *La Politique française à l'égard d'Israël, 1946–1949*; Hershco, *Entre Paris et Jérusalem*; Rucker, *Stalin, Israël et les Juifs*, 2015.

[27] See, for example, William Roger Louis, The End of British Imperialism: The Scramble for Empire, Suez, and Decolonization: Collected Essays (New York: I. B. Tauris, 2006); Louis, The British Empire in the Middle East, 1945–1951; and William Roger Louis,

The Establishment of the State of Israel: A Brief History

The following pages explore Israel's Moment in detail. Here, briefly, are key events in that history. In 1939 the British government, faced with Arab resistance to Jewish immigration to Palestine in the late 1930s resulting from longer-term Zionist goals as well as the shocks of Nazi persecution since 1933, issued a White Paper that restricted Jewish immigration to 1,500 persons a year. The White Paper not only represented a turn away from the promise of the Balfour Declaration of 1917 that Britain would support the establishment of a "Jewish national home" in Palestine but erected a major barrier to immigration that persisted throughout the years of persecution and mass murder of European Jewry. In April 1944 the British Labour Party passed a pro-Zionist resolution calling for the lifting of the White Paper restrictions. A month earlier the US House and Senate had both passed resolutions asking Britain to rescind the White Paper restrictions and offering support for the establishment of a Jewish state in Palestine. In summer 1944 the election platforms of both the Republican and Democratic parties called for an end to immigration restrictions. The Democrats went even further, proposing that Palestine be reconstituted as a "Jewish commonwealth."

President Franklin Roosevelt, in wartime meetings with the Saudi king, Ibn Saud, promised to consult with Arabs before taking a stance on the future of Palestine, yet also assured Jewish advocates in the United States that he would "find appropriate ways and means" of supporting Zionist aspirations "as soon as practicable." The liberal and leftist press in the United States focused attention on the wartime activities of Haj Amin al-Husseini, who had become world famous as a result of his radio broadcasts in support of Nazi Germany from 1941 to 1945.

Following their election victory of July 27, 1945 the government of prime minister Clement Attlee and foreign secretary Ernest Bevin reversed the Labour Party's wartime resolutions and sustained the White Paper restrictions. Bevin and his advisors in the British Foreign Office argued that the establishment of a Jewish state in Palestine, by inflaming Arab opposition, would undermine the British Empire in the Middle East, block access to oil, and enhance Soviet influence in the region. In August 1945, at a Zionist conference in Basel, Switzerland, David Ben-Gurion, leader of the Jewish Agency Executive in Palestine, emerged ascendant over Chaim Weizmann. Ben-Gurion captured the urgency, anger, and determination in the Jewish community in

"The Dissolution of the British Empire," in Judith Brown and William Roger Louis, eds., *The Oxford History of the British Empire*, vol. 4: *The Twentieth Century* (New York and Oxford: Oxford University Press, 2001), 329–378.

Palestine to quickly establish a sovereign Jewish state in Palestine as a way to end the centuries of stateless powerlessness in Europe that had pre-ceded the Holocaust and, the Zionists argued, made it possible. In August 1945 the Arab League informed the British government of its unequivocal opposition to that same project. British hopes for a binational state of Jews and Arabs with some sort of continued British presence dimmed.

On August 31, 1945, following receipt of a report by Earl Harrison, the US commissioner for immigration and integration, describing appalling conditions in which Jewish displaced persons were being held in Germany and Austria, President Harry Truman urged the Attlee–Bevin government to admit 100,000 Jewish refugees to Palestine, a request that angered Attlee and Bevin and inaugurated a period of tensions with the United States's closest ally. On October 31 the Haganah, the military arm of the Jewish Agency, blew up 153 railroad bridges in Palestine, a powerful expression of the growth of militancy and military effectiveness of the Jews in Palestine. In the first week in November antisemitic and anti-Zionist riots took place in Egypt, Syria, Lebanon, Iraq, and Libya. On November 13, in the hopes of finding a solution that would preclude a Jewish state in Palestine and find common ground with the Americans, Britain agreed to establish an Anglo-American Committee of Inquiry (AACI). On May 1, 1946, after hearing testimony and visiting Palestine and refugee camps in Europe, the twelve-member committee, six Americans and six Britons, issued a unanimous report that called for the admission of 100,000 Jewish refugees to Palestine, thus angering both the Arabs and Bevin, who sought to separate the issue of refugees in Europe from the future of Palestine via return of the refugees to countries in Europe, but pleasing the Zionists. Yet the committee also advocated the establishment of a binational state in Palestine, which pleased Bevin but angered both the Arabs and the Jews.

In Europe in 1945 and 1946 the hopes for postwar cooperation were strained by Stalin's decisions to impose one-party regimes in Eastern Europe. On February 26, 1946 George Kennan, then not well known outside foreign policy circles, sent an 8,000-word "Long Telegram" from Moscow to the secretary of state, James F. Byrnes, in Washington, addressing the sources of Soviet conduct and the need to contain Soviet expansion in areas deemed vital to US national security. On May 5, the now former prime minister Winston Churchill delivered his "Iron Curtain" speech in Fulton, Missouri, in which he described Soviet repres-sion in Eastern Europe and called for a unified Western response. The new "Cold War" would require unity of purpose between the United

States and Great Britain, a unity that was put to the test by differences over Palestine.

In summer 1945 details of the Nazi crimes filled newspaper front pages. Beginning in October 1945, and continuing for the following year, the Allies' International Military Tribunal in Nuremberg presented more facts, including details about the murders of European Jewry. Jewish and Zionist organizations in the United States, along with prominent American liberals in the press and politics, called on the United States, the Allied victors, and the United Nations War Crimes Commission (UNWCC) to list Haj Amin al-Husseini as a war criminal, indict him, and bring him to trial. None did so. On May 29, 1946, following a year of comfortable house arrest by the French government, Husseini "escaped" using an alias, and flew to Cairo. In June the Arab League meeting in Bloudan, Syria, formed a Palestine Committee to direct the struggle against Zionism and offer financial and military support toward that end. Britain, now with almost 100,000 troops in Palestine, cracked down on IZL, the Hebrew Resistance Movement composed of the Haganah, the Irgun, and Lehi (the latter were organizations that engaged in terrorist attacks on British forces). On July 22, 1946 the Irgun Zvai Leumi blew up the King David Hotel in Jerusalem, the military and civilian headquarters of the British Mandate in Palestine, with heavy loss of British, Arab, and Jewish lives.

The attack ended cooperation between the Haganah and the Irgun, led to intensified British repression of Jewish armed contingents, and reinforced British opposition to the Zionist project. On July 31 the Bevin Foreign Office announced the "Morrison–Grady" plan, which called for a binational state and linked support for the admission of 100,000 Jewish refugees to Zionist acceptance of a binational, not Jewish, state outcome. The Jewish Agency rejected it because it precluded a Jewish state. The Arab League rejected it because it allowed for some sort of Jewish political power in Palestine. In September the British Palestine Mandate authorities offered amnesty to the Mufti's associates.

On October 4, 1946 Truman, in response to the Harrison report as well as public sentiment in the United States, again urged Britain to admit 100,000 Jewish refugees to Palestine without conditions, a policy that again angered British decision makers hoping to link the admission of refugees to rejection of the Zionist project. In 1946 and 1947 the British Navy prevented ships organized by the Mossad Le'Aliyah Bet's clandestine emigration efforts from reaching Palestine with Jewish refugees from Europe. In January 1947 the Mufti and his associates consolidated control of the Arab Higher Executive, the political arm of Palestine Arabs. On February 18, faced with what its military viewed as the impossibility of repressing both Zionist forces led by Ben-Gurion and the Arab Higher Executive led by Husseini, and frustrated by Arab refusals to accept even a binational solution, the Attlee–Bevin government announced that it was handing the decision about the future of Palestine over to the newly created United Nations. Bevin and the British Foreign Office did so confident that the Zionists would be unable to find a two-thirds majority of the UN General Assembly to vote in favor of their goals. On March 12, 1947, in an address to a Joint Session of Congress, Truman announced what became known as "the Truman Doctrine" of economic and military assistance to countries, Greece and Turkey first of all, to oppose communism. American officials increasingly evaluated the advisability of a Jewish state in Palestine regarding its impact on Soviet and communist policy in the Middle East.

From April 28 to May 15, 1947 the first Special Session of the United Nations took place in Lake Success, New York to discuss the Palestine issue. The United States was noncommittal and supported the creation of a United Nations Special Committee on Palestine (UNSCOP) to study the matter and offer recommendations to the UN. On May 14, 1947 Andrei Gromyko, the Soviet ambassador to the United Nations, stunned the United States and Britain when he announced that if Arabs and Jews could not agree on a binational state, then the Soviet Union would support the partition of Palestine into separate Jewish and Arab states. Contrary to British expectations, the possibility of joint American and Soviet support for Zionist aspirations now seemed to exist. At the same session, the UN granted observer status to the two non-governmental organizations from Palestine. The Jewish Agency could speak for the Jews, and the Arab Higher Committee for the Arabs.

In summer 1947 the situation in Palestine focused less on the conflict between Jews and Arabs and more on that between the Jews and the British. British decisions to execute members of the Irgun found guilty of terrorism led to Irgun retaliation by hanging two British sergeants on July 30, infuriating British public opinion. That July and August the world press was filled with reports of the efforts of 4,500 Jewish refugees to run the British blockade on a ship renamed the *Exodus*. The events are famous, reported in the world press at the time, retold in the 1958 bestselling novel by Leon Uris and depicted in 1960 by Hollywood in film.[28] The British Navy seized the ship and transferred the passengers to three British vessels, which then sailed to the coast of France. When officials of the French Interior Ministry refused to use force to compel

---

[28] Leon Uris, *Exodus: A Novel of Israel* (New York: Doubleday, 1958; repr. 1983).

the passengers to disembark in one of France's southern ports, the British took them to camps near Hamburg in Germany. The result was an expansion of sympathy for Zionist aspirations and a blow to British relations with both the United States and the French government, which continued to assist rather than prevent Jewish immigration to Palestine.

On August 31 UNSCOP issued a majority report in favor of the partition of Palestine and a minority report in favor of a binational state. The imprimatur of a UN committee in favor of Zionist aspirations constituted an important success for Zionist efforts to defeat British policy and a further step in the internationalization of what had been a British-Arab-Zionist triangular conflict. On September 26, 1947 Britain publicly announced that it intended to withdraw from Palestine. On November 29, following extensive discussions in a committee of the whole called the Palestine Committee, a two-thirds majority of the UN General Assembly voted in favor of a Partition Resolution to create Jewish and Arab states in Palestine. The very next day the Mufti's forces in the Arab Higher Committee began a civil war with the Jews, attacking traffic on the roads to oppose the UN Partition Plan.

The UN resolution was bracketed by decisive American policy developments regarding Israel. In September and October 1947 leading diplomatic and military leaders of the United States met with their British counterparts at "the Pentagon talks" in Washington. They agreed that a Jewish state in Palestine would weaken Western influence in the Middle East and enhance that of the Soviets. They also agreed that it would threaten Western access to oil needed for the world economy and thus undermine the European recovery program, the Marshall Plan, which had been announced by the secretary of state on June 5, 1947 in a speech at Harvard University. On December 10, only a little more than a week after the UN resolution had passed, and when the Arab attacks on the Yishuv had already begun, the State Department announced an embargo on arms going to both sides in the Middle East. In January and February 1948 the State Department's Policy Planning Staff, led by George Kennan, articulated a policy opposed to the partition of Palestine. On March 18 the US ambassador to the UN, Warren Austin, announced a reversal of that policy. The United States now supported a "trusteeship" rather than the Partition Resolution which had proposed separate Arab and Jewish states. President Truman, angered by an effort to undermine his own support for partition, decided to bring more control over Palestine policy into the White House.

In spring 1948 the State Department used the machinery of UN Security Council truce resolutions to prevent further Jewish immigration, especially of military-age Jewish men, and to block delivery of any military equipment to the Jewish Agency. Though the Soviet Union itself did not send weapons directly to the Jews, the communist regime in Czechoslovakia began to send small arms and heavy weapons – tanks and planes – to the Yishuv.

On May 14, 1948 the British Mandate in Palestine ended, and David Ben-Gurion declared the existence of the state of Israel. That evening Truman granted de facto recognition to the new state. The next day Egypt, Iraq, Syria, and Transjordan, as well as Saudi Arabia and Yemen, invaded the new state of Israel, turning what had been a civil war between Jews and Arabs in Palestine into a war between Israel and six Arab states. On May 17 the Soviet Union granted Israel fuller – that is, de jure – recognition. The first Arab-Israeli war in 1948 was punctuated by periods of intense fighting interrupted by truce agreements negotiated by the United Nations. The war continued until armistice agreements between Israel and the Arab states were signed between January and July 1949. In July and September a UN "mediator," Swedish diplomat Count Folke Bernadotte, proposed a peace plan that would give the Negev desert to Transjordan, the Galilee to Israel, turn Haifa into a "free" port, and internationalize Jerusalem. His plan, supported by the United States and Great Britain, would have reduced the size of Israel below what it had been promised in the original UN Partition Plan. It accepted the existence of a small Jewish state. The Arabs rejected it. On September 17 Lehi terrorists assassinated Bernadotte, damaging Israel's cause at the United Nations.

On June 18, 1948 the Soviet Union began to blockade Berlin. The United States followed with an airlift of supplies to the city. In summer and fall 1948, as tensions between the Soviet Union and the West intensified in Europe, Israel's strongest and most persistent support came from the Soviet Union and Soviet bloc countries, which rejected the Bernadotte Plan as an instrument of British imperialism. Israeli offensives in October 1948 drove the Egyptian army out of the Negev. As the fall American presidential election approached, Truman reiterated support for the November 29, 1947 UN Partition Resolution and thus rejected the Bernadotte proposals. Nevertheless, the American embargo on arms to the Middle East continued throughout the course of the war of 1947–8. Throughout summer and fall 1948 Truman's support for the Zionists and the new state of Israel remained at odds with his own State Department, Pentagon, and CIA, all of which continued to believe that it undermined American national security interests in the region.

The war continued in several spurts of fighting and truces until early January 1949. The state of Israel survived, but the victory came at a great cost. The Yishuv suffered 5,700–5,800 dead, a quarter of them civilians, and about 12,000 seriously wounded, in a population that numbered 628,000 in November 1947 and 649,000 in May 1948. Palestinian losses may have been higher or slightly higher. Egyptian losses amounted to about 1,400 dead and 3,731 "permanently invalided." The Jordanian, Iraqi, and Syrian armies each suffered several hundred dead, and the Lebanese several dozen. The war also resulted in the creation of 700,000 Arab refugees.[29] Israel survived and signed armistice agreements in February 1949 with Egypt, in March with Lebanon, in April with Jordan, and in July with Syria. On January 29, 1949 Britain offered de facto recognition, and on January 31 the United States offered de jure recognition to the state of Israel. France waited until May 11 to do so. On May 11, 1949 the General Assembly voted in favor of admitting the new state of Israel to membership in the United Nations.

[29] Morris, *1948*, 406–407.

2　Zionist Momentum and the War Crimes Issue in the United States, 1944–1945

> The spirit in which Roosevelt mobilized the conscience of the world must be continued . . . We have an obligation toward Palestine that must be paid in full, and it must be met now.
>
> Senator Robert F. Wagner, "England's Responsibility and Ours," September 11, 1945

> Influences are at work to have Amin el Husseini whitewashed and eventually returned to the Middle East, there once again to become the main instrument of anti-Jewish intrigues and activities.
>
> American Zionist Emergency Council, Memorandum submitted to Secretary of State James Byrnes, December 12, 1945

In summer and fall 1944, as the Red Army came across the Nazi extermination camps in Poland, details about the murder of European Jewry boosted momentum in support of the Zionist project in Palestine both in public opinion and in the Roosevelt administration. On October 15, 1944 Franklin Roosevelt asked Senator Robert F. Wagner to convey the president's views to the annual convention of the Zionist Organization of America. The president referred favorably to the Democratic Party's election platform of July 1944, which supported the establishment of "a free and democratic Jewish commonwealth" in Palestine, and he concluded as follows: "I am convinced that the American people give their support to this aim and if re-elected I shall help to bring about its realization."[1]

In February 1945 Saudi Arabia's king, Ibn Saud, told the president in person what a terrible idea that would be. Roosevelt assured him that no decisions would be taken without consulting Arab leaders. In the Roosevelt White House the tug of war between FDR's support for Zionist aspirations and their association with the mentalities of wartime antifascism, on the one hand, and concerns about access to Arab oil both during and after World War II, on the other, remained

---

[1] "Statement of President Franklin D. Roosevelt to Senator Robert F. Wagner, October 15, 1944," Robert F. Wagner Papers, Box PA (Palestine) 733.

unresolved.[2] Yet in Congress, and in the liberal and left-leaning press, support for the Zionist project moved well beyond American Jewry into the leadership of both the Democratic and Republican parties. By 1944, especially for Roosevelt's liberal base in the Democratic Party, support for Zionism appeared as the logical extension of the anti-Nazi passions and mentalities of World War II in Europe. As we will see, in the United States in the last years of the war and the first postwar year, support for Zionism was one aspect of the move to the left that the war had fostered.

Senator Robert F. Wagner: A Liberal Leader for Zionism

Robert F. Wagner (1877–1953) (D-NY), emerged as the most important member of the United States Senate to support Zionist aspirations in Palestine (see Figure 2.1). Wagner, with good reason, is most remembered as one of the leading figures of American

Figure 2.1 Senator Robert F. Wagner, January 1, 1940. Source: Library of Congress/Corbis/VCG via Getty Images.

---

[2] On Roosevelt's "contradictory positions and vacillations" see Allis Radosh and Ronald Radosh, *A Safe Haven: Harry S. Truman and the Founding of Israel* (New York: HarperCollins, 2009), 16–35.

Figure 2.2 Congressman Emanuel Celler, April 5, 1943. Source: Library of Congress, Prints and Photographs Division, Washington, DC 20540.

liberalism during the era of the New Deal. In 1935 he sponsored the Social Security Act as well as the National Labor Relations Act (also known as the Wagner Act), both of which became law in 1936. He was also one of the founders and co-chair of the leading American religioud pro-Zionist organization the American Christian Palestine Committee, which, from 1938 to 1948, made the case for a Jewish state in Palestine. Together with Emanuel Celler (1888–1981) (D-NY) in the House of Representatives, Wagner became the most significant figure in American politics connecting the liberal antifascism of the Roosevelt years to support for Zionist aspirations both during and after World War II (see Figure 2.1).

On February 1, 1944 Wagner, drawing on the capital he had built up over eighteen years in the Senate, expanded the range of support for Zionism still further when he joined forces with Robert Taft, one of the most powerful and prominent Republican members of that body, to sponsor the "Wagner–Taft Resolution." It read: "That the United States avail of its good offices and take appropriate measures to the end that the doors of Palestine shall be opened for free entry of Jews into that country, and that there shall be full opportunity for colonization so that the Jewish people may ultimately constitute Palestine as a free and democratic Jewish commonwealth."[3] The two were an odd couple, as Taft had initially opposed intervention in the war in Europe, later attacked the Nuremberg war crimes trials, and was a conservative opponent of the labor movement.[4] Yet Taft's co-sponsorship and the fact that support for Zionist aspirations extended into the Republican Party were important because they undermined efforts made by the British government, the State Department, the Pentagon, and US intelligence officials to associate Zionism with the Soviet Union and communism in the early years of the Cold War.

Announcing the resolution, Wagner referred to the need "to right the tragic plight of the Jews of the Old World and help them rebuild their ancestral homeland where they may live as free men and useful citizens."[5] He recalled the Congressional Joint Resolution of 1922 (known as the Lodge Resolution), which lent American support to Britain's Balfour Declaration favoring a national home for the Jewish people. Wagner stated that during and after World War I Allied governments had hoped that the establishment of a "Jewish homeland in Palestine would solve an age-old problem," and that "the disgraceful era of economic and social persecution of the Jews of Europe would terminate, and that once again, this people, from whom we derive our Christianity, our basic literature and our basic laws, among many other contributions, would once again be allowed to work out their salvation in peace and freedom."[6] Yet more than two decades later, despite the remarkable progress Jews had made in Palestine, the hopes of the Balfour Declaration were not realized due to the rise of Hitler and Mussolini. During "the Munich period" in 1939 the British issued a White Paper restricting Jewish immigration, a "policy then as now – [that] shocked the sensibilities of men of good will everywhere," according to Wagner. He noted that no one was more outspoken in opposition to the policy than Winston Churchill, "the great statesman who guides the British Commonwealth."[7]

Wagner then turned to the beginning of World War II, when Hitler's "murder squads undertook their deliberate program of extermination of the Jewish population of Europe." At just the time when "Palestine should have been open to these unfortunate people ... the gates were virtually closed," as the Chamberlain government's White Paper restricted Jewish

[3] "Wagner–Taft Resolution for Jewish Palestine Commonwealth," Washington (February 1, 1944), Robert F. Wagner Papers, Box PA 733.

[4] See Brian Kennedy, "The Surprising Zionist: Senator Robert A. Taft and the Creation of Israel," *The Historian* 73, no. 4 (Winter 2011): 747–767.

[5] Robert F. Wagner, "For Press Release upon Introduction of Resolution in U.S. Senate: Wagner–Taft Resolution for Jewish Palestine Commonwealth," Washington (February 1, 1944), Robert F. Wagner Papers, Box PA 733, 1.

[6] Ibid.   [7] Ibid.

immigration to Palestine.[8] Though Britain had turned its back on the promises it made in the Balfour Declaration, the Jews in Palestine during World War II were firm allies of the anti-Hitler coalition:

Those Jews who were fortunate enough to be in Palestine have made and are making a glorious contribution to the Allied cause. While General Montgomery and his valiant Eighth Army were fighting with their backs to the Suez Canal, and Rommel had already invited guests to his contemplated first dinner party in Cairo, the Jews of Palestine were performing heroic deeds as commandos and as other shock troops. In Palestine the entire community of men and women dedicated their lives to the defense of their homeland and to the production of urgently needed materials of war for the allied forces. President Roosevelt, Mr. Churchill, and other Allied leaders have spoken most generously of their contributions.[9]

The "Jews of Palestine" had rendered service and sacrifice to the Allied war effort. When the war ended, Wagner predicted, Palestine would be ready to absorb those "destitute Jews who will survive Hitler's vengeance. The need then will be greater than ever before."[10]

Five weeks later, on March 9, the American Christian Palestine Committee held its annual dinner at the Statler Hotel in Washington, DC.[11] Wagner, as co-chair of the organization, was one of three main speakers. He regretted "the compromises and capitulations of the last two decades" and "a general retreat from the high purposes and ideals which motivated men in 1917 and '18," when the Balfour Declaration was signed. The British White Paper, he said, was part of an era of "compromise with evil" during the appeasement of Hitler in the 1930s.[12] "Few were far-sighted enough to realize that anti-Semitism was more than an attack on the Jew. It was a major weapon in the Nazi strategy of destroying democracy's internal defenses and isolating the democracies from one another." Wagner associated Nazi aggression in Europe with Nazi plans in the Middle East as he referred to "Palestine's Munich."

Even as Hitler conquered Czechoslovakia without firing a shot, by internally disrupting the country and by simultaneously alienating its professed friends and protectors, so Hitler's agents threatened a disastrous blow at Jewish Palestine – an outpost vital to democracy – by inciting the Arabs against the Jews and the British. And in 1939, Chamberlain yielded to terrorism in Palestine. In violation of the trusteeship imposed by the Palestine mandate and

---

[8] Ibid., 2.   [9] Ibid.   [10] Ibid.

[11] Robert F. Wagner, "Address by Senator Wagner: Delivered before Annual Dinner, American Palestine Committee," Washington (March 9, 1944), Robert F. Wagner Papers, Box PA 733.

[12] Ibid., 2.

in breach of the Balfour promise of 1917, he issued the White Paper of 1939, a document which threatens the complete liquidation of the Jewish national home.

The White Paper, limiting Jewish immigration to 75,000 over a five-year period and terminating it completely three weeks after tomorrow [March 9, 1944], was Palestine's Munich. It was conceived with the same disregard for equity and it was written in the same spirit of appeasement to aggression.[13]

The White Paper, according to Wagner, had denied Jews entry "into their own country, solely on the ground that they are Jews." It would freeze them "into a permanent one-third minority of a population" in what was proposed to be an Arab state. The Jews' rights promised by the League of Nations Mandate were "to be swept away" by a policy that Winston Churchill had "denounced as a breach and a repudiation" of the promise of the Balfour Declaration.[14]

"Freedom-loving men everywhere," Wagner said, needed to take a position on the issue and reaffirm "our stand of 1922," when Congress supported the establishment of a Jewish home in Palestine. In March 1944 "the argument for this declaration is a thousand times more cogent than it was in 1922; the overwhelming tragedy of the Jewish people of Europe pleads for it; the great colonization effort of the past 25 years vindicates it; the threatened repudiation in the White Paper demands it."[15] Victory in World War II had to be more than a military success but also one that pointed to a "lasting peace" and a "progressive order" in which the rights of people would be secured. The Jews had been denied those rights. Europe was "a vast graveyard for their dead." Now the Jews had "a right to ask us that they be counted in the ranks of tomorrow's society of free nations." While Hitler, "the monster" who engineered the Munich pact, was being "beaten into submission" the White Paper of 1939 remained in force. It had to be "torn to bits in order that the hopes of the Jewish people and of humanity may have a new birth of freedom."[16] Wagner's Statler Hotel speech of March 9, 1944 linked support for the Zionist project with opposition to Nazism. He made clear that the White Paper was of a piece with the mentality of appeasement, first of Hitler, then of Arab rejectionists. For Wagner, support for the Zionist project was at one with the purposes for which the Allies, also known then as "the united nations," were fighting against the Nazis.

---

[13] Ibid., 4. On Nazi strategy toward American domestic opinion see Jeffrey Herf, *The Jewish Enemy: Nazi Propaganda during World War II and the Holocaust* (Cambridge, MA: Harvard University Press, 2006).

[14] Wagner, "Address by Senator Wagner: Delivered before Annual Dinner, American Palestine Committee."

[15] Ibid.   [16] Ibid., 5.

Senator Taft, the standard-bearer of Republican conservatism and isolationism before 1941, also spoke at the American Christian Palestine Committee dinner.[17] "Nothing in modern history can equal the barbarity with which the Jews have been treated in axis countries," he asserted. The Jews of Europe needed a country to which they could immigrate, and Palestine was that place. While the Arabs might object, Taft did not believe that antagonizing them would harm Allied military goals, for by then "the war had gone beyond North Africa, and [thus] there would be no military effect" resulting from "American support for Jewish immigration to Palestine."[18]

Vice President Henry Wallace, whose popular-front sympathies led Roosevelt to replace him with Harry Truman as his vice-presidential nominee in summer 1944, also spoke at the Statler that evening.[19] He placed the Jewish catastrophe at the center of his left-leaning, folksy interpretation of the Jews in Western history. What FDR had called the "Four Freedoms," of religion and speech and from fear and want, meant "more to the Jewish people than anyone else. They began fighting for them 3,000 years ago and have never stopped since." No people had suffered so continuously in order to obtain freedom of religion and freedom of expression as the Jews, and none had "longed so passionately for freedom from fear and freedom from want." In their long search for "a haven," they had found one "among the democratic peoples fighting the axis," more so than "at any time since the prophets first raised their voices for social justice."[20] In Europe, the Axis powers in the preceding four years had treated the Jews "more barbarously than during all the rest of recorded history put together."

Just as Wallace associated the Jews with the Allies, so he welcomed their association with the United States. Hitler, he pointed out, taunted the United States as "a Jew-inspired nation." If by that he meant that "we are inspired by Jesus, the most famous of all the Jews, I am happy to admit the charge, and hope it is so." If he meant that "the 3 per cent of the people of the United States who are Jewish run this country," then, Wallace said, Hitler was "crazy."

But the Jews of America know what is going on in the world; they have fought the intolerant fascist aggressors since the time of Christ. The vast Hitler program of recent years is really a continuation on a great scale of that which has gone on in

---

[17] "Address by Robert H. Taft at the Dinner of the American Palestine Committee at Hotel Statler, Washington, D.C." (March 9, 1944), Robert F. Wagner Papers, Box PA 733.

[18] Ibid., 6.

[19] "Address of Vice President Henry A. Wallace at the Dinner of the American Palestine Committee at Hotel Statler, Washington, D.C." (March 9, 1944), Robert C. Wagner Papers, Box PA 733.

[20] Ibid., 2.

a smaller way in a thousand ghettoes through a thousand years. Small wonder that the Jews were the first to recognize Hitlerism for what it really is; small wonder they were among the first to try to awaken the democracies from their slumber; small wonder they feared the triumph of Fascism in America, even though we smash German military power, and hang Goebbels, Goering, Himmler and Hitler; small wonder they look askance at the devious Fascist maneuvering of a small military clique in Argentina.

For their deep perception of the Fascist danger, I say the Jews are deserving of the undying gratitude of all friends of democracy everywhere.[21]

Wallace connected the Jews in an unequivocally positive manner to Christianity, the Western tradition of democracy, the United States, and "the democratic peoples fighting the Axis," by which he implicitly meant all the powers of the anti-Hitler coalition, including the Soviet Union.

The three speeches at the Statler Hotel on March 9, 1944 provided evidence that momentum in favor of Zionist aspirations extended from Wallace's popular-front leftism to Wagner's New Deal liberalism to Taft's no-longer-isolationist conservatism. By March 1944, in reaction to reports about the ongoing war in Europe and the Middle East and to news of persistent Nazi efforts to murder Europe's Jews, a broad spectrum of support for Zionist aspirations had emerged among very significant figures across a broad spectrum in American politics.

The bipartisan support for Zionist aspirations was evident in the platforms of the Democratic and Republican parties in summer 1944. Issued on June 27, the Republican Party platform included a plank calling for "the opening of Palestine to their [the Jews'] unrestricted immigration and land ownership" so that "Palestine may be constituted as a free and democratic commonwealth."[22] The Democratic Party's platform, announced on July 19, went even further: "We favor the opening of Palestine to unrestricted Jewish immigration and colonization, and such a policy as to result in the establishment there of a free and democratic Jewish commonwealth."[23] The Democratic platform associated support for Zionist aspirations with the passions of World War II. It asserted, for example, that "the primary and imperative duty of the United States is to wage the war with every resource available to final triumph over our enemies, and we pledge that we will continue to fight side by side with the United Nations until this supreme objective shall have been attained

[21] Ibid., 2–3.
[22] "Excerpt from the Platform of the Republican Party, Palestine" (June 27, 1944), Robert F. Wagner Papers, Box PA 732.
[23] "The Democratic Party Platform 1944," in the American Presidency Project: www.presidency.ucsb.edu/documents/1944-democratic-party-platform.

and thereafter to secure a just and lasting peace." The term "United Nations" in the document referred both to the wartime coalition and to intentions to establish an international organization that "must be endowed with power to employ armed forces when necessary to prevent aggression and preserve peace."[24] According to their platform, the Democrats viewed the establishment of a Jewish state in Palestine as a logical consequence of Allied victory over Nazism and fascism (a victory that was still many months off) and envisioned it as part of a peaceful postwar order.

On May 18, 1945, ten days after Nazi Germany surrendered, Wagner and Taft collaborated again in support of Zionist aspirations. They co-signed letters to members of the Senate and House of Representatives asking them to sign a letter to be sent to President Truman. It urged that "immediate steps be taken to open Palestine to Jewish immigration and pave the way for a democratic Jewish Commonwealth." On July 2, 1945 fifty-four Senators and 261 members of the House of Representatives agreed to sign the following statement:[25]

The story of the monstrous atrocities perpetrated by the Nazis needs no repetition. The Jewish people were deliberately singled out for wholesale annihilation, and in this suffered beyond all other peoples. Civilization owes it to the Jewish people to see that the great work of reconstituting Palestine as the Jewish Commonwealth initiated at the end of the last war, with the endorsement of the League of Nations and of our Government and people, is brought to a successful conclusion.[26]

The statement reminded Truman that every president since Woodrow Wilson had reaffirmed US support for "the restoration of the Jewish National Home." Congress had endorsed the policy in 1922, and both major political parties did so as well in summer 1944. The legislatures of thirty-three states, representing 85 percent of the American population, adopted resolutions "in support of Jewish aspirations in Palestine."[27] All efforts to find refuge for the Jews of Europe had "been fruitless." It recalled the Jews' "single-minded devotion to the Allied cause, and their contribution of blood and toil which in Palestine" was "out of all proportion to their number," and which constituted "an outstanding chapter in the history of our common struggle." Now that the war in Europe was over, they urged that "all powers of our Government be exerted toward

---

[24] Ibid.

[25] Robert F. Wagner and Robert A. Taft, "Dear Senator," Washington (May 18, 1945), Robert F. Wagner Papers, Box PA 733.

[26] Members of the United States Senate and the House of Representatives to President Truman, Washington (July 2, 1945), Robert F. Wagner Papers, Box PA 733, 1–4.

[27] Ibid.

the immediate fulfillment of that policy to which America is so deeply committed." Doing so entailed using the president's influence with Britain "to open forthwith the doors of Palestine to unrestricted Jewish immigration and colonization" and to urge "all interested governments to join with the United States toward the end of establishing Palestine as a free and democratic Jewish Commonwealth at the earliest possible time."[28]

Upon entering office in July 1945, the Labour government in Britain reversed the party's pro-Zionist policy, which had been adopted only a year earlier. As prime minister Clement Attlee and foreign secretary Ernest Bevin had agreed to end Britain's imperial position in India, they, and Bevin in particular, were determined to preserve British influence in the Middle East, hopefully through what the historian of the British Empire William Roger Louis called a grand strategy of non-intervention and conciliation, primarily with the existing Arab regimes.[29] Bevin believed that the issue of Jewish refugees in Europe should be solved by their reintegration into European society, and thus be separated from the future of Palestine. In his view, and in the view of the dominant thinkers in the British Foreign Office and Colonial Office, a Jewish state in Palestine would antagonize the Arabs and lead to a decline in British influence in the region. American liberals reacted with anger to Attlee and Bevin's decision to place a left-of-center British government on the side of British imperialism and against Zionist aspirations.

Wagner became one of Bevin's leading American critics. On September 11, 1945 Wagner spoke on WTOP, the CBS radio affiliate in Washington, DC, on "Palestine – England's Responsibility and Ours."[30] He began by recalling the Nazi persecution and extermination of the Jews of Europe, noting their contributions "out of all proportion to their numbers, to medicine, to science, to literature, and to the ethical foundations of our religion and our laws. Though they are regarded as a people of the East, they are in the stream of Western civilization – and our Western culture would never have been the same without their contribution ... The whole world" was "irretrievably the loser because of the literal wiping out of so large a portion of the Jews ... In view of the disasters which the Jews have suffered, in view of what this means to all the free people of the world, the free peoples of the world owe <u>themselves</u>

---

[28] Ibid., 2–4.

[29] William Roger Louis, *The British Empire in the Middle East, 1945–1951: Arab Nationalism, the United States, and British Imperialism* (New York: Oxford University Press, 1984), 3.

[30] Robert F. Wagner, "'Palestine – England's Responsibility and Ours': Senator Robert F. Wagner (D-N.Y.) Demands U.S. Resolution on Palestine Problem Washington" (September 11, 1945), Robert F. Wagner Papers, Box PA 733.

an obligation to seek the maximum of justice for the Jews."[31] The attack on the Jews had dealt a heavy blow to the Western, and thus Christian, civilization to which the Jews had made such a central contribution.

Now that the war had been won, there was "no longer any expediency, no longer any political necessity, to justify the continuation of the British breach of faith" with the promises of the Balfour Declaration. Wagner asserted that "as surely as there is a tide in world affairs, Britain will suffer if her present policies toward Palestine continue – because these present policies do not commend themselves to the century of the common man." The British would strengthen their place in world affairs by "reverting to the Balfour Declaration" promise, "bringing it up to date, and carrying it forward" by "immediately" taking steps so that Palestine "may be the kind of Jewish homeland which the Jews have worked and sacrificed to make it."[32] With Attlee and Bevin's policy change in mind, Wagner called Britain's turn away from the Balfour Declaration a continuation of an old policy of colonialism and power politics. Conversely, his support for a Jewish state in Palestine perpetuated FDR's legacy. "The spirit in which Roosevelt mobilized the conscience of the world must be continued ... We have an obligation toward Palestine that must be paid in full, and it must be met now."[33] Zionism, for Wagner, was simultaneously a moral obligation on those who acknowledged Nazism's assault on the Jews as an attack on Western civilization and on Christianity and a continuation of the liberalism of the New Deal and Roosevelt's wartime leadership. Wartime antifascism and postwar support for Zionism reinforced one another.

Drawing on these arguments, Wagner, together with Taft and Senator David Walsh (D-MA), introduced a bipartisan resolution in Congress on October 26, 1945. The text asserted that "the ruthless persecution of the Jewish people in Europe had demonstrated the need for a Jewish home-land as a haven for the large number who have become homeless as a result of persecution" and supported Truman's "request for the imme-diate right of entry of one hundred thousand refugees" into Palestine.[34] The United States should support "free entry of Jews into that country" so that they could "reconstitute Palestine as a free and democratic com-monwealth in which all men, regardless of race or creed, shall enjoy equal rights."[35] The following week Wagner returned to his criticisms of British policy in a speech to a dinner of the International Christian Conference for Palestine at the Statler. "The infamy" of the British government's repudiation of the Balfour Declaration promise "now hangs over the

---

[31] Ibid., 2.   [32] Ibid., 2–3.   [33] Ibid., 4.
[34] Joint Resolution, S.J. Res. 112, In the Senate of the United States (October 22, 1945), Robert F. Wagner Papers, Box PA 733, 1–2.
[35] Ibid.

foreign policy of the Attlee government of 1945."[36] Oil concessions and Arab threats were responsible for the policy reversal. With the Anglo-American Committee of Inquiry (AACI) about to begin its work, Wagner dismissed the need for more commissions of inquiry. "Are not the death of 5,700,000 men, women and children conclusive proof of the necessity for a Jewish homeland?" He referred to the report by Earl Harrison to President Truman that documented "the misery and want of the shattered remnants of European Jewry."[37] The British government's "temporary and narrow considerations of imperialist expediency are unworthy of the British people." Wagner acknowledged that "all mankind" owed a debt to the British, who "stood alone against the Nazi hordes," while lamenting that Britain's "failure" since the end of the war "to repudiate the Chamberlain White Paper has shocked American public opinion."[38]

Wagner viewed Arab opposition to Zionist aspirations as due "largely to the manipulation of British foreign and colonial affairs." Wagner asserted that the Arabs owed their development to the Great Powers. "We must not forget that following World War I, the Arabs received virtually one million square miles – while the Jews were given that small dot on the map we call Palestine."[39] The future of Palestine had become "a testing ground of British good faith. For our sake and theirs," he hoped that "the British will thrust aside the fatal policy of appeasement." Wagner compared British and French appeasement in Munich in 1938 to British efforts to appease the Arabs after the war. Instead, Britain and the United States should affirm the "original purpose and intent of the Balfour Declaration and the Palestine Mandate ... abrogate all restrictions on immigration and colonization on the land ... [and] assist in the reconstruction of Palestine, as a free and democratic commonwealth in which all men regardless of race or creed shall enjoy equal rights." Doing so was "to obey the dictates of common decency," make good on past pledges, and refuse to repeat "the errors of the past."[40]

Critics of the Wagner–Taft Resolution denounced the Zionist project as an effort to establish a theocratic state. On December 6 Wagner and Taft wrote to Truman that their opponents had made "the astounding and baseless charge" that their Joint Resolution proposed to establish a "'theocratic' state based upon religious or racial discrimination."[41]

[36] Robert F. Wagner, "Address of Robert F. Wagner at the Dinner of the International Christian Conference for Palestine, Hotel Statler, Washington, D.C., November 2, 1945, Broadcast on ABC Network" (November 2, 1945), Robert F. Wagner Papers, Box PA 733, 2.

[37] Ibid. [38] Ibid., 2. [39] Ibid. [40] Ibid., 3.

[41] Robert F. Wagner and Robert A. Taft, "Text of Letter to President Truman From Senators Taft and Wagner," Washington (December 6, 1945), Robert F. Wagner Papers, Box PA 733, 1; "Zionism Traduced, Wagner, Taft Aver: Letter to Truman

Zionism did not envisage a theocracy but rather a "democratic state in which complete equality of rights and status shall obtain between all citizens, irrespective of race or faith, and between all religious groups within the state." A "Jewish Commonwealth" did not imply "any domination of the Jewish religion over the adherence of other faiths."[42] On December 17, 1945 Wagner and Taft won an overwhelming majority in the Senate in favor of their Joint Resolution.[43] From then on until the establishment of the state of Israel in May 1948, bipartisan Congressional support for Zionist aspirations remained intact, thus making it more difficult for Zionism's opponents to depict it as a vehicle for Soviet and communist influence in the Middle East. While the most passionate support for the Zionist cause lay in the Democratic Party, support from a significant sector of the Republican Party, the party of big business and conservative anticommunism, complicated efforts to associate Zionism with communism.

The issue of the prosecution of Arab leaders who collaborated with the Nazis played an important role in fostering momentum in the United States in support of the Zionist project. This was the case because Haj Amin al-Husseini (1895–1974), the Arab leader who sought to return to Palestine in order to spearhead opposition to founding a Jewish state there, had been a very prominent and famous collaborator. The possibility that "the Mufti," as the American press called him, might return to Palestine a free man enraged American liberals. Emanuel Celler led efforts in Congress to focus attention on the Husseini case. Celler, like Wagner, had been a leading supporter of the New Deal and a critic of the racist aspects of American immigration law. He also became one, if not the leading and most effective, of the advocates of Zionist aspirations in the House during the crucial years between 1945 and 1949. On March 22, 1945 the House of Representatives and Senate passed Concurrent Resolution 93. Celler was its primary sponsor.[44] The resolution called for the US government to appoint a commission to work with the already established United Nations War Crimes Commission (UNWCC) to prepare for "the punishment of war criminals of the Axis countries." War criminals were to be punished "regardless of whether their crimes have been against persons who are or were subjects of the

Protests Declarations that Racial or Religious Bias Is Aim," *New York Times*, December 8, 1945, 4.

[42] Wagner and Taft, "Text of Letter to President Truman," 3.

[43] Anthony Leviero, "Senate Vote Urges Opening Palestine: One-Sided Ballot Is Rebuff to Truman – Resolution Favors Free Entry, Commonwealth," *New York Times*, December 18, 1945, 1.

[44] See Emanuel Celler, *You Never Leave Brooklyn: The Autobiography of Emanuel Celler* (New York: John Day, 1953).

Axis nations, and regardless of whether such crimes were committed within the territory of the United Nations or that of the Axis countries."[45] American planning for a war crimes trial was understandably focused on the leaders and officials of the Axis powers. Celler, concerned that Husseini and other collaborators would escape judicial reckoning, urged a policy that would extend indictments beyond nationals of Germany, Italy, and Japan, to those of European and non-European collaborators.[46]

In hearings before the House Committee on Foreign Affairs, Celler asked what the US attitude would be "toward neutral countries who reserve the right to grant asylum to escaping war criminals." He noted that King Ibn Saud (1875–1953) of Saudi Arabia had "requested that the zone of holy shrines be declared neutral . . . If such a condition is accepted, Moslem war criminals like the Grand Mufti of Jerusalem, who at the present time, as a stooge for Hitler, is conferring in Berlin, can escape into these 'zones' and receive asylum therein."[47] Haj Amin al-Husseini was familiar to Americans as a result of his wartime radio broadcasts in support of the Nazis, sections of which were reported in the American press.[48] Celler declared that the work of the United Nations War Crimes Commission, a body that took its name from that of the anti-Axis coalition, had "been hamstrung by the British Foreign Office and/or by our State Department." The British government had turned back requests from a UNWCC official to include "Grand Mufti of Jerusalem" among those to be brought to trial.[49]

---

[45] House Joint Resolution 93, "Punishment of War Criminals: Hearings Before the Committee on Foreign Affairs, House of Representatives, Seventy-Ninth Congress, First Session on H. J. Res. 93" (March 22, 1945) (Washington, DC: US Government Printing Office, 1945).

[46] As was noted at the time, and as historians have documented in depth, the non-indictment of Husseini was only one chapter in the immediate postwar years of failure to bring Nazi collaborators to justice. Indeed, the United States recruited East Europeans in the early Cold War even though they included Nazi collaborators. On this see David Nasaw, *The Last Million: Europe's Displaced Persons from World War to Cold War* (New York: Penguin, 2020), 468–478 and 511–532; Richard Breitman and Norman J. W. Goda, eds., *U.S. Intelligence and the Nazis* (New York: Cambridge University Press, 2005).

[47] Emanuel Celler, "Punishment of War Criminals: Hearings Before the Committee on Foreign Affairs, House of Representatives, Seventy-Ninth Congress, First Session on H. J. Res. 93" (March 22, 1945) (Washington, DC: US Government Printing Office, 1945), 2–3.

[48] On Husseini's wartime collaboration with Nazi Germany see Jeffrey Herf, *Nazi Propaganda for the Arab World* (New Haven: Yale University Press, 2009); Klaus Gensicke, *The Mufti of Jerusalem and the Nazis: The Berlin Years* (London: Vallentine, 2014); and Joseph Schechtman, *The Mufti and the Führer: The Rise and Fall of Haj Amin el Husseini* (New York: T. Yoseloff, 1965).

[49] Celler, "Punishment of War Criminals," 4.

In spring 1945 Celler was not alone in thinking about the possibility of bringing Arab collaborators to trial. That June, American officials involved in planning the war crimes trials addressed the issue of whether to bring Husseini and other Arab Nazi collaborators to trial. On June 7, 1945 Supreme Court justice Robert Jackson (1892–1954), who had been appointed by President Truman to be chief counsel for the United States at the International Military Tribunal in Nuremberg, wrote to William Donovan (1883–1959), director of the Office of Strategic Services (OSS). He informed him that the prosecution team preparing the International Military Tribunal in Nuremberg prosecutors would work with the OSS "in all respects in preparing for the prosecution of the major European Axis criminals" including the "collection, evaluation, integration and presentation of evidence of all types."[50] On June 23, 1945 Donovan sent Jackson "On the Near East and the War Crimes Problem," a twenty-eight-page summary of OSS intelligence about pro-Axis activities and persons in Egypt, Iraq, Palestine, Iran, and Afghanistan; their collaboration with the Nazis; and the OSS assessment of the popular attitude in those countries toward putting those individuals on trial for war crimes.[51] It concluded: "In the Near East the popular attitude toward the trial of war criminals is one of apathy. As a result of the general Near Eastern feeling of hostility to the imperialism of certain of the Allied powers, there is a tendency to sympathize with rather than condemn those who have aided the axis." The OSS analysts were blunt about the political issues involved. In view of the anticipated postwar "inter-Allied rivalry in the area, the past and potential political usefulness of most, if not all, of the Near Eastern supporters of the Axis will preclude their trial as war criminals." In the context of "inter-Allied rivalry," "potential political usefulness" meant that US intelligence agencies might desire to use Arab former Nazi

---

[50] Robert Jackson to William Donovan, Washington (June 7, 1945), Papers of Robert H. Jackson, Library of Congress, Manuscript Division (hereafter LC Robert H. Jackson Papers), "Nuremberg War Crimes Trial, Office Files – U.S. Chief of Consul, Donovan, William J," Container 101, Reel 7. On the role of the OSS in assisting the conceptualization and fact finding of the IMT in Nuremberg see Kim Christian Priemel, *The Betrayal: The Nuremberg Trials and German Divergence* (Oxford: Oxford University Press, 2016).

[51] On "The Near East and the War Crimes Problem" see discussion in Herf, *Nazi Propaganda for the Arab World*, 233–238; and "'Near East and the War Crimes Problem': Office of Strategic Services, Research and Analysis Branch, R and A, No. 1090.116 23 June 1945, Situation Report: Near East, Analysis of Current Intelligence for the Use of OSS," 1–28, in United States National Archives in College Park (hereafter NACP), Record Group 84 Records of the Foreign Service Posts of the Department of State (hereafter RG 84), Syria: Damascus Legation, Confidential File, 1945, vol. 2, 711–800B, Classified General Records, Box 4.

collaborators in the event of rivalry with the Soviet Union in the Middle East.[52]

The OSS report assessed that "popular feeling against these people has never been strong," since they were regarded as "working for the freeing of their respective countries from British or French overlordship and the local population has had no direct experience with German occupation methods."[53] There was an "absence" of "popular pressure" in favor of prosecuting war crimes. The "political considerations" of both "local governments and the great powers" also led to opposition. Hence "the Near Eastern Axis collaborators will for the most part go unpunished and in so far as they have not already done so, will eventually return to the political life of their respective countries."[54] Conversely, efforts to put them on trial and reveal details of their Nazi collaboration would run up against opposition in a region that did not regard such collaboration with a revulsion equivalent to that common in the United States. These views would persist in American policy over the next several years.

In addition to the OSS report to Jackson, leaders of the State Department had access to the voluminous "Axis Broadcasts in Arabic" reports produced by the staff of the American Embassy in wartime Cairo.[55] Two US ambassadors to Egypt, Alexander Kirk (1941–4) and Pinckney Tuck (1944–5), had overseen this very significant project, and both continued to serve in the State Department. Beginning in 1941 and on a weekly basis from 1942 to the end of the war, "Axis Broadcasts in English," verbatim English translations of Nazi Germany's Arabic-language radio broadcasts to North Africa and the Middle East, were sent from the Cairo Embassy to the Office of the Secretary of State in Washington. The reports were then circulated throughout the relevant offices at the top levels of the State Department. They constituted a detailed record of radical antisemitism, anti-Zionism, enthusiasm for Nazism, hatred of the Allies, and open appeals for murderous violence against Jews. The broadcasts included a number that were specifically delivered by Haj

---

[52] On this see Breitman and Goda, eds., *U.S. Intelligence and the Nazis*; and Breitman and Norman Goda, *Hitler's Shadow: Nazi War Criminals, U.S. Intelligence, and the Cold War* (Washington: Military Bookshop, 2010).

[53] Cited in Herf, *Nazi Propaganda for the Arab World*, 234.   [54] Ibid.

[55] On the "Axis Broadcasts in Arabic" and US government files on Husseini see Herf, *Nazi Propaganda for the Arab World*; and Jeffrey Herf, "Haj Amin el-Husseini, the Nazis and the Holocaust: The Origins, Nature and Aftereffects of Collaboration," *Jewish Political Studies Review* 26, nos. 3–4 (2016): http://jcpa.org/article/haj-amin-al-husseini-the-nazis-and-the-holocaust-the-origins-nature-and-aftereffects-of-collaboration/.

Amin al-Husseini.[56] Husseini was intimately involved in the planning of the propaganda campaign.

When Husseini was in French custody from the time of his arrest by French occupation forces in May 1945 to his flight from France in May 1946, the United States, Britain, and France had the opportunity to indict him for war crimes. Yet neither in that year nor after he returned to political prominence in 1946 in Egypt and Palestine did the State Department reveal or publish selections from "Axis Broadcasts in Arabic"; nor did it urge that Husseini be put on trial for actions for which German Nazis, notably Reich press chief Otto Dietrich, were tried and convicted in Nuremberg.[57] During that important year the State Department did not use these or other documents to support his indictment or undermine his effort to revive his postwar political career in Palestine, even after he assumed a leading role as chair of the Arab Higher Committee. As we will see, Britain and France also refused to indict him for broadly similar reasons – that is, not to offend Arab opinion, to protect access to oil, and to maintain a military and economic presence in the Middle East. The Americans, and the British in particular, had extensive files on his wartime activities. The three Western Allied powers refrained from a public refutation of the apologetic and false testimony of Haj Amin's cousin, Jamal Husseini, before the AACI on March 12, 1946.[58] Incredibly, Jamal Husseini asserted that Haj Amin had not really collaborated with the Nazis but "was only seeking to get something out of them in case they were victorious," and was solely concerned "for the interests of his people who had no direct interest" in the "controversy" – that is, World War II. As J. C. Hurewitz, who had worked in the OSS, observed in 1950, if the British authorities in Palestine "did not elect to mete out punishment to the Mufti, his followers could hardly have been expected to do less than demand his recall ... The Mufti's reputation among the Palestine Arabs was now greater than at any time since his presidency of the first Higher Committee in 1936–37."[59]

The British, American, and also, as we shall see, French refusal to call Husseini to account for his actions in Nazi Germany represented a serious lost opportunity to foster peace and compromise in Palestine. By doing so they eased his path to remaking himself from "Nazi collaborator" to

---

[56] See for example, Haj Amin el-Husseini, "The Protests of Moslems of Europe against the Balfour Declaration," cited in Herf, *Nazi Propaganda for the Arab World*, 185–188.

[57] On the trial of Otto Dietrich in the Nuremberg Military Tribunal "successor trials" see Herf, *The Jewish Enemy*, 272–274.

[58] See discussion in J. C. Hurewitz, *The Struggle for Palestine* (New York: W. W. Norton, 1950; repr. Greenwood Press, 1968), 252.

[59] Ibid.

a symbol of the Arab struggle against Zionism, imperialism, and the West. The inclination to displace the history of actual collaboration with narratives of national heroism and resistance was an important aspect of political culture in the immediate postwar years in Europe, one that contributed to the rapid shift of alliances, passions, and mentalities from those of the wartime antifascism of the anti-Hitler coalition to those of the emergent Cold War.[60] That same shift, exacerbated by desires to curry favor with the Arab states and the Palestine Arabs, made it possible for the Mufti to offer apologetics for his Nazi years and play an important political role without having to break with the racist and antisemitic beliefs he had expressed in the 1930s, which aroused the Nazis' interest in his political efforts, and which led to his famous and consequential years of collaboration with Hitler from 1941 to 1945.

In summer 1945 Peter Bergson of the Hebrew Committee for National Liberation, an American organization supporting the Irgun in Palestine, wrote to H. V. Evatt, Australia's foreign minister and member of the UNWCC, and to the government of Yugoslavia, urging both to bring Husseini to trial. Copies of the memo are in the files of Green H. Hackworth, the State Department's legal advisor. Summarizing what he called "the principal crimes instigated and committed by the ex-Grand Mufti of Jerusalem, Haj Amin al-Husseini" in Berlin as well as "on the territory of Yugoslavia," he asked the Yugoslav government and the UNWCC to place him on the latter's list of war criminals. On July 5 Yugoslavia informed Hackworth that it had done so.[61] The Yugoslav decision offered Britain, France, and the United States an opportunity to seize the moment to investigate him further.

Bergson, with his ties to the Irgun, was not an effective messenger to the US government. The State Department kept him at a distance. It was, however, willing to meet with mainstream Zionist representatives. On August 17, 1945 Loy Henderson, director of the State Department's Near East and Africa Division and a vigorous opponent of Zionist aspirations, chaired a meeting with Eliahu Epstein (1903–90), the head of the Jewish Agency's political office in Washington, and Benjamin Akzin

---

[60] On narratives of national resistance in postwar Europe that obscured the extent of collaboration see Tony Judt, *Postwar: A History of Europe since 1945* (New York: Penguin, 2006). On the Low Countries see Pieter Lagrou, *The Legacy of Nazi Occupation: Patriotic Memory and National Recovery in Western Europe, 1945–1965* (Cambridge and New York: Cambridge University Press, 2007). On France see Henry Rousso, *The Vichy Syndrome* (Cambridge, MA: Harvard University Press, 1991).

[61] Peter H. Bergson to H. V. Evatt, Minister of Foreign Affairs, Australia, Washington (July 28, 1945), NACP RG 59, General Records of the Department of State, Records of the Legal Adviser Relating to War Crimes, 21. War Crimes – Jewish Atrocities, [Lot File No. 61D 33] Records Relating to German War Crimes, 1942–1946, Box 4.

(1904–85), political advisor to the American Zionist Emergency Council (AZEC), one of the leading umbrella organizations supporting Zionist aspirations.[62] Akzin asked if the State Department "had any information regarding the whereabouts of the Mufti, as it was rumored that the French authorities were reluctant to hand the Mufti over to the British." He observed that "the Mufti had been placed on the list of war criminals by the Yugoslav Government" and asked what the US policy was. Henderson replied that the United States had taken no position on the Mufti "since [his] Palestinian nationality would make him a primary responsibility of the British Government." Akzin said that the Zionists were concerned because "they had 'evidence' that it was the Mufti who was originally and directly responsible for the slaughter by the Nazis of 7,000,000 Jews. Perhaps if the French Government were to be told that opinion in this country was strongly in favor of classing [sic: classifying] the Mufti as a war criminal, the French would expedite the turning over of the Mufti to the British." Though Husseini was not "originally and directly" responsible for the Holocaust, the State Department had enough incriminating evidence in its files to charge him with crimes against humanity, an indictment that would have led to further investigations to assess the extent of his collaboration with the Nazis. Instead, the State Department legal experts replied that since Husseini was not an Axis (German, Italian, or Japanese) national, he would not be subject to prosecution for war crimes.[63]

AZEC persisted in its efforts to see that Husseini would be prosecuted for war crimes. On December 13, 1945 Rabbi Stephen Wise (1874–1949), president of the World Jewish Congress and co-chair of AZEC, sent

---

[62] "Memorandum of Conversation," Washington (August 17, 1945), "Palestine," NACP RG 59, Records of the Legal Adviser Relating to War Crimes, 21. War Crimes – Jewish Atrocities, [Lot File No. 61D 33], Box 4. Epstein became the first Israeli ambassador to the United States and, following a diplomatic career, was the president of Hebrew University from 1962 to 1968: https://en.wikipedia.org/wiki/Eliahu_Eilat; Benjamin Akzin was a graduate of Harvard Law School, served on the US War Refugee Board during World War II, and was political advisor to AZEC from 1945 to 1947. He emigrated to Israel in 1949, where he became a professor at the Law School of the Hebrew University and founded its Department of Political Science in the 1950s, which he chaired until the early 1960s. He then went on to become a founder of the University of Haifa in 1963: https://en.wikipedia.org/wiki/Benjamin_Akzin. AZEC, formed during World War II, was the precursor to the American Israel Public Affairs Committee. See Daniel H. Shapiro, *From Philanthropy to Activism: The Political Transformation of American Zionism in the Holocaust Years, 1933–1945* (New York and Oxford: Pergamon Press, 1994); and Walter Hixson, *Israel's Armor: The Israel Lobby and the First Generation of the Palestine Conflict* (New York: Cambridge University Press, 2019).

[63] On postwar trials outside Germany see Istvan Deak, Jan T. Gross, and Tony Judt, eds., *The Politics of Retribution in Europe: World War II and Its Aftermath* (Princeton: Princeton University Press, 2000).

a lengthy memorandum dated the day before to secretary of state James Byrnes concerning Husseini.[64] The memorandum included some errors about the Mufti's activities, but on the whole offered considerable detail that scholars subsequently confirmed about the extent and nature of his collaboration with the Nazi regime. It could have been a sound basis for opening an inquiry into whether Husseini should be indicted for war crimes or crimes against humanity. The memo was handled in the office of the department's legal advisor, Green Hackworth.

Wise's memo expressed concern over the Arab League's efforts to bring about Husseini's "exoneration from his crimes" and "even his eventual re-instatement in a position of power and influence in Palestine or elsewhere in the Middle East." As he had been "the chief instigator of all the anti-Jewish pogroms and disturbances in Palestine for a period of twenty years, these efforts have aroused the utmost concern."[65] The AZEC memo accurately stated that "the Mufti became the supreme leader of all the fascists and pro-Axis forces in the Middle East. Following the pattern adopted later by Hitler in Europe, Amin el Husseini directed his first attacks against the Jews, while he prepared himself for the future onslaught on Britain and British influence in the Middle East."[66] It was correct as well in pointing out that he had "organized anti-Jewish pogroms in Palestine in 1920, 1929, 1933 and 1936–1939." To "establish his domination over the entire Arab population of Palestine, he employed intimidation and murder against his political opponents among the Arabs." The memo referred to a newspaper report in Cairo of March 2, 1939 listing the names of twenty-four Arab "political and spiritual leaders" and an additional nine family members "murdered by the Mufti's gangsters up to 1939."[67] It cited a 1942 article in *Foreign Affairs* by C. L. Sulzberger, then foreign correspondent for the *New York Times*, on Husseini's pro-Axis activities in Syria in 1937, his welcome in Iraq, and financial support from Arab governments, Nazi Germany, and Fascist Italy.[68] Wise recalled Husseini's role in the pro-Axis government of Rashid Ali Kilani in Iraq, suppression of that government by the British, his escape to Iran, and then to Fascist Italy and Nazi Germany.

Wise and his fellow authors presented the following account of Husseini's collaboration with the Nazis. He advised Hitler and

---

[64] American Zionist Emergency Council, "Memorandum Submitted to the Secretary of State" (December 12, 1945), NACP RG 59, Records of the Legal Adviser Relating to War Crimes, 21. War Crimes – Jewish Atrocities, [Lot File No. 61D 33], Box 4.
[65] Ibid.   [66] Ibid., 2.   [67] Ibid.
[68] See C. L. Sulzberger, "German Preparations for the Middle East," *Foreign Affairs* 20, no. 4 (July 1942): 663–678.

Mussolini on Arab and Muslim affairs, urged Arabs and Muslims to join the Axis powers in World War II, and mobilized Muslims in Bosnia into a "special Moslem Mountain Divisions forming part of the S.S." He "employed terror against those who refused to join the Wehrmacht." Under his "instigation and under his management" many "Yugoslavs were killed in cold blood."[69] The AZEC memo quoted a telegram Husseini sent to Hitler on June 4, 1942:

Allow me, Fuehrer, to express to you the sincere joy of the Arabian people and my best wishes on the occasion of the Axis victory in North Africa. These successes were crowned by the solemn declarations of the German and Italian Governments, in which the sovereignty and independence of Egypt were recognized and assured. These wise policies of the Axis powers, which guided the German-Italian armies from victory to victory, will produced a very good echo not only in Egypt but also in all the other Arab lands and the entire Orient, for they offer the best proof of the noble aims of the Axis governments and assure the other Arab lands of their liberty and independence. The Arab people will further continue to fight on your side against the common enemy up to ultimate victory.[70]

Hitler replied to express "his heartfelt thanks for your friendly congratulations."[71]

Given Husseini's wartime record, the AZEC authors wrote, "there was little doubt" that after the democracies won the war "he would be included among the leading war criminals to be punished by the Allies. However, for mysterious reasons his name does not appear on the list of war criminals." Referring to the previously mentioned statement of the Yugoslav government, the memo noted, "here we have the first official confirmation of the fact that the crimes of the ex-Mufti have been made the subject of behind-the-scenes political negotiations. Influences are at work to have Amin el Husseini whitewashed and eventually returned to the Middle East, there once again to become the main instrument of anti-Jewish intrigues and activities."[72] The French government was treating him "with utmost consideration," supplying him "with every comfort" while it facilitated his correspondence with Arab leaders in

[69] American Zionist Emergency Council, "Memorandum Submitted to the Secretary of State" (December 12, 1945), 6–7. On Husseini in the Balkans during World War II see most recently David Motadel, *Islam and Nazi Germany's War* (Cambridge, MA: Harvard University Press, 2014).

[70] American Zionist Emergency Council, "Memorandum Submitted to the Secretary of State," 7. The memo did not indicate how the AZEC authors received this and other documents.

[71] Ibid., 7–8. Husseini made similar remarks when he met Hitler in person in Berlin on November 28, 1941. See Herf, *Nazi Propaganda for the Arab World*, 76–77.

[72] American Zionist Emergency Council, "Memorandum Submitted to the Secretary of State," 8.

the Middle East. The Arab League and other Arab associations, which "didn't dare to bring up the question of the Mufti because of his obvious involvement with the Axis, now openly demand his return to power." There were reports that a delegation from Palestine and Egypt traveled to France "in order to negotiate secretly either the official release of the ex-Mufti or his escape to the Middle East with the acquiescence of the French authorities."[73] As we will see, the AZEC authors were well informed about the broad outlines of Husseini's relations with the French government.

Wise and his fellow AZEC authors understood that the governments concerned were not showing much interest in bringing Husseini to account. The December 12 memo concluded that it was "difficult reasonably to explain" the "extraordinary indulgence" toward Husseini by various parties "without analyzing the motives of the governments concerned." The British government, "having apparently learned nothing from past lessons" regarding its early indulging of Husseini, seemed to "be taking the lead in refusing to indict the former Mufti either as a traitor or as a war criminal." It was "using its influence also to prevent other governments from indicting him" and appeared "to be preparing the ground to enable Amin el Husseini once again to play an active political part." The French government, "deeply resentful as it is of Great Britain's part in the Syrian-Lebanese affair, regards the ex-Mufti as a possible anti-British tool in the future and is, therefore, also for its part treating him with kid gloves." The government of Yugoslavia was aware of British and French views. It did not want to further "complicate its already uneasy relations with the Western powers" over a question which, from the Yugoslav point of view, was "of relatively minor importance."[74]

Wise and his fellow AZEC authors then drew attention to the importance of the Jews' lack of sovereignty and power to influence events. "The Jewish people" lacked a state and membership in the UN, and was therefore unable to indict Husseini on war crimes charges. "It must depend on the good will of some state which is a member of the United Nations," and on the United States, in particular.[75] They urged the United States "to take the initiative to indict as a war criminal this man who has been a major supporter of the Axis and who is directly involved in the murder of millions of Jews of Europe" and to instruct American representatives on the UNWCC to do so as well.[76] The memorandum concluded by pointing out the consequences of an American and Allied

[73] Ibid., 10–11.   [74] Ibid.   [75] Ibid., 11–12.   [76] Ibid., 12.

failure to indict Husseini or at least to prevent him from returning to political prominence:

In the case of practically all of the Axis criminals [in Germany and Europe] an end has, as far as we know, been put to their ability to cause additional damage in the future and their punishment now appears mainly a matter of just retribution for past crimes. But the ex-Mufti, should he escape punishment and remain a free and ostensibly respectable person, will undoubtedly be in a position to stir up further trouble and to cause more massacres of Jews. It is earnestly hoped that our Government will realize the serious moral responsibility, which in common with other governments, it would share for the loss of human lives and for the other grave consequences which would result from a policy of allowing the Mufti to go unpunished for his past crimes and free to commit new ones. It is urged that the Government of the United States will take its stand accordingly, at the same time drawing the attention of the British and French Governments to responsibilities which they would incur in the eyes of the world and of history should they continue to shield Amin el Husseini.[77]

Hackworth was noncommittal. He forwarded the AZEC memo to (the future senator) Claiborne Pell, the US representative at the UNWCC in London,[78] but accompanied it with a note stating that an unnamed "Chief Research Officer" of the UNWCC had "advised that the ex-Grand Mufti would probably not come within the category of war criminals with which the Commission is concerned." The Yugoslav government had placed him on its list of war criminals, but "no further action is contemplated until the outcome of the current inter-Governmental communications, regarding the possible political implications of the ex-Grand Mufti's arrest, is [sic] known."[79]

On March 22, 1946 Secretary of State Byrnes informed Wise that no charges had been filed against Husseini "by any government with the United Nations War Crimes Commission." It was "the usual practice" of the commission to list as war criminals only those against whom a member government had filed charges with it. Byrnes told Wise that it was American policy to file war crimes charges "only in cases where there is evidence establishing the commission of crimes against American nation-als," an assertion that was contradicted by the American prosecution of the

[77] Ibid., 12–13.
[78] Green H. Hackworth to Dr. Stephen S. Wise, Washington (December 29, 1945) and "To the United States Commissioner on the United Nations Commission for the Investigation of War Crimes, Care of American Embassy, London," NACP RG 59, Records of the Legal Adviser Relating to War Crimes, 21. War Crimes – Jewish Atrocities, [Lot File No. 61D 33], Box 4.
[79] Hackworth to the United States Commissioner on the United Nations Commission for the Investigation of War Crimes, Care of American Embassy, London, Washington (December 29, 1945), NACP RG 59, Records of the Legal Adviser Relating to War Crimes, 21. War Crimes – Jewish Atrocities, [Lot File No. 61D 33], Box 4.

defendants in the Nuremberg trials of German nationals accused of committing war crimes and crimes against humanity primarily against Europeans, that is, non-American citizens.[80]

AZEC's efforts in 1945 did not sway the State Department, but indicting the Mufti became a *cause célèbre* in 1945 and 1946 in the liberal and left-leaning press in New York, including the mass-circulation *New York Post*, the smaller, more leftist daily *PM*, and the flagship journal of the non-communist left, *The Nation*. Under its editor and general manager, T. O. Thackrey, the *Post* advocated a left-liberal opposition to communism. As he put it in an editorial of May 29, 1946, "Communism grows strong on unresolved problems, unemployment, hunger and bankrupt reaction. Chaos is the real appeasement of Communism." He opposed "the tendency to switch away from last year's determination to destroy German heavy industry, and to swing toward the rebuilding of the German state to counter Russian expansionist pressure exerted through the German Communist Party in the eastern zone." Communism could not be checked by "rebuilding a reactionary German state."[81]

Given Thackrey's views that American denazification in Germany was too mild, it was not surprising that the *Post* ran a series of articles about Husseini by journalist Edgar Ansel Mowrer in June 1946. Mowrer had reported from Germany during the 1930s and then worked in the US government's wartime Office of War Information. His series began on June 1, 1946 with "The Rise of Another Mass Murderer – Mufti's Career Rivals Hitler."[82] He was not subtle. Husseini was "a great criminal" who "did more than any other single individual to win the war for the Axis – and nearly succeeded. As an enemy of the United Nations he was surpassed only by Hitler," but only because Hitler's power "surpassed his." His "unbridled extremism of speech" and the violence of his "verbal attack upon the Jews ... soon made him the leading anti-Zionist."[83] A few days later, the *Post*'s front-page subheadline read, "Edgar Ansel Mowrer Reveals: '41 Iraqi Revolt Led by Mufti Near Won War for Hitler." Mowrer mixed hyperbole with a plausible account of the significance of the pro-Axis government in Iraq of Rashid Ali Kilani.[84] Mowrer

---

[80] Secretary of State James F. Byrnes to Stephen Wise, Washington (March 22, 1946 and April 5, 1946), NACP RG 59, Records of the Legal Adviser Relating to War Crimes, 21. War Crimes – Jewish Atrocities, [Lot File No. 61D 33], Box 4.

[81] "What Is Appeasement?" *New York Post*, May 29, 1946.

[82] Edgar Ansel Mowrer, "The Rise of Another Mass Murderer – Mufti's Career Rivals Hitler," *New York Post*, June 1, 1946, 2, Library of Congress [LC], *The New York Post*, microfilm 1348, June 1, 1946 thru June 30, 1946.

[83] Ibid.

[84] "Edgar Ansel Mowrer Reveals: '41 Iraqi Revolt Led by Mufti Near Won War for Hitler," *New York Post*, June 4, 1946, 1–2, LC, microfilm 1348.

argued that if a pro-Axis government had persisted in Iraq, the Nazis could have moved south, seized Middle East oil, and struck a devastating blow to Britain, then fighting alone against the Nazis. In other words, the issue of Arab collaboration and Husseini's role was not an unimportant sideshow in the drama of World War II. Rather, it was one that, if not defeated by a British invasion, could have aided the Axis efforts to win World War II.

The next week, following reports that Husseini had left France and arrived in Egypt, the *Post* led with the headline "Paris Report: French Fire Official who Let Mufti Flee."[85] On June 12 Mowrer asked, "What Was the Mufti's Secret Power That Let Him Escape Trial?"[86] In August 1945, he noted, Yugoslavia placed the Mufti on the UN list of war criminals. "By January 1946, somebody had taken his name off the list. Who?" Mowrer mused that it might have been the Soviet Union, "seeking a card to play in the Middle Eastern game." Or had the British asked the French to refuse Britain's public request for his extradition? He compared French appeasement of Hitler, Mussolini, "and Franco" to its "policy of appeasing the Arabs." Now he surmised that "the Mufti provided a tool" that the French might use "to undermine Anglo-Saxons in the Middle East."[87]

Mowrer's article raised a number of troubling questions about the Mufti. Why were the Allies not indicting Husseini for war crimes? Why was he not indicted as a British traitor or, for that matter, under the Palestinian Criminal Code under the British Mandate? Why would his release from house arrest in Paris suit the British and US governments? Why would they credit his denials that he knew Adolf Eichmann or had any part in the "wholesale slaughter of Jews"? The Mufti was "a notorious liar." "Why was no attempt made to get to the truth? Recently the Chief Gestapo file on the Mufti was found. It is now in the hands of the Americans in Frankfurt. Why has this material not been made public? Is somebody afraid of what Haj Amin might say when he faces his judges?" "On the face of it," he had "committed abominable crimes." It was "against civilized ethics to shoot him without a hearing. It is equally wrong and cowardly to boot – not to bring him to trial."[88]

Mowrer suggested that the Allied prosecution in Nuremberg could indict Husseini as a contributor to crimes against peace, war crimes, and crimes against humanity. "Is the man who spread the war to Iraq to enjoy immunity? Is the rabble-rouser who howled over the international

[85] "Paris Report: French Fire Official who Let Mufti Flee," *New York Post*, June 10, 1946, 1–2, LC, microfilm 1348.

[86] "What Was the Mufti's Secret Power That Let Him Escape Trial?" *New York Post*, June 12, 1946, 21, LC, microfilm 1348.

[87] Ibid.   [88] Ibid.

radio: 'Kill the Jews wherever you find them' not responsible for the 'murder, extermination, enslavement, deportations and other inhumane acts committed against civilian populations before and during the war' – to quote the Nuremberg Number 1?" – that is, the language of the Nuremberg war crimes indictment. Yet when evidence "allegedly implicating the Mufti in the murder of millions of Jews" was presented to the US prosecution staff in Nuremberg led by Supreme Court justice Robert Jackson, they ignored it. "Mr. Jackson, President Truman, Prime Minister Attlee, Marshall Stalin ... this will not do. If Haj Amin el Husseini escapes trial at Nuremberg, then Allied justice is a whore."[89]

Mowrer sought to translate his words into action. The next day he telegraphed Robert Jackson to say that he was publishing "proof – I say proof – Mufti's complicity in and responsibility for murder European Jewry" and was "prepared fly Nurnberg immediately to present conclusive documentary evidence ex-Mufti's complicity."[90] Jackson quickly replied that, in accord with the rules defining the prosecution in Nuremberg, he would be interested in his documentary evidence "if it even remotely incriminates any of the defendants at Nuremberg or the Hitler regime in general," but "if it incriminates only the Mufti, it could not be used in this trial" because the International Military Tribunal had "jurisdiction to try criminals of only European Axis countries. Any change to include Asiatic [defendants] in subsequent proceedings would have to be made in Washington and would require concurrence of all interested powers."[91]

Though stymied in Nuremberg, Mowrer still had access to the *Post*'s readers. That same day, in an article headlined "Official Documents Convict Mufti of Complicity in 6,000,000 Murders," he claimed there was "documentary proof" that Husseini "was party to the murder of nearly six million European Jews," knew about them, and encouraged them. "His chief worry was that some Jews should escape the horrible death by gas or chemicals or burning alive that awaited the rest in Polish slaughter camps like Oswiecim, Treblinka and Maidanek."[92]

---

[89] Ibid.

[90] Edgar Ansel Mowrer to Robert Jackson, New York (June 13, 1946), "Nuremberg War Crimes Trial, Office Files-U.S. Chief of Consul, Grand Mufti of Jerusalem (Haj Amin El-Husseini)," LC, Robert H. Jackson Papers, Nuremberg War Crimes file, Container 102, Reel 8.

[91] Nielsen to SECSTATE, No. 397, Oslo (June 13, 1946), "Following for Edgar Ansel Mowrer New York Post from Justice Jackson," NACP RG 59, Records of the Legal Adviser Relating to War Crimes, 21. War Crimes – Jewish Atrocities, [Lot File No. 61D 33], Box 4. On debates about the prosecution indictment decisions for the IMT in Nuremberg see Priemel, *The Betrayal.*

[92] "Official Documents Convict Mufti of Complicity in 6,000,000 Murders," *New York Post*, June 13, 1946, 2, LC, microfilm 1348.

The proof consisted of a fragment of a telegram from Himmler to Husseini reminding him that Nazism "from the beginning has inscribed on its banner the war against world Jewry." The *Post* also published excerpts from Husseini's letters to the foreign ministers of Hungary, Romania, and Bulgaria about the "necessity of preventing these Jews from leaving your country to Palestine." Instead, he urged that they be sent to Poland, "where they would find themselves under active surveillance." He also told the Bulgarian authorities that refusing to send Jews to Palestine "would accomplish a good and gracious act toward the Arabian people, who will be permanently grateful to you, and you will make friendly relations between Arabs and Bulgarians ever more close."[93]

On June 12, 1946 the press campaign in the *Post* – and as we will see *The Nation* and *PM* – combined with the efforts of Zionist organizations such as AZEC and the American Jewish and local politicians, led to a mass rally at Madison Square Garden that focused on the Mufti (see Figure 2.3). Banners in the hall stated: "Escape for the Nazi Mufti – But no Rescue for Nazi Victims"; "Padlocked by British Imperialism and US State Department"; "The Liberated Jews Still Plead for Liberation"; and "Rescue the Jews from the DP Camps."[94]

Bartley Crum, a member of the Anglo-American Committee of Inquiry on Palestine, who was developing a public role as a lawyer defending leftist causes, told the Madison Square Garden audience that the *Post* was "prepared to offer a $5,000 [over $65,000 in 2019 dollars] award for the Mufti of Jerusalem if he can be found and placed on trial as a war criminal."[95] The reward "depended on whether Justice Jackson at Nuremberg could give assurance the Mufti would be tried." Edgar Mowrer was prepared to fly to Nuremberg "with documents proving the Mufti's war guilt." According to *Post* editor Thackrey, "it was questionable whether any of the powers involved in the Palestine question wanted to find the Mufti of Jerusalem."[96] As of mid-June 1946, despite the existence of this extensive confirming evidence, none of the Allied victors indicated an interest in bringing Husseini to trial while the push to

[93] Ibid.

[94] "Bevin Assailed at Garden Rally, His Speech Is Called Anti-Jewish," *New York Journal Tribune*, June 13, 1946, Robert F. Wagner Papers, Box PA 732.

[95] For his account of the Anglo-American Committee see Bartley Crum, *Behind the Silk Curtain: A Personal Account of Anglo-American Diplomacy in Palestine and the Middle East* (New York: Simon & Schuster, 1947). Also see Patricia Bosworth, *Anything Your Little Heart Desires: An American Family Story* (New York: Touchstone, 1998), a family memoir by his daughter.

[96] "Post Ready to Offer Reward for Bringing Mufti to Trial," *New York Post*, June 14, 1946, 2, LC, microfilm 1348.

Figure 2.3 Mass demonstration, sponsored by American Zionist Emergency Council and American Jewish Conference, Madison Square Garden, New York City, June 12, 1946. Banners state: "Are the Four Freedoms for all but the Jews?" and "Escape for the Nazi Mufti, but no rescue for the Nazi victims." Source: Robert F. Wagner Papers: Palestine Files, Georgetown University, Booth Family Center for Special Collections, digital photo by author.

do so was now associated both with Zionists and liberals and leftists in New York.

The plight of Jewish survivors of the Holocaust languishing in displaced-persons camps in Germany and Austria became another, probably even more important, source of momentum in favor of Zionist aspirations. In summer 1945, in response to public concern, President Truman had sent Earl Harrison, dean of the University of Pennsylvania Law School, to Europe to examine the conditions of Jews in these camps. Harrison's report, delivered to Truman at the end of August, offered a powerful account of the Jews' continued suffering and contributed to Truman's decision to urge Britain to allow 100,000 Jews to emigrate to Palestine.[97] In response, Foreign Secretary Bevin proposed an Anglo-American committee. Bevin and the British Foreign Office expected that Americans would agree that the territory of Palestine was too small to provide a solution to the problem of Jewish refugees in Europe and would support a binational state there.[98] That November the United States agreed with Britain to establish the Anglo-American Committee of Inquiry into the Problems of European Jewry and Palestine.

With the findings of the Harrison report fresh in his mind, Truman insisted that the committee connect the refugee issue to that of the future of Jews in Palestine.[99] The committee, composed of six Americans and six Britons, was "to examine the position of Jews in those countries in Europe where they have been the victims of Nazi and Fascist persecution, and the practical measures taken or contemplated to be taken in those countries to enable them to live free from discrimination and oppression and to make estimates of those who wish or will be impelled by their conditions to migrate to Palestine or other countries outside Europe."[100] From January to April 1946, accompanied by much publicity, the committee held hearings with Arabs and Jews in Palestine and visited refugee camps in Europe. On April 20 it completed a report with unanimous recommendations that called for both the immediate admission of 100,000 Jews

[97] On the displaced persons see Atina Grossmann, *Jews, Germans and Allies: Close Encounters in Occupied Germany* (Princeton: Princeton University Press, 2007); and "The Plight of the Jewish DPs: The Harrison Report," in Radosh and Radosh, *A Safe Haven*, 91–111.

[98] Louis, *The British Empire in the Middle East, 1945–1951*, 388.

[99] See Amikam Nachmani, *Great Power Discord in Palestine: The Anglo-American Committee of Inquiry into the Problem of European Jewry and Palestine, 1945–1946* (London: Frank Cass, 1987), 61–66; Michael J. Cohen, *Palestine and the Great Power, 1945–1948* (Princeton: Princeton University Press, 1982); and Norman J. W. Goda, Barbara McDonald Stewart, Severin Hochberg, and Richard Breitman, eds., *To the Gates of Jerusalem: The Diaries and Papers of James G. McDonald, 1945–1947* (Bloomington: Indiana University Press, 2015).

[100] Cited in Nachmani, *Great Power Discord*, 62–63.

into Palestine and a Palestine that "shall be neither a Jewish state nor an Arab state." The committee rejected the view that Jewish immigration could continue only with Arab acquiescence, as that "would result in the Arab dominating the Jew" and would lead to Jewish efforts to force immigration "to produce as quickly as possible a Jewish majority and a Jewish state."[101] To the disappointment of the British Foreign Office, the report rejected the British White Paper restrictions on Jewish immigration to Palestine, but also, to the disappointment of Zionists, it rejected calls for partition and establishment of a Jewish state.[102] Though the report's option for a binational solution precluded a Zionist outcome, simply by linking the refugee issue to the future of Palestine and agreeing with Truman's support for the admission of 100,000 Jews into Palestine, it added to political momentum in the United States for the Zionist cause.

Ernest Bevin gave his critics, especially those in New York, reason to wonder if antisemitism was influencing his geopolitical views. At the Labour Party's annual conference in Bournemouth in early June 1946 he took note of the "agitation ... particularly in New York, for 100,000 Jews to be put into Palestine. I hope I will not be misunderstood in America, if I say that this [100,000] was proposed with the purest of motives. They did not want too many Jews in New York."[103] On June 12, after Bevin rejected the Anglo-American Committee's recommendation to admit 100,000 Jews into Palestine, the *Post* declared: "Bevin Rejects Palestine Report, Lays Agitation in U.S. to Fear of Too Many Jews in New York."[104] From June to August other headlines expressed the paper's sympathy for Zionist aspirations and criticism of British policy: "British Arrest Whole Jewish Village"; "Refugee Ship Halted at Haifa"; "British Fire on Haifa Crowd, Kill 3 Jews"; "Haifa Exiles Defy British Troops"; "Arab Troops Bolster British in Jerusalem."[105]

The issues raised in Madison Square Garden resonated deeply with American Jewish veterans. Over 500,000 had served in the US armed forces in the war and were organized in Jewish War Veterans of the United States. On June 20, 1946, with Mowrer's reporting in mind, Maxwell

---

[101] *Report of the Anglo-American Committee of Inquiry Regarding the Problem of European Jewry and Palestine,* cited in Goda, et al., eds., *To the Gates of Jerusalem,* 224–225.

[102] On reactions to the report see Nachmani, *Great Power Discord,* 234–269.

[103] Ernest Bevin, cited in Louis, *The British Empire in the Middle East, 1945–1951,* 428.

[104] "Bevin Rejects Palestine Report, Lays Agitation in U.S. to Fear of Too Many Jews in New York," *New York Post,* June 12, 1946, 1, LC, microfilm 1348.

[105] "British Arrest Whole Jewish Village," *New York Post,* June 17, 1946, 1; "Refugee Ship Halted at Haifa," August 12, 1946; "British Fire on Haifa Crowd, Kill 3 Jews," August 13, 1946; "Haifa Exiles Defy British Troops," August 17, 1946; "Arab Troops Bolster British in Jerusalem," August 19, 1946, LC, microfilm 1348.

Cohen, that organization's leader, wrote to President Truman, Secretary of State Byrnes, House Majority Leader John W. McCormick, and the majority leader in the Senate, Joseph W. Martin, to urge them to indict Husseini for war crimes.[106] He urged the president to indict Husseini for war crimes. Cohen again referred to "documentary proof definitely establishing the complicity" of Husseini "in 6,000,000 murders and collaboration with Hitler and Nazi and Fascist leaders" that had "been uncovered by the Allied military authorities in Bavaria." He urged that "this Nazi agent," who had been involved in the Arab revolt in Iraq in 1941, raised Arab and Muslim legions to fight the Allies, and

conducted vicious campaigns from Axis radio stations against allied governments, who actively cooperated with Hitler, Himmler and Eichmann to organize extermination of European Jews be brought before the bar of world justice to stand trial for his crimes. To allow this criminal to escape trial is to condone treachery, organized murder and defiance of the cause for which our country fought.[107]

Cohen also wrote directly to Robert Jackson in Nuremberg urging an indictment of "the Mufti" and that "various Allied governments" be asked to cooperate in extraditing him to stand trial.[108] Although the efforts by AZEC, Jewish War Veterans, and Emanuel Celler to indict Husseini had been reinforced by the *Post*'s multi-pronged press campaign, they were not successful.

The Husseini case was a point at which American judicial reckoning with Nazi war crimes and crimes against humanity intersected with issues of US foreign policy in the Middle East. Even at this early point, a year before Truman declared the Truman Doctrine, the priorities of American foreign policy in the Middle East outweighed issues of postwar accountability for Nazi collaborators. On June 25, 1946 Telford Taylor, counsel for the US prosecution in Nuremberg, wrote to Robert Jackson that "in the existing diplomatic situation and in the light of public opinion in the United States, Mr. Mowrer and the view he represents must be given

---

[106] Maxwell Cohen, National Commander Jewish War Veterans of the United States to Honorable John W. McCormick, New York (June 20, 1946), NACP RG 59, Confidential US State Department Central Files: Palestine-Israel Internal and Foreign Affairs, 1945–1949, LM 163, Roll 24, 867N.404/6–2246. McCormick forwarded Cohen's letter to Byrnes. See John W. McCormick to James F. Byrnes, Washington (June 22, 1946), NACP RG 59, Palestine-Israel Internal and Foreign Affairs, 1945–1949, LM 163, Roll 24, 867N.404/6–2246.

[107] Ibid.

[108] Maxwell Cohen to Robert H. Jackson, LC, Papers of Robert H. Jackson, Nuremberg War Crimes file, "Nuremberg War Crimes Trial, Office Files-U.S. Chief of Consul, Grand Mufti of Jerusalem, (Haj Amin El-Husseini)," Container 102, Reel 8; also in Maxwell Cohen to John W. McCormick, New York (June 20, 1946), NACP RG 59, Confidential US State Department Central Files: Palestine-Israel Internal and Foreign Affairs, 1945–1949, LM 163, Roll 24, 867N.404/6–2246.

'gentle treatment.'"[109] Taylor, following conversations with Benjamin Cohen, a State Department representative in Paris who had been a legal advisor in the State Department and an advisor to President Franklin Roosevelt and was generally sympathetic to Zionist aspirations, wrote that Cohen thought "that a trial of the Grand Mufti would be out of our usual line of activity and would present prodigious diplomatic embarrassments. He feels that somewhere along the way it should be possible to shelve the matter gracefully."[110] Judging from press accounts, Taylor continued, "the King of Egypt may help us out by giving the Mufti sanctuary under circumstances which clearly indicate that they would not surrender him for trial. In the meantime, there is no reason that I can see why we should not examine Mr. Mowrer's evidence."[111] But examination of the evidence did not lead to indictment. Given the important cooperation offered by the OSS to Jackson's prosecution staff in Nuremberg, Jackson, and most probably Taylor as well, was aware of the June 1945 OSS assessment of Arab opposition to bringing Arab collaborators with the Nazis to trial.

Hence, the diplomatic embarrassments to which Taylor referred were the expected objections of the Arab governments to an indictment and the resulting difficulties for the United States in the postwar Middle East. Taylor's rejection of efforts to indict Husseini appeared to mirror the concerns voiced by the OSS a year earlier, namely that the case of Husseini was also important because other Arab leaders with whom the United States was eager to have good relations were firmly opposed to a trial that would reveal evidence of the extent of his Nazi collaboration and thus the continuity of his views before and after 1945.

But AZEC was not willing to let the matter drop. On July 19, 1946 its representative Benjamin Akzin was again at the State Department, this time meeting Katherine Fite in the department's Office of the Legal Adviser, to discuss the issue of indicting the Mufti. He repeated that Husseini, along with Hitler, Himmler, and Eichmann, was "responsible

---

[109] Telford Taylor to Robert Jackson (June 25, 1946), "Memorandum for Mr. Justice Jackson: Subject: The Grand Mufti of Jerusalem," LC, Robert H. Jackson Papers, "Nuremberg War Crimes Trial, Office Files-U.S. Chief of Consul, Grand Mufti of Jerusalem (Haj Amin El-Husseini)," Container 102, Reel 8.

[110] Ibid. It should be noted that Cohen did support Zionist aspirations and then the new state of Israel. See Papers of Benjamin V. Cohen, LC Manuscript Division, Box 12, the files on "Franklin D. Roosevelt, 1944–1945" and "Palestine and Israel."

[111] Telford Taylor to Robert Jackson, (June 25, 1946), "Memorandum for Mr. Justice Jackson: Subject: The Grand Mufti of Jerusalem." Taylor does not discuss the issue of whether to indict Husseini in his *The Anatomy of the Nuremberg Trials: A Personal Memoir* (New York: Knopf, 1992).

Figure 2.4 Rabbis Stephen S. Wise (right) of New York, and Abba H. Silver of Cleveland, Ohio, co-chairmen of the American Zionist Emergency Council, after they conferred with President Roosevelt at the White House, March 9, 1944. Source: Bettman/Getty Images.

for the extermination of European Jews."[112] He called the US policy of leaving the indictment decision to the UNWCC "an obvious run-around," while the limitation of charges only to persons of European Axis nationality was "another obvious run-around." In response to his comment that "it would be shocking" for the Department to take a position without considering the evidence AZEC was providing, Fite replied that the decision would be made at "a higher level" than the Office of Legal Adviser, presumably by the secretary of state.[113] On September 13 the State Department's Political Division sent Robert Jackson in Nuremberg a memo from Abba Silver and Stephen Wise of AZEC "outlining the alleged responsibility of the Mufti of Jerusalem as a war criminal" (see Figure 2.4). It was the same memo Akzin had shown Fite in July. The State Department's cable to Jackson stated that

[112] Katherine Fite, Washington (July 19, 1946), "Memorandum of Conversation: The Grand Mufti of Jerusalem," NACP RG 59, Records of the Legal Adviser Relating to War Crimes, 21. War Crimes – Jewish Atrocities, [Lot File No. 61D 33], Box 4. On Fite see the entry at the Robert Jackson Center website: www.roberthjackson.org/article/ka therine-b-fite/
[113] Ibid., 2–4.

as the Mufti was the subject of a territory under the British Mandate, Palestine, Jackson "may wish to determine through prior discussion with the British representative at the Military Tribunal whether or not action in the matter would be advantageous or permissible under the terms of the agreement setting up a war crimes tribunal."[114] Suggesting that Jackson consult with the British could have been what Akzin called "another obvious run-around," or it may also have been an effort to engage the British in an issue that did, in fact, concern them directly as they had pursued Husseini for his terrorist activities in 1936-9 and were well informed of his Nazi-era collaboration. Spreading the burden of decision making about the indictment decision was compatible with both interpretations.

The "Memorandum on the Responsibility as a War Criminal of Haj Amin El-Husseini, Former Mufti of Jerusalem," presumably the work of Akzin, Silver, and Wise, dated July 16, 1946, was a remarkable document. One would think that Jackson and Taylor, and perhaps their British counterparts, would find that it merited very serious consideration, as it continues to do.[115] It comprised about 5,000 words plus an additional twenty pages of documents, including witness statements by Andrei Steiner and Rudolf Kastner, Jewish representatives who had negotiated in Europe with Dieter Wisliczeny, an SS officer who had worked with Adolf Eichmann and was the "German Adviser on Jewish Affairs in Slovenia, Greece and Hungary."[116] The negotiations had concerned the possibility of allowing Jewish children to go to Palestine during the Holocaust. Steiner quoted Wisliczeny as saying that Husseini was "in closest contact and collaboration with Eichmann ... had always been a protagonist of the idea of the annihilation of the Jews ... and was one of the initiators of the systematic extermination of European Jewry by the Germans."[117]

---

[114] State Department, Political Division to the Office of the United States Chief of Consul for the Prosecution of Axis Criminality, Nuremberg Germany, Care of the United States Political Adviser, Berlin, Washington (September 13, 1946), LC, Robert H. Jackson Papers, Nuremberg War Crimes file "Nuremberg War Crimes Trial, Office Files-U.S. Chief of Consul, Grand Mufti of Jerusalem, (Haj Amin El-Husseini)," Container 102, Reel 8.

[115] "Memorandum on the Responsibility as a War Criminal of Haj Amin El-Husseini, Former Mufti of Jerusalem" (July 16, 1946), LC, Robert H. Jackson Papers, Nuremberg War Crimes file "Nuremberg War Crimes Trial, Office Files-U.S. Chief of Consul, Grand Mufti of Jerusalem, (Haj Amin El-Husseini)," Container 102, Reel 8.

[116] On Wisliczeny's links to Eichmann, his role in the Holocaust, and his testimony in Nuremberg see Hans Safrian, *Eichmann's Men*, trans. Ute Stargardt (New York: Cambridge University Press, 2010); and David Cesarani, *Becoming Eichmann: Rethinking the Life of a "Desk Murderer"* (London: De Capo Press, 2004).

[117] "Exhibit A: Affidavit of Andrei Steiner with Appended Confirmation by SS Hauptsturmbahnführer Dieter Wiscliczeny," Memorandum on the Responsibility as a War Criminal of Haj Amin El-Husseini, Former Mufti of Jerusalem (July 16, 1946),

Wisliczeny's assertion that Husseini was "one of the initiators" of the Holocaust was wrong. While the Mufti fanned the flames of antisemitic hatred in his work as a propagandist, he was not a central decision maker in the Nazi regime.[118] Kastner, leader of the Jewish Rescue and Relief Committee in Budapest, based on his conversations with Wisliczeny, believed that Husseini had "played a role in the decision of the German government to exterminate the European Jews" by proposing the idea to Hitler, Ribbentrop, and Himmler. "He considered this as a comfortable solution for the Palestine problem." Wisliczeny said that Husseini's radio messages from Berlin "surpassed us in anti-Jewish attacks." He was "one of Eichmann's best friends and has constantly incited him to accelerate the extermination measures" and had claimed to have "visited incognito the gas chambers in Auschwitz."[119] In reality, the Nazis needed no encouragement from Husseini to carry out the Final Solution. Subsequent research indicates that while Husseini knew Eichmann, his contacts with Heinrich Himmler were more extensive. It does not confirm that the Mufti visited Auschwitz.[120] On the other hand, the AZEC July 18 memo accurately cited one of Husseini's radio broadcasts of March 1944 urging listeners to "kill the Jews wherever you find them. This pleases God, history and religion."[121]

The memo included translations of letters that Husseini had sent to Joachim von Ribbentrop, Himmler, and the foreign ministers of Italy, Bulgaria, and Hungary during the war, urging them all not to allow Jews to enter Palestine. In a letter to the foreign minister of Bulgaria of June 5, 1943, Husseini recommended that Jews be sent to places where they will be "under stringent control, as for instance in Poland." The AZEC authors wrote that "what stringent control of the Polish type meant in 1943 was an open secret both for the writer and the addressee, and *Der Grossmufti* could well afford the innuendo of an understatement."[122]

LC, Robert H. Jackson Papers, Nuremberg War Crimes file "Nuremberg War Crimes Trial, Office Files-U.S. Chief of Consul, Grand Mufti of Jerusalem, (Haj Amin El-Husseini)," Container 102, Reel 8.

[118] On the importance and limits of Husseini's political position in Nazi Germany see Herf, "Haj Amin al-Husseini, the Nazis and the Holocaust."

[119] Wiscliczeny cited by Rudolf Kastner in "Memorandum on the Responsibility as a War Criminal of Haj Amin El-Husseini, Former Mufti of Jerusalem."

[120] On Husseini's contacts with Himmler and his pleas to not permit Jewish immigration to Palestine see Herf, *Nazi Propaganda for the Arab World*, ch. 7; and Klaus Gensicke, *Der Mufti von Jerusalem und die Nationalsozialisten* (Darmstadt: Wissenschaftliche Buchgesellschaft, 2007).

[121] According to the American monitoring of Axis radio, the broadcast was on March 1, 1944. See Herf, *Nazi Propaganda for the Arab World*, p. 213.

[122] "Memorandum on the Responsibility as a War Criminal of Haj Amin El-Husseini, Former Mufti of Jerusalem," 8.

Citing these letters, Akzin, Silver, and Wise wrote that Husseini's efforts were not limited to preventing Jewish immigration to Palestine. He also "actively encouraged the deportation of Jews from other countries to the Polish extermination camps."[123] The AZEC authors annexed a letter from Husseini of June 28, 1943 to the Romanian government in which he urged that it oppose the emigration of 1,800 Jewish children to Palestine.[124]

The AZEC authors added that, since their previous letter to the State Department of December 13, 1945, "new material of a different nature and involving entirely new charges has come to light" concerning Husseini's wartime activities in Germany. It appeared "to establish conclusively that the Mufti played a role of some importance in the extermination of the Jews of Europe and that he is guilty of complicity in organized mass murder and of other crimes against humanity," crimes that fell within the purview of the Charter of the International Military Tribunal in Nuremberg. Husseini had urged the Italian government to prevent the escape of Jews from Bulgaria, Hungary, and Romania. Citing letters by him to Hitler, Ribbentrop, and Himmler, they wrote:

> The destruction of the Jews was indeed the avowed and official basis of the alliance between the Mufti and Hitler. On November 3, 1943, on the radio, he said the Germans "never harmed Moslems, and are fighting our common enemy ... *But most of all they have definitely solved the Jewish problem*. These ties, and *especially the last one, the common war against the Jews*, make of our friendship with Germany not a provisional friendship dependent upon conditions but a permanent and lasting one based on mutual interests.[125]

Akzin, Silver, and Wise then raised an issue central to the program of denazification in Germany, namely that of preventing former officials of the Nazi regime and Nazi collaborators from reviving Nazism in some form after its military defeat in 1945. Indicting Husseini, they wrote, "would also secure, more than in any other case before the [UN War Crimes] Commission, one of the basic purposes of criminal law, that of incapacitation. Every member of the United Nations shares in the grave responsibility of leaving this dangerous war criminal unpunished and free to renew his murderous activities." Husseini's return to political activity would have "the most dangerous implication for the physical safety of every Jewish community," not only in Palestine but in the various Arab countries of the Near and Middle East.[126]

The AZEC authors correctly pointed out that the policy of filing charges only when there was evidence of crimes against American

---

[123] Ibid.   [124] Ibid., 7–8.   [125] Husseini, cited in ibid., 10–11 (emphasis in original).
[126] Ibid., 14.

nationals "does not apply in the case of 'major' war criminals." While it was true that the Four Power agreement on war crimes prosecution referred to "European Axis war criminals ... it surely was not intended thereby to lay down a racial criterion and thus to authorize the indictment only of persons of European stock."[127] Rather, it was to distinguish between Axis criminals in Europe and those in the Pacific theater. Though Husseini was not a member of one of the Axis governments, "he can be classed as a member of the Nazi Conspiracy insofar as this Conspiracy refers to the annihilation of the Jewish people in Europe, as well as in connection with waging of a war of aggression." The Mufti, they continued, fell under the purview of the War Crimes Commission because of his contribution to acts of murder, extermination, enslavement, and deportation against civilian populations on "political, racial or religious grounds" as well as the Axis goal of world domination. He was "the active collaborator and the tool of the Axis."[128]

The AZEC memo asserted that the United States should take the initiative in submitting charges against Husseini to the International Tribunal. "So far as the massacre of Jews as Jews" was concerned, there was no state to represent their interests. "The Jewish people as such is unrepresented in the councils of the nations and is without *locus standi* in regard to the War Crimes Commission." For political reasons, Britain would not indict the Mufti. "Time and again in the past the British Government has failed, when opportunity offered, either to bring him to justice, or, as at present, to prevent his escape." The US government should act in part because "the largest surviving Jewish community in the world today is in the United States." Even more important, the US government had "in the past in most vigorous terms condemned and protested the unparalleled outrage perpetrated during the war against the Jewish people. On numerous occasions" Roosevelt had expressed "in unequivocal terms" a determination to bring those responsible to justice. "These protests and declarations will remain idle words as far as one of the arch-criminals of them all is concerned, unless action is now taken to secure the Mufti's apprehension and trial."[129]

The AZEC memos of 1945 and 1946 constituted an impressive record of the Mufti's collaboration with the Nazi regime in matters related to the

---

[127] Ibid., 15–17.   [128] Ibid., 16.

[129] Ibid., 17. Husseini's letters to the governments of Italy, Bulgaria, Hungary, and Romania, and to Ribbentrop and Himmler, were in "Exhibits annexed to Memorandum on the Responsibility as a War Criminal of Haj Amin El-Hussein, Former Mufti of Jerusalem," Washington (July 16, 1946), LC, Robert H. Jackson Papers, Nuremberg War Crimes file "Nuremberg War Crimes Trial, Office Files-U.S. Chief of Consul, Grand Mufti of Jerusalem, (Haj Amin El-Husseini)," Container 102, Reel 8.

extermination of the Jews of Europe based on the evidence available at the time. At this preliminary stage of investigation they included some errors, but more importantly they offered the beginnings of a road map that, on the whole, included plausible hypotheses for further investigation for Allied prosecutors in Nuremberg, investigators in the UNWWC, and American officials in the State Department if they wished to go down that road. Had the State Department leadership ordered the Nuremberg team to pursue the case against Husseini, its diplomatic, military, and intelligence files had abundant material on which to build a compelling case for indictment and possible conviction. The political decisions against indicting Husseini in 1946 and against revealing the extent of US government knowledge of the collaboration on his part and that of his associates benefited from a broader reluctance to place even European collaborators on trial. The willingness in Washington (and London and Paris) to look away from the Mufti's Nazi years revealed a similar policy. As Taylor's prosecution of Reich propaganda chief Otto Dietrich indicated, activities similar to those of Husseini were thought worthy of prosecution when committed by German officials of the Nazi regime.[130]

The absence of a trial of Husseini had important consequences for the future of Jews and Arabs in Palestine after World War II. Such a trial would have brought to world attention the Allies' extensive evidence of Husseini's collaboration with the Nazis. In so doing, it would have made it more difficult for him to revive his political career and emerge as the leader of postwar Palestinian nationalism, and would have made it far more difficult for the United Nations in 1947 to allow him and the Arab Higher Committee to represent the Palestine Arabs. As it was, the absence of a trial and punishment enabled the leading voice of Arab extremism and radical antisemitism to be welcomed home to the Middle East as a hero of an anti-imperialist struggle rather than as a disgraced collaborator with Nazism and its crimes against the Jews.

From the weeks following his arrest in Switzerland in summer 1945 to late spring 1946 the French government held Husseini under house arrest in a suburb of Paris. In the second week of June 1946 the press reported that the Mufti had "escaped" from Paris and arrived in Cairo. On June 13, 1946 Jean-Pierre Bénard of the French Embassy in Washington told Henry Willard, the acting deputy director of the Division of Near Eastern and African Affairs, that Husseini had departed using an alias

---

[130] Taylor, for example, led the prosecution in one of the successor trials that resulted in a guilty verdict for Otto Dietrich, the Reich press chief, for his role in spreading Nazi propaganda. On Dietrich's trial and conviction see Herf, *The Jewish Enemy*, 272–274; and Alexander Hardy, *Hitler's Secret Weapon: The "Managed" Press and Propaganda Machine of Nazi Germany* (New York: Vintage, 1967).

on a TWA flight, and that the "French had only undertaken to protect him from harm and not to watch or control his movements in any way. The Grand Mufti was under no obligation to ask permission or report in regard to his comings and goings."[131] In other words, as we will see in Chapter 4, his departure was facilitated by very light surveillance.

Following the Mufti's arrival in Cairo in June, US ambassador to Egypt Pinckney Tuck sent detailed reports about the reaction in the Egyptian press to his arrival.[132] Tuck had begun his service in Cairo in 1944 and was thus familiar with the "Axis Broadcasts in Arabic" reports of Nazi radio begun under his predecessor, Alexander Kirk. Tuck used the response of the Cairo press, then the intellectual capital of the Arab countries, to gain insight into how leading journalists and editors assessed Husseini's involvement with the Nazis.[133] Tuck wrote that the "news of his escape from France and his alleged presence in the Middle East has greatly excited the Egyptians. Sketches of past accomplishments in Palestine with stress on his escapes from the British in Palestine and Iraq continue to be published although his activities in Germany are glossed over."[134] Cairo political circles were divided. "The rank and file are held to be highly entertained by the slip given the French and British by Haj Amin." Opponents of Zionism welcomed his "escape" as providing a "timely leader for the Arabs against the Zionists." Others, hoping to avert bloodshed, found his appearance "ill-timed." "They hope, in any event, that he will not attempt to approach Russia as he did the Nazis, on behalf of the Arabs."[135] Tuck then summarized reaction in various Egyptian papers such as *al-Kutla*, *al-Misr*, *al-Mokattam*, *Akhbar al-Yom*, and *Misr al-Fatat*:

The charge that Haj Amin collaborated with the Nazis is apparently of no concern to Arabs either in Egypt or elsewhere. *Al Mokattan* declares, "It is not Haj Amin who is a war criminal but others. He acted in the best interests of his country." *Akhbar At Yom* declares, "If the British consider the Mufti a war criminal because he made speeches against Zionism, the Arabs consider Churchill a criminal

---

[131] "Memorandum of Conversation: Escape of the Grand Mufti of Jerusalem," Washington (June 13, 1946), NACP RG 59, Palestine-Israel Internal and Foreign Affairs, 1945–1949, LM 163, Roll 24, 867N.404/6–1146.

[132] On the Tuck reports see Herf, *Nazi Propaganda for the Arab World*, 241–245.

[133] On the Arab political and journalistic response to news of the Holocaust see Meir Litvak and Esther Webman, *From Empathy to Denial: Arab Responses to the Holocaust* (New York and London: Columbia University Press/Hurst, 2009). On the postwar "general amnesty" regarding Husseini's collaboration with the Nazis see Matthias Küntzel, *Nazis und der Nahe Osten: Wie der Islamische Antisemitismus Entstand* (Berlin and Leipzig: Hentrich & Hentrich, 2019), 140; and Schechtman, *The Mufti and the Führer*.

[134] S. Pinckney Tuck to Secretary of State, A-261 (June 17, 1946), NACP RG 59, Palestine-Israel Internal and Foreign Affairs, 1945–1949, LM 163, Roll 24, 867N.404/6–2247.

[135] Ibid.

because he broke his promises. [British ambassador to Egypt] Killearn is one also because he used tanks in the February 4th incident. [On February 4, 1942 the British ambassador ordered tanks and armored cars to surround Egypt's King Farouk's palace to pressure him to appoint a prime minister sympathetic to the Allies, not the Axis.] If the Americans call the Mufti a war criminal, then Americans must consider George Washington a war criminal for they both fought for the freedom of their country." *Misr Al Fatat*, mouthpiece of the Young Egypt movement, climaxes such exaltation, as evident from a cursory reading of the editorial written by Ahmed Hussein, head of the organization. Especially indicative of the ill-balanced thinking of this organization are the phrases, "Germany and Hitler are gone but Haj Amin Al Husseini will continue their struggle ... He is but one man, but Mohammed was also one man and so was Christ and they achieved great results ... Amin has a divine spark in his heart? which make him above human beings ... his battle has begun, and it is easy to foresee the result. The Lord Almighty did not preserve Amin for nothing."[136]

Tuck reported that newspapers such as the *Egyptian Gazette*, which viewed him as being as much of a danger as the Stern Gang and spoke up for good relations with Britain, were subjected to sharp criticism from *al-Balagh*, a paper close to the Wafd Party. "If it [the Gazette] wishes to flaunt its Zionism, then it had better move to London or Washington where it will find many supporters who believe in dreams of domination more arrogant than any indulged by the Nazis."[137]

On June 21, 1946 Tuck reported that Egypt's King Farouk had granted Husseini sanctuary. The communiqué announcing the decision made "surprising reference to Mufti's past by stating that this is no time to discuss political errors attributed to Mufti in the past but rather occasion to extend help and protection which no generous man could refuse."[138] It was a popular decision. To emphasize the importance and enthusiasm of the reception of Husseini, the following day Tuck sent a second memo with extensive selections from editorials from *al-Mokattam*, *al-Misr*, *Mussamarat al-Gaeb*, *Akhbar al-Yom*, *al-Kutla*, *Misr al-Fatat*, the *Egyptian Gazette*, and *al-Balagh*, along with a cartoon from *Akhbar al-Yom*.[139] He concluded that "the universality of the exuberance of the press ... would seem to indicate that the welcome is widespread and genuine."[140]

---

[136] Ibid., 2. On the February 4 incident see Herf, *Nazi Propaganda for the Arab World*, 94.

[137] Tuck to Secretary of State, A-261, 3.

[138] Tuck to Secretary of State, No. 1103 (June 21, 1946), NACP RG 59, Palestine-Israel Internal and Foreign Affairs, 1945–1949, LM 163, Roll 24, 867N.404/6–1746.

[139] Tuck to Secretary of State, No. 1644, Cairo (June 22, 1946), "Press Comment on the Escape of Haj Amin El Husseini," NACP RG 59, Palestine-Israel Internal and Foreign Affairs, 1945–1949, LM 163, Roll 24, 867N.404/6–2246. Also see discussion of the reception in Herf, *Nazi Propaganda for the Arab World*, 240–245.

[140] Tuck to Secretary of State, No. 1648 (June 24, 1946), "Editorial comments from the Cairo press concerning the appearance of the Mufti in Egypt," NACP RG 59, Palestine-Israel Internal and Foreign Affairs, 1945–1949, LM 163, Roll 24, 867N.404/6–2446.

In Tuck's view, the journalists at the *New York Post* and *Manchester Guardian* were mistaken that Husseini "occupies a more important place in the eyes of American and British officialdom than he does among the Arabs," and that such standing among Arabs "has, in fact, been created by the attention given to him abroad by American and British press."[141] In fact, Tuck's memos of June 1946 echoed the OSS analysis of the previous year on the war crimes issue in the Arab states. In those states, Husseini's collaboration with the Nazis presented no barrier to reviving his political career. For at least some of his supporters it was an asset, not a liability. Tuck drew attention to an editorial in *al-Kutla* that criticized the Egyptian government communiqué for referring to Husseini's past "political errors." On June 21, 1946 *al-Kutla* expressed "disgust" about the government's comment. "It is bad taste and indecent to refer to 'mistakes' which are considered by Arabs to be acts of gallantry."[142] The editorial was an early postwar expression in parts of Arab political life of admiration for Nazism and Hitler.[143]

Pinckney Tuck's reporting demonstrated again why the Husseini case had such great political significance. As the OSS had understood the year before, there was a significant aspect of Arab public and published opinion that constituted an exception to the norm of revulsion with Nazism and Hitler among the Allied victors and in many other countries. Rather than view Husseini's years in Berlin as a disqualification for continued engagement in public life, there existed a politically significant body of Arab opinion that, knowing very well that he had supported Nazi Germany, actively sought his return to political activity. The question for American – and British, and French – policy makers was how to respond to such a political culture, one in which apologia or even enthusiasm for Nazism went well beyond the political fringe. During the war the United States had refrained from focusing on the antisemitic aspects of Nazi policy out of fear that doing so would lend credence to the Nazi accusations that the United States was fighting a "Jewish war."[144] Tuck's assessment of Egyptian political and intellectual responses to Husseini's

---

[141] Ibid.

[142] "Bad Diplomacy," *al-Kutla* (June 21, 1946), cited in Tuck, No. 1648 (June 24, 1946), "Editorial comments from the Cairo press concerning the appearance of the Mufti in Egypt," 5. For the text of the Egyptian government communiqué see Tuck, No. 1637, Cairo (June 27, 1946), "Text of communique on Haj Amin Al Husseini," NACP RG 59, Palestine-Israel Internal and Foreign Affairs, 1945–1949, LM 163, Roll 24, 867N.404/6–2746.

[143] On this see Litvak and Webman, *From Empathy to Denial*.

[144] On this see discussion of the US Office of War Information in Herf, *Nazi Propaganda for the Arab World*, 83–84.

return indicated that antisemitism and even enthusiasm for Nazism were indeed important causal factors in Arab politics and in the warm welcome home Husseini received in some quarters.

This continuity of policy from World War II to the postwar years was one factor that led the US government to decide against both calling for the indictment of Husseini and attempting to delegitimize and undermine those Arabs tainted by their past Nazi associations who were now leading the Arab opposition to Zionist aspirations. The Western Allies' implicit decision to limit "denazification" efforts to postwar Germany and Japan meant that the collaboration with Nazism by some Arab leaders would remain marginal in postwar American government discussions about the Palestine issue. Instead, American policy makers opted for silence and amnesia in efforts to foster good will in the Arab states. American liberal critics of the State Department argued that leniency was short-sighted, both in Europe and in the Middle East. Other factors, such as access to oil and containing communism, were weighing more heavily in decision making in Washington.

In February 1947 the State Department received still more very public evidence about the presence of antisemitism and racism within the leadership of the Arab Higher Committee. On February 3 G. Lewis Jones, the second secretary in the US Embassy in London, sent "Initial Text of Jamal Husseini at the Opening of the Palestine Conference in London, January 27, 1947" to the Office of the Secretary of State, an office that George Marshall had assumed earlier that week.[145] Husseini, a cousin of Haj Amin, represented the Arab Higher Committee at the conference. He spoke at length about what he regarded as the injustice of the Balfour Declaration, the violation of Arab rights of self-determination it caused, and the unacceptability of the recommendation by the Anglo-American Committee of Inquiry to support the admission of 100,000 Jews in Europe to Palestine. The Arabs of Palestine would resist partition

with all the means at their disposal. To the Arab world, partition presents a further menace. The Arab world is a territorial continuity inhabited by a homogenous population with one national outlook. As such it is free from serious frictions and a natural bulwark for peace. Homogeneity in race has always been the natural basis for mutual understanding and community of interests. The creation of an alien Jewish state in Palestine means the destruction of this territorial continuity and national homogeneity and the creation of a running sore that will undoubtedly become a permanent source of trouble in the Middle East. Such a move,

---

[145] Jamal Husseini, "Statement at the Opening of the Palestine Conference in London on January 27, 1947," quoted in full in G. Lewis Jones to Secretary of State, No. 3594, London, "Initial Text of Jamal Husseini at the Opening of the Palestine Conference in London, January 27, 1947," NACP RG 59, M1390 501BB.Palestine 867N.01/2-347.

which in fact entails the creation of another Balkan in the Middle East, the Arabs can never tolerate.[146]

Jones's report went to Marshall, Deputy Secretary of State Robert Lovett, and the officials in Department's Division of Near Eastern and African Affairs.

As a result of Jones's report the State Department knew that this leader of the Arab Higher Committee and close associate of Haj Amin al-Husseini had publicly asserted that the Zionist project would undermine the "homogeneity in race" of the Arab world, a homogeneity which, he claimed, was the basis for mutual understanding and peace in the Middle East. Rather than denounce Nazi Germany's efforts to establish homogeneity of race in Europe, Jamal Husseini – in London, in January 1947 – felt free to state that he shared the goal of homogeneity, and that heterogeneity, or, in the discourse of recent decades, diversity, of religion and ethnicity, was an evil to be denounced and avoided. In other words, his opposition to a Jewish state in Palestine perpetuated the racist views of homogeneity that the Allies had recently waged war to defeat. The racism and antisemitism of Jamal Husseini and of the Arab Higher Committee was a cause more than a consequence of the conflict with the Zionists. Peace and compromise presupposed fighting against those hatreds. Yet the top leadership of the State Department chose not to draw attention to such themes being voiced by this leader of the Arab Higher Committee. It did not engage in a diplomatic and political campaign to raise these issues in the hopes of blunting extremism and fostering moderation in the Arab Middle East.

Five months later, on June 6, 1947, Senator Robert Wagner wrote to Secretary of State Marshall to again raise the issue of this road not taken. He believed that the State Department possessed "a number of documents pertaining to the wartime activities of Nazi and Fascist leaders and collaborators, particularly material relating to the former Mufti of Jerusalem, who now serves as Chairman of the Arab Higher Committee of Palestine, and his collaborators with the Axis powers during the war." Because it was "of such unquestioned interest to the Congress and to the American people, and because the United Nations is now investigating the Palestine question," Wagner deemed it

most urgent that the Department of State should publish all the material it has in its possession regarding this important matter. I am particularly anxious that the extent of the ex-Mufti's role in the Iraqi revolt of 1941, be disclosed, as well as his activities as an agent of the Axis since 1941, and his role in the extermination of

---

[146] Ibid., 2.

the Jews, as revealed in documents discussed by Bartley C. Crum in his recent book, "Behind the Silken Curtain" . . . Since the facts presented by the publication of the material will, I feel sure, help the United States and other members of the United Nations to reach a decision on Palestine at the United Nations Assembly and will help to determine our course of action in the Middle East, I am counting on your help and cooperation.[147]

On June 18 Marshall replied that the US, British, and French governments had agreed to publish material "in a manner which will give an accurate and complete picture of the events, personalities and developments during the Nazi-Fascist period. It is understood that a number of these documents relate or refer to the former Mufti."[148] Marshall followed up on June 30, adding:

At the present time numerous documents bearing on the activity of the Nazi and Fascist parties, their leaders and collaborators, which were seized during the conquest of the Axis countries by the Allied Armies, are being examined, analyzed, translated, and classified by teams of historians represented the United States, British and French Governments. The three governments have agreed that this material will be published just as soon as the work on it, which is necessarily slow and arduous, has advanced to a stage that will permit its presentation in a manner which will give an accurate and complete picture of the events, personalities and developments during the Nazi-Fascist period. It is understood that a number of those documents relate or refer to the former Mufti.[149]

In fact, documents in the files of the State Department, such as reports of the "Axis Broadcasts in Arabic," were not declassified until 1977. Though declassified, they and other documents related to Arab collaboration with Nazi Germany were never published by the US government. In his reply to Wagner, Marshall confirmed what became subsequently evident, namely that the relevant documentary evidence held by the United States on collaboration with the Nazis by Husseini and other leaders of the Arab Higher Committee was extensive. Following Husseini's return to the Middle East in 1946 it was unlikely that the United States could convince the Arab states to extradite him for trial in the successor trials in Nuremberg. Yet there was time to bring the documentary evidence to the attention of the United Nations and thus undermine efforts by the Husseini-controlled Arab Higher Committee to speak

[147] Wagner to George Marshall (June 6, 1947), Robert F. Wagner Papers, Folders 35–50, Box 3 of 4. See also Crum, *Behind the Silk Curtain*.

[148] Marshall to Wagner, Washington (June 18, 1947), Robert F. Wagner Papers, Palestine Files 1945–1948, Folders 35–50, Box 3 of 4.

[149] Marshall, Washington (June 30, 1947), "Reply to Senator Wagner," NACP RG 59, Palestine-Israel Internal and Foreign Affairs, 1945–1949, LM 163, Roll 24, 867N.404/6–2647.

at the UN as the representative of the Palestine Arabs. Had the Arab Higher Committee been denied that honor, perhaps other, moderate, forces willing to accept partition in Palestine would have had more opportunities to counter the power of the rejectionists that Husseini had reassembled. It was a powerful card in the American diplomatic arsenal which the State Department decided not to play.

The decisions not to indict Husseini, along with the classification and non-publication of these documents, constitute an important chapter in the rapid shift of mentalities from the antifascism expressed in the Democratic Party's election platform of 1944 to the very different priorities of gaining the good will of Arab oil producers and Arab support for containment of the Soviet Union and communism in the early months and years of the Cold War. Husseini and his associates benefited as well from a European reluctance to look closely at the record of collaboration in general. By refusing to reveal the full record of his Nazi collaboration and its aftereffects, American – and British and French – leaders made it more likely that the Mufti and his associates could return to the political stage, both in Palestine and on the international stage at the UN, oppose any compromise with the Jews, start the war against the Jews in November 1947, urge the Arab states to invade the new state of Israel in May 1948, and stimulate hatred of the United States and the Western democracies.

There was a particular and bitter irony in the fact that it was the State Department led by George Marshall, formerly General George Marshall, the army chief of staff in World War II, that refused to take this course and instead adopted a policy of leniency and deliberate forgetfulness about Arab collaboration with the Nazis. It is not the wisdom of hindsight that leads to these conclusions. It was evident among American liberal and left-liberal advocates of the road not taken by the State Department.

In 1945 and 1946 the battle had been joined between support and opposition to the Zionist project. The State Department, and, as we will see, most of the British and American foreign and military leadership even in these immediate postwar months, was in the early stages of opposition. It was in the public sphere, in the press and in politics, where momentum in favor of the Jewish state in Palestine was found. We turn now to those who fostered momentum in favor of the Zionist project. They recalled past promises made to the Jews. They voiced fresh and vivid memories of the Holocaust, expressed empathy for its survivors, and a determination to bring perpetrators to account. For the liberals and leftists of 1945–6 in New York, the Zionist project was the logical extension of their core beliefs.

3   American Liberals and Leftists Support Zionist Aspirations, 1945–1947

The rich annals of appeasement contain no more striking story than that of Haj Amin el Husseini, no more convincing testimony to the readiness of the British government to be gulled.

> I. F. Stone, "The Case of the Mufti," *The Nation*, May 4, 1946

The Arab Higher Committee is an almost exact equivalent, in Middle Eastern terms, of the cabal that ruled Hitler's Germany.

> "The Mufti's Henchman," *The Nation*, May 17, 1947

From 1945 to 1949 support for the Zionist project became a defining issue for liberals and leftists in the United States. It was, in the view of its most articulate advocates, a logical continuation of the anti-Nazi and antifascist passions of World War II. During the public controversy in the United States about policy toward post-Mandate Palestine the venerable weekly *The Nation* (founded in 1865) and the spirited daily *PM*, published in New York from 1940 to 1948, were the defining, agenda-setting, noncommunist journals of leftist opinion and reporting in the United States. Both became leading advocates of Zionist aspirations and equally forceful critics of the policies pursued by Britain and the State Department. They supported the policies of the New Deal, denounced the antisemitism of those opposed to American intervention in the war in Europe, denounced racism and segregation, and reported extensively on the war in Europe and then on the Nazis' anti-Jewish policies. They called for trials for German and Japanese "war criminals" and worried that denazification in Germany was giving way prematurely to desires to rebuild the German economy and polity as an anticommunist bulwark against the Soviet Union. Though they did not publish articles celebrating Stalin or communism in the Soviet Union and Eastern Europe, they did not focus on the evils of Soviet rule and communist dictatorship. For the editors of *PM* and *The Nation*, the Soviet Union's decision in May 1947 to support the partition of Palestine into Jewish and Arab states appeared to be the logical outgrowth of the moral and political causes for which World War II had been fought. Rather than criticize the Zionists for receiving support from the communists, they asked instead why the United States was not supporting the Zionists just as firmly.

The more mainstream liberal magazine *The New Republic* (*TNR*) was also favorable to the Zionists. On July 1, 1946 *TNR*, then edited by Bruce Bliven, published Richard Crossman's "Britain, the Arabs and the Jews."[1] Crossman (1907–74), a British member of the Anglo-American Committee of Inquiry and Member of Parliament from 1945 to 1970, emerged as one of the foremost critics of Bevin's Palestine policy in the British Labour Party.[2] The British, he wrote, had an "inclination to fall in love with all that is decadent in Arab civilization and to disregard or dislike the new, less charming and less subservient features," which British officials associated with the Jews. Such views were, Crossman observed, less a form of pro-Arabism than a "concealed anti-Semitism even more insulting to the Arabs than the Jews."[3] In November *TNR* ran a piece by British political theorist and member of the Labour Party Harold J. Laski pointing out that British prime minister Clement Attlee and his colleagues "have given no ostensible weight to the very great services rendered to the Allied cause by the Jews in Palestine during the war," including those of the Jewish Agency's foreign affairs speaker, Moshe Shertok.[4]

In December 1946 Henry Wallace, vice-president of the United States from 1940 to 1944, began a term as editor of *The New Republic* that lasted until July 1948. Truman had fired him as secretary of commerce for what he viewed as Wallace's overly conciliatory policies toward the Soviet Union. Under Wallace's editorship *TNR* became a critic of Truman's hard line toward the Soviet Union. He published a number of editorials that expressed his support for Jewish immigration to Palestine, the UN Partition Resolution, and his enthusiasm for agricultural development in the Jordan Valley modeled on the New Deal Tennessee Valley Authority.[5] Though Wallace's sympathies were with the Zionists, *TNR*

---

[1] R. H. S. Crossman, "Britain, the Arabs and the Jews," *The New Republic*, July 1, 1946, 932–933.

[2] See Amikam Nachmani, Great Power Discord in Palestine: The Anglo-American Committee of Inquiry into the Problems of European Jewry and Palestine, 1945–1946 (London: Frank Cass, 1987); and Richard Crossman, Palestine Mission: A Personal Record (New York: Harper, 1947). On Crossman's assessment of the Anglo-American Committee, his support for Zionism, and criticism of Bevin's policies see William Roger Louis, The British Empire in the Middle East, 1945–1951 (New York and Oxford: Oxford University Press, 1984), 397–419.

[3] Crossman, *Palestine Mission*, 932–933.

[4] Harold J. Laski, "Truman v. Attlee on Palestine," *The New Republic*, November 4, 1946, 585.

[5] See, for example, Henry Wallace, "The Problem of Palestine," *The New Republic*, April 21, 1947, 12–13; "First Impressions of Palestine," *The New Republic*, November 3, 1947, 11–12; and "Conquerors of the Negev," *The New Republic*, November 10, 1948, 4, 10–12.

under his editorship did not offer the same amount of investigative journalism and analysis evident in the pages of *The Nation*, *PM*, and the *New York Post*.

With an average circulation of 165,000,[6] *PM* combined a tabloid format – bold headlines and plentiful photos – with a consistent left-liberal but noncommunist perspective on events. Its location in the New York media market and ability to attract excellent journalists and commentators contributed to its impact. I. F. Stone[7] was its most prominent contributor addressing Palestine-related issues, but others offering frequent commentaries on those issues included well-known veteran journalists Victor Bernstein, Max Lerner,[8] John P. Lewis, Saul Padover, and Alexander Uhl. Together they offered *PM*'s readers reporting and commentary sympathetic to Jewish aspirations for a state in Palestine, in contrast to the generally more reserved stance of the *New York Times*.

PM devoted a remarkable amount of coverage to the fate of the Jews after the war and to the prospect of a Jewish state in Palestine. From July 1, 1945 to June 1, 1948 some 145 (15 percent) of its front-page headlines referred to articles dealing with Jewish displaced persons, antisemitism, or the conflict in Palestine at the United Nations and in Palestine itself. I. F. Stone alone wrote 44 of those front-page stories. In just two months, July and August 1946, *PM* published 25 of Stone's reports in a series entitled "Underground to Palestine," which dealt with the efforts of Jewish refugees in Europe to reach Palestine. The reports became the basis for the book of the same title.[9]

In the 1940s Victor Bernstein (1905–92) served as *PM*'s foreign editor, and from 1945 to 1948 his own articles appeared on the front page seventeen times. His focus was on the Nuremberg war crimes trials and US policy in postwar Germany, and then on Palestine.[10] In those same three years *PM* ran eighteen stories on Nazi war crimes and the war crimes trials. From

---

[6] See Paul Milkman, *PM: A New Deal in Journalism 1940–1948* (New Brunswick, NJ: Rutgers University Press, 1997).

[7] On Stone's views on Zionism and Israel see Susie Linfield, "I. F. Stone: The Limits of Isaiah," in *The Lions' Den: Zionism and the Left from Hannah Arendt to Noam Chomsky* (New Haven: Yale University Press, 2019), 229–261.

[8] Lerner was a frequent contributor. See Max Lerner, "Fate of Jews Index to Fate of us all: The Jew and the Western Conscience," *PM*, October 2, 1945, 1–2. Lerner also wrote a column for the *New York Post*. From 1949 to 1973 he taught in the program in American Studies at Brandeis University, and in 1957 he published *America as a Civilization: Life and Thought in the United States Today* (New York: Simon & Schuster, 1957).

[9] I. F. Stone, *Underground to Palestine* (New York: Pantheon, 1978 [1946]).

[10] See, for example, Victor Bernstein, "What's Behind the Go Easy on Germany Policy," *PM*, October 12, 1945, and "How Giving Germany Back to the Germans Is Working Out," *PM*, November 12, 1945.

1937 to 1939 Bernstein had been the Berlin correspondent for the Jewish Telegraphic Agency. In 1945 he returned to Berlin for *PM* and covered the liberation of the Nazi concentration camps. Drawing on his experience covering the Nuremberg trials, he explored thousands of captured documents in his 1947 work *Final Judgment: The Story of Nuremberg.*[11]

On October 1, 1945, following the public release of the Harrison report on the condition of Jews in displaced persons camps, *PM* led with an editorial by Stone.[12] He applauded Truman for his appeal to the British to allow 100,000 Jewish displaced persons to go to Palestine and noted that since the 1,200,000 Arabs outnumbered the 600,000–700,000 Jews in Palestine, "it would not prejudice later settlement of the question of unlimited immigration or of a Jewish state. It is an immediate emergency measure of the utmost urgency that leaves ample leeway for the solution of broader questions." Yet, Stone continued, the matter was not only a Jewish question. He agreed with Truman that the USA had no better way to demonstrate its determination to wipe out Nazism than "by the way in which we ourselves treat the survivors remaining in Germany."[13]

PM expanded its focus on the Palestine/Israel issue by reporting on the Middle East more broadly, and on sources of opposition to Zionism in the region. On November 2, 1945 Gerald Frank, *PM*'s foreign correspondent in the region, referred to "the fascist Moslem Brotherhood" that was stirring up "riots" in Egypt.[14] He reported that Hassan al-Banna, the head of the Muslim Brotherhood, had made a request "to free the ex-Mufti, now held in Paris as a war criminal." In recent months al-Banna had "published many pamphlets to prove that Islam has always supported totalitarianism and has always magnified the principle of the leader." He described the mainstay of the Brotherhood's membership as "young religious students who attend El Azhar, Cairo's 1000-year-old theological college. It was these students, with el-Banna himself at their head, who had recently marched upon Jewish synagogues and looted them, and then went on to loot British and Greek shops." American diplomats and intelligence agents in Cairo were sending classified reports along similar lines.[15]

---

[11] "Victor Bernstein, a Retired Editor Dies," *New York Times*, November 19, 1992; Victor Bernstein, *Final Judgment: The Story of Nuremberg* (New York: Boni & Gaer, 1947). Bernstein was the managing editor of *The Nation* from 1952 to 1963.

[12] I. F. Stone, "The Harrison Report: A Revelation and a Challenge," *PM*, October 1, 1945, 2.

[13] Ibid.

[14] Gerald Frank, "The Inside Story: Fascist Moslem Brotherhood Stirs Riots in Egypt," *PM*, November 2, 1945, 3.

[15] Ibid. For contemporaneous reports by American diplomats and military intelligence agents on the riots and on affinities between the Nazis and the Muslim Brotherhood

On November 15, 1945, in response to British plans to appoint a committee of inquiry to examine options for the future of Palestine, Stone published "Palestine has had Enough of 'Inquiries.'"[16] "People abroad must remember that there is hardly a Jewish family here which did not lose friends or loved ones in the Hitler holocaust and many are striving to bring scattered relatives and survivors here [to Palestine]."[17] The following month Stone wrote five more articles on Palestine, each with a front-page headline. On December 4 he argued that Palestine was indeed a home to the Jews.[18] Under the headline "There the Rejected and Despised Find Freedom, Equality Denied them Elsewhere" he described the emotional, religious, and secular reasons why Jews felt bound to Palestine:

Hitlerism, the homelessness of the little remnant of Central and East European Jewry, the increased anti-Semitism in the wake of the war, the disheartening hesitations of the democratic powers, have left few Jews, rich or poor, secure or insecure, in any mood for elaborate theoretical pros-and-cons about Palestine. For several hundred thousand Jews, the choice is emigration to Palestine or emigration to Mars via the Pearly Gates. If Jewish and non-Jewish opinion can help them find a home in Palestine that portentous perennial, The Jewish Problem, can be left to the leisurely if sometimes cruel processes of history.

I am not objective about the plight of Central and East European Jewry. As a newspaperman I have never sought to be "objective" about injustice or inhumanity anywhere.

In Palestine, whether among Jews or Arabs, a Jew is a Jew, and no one asks him why. No apologetics, spoken or unspoken, are necessary, no lengthy and defensive dispositions on whether Jews are a race, [or] a religious myth ... The sense of no longer being a minority in a world of hostile [powers] is like the lifting of a neurosis and explains why Jews who enjoyed standing and wealth elsewhere are often happier with a much harder Zion.[19]

Stone wrote that the Jews, especially those of Central and Eastern Europe had tried unsuccessfully the way of assimilation. They had "never known Western freedom and equality," Stone pointed out; yet they had been "loyal citizens of their fatherlands, fought for them and died for them and still been despised and rejected. Until one understands this, one cannot understand either Palestine or the present mood of the Jews there and in

see Jeffrey Herf, "Postwar Aftereffects," in *Nazi Propaganda for the Arab World* (New Haven: Yale University Press, 2009), 239–260. On the ideological as well as practical links between Nazis and the Muslim Brotherhood see Matthias Küntzel, *Nazis und der Nahe Osten: Wie der Islamische Antisemitismus Entstand* (Leipzig: Hentrich & Hentrich, 2019).

[16] I. F. Stone, "Palestine has had Enough of 'Inquiries,'" *PM*, November 15, 1945, 1 and 3.

[17] Ibid., 3.

[18] I. F. Stone, "Why Palestine Is 'Home' to Jews: There the Rejected and Despised Find Freedom, Equality Denied them Elsewhere," *PM*, December 4, 1945, 4.

[19] Ibid.

Central and Eastern Europe, who are determined to die fighting, if necessary, for the right to go home."[20]

In the emerging conflict between Jews attempting to get to Palestine and British government efforts to prevent them from doing so, Stone and *PM* emphatically took the side of the Jews. On December 6 he wrote that it was "not surprising" that Jews felt "as bitterly about the White Paper restrictions" on Jewish immigration to Palestine from 1939 to 1945 "as they did about the deliberate bestialities of the Nazis." It was "not difficult to understand the deliberate, systematic, organized, and admitted smuggling of refugees 'illegally' into Palestine, activities which continue despite British naval patrols, curfews and a veritable army of occupation."[21] Stone expressed sympathy for the efforts of "the Yishuv" to intensify "illegal immigration" and establish new colonies "where Jewish settlement was forbidden by the White Paper." He particularly empathized with Jewish bitterness at the British who had repaid Jewish support for the Allies during the war with the blockade of Palestine. "The Jewish forces with which the British now must contend are made up in part of the same men who worked for the British in underground intelligence tasks in Vichy-controlled Syria and in Axis Europe during the war."[22] The Jews in Palestine included veterans who had been anti-Nazi partisans in Europe. They were not going to be deterred by British efforts prevent Jewish immigration to Palestine. Stone was, he wrote, not a Zionist but neither was he an anti-Zionist.[23] Here again, Stone's fresh memories not only of the Holocaust but of Jewish participation in the Allied war against Nazi Germany fueled his empathy for the Zionists.[24]

On December 9 Stone attributed Attlee and Bevin's adoption of the anti-Zionist views of the British Foreign Office to distortions of British class snobbery.[25] After serving in the wartime British cabinet, he wrote,

---

[20] Ibid., 5.

[21] I. F. Stone, "Why Palestine Jews are in 'Revolt': They Feel Strongly on Legal and Moral Objections to the White Paper," *PM*, December 6, 1945, 8.

[22] Ibid., 9.   [23] Ibid.

[24] Since the 1990s an extensive scholarship and journalistic commentary has been published regarding whether, and if so in what manner, I. F. Stone had contact with or engaged in espionage for the Soviet intelligence service, the KGB. For an extensive overview see Max Holland, "I. F. Stone's Encounters with Soviet Intelligence," *Journal of Cold War Studies* 11, no. 3 (Summer 2009): 144–205. Also see D. D. Guttenplan, *American Radical: The Life and Times of I. F. Stone* (New York: Farrar, Strauss & Giroux, 2009); and Alexander Vassiliev, John Earl Haynes, and Harvey Klehr, *Spies: The Rise and Fall of the KGB in America* (New Haven: Yale University Press, 2009). Stone wrote his first articles in support of the Zionist project in fall 1945 and many more in 1946 and early 1947, that is, before the Soviet Union publicly announced its support for the Partition Plan at the United Nations in May 1947. Holland's review of the controversy does not discuss Stone's essays on Zionism and Israel.

[25] I. F. Stone, "Why British Labor Switched on Palestine," *PM*, December 9, 1945, 2.

they began to adopt views "molded by snobbery, imitation and conformity to the upper class largely Tory and imperial point of view. These subordinates provide the Cabinet officer with information, past precedents and that most awful deterrent of all, the silent disapproval that says we-just-don't-do-things-that-way-here."[26] The following week he attributed the generally pro-Arab sentiments among "most British officials in Palestine" to their "autocratic, colonial mentality." They thought it easier to deal with Arabs than Jews because they viewed the former as "natives, the latter as European equals who did not accept assumptions of colonial superiority."[27]

On December 11, in an article entitled "Russia-and the British Policy in Palestine: Nurture Arab Anti-Zionism to Help Build Bloc," Stone pointed out that the British government feared that the Arabs would "go over to the Russians" if Jewish immigration continued. But Stone doubted they would turn to the Soviets. The "Pashas who fear the social effects of Zionism are 10 times as fearful of Communism." Britain's policy in the Middle East was to "build a bloc there under British tutelage" to counter influence of both the Soviet Union and the United States, though "their more urgent concern is with the USSR, which they fear and distrust." To build such a bloc the British needed support from Arabs, and to gain that support they were willing to exact concessions "at the expense of others," who in this case were "the French, the Jews, and the Christian minorities."[28] British imperial strategy in the Middle East and Mediterranean aimed to retain access to oil and military bases.

The British are using anti-Zionism in the Middle East to unite the Arab world under British leadership and to divert Arab nationalist agitation from an anti-British to an anti-Jewish basis. If this policy requires the abandonment of the Balfour Declaration, the stoppage of Jewish immigration to Palestine, the relegation of the Yishuv to the precarious status of another ghetto in the Arab world, these British officials are fully prepared to pay the price. It's no skin off their elbows ... This ... is the essence of British policy in the Middle East.[29]

The British tilted toward the Arabs because of oil, access to military bases, fear of communism, and a belief that the religious and traditional Arabs, presumably in contrast to the modern Jews, who were far more immune to communism. In Stone's view, anti-Zionism – that is, opposition to the establishment of a Jewish state in Palestine and support for Arab rejection

---

[26] Ibid., 3.
[27] I. F. Stone, "Why Most British Officials in Palestine Are Pro-Arab: Cold Fish Atmosphere Pervades Colonial Service," *PM*, December 10, 1945, 6.
[28] I. F. Stone, "Russia-and the British Policy in Palestine: Nurture Arab Anti-Zionism to Help Build Bloc," *PM*, December 11, 1945, 7.
[29] Ibid.

of the promises of the Balfour Declaration – was central to Britain's efforts to sustain, not undermine, its imperial power in the Middle East.

Another *PM* contributor, the foreign editor Alexander Uhl (1899–1976), emphasized France's role in placing obstacles in the Zionists' path, focusing on the implications of Husseini's return to the Middle East in a series of articles published in winter and spring 1946.[30] On February 15 his piece "Plot to Get Grand Mufti to Middle East Reported" appeared, accompanied by two photos, one of Husseini's meeting with Hitler on November 28, 1941 (captioned "The Grand Mufti Visits Hitler") and the other of Husseini reviewing troops in the Balkans. The caption of that photo read: "This picture which appeared in the *Berlin Illustrated News* shows the Grand Mufti reviewing Bosnian (Yugoslav) troops which had been incorporated into the SS troop detachments." Uhl, like Stone, predicted that the Grand Mufti, "who played stooge for Hitler is going to 'escape' from forced residence in France and turn up in the Middle East," and he explained why. Negotiations were underway between the British and French governments, both of whom "see the Mufti as a powerful weapon to keep the Arab world united against possible Soviet expansion."[31] "The Arab League wants him back, especially to play him off against the Zionists, and already started a propaganda campaign to whitewash him. Neither the French nor the British want anything to happen to him because of possible effects on their Moslem subjects – and he can be a valuable tool wherever the Moslem world involves with the British or French empires." Uhl noted that Husseini's nephew Jamal Husseini, whom he described as an "Arab terrorist leader, recently turned up in Jerusalem from Rhodesia, a free man despite his record of pro-Axis intrigues." According to Uhl, the return of these leaders "brought bitter protests" from the American Zionist Emergency Council (AZEC), which saw it as "another step in British imperialist intrigue in the Middle East … The British Colonial Office is now engaged in bolstering pan-Arabism and the Arab League, which are meant to be instruments in the perpetuation of Britain's sole control over the Middle East," said an AZEC spokesperson.[32]

On April 10 Uhl warned that France was letting the Mufti, "one of the men most responsible for the slaughter of millions of Jews, … slip out

---

[30] As bureau chief of the Associated Press in Madrid from 1935 to 1938, Uhl directed the AP's coverage of the Spanish Civil War. He also covered World War II in Europe and was awarded the French Legion of Honor: "Alexander H. Uhl, Long a Newsman, Dies in Spain at 77," *New York Times*, August 25, 1976, 32: www.nytimes.com/1976/08/25/arc hives/alexander-h-uhl-long-a-newsman-dies-in-spain-of-77.html

[31] Alexander Uhl, "Plot to Get Grand Mufti to Middle East Reported," *PM*, February 15, 1946, 3.

[32] Ibid.

free" because Britain and France were engaged in "an enormous game of diplomatic hocus-pocus."[33] Though the French government asserted that it "had never received a formal demand from Britain for the Mufti's extradition," Foreign Minister Bevin stated in the House of Commons that Britain had in fact done so, but "the French had not complied." Uhl concluded that

> what is behind all this, is that neither the French nor the British Colonial Offices want to upset their Moslem relations by doing anything unpleasant to the Mufti despite his pro-Axis activities. While they are therefore going through diplomatic motions, the Mufti is slipping through the hands of the War Crimes Commission and once he gets to Saudi Arabia all chances of punishing him will be gone.[34]

As we will see in the following chapter, Uhl was right that neither Britain nor France was willing to put Husseini on trial, and in fact the French government saw benefits in allowing his return to the Middle East. The Zionists, on the other hand, regarded him "as a threat to any peaceful settlement of the relations between Jews and Arabs in Palestine."[35]

I. F. Stone, *The Nation, PM* and "Underground to Palestine"

Support for Jewish immigration to Palestine, in opposition to British efforts to prevent it, energized these left-leaning journalists between 1945 and 1948. Stone traveled to Europe to follow the path of Jewish clandestine immigration to Palestine. In summer 1946 he published a series of articles in *PM* about the refugee drama. The Brichah, a Zionist organization meaning "flight," assisted Jews leaving Eastern Europe. By late 1946 about 250,000 Jewish refugees were in the Allied occupation zones of Germany and Austria and in Italy.[36] In fall 1945 the Haganah, the Zionist military organization representing the majority of the Jews in Palestine from 1920 to 1948, established Mossad Le'Aliyah Bet (Institute for Immigration, B). From its headquarters in Paris it opposed the British White Paper restrictions on Jewish immigration to Palestine by organizing a network that arranged illegal refugee ships seeking to transport Jews to Palestine.[37] By the spring of 1948 it had moved up to 80,000 Jews from

---

[33] Alexander Uhl, "France Letting Grand Mufti Slip out Free: Hitler's No. 1 Arab Collaborator May Now Be in Middle East, " *PM*, April 10, 1946, 7.

[34] Ibid.   [35] Ibid.

[36] See Yehuda Bauer, *Flight and Rescue: Brichah* (New York: Random House, 1970); Atina Grossmann, *Jews, Germans and Allies: Close Encounters in Occupied Germany* (Princeton: Princeton University Press, 2007).

[37] On the Haganah see Anita Shapira, *Land and Power: The Zionist Resort to Force, 1881–1948* (Stanford: Stanford University Press, 1999).

Europe.[38] Doing so involved organizing Jewish survivors of the Holocaust for clandestine journeys by foot, truck, and train when possible, many from Eastern and Central Europe, others from displaced-persons camps in occupied Austria and Germany, to ports mostly in Italy, France, Romania, and Bulgaria. From those ports the Jews boarded ships seeking to break the British blockade of Palestine.[39] According to Ze'ev Hadari, the deputy of the Zionist immigration operations in Marseille, the Mossad Le'Aliyah Bet transported about 70,000 Jews on its ships, of whom the British Navy captured 52,500, detaining them in camps on Cyprus, where they were held until Israel attained its independence in May 1948.[40] Of the sixty ships that challenged the British naval blockade, only thirteen reached the shoreline of Palestine, and half of those landings took place prior to January 1946.[41]

The organizers of Mossad Le'Aliyah Bet and their supporters in Europe and the United States purchased seventy-five ships to transport Jews to Palestine and break the British naval blockade seeking to prevent the entry of what the British called "illegal immigrants." From summer 1945 to May 1948 they dispatched sixty ships from several ports in Europe.[42] The first left Italy for British Mandate Palestine on August 28, 1945 and the last also left from Italy and arrived in the new state of Israel on May 29, 1948. Five ships left Europe for Palestine in 1945, twenty-four in 1946. Though the headquarters of the Mossad Le'Aliyah Bet was in Paris and its most important transit camps were in and near Marseille, thirty-one ships left from ports in Italy, seventeen from France, fourteen from Romanian and Bulgarian harbors, four from Greece, three from Yugoslavia, two from Algiers, one each from Sweden, Belgium, and (with arms) from Czechoslovakia.

Most were intercepted by destroyers of the British Royal Navy and, as noted above, the passengers were then taken to detention camps in Cyprus. The British held them there until Israel attained its independence in May 1948. Most of the time the immigrants did not physically resist

---

[38] See Idith Zertal, *From Catastrophe to Power: Holocaust Survivors and the Emergence of Israel* (Berkeley and Los Angeles: University of California Press, 1998).

[39] See the account in Ze'ev Venia Hadari, *Second Exodus: The Full Story of Jewish Illegal Immigration to Palestine, 1945–1948* (London: Vallentine Mitchell, 1991).

[40] Stuart A. Cohen, "Imperial Policy against Illegal Immigration: The Royal Navy and Palestine, 1945–48," *Journal of Imperial and Commonwealth History* 22, no. 2 (May 1994): 275–293; Arieh Kochavi, "The Struggle against Jewish Immigration to Palestine," *Middle Eastern Studies* 34, no. 3 (July 1998): 146–167, at 163; Arieh Kochavi, "Britain and the Illegal Immigration to Palestine from France following World War II," *Holocaust and Genocide Studies* 6, no. 4 (December 1991): 383–396; Fritz Liebreich, *Britain's Naval and Political Reaction to the Illegal Immigration of Jews to Palestine, 1945–1948* (London and New York: Routledge, 2005).

[41] Cohen, "Imperial Policy against Illegal Immigration," 277.   [42] Ibid.

orders to disembark, but on those few occasions when they did, launching volleys of canned food at their captors, there were multiple injuries and some deaths among the passengers as British sailors responded with tear gas and, several times, even live machine-gun fire. According to Hadari, 2,260 Jewish survivors of the Holocaust attempting to reach Palestine in those three years were killed or drowned.[43]

As we shall see, the Zionist challenge to British policy and American public support for the plight of the refugees became an American preoccupation for two reasons. For State Department officials who stressed the primacy of the Anglo-American alliance, the Zionist challenge to British policy and support for that challenge among American politicians put strains on Anglo-American strategic relations. But at the same time, American liberals whose sympathies lay with Jewish survivors of the Holocaust depicted British policy as blundering at best and heartless at worse. American journalists and representatives of American Jewish organizations such as the Joint Distribution Committee, the Jewish World Congress, and Hadassah reinforced one another in bringing their dire circumstances to the attention of the American public, as did the release of the Harrison report in fall 1945.

In a series of reports in *PM* in summer 1946 entitled "Underground to Palestine," I. F. Stone led the way in bringing "the second exodus" to the attention of American readers (see Figure 3.1). By July 11, 1946, when he published the first of his reports, eleven of the refugee ships had left European ports for Palestine. From July 22 to August 29, 1946 *PM* published eighteen front-page articles by Stone describing harrowing nighttime border crossings in Central and Eastern Europe on the way to ports such as Marseille and Genoa, and then the crowded, hot, and oppressive voyages that mostly ended with seizure by British naval vessels. The "Underground to Palestine" series was the lead story in *PM* that summer.

Stone reported on frustrating months waiting for permission to cross into the American zones in Germany and Austria; the antisemitism faced by Jews who tried to return to their homes in Poland; their despair at learning of the deaths of loved ones; nightmare memories of concentration and death camps and the persistence of antisemitism in Europe.[44] He

---

[43] Hadari, *Second Exodus*, xiv.
[44] I. F. Stone, "Starting Today: By I. F. Stone, Through Europe's Underground to Palestine," *PM*, July 22, 1946, 3. Articles that followed in the series include: "Border Passage for Group: A Carton of Cigarettes," *PM*, July 24, 1946, 3; "First Night on the Train: Enroute to the 'Promised Land,'" *PM*, July 25, 1946, 3; "We All Expected to Be Sent to the Crematoria," *PM*, July 26, 1946, 3; "Vienna's Ring – the Heart of a Vanished Empire," *PM*, August 4, 1946, 8; and "The Model Camp for Refugees in Austria," *PM*, August 6, 1946, 9.

Figure 3.1 I. F. (Isidor Feinstein) Stone, New York City, January 1, 1955. Photo by Lotte Jacobi. Source: University of New Hampshire/ Gado/Getty Images.

described their relief at arriving in the American zones in Germany and Austria, where the Jews "at last" met "a friendly reception" and received identification papers that allowed free movement around the American zone. "The U.S. Army, despite what you may read of complaints and occasional clashes between DPs and military police, is the best friend the Jewish people have in Europe today," Stone wrote.[45] Yet his reports culminated in articles on the confrontation of the refugee ships with warships of the British Navy, which seized the ships, forced to the Jews to disembark in Haifa and transferred them to other ships, which then took them to Cyprus.[46] His stories of Jews reaching the shores of Palestine only to be turned away by the British deepened sympathy for the refugees in Europe and the United States.

On returning to the United States at the end of August 1946 after his in-depth reporting in Europe and the Mediterranean, Stone expressed his anger at British policy in a signed editorial that began on the front page of *PM*: "What's Behind British Policy in Palestine?"[47] The British were "not playing a pro-Arab game"; rather, they were "trying to build an alliance

---

[45] Stone, "Vienna's Ring," 8.

[46] I. F. Stone, "About 3 Boats among Fleet Captured by the British," *PM*, August 7, 1946, 13; "The Crew Spoke a Sailor's Brooklynese," *PM*, August 5, 1946, 9; and "Night of Horror in Refugee Ship's Hold," *PM*, August 23, 1946, 3.

[47] I. F. Stone, "What's Behind British Policy in Palestine? They Have Taken Crafty Counsel against thy People," *PM*, August 29, 1946, 6.

with the Moslem upper classes in the Middle East against the Soviet Union, and also against France and the United States. They want to keep the whole area under their control" and were "prepared to sacrifice not only the Jews, but the Christian minorities of the East in that program."[48] Stone stated that he was "convinced that the Jewish people can expect nothing whatsoever from the British government except disappointment, betrayal and attack."[49] The British Empire was "now waging a war designed to smash what the Jews have accomplished in Palestine, and to break the hearts of the homeless in DP camps and elsewhere by shutting off their one hope – the so-called illegal immigration." In doing so, Britain was violating its obligations under the League of Nations Mandate that gave it temporary trusteeship in order to establish a Jewish national home. "To bar the Jews from the Holy Land is to violate the mandate and the treaty."[50] The British were

> too humane a people to send the Jews of Europe to gas chambers as the Nazis did, but their government can be very cruel in an almost absent-minded and complacent way when the supposed needs of the Empire are at stake. [Britain] did not intend to kill the homeless Jews of Europe – it just wants to destroy their hopes, but that amounts to the same thing. As one Jewish ex-partisan said to me on shipboard: "The Germans killed us. The British don't let us live . . . " The Moslem upper class on the whole – with the exception of some far-sighted men – share with the British: the phobia about the USSR; fear of unrest among miserable Arab masses, and dislike for the modern ideas and methods brought to the ancient East by the returning Jews.[51]

The British government "wants the Middle East to remain an area of backwardness" where "native rulers" could be easily handled in the traditional imperial manner, but Britain offered "freedom neither to the Arabs nor the Jews." To Stone, Britain's campaign against Jewish immigration to Palestine was a "struggle from which Britain will emerge with shame, but not with victory."[52]

Around the same time, *PM*'s Alexander Uhl wrote that the USA was also complicit in dashing Jews' hopes for a homeland. On August 25 he penned a front-page editorial on "FDR and British Imperialism" in which he denounced what he saw as an apparent shift of US foreign policy in favor of British policy in the Middle East.[53] He regretted that "the State Department, in fear of Russia, has accepted bag and baggage the thesis that the defense of American interests in the world today means defense of the British imperial system." The policy was unrealistic and likely to lead to war. Uhl criticized Truman for accepting the kind of Anglo-American alliance against Russia that Churchill had called for in his Iron Curtain

---

[48] Ibid.   [49] Ibid.   [50] Ibid.   [51] Ibid.   [52] Ibid.
[53] Alexander Uhl, "FDR and British Imperialism," *PM*, August 25, 1946, 1 and 2.

speech in Fulton, Missouri the previous March. While FDR certainly did not intend to destroy the British Empire, his priority in World War II was defending British democracy, not the British Empire. The State Department, on the other hand, supported "the thesis that the Russians must be held back, which has meant in practice maintaining the British position throughout the world." Its policy toward the Middle East was "made by the same kind of commercial and industrial interests that make British imperial policy." While it was in American interests to "defend British democracy," it was "**NOT** in the interests of the American people to defend the British imperial system. FDR had made that distinction. We are not making it today."[54]

With the arguments made by Stone and Uhl, *PM*'s partisanship toward the Jewish state in Palestine and the associated criticism of British imperialism put it at odds with the fault lines of the emerging political contest between the West and the Soviet Union and communist states. The emerging Cold War called for close cooperation between the United States and Britain in order to contain the expansion of communist influence, and toward that end, US support for a continued strong British presence in the Middle East. Stone and Uhl's attacks on British policy put them at odds with that view. Because the Soviet Union also sought to diminish British influence in the Middle East, in the halls of power in Washington and London important advocates of the new hard line against the Soviet Union began to make the case that there was a connection between support for the Zionist project and Soviet policy.

Zionism and *The Nation* in 1945 and 1946

While *PM* was influential in the New York area, *The Nation* had a national reach and served as the flagship of Roosevelt-era liberalism and the non-communist left. Its editor, Freda Kirchwey (see Figure 3.2), made Zionist aspirations one of the defining aspects of both her own writing and that of authors she invited to appear in the magazine.[55] On September 15, 1945, four months after the end of the war in Europe, *The Nation* published Senator Robert Wagner's essay "Palestine – a World Responsibility."[56]

Palestine should no longer be discussed dispassionately. The period of inquiry, investigation, and calm debate is long behind us. Detachment has ceased to be a virtue. Today Palestine cries aloud in indignation. In Palestine international

---

[54] Ibid., 2 (emphasis in original).
[55] On Kirchwey see Sara Alpern, *Freda Kirchwey: A Woman of "The Nation"* (Cambridge, MA: Harvard University Press, 1987).
[56] Robert Wagner, "Palestine – a World Responsibility," *The Nation*, September 15, 1945, 247–249.

Figure 3.2 Freda Kirchwey, January 1944 in Vogue. Source: Constantin Joffe/Conde Nast Collection Editorial/Getty Images.

promises have been broken, loyalty and fidelity have been unrequited, hostility has been appeased and human life has been subordinated to the mysterious demands of imperial policy. The miracle is that, despite all this, Jewish Palestine has throughout the war been a bastion of security to the United Nations and is today the most successful pioneering effort in human history.[57]

The "imperial policy" that Wagner had in mind was Britain's determination to sustain its presence in the Middle East. Now that the war was over, "the military considerations which have restrained official expression of America's views on Palestine are no longer germane." That is, fears were now moot that the Arab states would support the Axis or undermine the Allied war effort if the Allies announced a firm policy in favor of implementing the promises of the Balfour Declaration. It was time for "plain speech and forthright action." In the pages of *The Nation* Wagner recounted the longstanding American political consensus in support of establishment of a Jewish state in Palestine and extolled the accomplishments of the Jewish community there in recent decades.

Wagner's judgment on British policy was harsh. He called the White Paper of 1939 a "mortal blow" that limited immigration to Palestine in the very years "when European Jewry was undergoing martyrdom at the

---

[57] Ibid., 247. He is referring to the term used for the coalition of allies during World War II.

hands of Hitler, when refugees fortunate enough to escape the torture chambers and crematoriums were naturally turning toward Palestine as a sanctuary and a haven ... By thus yielding to Nazi propaganda Great Britain hoped to win Arab support. It succeeded only in losing Arab's respect."[58] The White Paper had been an act of "moral bankruptcy": Wagner applied that judgment with sadness to the policy of Britain, "a great and brave ally with whom we have just fought shoulder to shoulder to save civilization." The White Paper restrictions on Jewish immigration to Palestine took place when the British government "counseled its people to stray after the false idols in the groves of appeasement." While appeasement was discredited, the policy it fostered toward Palestine continued. There were no military considerations anymore "to obscure the cruelty of this illegal policy," yet the "gates of Palestine are still barred to the Jews."[59]

Now that the war in Europe had ended, Wagner argued, the United States should see that "the Balfour Declaration should be executed fully, expeditiously, and faithfully." It was "heartbreaking to consider how many human lives might have been saved had Palestine remained wide open." The "tragedy which is behind us ought to spur us on to more responsible action with respect to the small remnant of European Jewry which has escaped." Palestine was a "world problem" and was "the crucible" that would test "the ability of the powerful to deal faithfully with the weak. The Christian world has Palestine on its conscience. If it would regain its moral self-respect, it must promptly do justice to Palestine."[60] By "justice for Palestine" Wagner meant establishing a Jewish state there and bringing an end to what he called a policy of appeasement of the Arabs which Britain had inaugurated.

The Nation also provided a national platform for I. F. Stone. On October 6, 1945, in his first postwar essay in that journal, Stone wrote that the revelations of the Harrison report demonstrated that the Anglo-American world was not living up to the moral traditions of wartime antifascism.[61] Rather than "resolute action" to fight antisemitism or a "great and graphic act of justice to the homeless of Jewry as an object lesson to the Nazi-infected peoples," the report was "only likely to convince the enemies of world order in Central Europe, at home and elsewhere, that the democratic forces of the Anglo-American world are weak and irresolute, too half-hearted to live up to their grandiose moral pretensions, not genuinely anti-fascist, easily gulled, and perhaps next time,

---

[58] Ibid., 248.   [59] Ibid.   [60] Ibid., 249.

[61] I. F. Stone, "The Plight of the Jews," *The Nation*, October 6, 1945, 330. For Stone's articles in *The Nation* during World War II see I. F. Stone, *The War Years, 1939–1945* (Boston: Little, Brown: 1988).

with more luck, to be defeated."[62] Stone cited Harrison's conclusion that there was "nowhere else [but a Jewish state in Palestine] for them [the Jews] to go; covert anti-Semitism and xenophobia greet them even in America and England." With Attlee and Bevin's reversal of the British Labour Party's previous policy in support of Zionist aspirations in mind, Stone wrote that, like Wagner, he viewed British policy as another example of appeasement, this time in an effort to gain good will from the Arabs by opposing the Zionists.

As early as that October Stone sensed a shift away from the passions of World War II. "The problem of Jewish immigration into Palestine is similarly part of the greater problem of substituting Allied cooperation for power politics." For Stone, "allied cooperation" referred to a continued willingness to work with the Soviet Union. "Pledges to the Jews on Palestine are being broken because of British imperialist desires to use the thin layer of the Arab ruling class as a pawn in a game of oil politics with America and power politics with the Soviet Union." As the Arab League was "the creation and the tool of the British Foreign Office," Stone argued that "a Palestine settlement benefitting both Jews and Arabs" was "possible any time the British government wants it."[63] Yet British efforts to convince the Arabs to accept the binational solution recommended by the Anglo-American Committee of Inquiry ran up against a wall of Arab rejection far higher than suggested by the powers he attributed to Britain in that comment.[64]

On December 8, 1945 *The Nation* published a report by Stone from Palestine, his first from the region. Stone then favored a binational state rather than a Jewish state. Nevertheless, he wrote that "it would be foolish, and it would be completely to misunderstand how history and human beings work to disparage Zionism." Yet this secular Jewish leftist found himself

immensely attracted by the life of the Yishuv, the Jewish community of Palestine. It is the one place in the world where Jews seem completely unafraid ... In Palestine a Jew can be a Jew. Period. Without apologies, and without any lengthy arguments as to whether Jews are a race, a religion, a myth, or an accident. He needs explain to no one and he feels profoundly at home; I am quite willing to attribute this to historic sentimentality, but it remains none the less a tremendous and inescapable fact.[65]

Stone's admiration for the Yishuv as "the one place in the world where Jews seem completely unafraid" was of a piece with his general rejection of racism and antisemitism.

---

[62] Stone, "The Plight of the Jews," 330.   [63] Ibid.

[64] On the Arab opposition both to Zionism and to the recommendations of the Anglo-American Committee of Inquiry see chapters 16–20 in J. C. Hurewitz, *The Struggle for Palestine* (New York: W. W. Norton, 1950; repr. Greenwood Press, 1968).

[65] I. F. Stone, "Palestine Pilgrimage," *Nation*, December 8, 1945, 615–616.

Two months later *The Nation* published Stone's first report from Palestine. Though he personally was not in favor of a Jewish state in Palestine, he repeated that "it would be foolish, and it would be completely to misunderstand how history and human beings work to disparage Zionism." He found himself "immensely attracted by the life of the Yishuv, the Jewish community of Palestine." He repeated the sentiments he had expressed in *PM*, but now to a national audience. Palestine was "the one place in the world where Jews seem completely unafraid," and where "a Jew can be a Jew" and can feel "profoundly at home."[66]

In these first months after the war Stone contributed to making support for Zionist aspirations a part of the worldview of the American liberals and leftists.

In "The Case of the Mufti," a May 4, 1946 article in *The Nation*, Stone called "the case of the Mufti number-one business for those who desire a peaceful solution to the Palestine problem." If this "Arab war criminal" was permitted to return to Palestine, "the stage will be set for trouble."[67] Those who sought a peaceful solution "must prevent his return or see their hopes blasted." If Husseini and his followers returned, they would "again terrorize the moderate Arab leaders, as they did during the 1936–39 uprising." Following, the press reports that the Mufti was "one of the initiators of the systematic extermination of European Jewry by the Germans," a British decision to allow him to return would deepen bitterness among Palestine Jews and "strengthen the terrorist minority" responsible for "outrages" that "shamed every friend of Palestine."[68]

Stone wrote that "the rich annals of appeasement contain no more striking story than that of Haj Amin el Husseini, no more convincing testimony to the readiness of the British government to be gulled." Despite his role in producing Nazi propaganda and in organizing SS units in Yugoslavia, "for some mysterious reason the Yugoslavs have taken him off their war criminals list."[69] The French government, Stone continued, was "playing the same kind of stupid, dirty role in connection with the Mufti that it played in 1937" when it gave him refuge in Syria as the British were pursuing him. Stone predicted that the French would permit the Mufti to leave comfortable house arrest in France for the Middle East, and indeed, several weeks later Husseini "escaped" to Egypt.[70] For Stone, Husseini's return served as a prime example of how the British and French governments were placing imperialist interests ahead of the purposes for which World War II had been fought and won.

---

[66] Ibid., 616.
[67] I. F. Stone, "The Case of the Mufti," *The Nation*, May 4, 1946, 526–527.
[68] Ibid., 526.   [69] Ibid., 527.   [70] Ibid.

In summer 1946 Freda Kirchwey herself traveled to Palestine, and "Palestine and Bevin," her first article in *The Nation* based on her onsite reporting, appeared on June 22. If "real trouble" started, she wrote, it would not be because 100,000 Jews came to Palestine but because many of Britain's "agents, military and civilian" were doing "everything but openly invite an Arab revolt." She argued that in view of Bevin's refusal to endorse the recommendations of the Anglo-American Committee of Inquiry to admit 100,000 Jews into Palestine, "the Moslem world becomes more and more convinced that blackmail pays and that the Western powers can be frightened into sacrificing the Jews just as they have already abandoned the Christians in Lebanon."[71] How could Britain achieve order in Palestine while "encouraging the Arabs to resist even the recommendations of its own [Anglo-American] Committee of Inquiry"?[72]

In "Will the Arabs revolt?" of July 13, Kirchwey echoed the arguments of Stone and Wagner regarding the meaning of appeasement in this context. She attributed British fears of Arab revolt to the "history of Arab blackmail and British appeasement."[73]

During the years before the outbreak of war, Nazi agents in every Arab country spread the charge that the British intended to subject Moslems to Jewish domination. Arab attacks on Jewish settlements in the late 30s were largely the product of this untiring propaganda, and by the end of 1938 the Colonial Office had pretty well convinced the government that the loyalty of Jewish Palestine would be more than offset, in case of war, by the hostility of the Arab chieftains. Quite abruptly, and without regard for past commitments, the British instituted a sweeping program of appeasement. For the first time Arab notables were invited to join in discussions of the Palestine problem. Then the whole policy based on the Balfour declaration and embodied in the Mandate was reversed by the provisions of the White Paper. Through these moves the British hoped to counter Axis propaganda and insure the loyalty of the Arabs.[74]

The results of British appeasement policy were that, "with very few exceptions Arab leaders in Palestine and outside were either openly pro-Axis or unreliable and shifting in their allegiance. The behavior of the Mufti – today again at large and ready to resume his dominant role in the Middle East – was only a dramatic expression of the general Arab attitude." In the postwar years the "engineers of Britain's colonial policy" saw "the looming threat of Soviet power pressing toward the warm-water ports and oil resources of the Middle East." A bloc of Arab states "linked

[71] Freda Kirchwey, "Palestine and Bevin," *The Nation*, June 22, 1946, 737–778.
[72] Ibid., 739.
[73] Freda Kirchwey, "Will the Arabs Revolt?" *The Nation*, July 13, 1946, 36–39.
[74] Ibid., 38–39.

to Britain by concessions, favors, and a well-grounded fear of communism still seems to the conventional colonial mind the best available bulwark against Russia's penetration."[75] British appeasement of the Arabs during World War II persisted into the postwar years.

Kirchwey interpreted the conflict in Palestine as one pitting the British Empire allied to conservative Arab elites against currents of modernity and social change that the Jews were bringing to Palestine. She thought that the "growth of Jewish strength in Palestine" posed problems for the hopes of the British colonial mind. The Jews' energy and "progressive social programs menace, far more imminently than does Russia, the hierarchic feudalism of the Moslem world from which the Arab ruling class derives its wealth and power. To encourage the Jews would be to plant dynamite under the decadent system. It would make further appeasement impossible." The Arabs, on the other hand, might call on Russia for help. Seeing these possibilities, "the frightened colonial official" has a "single impulse," that is, to "step on the Jews." He does not want social change but the "old system and men on top with whom he can make satisfactory deals." If he can do it with military force "he will wipe out the Jewish defense forces while there is still time and stop the smuggling of D.P.'s [displaced persons] from Europe."[76] The consequence of liberal and leftist anticolonialism and support for progressive modernity was support for the Jews – that is, the Zionists – in Palestine.

On August 3 Kirchwey published "The Battle of Palestine," a report and commentary on the Anglo-American Committee of Inquiry report, British repression of the Haganah, and of the Irgun's bombing the King David Hotel on July 26, 1946. She denounced the attack.[77] Kirchwey wrote that the Holocaust had left a deep impression on the Jews in Palestine. "The horror of the past six years is alive in every Jew in Palestine whether he suffered it in his own person or through the bodies and minds of his fellow Jews in Europe. His feeling is inflamed by every sign of easy indifference, in Britain or elsewhere, to fate of the remnant of refugees in Europe. It is reinforced by each boatload of survivors that slips into Haifa harbor." The Jews were "now all militants" who were "prepared to fight for the right to control their own institutions and decide their own destiny."[78]

By summer 1946 the combination of the tabloid headlines in the *New York Post*, the mixture of reporting and opinion in *PM*, and the longer-form journalism in *The Nation* had established the coordinates of

---

[75] Ibid., 39.   [76] Ibid.
[77] Freda Kirchwey, "The Battle of Palestine," *The Nation*, August 3, 1946, 117–120.
[78] Ibid., 119.

opinion in these leading organs of American liberal and leftist sentiment. They argued that anti-Zionism, opposition to Jewish emigration to Palestine, and efforts to erase or dismiss the history of Husseini's collaboration with the Nazis represented a turn away from the purposes of the wartime allies and toward new conservative, even reactionary, currents that focused on the threat of communism and efforts to appease traditional elites in the Arab states. Such efforts constituted forms of appeasement of reactionary forces in the Arab societies. The memory of the Holocaust, both in Palestine and among the Zionists' supporters in the United States, was vivid and fresh, but often in these early years it took the sublimated form of emphatic support for Zionist aspirations in Palestine.[79]

In London in July British colonial officials argued that the recommendations of the Anglo-American Committee to admit 100,000 Jews into Palestine would estrange the Arabs, endanger Britain's position in the Middle East, and involve financial and military commitments that Britain could not meet.[80] Instead, they proposed a scheme for provincial autonomy in Palestine that called for semi-autonomous Jewish and Arab cantons, both under a trusteeship run by the British. While the Jews could move 100,000 refugees to their small part of Mandate Palestine, the Arabs would receive most of the land. State Department official Henry F. Grady led a US delegation to London seeking to find common ground on Palestine policy with the British. On July 25 his team endorsed the British provincial autonomy proposal in what became known as the Morrison–Grady plan, co-named for Britain's deputy prime minister, Herbert Morrison, who introduced the plan in the House of Commons on July 31, 1946.[81] It called for a British high commissioner to control an area around Jerusalem, Haifa harbor, and the Negev, as well as defense and railways. The Jewish area would comprise 10 percent of the land, the Arab area 40 percent. The entry of the 100,000 Jews would be contingent on approval of the autonomy scheme by both Jews and Arabs. There would be no Jewish state in Palestine.

On July 27 James McDonald, one of the American members of the Anglo-American Committee of Inquiry, met with President Truman, together with Senators Robert Wagner and James Mead of New York, at the White House.[82] In a memorandum prepared beforehand,

---

[79] On the fresh memory of the Holocaust among the Jews in Palestine and its impact on support for imminent realization of Zionist goals see Shapira, *Land and Power*, 277–352.
[80] See Louis, *The British Empire in the Middle East, 1945–1951*, 397–419; and Norman W. Goda, Barbara McDonald, Severin Hochberg, and Richard Breitman, eds., *To the Gates of Jerusalem: The Diaries and Papers of James G. McDonald, 1945–1947* (Bloomington: Indiana University Press/United States Holocaust Memorial Museum, 2015), 239–243.
[81] Goda et al., eds., *To the Gates of Jerusalem*, 240–241.   [82] See ibid., 244–249.

McDonald argued that the Morrison–Grady plan would, in effect, "establish in Palestine a Jewish ghetto wholly unacceptable to the Jews throughout the world and to the conscience of mankind."[83] It would repudiate Truman's call for the immediate admission of 100,000 displaced Jews "because their admission is made contingent upon Arab acceptance of the new scheme which I am almost certain will not be given [and] it is contingent upon Jewish acquiescence which can never be given because acceptance would involve the surrender of Jewish rights under the Balfour Declaration and the Mandate and all of their historical hopes." The plan amounted to a repudiation of Britain's obligations under the Balfour Declaration and was "the culmination of Britain's persistent policy of a quarter century of whittling down the territory of the Jewish National Home." It would leave to the Jews "but one thirtieth of the original Palestine envisioned under the Balfour Declaration . . . All of this is in violent opposition to the position twice taken by the Congress of the United States, by the Democratic Party, and by your distinguished predecessor, Franklin Delano Roosevelt."

In response to Truman's irritation at this criticism, McDonald, with Loy Henderson, the director of the Division of Near Eastern and African Affairs, and the State Department team in London in mind, told the president that "you have been badly served. You sent bad men" to London to negotiate what became the Morrison–Grady plan.[84] McDonald's July 27 meeting with Truman was consequential. Three days later Truman rejected the Morrison–Grady plan and recalled the Grady team from London. On October 3 he wrote to British prime minister Attlee expressing his opposition to the plan.[85] He observed that the Jewish Agency in Palestine had accepted "the creation of a viable Jewish state in control of [a part of] Palestine instead of the whole of

[83] "Memorandum for President Truman from James G. McDonald, Formerly Member of the Anglo-American Committee of Inquiry, July 27, 1946, McDonald Papers, Columbia University, Box 5, Folder 1; also in TL, Papers of Harry Truman, President's Secretary's Files, Box 162, Folder Committee on Palestine and Related Problems," cited in Goda et al., eds., *To the Gates of Jerusalem*, 247.

[84] Truman appreciated his candor. After McDonald told him that "I had no object in coming except to tell the truth," the president replied that "I want to hear it. I hear it too seldom": James G. McDonald to Eddie Cantor, August 6, 1946, McDonald Papers, Columbia University, Box 1, Folder 24, cited in Goda et al., eds., *To the Gates of Jerusalem*, 249.

[85] "President Truman to British Prime Minister (Attlee)," Washington (October 3, 1946), *Foreign Relations of the United States* (hereafter *FRUS*), *The Near East and Africa*, 1946, vol. 7: https://history.state.gov/historicaldocuments/frus1946v07/d548; also in the *New York Times*, October 5, 1946, 2. See the discussion in Allis and Ronald Radosh, "Conflict between Allies: The Morrison-Grady Plan," and "Truman's October Surprise," in *A Safe Haven: Harry S. Truman and the Founding of Israel* (New York: HarperCollins, 2009), 171–206.

Palestine" and proposed "immediate issuance of certificates for 100,000 Jewish immigrants."[86] Truman noted the support the Jewish Agency proposals had received in the press and public forums in the United States and indicated that "from the discussion which has ensued it is my belief that a solution along these lines would command the support of public opinion in the United States, and [Atlee's] support as well."[87]

The Nation at the United Nations

Truman's support for "a viable Jewish state in control of part of Palestine" contradicted Attlee and Bevin's efforts to prevent it in hopes of sustaining Arab support for a binational federation and a continued British role in the region. British opposition to Zionist aspirations was now coming at the cost of tensions with its most important ally, the United States. Bevin was unwilling either to support the Jewish Agency's proposals or even to urge the Arabs to accept the admission of 100,000 Jewish refugees without conditioning it on acceptance of a proposal for provincial autonomy. Finally, on April 2, 1947 the British government, admitting that it could not find a solution to the Palestine conflict, requested that the issue be placed on the agenda of the United Nations General Assembly in the coming fall. On April 13 a majority of UN members agreed to call a Special Session of the General Assembly to address the Palestine question. It took place from April 28 to May 15, 1947.

In the weeks preceding the UN Special Session the Nation Associates, directed by Freda Kirchwey, prepared and distributed to all fifty-five delegations in the General Assembly copies of *The Arab Higher Committee: Its Origins, Personnel, and Purposes*.[88] This lengthy report on Haj Amin al-Husseini's pro-Axis activities drew on classified US government files. In *The Nation*'s May 17, 1947 issue the editors published a summary of the report: "The Palestine Problem and Proposals for its Solution."[89] *The Nation*'s editors "earnestly suggested" that the UN General Assembly should support a plan of partition for Jews and

[86] Cited in Radosh and Radosh, *A Safe Haven*, 189.
[87] "President Truman to British Prime Minister (Atlee)" (October 3, 1946).
[88] For the unabridged version that *The Nation* sent to the United Nations see The Nation Associates, *The Arab Higher Committee: Its Origins, Personnel and Purposes, the Documentary Record Submitted to the United Nations, May 1947* (New York: The Nation Associates, 1947).
[89] Freda Kirchwey et al., "The Palestine Problem and Proposals for Its Solution: An Abridged Version of a Memorandum to the General Assembly of the United Nations," *The Nation*, 164, no. 20, May 17, 1947, 585–615. The magazine listed six authors: Freda Kirchwey, publisher of the magazine; Henry A. Atkinson, secretary of the Church Peace Union; Raymond Swing; James G. Patton, president of the Farmers Educational and Cooperative Union; Frank P. Graham, chairman of *The Nation*'s Advisory Council;

Arabs, an interim plan for a UN trusteeship, and "the immediate facilitation of immigration into the Jewish area of Palestine for the Jewish population now in the camps of Europe." The scheme would not "satisfy all or any of the elements in the conflict but given a spirit of tolerance and the firm backing of the United Nations authority, we feel it can be made to work."[90]

The Nation authors juxtaposed to a spirit of tolerance the views of Husseini and the leaders of the Arab Higher Committee (AHC). They opposed the UN decision to allow the AHC to represent the Palestine Arabs in the UN. The AHC was "totally dissimilar" to the Jewish Agency "and the distinction between the two should have been recognized."[91] The Jewish Agency was an elected body, democratically controlled. "By contrast, The Arab Higher Committee represents nothing more stable than a deal among leaders of the various Arab factions in Palestine – and the will of the Grand Mufti." The AHC had "no legal status, no representative character, and the maneuvers that finally landed it on the same juridical level with the Jewish Agency have created a precedent which may cause plenty of trouble later on." Kirchwey et al. concluded that, upon examination, "the Arab Higher Committee is an almost exact equivalent, in Middle Eastern terms, of the cabal that ruled Hitler's Germany."[92]

The editors wrote that their memorandum about the Mufti was based on documents selected from "many thousands found at the end of the war by American authorities in Germany," most of which "are in the possession of the Department of State. They substantiate to the last detail the charge that the Mufti not only was an Axis agent throughout the war but was himself largely responsible for the Nazi policy of exterminating the Jews of Europe."[93] As we have noted in the discussion of the AZEC memoranda, these early statements mixed fact with exaggeration about Husseini's decision-making powers.[94]

Nonetheless, *The Nation* editors were able to offer credible documentation about what Husseini and "the Mufti's henchmen" – now members of the AHC – had done in the Nazi years. Jamal Husseini, for example,

Philip Murray, president of the Congress of Industrial Unions (CIO); and Frank Kingdon, co-chairman of the Progressive Citizens of America.
[90] The Editors, "The Shape of Things to Come," *The Nation*, 164, no. 20, part I, May 17, 1947, 557.
[91] The Editors, "The Mufti's Henchmen: A Who's Who," *The Nation*, 164, no. 20, part I, May 17, 1947, 561.
[92] Ibid.   [93] Ibid.
[94] See Herf, *Nazi Propaganda for the Arab World*; Jeffrey Herf, "Haj Amin al-Husseini, the Nazis and the Holocaust: The Origins, the Nature and the Aftereffects of Collaboration," *Jewish Political Studies Review* 26, nos. 3–4 (Spring 2016): http://jcpa.org/article/haj-ami n-al-husseini-the-nazis-and-the-holocaust-the-origins-nature-and-aftereffects-of-collaboration/

"organized a pro-Axis fifth column which brought about the Iraqi rebellion of 1941." He was interned by the British in Rhodesia "on account of his pro-Axis activities," yet the British allowed him to go to Palestine, where he became vice-chairman of the AHC. Another member, Emil Ghouri, was a leader of the "underground Arab army and ... alleged to be one of those responsible for internal terror against Arab opponents of the Mufti and Arabs who sell land to Jews." During the Iraqi revolt he had been "in charge of propaganda for the Mufti." He advocated that "all Jews who came to Palestine after 1918 be regarded as foreigners and be deprived of rights in an independent Arab Palestine."[95]

The descriptions of two other members of the AHC, Rasem Khalidi and Wassef Kamel, added information about connections between leaders of the AHC and the Axis powers. In 1936 Khalidi, "at the outbreak of the Axis-sponsored Arab uprisings in Palestine ... was a member of the most intimate circle of Haj Amin al-Husseini." In 1937 he "was a member of a committee that directed Arab terrorism in Palestine." He joined the Mufti in organizing the Iraqi rebellion of 1941. "After its failure he escaped to Ankara and thence to Italy and Germany. During the war, in 1943, he served as an announcer on the Axis-Arabic radio station in Athens. Since 1944 he has been a member of the Mufti's personal entourage, first in Berlin and later in Paris and Egypt. He has recently been refused an American visa by the State Department."[96] Kamel had the same political trajectory from the 1936 riots, flight to Iraq, participation in the Iraqi rebellion of 1941, escape to Turkey, "where he served as a paid agent of the German Secret Service," and then to Italy and Germany, "where he continued his work as one of the closest collaborators of the Mufti." He returned to Syria in 1946. In April 1947 the AHC appointed him to be part of "the propaganda delegation to the United Nations" and he had been attending UN sessions.[97]

The Nation editors drew a straight line from wartime collaboration with the Nazis to postwar leadership of the AHC. The acts of the men seeking recognition as representatives of the Palestine Arabs "establish their place among the worst of the Axis war criminals." Their "political credentials" were "unspeakable." For the UN "to accept these henchmen of the Mufti as official spokesmen of the Arab cause is to deal with its enemies and the allies of its enemies. The consequences will become even more evident in the months ahead."[98] Husseini and his "henchmen" had been enemies of the United Nations that fought against Nazi Germany. *The Nation* editors asserted that they did not deserve recognition from the UN.

---

[95] "The Mufti's Henchman," 561.   [96] Ibid., 561–562.   [97] Ibid., 562.   [98] Ibid.

"The Palestine Problem" examined a number of essential issues: the partition plan; the need for migration; the prospects of other countries to which Jews could migrate; the Jewish claim to Palestine; subversion of the Mandate; Jewish achievements in Palestine; benefits to the Arabs; Arabs and Jews in World Wars I and II; the Grand Mufti in World War II; Britain and the Arab League; the British Labour Party's pledges on Palestine; oil, communication, and bases; American support for a Jewish national home; the Anglo-American Committee and what followed; immigration and repression; some proposed solutions; whether a Jewish state could be established; and possibilities for expansion.[99] In the introduction the editors placed Nazism and the massacre of Europe's Jews front and center. They noted that at the same time as the UN was meeting in New York for a Special Session to address the Palestine issue, "in Germany Allied war tribunals are still condemning Nazis responsible for the massacre of the Jews."[100] They recalled that "the mass slaughter of the Jewish people was accomplished by the Nazis without effective interference from other nations." As the Nazis carried out the murder of Europe's Jews, "no country was willing to open a single door to rescue a single life."[101] Only "one people in one country was prepared to welcome these victims – the Jewish community in Palestine." Yet "the doors of Palestine too were slammed shut in the face of supplicants" by the British White Paper of 1939, which limited immigration to 75,000 persons over five years. That "restrictive order ... was enacted, quite frankly, in an effort to appease the Arabs."[102] That "act of appeasement, like other acts of the Chamberlain government, resulted in failure." It violated the terms of the British Mandate, but "did not buy the loyalty of the Arabs. Their war record was one of enmity and double-dealing. The Jews, on the other hand, though injured and betrayed by the restrictions imposed in the White Paper, played a notable role in the defeat of the Axis."[103] The nations in the world had endorsed the promise of a Jewish state in Palestine to "the Jews of the world," a promise broken by the White Paper and then the current policy of the British government. Still, in spring 1947 there was "no hope of rescue for the survivors of Hitler's extermination program apart from Palestine."[104]

Kirchwey and her colleagues wrote that Britain's current policy was "based on the mistaken belief that only by continued support and appeasement of the Arab rulers and politicians can their [Britain's] threatened position in the Middle East be safeguarded." Such a policy

---

[99] "Contents: The Palestine Problem," *The Nation*, 164, no. 20, part II, May 17, 1947, 585–615.
[100] "Introduction: The Palestine Problem and Proposals for Its Solution," 585–586.
[101] Ibid.   [102] Ibid.   [103] Ibid.   [104] Ibid.

ignored that fact that "the intimidation program of the Arabs is led by men who organized and carried out the Arab campaign of sabotage against the United Nations."[105] In 1947 the phrase "Arab campaign of sabotage against the United Nations" could refer to the dual meaning of that term, that is, both Arab opposition to the United Nations at war with Nazi Germany during World War II and opposition from these same figures to a possible United Nations plan for partition of Palestine into a Jewish and an Arab state.

The editors then turned to Britain's refusal to allow Jewish immigration to Palestine "except in insignificant numbers." Britain had used "every method of exclusion and repression" to prevent entry of more Jews into Palestine, they wrote. "Behind this policy is the larger purpose of seeking support for British imperial interests, both material and strategic, from the ruling elements among the Arabs, even at the cost of defending a decadent feudal and hierarchical social system and at the same time violating the commitments embodied in the Palestine Mandate."[106] The political conflict between the Zionists and the British positioned the Jews' anti-imperial struggle against a Britain aligned with forces of reaction in the Arab countries.

According to *The Nation* editors, a "permanent solution" for the conflict in Palestine required two independent states, one Jewish, one Arab. The Jewish state should be large enough "to constitute a national territory and to allow for the absorption of as many of the surviving Jews of Europe as wish to immigrate." Both states should "guarantee equality of rights to all inhabitants without distinction of race or religion." The Jewish state should grant official recognition to the Arabic language and to Arab schools. Both the Jewish and Arab states should be admitted to the UN. The editors supported two territorial plans. "Since historically Transjordan has always been a part of Palestine," the option was left open as to whether the new Arab state would be part of Transjordan or not. Until the Jewish state was created, "authority should be transferred to the Jewish Agency to regulate immigration," and it "should be recognized as the official provisional representative of the Jewish state to be established." While these proposed solutions "will not be wholly satisfactory to Great Britain, to the Arabs, or to the Jews," they were "capable of fulfilling, at least in part, the fundamental aspiration of both Jews and Arabs – the aspiration to independent statehood."[107]

In its discussion of Jewish immigration to Palestine, *The Nation* authors mentioned "the 500,000 Jews, almost half the surviving Jewish population" in Europe who may wish to migrate to Palestine. It referred

---

[105] Ibid.   [106] Ibid.   [107] Ibid., 586–587.

to Anglo-American Committee of Inquiry report that "an active anti-Semitism which, added to the impoverishment and the psychological horror of living in countries responsible for the slaughter of their families and friends, has produced a desire, as well as a need, to emigrate."[108] They quoted Judge Simon H. Rifkind, adviser on Jewish affairs to the Commanding General of the American Forces in the European Theater, that "the problem of these Jews of Europe is insoluble without Palestine. It is the one place available for mass migration."[109] Most Jewish displaced persons wished to go to Palestine but those who wished to go elsewhere faced immigration restrictions in Australia, Canada, New Zealand, South Africa, the United States, Argentina, Brazil, Mexico, Chile, and Colombia. Just as antisemitism had not ended in post-1945 Europe, so the world's knowledge about the Holocaust in the two years since then had not led other countries to terminate their restrictions against immigration of Jews.[110]

In one section of the report, "Arabs and Jews in Two Wars," the authors wrote that "the record of the Arabs in and out of Palestine and of the Jews throughout the world in both wars discloses the sharpest contrast."[111] In World War II 1.3 million Jews were in uniform "in the armed forces of the United Nations," 550,000 in the armed forces of the United States, 500,000 in those of the Soviet Union, and 65,000 in those of the British. In wartime Palestine, they reported, "85,800 men and 50,400 women *volunteered* for war service; 27,028 Palestine Jews served with the British forces in Palestine and France, Egypt, Sudan, Eritrea, Abyssinia, Liberia, Greece, Crete, Iraq, Italy, Austria, and the Low Countries" (emphasis in original). Moreover, the Anglo-American Committee of Inquiry had pointed out that during World War II Palestine had become "a base as well as an arsenal," and that "the Jewish community of Palestine furnished the skill, the inventiveness, and the energy to provide [for] the needs not only of Palestine but of the surrounding countries" during the war.[112]

Conversely, the authors stated, during World War II "the Arab community of Palestine assumed a most indifferent attitude. The Arab states were in largest part pro-Axis, and the Grand Mufti of Jerusalem, still the most popular leader of Palestine Arabs, played an active role as an ally of the Axis." Again citing the Anglo-American Committee, the authors noted that from a population twice as large as the Jewish community,

---

[108] Ibid., 587.   [109] Ibid., 588.

[110] Ibid., 590–595. On immigration restrictions to the United States see David Nasaw, *The Last Million: Displaced Persons from World War to Cold War* (New York: Penguin Press, 2020).

[111] "Arabs and Jews in Two Wars," in "The Palestine Problem," 596.   [112] Ibid.

"only 12,455 persons were recruited for military service, a figure less than half the Jewish total."[113] Of the Arab states, only Transjordan declared war on Germany in 1939, and that could be attributed to its dependence on aid from Britain. Iraq declared war on Germany in January 1943 only "after it was clear that the Nazis were losing. Egypt, Saudi Arabia, Syria, and Lebanon failed to declare war on Germany until February 1945, three months before the war ended and when the victory of the Allies was certain." These governments took no direct part in military operations.[114]

The Nation authors discussed the Iraqi revolt of April 1941, when Rashid Ali Kilani revolted against the British and formally declared war on Great Britain. "The Iraqi revolt, fundamental to German strategy," took place when British prospects in the war were dark. German and Italian planes "entered the fight." The Vichy high commissioner in Syria and Lebanon "rushed trainloads of French arms to Iraq," while "the ex-Mufti," working with Iraq's military forces, mobilized "subversive elements throughout the Middle East." The rebels received congratulations from King Farouk of Egypt; Hashim Atasi, president of Syria from 1936 to 1939; and Riad as-Sulh, the past and present premier of Lebanon. "The Palestine Arabs made their contribution through the participation of their émigré leaders in Iraq. In Syria and Lebanon Arab Nazi organizations flourished throughout the entire period of the Nazi development." The authors named those organizations: "Iron Shirts, the An-Nadi al-Arabi Club of Damascus, the Council for the Defense of Arab Palestine, the Syrian Popular Party, the National Bloc, and the Istiqlal Club." Further, "Baldur von Schirach, head of the Hitler Youth Movement," visited Syria and established contact with Arab youth organizations. The authors then cited at length a report from the British General Intelligence Service dated December 1, 1941, which referred to payments to the ex-Mufti of Jerusalem from the German and Italian governments.[115]

Turning to "The Grand Mufti in World War II," the editors wrote that Husseini had "a long-time record of complicity in terrorism." The British had failed to hold him accountable for riots in 1929, "with the result that in 1936 he again was responsible for attacks on the Jews of Palestine. At the same time he caused the assassination of hundreds of prominent Arabs, including twenty-four leading Palestine Arabs who refused to accept his leadership."[116] Referring to captured files of the German High Command, the authors wrote that they revealed that "the Arab

---

[113] These figures regarding Palestine and the core Arab states in the Middle East have been confirmed by recent scholarship. In French North Africa 233,000 men enlisted to fight against Nazi Germany. See David Motadel's summary of recent scholarship in his *Islam and Nazi Germany's War* (Cambridge, MA: Harvard University Press, 2014), 115.

[114] "The Palestine Problem," 596–597.   [115] Ibid.

[116] "The Grand Mufti in World War II," in ibid., 597.

riots of 1936 in Palestine were carried out by the Mufti with funds supplied by the Nazis." Further, the Mufti and "his henchmen were directly responsible for the anti-Jewish pogrom, in which almost four hundred Jewish men, women, and children were stabbed or brutally clubbed to death in the streets of Baghdad." Following the failure of the Iraqi revolt, Husseini "found refuge in the Japanese embassy." In October 1941 he escaped to Italy, and in December he went to Berlin. This "agent of the Axis" received a special office from the Nazis.

The authors then presented details of Husseini's collaboration with the Nazi regime, details which have been confirmed by subsequent scholarship as more archives became available:

His activities included propaganda, espionage, organization of Moslem military units in Axis-occupied countries and in North Africa and Russia, establishment of Arab legions in an Arab brigade, and organization of fifth-column activities in the Middle East, including sabotage and parachutist expeditions.

In the course of his propaganda work the Grand Mufti had at his disposal not only German-controlled radio but radio stations in Bari, Rome, Tokyo, and Athens. In addition, he was responsible for sending to the Middle East various propaganda publications in Arabic.

His espionage service extended throughout the Middle East. He had a sub-office in Geneva linking him to Egypt and Turkey, and another in Istanbul, branching out all along the Syria-Turkish frontier in Mersine, Alexandretta, Antioch, Adana, and Diarbekr. These stations received information directly from the Mufti's agents in Palestine, Syria, and Iraq, and maintained close contact with German Intelligence in Turkey.

In Athens, the Mufti established a parachutist and sabotage school for Arabs.

At the Hague, under his direction, Arab students were trained in wireless transmission, high explosives, and demonstrations. The Mufti's agents were parachuted into Turkey, Syria, and Iraq. A number of them were caught by the British. On a number of occasions these agents, with the help of local Arabs, cut telephone lines and pipelines in Transjordan and Palestine and sabotaged railways and bridges in Iraq.

Another of the Mufti's accomplishments was the organization of Moslem military units. He attempted to recruit for the German military command some 500,000 soldiers from Morocco, Tunisia, and Algeria. In Asiatic Russia he collaborated with Moslem Russian quislings and White Russian traitors, whom he helped to form pro-Axis legions.

In 1942 he started to organize Axis Arab legions of Arab students in Germany and Arab prisoners of war who had followed him to Germany. His legionnaires wore the German uniform with "Free Arabia" patches on their shoulders.[117]

This level of detail went beyond anything that had been reported in the press. It suggested that there were officials in the US and/or British

[117] Ibid., 598.

governments, perhaps former officials in the OSS, who were leaking files about Husseini's wartime activities. While much of the information, especially some of his radio broadcasts, had been publicly known during and after the war, "The Palestine Problem" presented what was then the most comprehensive public account of Husseini's collaboration with the Nazi regime. The authors cited Edgar Mowrer's previously mentioned reporting in the *New York Post* regarding Husseini's "anti-Russian broadcasts," which "attempted to incite the Moslems of the Caucasus and eastern Russia to turn against Moscow and join the Axis."[118]

The Nation authors also cited the reporting of Mowrer and of Bartley Crum regarding "the Mufti's role in extermination of the Jews." They pointed to Crum's conclusions, based on research in the archives of the Allied Tribunal at Nuremberg, in which he cited the Rudolf Kastner testimony based on conversations with Dieter Wisliczeny, who "was this this moment held in a cell in Nurnberg as a war criminal and an important witness," as saying that "the Grand Mufti has repeatedly suggested to the Nazi authorities – including Hitler, von Ribbentrop, and Himmler – the extermination of European Jewry." According to Crum, "it was the Mufti who insisted to the Nazi leaders that no matter what deals were made, no matter what moneys were paid for the ransom of the Jews, no Jews should be permitted to go to Palestine." Crum stated that the negotiations broke down "because the Mufti refused to countenance their being ransomed, and as a result the entire [Jewish community of Bratislava] was liquidated." Crum referred to letters from Husseini to German officials encouraging "the deportation of European Jews to Polish extermination camps" and another to Heinrich Himmler accusing him and von Ribbentrop of being "too lenient toward the Jews."[119] Crum exaggerated Husseini's decision-making power. The Mufti was not in a position to determine the outcome of negotiations between the Nazis and Jews. That said, he did encourage the Nazis and collaborationist regimes in Eastern Europe to send Jews to Poland. "The Palestine Problem" erred in overstating Husseini's decision-making power, but it was accurate in its basic claims regarding his consequential collaboration with the Nazi regime.

The Nation authors regretted that Husseini had not been called to account. Instead, he had escaped to comfortable house arrest in France in May 1946, received asylum from Egypt's King Farouk and money from the Arab League, and was therefore able to resume his role as a leader of the Palestine Arabs and "unofficial head of the Arab League. The record of the Grand Mufti lost him no followers." Jamal Husseini had stated that

---

[118] Ibid.   [119] Ibid.

it was the Mufti alone who could speak for the people of Palestine, the authors said, quoting him about the Mufti's wartime activities as follows: "The Grand Mufti in Germany was working for the interests not of the English, who were warring with the Germans, but of his people, who had no direct interest at least in the controversy."[120] The Arab governments and press had welcomed this Nazi collaborator. In so doing, in the view of *The Nation* editors, they were at odds with the nations that had united to defeat the Nazis and Fascist Italy. These authors and other American liberals criticized France and Britain for failing to prevent Husseini's return to the Middle East, and the United States for refusing to indict him for war crimes in Nuremberg.

The Nation authors viewed the Arab League, which took a leading role in opposing the establishment of a Jewish state in Palestine, as compromised by its close relationship with Husseini.[121] The League had lobbied for his release from French custody and facilitated his emergence as the leader of the Arab Higher Committee in June 1946.[122] After his escape from France, the Palestine Arab Higher Committee and the member states of the Arab League "began insistent agitation to demand that an invitation be extended by the British to the Grand Mufti to attend the London conference on Palestine." On December 13, 1946 Jamal Husseini announced that the Arab League demanded that Great Britain permit the return of the Grand Mufti to Palestine.[123] *The Nation*'s report indicated that a year after the Arab League had been granted official recognition at the founding conference of the UN in San Francisco in April and May 1945, it was promoting the career and advocating the policies of the Arab world's most famous and important collaborator with Nazi Germany. In so doing, the UN had lent legitimacy to an organization whose leading figure had fought against the "United Nations," that is, the Allies, during World War II.

The authors of "The Palestine Problem" recalled that the British Labour Party "since 1917" had "taken a firm stance in favor of a Jewish National Home and the establishment in Palestine of a Jewish Commonwealth." In 1944 the party had adopted a plank calling for opening the doors of Palestine to Jewish immigration and favoring a national home. It even called for a transfer of population: "Let the Arabs be encouraged to move out as the Jews move in" by being "compensated handsomely for their land ... The Arabs have many wide territories of their own; they should not seek to exclude Jews from this

---

[120] Ibid.   [121] "Britain and the Arab League," in "The Palestine Problem," 599.
[122] Ibid., 600.   [123] Ibid.

small area of Palestine."[124] In April 1945 the Labour Party again called on the British government to "remove the present unjustifiable barriers on immigration and to announce without delay proposals for a future Palestine, in which it has the full sympathy and support of the American and Russian governments."[125] *The Nation* authors regretted its reversal of policy after coming to power in July 1945. The reversal, they pointed out, was in accord with British imperial strategy. The "imminent withdrawal" of British forces from Egypt gave Palestine even greater strategic importance. "To protect this key position, the Labour government has continued the Tory policy of placating and supporting the Arab rulers and in so doing has violated its pledge to the Jews of Palestine and its obligation to the displaced Jews of Europe."[126] British determination to protect access to her major source of oil was at the root of the decisions to maintain a foothold in the Middle East. "Only such a purpose can explain why the British armed forces in Palestine now number 120,000," in contrast to the 2,000 in 1935 or even at most 25,000 during World War II. Britain's desire to preserve military bases on Jordan's territory as well as access to bases in Iraq and Saudi Arabia was, they wrote, another source of Attlee and Bevin's reversal of policy.[127]

Oil was a key factor in American decision making as well. "An Anglo-American political and military policy is a distinct possibility as a result of merged economic interests in the Middle East. A world monopoly on oil is being established by British and American interests, with the participation of the British government and the knowledge and consent of the American government."[128] Yet the vast wealth accumulated in the oil industry had not changed the fact that "the economy of the region is still based on a feudal land system which keeps the populations in a state of destitution, ignorance, and misery. Two per cent of the population controls the wealth and the power of all the Arab states."[129] The editors noted that Anglo-American economic interest in oil created close connections with conservative elites in the Arab states who were firmly opposed to the establishment of a Jewish state in Palestine. Powerful economic interests in the United States and Great Britain stood in opposition to Zionist aspirations.

Britain was not the only target for *The Nation*'s disapproval; the United States also came in for its share. In a section of the report entitled "American Support for the Jewish National Home," the authors narrated

---

[124] British Labour Party plank, cited in "The Palestine Problem," 600.   [125] Ibid.
[126] "Oil, Communications and Bases," in "The Palestine Problem," 601.
[127] Ibid. The number of British troops in Palestine peaked at 100,000 before evacuation from Palestine. See Louis, *The British Empire in the Middle East, 1945–1951*, 10.
[128] "Oil, Communications and Bases," 602.   [129] Ibid., 603.

the long history of favorable US policy which was now in danger of being reversed. They recalled that since Wilson, presidents and successive Congresses had endorsed the Balfour Declaration. In 1944 both the Democratic and Republican party platforms included resolutions favoring the establishment of a Jewish commonwealth in Palestine.[130] Franklin Roosevelt expressed support for Zionist aspirations in 1944 and 1945. So did a majority of both members of Congress in the resolution sent to President Truman on December 19, 1945 urging American assistance to establish Palestine "as a free and democratic Jewish commonwealth" and in a concurrent resolution of December 19, 1945 of the House and Senate to establish Palestine as a Jewish National Home "as a democratic commonwealth in which all men, regardless of race or creed, shall have equal rights."[131] The authors noted Truman's statement of support in summer and fall 1946 for the entry of 100,000 Jews into Palestine.

Kirchwey and her colleagues reminded readers of the recommendations of the Anglo-American Committee of Inquiry of April 1946 in favor of issuing 100,000 certificates for entry into Palestine for Jews "who have been victims of Nazi and Fascist persecution."[132] Britain had rejected the proposal, but the United States accepted it. This, the authors said, was understandable in light of what Richard Crossman had written in *Palestine Mission*, namely that the British in Palestine "are anti-Jewish and are either pro-Arab or strictly impartial in detesting both."[133] Under the rubric "Immigration and Repression," the authors referred to "boatload after boatload" of Jewish immigrants who tried to get to Palestine "only to be forcibly removed" by the British Navy and sent to the island of Cyprus. British rule in Palestine had become a "police state" where censorship was "absolute ... civil liberties are non-existent" and martial law was imposed.[134] But what accounted for the American turn away from Zionism? They held "State Department Prejudice ... responsible for decisions which contradicted the publicly announced policy of the American government with respect to Palestine, as well as the viewpoint of Truman."[135]

Kirchwey and her colleagues were emphatic in their support for the partition of Palestine into Jewish and Arab states. They pointed out that the Jewish Agency accepted partition, while the Arabs insisted on one

[130] "American Support for the Jewish National Home," in "The Palestine Problem," 604.
[131] Ibid., 604–605.
[132] "The Anglo-American Committee and What Followed," in "The Palestine Problem," 606.
[133] Ibid., 608. See also Crossman, *Palestine Mission*.
[134] "Immigration and Repression," in "The Palestine Problem," 608–609.
[135] Ibid., 608.

state. In such a state, they wrote, "the Jewish population, progressive and technically advanced, would be at the mercy of a backward and antagonistic Arab majority led by the arch-enemy, the Mufti," with the backing of the other Arab states.[136] They were not reassured about how Jews would fare in an Arab-dominated state. "An examination of the record, however, clearly indicates that there is nothing to justify confidence in the attitude of the Arab states toward any minority in their population. The experience of the Kurds, Christian Lebanese, Copts, Armenians, and Jews offers striking refutation of such assurances."[137] Pogroms had recently taken place in Bagdad, Tripoli, and Cairo, and in March 1947 the Syrian government announced that the death penalty would be imposed on Jews unless they publicly denounced Zionism and surrendered all Jewish refugees attempting to reach Palestine. If Palestine were an Arab state, no Jewish immigration would be possible, as Arab representatives viewed it as a form of conquest.

The editors called for Arab and Jewish political and economic cooperation, but according to Raghib al-Nashashibi, the moderate mayor of Jerusalem, this possibility had been undermined by British appeasement of Haj Amin al-Husseini, who purged moderate Arab leadership through terror and murder. Kirchwey and her colleagues concluded that "Arab kings and effendis on the one hand and British imperialism on the other" militated "against Arab-Jewish understanding." The "rich Arabs" were opposed to Zionism because "Jewish social and technical innovations mean lifting the masses from their ignorance and serfdom."[138] Given these conditions, only a Jewish state made sense. Despite the obvious challenges involved, the authors concluded that establishment of such a state was possible.

The Nation's "The Palestine Problem" was a defining statement of liberal and left-liberal American views about Palestine and Zionism in spring 1947. While American public support for Zionist aspirations spanned both major political parties and the political spectrum from left to center right, its most passionate support, outside of Jewish organizations, came from liberals, left-liberals, and, until 1949, from leftists as well. Indeed, support for Zionism was a defining feature of "progressive" politics. For *The Nation* authors Zionist aspirations were a continuation of the passions and ideas for which the "united nations" had fought to defeat Nazism and fascism. This anticolonial left of 1947 was emphatically pro-Zionist. It described those leading the opposition to those Jewish hopes, from the Arab Higher Committee to British imperial interests, early

---

[136] "Some Proposed Solutions," in "The Palestine Problem," 611.   [137] Ibid.
[138] Ibid., 612.

advocates of the containment of communism, and Anglo-American oil concerns, as opponents of this broad progressive sentiment. They demonstrated that arguments for preserving British imperial interest in the Middle East and containing communism fostered opposition to Zionist aspirations. "The Palestine Problem" became a key text in defining the meaning of left and right, progress and reaction concerning the question of Palestine and Zionism in 1947.

Zionism had one supporter who came from within the American diplomatic establishment. He was Sumner Welles, the under secretary of state in the Franklin Roosevelt administration from 1937 to 1943.[139] In the Roosevelt administration Welles was primarily involved in US foreign policy toward Latin America, but after 1943, with Roosevelt's support, he worked on drafting the United Nations Charter. In the last months of World War II he spoke frequently to Jewish organizations about the Nazi crimes in Europe and the need to support a Jewish state in Palestine.[140]

Like Robert Wagner, Welles engaged in Christian pro-Zionist activism. On May 14, 1946 he spoke to the American Christian Conference on Palestine in Baltimore.[141] After recalling "the millions of persons of the Jewish faith who had been exterminated by Hitlerism" and the "poisons engendered by Nazism" that had prevented "an overwhelming majority of their survivors to return to the homes of their origin," he said that "the only possible solution" for their plight, "under present world conditions, lay in their chance to leave Europe for new places of security and hope."[142] The United Nations had a role to play in facilitating "the establishment of a Jewish Commonwealth in Palestine."[143] Welles regarded the Jews' free and willing "return to their former homes" in Palestine as a fulfillment of the UN's support for human rights.[144] The United States had an "inescapable moral obligation" to use its influence at the UN and elsewhere to "press for the establishment of a free and democratic Commonwealth of Palestine which will afford security and equal rights to all of its citizens, whatever

---

[139] On Welles and Zionism see "Postmortem Appraisal of the United Nations Game: Sumner Welles and the Zionists," in Louis, *The British Empire in the Middle East, 1945–1951*, 487–493; and Benjamin Welles, *Sumner Welles: FDR's Global Strategist: A Biography* (New York: St. Martin's Press, 1997).

[140] Welles spoke to the American Jewish Committee on February 4, 1945 and to the New York chapter of Hadassah on April 15, 1945; transcripts in Franklin Delano Roosevelt Library and Museum, Sumner Welles Papers, Series 10: Speeches and Articles, 1928–1951, Box 197.

[141] Sumner Welles, "Palestine's Rightful Destiny," Address to the American Christian Conference on Palestine, Baltimore (May 14, 1946), Robert F. Wagner Papers, Palestine Files, Georgetown University, Booth Family Center for Special Collections: Research Center. Also see Sumner Welles, "Palestine and World Peace," *The Nation*, October 23, 1947, 439–440.

[142] Welles, "Palestine's Rightful Destiny," 5.   [143] Ibid., 7.   [144] Ibid., 10.

their faith and whatever their race may be."[145] In this and subsequent speeches, newspaper columns, essays, radio addresses, and books, Welles associated the Zionist project with American values of democracy and liberty. In so doing, he became a sharp critic of the State Department's policies toward Palestine and Zionism.

Between 1945 and 1947 liberal and left-leaning writers and political leaders in the United States – Victor Bernstein, Emanuel Celler, Freda Kirchwey, I. F. Stone, Alexander Uhl, Robert Wagner, Sumner Welles, and the writers and editors of *PM*, the *New York Post*, and *The Nation* magazine, as well as Zionist advocates in the American Zionist Emergency Committee, articulated the political coordinates of left and right as they concerned the Zionist issue. They viewed the effort to establish a Jewish state in Palestine as a project of liberalism and as a leftist project as well, one that rejected imperialism – in this case that of Britain – and the temptations of appeasement of reactionary powers, the Fascists and Nazis in the 1930s, and Husseini and the Arab Higher Committee in the immediate postwar years. In so doing, they contributed significantly to making support for the Zionist project a defining feature of the meaning of postwar liberalism, especially left liberalism, and leftism in the United States.

American debate about the Zionist project and the Husseini case, though passionate and important, concerned a figure then held by the government of France under house arrest near Paris. There the Husseini case became a matter of foreign policy. France was beginning to tell itself a story about a nation of resisters that obscured the realities of collaboration. As we will see in the following chapter, the desire to preserve French influence in the Arab world extended that inclination to leniency about collaboration to Arab collaborators.

---

[145] Ibid., 11.

4   Haj Amin al-Husseini and the French Government: May 1945–May 1946

> I am aware of the importance of the debt which I owe to you. Rest
> assured that my action in your favor will match the scale of this debt.
>
> Haj Amin al-Husseini in conversation at the French
> Embassy in Cairo, October 11, 1946

In May 1945 French soldiers in their occupation zone in Germany
arrested Haj Amin al-Husseini. French officials brought him to Paris
and held him in custody until June 1946, when he made a famous and
suspicious "escape" on a commercial flight to Cairo. This chapter draws
on the files of the French Foreign Ministry (MFA) to examine the crucial
decisions made by the government of France in those twelve months that
allowed Husseini to avoid a trial for Nazi-era war crimes and that facilitated his return to political life in Palestine. Members of the MFA debated
about how to respond to British requests for his extradition and to public
calls in the United States for his indictment on war crimes charges. The
ministry, under the leadership of foreign minister Georges Bidault, and
due to the urging of officials eager to foster good will toward France in
North Africa and the Middle East, treated Husseini as a respected and
respectable political prisoner.[1] Officials at the Quai d'Orsay (a common
sobriquet for the Foreign Ministry) rejected Britain's extradition
requests, refused to indict him for war crimes, and offered conditions of
house arrest so lax that he was able to escape with relative ease and return
to the Middle East.[2] France received the good will it sought. Many Arabs
welcomed home the former Nazi collaborator to lead the fight against the
Jews in Palestine.

    Shortly after French troops had captured Husseini, details of his war-
time activities began to arrive at France's Ministry of the Interior as well

---

[1] Tsilla Hershco, "*Histoire d'une évasion: Le grand mufti de Jérusalem en France,*"
Controverses 10, no. 2 (2006): 244–273. Also see her *Entre Paris und Jerusalem: la
France, le sionisme et la création de l'état d'Israel* (Paris: Honore Champion Éditeur, 2003).
[2] Ministres des Affaires Étrangènes et Européennes (hereafter MAE), Direction Afrique-
Levant, Généralités Proche-Orient (hereafter DAL, GPO), CADC, MAE214QO 38,
MAE-CADC.

as its Foreign Ministry. On May 11 Adrien Tixier (1893–1946), the first postwar director of the Interior Ministry and a veteran of the Resistance, informed Bidault that under interrogation in Germany an officer of the Gestapo had described the Mufti as "the brains of German espionage in all the Muslim countries and especially in Arab language countries."[3] But his reputation in the Middle East was very different. On May 12 Jean Lescuyer, the French ambassador in Cairo, wrote to the Foreign Ministry about reaction in the Egyptian press to the news that Husseini was in French custody. The Grand Mufti, he said, "enjoys a very great name in the Near East." He had come to define Palestinian aspirations and was "actually considered to be one of the rare leaders who as a result of his religious character was able to prevail in the Muslim community, particularly in the Arab League."[4] Lescuyer recalled examples of Husseini's "cooperation" with the French, presumably when he was in Lebanon in 1937–9, the echoes of which "could be favorable to our cause in Muslim countries." The Mufti "had certainly betrayed the cause of the Allies, but he especially betrayed England without affecting our interests directly. Nothing seems to compel us to take action against him, as doing so would only cause us harm in the Arab countries."[5]

On May 15 the French Embassy in Beirut, then led by Charles Lucet, reported that Husseini's "close relations with the authorities of [the Nazi] regime had not diminished his moral standing" in Lebanon. The French diplomats in Beirut wanted to know details of his incarceration so they could "reassure his friends" about his situation. Sami Solh, a past and current prime minister of Lebanon, asked if it would be possible to send money to the Grand Mufti to meet his personal needs. The author of the unsigned memo from the Beirut embassy wrote that he "would be happy to be able to give a positive reply."[6] It was an early notice that some prominent Arab leaders supported Husseini despite his record of collaboration with the Nazis, and some French diplomats in

---

[3] Le Ministre de L'Interieur, Direction Generale de la Sureté Nationale to MAE, Paris (May 11, 1945), "Le Grand Mufti de Jerusalem," CADC, MAE, DAL, GPO, 214QO 38 (a), 1943–1945, 4. On Tixier see Gilles Morin and Pascal Plas, *Adrien Tixier, 1893–1946: l'Heritage méconnu d'un reconstructeur de l'état en France* (Le Geneytouse: Lucien Soumy, 2012).

[4] Jean Lescuyer to MAE, Cairo (May 12, 1945), No. 580/581, CADC, MAE, DAL, GPO, 214QO 38(a), 1943–1945, 6.

[5] Ibid.

[6] Beyrouth to MAE, Beirut (May 16, 1945), No. 1089 à 1091, CADC, MAE, DAL, GPO, 214QO 38(a), 1943–1945, 8. Charles Lucet went on to a successful diplomatic career serving as France's representative on the United Nations Security Council, ambassador to the United States, and head of the Political Department in the French Foreign Ministry. See *Annuaire diplomatique et consulaire de la République Française* (Paris: Imprimerie Nationale, 1947).

the Middle East saw favorable treatment toward him as an opportunity France should seize.

The Mufti in Custody: A Balancing Act

On May 18 the Arab concerns about Husseini's well-being that Bidault was hearing from his diplomats in the field led him to inform his counterpart in the Ministry of War, André Diethelm, that the Grand Mufti "enjoys a great reputation ... Despite, and perhaps because of his attitude during the war and running afoul of the British authorities, his prestige has remained intact in the Arab population."[7] As "all measures taken regarding the Grand Mufti therefore risk repercussions in the Orient and consequently in our protectorates in North Africa," it was essential to ensure that French troops did no harm to the Mufti. Bidault requested that the War Ministry coordinate its handling of Husseini with him.[8] On the same day René Chauvel, the secretary general of the MFA, reported that Emile Ghoury (Emil Ghouri), the secretary of the Arab Higher Committee and general secretary of the Palestine Arab Party, had emphasized the continuing "influence and esteem" that Husseini retained in Palestine, and he, too, wanted to be able to reassure Husseini's supporters who were viewing his condition "with anxiety."[9] While Ghoury recognized that France could not release Husseini, "the assurance that he is welcomed to French territory with the respect due to his religious personality would be sufficient to foster the recognition and appreciation of the Arabs of Palestine."[10] On May 22 the MFA received a diametrically opposite request from the British Embassy in Paris, the first of several, asking that the French hand Husseini over to the Supreme Allied Command offices in Paris, so that he could be either placed on trial for war crimes or deported to a British possession outside the Middle East.

On May 24 Chauvel informed the French Embassies in Cairo, Beirut, Jeddah, Rabat, Tunis, London, and Washington that Husseini was now in a villa in the Paris area. He assured them that "despite the heavy charges against him, Haj Amin is treated with respect as the Government wishes to take into account in his favor the religious prestige

---

[7] Le Ministre des Affaires Étrangères à Monsieur le Ministre de la Guerre, Paris (May 18, 1945), "a.s. du Grand Mufti de Jerusalem," CADC, MAE, DAL, GPO, 214QO 38(a), 1943–1945, 9.

[8] Ibid.

[9] René Chauvel, "Urgent s.s. du Grand Mufti de Jerusalem," Le Ministre des Affaires Étrangères à Monsieur le Ministre de la Guerre, Paris (May 18, 1945), MAE, DAL, GPO, 214QO 38(a), 1943–1945.

[10] Ibid.

attached to his function as the Grand Mufti of Jerusalem."[11] On May 26 Lucet wrote from Beirut in response to reports that the French government would investigate Husseini's "anti-French activity." He thought it would "be to our advantage to abstain" from doing so, and rather "let the British bear the consequences of such an initiative."[12] Bidault now found himself caught between the British extradition request, on the one hand, and pleas from Arab capitals not to do so, on the other. His note to Tixier of May 26 indicated where he struck the balance:

Due to the quality of his birth (*la qualité de sa naissance*), the authority conferred on him by his faith and his nationalist convictions, Hadj Amin el Hussein has acquired a great name not only in the Middle East but also in all of the Arab world. His conflict with the British authorities and his comportment during the war have not diminished the consideration and esteem he enjoys among his coreligionists.[13]

On the other hand, France had to take into account the "resentment of our allies," that is, the British, as well as the "repercussion" of our decisions "among the Muslim population in the territories for which we are responsible." To avoid angering the British, the Ministry of the Interior should adopt a "regime of narrow surveillance and prevent all connections between him and his coreligionists." To avoid antagonizing the Arabs and Muslims, "no measure of special rigor should be used against him."[14] In the coming months Bidault's balancing act would tilt toward more leniency to the Mufti.

Initially, the Ministry of the Interior had Husseini in its custody. Under Tixier it became known as a bastion of the democratic left, and thus of a ministry that might facilitate a judicial reckoning with Husseini. On June 2 Tixier confirmed that as of May 19 Husseini and two secretaries were in the custody of the Paris police at a house in the Paris region. The Interior Ministry provided them with a cook approved by the Central Mosque in Paris but prevented Husseini from receiving visitors.[15] On June 18

---

[11] Jean Chauvel, "au sujet du Grand Mufti du Jérusalem," Paris (May 24, 1945), MAE, Afrique Levant à Caire, Beyrouth, Djeddah, Rabat, Tunis, Londres, Washington, CADC, MAE, DAL, GPO, 214QO 38, 1943–1945, 13.

[12] Beyrouth to MAE, Beirut (May 26, 1945), No. 1251, CADC, MAE, DAL, GPO, 214QO 38, 1943–1945, 15.

[13] Bidault to Tixier, "Au sujet due Grand Mufti de Jérusalem," Paris (May 28, 1945), No. 363, CADC, MAE, DAL, GPO, 214QO 38, 1943–1945, 16.

[14] Ibid.

[15] Le Ministre de L'Intérieur (Adrien Tixier) à Monsieur le Ministre des Affaires Étrangères (Georges Bidault), Paris (June 2, 1945), "Objet: Au sujet du Grand Mufti de JERUSALEM, Référence: Votre letter no. 363 du 26 ai 19.5," CADC MAE, DAL, GPO, 214QO 38, 214/38(a), 1943–1945, 21; and Georges Bidault to LEGAFRANCE LE CAIRE, Paris (June 11, 1945), No. 702, CADC, MAE, DAL, GPO, 214QO 38, 214/38(a), 1943–1945, 24.

Bidault heard an appeal for lenient custody for the Mufti from General Paul Beynet, commanding general of the French Legion of Honor and Plenipotentiary of France.[16] On June 22 the Department of European Affairs in the MFA refused a second British extradition request. In so doing, it cited Husseini's claim that he "was innocent of all the charges made against him," which it minimized as "his Germanophile tendencies." Moreover, the government of Egypt was pressing France to return the Mufti to Palestine. France desired to "see its relations with the Arab world in general to be ameliorated."[17] Making Husseini's custody as comfortable as possible was one way to do that. On July 31 Bidault wrote to Tixier that the Ministry of the Interior should pay the expenses of placing Husseini in a residence "some distance from Paris, in a comfortable country house surrounded by a garden or park in which he can wander freely under discreet surveillance by a guard attached to his person."[18]

Interrogating the Mufti

Husseini's first extended conversation with French officials took place on June 26, 1945.[19] According to these officials, Husseini was captured by French troops on May 5, 1945 in Germany and then brought to France. He thereby avoided interrogation by American and British officials working on preparations for the Nuremberg trials and on the many other Allied interrogations of former officials and collaborators of the Nazi regime.[20] Husseini made a good first impression on the French officials. The report observed that "the man does not lack charm. He has an agreeable face, fine features, high forehead, spiritual eyes and a certain air of dignity and aristocratic grace."[21] The officials noted that the Mufti expressed his "gratitude to France" and "appreciated its hospitality for the second

---

[16] Le Général d'Armée P. Beynet to Georges Bidault, Paris (June 18, 1945), "du Grand Mufti de Jérusalem," MAE, CADC MAE, DAL, GPO, 214QO 38, 214/38(a), 1943–1945, 32.

[17] MAE, Département des Affaires Européennes, RT/56/81, "Note Soumise au Ministre des Affaires Étrangères," Paris (June 22, 1945), CADC MAE, DAL, GPO, 214QO 38, 214/38(a), 1943–1945, 42.

[18] Bidault to Tixier, "Le Ministre des Affaires Étrangères au Ministre de L'Intérieur: Au sujet du Grande Mufti de Jérusalem," Paris (July 31, 1945), Direction d'Afrique-Levant-Affaires musulmanes," CADC, MAE, CADC MAE, DAL, GPO, 214QO 38, 214/38(a), 1943–1945.

[19] "Visite au Grand Mufti de Jérusalem," Paris (June 26, 1945), CADC, MAE, CADC MAE, DAL, GPO, 214QO 38, 214/38(a), 1943–1945, 33.

[20] On the investigations of former officials of the Nazi regime and foreign collaborators see Jeffrey Herf, *Divided Memory: The Nazi Past in the Two Germanys* (Cambridge, MA: Harvard University Press, 1997).

[21] "Visite au Grand Mufti de Jérusalem," Paris (June 26, 1945), 33.

time." He recalled that when he left Palestine "after the insurrection in 1936 ... French authorities welcomed him then in Beirut." The Mufti narrated his travels to Iraq, Iran, Turkey, Italy, and Germany. When the Allied armies invaded "the territory of the Reich, he thought it prudent to escape British authorities and seek refuge in France." He said nothing about his activities in Berlin from 1941, and it appears that the French did not press the issue.

Instead, Husseini complained that Britain had been responsible for the growth of the Jewish population in Palestine from 50,000 to 500,000 in the preceding twenty years. Britain "was unable to free itself from the influence of the Jewish world on its policies."[22] He foresaw a "community of interests between France and the Arab countries."[23] Indeed, such agreement "could take the form of an 'alliance'" which Husseini was "ready and qualified to arrange" in one of the following two forms: The "positive" one would foster French links to Syria, while the "negative" was one in which Husseini would provoke a crisis in Palestine, Egypt, Iraq, and also in Transjordan that would "divert the attention" of the countries of the Levant and the Arab world to Britain and thus benefit France. In other words, just over a month after the Allies' defeat of Nazi Germany, Husseini informed French officials that he would be glad to discuss modalities of an alliance between France and Arab regimes that would damage France's ally, Great Britain, and oppose the growing presence of Jews in Palestine.[24] The French could gain his good will by opposing Jewish immigration to Palestine. Rather than speak as a man on the run worried about a possible indictment for war crimes, Husseini in June 1945 thought he had a bright political future ahead, perhaps in an alliance with France to counter the presence of the Jews and the British.

That summer, Henri Ponsot (1877–1963), the former French ambassador to Syria and Lebanon and the specialist in Middle East affairs in the Foreign Ministry, had several discussions with Husseini, in the course of which he became Husseini's leading advocate in the MFA.[25] In their first meeting, on July 1, Husseini requested that he receive the same amount of liberty that the French had given him in Lebanon in 1937–8, that he be treated as a political refugee, and that his two secretaries, "M. Derviche [Derwish] and M. Khalidi," be given the same status. He mentioned "multiple interventions in his favor," including from the All-India Muslim League and the Arab League. He sought to capitalize on French resentments toward the British. With British demands for his extradition in mind, Husseini referred to "the protection that the English have always

[22] Ibid., 34–35.   [23] Ibid., 35.   [24] Ibid., 35–36.
[25] On Henri Ponsot see Hershco, "Histoire d'une évasion," 249–252.

given to enemies of France." He promised not to "abuse the hospitality" offered by France. He had not forgotten the country's "hospitality," which he had received for those two years in Lebanon.

Husseini played to Vichy France's resentment of British elimination of its wartime influence in the Lebanon and Syria. He told Ponsot that the English had not forgotten that the success of their policy in Palestine, "with a view to their Jewish establishment, had worked for a long time to eliminate French influence in the Levant."[26] He appeared to assume that Ponsot would share his anger at the British defeat of the forces of Vichy France in the region during World War II. He referred to the Iraqi coup in 1941 as "a revolt against the English" and said nothing about the pro-Axis sympathies of the Rashid Kilani regime in which he had participated. He complained that his efforts to find refuge in Iran and Turkey were made impossible due to the influence of the English. Skipping over the years in Nazi Germany, he turned to Palestine, "the heart of the Arab problem" caused by the "installation of foreign colonialists" (*colons étrangères*).

We [i.e. Husseini and his allies] can collaborate with the French, for confidence and trust exists between us. French cultural influence in Levant is profound despite its provisional setback in Palestine under English influence. You have not tried to implant an alien population among us, as the English have done in Palestine. We do not lose territory to you. Your actions are more disinterested [than those of the British].[27] Ponsot's report did not include reactions to Husseini's assertions.

Meeting with Ponsot again for over two hours on July 29, 1945, Husseini declared himself innocent of accusations of war crimes in Yugoslavia.[28] Instead, he presented himself as the defender of Muslims faced with extermination in Yugoslavia by the Serbs and Tito. He spoke as if Nazi Germany had not waged a racist war of extermination on its Eastern Front,[29] claiming instead that he had appealed to the Italians and the Germans and formed a division of Muslim soldiers in order to protect the Muslims of Yugoslavia from such an assault.[30] The notes indicate that Ponsot listened but did not express comment about Husseini's version of events.[31]

---

[26] "Premier entretien de M. Ponsot avec le grand Mufti, Amin Husseini," Paris (July 1, 1945), CADC, MAE, CADC MAE, DAL, GPO, 214QO 38, 214/38(a), 1943–1945, 44–45.

[27] Ibid., 47.

[28] M. H. Ponsot, "Second entretien avec le Mufti de Jérusalem, Amin Husseini," Paris (July 29, 1945), CADC, MAE, CADC MAE, DAL, GPO, 214QO 38, 214/38(a), 1943–1945, 58–62.

[29] The scholarship on the war of extermination on Nazi Germany's Eastern Front is vast. See, for example, Rolf Dieter Müller and Gerd R. Ueberschar, *Hitler's War in the East: A Critical Assessment*, trans. Bruce D. Little (New York: Berghahn Books, 2002).

[30] Ibid., 2.

[31] On Husseini and the Muslim SS Division see, most recently, David Motadel, *Islam and Nazi Germany's War* (Cambridge, MA: Harvard University Press, 2014).

On August 3 Ponsot sent Bidault a statement by Husseini declaring his innocence of war crimes accusations made by Yugoslavia along with the Mufti's reference to expressions of support for him from Egypt's King Farouk, the Arab League, and Emile Ghoury, general secretary of the Palestine Arab Party.[32] In the Balkans he had defended the Muslims of Bosnia-Herzegovina against "abominable acts." To stop "acts of extermination" by Serb forces, he had appealed to the German and Italian governments to assist in protecting Balkan Muslims.[33] Though the German and Italian authorities refused to intervene directly, they formed the Muslim division in order to offer defense against the Serb attacks.[34] His version was that he had collaborated with the Germans to defend Muslims from attack, not to assist in the implementation of a Nazi race war.

On August 7 Ponsot urged the French occupation in Austria and the Tyrol to "facilitate the return to Egypt or Syria" of sixteen "collaborators of the Mufti" being held there. They had been with him in Nazi Germany, but since the Grand Mufti was "in our hands," it would be advisable to pursue the matter "with diligence to obtain the expected benefits," presumably in the form of good will toward France on the part of Husseini's advocates in the Arab states.[35] Three days later Ponsot penned another memo, this time referring to persistent requests from Egypt and Saudi Arabia that Husseini be permitted to return to Egypt. The French government needed to arrive at a "politically equitable decision. It must conserve good will and benefit in the Muslim world."[36] It could do so by facilitating the return of the Mufti and his fellow former Arab Nazi collaborators to the Middle East.

On August 13 Bidault wrote to the French Embassies in Washington, London, Beirut, Cairo, and Jerusalem that, due to France's "obligations"

[32] Haj Amin el-Husseini, "Declaration du Grand Mufti de Jérusalem à Monsieur Ponsot," Paris (July 29, 1945); and Henri Ponsot to Georges Bidault, "Réponse du Grand Mufti de Jérusalem à la demande d'extradition de la Yugoslavie," Paris (August 3, 1945), CADC, MAE, CADC MAE, DAL, GPO, 214QO 38, 38(a), 1943–1945, 71–72.

[33] El-Husseini, "Declaration du Grand Mufti de Jérusalem à Monsieur Ponsot."

[34] "Annex 2," Henri Ponsot to Georges Bidault, Paris (August 3, 1945), CADC, MAE, CADC MAE, DAL, GPO, 214QO 38, 38(a), 1943–1945, 75.

[35] Henri Ponsot, Paris (August 7, 1945), "Liste des partisans du Grand Mufti, Note: Rapatriment d'Autriche des collaborateurs du Grand Mufti de Jérusalem," CADC, MAE, CADC MAE, DAL, GPO, 214QO 38, 214/38(a), 1943–1945, 80. The sixteen "partisans of the Grand Mufti" were: Dr. About Seoud; Hassan Aboul Seoud; Saaduldyn Abdul Latif; Safwat al-Husseini; Salim al-Husseini; Ramsi Alajati; Zafer Rifai; Youssef Al Jassem; Baheri Dyn Tabba; Farhan Jandali and family; Fauzi Koutb; Haji Chawkat; Mohamed Afifi; Wassef Kamel; Akram Jaouni; Mohamed Charaf; and Nadat Alchawaf.

[36] Ponsot, Paris (August 10, 1945), "Note: Le Grand Mufti 'Criminel de Guerre,' Entretien avec le Ministre d'Égypte," CADC, MAE, DAL, GPO, 214QO 38, 214/38 (a), 1943–1945, 81–83.

to its British and American allies, it would be difficult for France to come to Husseini's defense if the Yugoslav government indicted him for war crimes. Yet France's interests in the Arab world required that it facilitate Husseini's communications and thus "reassure" his allies in Saudi Arabia and Egypt.[37] The Arab states should be informed that the French government was treating Husseini as a "political prisoner" and had decided to "ameliorate" his condition. France viewed him as "a personality who was representative of Islam" and was aware of the "favorable disposition" toward him in the Arab world. Hence France wanted to make his stay more comfortable, offer him more liberty, and permit him to see more visitors. However, it would not support requests for the return of the Mufti's "partisans" who were now held by the Americans and the British in Central Europe. Nor could France "deliver him to Great Britain" in view of the reaction that would unleash among the Arabs. "His political presence in France offers us no advantages. We must facilitate his departure to an Arab country, preferably to Egypt or Saudi Arabia."[38] Saudi Arabia was offering Husseini a place of refuge precisely to avoid his indictment for war crimes in a trial in Yugoslavia. The French government could agree to send him to Saudi Arabia on the pretext that, as a member of the United Nations, the Saudis would have the same obligations as the French to return him to an international tribunal dealing with war crimes.[39] Bidault adopted this balancing act for the next nine months.

In a memo to Bidault of August 24, Ponsot presented Husseini's more detailed response to the war crimes accusations made by the government of Yugoslavia and the right-wing Zionist Hebrew Committee for National Liberation in the United States, along with his own, sympathetic, summary.[40] In accepting Husseini's version of events, Ponsot functioned as Husseini's advocate within the MFA. Husseini claimed that "no Jew" had been harmed during his presence in Iraq in 1941. It was the Jews' "zeal in welcoming the English return to Baghdad that marked them for the Arabs' vindictive actions." Further, according to Ponsot, Husseini did not "know anything about extermination camps for Jews or others, just as

---

[37] Bidault to LONDRES, WASHINGTON, BEYROUTH, LE CAIRE, JERUSALEM (August 13, 1945), CADC, MAE, DAL, GPO, 214QO 38, 214/38(a), 1943–1945, 84.

[38] Bidault, "Note, A/s du Grand Mufti," Paris (August 13, 1945), CADC, MAE, DAL, GPO, 214QO 38, 214/38(a), 1943–1945, 100–102.

[39] Ibid.

[40] Ponsot to Bidault, Paris (August 24, 1945), "Le Grand Mufti répond aux Accusation dont il es l'objet," and "Note remise à Monsieur PONSOT par le GRAND MUFTI, le 23 août 1945," CADC, MAE, DAL, GPO, 214QO 38, 214/38(a), 1943–1945, 103–104 and 105–106. On communication by Peter Bergson of the Hebrew Committee for National Liberation in the United States to the French government about Husseini, see AMBAFrance, No. 3.050 to 3.052 Washington (May 10, 1945), CADC, MAE, DAL, GPO, 214QO 38(a), 1943–1945.

he has never known or heard of Karl Hichman [*sic*: Adolf Eichmann]."[41] Yet the accusations against Husseini were not that he had been involved in killing Jews in Auschwitz but that he had urged Nazi officials to send Jews to Poland rather than allowing them to go to Palestine. Rejecting accusations that had not been made was the tactic of a political supporter, not an official seeking the truth about Husseini's wartime activities.

On August 23 Husseini wrote a statement for the French about his political activities. It would probably have been his line of defense had he been brought to trial, but, short of this, it still formed the basis for his subsequent evasions and apologia about his years of Nazi collaboration. Regarding the events in Palestine from 1936 to 1939, in which Husseini had led armed attacks on the Jews and on Arabs who rejected his views, Husseini said that as president of the High Muslim Council his actions were "consecrated purely to religious affairs" and that the Arab Higher Committee "represented all the Arab political parties." These two institutions "were never the object of accusations of acts of terrorism."[42] In fact, Husseini had been deeply involved in politics. The Arab Higher Committee did not represent all political parties and was known for its attacks on Jews and on other Arab leaders. Yet in reporting his conversations with Husseini, Ponsot, who had been a French diplomat in Lebanon in the 1930s and thus had to have known what had gone on, did not challenge any of these assertions.

Husseini repeated that no hostilities took place against Jews while he was in Iraq in 1941, claiming that they occurred only after he departed for Iran following the occupation of Baghdad by British troops. The Jews, he said, became the object of hostility "due to their manifestations of enthusiasm when the English troops entered Baghdad. The Jews outraged the population by prominently offering flowers to the English troops as the Iraqi troops were retreating. They thus pushed the public and the Iraqi army to open fire on them and there were victims."[43] In this way, Husseini justified the Iraqi pogrom of 1941: The Jews had only themselves to blame because they welcomed the British who overthrew a pro-Axis regime. Ponsot offered no word of criticism of what was, in effect, an antisemitic interpretation of the course of events in Iraq. Husseini repeated what became his standard explanation of his involvement with the Bosnian SS Division: he had helped to organize it only to come to the defense of Muslims facing "massacres" at the hands of the Serbs. He said nothing about the substance of the charge that he had collaborated with the Nazis to form a Muslim SS division.[44] But Ponsot did not confront

---

[41] "NOTE remise à Monsieur PONSOT par le GRAND MUFTI, le 23 Aout 1945," 106.
[42] Ibid.   [43] Ibid.   [44] Ibid.

Husseini with contrary evidence. Instead, he accepted Husseini's denials, writing that that the Mufti "was not aware of the extermination camps for the Jews or others and that likewise he has never known or heard of Karl Hichman [sic: Adolf Eichmann]."[45]

As we have seen, French hospitality to Husseini aroused suspicion and criticism in the United States. On August 24, 1945 Henri Bonnet, the French ambassador to the United States, informed Bidault that Husseini had recently been denounced by representatives of the Jewish Agency in Washington.[46] On August 10 the Jewish Telegraphic Agency press service had asserted that "it is doubtful ... whether the French are prepared to hand over the ex-Mufti with whom they have had good relations over a period of years and whom they once sheltered in Syria when he was compelled to flee Palestine." The press service reported that he was in custody in a "sumptuous villa," as "the French government does not regard the ex-Mufti as a war criminal, and he is being accorded the treatment due to a great political and religious leader, and one belonging to an old and illustrious family."[47] By the end of August Husseini's two secretaries, Isaac Derwish and Hasam Khalidi, were free to come and go from the residence, where they were staying, while Husseini himself was allowed to move about the villa as he pleased.[48] By the end of September 1945 the French had provided Husseini with a chauffeur, allowing him to leave the residence. His two secretaries had complete liberty, thus facilitating his contact with supporters in the Arab states. The police had requested 300,000 francs for renovations on a different villa.[49]

On August 28 Ponsot met with Husseini for the fourth time to hear his response to the Yugoslav war crimes accusations.[50] The Egyptian and Syrian ambassadors, along with the Arab League, continued to protest the accusations against Husseini and the possibility that he would be extradited to stand trial for them. The Egyptian government had

---

[45] Ibid.

[46] Henri Bonnet to Georges Bidault, Washington, DC (August 24, 1945), MAE, DAL, GPO, 214QO 38, 214/38(a), 1943–1945, 107.

[47] "Jewish Telegraphic Agency News Bulletin: France not prepared to hand over the ex-Mufti: Does not regard him a 'war criminal'" (August 10, 1945), cited in Henri Bonnet à Georges Bidault, Washington, No. 1238 (August 23, 1945), "Hadj Amin el Husseini Grand Mufti de Jérusalem," CADC, MAE, DAL, GPO, 214QO 38, 214/38(a), 1943–1945, 109.

[48] Georges Bidault to Adrien Tixier, Ministre de l'Interieur, Cabinet due Ministre, Paris (August 31, 1945), No. 611, "Reference: Votre note n. 6950/45 XV. SU 2 JUIN 1945, Au sujet du Grand Mufti de Jerusalem," CADC, MAE, DAL, GPO, 214QO 38, 38(a), 1943–1945, 133–134.

[49] "Note," Paris, n.d., CADC, MAE, DAL, GPO, 214QO 38, 38(a), 1943–1945, 159–160.

[50] Ponsot, Paris (August 28, 1945), "4 ème entretien de Monsieur Ponsot avec le Grand Mufti," CADC, MAE, DAL, GPO, 214QO 38, 214/38(a), 1943–1945, 127–129.

contacted Yugoslavia to "request that it reject extradition of the Mufti as a war criminal."[51] Husseini was ready to break his previous silence and respond to accusations made "by the committees of the Jews of the United States, the promoters of the Yugoslav's decision" to accuse him of war crimes. He asserted that "Jewish propaganda was obviously trying to discredit him in the eyes of the Allies."[52]

On September 13 Bonnet informed Bidault that France's treatment of the Mufti had caused "increasing discontent" in Zionist and liberal circles in the United States. The World Jewish Congress was "astonished" that France was offering protection to someone now on a list of war criminals. France had become the source of "resentment" among Zionists and Jews in the United States, as well as among moderate Arabs and young communists in Lebanon and Syria. The American political establishment would see the protection of Husseini as sign of weakness by France, while the liberal press had become very critical of France.[53] On October 17 the British Foreign Office repeated its request of May 22 that Husseini and his secretaries be delivered to Supreme Allied Command headquarters in Paris for extradition to Britain.[54] On October 18 Chauvel acknowledged that the British had sent "urgent instructions" that Husseini and his two secretaries "be delivered without delay to the British Military Authorities in Paris." Yet the British, he wrote, knew that "it is impossible for us to deliver the Grand Mufti."[55] "Impossible," that is, in Chauvel's view, if France was to retain good relations with the Arab governments.

On October 25, 1945 the Department for Africa and the Levant in the Quai d'Orsay sent a five-page unsigned memo to Chauvel and Bidault summarizing the government's contact with and policy toward Husseini since his capture by French troops in Germany on May 5, 1945.[56] Given the detail and familiarity with the case, it was likely written by Ponsot. Over the summer, the memo stated, the Yugoslav government had publicly asked the French to send Husseini there to stand trial for his collaboration with German forces during World War II. Yugoslavia did not, however, make a formal request to France for his extradition, and as of October, presumably in response to pressure from the Arab regimes and the Arab League, the Yugoslav government had abandoned that effort. Conversely,

---

[51] Ibid., 128.   [52] Ibid., 127.

[53] Bonnet to Bidault, Washington (September 13, 1945), No. 1376, "a.s. Grand Mufti de Jerusalem," CADC, MAE, DAL, GPO, 214QO 38, 214/38(a), 1943–1945, 142–143.

[54] British Embassy Paris, "Aide Memoire," Paris (October 16, 1945), CADC, MAE, DAL, GPO, 214QO 38, 214/38(a), 1943–1945, 159–160, and 172–173.

[55] Chauvel, Paris (October 18, 1945), CADC, MAE, DAL, GPO, 214QO 38, 38(a), 159–160, 174–175.

[56] Direction Afrique-Levant to Jean Chauvel and Georges Bidault, "Note," Paris (October 25, 1945), CADC, MAE, DAL, GPO, 214QO 38, 38(a), 159–160, 174–175.

on October 16 the British had sent another written request that Husseini, Derwish, and Khalidi should be given to "British military authorities in Paris without delay."[57] In response, this remarkably frank memo presented the reason why the French government should not extradite Husseini either to Yugoslavia or Britain to face war crimes accusations:

Though that is our legal obligation, it is politically impossible to consent to such a delivery. Our representatives in Beirut, Jerusalem, Cairo, and Jeddah have voluntarily and on several occasions informed us how intact the Mufti's prestige remains among his coreligionists. We have received gratitude in all the countries of Islam for having welcomed and treated with humanity a person considered to be a true hero of Arab patriotism. If, after six months of reflection, we delivered him, it would be difficult to explain [our decision] throughout the Middle East. Were we to do so, we would unleash a new wave of hostility against us in all the Arab countries, and would also deprive ourselves of the interesting and fruitful contacts that the Mufti maintains with important figures from the Arab world including Sami Solh, prime minister of Lebanon, and Abdul Hahman Hassan Azzam Bey, secretary general of the Arab League. We suggest that we make it clear to the British government that for political reasons it is impossible for us to deliver the Mufti and his secretaries [to the British, the Yugoslavs, or the Allies].[58]

To respond to British concerns that the French were going to deliver Husseini to his supporters in the Middle East, the October 25 memo suggested offering "partial satisfaction" to the British. Acknowledging the lenient terms of his custody up to that point, the memo suggested no longer allowing visitors to see him or allowing him to leave his residence unaccompanied.[59] On November 6 Tixier noted that control of Husseini's custody had passed from the Interior Ministry to the Foreign Ministry and the Paris police. He no longer knew where Husseini was, but thought that "Ambassador Ponsot" would.[60]

On November 1 the British had expressed concerns that the French government was assisting Husseini's efforts to return to the Middle East.[61] The British Air Ministry had received a request from its French counterpart "to afford facilities to an aircraft which the French authorities wish to send from Algiers to Jedda on the 4th November, carrying 27 Muslim passengers from French North Africa for the pilgrimage." Concerned that the flight from North Africa might first fly to France, the British wrote that "they cannot overlook the possibility that this flight

---

[57] Ibid., 182.   [58] Ibid.

[59] Afrique-Levant to René Chauvel, Paris (October 25, 1945), "Note," CADC, MAE, DAL, GPO, 214QO 38, 214/38(a), 1943–1945, 159–160, 181–182.

[60] Tixier to Bidault (October 29, 1945), CADC, MAE, DAL, GPO, 214QO 38, 214/38(a), 1943–1945, 189.

[61] British Embassy Paris to Ministry of Foreign Affairs, Paris (November 1, 1945), CADC, MAE, DAL, GPO, 214QO 38, 214/38(a), 1943–1945, 190.

might be used, without the knowledge or approval of the French Provisional Government, as a means of facilitating the return of the ex-Mufti of Jerusalem to the Middle East." The British thus sought "an assurance that the French Provisional Government will take every precaution against this contingency."[62]

On December 7 Ambassador Lescuyer reported in a dispatch from Cairo that leading newspapers in Cairo (*al-Ahram*, *al-Siassa*, *al-Mokattam*, *Egyptian Gazette*) were claiming that the Arab League officials regarded the accusations against the Mufti as "the result of a large Zionist conspiracy."[63] Emile Ghoury, a leading figure in the Arab Higher Committee, wrote to Lescuyer to express his fears that the Stern Gang (associated with the Irgun in Palestine) in Paris was preparing to assassinate Husseini, and to request that the French take measures "to protect the Mufti against a possible assassination attempt." Lescuyer promised to forward Ghoury's apprehensions to the Foreign Ministry in Paris.[64]

On December 8, 1945 Alexander Cadogan, the permanent under secretary in the British Foreign Office, informed René Massigli (1888–1988), France's ambassador in London, that Britain continued to insist that the French hand the Mufti over to them. Cadogan assured the French that "we do not propose to bring him to trial, and that there is therefore no question of his being put to death." If the French government feared it "might incur criticism for having handed this man over to us to be put to death, I am able to assure you that this fear is unfounded." Rather, Britain's "intention is to send the Mufti to some British territory far from the Middle East, where he will have no opportunity to cause further trouble." The British would be glad to learn whether, with "this understanding, your Government would be prepared to hand him over."[65]

Cadogan's promise not to put Husseini on trial was significant. Trying Husseini would have given the prosecution the opportunity to examine witnesses as well as the files of the Nazi regime and of the American, British, French, Soviet, and Yugoslav governments, and perhaps of those of the Jewish Agency and Arab governments as well, about Husseini's years of Nazi collaboration. The witness list could have brought Husseini's network and his surviving connections with the Nazis to testify. The resulting revelations would have made it more difficult for

---

[62] Ibid.
[63] Lescuyer to Bidault (December 7, 1945), CADC, MAE, DAL, GPO, 214QO 38, 214/38 (a), 1943–1945, 216–218.
[64] Ibid.
[65] Alexander Cadogan to René Massigli, London (December 8, 1945), No. 9301/3032/G, and René Massigli to Bidault, London, No. 3804, "a.s. Mufti," CADC, MAE, DAL, GPO, 214QO 38, 214/38(a), 224–226 and 223.

France, or any of the Allied powers, to allow Husseini to return to the Middle East, and could have ended or severely damaged his political career. Those revelations would have also undermined the ability of the Arab Higher Committee to represent the Palestine Arabs at the United Nations. Both at the UN and in Palestine, such a trial could have aided more moderate Arab leaders in Palestine who might have accepted, not rejected, the various partition plans being proposed, culminating in the one ultimately adopted, without the support of more militant Arabs, by the United Nations in November 1947.

Instead, by December 8, 1945 Britain had decided not to bring war crimes charges against Husseini, and the next month Yugoslavia also dropped the effort to bring him to trial in Belgrade.[66] On February 11, 1946 Sir Harold Orme Sargent (1884–1962), Cadogan's successor as the permanent under secretary of the British Foreign Office, presented Massigli with arguments intended to strike a nerve in post-Vichy France. He described Husseini as a "Quisling," that is, a "traitor to his country," in this case British Mandate Palestine, comparing his treason to that of Pierre Laval and others who were brought to court "for having supported Germany during the war." Britain had delivered persons in its custody to other Allied governments when they were accused of treason to those states; the same principle of treason to an Allied government should apply in the case of the Mufti and oblige France to extradite him to Britain.[67] But the French Foreign Ministry again rejected Britain's request for extradition.

The View from the United States

The very different mood in the United States propelled Henri Bonnet, France's ambassador in Washington, to recommend that his government adopt a firmer approach to Husseini. Bonnet took note of the anger toward France among Zionists and their supporters in the New York press. On January 17, 1946 he sent the MFA the full text of the previously discussed American Zionist Emergency Council (AZEC) memorandum that Stephen Wise and Abba Silver had sent to secretary of state James F. Byrnes on December 13, 1945. The following day Bonnet added that "the most important Zionist organizations" in the United States were worried that a man they viewed as a war criminal would "yet again escape and return to an Arab country." Jewish organizations in the United States were focused on "the question of the Mufti," though "liberal and

---

[66] Bonneau to Washington, Paris (January 28, 1945), No. 674, CADC, MAE, DAL, GPO, 214QO 38, 214/38(b)-230 to 489, 1946, 266.
[67] Ibid., 351–352.

anti-German opinion in the United States was equally hostile to him."[68]
On February 19 Bonnet again wrote to Bidault about the attention that
the "liberal milieu" in United States was devoting to the "ex-Mufti of
Jerusalem,"[69] referring to the article in *PM* by Alexander Uhl dealing with
possible forms of escape ("evasion") by Husseini. Bonnet reported Uhl's
view that both Britain and France were negotiating about how best to
arrange his "escape" to the Middle East, and that both powers viewed the
"ex Grand Mufti as an instrument" that could help establish the Arab
world as "a rampart against Soviet influence in the Middle East."[70] *PM*
had reported that in Paris the Mufti had numerous Arab visitors, "including Yunus al-Bahri, former announcer for radio Berlin" in the Nazi years.
Bonnet relayed Uhl's critical assessment that it was "evident" that
Husseini was "assured of impunity if he would be able to return to a
Muslim country. In Uhl's view, neither the French nor the British desire
that he be subject to sanctions because of the probable impact that such
measures would have on their Muslim subjects."[71] Though Uhl did not
fully understand the nuances of the British position of deportation away
from the Middle East without a war crimes trial, the French files indicate
that his interpretation of France's policy was correct.

On April 11 Bonnet sent Bidault a Reuters report on the circumstances
of Husseini's custody, along with a copy of a recent related article by Uhl
in *PM*. Reuters reported that Husseini's "movements were practically
free" and that "France would place no obstacle in the way of his departure
to an Arab country disposed to welcome him."[72] The report had caused
"a strong reaction" among Zionist leaders, including Nahum Goldmann,
Stephen Wise, Abba Silver, and Louis Lipsky. In the event that France
allowed Husseini to return to the Middle East, they were ready to issue a
public statement attacking the French position not only because France
had freed him but also because "for many months it facilitated personal
and permanent contacts with the political milieu in the Middle East." The
Zionist leaders were convinced that the Mufti's contacts with Arab leaders had been organized with the "'aid and complicity' of French

[68] Bonnet to MAE, Washington, DC (January 17, 1946), CADC, MAE, DAL, GPO,
214QO 38, 214/38(b)-230 to 489, 1946, 365–366.
[69] Bonnet to Bidault, Direction d'Afrique-Levant, Washington (February 19, 1946), No.
468, "a.s Haj Amin el Husseini," CADC, MAE, DAL, GPO, 214QO 38, 214/38(b)-230
to 489, 1946, 274–275.
[70] Ibid.   [71] Ibid., 275.
[72] Bonnet to Bidault, Washington (April 10, 1946), No. 806, "a.s. Hadj Amin el Husseini,"
CADC, MAE, DAL, GPO, 214QO 38, 214/38(b)-230 to 489, 1946, 300–303. Bonnet
included the Reuters report and Alexander Uhl, "France Letting Grand Mufti Slip out
Free: Hitler's No. 1 Arab Collaborator May Now Be in Middle East," *PM*, April 10,
1946, 304–305.

authorities" so that he could direct the Arabs' battle against Zionism, and that he had been in touch with Rashid Ali Kilani and Yunus al-Bari, both free in their movements as well. The Zionist leaders sought to prevent his return to the Middle East because he would seek to fan anti-Jewish sentiment in the Arab states at a time when the report of the Anglo-American Committee of Inquiry might recommend the partition of Palestine and establishment of separate Jewish and Arab states.[73]

In conversations with Bonnet in Washington, Goldmann and Wise both expressed admiration for France as a "guardian of liberty and democracy." France, they said, also stood in contrast to the USSR, "which was a form of totalitarian government that was contrary to all the traditions of the Jewish people." However, there would be "indignation and anger" at the French government among the majority of seven million American Jews if Husseini "directly or indirectly benefited from its assistance" in escaping judicial reckoning and then returning to the Middle East. Husseini's "intimate collaboration with the Nazis" remained central in this campaign. Liberal opinion, as expressed in *PM* as well as in Congress, was an important source of support for France in the United States.[74]

On April 15 Bonnet sent more information about anger at French policy among American liberals and American Jewish opinion.[75] Congressman Emanuel Celler had described the ex-Mufti's career in Congress and "expressed his astonishment that the French government, to its great shame, had refused to deliver the Mufti, allowed him freedom of movement and may be preparing to authorize his return to the Middle East." Celler appealed personally to French prime minister Léon Blum, known for his sympathies for Zionism, as well as to the ambassador, to intervene with the Foreign Ministry "so that the Mufti stays in prison, is placed on a list of war criminals and is judged as such." Celler added that France needed American friends and American economic aid. She would only receive that aid if she "conformed to the rules of justice. Those rules demand that the Mufti be punished."[76] Bonnet added a copy of Edgar Mowrer's *New York Post* article citing the affidavit of Dieter Wisliczeny. Bonnet concluded that in view of these "new elements of information" and the passionate reactions they were unleashing in the United States, "it would be very useful now" to state that it would be "impossible" for the

[73] Bonnet to Bidault, "a.s. Hadj Amin el Husseini," 301.   [74] Ibid., 302–303.
[75] Bonnet to MAE, Washington (April 15, 1946), No. 2027–20–29, CADC, MAE, Direction Afrique-Levant, Généralités Proche-Orient 214QO 38, 214/38(b)-230 to 489, 1946, 311.
[76] Ibid.

Mufti to return to the Middle East now.[77] That is, with American reaction in mind, he took issue with the views of Ponsot, Chauvel, and the French ambassadors in Cairo and Beirut.

On April 18 Bonnet sent another dispatch to Paris informing officials there that the "Zionist milieu and their supporters" in the USA were preoccupied with the possibility that France and Britain would agree to send Husseini back to the Middle East. The opposition now came not only from Zionist organizations and their liberal supporters in the press, but also from "numerous members of the Senate and the House of Representatives, Republicans as well as Democrats, [who] used many opportunities to support Zionist themes. Few among them take a different view. The situation is the same in the press." It was "no exaggeration" to say that "the majority of American public opinion would disapprove of our policy" if it led to Husseini's release and return to the Middle East. Bonnet stressed that these factors must "not be lost from view." While keeping France's interests in North Africa and the Middle East in mind, it was important that "we not alienate American opinion."[78]

On April 20, 1946 Lescuyer informed Bidault that a delegation from the Muslim Brotherhood had come to the embassy in Cairo to express in person that "the Arab world was touched by our attitude and all the hopes it placed in our future action toward the world of Islam." Lescuyer included a letter of April 17, 1947 from Hassan al-Banna, the leader of the Muslim Brotherhood in Egypt, "in case you think it would be useful for propaganda in North Africa."[79] Al-Banna's note to the French Embassy in Cairo read as follows:

The attitude of your government toward his Eminence Mohammed Haj Amin el-Husseini, Grand Mufti, and the premier leader of Palestine, has produced the best impression among us. Your solicitude toward him and your refusal to deliver him to Great Britain comprises in our view the element of a laudable first step towards the establishment of good relations between France and the Arab and Muslim peoples . . .
In the name of the Arab and Muslim world, the Muslim Brothers thank the French Government for its generous stance toward his Eminence the Grand Mufti and expect to see the same attitude toward Emir Abdel Kermi and other deported Arab leaders.
Please accept the expression of my profound respect, Hassan al-Bana.[80]

---

[77] Bonnet to MAE, Washington (April 15, 1946), No. 2027–20–29, CADC, MAE, DAL, GPO, 214QO 38, 214/38(b)-230 to 489, 1946, 311.

[78] Bonnet to MAE, New York, (April 17, 1946), No. 32 à 34, CADC, MAE, DAL, GPO, 214QO 38, 214/38(b)-230 to 489, 1946, 313–314.

[79] Lescuyer to MAE, Direction d'Afrique-Levant, Cairo (April 20, 1946), "Objet: Grand Mufti de Jerusalem," CADC, MAE, DAL, GPO, 214QO 38, 214/38(b)-230 to 489, 1946, 319.

[80] Hassan al-Bana to Légation de France, Cairo (April 17, 1946), "Traduction d'une Lettre Remise par le Groupement des 'Frères Muselmans' à la Légation de France le 17.4.46," CADC, MAE, DAL, GPO, 214QO 38, 214/38(b)-230 to 489, 1946, 320.

Al-Banna's letter indicated that the policies of the Foreign Ministry had succeeded in generating good will in the world's leading organization of Islamist fundamentalism, one that made no pretense of distinguishing between hatred of Jews and rejection of Zionism.

On May 1, 1946 the British Foreign Office again wrote to Massigli, reminding him that the Quai d'Orsay had not responded to British requests to hand over the Mufti.[81] Further, the British were surprised to learn that Husseini was living freely, with considerable privileges. The British concluded that the French would not extradite him to Britain "and that this Axis collaborator will enjoy complete liberty and comfort on French territory." That was a situation that the British found "difficult to accept," and it led them to ask what the intentions of the French government were "concerning the future surveillance of the Mufti."[82] On May 7 an unsigned memo in the MFA reflecting Ponsot's views offered elements of a response.[83] It stated that Husseini was a political refugee and that the British had never classified him as a war criminal; hence, extradition would be arbitrary. By not having made such a formal declaration the British had placed the French government "in an indefensible position," for if it refused to extradite Husseini it would anger its close ally the British, but if it complied it would harm French relations with the Arabs. As both France and Britain sought good relations with the Arabs, the author hoped that a solution could be found that would be satisfactory to "all parties," that is, France, Britain, the Arab League, and Arab states.[84] The author did not mention a fourth "party," the Jews in Palestine. Following seven exchanges between the British Foreign Office and the Quai d'Orsay from May 22, 1945 to April 30, 1946, it was evident that the MFA placed priority on good relations with Arabs, including those who defended Husseini, ahead of demands by the British for extradition and the Zionists to bring the Mufti to trial.[85]

On May 29, 1946, using a false passport and an alias, Haj Amin al-Husseini "escaped" from France on a TWA flight from Paris to

---

[81] C. Paris, Translation M. Sargent to (René) Massigli, London (May 1, 1946), No. I562/ I564, CADC, MAE, DAL, GPO, 214QO 38, 214/38(b)-230 to 489, 1946, 328–329.

[82] Ibid., 328.

[83] "Situation actuelle du Muphti de Jerusalem, Observations formulées en vue d'une réponse au Gouvernement Britanique," Paris (May 6, 1946), CADC, MAE, DAL, GPO, 214QO 38, 214/38(b)-230 to 489, 1946, 332–337.

[84] Ibid., 337.

[85] Direction d'Afriques-Levant sous-direction du Levant, Paris (May 24, 1946), "Note," CADC, MAE, DAL, GPO, 214QO 38, 214/38(b)-230 to 489, 1946, 349–352. This document summarizes memoranda of May 22, October 16, October 18, and December 8, 1945, and those of February 11 and April 30, 1946.

Cairo.[86] On June 13 the Foreign Ministry informed thirty French Embassies (in Europe, the Middle East, Jerusalem, and Washington, DC) that the Grand Mufti, using a false Syrian passport, had made his "clandestine" departure and arrived in Cairo.[87] On June 18 Lescuyer reported that Husseini's return to Egypt was greeted with "joy" and accompanied by "gratitude" toward France.[88] He wrote that "France benefits from the general elation. The Arab press does not refrain from emphasizing the friendly manner in which France treated the Mufti in Paris." The same was the case in political circles.[89] The year of preventing Husseini's extradition to Yugoslavia, Britain or the Supreme Allied Command headquarters in Paris, treating him like an honored political refugee, and loosening "surveillance" had culminated in a French diplomatic triumph. The Mufti's "escape" was attributed in many Arab eyes to a decision by the French government to facilitate it. The result would, hopefully, be Arab good will toward France, a rebuke to the British, and a defeat for the Zionists.

Soon afterward the Quai d'Orsay received further confirmation about the Mufti's actions during World War II. On July 8, 1946 Jacques Tarbé de Saint Hardouin, France's political ambassador at the headquarters of the French military occupation in Germany, sent a French translation of "History and Origins of SS Mountain Division of Volunteers of Bosnia and Herzegovina" to Foreign Minister Bidault. It was written in the office of "Reichsführer SS" Heinrich Himmler and dated November 30, 1943.[90] Bidault and other officials in the MFA could now read that Himmler had organized the Waffen SS so that "Europeans of a good race" could participate in creating a "National Socialist Europe" – and that the Mufti had assisted him. In February 1943 Himmler decided to create a Waffen-SS division composed "exclusively of volunteers from Bosnia of the Muslim faith," and called upon the Mufti to help. The

---

[86] Préfecture de Police, Le Directeur-Adjoint de le Police Judiciare à Directeur des Affaires d'Afrique et du Levant au MAE, CADC, MAE, DAL, GPO, 214QO 38, 214/38(b)-230 to 489, 1946, 386.

[87] R. Offroy, Paris (June 13, 1946) "Télégramme au Depart," MAE, Service d'Information et de Presse, Paris (June 13, 1946), CADC, MAE, DAL, GPO, 214QO 38, 214/38(b)-230 to 489, 1946, 401–402.

[88] Chargé d'Affaires de France en Egypte à Ministre des Affaires Étrangères, Direction, d'Afrique-Levant, Georges Bidault, No. 242/AL, Cairo (June 18, 1946), CADC, MAE, DAL, GPO, 214QO 38, 214/38(b)-230 to 489, 1946, 418–420.

[89] Ibid.

[90] Reichsführer S.S., Berlin (November 30, 1943), "Histoire et Origine de la Division de Montagne SS de Volontaire de Bosnie et d'Herzègovina (SS Freiwilligen-B.H.-Geb. Division SS Division," sent by M. J. Tarbé to Georges Bidault, Ministre des Affaires Étrangères, Direction d'Afrique-Levant, Baden-Baden (July 8, 1946), No. 5573, "Objet: Le Grand Mufti de Jérusalem et la division muselman de volontaires bosniaques," CADC, MAE, DAL, GPO, 214QO 38, 214/38(b)-230 to 489, 1946, 440–443.

account explained the need for such a division, which would help the Bosnians to

conquer their liberty. In addition it would show the rest of the Muslim world, which was a resolute enemy of Judaism, the Anglo-Americans and Bolshevism, that the Reich [Nazi Germany] stood for its protection and had decided to undertake and to fight closely and intimately together in combat with the Muslim world. In view of the Head of the General Direction [i.e. Heinrich Himmler] of the SS, the Grand Mufti of Palestine is the most qualified representative of the Muslim world to this action and engagement.[91]

In March 1943, accompanied by officials of the SS Main Office – that is, the Reich Security Main Office – the Mufti went to Bosnia to participate in producing propaganda, assist Muslim clergy, and help recruit Muslims for the SS division there. The account noted:

In November 1943, the Grand Mufti of Palestine and the Reichsführer SS [Heinrich Himmler], Minister of the Interior, inspected several units of the Division who received the Reichsführer SS in the name of the SS Mountain Division of Volunteers of Bosnia Herzegovina … This SS division must serve as an example and a beacon to the rest of the Muslim world in the battle against the common enemies of National Socialism and of Islam.[92]

In other words, Husseini had traveled to the Balkans with Himmler to support the Nazi war effort against "Judaism, the Anglo-Americans, and Bolshevism." By the time the leadership of the MFA received this information, which came from the captured files of the Nazi regime, it was too late for it to do much good. By then, with at least French carelessness and at most French assistance, Husseini was now in the Middle East, where none of the Arab governments intended to hand over a man receiving a hero's welcome to a court that would put him on trial for crimes against humanity committed while he collaborated with the Hitler regime.

Remarkably, a few months later Haj Amin al-Husseini had an extended conversation with an official in the French Embassy in Cairo to explain why he had left Paris.[93] Initially he had written to Bidault to "express my gratitude for the welcome that I received in France." But he began thinking about escaping when the Foreign Ministry announced that Bidault "would not oppose my return to the Middle East if an Arab state requested it. For me this news was a tacit approval for my departure, one that could not be officially expressed." Therefore, he thought he "could with a free conscience return to the land of Islam." He could not

[91] Ibid., 441–442.   [92] Ibid., 443.

[93] Haj Amin el Husseini, "Declaration de El Haj Amine El Husseini, Grand Mufti de Jérusalem, à un membre de cette Légation," Cairo (October 11, 1946), CADC, MAE, DAL, GPO, 214QO 38, 214/38(b)-230 to 489, 1946, 471–474.

ask the French for formal permission to leave as he knew that France, "in order to maintain your good relations with London ... would have been obliged to reject my request."[94] His note combined excessive flattery with gratitude. "I am aware of the importance of the debt which I owe to you. Rest assured that my action in your favor will match the scale of this debt ... the only country in the world that is truly democratic is yours [i.e. France]."[95]

Husseini's statement made clear that he understood the MFA to be giving him tacit approval to escape to the Middle East. His political experience and solicitude for France's balancing act between Britain and the Middle East was evident in his appreciation of France's desire not to publicly offend its British ally by openly supporting his return to the region. In view of their support, his expression of gratitude, especially to Ponsot and Lescuyer, was most appropriate. He owed Ponsot a great deal. He understood very well that France had shielded him from extradition to Britain and had resisted calls to indict him for war crimes in Nuremberg. Husseini's statement demonstrated that French policy toward him since May 1945 had produced the hoped-for result: gratitude to France. It is likely that experienced diplomats like Bidault, Ponsot, Lescuyer, and Chauvel would have seen Husseini's declaration that France was the only democracy in the world as the excessive and cynical flattery that it certainly was.

In the same October 11 conversation Husseini went beyond the niceties of his written statement to explain how his future intentions fitted into what he viewed as France's strategic interests in the Middle East. In the strategic competition between "the Anglo-Saxons" and "the Russians," the former were "officially obliged" to support Zionism for religious reasons and to oppose the Arab cause. "But they [the Anglo-Saxons] are equally eager to find sympathy among Muslims in order to establish a check to Bolshevism." Due to their "religious incompatibility and to save their traditions" the Arab governments were inclined to the Anglo-Saxons. Communism constituted a "psychological shock" that was unlikely to arouse support among Muslims. Husseini had the impression that the Arabs "strongly desire a rapprochement with France."[96] Nevertheless, while the Arabs were inclined to the West, American and British support for Zionism pushed them to consider tilting toward the communists, despite the fact that they had nothing in common with them. Husseini's message was that France could play a special role as it was free of the Anglo-Saxon support for Zionism and therefore could draw the Arab world away from the communists.

[94] Ibid., 471.   [95] Ibid., 471–472.   [96] Ibid., 473.

France, the Mufti continued, had no serious problems in North Africa compared to those of the Anglo-Saxons in the Middle East. What stood in the way of the Arabs' good relations with the Americans and the British "was that Jewish action has taken a preponderant place in their governments. It was the same in Germany where, thanks to its leaders' natural simplicity [in the era of the Weimar Republic] the Jews, had taken control of the reins of command before Hitler came to power."[97] In the Latin countries, such as France, the Jews had sometimes attained important positions, "but the spontaneous reaction of Catholicism meant that they never were able to guide the destinies of these countries" or of the countries of North Africa. "It seems therefore that the issue is one of an entente between the Muslims of Tunisia, Algeria, Morocco and you [i.e. France]. Everything – your civilization, your spirituality, your liberalism – contributes to making such an entente possible."[98]

Husseini's antisemitic interpretation of politics was on full display. He attributed the governments' support for Zionism to the supposed power of the Jews in Britain and the United States, which, for Britain at least, was odd in view of the Attlee–Bevin government's emphatic opposition to the Zionists and support for the Arabs. Husseini sympathetically referred to the "spontaneous reaction of Catholicism" in France that placed a check on Jewish power and thus on support for Zionism. According to Husseini, France's predominant Catholicism formed a foundation for a rapprochement between France and the Arabs. It was obvious that the defeat of Nazism and the revelations of the Holocaust in summer 1945 had not led him to abandon the hatred of Jews he had expressed before and during the years of Nazi collaboration, but now he was, in effect, also attributing it to the French (or assuming that they shared it).[99]

Husseini continued his efforts to maintain cordial relations with France. At the end of November he met in Cairo with the new French ambassador, Gilbert Arvengas. He appealed to France to help stop a possible – in reality, at that point nonexistent – British plan to partition Palestine and create a Jewish state. If he did not receive a positive response, he "was ready to consider" turning to Russia. He told Arvengas that "without immediate support the entire Middle East risked turning to Russia." The Arabs needed arms. If France delivered them, he promised that "North Africa would remain obedient to the French."

---

[97] Ibid., 474.   [98] Ibid.

[99] As his 1937 essay "Islam and the Jews" made clear, Husseini's hatred of the Jews was not originally due to the impact of Nazism. On this see Jeffrey Herf, "Introduction," in *Nazi Propaganda for the Arab World* (New Haven: Yale University Press, 2009); and Matthias Küntzel, *Nazis und die Nahe Osten: Wie der Islamische Antisemitismus Entstand* (Berlin: Hentrich & Hentrich, 2019).

Arvengas thought it was "without question necessary to give full weight to the Mufti's apprehensions."[100] In November the man full of expressions of gratitude to France just a month earlier was willing to threaten a turn to the Soviet Union it if he did not receive what he wanted. From being a man under arrest and facing possible indictment for war crimes, Husseini now spoke as a political actor willing and able to threaten the government of France.

A review of the policy of the MFA toward and contact with Haj Amin al-Husseini in the eighteen months from May 1945 to November 1946 leads to the following conclusions: First, French officials never critically examined the record of his collaboration with Nazi Germany. Henri Bonnet's dispatches from Washington in 1945 and 1946 alone contained enough evidence offered by the American Zionist Emergency Committee to justify probing deeper into the captured German records to ascertain the truth of the matter. But the MFA did not do so. Instead, soon after he was taken into custody, French officials decided to give priority to good relations with the Arab states and Muslim world more broadly over a careful examination of Husseini's Nazi years. That priority, evident especially in the conversations and recommendations of Henri Ponsot, remained constant. It led to removing control of Husseini's surveillance from Adrien Tixier's Ministry of the Interior to Georges Bidault's Foreign Ministry in October 1945. That change led in turn to a relaxation of surveillance that made it possible first for his two secretaries and then for Husseini himself to travel around France and meet with supporters from France and the Arab states. He was a political "prisoner" in name only. And ultimately, the relaxation of surveillance enabled him to "escape."

Second, although Britain did not formally accuse Husseini of war crimes, it made plausible arguments in favor of his extradition, and thus the prevention of his return to the Middle East. By contrast, at no time during their control over Husseini did the MFA view his return to the region with trepidation. On the contrary, its leading officials, especially Henri Ponsot and Jean Chauvel, saw it as an opportunity to enhance French influence in the Arab and Muslim world. Husseini's departure to Cairo in May 1946 was one result of French efforts to curry favor with Arabs and Muslims.

Third, during the entire time he was in their custody, French officials never made Husseini's collaboration with the Nazis and his continuing antisemitic views central issues of public discussion or diplomatic

---

[100] M. Gilbert Arvengas to Georges Bidault, President du Gouvernement Provisoire de la Republique Francaise, Ministre des Affaires Étrangères, Cairo (November 30, 1946), "Entretien avec le Mufti," CADC, MAE, DAL, GPO, 214QO 38, 214/38(b), 1946, 485–489.

strategy. The Zionists' efforts to raise these issues in the United States and in France failed to exert any impact on the foreign policy of France, focused as it was on relations with the Arab states and the Muslim world. The sequence of decisions by the MFA in the twelve months from the time of Husseini's capture to his "escape" to Cairo was but one example of the inclination, evident within postwar France and postwar Europe, to obscure or ignore the history of collaboration with the Nazis during World War II and the Holocaust.

The year-long episode of Husseini's lenient custody in France was part of the larger history of the transition from World War II to the Cold War, and the willingness to enlist former Nazis and Nazi collaborators into the emerging anticommunist consensus. As was the case in Britain, the policies of empire or imperial presence, this time in France, were at odds with Zionist aspirations. By early 1947 the foreign policies of the French government, along with those of the USA and the British, had converged to constitute a formidable barrier both to Zionist aspirations and to a necessary judicial and political reckoning with the crimes of the Nazi regime and its supporters.

5 The "Question of Palestine" at the United Nations General Assembly's First Special Session: April–May 1947

> But there is also another bond, a most tragic bond, which has been formed between my nation and the Jews. This bond was created by the Nazis.
>
> Alfred Fiderkiewicz, Polish representative to the United Nations and vice-president of the General Assembly, New York, May 12, 1947.

> The fact that no western European State has been able to ensure the defence of the elementary rights of the Jewish people and to safeguard it against the violence of the fascist executioners, explains the aspirations of the Jews to establish their own State.
>
> Andrei Gromyko, Soviet representative to the United Nations, New York, May 15, 1947.

By late April, 1947 the British government, frustrated with its inability to achieve a binational compromise but confident that there would not be a two-thirds majority in the UN General Assembly in favor of a Jewish state in Palestine, handed the problem over to the newly established international organization.[1] From 1945 to 1947 Britain and the Jews and Arabs of Palestine had been the primary actors involved in determining that territory's future. When the problem became one for the United Nations at its first Special Session from April 28 to May 15, the number of actors who expressed views and sought to influence events in Palestine expanded dramatically. With the shift to the UN, the future of Palestine became an issue of international politics rather than one primarily of concern to the British, the Arabs, and the Jews.

The session's purpose was to establish a committee, this time under the auspices of the UN, to consider yet again "the question of Palestine" and offer recommendations to the regular General Assembly meeting in the

---

[1] On Britain's decision to send the issue to the UN and the first Special Session see chapters 9 and 10 in Michael J. Cohen, *Palestine and the Great Powers, 1945–1948* (Princeton: Princeton University Press, 1982); and chapters 4 and 5 in William Roger Louis, *The British Empire in the Middle East, 1945–1951: Arab Nationalism, the United States, and Postwar Imperialism* (New York and Oxford: Oxford University Press, 1984).

131

coming fall.[2] At the same time that Truman and Marshall were laying the foundation for an American policy of containment of the Soviet Union and communism, the Special Session revealed political coordinates regarding Zionist aspirations that did not neatly overlap with the emerging divisions between the Western democracies and the Soviet Union. When the Soviet Union indicated that it concurred with Truman's support for the admission of 100,000 Jewish refugees to Palestine, it first appeared as though the two superpowers were in full agreement on this issue – a striking exception amidst the deepening East–West tensions in the early months of the Cold War. But a close reading of the Special Session records indicates that the Soviet Union and its East European allies expressed their support for a Jewish state in Palestine with a passion and intensity that stood in contrast to the careful legalisms and ambiguities coming from the representatives of the United States, as the latter balanced the State Department's concerns to sustain close bonds with Britain against popular pressure in favor of the Zionists.[3]

Before the session began, the Arab states – Egypt, Iraq, Syria, Lebanon, and Saudi Arabia – announced their opposition to any Jewish state in Palestine. Instead, they favored the termination of the British Mandate over Palestine and its replacement with a unitary independent state, one with an Arab majority and strict limits on Jewish immigration.[4] The Arab states contended that there was nothing further to discuss as, in their view, the Balfour Declaration had violated the principles of self-determination of the League of Nations Covenant and amounted to foreign imposition without the Arabs' consent. They claimed that "all that was necessary in Palestine was to apply the principles of the [UN] Charter and declare an independent Palestine along democratic lines with equal rights for all citizens." As "the Jewish question" and thus that of refugees in Europe "was a completely separate one from the Palestine problem," and as the Arabs opposed Jewish immigration to Palestine, their proposal amounted to establishment of an Arab-majority state in all of Mandate Palestine.[5]

The surprise of the first session consisted in the fact that, other than the Jewish Agency, the primary opposition to the Arabs came from the representatives of the Soviet Union, Poland, and Czechoslovakia. On

---

[2] "First Special Session," *Yearbook of the United Nations 1946–47* (New York: United Nations, 1947), 277.

[3] On the balancing act between the emerging Cold War and support for Zionist goals see "Ambivalence: Truman's Policy toward Palestine, 1945–1947," in Peter L. Hahn, *Caught in the Middle East: U.S. Policy toward the Arab-Israeli Conflict, 1945–1961* (Chapel Hill and London: University of North Carolina Press, 2004), 32–41.

[4] "First Special Session," 278.   [5] Ibid.

April 29, 1947, Józef Winiewicz, head of the Polish delegation, addressed the UN's First Committee, which had been assigned the task of discussing the question of Palestine before the full General Assembly took it up. Winiewicz opposed the Egyptian proposal to terminate the Mandate and establish a unitary independent state "even before we have heard the opinion of the most interested party, the Jewish people, for which the mandate in Palestine provided special rights."[6] He urged the First Committee "to take up as soon as possible the admission of a Jewish representative body for consultation with the Assembly."[7] On May 2 Winiewicz urged that the "General Assembly ... give careful consideration to the point of view of the Jewish people on the Palestine question." He then accepted an amendment by the Czechoslovak delegation rewording his second paragraph to read that the General Assembly "decides to invite the representative of the Jewish Agency for Palestine to appear before the General Assembly for consultation."[8] Winiewicz stressed the connection between the Jewish population and Palestine that had developed since the Mandate was established and explained that Poland was particularly interested in the issue because many of the Palestine Jews had come from Poland.[9]

Communist orthodoxy before World War II had regarded Zionism as a divisive, nationalist competitor. Yet, at the United Nations in May 1947, Andrei Gromyko (1909–89), the head of the Soviet delegation, struck a very different note.[10] On May 2 he told the First Committee that he wanted "representatives of Jewish organizations" to be allowed to attend the General Assembly's plenary meetings as well as at those of the First Committee. Barring them from doing so "would be especially unjust from the point of view of the Jewish population in Palestine which is vitally concerned with this matter."[11] Here he was implicitly challenging the United States, which had agreed with the Arab states' position that only states could be represented in General Assembly. Were that to remain the case, the Jewish Agency would be able to speak to the First Committee but not to the General Assembly, in which the Arab states had ample representation.

---

[6] Józef Winiewicz, cited in [US] Central Intelligence Agency, "Communist Bloc Opposition to Arab Aspirations in Palestine: An Analysis of the Communist Position on the Palestine Question," Washington (June 23, 1953), CREST (Document Release Date, July 8, 1998): CIA-RDP62-0086SR000200180002-1, 16–17.

[7] Ibid.   [8] Ibid., 5. Also see *Yearbook of the United Nations, 1946–47*, 281.

[9] *Yearbook of the United Nations, 1946–47*, 281–282.

[10] On the evolution of Stalin's policies, including on the Soviet Union at the United Nations, see Laurent Rucker, *Stalin, Israël et les Juifs* (Paris: Presses Universitaire Française, 2001).

[11] Andrei Gromyko, New York, cited in CIA, "Communist Bloc Opposition," 6.

The previous January Truman had appointed Warren Austin, a former Republican governor of Vermont, to be the United States's first ambassador to the UN. Austin served in that post until 1953. During the crucial years of 1947–8 he was in frequent, at times daily, contact with Secretary of State George Marshall and Under Secretary of State Robert Lovett, who had primary responsibility for the Palestine issue in the State Department. Austin's views were aligned closely with the leaders of the State Department, who directed him to submit a resolution postponing consideration of inviting the Jewish Agency to speak to the General Assembly. Gromyko criticized the proposal because it "not only makes no provision for inviting Jewish organizations to the General Assembly's plenary meetings but does not provide for inviting representatives of the Jewish organizations at all."[12] Dr. Alfred Fiderkiewicz (1886–1972), Poland's UN ambassador, concurred. The problem of Palestine, he said, could not be solved "without a Jewish voice being heard before the Assembly."[13]

On May 3, 1947 the 73rd UN General Assembly Plenary debated whether to allow representatives of the Jewish Agency to address it. Fiderkiewicz spoke in favor.[14] The UN Charter did not contain any prohibition, he asserted, while its articles 70 and 80 expressly permitted hearing representatives of "non-governmental bodies" when required. No solution to the Palestine issue could be reached "without hearing the views of the most interested parties in the case, the Jewish people." Fiderkiewicz favored a Polish resolution, as amended by the Czechoslovak delegation, that the General Assembly decide "to invite representatives of the Jewish Agency for Palestine to appear before the plenary meeting of the General Assembly for the purpose of stating their views on this question."[15] Austin retorted that allowing the Jewish Agency to address the General Assembly would "warp this Constitution," that is, the UN Charter, "if we were to accord privileges to non-member, non-states, to appear before any other body than the Security Council; to wit, the General Assembly."[16]

Gromyko disagreed with Austin. The UN had not heard the voice of "those organizations which speak for a considerable part of the Jewish population of Palestine." It was not "normal" that no such representatives had spoken at the UN. It could not be overlooked or ignored that the

---

[12] Ibid.

[13] Alfred Fiderkiewicz, New York (May 2, 1947), cited in CIA, "Communist Bloc Opposition," 8.

[14] Mr. Fiderkiewicz (Poland), 73rd Plenary Meeting, United Nations General Assembly (hereafter UNGA), 70–72: https://documents-dds-ny.un.org/doc/UNDOC/GEN/NL4/727/11/pdf/NL472711.pdf?OpenElement.

[15] Ibid., 71.   [16] Mr. Austin (United States of America), in ibid., 72–73.

Palestine problem "primarily concerns and furthermore, alarms the Jewish population of Palestine." To facilitate an "objective and thorough consideration of the Palestine problem, even in this first stage, it would be perfectly just to invite representatives of the Jewish organizations to give expression to the point of view of the Jewish population of Palestine," and it "would be unjust to deprive" them of that opportunity.[17] With Austin's comments in mind, Gromyko pointed out that the UN Charter did not contain clauses preventing representatives of such non-governmental organizations from being invited to speak to the General Assembly. Austin had argued that doing so would undermine its prestige as a representative parliamentary entity, and thus that of the entire UN as well. Gromyko replied with sarcasm: "the reason why an invitation to the Jewish representatives may be prejudicial to the prestige of the General Assembly . . . remains the secret of those who put forward and defend such arguments."[18] Allowing representatives of "qualified Jewish organizations" to speak to the General Assembly, rather than being "prejudicial to the prestige of the General Assembly and the United Nations . . . can to a certain extent help to strengthen the General Assembly's authority and prestige" by facilitating a more thorough examination of the facts "which are unknown to many, and to hear the needs of a large part of the population of Palestine, of the needs of the Jewish population, of which so far, we are in fact aware only from fragmentary and often mutilated press reports."[19]

Gromyko pointed out that the Arab states had the opportunity to make the case against the Zionists in the General Assembly, but the Jewish organizations did not. "If this question is to be approached justly and objectively, the representatives of the Jewish organizations to the General Assembly should be admitted and given an opportunity of setting forth their views at the plenary session." To those who claimed that doing so would set a precedent and open the floodgates to making a norm of inviting non-governmental organizations, Gromyko countered that "usual practice would remain usual, not become unusual; on the contrary, the unusual could be considered exceptional." Inviting the Jewish organizations to the General Assembly "would be considered . . . an exception, justified by the special character of the Palestine problem."[20]

If the Jewish organizations were denied the opportunity to speak, Gromyko continued, they and "the whole Jewish population" might interpret that to mean that the UN "does not want to give consideration to a considerable part of the Palestine population." It would not be in the

[17] Mr. Gromyko (Union of Soviet Socialist Republics) (hereafter USSR), in ibid.
[18] Ibid., 79.   [19] Ibid.   [20] Ibid., 80.

interests of the UN "if such an impression, or even such a conviction, were to be created among the Jewish population, and among others besides the Jewish population."[21] Therefore, they "or any other Jewish organizations" that could make a useful contribution should be invited to speak to the General Assembly. The submission of written communications and documents to the First Committee was not a substitute for the right to speak in person to the entire membership of the United Nation assembled in a plenary of the General Assembly.[22] The contrast between Soviet support and American opposition to inviting the Jewish Agency the right to address the General Assembly was striking.

Austin's opposition to allowing representation by the Jewish Agency did not go unnoticed by Zionists in the US Congress. On May 3 Emanuel Celler (D-New York) issued a press statement criticizing Austin's position.[23] The Arabs, he said, "had a monopoly of argument on Palestine in the United Nations. They have greatly distorted the truth while the Jews have been gagged and cannot refute the untruths." Austin, "with unwarranted concern for protocol," refused to allow the Jews in the General Assembly and relegated them to the Political and Security Committee. Celler regarded Austin's position as symptomatic of the State Department's overall treatment of Zionism, which he firmly rejected. Celler called on Marshall "to end silence on Palestine," which he interpreted as tantamount to a "negation" of the Truman administration's policy and of US support since the 1920s for establishment of a Jewish state in Palestine. Marshall's "silence" created "confusion and makes the Arabs more intransigent." The secretary of state "cannot and dare not retreat from the declared policy of the United States" by every president since Woodrow Wilson in support of establishing a Jewish state in Palestine. Marshall should "openly reinforce" Truman's request for the immediate admission of 100,000 Jews into Palestine "and demand that Britain abrogate the nefarious white paper of 1939. Austin must be reversed in the interest of fair play to permit representation of the Jewish Agency so that all sides may be heard. The Arabs and the British are permitted the dual role of claimant and judge while the Jews as vitally interested parties are excluded. Our delegate should be so instructed."[24]

---

[21] Ibid., 81.   [22] Ibid., 82.

[23] Emanuel Celler to Associated Press et al., Washington (May 3, 1947), Library of Congress (hereafter LC), Emanuel Celler Papers, Box 23. He also sent the statement to United Press, the Jewish Telegraphic Agency, the Independent Jewish Press Service, the New York Herald Tribune, the New York Post, the New York Times, the New York World Telegram, and PM.

[24] Celler to Associated Press et al., Washington (May 3, 1947), LC, Emanuel Celler Papers, Box 23.

But the United States did not change its position. In the Special Session the representatives of the Soviet Union, Czechoslovakia, and Poland referred to the murder of six million Jews in Europe; Britain, France, and the United States did not. On May 12 Fiderkiewicz, who had survived imprisonment in Auschwitz from 1943 to 1945, told the First Committee that he thought it "most regrettable that during the debate before this Committee some of the most important aspects of the question have been lost sight of."[25] He then proceeded to deliver the most extensive statement made by anyone at the UN in 1947–8 on the connection between the Holocaust and Zionist aspirations in Palestine (see Figure 5.1).

He began by noting that on April 26, 1946 Poland's prime minister, Edward Osóbka-Morawski, had stated before Poland's

Figure 5.1 Alfred Fiderkiewicz, Polish representative and vice-president of the United Nations General Assembly (center), speaking with Soviet representative Andrei Gromyko (left) and UN General Secretary Trygve Lie (right), UN General Assembly, first Special Session, May 15, 1947. Source: UN7552630, May 15, 1947, UN Photo MB.

---

[25] Dr. Fiderkiewicz (Poland), Lake Success, New York (May 12, 1947), 54th Meeting, First Committee, United Nations, 243: https://documents-dds-ny.un.org/doc/UNDOC/GEN/NL3/254/63/pdf/NL325463.pdf?OpenElement.

communist-dominated National Council that "in view of the greatest tragedy which has befallen the Jewish people, help should be extended to those Jews who are trying to realize their national aspirations in Palestine." According to Fiderkiewicz, Osóbka-Morawski's statement was no accident. Rather, it resulted "from the close relations which Poland enjoyed and continues to enjoy with the Jewish people."[26] The "Jewish life, economy and institutions" that had been built up in Palestine "resulted to a large extent from the work and efforts of Polish Jews who were citizens of our country, Jews who speak the Polish language and whose life has been closely connected with that of our own nation." These connections had created "an inevitable bond of sympathy between my nation and the Jewish people and their national aspirations in Palestine." The Polish government felt "very bitter about the fact that brutal force is used by the [British] Palestine administration to destroy the accomplishments which have often changed deserts into blooming lands."[27]

The bitterness had to do as well with bitter memories:

During this war [World War II] a very close bond was formed between Jews and Poles in their common struggle against the Nazi oppressors, whose ultimate aim was the extermination of Jews and Poles alike. Jewish partisans in the forests of Lublin, the uprisings of Jews in the Warsaw ghetto, as well as the accomplishments of the Jewish soldiers who fought with the Polish armies on all fronts, played a considerable part in the struggle for independence.

But there is also another bond, a most tragic bond, which has been formed between my nation and the Jews. This bond was created by the Nazis. You are very well aware of the tragedy of extermination of three million Polish Jews, citizens of our Republic, in the notorious extermination camps of Maidanek, Oswiecim, Treblinka and others. Polish Jews were not the only Jews to be exterminated there. Hitler and his accomplices in mass murder chose Poland as the place where all the Jews who fell under Nazi rule were to be exterminated. From all over Europe, from Germany, the Union of Soviet Socialist Republics, Czechoslovakia, Austria, France, Holland, Hungary and other countries, Jews were brought into the extermination camps erected by the Nazis on Polish soil and perished there in the gas chambers. *I was there myself and I saw one and a half to two million burned in crematoriums* [emphasis added].

Our people were witnesses of this mass tragedy. We cannot forget it and we shall not forget it. With the memory of this mass tragedy of a people deeply engraved in the mind and soul of our nation, we cannot help being interested in the fate of those unfortunate displaced persons who lost their families and who find it psychologically impossible to return to the places which to them are cemeteries where they are haunted by the memories of their dear ones killed by the Nazi barbarians. We sympathize with these displaced persons. We understand

---

[26] Ibid., 244.   [27] Ibid.

their situation, their mentality, and their aspirations. We understand their desire to begin a new life in a new land. We shall therefore support their right to establish new lives in countries in every part of the world.

We understand that by linking the Palestine problem with that of the Jews in displaced persons' camps in Europe, we make this already difficult problem even more complicated. No doubt if we could discuss these two problems separately the solution would be easier. Unfortunately, however, it is impossible to separate these two problems, because a great majority of the Jews in the displaced persons' camps desire to go to Palestine; moreover, the Palestine Jewish community is the only one which is prepared to accept Jews in great numbers.[28]

The Polish government, Fiderkiewicz continued, was "doing all it can" to encourage "all Polish Jews to return and establish themselves in Poland." Yet it also understood that many of the displaced persons found it "psychologically impossible to return to their country of origin or to go to any other country but Palestine, where, among their own people, they expect to build a new Jewish national life of their own. They consider Palestine as the historical homeland of the Jewish people. We sympathize with their aspirations and we give them our full support." Therefore, the Polish government considered it "essential" to support "the right of extended immigration of Jews into Palestine" that had been supported both by the Anglo-American Committee of Inquiry and by Truman.[29] Poland's was "a practical position, born of the practical consequences of the mass extermination of the Jews by the Nazis, and of the special position of the Jews among other displaced persons. It is a requirement of life more powerful than political doctrines of which we may approve or disapprove," Fiderkiewicz explained. That was why "we favor Jewish immigration and Jewish national aspirations in Palestine"; but, he added, indicating that he also understood the complexities of the situation, he did not want these aspirations "to encroach upon the rights and privileges of the Arab inhabitants of that country."[30] He expressed sympathy as well for Arab aspirations for "national freedom and independence" for the Arab population of Palestine.

Fiderkiewicz went on to say that Arab freedom and independence also meant independence from

certain great Powers and [freedom] from subservience to foreign oil interests, an independence which is based, to quote a recent statement by President Truman, "on representative government, free elections, guarantees of individual liberty, freedom of speech and religion, and freedom from political oppression." And, may I add, economic freedom as well. Any struggle of the Arab people for such national independence will always have our fullest sympathy and support.[31]

---

[28] Ibid., 245.   [29] Ibid., 246.   [30] Ibid., 247.   [31] Ibid.

Fiderkiewicz said that he hoped for collaboration between Jews and Arabs in Palestine, with equal rights for both in a free democratic state under a trusteeship for a limited period followed by either one independent state, Poland's preferred solution, or "the formation of a separate Arab and a separate Jewish State in Palestine."[32]

Fiderkiewicz then turned to the matter of the Nazi collaborationist past of leaders of the Arab Higher Committee who were seeking the right to represent the Palestine Arabs at the UN. He insisted that the UN investigating committee that was to be established by the First Special Session

> must examine the credentials of various political groups which claim to speak in the name of different sections of the population of Palestine. In particular, it is necessary to examine the political role and influence of former Nazi collaborators whose very political records make Arab-Jewish co-operation impossible, and whose political records forbid any real co-operation with them by the United Nations. The position of political ostracism which our Organization has imposed on Franco and his pro-Nazi regime must apply to all Nazi collaborators, whoever and wherever they may be.[33]

The proposed UN committee, in addition to considering the situation in Palestine, "must examine the position of the Jews in the displaced persons' camps and recommend as soon as possible the transfer of those Jews to Palestine who desire to go there," raise the standard of living of the non-Jewish inhabitants of Palestine, and "facilitate Jewish immigration." It was "necessary to remove Palestine from the game of big power politics and from questions having to do with strategic outposts or monopolistic oil interests." Fiderkiewicz called on Britain to release "the many hundreds of political prisoners" in Palestine, suspend all death sentences, and open the door to immigration. In doing so, Britain would "make its greatest contribution to the proper solution of the problem." The people of Palestine deserved "to be treated not as pawns on the chessboard of big Power politics, but as human beings about whose welfare we are deeply concerned ... Let us not think of strategic considerations and of oil. Let us think of the common people of Palestine – Christians, Jews, Muslims – and let us keep their welfare always in our minds."[34] Fiderkiewicz argued that "the chessboard of big power politics," by which he meant currents of policy in the United States and Great Britain, tilted in opposition to the Jews' aspiration for a state in Palestine.

Fiderkiewicz's statement about the Holocaust, his empathy for and understanding of why the Jewish refugees wanted to build a state in Palestine, and his solidarity and support of that effort made it one of the

[32] Ibid., 248.   [33] Ibid., 250.   [34] Ibid.

most extensive and powerful to be delivered in the flood of oratory at the UN debates in 1947–8. That he spoke from his personal experience as a survivor of Auschwitz deepened its impact. To be sure, the Soviet bloc representatives believed that the Zionist project would serve to reduce British influence and to increase Soviet influence in post-Mandate Palestine. They were playing power politics no less than Britain and the United States, a fact that underscored both the pro-Zionist implications of communist "anti-imperialism" in 1947 and the politically indeterminate consequences of Fiderkiewicz's sharp and vivid memories of the Holocaust. Yet Fiderkiewicz, though aware of the East–West conflict that had intensified that spring, obviously spoke from the heart and from his own experience. He recalled the Jews as victims of Nazi barbarism but also, and very importantly, as comrades in the shared armed resistance to the Nazis. Like the liberals and leftist pro-Zionists in New York, he evoked the passions of the war that had ended in 1945.

Having gained the opportunity to speak that same morning, Moshe Shertok, the Jewish Agency's representative at the United Nations and a future foreign minister and prime minister of Israel, argued against a unitary, Arab-dominated state. He pointed out that an Arab minority in a Jewish state would be secure because it "will forever remain surrounded by Arab countries with which it will be vitally interested to be at peace," but the situation for Jews was quite different. "There will always be Jewish minorities in other lands. But a Jewish minority in an Arab state will have no such security at all. It will be at the mercy of the Arab majority, which would be free from all constraints." The question of cooperation between Jews and Arabs was, "of course, the dominant question of the future."[35] Arab refusal to accept the Jews' national aspirations undermined that goal. Shertok then associated that refusal with Husseini's political role. "At the head of the Arab Higher Committee of Palestine stands a man who, apart from other well-known aspects of his activity, was directly involved during the war in the nazi policy of the extermination of the Jews of Europe."[36] Neither Austin nor Alexander Cadogan, the British ambassador to the UN, nor US or British officials in Washington or London, seized the opportunity to address the Husseini issue at this early date of UN deliberations. Their silence was a serious lost opportunity to enhance the prospects for compromise and lasting peace.

In the afternoon session on May 12 Emile Ghoury (1907–84), the secretary of the Palestine Arab delegation speaking for the Arab Higher

---

[35] [Moshe] Shertok, The Jewish Agency of Palestine, Lake Success (May 12, 1947), United Nations, 54th Meeting, First Committee, 257: https://documents-dds-ny.un.org/doc/U NDOC/GEN/NL3/254/63/pdf/NL325463.pdf?OpenElement.

[36] Ibid., 258.

Committee, responded to Shertok's accusation about the Mufti.[37] As the Arabs had "never recognized the mandate, the Balfour Declaration, or anything deriving from either, there can be no question of collaboration with a body which is a creature of the mandate and which has as its object the realization of Zionist aims in Palestine." Before the Balfour Declaration, Arabs and Jews had a relationship in Palestine "based on cordiality and mutual respect." The Balfour Declaration disturbed "this harmonious relationship to the extent of recourse to armed conflicts." Harmony could "be restored once the Zionists relinquish their political designs and ambitions in Palestine" and an independent state is created in Palestine that would not support "such political designs and ambitions of an alien minority against the majority of the inhabitants." Arab opposition to immigration and the establishment of a Jewish national home in Palestine was "not based on any racial prejudice against the Jews as such, but would be equally strong whatever the race or religion of any group which might attempt to wrest the country from its Arab inhabitants, or to force immigrants into it against the will of the Arabs." The Arab Higher Committee urged an "immediate and complete stoppage of all immigration in the meantime" and urged that the UN make a recommendation to Britain to do so. He declared that the Arab Higher Committee would "continue to resist all Jewish immigration to Palestine under all circumstances."[38]

Ghoury then offered the following apologia about Husseini's collaboration with the Nazis. He could understand "that the acts of anyone who seemed to cast his lot with the Axis during the war must seem to be wicked and detestable" and "how difficult it is for some of you at this moment to see the Grand Mufti in any other light than this." Yet "if the reasons that drove him to take the course he took were fully known, fair-minded men would at least see that there was another side to this matter; that in fact, it was the policy that was adopted in Palestine that finally forced this course of action on the Mufti." He had been driven from Palestine in 1937, then Syria, Iraq, and Persia, and refused asylum in Turkey, so, "having no alternative, [he] sought refuge in Germany, not because he believed in Nazism, but because he had despaired of justice."[39]

It was true, Ghoury conceded, that the Mufti had been "the most inveterate enemy of British policy in the Middle East," but was "there anything to be wondered at in that?" He asked the delegates to "put

---

[37] Emile Ghoury, Secretary of the Palestine Arab Delegation, Lake Success (May 12, 1947), United Nations, 55th Meeting, First Committee, 265–272: https://documents-dds-ny.un.org/doc/UNDOC/GEN/NL3/254/64/pdf/NL325464.pdf?OpenElement.
[38] Ibid., 266–267.   [39] Ibid., 267.

yourselves in the place of the Arabs of Palestine in the period between the two wars."

You are, of course, convinced that the Axis represented something evil, and that you and your allies were fighting not only for your survival, but also for certain moral values which made your cause the cause of decency and justice and of right versus wrong in the world at large. However, that was not at all evident to the Arabs of Palestine. For twenty years, Britain, as it seemed to them, had been pursuing a monstrous policy aimed at taking their country away from them and giving it to another people. All their protests against this violation of their elementary rights had gone unheeded. All the promises made to them had been broken. When they attempted to offer resistance in defence of their native land and natural rights, they were machine-gunned, their villages were bombed, and more Jewish immigrants were brought in ... I would say that the attitude of the Mufti represented a natural stand taken in self-defence, a stand which any threatened nation would have taken in order to protect itself. He had to escape to Europe in order to avoid arrest by the British as a result of Zionist propaganda. As regards his taking refuge in Germany, that was the only alternative to arrest and exile which were being urged on Great Britain by the Zionists. His sole crime was that he had stood in the way of Zionist aims.[40]

Ghoury's description of Husseini as an innocent victim unjustly pursued by the British became a standard theme made by his apologists. As officials of the State Department and the British Foreign Office knew very well, Husseini's "sole crime" was not to have opposed Zionism, as if that would have been a crime at all. They knew, or had ready access to, other officials who were well aware that his "crime" was to have lent enthusiastic, eager, and willing moral and intellectual support to the war waged against the Jews of Europe and in favor of Nazi Germany's efforts to win World War II. To claim that the Arabs of Palestine were unaware of the evils of Nazism obscured the extent to which Husseini's enthusiasm for Hitler and Nazism was shared by his followers who heard his ranting about killing the Jews on Nazi radio broadcasts. Ghoury's version of events was a whitewash of Husseini's emphatic enthusiasm for Nazi Germany based on agreement on political fundamentals; of his long-standing religiously grounded hatred of Judaism and the Jews, which was the basis of his opposition to the Zionist project in Palestine; and of his use of terror to suppress Arabs in Palestine interested in compromise with the Zionists. Husseini's hatreds had been a matter of public record in the Middle East since his iconic statement "Islam and Jews" of 1937. His enthusiasm for Hitler's attack on the Jews was a key theme in his radio broadcasts from and for Nazi Germany between 1941 and 1945. Yet again, neither Austin nor Cadogan commented on the accusation made

[40] Ibid., 268.

by Shertok and denied by Ghoury. Both supported giving the Arab Higher Committee the right to represent the Palestine Arabs at the UN.

On May 14, 1947 Andrei Gromyko delivered the most famous and surprising speech of the Special Session. He said that "the aspirations of a considerable part of the Jewish people are linked with the problem of Palestine and of its future administration." For Gromyko to use the phrase "the Jewish people" was a departure from communist – and certainly Stalinist – orthodoxy. It was to accept that the Jews were indeed a "people," and hence a "nation," which, like all others, had a right of self-determination and statehood. He added that the great attention given to the issue at the UN was "understandable and fully justified." Yet it should be considered in light of the fact that "during the last war, the Jewish people underwent exceptional sorrow and suffering ... The Jews in territories where the Hitlerites held sway were subjected to almost complete physical annihilation. The total number of members of the Jewish population who perished at the hands of the Nazi executioners is estimated at approximately six million. Only about a million and a half Jews in Western Europe survived the war."[41] In the aftermath of the war "large numbers of the surviving Jews of Europe" had been "deprived of their countries, their homes and their means of existence." Hundreds of thousands were wandering in various countries of Europe "in search of means of existence and in search of shelter." Many were in displaced-persons camps and were still enduring "great privations."[42] The time had come "to help these people, not by word, but by deeds. It is essential to show concern for the urgent needs of a people which has undergone such great suffering as a result of the war brought about by Hitlerite Germany. This is a duty of the United Nations." In other words, the United Nations now had to do what the British Empire and the countries of Western Europe had failed to do, namely, come to the aid of Hitler's primary victims.

Past experience, particularly during the Second World War, shows that no western European State was able to provide adequate assistance for the Jewish people in defending its rights and its very existence from the violence of the Hitlerites and their allies. This is an unpleasant fact, but unfortunately, like all other facts, it must be admitted. The fact that no western European State has been able to ensure the defence of the elementary rights of the Jewish people and to safeguard it against the violence of the fascist executioners, explains the aspirations of the Jews to establish their own State.[43]

---

[41] Andrei Gromyko (USSR), Lake Success (May 14, 1947), 77th Meeting, UNGA, 131: https://documents-dds-ny.un.org/doc/UNDOC/GEN/NL4/727/15/pdf/NL472715.pdf? OpenElement.
[42] Ibid.   [43] Ibid., 131–132.

Gromyko was the first UN ambassador to refer to these events and their implications for the future of Palestine in a speech before the UN General Assembly (Fiderkiewicz had spoken at a First Committee hearing). While the Western powers had not intervened in 1944 to bomb Auschwitz, neither had the Soviet Union tried to stop the Holocaust when the tide of battle turned in 1943.[44] That said, it is important to note, especially in light of subsequent Soviet antagonism to Israel, that in 1947 at the United Nations, discussion of the Holocaust came first and most extensively from two communist countries: the Soviet Union in the General Assembly and Poland in the First Committee.

Gromyko listed four policy options for the future of post-Mandate Palestine. These included either establishment of a single Arab–Jewish state, with equal rights for Arabs and Jews; partition of Palestine into two independent states, one Arab and one Jewish; establishment of an Arab state in Palestine, without due regard for the rights of the Jewish population; or establishment of a Jewish state in Palestine, without due regard for the rights of the Arab population. He rejected a Jewish or Arab state in all of what was British Mandate Palestine. In remarks that contradicted assertions made by the Arab-state ambassadors and the Arab Higher Committee's Ghoury, Gromyko said that "both" Arabs and Jews were "peoples" who had "historical roots in Palestine. Palestine has become the homeland of both these peoples, each of which plays an important part in the economy and the cultural life of the country."[45]

Gromyko rejected the options of both "an independent Arab State, without consideration for the legitimate rights of the Jewish people" or "an independent Jewish State, while ignoring the legitimate rights of the Arab population." Neither of those "extreme decisions would achieve an equitable solution of this complicated problem, especially since neither would ensure the settlement of relations between the Arabs and the Jews, which constitutes the most important task."[46] The Soviet Union's preferred option – ironically it was identical to the preferred option of Bevin and the British Foreign Office – was "establishment of an independent,

---

[44] Gromyko did not mention that the Red Army and Air Force, which were far closer to the Nazi death camps, also failed to seize the opportunity to bomb them. On this see Danny Orbach and Mark Solonin, "Calculated Indifference: The Soviet Union and Requests to Bomb Auschwitz," *Holocaust and Genocide Studies* 27, no. 1 (Spring 2013): 90–113; and Jeffrey Herf, "The Nazi Extermination Camps and the Ally to the East: Could the Red Army and Air Force Have Stopped or Slowed the Final Solution?" *Kritika: Explorations in Russian and Eurasian History* 4, no. 4 (September 2003): 913–930. On the response of the Western allies see Bernard Wasserstein, *Britain and the Jews of Europe, 1939–1945*, 2nd ed. (New York: Leicester University Press, 1999); and Richard Breitman and Allan J. Lichtman, *FDR and the Jews* (Cambridge, MA: Harvard University Press, 2013).

[45] Andrei Gromyko (USSR), Lake Success (May 14, 1947) 77th Meeting, UNGA, 133.

[46] Ibid.

dual, democratic, homogeneous Arab-Jewish State ... based on equality of rights for the Jewish and the Arab populations" that would foster "co-operation between these two peoples."[47] However, if that "plan proved impossible to implement, in view of the deterioration in the relations between the Jews and the Arabs ... then it would be necessary to consider the second plan," that is, "the partition of Palestine into two independent autonomous States, one Jewish and one Arab." It would be preferable "only if relations between the Jewish and Arab populations of Palestine indeed proved to be so bad that it would be impossible to reconcile them and to ensure the peaceful co-existence of the Arabs and the Jews."[48]

Gromyko's speech placed the Soviet Union, and thus the international communist movement, on the side of the establishment of a Jewish state in Palestine. He rejected Arab claims that the Jews had no roots in Palestine and that a Jewish state would be a product of British imperialism. Yet viewed through the lens of the policy of containment of communism, which by then had become a consensus in the diplomatic and military establishments in London, Paris, and Washington, his speech lent credence to the view that Zionist aspirations overlapped with Soviet efforts to eliminate or reduce British – and Western – influence in the strategically vital Middle East. From that perspective, Gromyko's speech could be seen, not as an accurate statement about World War II and the Holocaust and its implications for the problem of Palestine, but rather as a clever and cynical effort to place the memory of the Holocaust at the service of Soviet expansion in the Middle East (see Figure 5.2).

On May 15 the General Assembly voted forty-five to seven with one abstention in favor of resolution A/307 establishing a United Nations Special Committee on Palestine (UNSCOP). It was assigned the task of issuing a report and recommendations on the various options by September 1. The members of the committee were representatives of Australia, Canada, Czechoslovakia, Guatemala, India, Iran, Netherlands, Peru, Sweden, Uruguay, and Yugoslavia. At that point, only Czechoslovakia had emerged as an emphatic supporter of the Zionists. Both the leading democracies – the United States, Britain, and France – as well as communist dictatorships in Europe, including the Soviet Union, Czechoslovakia, and Poland, voted in favor of establishing UNSCOP. The seven "no" votes came from Afghanistan, Egypt, Iraq, Lebanon, Saudi Arabia, Syria, and Turkey, indicative of Arab – and in the case of Afghanistan and Turkey, Muslim – opposition both to the UN's role in finding a resolution to the Palestine question and to a possible partition plan that made room for a

[47] Ibid., 134.   [48] Ibid.

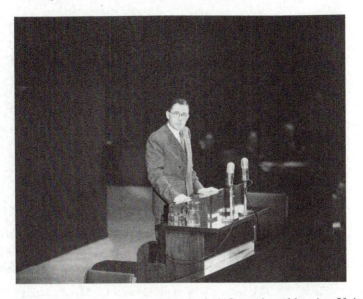

Figure 5.2 Soviet representative Andrei Gromyko addressing United Nations, November 29, 1947, speaking in favor of an immediate vote on the Palestine Partition Plan to the UN General Assembly at Flushing Meadows. Source: Bettman/Getty Images

Jewish state in Palestine.[49] Though the strongest support for the Zionists came from the Soviet Union, Poland, and Czechoslovakia, the overwhelming majority in support of the establishment of UNSCOP indicated that there was a broad willingness in the UN to consider a partition plan as a possibility.

Throughout the session, Ambassador Austin was in almost daily contact with Secretary Marshall and other State Department officials in Washington (see Figure 5.3). On May 22 he wrote to Marshall that American support for the creation of UNSCOP did not mean support

[49] 79th Plenary Session, UNGA, New York (May 15, 1947), 176–177: https://documents-dds ny.un.org/doc/UNDOC/GEN/NL4/727/17/pdf/NL472717.pdf?OpenElement. The votes in favor of establishing UNSCOP were: Argentina, Australia, Belgium, Bolivia, Brazil, Byelorussian Soviet Socialist Republic, Canada, Chile, China, Colombia, Costa Rica, Cuba, Czechoslovakia, Denmark, Dominican Republic, Ecuador, El Salvador, Ethiopia, France, Greece, Guatemala, Honduras, Iceland, India, Iran, Liberia, Luxembourg, Mexico, Netherlands, New Zealand, Nicaragua, Norway, Panama, Paraguay, Peru, Poland, Sweden, Ukrainian Soviet Socialist Republic, Union of South Africa, Union of Soviet Socialist Republics, United Kingdom, United States of America, Uruguay, Venezuela, and Yugoslavia. Those opposed were Afghanistan, Egypt, Iraq, Lebanon, Saudi Arabia, Syria, and Turkey. Siam abstained; Haiti and the Philippine Republic were absent.

Figure 5.3 US secretary of state George C. Marshall and US UN representative Warren R. Austin at the Opening Session, General Assembly, United Nations, Flushing Meadows, September 16, 1947. Source: Bettman/Getty Images.

for the creation of a Jewish state in Palestine.[50] It was important that "we agree amongst ourselves at the earliest possible moment upon a working hypothesis" for the United States to present to UNSCOP in the coming summer months. In an undated memorandum to Marshall, deputy secretary of state Dean Acheson wrote that "our views, which have been discussed with [former] Senator [and current ambassador] Austin, are reflected in Austin's letter."[51] Austin wrote that this "working hypothesis" would be to aim at "an independent Palestinian state which would be admitted as a Member of the United Nations" but "would *not* be a state based on religious or racial factors. It would be *neither* a Jewish state *nor* [emphasis in original] an Arab state." There would be "full guarantees of the civil and religious rights and liberties of all minority groups, full account being taken of the special status of the holy places." Immigration might be as high as 2.5 percent of the total population of Palestine for the

---

[50] Warren Austin, "The United States Representative (Austin) to the Secretary of State," New York (May 22, 1947), *Foreign Relations of the United States* (hereafter *FRUS*), 1947, *The Near East and Africa*, vol. 5: https://history.state.gov/historicaldocuments/frus1947 v05/d767; Warren Austin to George Marshall, New York (May 22, 1947), NARA RG 59 Department of State, Decimal File, 1945–1949, 501.BB Palestine/5–2247, Box 2114.

[51] Cited in ibid.

first two years, and 1 percent per year thereafter. "Immigration should be on a non-discriminatory, non-privilege basis" except for relatives of families already living in Palestine. There should be a period "of perhaps five to ten years of preparation for independence. During this period Palestine should be placed under a United Nations trusteeship."[52] Notably, the "working hypothesis," which had drawn on a May 26 memorandum by Loy Henderson, director of the State Department's Division of Near Eastern Affairs and one of the leading opponents of the Zionist project, precluded creation of a Jewish state in Palestine.[53]

Austin thought that his proposal was "the most objective one and should be the most appealing to all reasonable people." He anticipated that the Soviet Union "would go along," though he admitted that his "optimism" on that score may have been unwarranted. His proposed solution "might be acquiesced in by the Arab states" and, he thought, it "would commend itself to the more reasonable and better-balanced elements of the Jewish population of the United States and other countries." The implication of Austin's "working hypothesis" was that the Zionists and their supporters were "less reasonable" and less well balanced than those Jews in the United States and Europe who favored a binational state rather than partition and a Jewish state. Objectively, Austin's hypothesis was one that favored the Arab rejection of a Jewish state, but he was skilled at obscuring the anti-Zionist implications of his proposal in a fog of procedural detail. The Soviet Union and Poland had spoken clearly in favor of partition into Jewish and Arab states in Palestine. Britain's anti-Zionism was a matter of public record. France sat on the fence, torn between its pro-Arab Foreign Ministry and the sympathy for the Zionists from the Ministry of the Interior, and much of French public opinion.

George Marshall's priority was to aid in the economic recovery of Western Europe and thereby prevent further Soviet expansion in Europe. On June 5, 1947 he delivered what became known as "the Marshall Plan Speech" at Harvard University, in which he presented the broad outlines of an American policy designed to accomplish those goals.[54] Several weeks earlier Marshall had appointed George F. Kennan – by then well known as the author of the "Long Telegram" of February 1946 on the sources of Soviet conduct – as the first director of the Policy Planning Staff, an

---

[52] Ibid.
[53] See Loy Henderson, Director, State Department Division of Near Eastern Affairs: Mr. Green to Mr. Rusk, "A Plan for the Future Government of Palestine," Washington (May 26, 1947), NARA RG 59 CDF, 501.BB Palestine/5–2647, Box 2114.
[54] "The Marshall Plan Speech" (June 5, 1947): www.marshallfoundation.org/marshall/the-marshall-plan/marshall-plan-speech/.

institution Marshall had established that spring in the State Department. Marshall's speech was an economic complement to the president's "Truman doctrine" articulated in a speech on March 12 to a Joint Session of the US Congress. The president, secretary of state, and the new director of the Policy Planning Staff all agreed on the fundamentals of a policy aimed at deterring and containing Soviet expansion, especially in Europe. In the very same months that the USA was adopting a policy that blended the Truman doctrine and the Marshall Plan, the Soviet Union and several of its Soviet bloc allies were becoming the leading voices in support of Zionist aspirations at the United Nations. On June 10 Marshall replied to Austin to thank him for his "courageous and effective leadership." He said he had found Austin's suggestions "extremely helpful." They were "being carefully studied."[55] In other words, Marshall retained the possibility that the goal of US policy should be a unitary binational state in Palestine.

The pro-Zionist liberals, both on the UN delegation and in the press, noted with alarm Austin's suggestion to replace a plan for partition with one for some sort of Great Power trusteeship. Eleanor Roosevelt, then a member of the United States UN delegation, was sufficiently worried that she wrote to Marshall on May 26:

I cannot help feeling that our own policy [about Palestine] has been very weak. Either we think it is right to uphold certain things in Palestine, in spite of the Arabs who cannot, after all, cause very serious trouble from the military standpoint if we wish to use planes and tanks or are we going back on something which it seems to me we pledged ourselves to many years ago, tacitly if not in clear words.

By this she meant the promises of the Balfour Declaration and repeated American affirmations of support for them.[56]

On June 11 Freda Kirchwey conveyed her criticism of US policy to Emanuel Celler.[57] The American delegation, she wrote, seemed to have "forgotten entire[ly] the existence" of Truman's policy of support for the establishment of a Jewish state and appeared "more concerned with pulling the British chestnuts out of the fire" than securing what she viewed as a decent solution. "Under the guise of alleged neutrality, the American delegation" had led the effort to "prevent participation rights

[55] George Marshall to Warren Austin, Washington (June 10, 1947), NARA RG 59 CDF, 501.BB Palestine/5–2247, Box 2114.

[56] Eleanor Roosevelt to Marshall, New York (May 26, 1947), NARA RG 59 CDF, 501.BB Palestine/5–2647, Box 2114.

[57] Freda Kirchwey to Emanuel Celler, "Confidential Memorandum," New York (June 11, 1947), LC, Emanuel Celler Papers, Box 23. In January 1948 *PM* reported on Kirchwey's initiative: "Anglo-State Dept. Plot on Partition Charged," *PM*, January 29, 1948, 7.

for the Jewish Agency for Palestine" in the UN General Assembly. It "was responsible for extending an invitation to the Arab Higher Committee, although it knew full well that the Chairman of the Arab Higher Committee is the notorious Mufti whose record of association with the Axis is exposed in the files of the State Department."[58] It had agreed with the efforts of "the pro-Arab [British] Foreign Office representative" to separate the refugee issue from the Palestine problem, even though Truman had already expressed support for the immigration of 100,000 Jewish refugees. Kirchwey accused the US delegation at the UN of being "a leader in the appeasement of the Arab states and their blackmailing threats of a Holy War against the Jews if the independence of Palestine as an Arab state were not authorized."[59]

Kirchwey regarded "the whole demeanor" of the delegation led by Austin as a "painfully embarrassing expression of ineptness and unwillingness to take a decent position." Had the United States at the UN shown "leadership," that is, a firm position in favor of parti-tion, it could have found "widespread acquiescence in the proposals to which our government is committed. Instead, the moral leadership of the United Nations on this question was left to the Soviet Union, other Slavic states, and several Latin American states. More recently, Secretary Marshall has stated it is too early to present a policy."[60] Kirchwey claimed that many people were seeing through Austin, interpreting his public pose of neutrality as in reality a change in US policy "without the knowledge or sanction of the Congress of the United States or the people of this country." Kirchwey thought Truman had erred in turning Palestine policy over to the State Department. He needed to be told the truth that the "strengthening of the democratic Jewish community – the only democratic community in the feudal Middle East – can be the most leavening of influence in spreading democracy in this area and preventing the understandable urge of have-not peoples to support other movements which promise them something instead of nothing."[61]

Implicit in Kirchwey's letter to Celler was the idea that a Jewish state in Palestine would be a bulwark against, rather than a lever for, Soviet influence in the Middle East. Over the next twelve months Celler and others repeatedly articulated that view. Yet from May 1947 to May 1949 the Soviet Union and the communist regimes in Eastern Europe became the Zionists' most emphatic and most important supporters at the United

---

[58] Kirchwey, "Confidential Memorandum."   [59] Ibid.
[60] The Nation Associates, "Confidential Memorandum," New York (June 11, 1947), LC, Emanuel Celler Papers, Box 23, 1–3.
[61] Ibid., 5.

Nations. As the interventions of Fiderkiewicz and Gromyko had made very clear, that support was clear and unambiguous, especially compared to the ambiguity and ambivalence of US policy. The Marshall-era State Department, the leadership of the Pentagon, and the analysts at the Central Intelligence Agency took notice of the Soviet bloc enthusiasm for Zionist aspirations at the UN.

The Truman Doctrine, the Cold War,
      and Jewish Refugees, Spring 1947

I believe it must be the policy of the United States to support free peoples
who are resisting attempted subjugation by armed minorities or by
outside pressures.
President Harry S. Truman in the Truman Doctrine speech
to a Joint Session of Congress, March 12, 1947.

It is not easy to determine the reasons for internment in Nazi concentration camps.
Marshall M. Vance, American consul general General in the Office
of the US Political Adviser for Germany in Berlin
to all US consular offices in Germany, March 20, 1947.

After the British White Paper restrictions on Jewish emigration to
Palestine, Zionism conflicted with British policy. In spring 1947 the
Mossad Le'Aliyah Bet's efforts to bring Jewish survivors of the
Holocaust to Palestine met another obstacle: Anglo-American suspicions
that they were part of a Soviet and communist bloc attempt to infiltrate
Palestine. While the internationalization of the Palestine question at the
United Nations played out in full view and on the front pages of news-
papers around the globe, the particular conflict between Britain and the
Yishuv, the organized Jewish community in Palestine, took place at times
in public and at times behind the scenes. The Mossad Le'Aliyah Bet
(Hebrew for "Institute for [illegal] Immigration 'B'"), a national institution controlled by the Jewish Agency, was responsible for organizing the
Brichah (Hebrew for "flight"), the clandestine and, in Britain's view,
illegal, immigration to Palestine.[1] To defeat that effort, Britain continued
to employ its diplomats and the British Navy. The State Department's
files on Palestine from 1945 to 1949 are massive. A significant proportion
of these files deal with the American response to what the British called

[1] See Yehuda Bauer, *Flight and Rescue: Brichah* (New York: Random House, 1970); and
Ze'eve Venia Hadari, *Second Exodus: The Full Story of Jewish Illegal Immigration to Palestine,
1945–1948* (London: Vallentine Mitchell, 1991). The Mossad, Israel's intelligence
agency, was established in 1951.

"illegal" immigration and what the Zionists viewed as an essential flow of people to bring about the establishment of a Jewish state in Palestine.

Beginning in 1946, British officials, both from the Foreign Office in London and in the British Embassy in Washington, sent a steady stream of messages to the State Department ranging from assertions of general policy to detailed reports about particular ship sailings and clandestine refugee movements. They called on their American allies to assist in preventing ships that were believed to be preparing to carry Jewish immigrants to Palestine from leaving American ports. The State Department leadership repeatedly decided that the alliance with Britain took priority over the Mossad Le'Aliyah Bet's clandestine efforts to bring Jewish survivors in Europe to Palestine.

On March 14, 1947, for example, Thomas Bromley at the British Embassy wrote to Gordon Merriam at the State Department's Division of Near Eastern and African Affairs (NEA) to ask whether the department had information about the possible departure of the *President Warfield* from Norfolk, Virginia and two other ships "now in Baltimore" that "may also be intended for the purpose of carrying illegal immigrants to Palestine."[2] Bromley also asked if the department had taken a position regarding "advertisements appearing in the American press soliciting funds on behalf of organizations endeavoring to aid and support illegal immigration into Palestine and illegal activity there."[3] Many similar requests were to follow in the next year.

The Division of Near Eastern and African Affairs was sympathetic to the British position. Its contributions to the Department's "Palestine File" document American efforts to surveille and, if possible, prevent the departure of those vessels, efforts that drew in the participation of the FBI. On April 25, 1947 William R. Vallance of the State Department's Office of Legal Adviser sent a twenty-two-page memo to the NEA on "certain ships departing from American ports for destinations in the Mediterranean."[4] He offered a detailed account of American legislation opposing exports of arms and ammunition, recruitment of persons to participate in conflicts abroad, and solicitation of funds for ships used in transporting "illegal immigrants." In light of the reports about the SS *President Warfield* and other ships, he recommended that the

[2] "Memorandum of Conversation: Matters Relating to Palestine," Washington (March 14, 1947), United States National Archives in College Park (hereafter NACP) RG 59, M1390, Records of the Department of State Relating to Internal Affairs of Palestine, 1945–1949, Roll 8, 867N.01/3–147.

[3] Ibid.

[4] William R. Vallance to Fraser Wilkins, Washington (April 25, 1947), "Subject: Certain ships departing from American ports for destinations in the Mediterranean," NACP RG 59, M1390, Roll 8, 867N.01/.

memo and British Embassy requests be sent to the attorney general, Thomas Clark, "requesting that immediate steps be taken to cause a complete investigation to be made with respect to these activities and appropriate action taken to punish persons or organizations found to be violating the laws of the United States." The Treasury Department should also be contacted "to exercise vigilance to prevent any violation of our laws with respect to these activities."[5]

Beginning in 1946, the British Embassy also raised the issue with the State Department of the tax-exempt status of the Zionist organizations in the United States. In a memo of May 21, 1947 Leonard Meeker of the US Treasury Department observed that "repeated British representations to the Department of State on this problem have gone unanswered for almost a year."[6] Meeker offered examples of Zionist organizations that enjoyed tax-exempt status yet were engaged in a type of political advocacy that was not covered by the exemptions offered for charitable, religious, or educational purposes. Support for "organized illegal immigration" had both charitable and non-charitable, political, aspects – that is, engagement in "opposition to British rule" in Palestine. Nevertheless, the Department of Treasury had neglected problem for nearly a year. Meeker concluded that the Treasury Department should reconsider the tax-exempt status of the American League for a Free Palestine and other organizations assisting "illegal immigration into Palestine."[7]

American supporters of the Irgun, then engaged in a violent campaign that included terrorist attacks to drive the British out of Palestine, aroused the interest of the Director of the FBI, J. Edgar Hoover.[8] In the State Department, the Division of Foreign Activity Correlation (DFAC) examined organizations in the United States that lobbied or supported foreign countries. On April 7, 1947 Hoover forwarded a report to Jack Neal, head of the DFAC, about a fund-raising request sent by well-known Hollywood figures Ben Hecht, Will Rogers, and Louis Bromfield on behalf of the American League for a Free Palestine, an organization supporting the Irgun. A Pennsylvania businessman who received a request for funds to support ships in "Armada proportions to force world opinion and implement Truman's expressed policy" contacted

---

[5] Ibid., 22.
[6] Leonard Meeker to Mr. Foly, Washington (May 21, 1947), "Subject: Income-tax Status of Certain Zionist Organizations," NACP RG 59, M1390, Roll 9, 867N.01/5–2147.
[7] Ibid.
[8] On the Irgun and terror see Bruce Hoffmann, *Anonymous Soldiers: The Struggle for Palestine, 1917–1947* (New York: Vintage, 2015). Also see the memoir by Menachem Begin, then the leader of the Irgun, *The Revolt* (New York: Nash Publishing, 1951).

the FBI about the matter. The activity raised the possibility of violation of the US Foreign Agents Registration Act.[9]

In May and June the League placed a series of advertisements in newspapers denouncing British policy and seeking to raise funds. "Letter to the Terrorists of Palestine," a piece by Ben Hecht, sponsored by the Palestine Resistance Fund, which was organized by the League, appeared in the *New York Post* on May 14, and in *PM* on May 17 and again on June 3. The British Embassy was outraged. On May 21 the British ambassador, Archibald Clark Kerr, Baron Inverchapel (1882–1951), quoted from one of the ads in a message to the State Department: "Every time you blow up a British arsenal, or wreck a British jail, or send a British railroad train sky high, or rob a British bank or let go with your guns and bombs at the British betrayers and invaders of your homeland, the Jews of America make a little holiday in their hearts."[10] It was "quite clear that this passage can only be regarded as a direct incitement to the murder of British officials and troops in Palestine," Inverchapel observed. The British government "regard it as intolerable that such a statement should appear in the press of a friendly country." Inverchapel pointed out that the statement also conflicted with a recently passed UN resolution "that all governments and peoples refrain from any action which might create an atmosphere prejudicial to an early settlement of the Palestine question."[11] Accordingly, the British requested that the US government stop the advertisements immediately. Secretary of State James Byrnes, George Marshall's predecessor, had previously informed Inverchapel that there were "no legal means open" to the US government "to prevent the appearance of such advertisements." However, Inverchapel argued that, in view of the fact that the UN was now "formally seized of the Palestine question, a statement should be issued by the United States Government condemning in the strongest terms the present advertisement and the activities of which complaint has already been made."[12] On May 27 Secretary of State Marshall replied that he "deeply regrets the appearance in the American press of the advertisements" to which Inverchapel referred. "Earnest attention is presently being given to this matter." Though the ads were

[9] John Edgar Hoover, Director, Federal Bureau of Investigation to Jack D. Neal, Chief, Division of Foreign Activity Correlation, State Department (Washington, April 7, 1947), "Subject: American League for Free Palestine," NACP RG 59, M1390, Roll 8, 867N.01/4–747.

[10] Ben Hecht, "Letter to the Terrorists of Palestine," *PM* (June 3, 1947), NACP RG 59, M1390, Roll 9, 867N.01/10–247.

[11] "Aide Memoire," British Embassy, Washington, DC to Department of State (May 19, 1947), NACP RG 59, M1390, Roll 9, 867N.01/10–247.

[12] Ibid., 2.

protected by freedom of the press and speech, the State Department was giving careful consideration "to determine whether preventive action of some character might not be formulated."[13]

On June 27 Bevin reminded Marshall that Inverchapel had expressed "our grave concern at the persistent and successful attempts of Jewish organizations to send Jewish illegal immigrants to Palestine from various European countries" and "how much we regret that the funds for this illegal immigrant traffic are largely subscribed in the United States."[14] He alerted Marshall that he was also seeking support from members of the United Nations

to take the strictest precautions to prevent the transfer through their territory and the departure from their ports of Jews attempting to enter Palestine illegally, [and to] discourage the activities of organizers of this traffic, who are using Jewish refugees as a means of exerting political pressure on the Government of Palestine at a moment when the future of that country is under consideration by the United Nations.[15]

He sought assistance from the US government and "representatives of charitable and refugee organizations in Europe" to "discourage the unauthorized movement of Jewish refugees leading to the departure of illegal immigrant ships for Palestine. My colleagues and I feel very strongly that the organizers of this traffic are not only endangering the peace and security of the Middle East but are now flouting the authority of the United Nations."[16] The assertion that the refugee stream was a threat to peace in Palestine remained a continuing theme of British protests.

On July 8, 1947 the British Embassy informed the NEA that the ship *Colony Trader*, "implicated in the illegal immigration traffic to Palestine," flying a Costa Rican flag but owned by a company in New York, had been detained by the British Navy in Gibraltar. The British requested that the State Department prevent the sale of World War II surplus landing craft (LSTs) to Zionist organizations.[17] The State Department complied. Two days later NEA director Loy Henderson, writing for Marshall, advised Admiral William W. Smith, chairman of the United States Maritime Commission, of the policy change, stating that the sale and then export

---

[13] George Marshall, "Aide Memoire," Washington (May 27, 1947), NACP RG 59, M1390, Roll 9, 867N.01/5–1947.

[14] Ernest Bevin to George Marshall, No. E 5001/48/G, London (June 27, 1947), NACP RG 59, M1390, Roll 9, 867N.01/6–2747.

[15] Ibid.   [16] Ibid.

[17] W. D. Allen, British Embassy, Washington, DC to Gordon Mattison, Assistant Chief, Division of Near Eastern Affairs (July 8, 1947), NACP RG 59, M1390, Roll 9, 867N.01/7–847.

of World War II LSTs "would be contrary to the national interests" of the United States. Therefore, the State Department had revoked licenses that had been previously approved earlier in June and would reject any recently submitted applications.[18]

More "Intelligence" on "Soviet Infiltration" among Jewish Refugees

Beginning in fall 1945, Soviet infiltration via the Jewish refugee stream became a core theme in British and American intelligence about clandestine Jewish emigration to Palestine in these years. The tone is captured in one of the early reports forwarded to Secretary of State Byrnes by the Office of the US Political Adviser to the Supreme Allied Commander in the Mediterranean on November 4, 1945.[19] In it, British colonel C. R. Tuff, citing Polish military sources, wrote that it was "alleged that the N. K.G.B" was sending "agents into Palestine for diversionary and propaganda purposes." The agents were "recruited from Polish Jews" and were to enter Palestine through Czechoslovakia, Austria, and Italy. "The story these agents tell is that they have come from German Concentration Camps and they do NOT wish to return to Poland for fear of anti-Semitism, and are most anxious for this reason, to enter Palestine." Once in Palestine they had five main tasks: "spread hatred" of the British among the Jews because of the White Paper restricting Jewish immigration; "stir up the Jews to armed revolt against the British authorities and the Arab population; ... spread the rumor that the British are unfairly supporting the Arabs to the detriment of the Jewish cause; ... state emphatically to all Jews that Russia supports the Jewish cause in Palestine"; and work in close cooperation with the Jewish Communist Party in Palestine.[20] While the reports offered a plausible account of what communists in Palestine would try to do, the question of the weight of such views within the larger Zionist political scene in Palestine was left unanswered.

The association between the refugee stream and communist infiltration remained a continuing theme in such reports. On March 20, 1947 Marshall M. Vance, the American consul general in the Office of the

---

[18] Loy Henderson for the Secretary of State to Vice Admiral William W. Smith, Washington (July 10, 1947), NACP RG 59, M1390, Roll 9, 867N.01/7–1047.

[19] C. Offie, Deputy U.S. Political Adviser to Secretary of State, Berlin (November 4, 1945), "Subject: Soviet Agents in Palestine"; and C. R. Tuff, "Soviet Agents in Palestine," NACP RG 84, Foreign Service Posts of the Department of State, Records of the U.S. Political Adviser to the Supreme Allied Commander, Mediterranean, "Top Secret" File, 1944–47, 711.9–711.10, Box 2.

[20] Tuff, "Soviet Agents in Palestine."

US Political Adviser for Germany in Berlin, sent a thirteen-page memo to all US consular offices in Germany in response to a State Department request to his office of March 3 to examine "the adequacy of security screening as a safeguard against infiltration of subversive agents and undercover operatives." At issue was screening of "immigrants receiving visas in Germany and Austria, especially under the displaced persons program."[21] The report followed discussions with the staff of the consulate general in Berlin and members of the US Counter-Intelligence Corps (CIC) in Germany.

The stated task of the screeners was to detect "imposters making false claims to 'displaced person' and 'persecutee' status with fictitious names or forged papers, applicants with Nazi backgrounds, and black marketeers." Prior to examination by US officials, those claiming displaced-person (DP) status were first screened by American religious and welfare agencies including the American Joint Distribution Committee (AJDC), the Hebrew Immigrant Aid Society (HIAS), the International Refugee and Rehabilitation Committee (IRRC), and the American Christian Committee for Refugees (CCR). Vance wrote that some of those organizations depended heavily on local organizations, Jewish community organizations, and political gatherings of "victims of fascism" to evaluate claims to receive DP status. However, "due to the irregular nature and questionable value of most available sources of information," that is, presumably, from these organizations, the screening team had to rely on "direct questioning of applicants."[22]

Vance concluded that "it must be frankly stated that no <u>systematic</u> screening is being conducted at the present at this office for the specific purpose of preventing infiltration into the United States of subversive agents and undercover operatives under the displaced persons program."[23] During the Nazi invasion of Poland in 1939 thousands of Jews had fled to the east and sought refuge in the Soviet Union. They were among the many now claiming DP status. They had "lived four to six years in the Soviet Union, and within the past two years have returned to Poland and other Eastern European countries where they found conditions so difficult that they decided to infiltrate into Germany and reach Palestine or the United States, if possible." The CIC teams believed that many of these "infiltrees from the East" had entered Berlin in 1947 with

[21] Marshall M. Vance, American Consulate General, Berlin to All Consular Offices in Germany, Memorandum No. 32, "Adequacy of Security Screening as a Safeguard against Infiltration of Subversive Agents and Undercover Operatives," Berlin (March 20, 1947), NACP RG 84, Foreign Service Posts of the Department of State, Munich Consulate General, Classified General Records, 1943–1951, 1947 (800–820), Box 4.
[22] Ibid.   [23] Ibid., 3.

"fraudulent documents" asserting that they had resided in the American Sector of Berlin since December 1945 as required. The CIC "suspected that many such persons have been 'briefed' by sponsoring organizations as well as legal welfare organizations, and a few have admitted as much." Hence it "must be assumed at least a few" of such individuals "are subversive agents and undercover operatives." Those claiming to have been in Nazi concentration camps "cannot be investigated by any means now available," as few had any documents and, if they did, their authenticity was doubtful.[24]

The suspicion and skepticism with which Vance and his fellow counter-intelligence screeners viewed those claiming to have survived the Holocaust is evident in the following:

(f) The very qualifications of persons claiming "persecutee" status imply political backgrounds which render many of the applicants suspicious. At least a few of them were interned because of membership in German political groups of the extreme left, or because of extremist activities, [and] now can be expected to serve their revolutionary causes willingly or even fanatically.

(g) It is not easy to determine the reasons for internment in Nazi concentration camps. On the one hand, many former inmates who were locked up for common crimes now claim they were political prisoners, whereas, on the other hand, it must be assumed that some of those who were actually interned for revolutionary views and activities, when they learn that this might prove the obstacle to immigration, claim that they were put away for listening to British broadcasts or other reasons that would not stigmatize them.[25]

Vance regretted that the number of screening agents was too few. Most focused their attention on investigating individuals suspected of having Nazi backgrounds or engaging in black market activities. In sum, "a large proportion, if not a majority, of claimants to American citizenship who remained in enemy countries during the war are persons of extremely doubtful loyalty to the United States," and many were "opportunists who would serve any cause or interests" through material interests, ideological appeals, or coercion. Vance concluded that current security screening was "not an adequate safeguard against infiltration of subversive agents and undercover agents among immigrants receiving visas at this office."[26]

As the International Military Tribunal in Nuremberg, which ran from October 1945 to October 1946, had presented overwhelming evidence about the extermination and death camps, Vance had had abundant opportunity to understand why Nazi Germany sent people, Jews above all, to concentration and death camps. Yet he appeared to have scant knowledge of the way the Gestapo had used the law to charge political

[24] Ibid., 4.   [25] Ibid.   [26] Ibid., 11 and 13.

opponents with a variety of common crimes, and little appreciation of Nazi anti-Jewish policies that led to the arrest and deportation of Jews simply because they were Jewish. Suspicion, not empathy, was evident in this and other reports being sent to Washington about the Jewish refugees trying to get to Palestine.

The Vance memo of March 24 could be summarized as follows: thousands of Jews, aided by primarily Jewish liberal or left-leaning aid organizations, were being coached to lie to American officials. Their tales of suffering due to Nazi persecution were in fact clever ruses used by leftist political operatives and opportunists. The effort of Jewish organizations and of the Mossad Le'Aliyah Bet to move refugees to Palestine was being used by the Soviet Union to infiltrate communist agents into Palestine. As the refugees came from Eastern Europe and the Soviet Union, it was likely that they were bringing with them leftist or even communist politics.

The Vance memo displayed little understanding of the Holocaust or of the presence of antisemitism in postwar Eastern Europe. His skepticism about the truthfulness of refugee stories of persecution was not unique. As was evident in other reports from these years, many American officials observing the Jewish exodus from Europe to Palestine shared Vance's suspicions about the connections between Jews, the Soviet Union, and communism. The past connection between the Jews and communism surfaced in American and British intelligence reports portraying the evolution of clandestine immigration into a plot between Zionists, the Soviet Union, and the communists.[27]

The State Department in these years received frequent reports from US embassies and consulates in Europe on the efforts of Jewish refugees to travel to ports in France and Italy and from there to embark on ships to Palestine. On April 13, 1947 James R. Wilkinson, the American consul general in Munich, informed the secretary of state that 270 Jews had been returned to the US Zone in Germany by French authorities; they had been attempting to get to Marseille and from there to go to Palestine. "They had managed to travel in railroad cars from Munich to Ludwigshafen, a fact which indicates some rather high connections in the organization of the flight." This was said to be "the beginning of what is planned to become a mass exodus of Jewish displaced persons from

[27] In these same months former Nazis, including members of the SS directly involved in the Holocaust, also traveled on routes from Germany and Austria, south to Italy. On the willingness of US intelligence officials to aid the travel plans of former Nazis in order to gain their assistance in the coming Cold War with the communists see Richard Breitman and Norman J. W. Goda, eds., *U.S. Intelligence and the Nazis* (New York: Cambridge University Press, 2005); and Gerald Steinacher, "The Intelligence Service Ratline," in *Nazis on the Run: How Hitler's Henchmen Fled Justice*, trans. Shaun Whiteside (New York: Oxford University Press, 2011), 159–210.

Germany to Palestine." "Jewish sources" in Munich, he continued, said that half of the DPs planned to leave for Palestine "in the next six months and that they are not going to let anything stand in their way." In view of reports of 2,000 Jewish DPs "in the area of Bad Reichenhall near the Austrian border ... the constabulary here [in Munich] has been ordered to stop this departure by whatever means may be necessary, even by the use of force."[28]

American authorities, responding to British concerns, were also worried about efforts of military-age Jewish men to reach Palestine. On April 1 William P. Cochran, Jr., the political officer in the US Consulate in Frankfurt am Main, reported "movement of young male Polish Jews through Czechoslovakia and the American occupied zone of Germany, to France and presumably to Palestine."[29] "These Jews," he wrote,

are men of military age who have served recently in the Soviet army or in the "Soviet sponsored" Polish army. Obviously, in view of the reported inadequacy of the screening performed by the American Joint Distribution Committee (which sponsors these movements of persons), the inclusion of Soviet agents destined to Palestine, to join the underground there, or for possible debarkation in the American zone en route, is a distinct possibility.

Cochran conveyed reports that "a movement of 30,000 Polish Jews through these channels is anticipated in the next few months."[30]

Cochran included "Movement of Jews in and through Czechoslovakia," a more detailed report from Captain M. E. Kryston, the US military attaché in Prague, stating that such movement "is an organized movement sponsored by the American Joint Distribution Committee."[31] Transportation by rail was paid for by the AJDC before going to the Russian Zone in Austria. An AJDC transit camp in Prague offered food, "presumably distributed by UNRRA," and temporary lodging. "A special train was dispatched from Prague with four (4) or five (5) ex-soldiers, Jews fighting with the Russian or Polish (Russian) Army. Destination of this train was Marseilles, France. Visas were issued for 3 months by the French consulate in Prague." The train itself was provided by the Czech government. It was possible

[28] James R. Wilkinson to Secretary of State, "Attempt of Jewish Displaced Persons to Go to Palestine" (April 23, 1947), NACP RG 59, M1390, Roll 9, 867N.01/4–2347.
[29] William P. Cochran, Jr. to Secretary of State, Washington, D.C., No. 143, "Report on Repatriation of Young Male Jews to Palestine," Frankfurt (April 1, 1947), NACP RG59, M1390, Roll 9, 867N.01/4–147–7–3147.
[30] Ibid.
[31] M. E. Kryston, "Movement of Jews in and through Czechoslovakia" (March 15, 1947), NACP RG 59, M1390, Roll 9, 867N.01/4–147–7–3147.

that these Jews were sending these special ex-soldiers to Palestine to bolster the resistance parties now causing the British considerable trouble in Palestine. There is also a possibility of Russian agents being included in the infiltree program because screening made by the AJDC is not very thorough. Since this train passes thru the U.S. zone, Germany, it is quite possible that one of the supposed agents could easily detrain at one of the several stops in Germany, thereby infiltrating Soviet agents into the US Zone.

A train of 370 Jewish children and 30 other Jews, ranging in ages 18–35 left Prague, 6 March 1947 for Marseille, France for subsequent shipment to Palestine. Visas were issued by the French consulate in Prague for a 3-month period. British approved shipment to Palestine under their monthly quota program. Czech furnished the rolling stock and the AJDC provisioned the train for six days. The children were mostly born in Russia and Poland.[32]

Kryston's report indicated the support by the Czech government and the French Embassy in Prague in cooperation with the AJDC for the "infiltrees," who included military-age Jewish men whom the British were trying to keep out of Palestine. Only two years after the end of the Holocaust, Cold War suspicion and fears of communist infiltration had overcome empathy for its victims (see Figure 6.1).[33]

Truman, His State Department, and Britain

Such antipathy contrasted sharply with the emotions of President Truman, who frequently displayed public empathy for the survivors of the Holocaust and moral sympathy for the Zionist cause. However, as author of the Truman Doctrine he was also the decisive actor in shaping the policy of containment and deterrence against Soviet expansion and communist movements. On January 8, 1947 Truman nominated George Marshall, the former chief of staff of the Army during World War II, to replace James Byrnes as secretary of state, and on January 21 the Senate unanimously approved the appointment. Marshall served as secretary of state until January 20, 1949, that is, during the most crucial period of the Zionist confrontation with Britain, the civil war between the Jewish Agency and the Arab Higher Committee from December 1947 to May 15, and the first Arab-Israeli war from mid-May to the tense truce in March 1949. He had deep reservations about the wisdom of a Jewish state in Palestine. In May 1947 Marshall appointed George Kennan, by

---

[32] Ibid., 2.

[33] On the political sentiments and organizations, including leftist and pro-Sovietism among some Jewish survivors of the Holocaust in Eastern Europe, see Bauer, *Brichah*, 1–42.

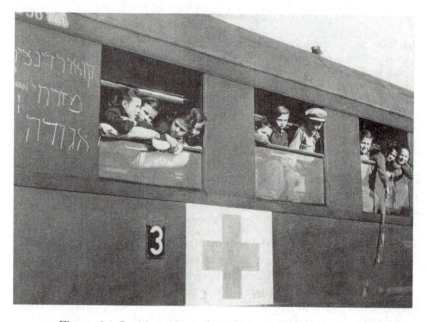

Figure 6.1 Jewish orphans from Belsen displaced-persons camp in Germany arriving at Marseille to immigrate to Palestine, January 1948. Source: Keystone-France/Gamma-Keystone/Getty Images.

then well known as the author of the "Long Telegram" of February 1946 on the sources of Soviet conduct, as the founding director of a new institution, the Policy Planning Staff in the State Department (see Figure 6.2). For these and other American policy makers, Zionist aspirations, strongly linked in their origins and support to Jews from Central and Eastern Europe, appeared to be at odds with, if not opposed to, the massive shift of policy away from the mentalities and passions of "the United Nations" fighting Fascism and Nazism to a Western alliance focused on the containment and deterrence of the Soviet Union and communism.

Concerns about Soviet expansion in the civil war in Greece and instability in Turkey were the immediate events that led Truman to declare the Truman Doctrine of American opposition to communist expansion in a speech to a joint session of Congress on March 12, 1947.[34] Britain's Attlee

---

[34] "The Truman Doctrine: President Harry S. Truman's Address Before a Joint Session of Congress, March 12, 1947," Yale Law School, The Avalon Project, Documents in History, Law and Diplomacy: https://avalon.law.yale.edu/20th_century/trudoc.asp.

Figure 6.2 US president Harry Truman and secretary of state George Marshall shake hands, Washington, May 29, 1947. Source: Hulton Archive/Getty Images.

and Bevin were in fundamental agreement with Truman's anticommunist policy. A strong Anglo-American alliance, deepened over the course of World War II, was a central component of the emerging policy of containment. The difference with Truman emerged, however, when Bevin applied the logic of anticommunism as well as arguments for perpetuating British military and political presence in Palestine. Moreover, as we have seen, when Britain used diplomatic pressure and its naval power to prevent-large scale Jewish immigration to Palestine after 1945, criticism of its anti-Zionist policy expanded in the liberal press and politics in the United States.[35]

But Truman's sympathies did not carry over to his State Department. Under Marshall, that branch of the Truman administration leaned toward Britain and its continued presence in the Middle East rather than to the non-state actors of the Zionists of the Jewish Agency in Palestine. After all, Britain, though economically weakened by its wartime exertions, was still in possession of a potent navy and a diminished but still strategically vital empire. Further, Britain was the emotional and strategic linchpin of both the American wartime alliance in World War II

---

[35] On the views of the British chiefs of staff on the strategic importance of the Middle East for Britain see William Roger Louis, *The End of the Palestine Mandate* (Austin: University of Texas Press, 1986), 16–35.

in Europe and of the emerging Cold War with the Soviet Union. The Anglo-American alliance and its multiple personal connections, friendships, and strategic commonalities dated from the Atlantic Charter of 1941 signed by FDR and Winston Churchill to the Truman Doctrine and Churchill's "Iron Curtain" speech in Fulton, Missouri of March 5, 1946.[36]

Zionism, on the other hand, was led by Jewish immigrants from Eastern Europe who included survivors of a mass murder that took place overwhelmingly on the Eastern Front in World War II. Neither the Eastern Front nor the Holocaust fitted comfortably into the Western-centric narrative of the war.[37] Indeed, in the face of the Stalinization of Eastern Europe after the war, the architects of the Cold War recalled the alliance with the Soviet Union with growing reluctance. Support for the Zionists was coming from governments who were building dictatorships behind what Churchill called an "iron curtain."[38] In addition to the obvious disparity of power between the British ally and the Zionists in Palestine, the Zionists' presence angered the Arabs sitting on top of oil deposits – access to which the British, especially, but also the Americans viewed as essential to the economic recovery of war-torn Western Europe. From 1946 to 1948 the British government repeatedly urged both the United States and France to do all they could to prevent what it called "illegal Jewish immigration" to Palestine and block the Zionists from obtaining weapons. The officials of both NEA and the Policy Planning Staff shared Britain's view of the matter and sought to assist British policy.

The mood in the US Congress was quite different. On February 17, 1947 Republican senator Robert Taft from Ohio wrote to Marshall criticizing the British for "not providing for the admission of a hundred thousand immigrants to relieve the situation in German camps." He sought a clearer American position in support of a partition plan that would lead to separate Jewish and Arab states. As British policy did not "comply with the policy of the American government in any way," Taft suggested that "proper representation to that effect should be made to the British government."[39] The following day Senator Estes Kefauver, a

---

[36] On the cultural meaning of the Anglo-American alliance see Michael Kimmage, *The Abandonment of the West: The History of an Idea in American Foreign Policy* (New York: Basic Books, 2020).

[37] On the lack of fit between the memory of the Holocaust and the emerging Cold War see Jeffrey Herf, *Divided Memory: The Nazi Past in the Two Germanys* (Cambridge, MA: Harvard University Press, 1997).

[38] On the Soviet Union in Eastern Europe see Anne Applebaum, *Iron Curtain: The Crushing of Eastern Europe, 1944–1956* (New York: Doubleday, 2012).

[39] Robert A. Taft to George C. Marshall, Washington (February 17, 1947), NACP RG59, M1390, Roll 8.

Democrat from Tennessee, wrote to Marshall that the principles of "law and justice" demanded that "the full force of our Government should be thrown immediately behind the Hebrew people in their efforts to secure a just execution of the solemn pledges made in the League of Nations Mandate." To date the US had "done nothing but politely request" that Britain carry out its pledges. A just settlement of the Palestine problem required "revocation of the White Paper restrictions." Indeed, "the displaced and imprisoned persons in Europe" could not "await the final determination of this matter in the United Nations." In the interim, "the force of this Government should be used toward enabling them to find refuge in Palestine."[40] On February 20 Senator Alexander Wiley, a Democrat from Wisconsin, wrote to Marshall urging the State Department to make "its strongest representations to the British Government for the immediate admission into Palestine of 100,000 Jewish displaced persons." He referred to "the long history of American support and sympathy with this objective and ... the long record of the British Government in barring the doors of Palestine to immigration of the people of Israel. There has been more empty talk and broken promises on upon this subject than perhaps on almost any other in the whole field of foreign relations." Wiley urged Marshall to "take action in order that the humanitarian objective of Jewish immigration may be realized, and in order that the good word of the United States may be fulfilled."[41]

The *Exodus* and Its Aftermath

The strains in US relations with Britain became even more evident during what became known as "the *Exodus* Affair" of July–August 1947. The Baltimore steamship *President Warfield*, renamed *Exodus 1947*, departed from the French port of Sète on July 11 with 4,500 Jewish immigrants on board intent on reaching Palestine. On July 18 it was seized by the British Navy off the coast of Palestine in an operation that caused the deaths of one crew member and two passengers. The British transferred the passengers to three other ships, which arrived on July 19 at Port-de-Bouc, on France's southern coast. Britain urged the French government to take the passengers off the ship, by force if necessary, but French officials, who had jurisdiction in the matter, refused to do so. After a stand-off lasting three weeks the British then took the ships to Hamburg, forcibly removed the passengers, and sent them back to camps in Germany. The episode was a

---

[40] Estes Kefauver to Georges C. Marshall, Washington (February 18, 1947), NACP RG 59, M1390, Roll 8.

[41] Alexander Wiley to Georges C. Marshall, Washington (February 20, 1947), NACP RG59, M1390, Roll 8.

public-relations disaster for Britain, but it deepened sympathy, especially in France and the United States, for the plight of the refugees and for their efforts to reach Palestine.

Jefferson Caffery, the US ambassador in France, told the State Department on July 24 that France's refusal to force the refugees off the ships reflected support for them in its press and in public opinion. It was "obvious," he wrote, "that the French Government has never lived up more than halfheartedly to their agreements with the British to prevent illegal immigration to Palestine through France."[42] Though the British gave early warning to French authorities that the *Exodus* was in Sète and intended to leave for Palestine, "nevertheless, the ship had little difficulty in escaping from the port, in spite of the fact that it had been declared *unseaworthy for passenger transport and that it was obvious that it might not reach* its supposed destination in Columbia with 4,500 passengers on board. Moreover past experiences might have caused the French to regard with some doubt [the] Colombian visa which the passports had."[43] Despite British pleas, the French government took the view that those passengers who wished to land in France could do so, but "no passengers would be forced to leave the ship."[44] According to Caffery, French public opinion was critical of British policy for its unsympathetic "treatment of poor Jews who have escaped from German crematoriums," and he concluded that the French government, or at least the Ministry of the Interior, was undermining British efforts to prevent immigration to Palestine. It did so by deficient examination of the validity of both the refugees' passports and the certificates of seaworthiness of the departing ships.[45]

On August 22 Eliahu Epstein, the Washington representative of the Jewish Agency, wrote to the secretary of state to protest the proposed transfer of refugees to Germany, "the graveyard of their families and of millions of their fellow Jews." Doing so "would be a final act of callousness and brutality." He urged the American government to "seek a change of policy on this issue in London on grounds of common humanity" and insist that "Britain be no longer false to her own past tradition of sympathy towards the suffering, the downtrodden and the oppressed."[46] Four days later the acting secretary of state, Robert Lovett, in a memo to

[42] Jefferson Caffery to Secretary of State, "French Attitude Regarding Jewish Refugees on S.S. Exodus," Paris, No. 2995 (July 24, 1947), NACP RG59, M1390, Roll 9, 867N.01/7–2447.

[43] Ibid. (emphasis in original).   [44] Ibid.

[45] Department of State to US EMBASSY, PARIS, No. 3282 (August 29, 1947), NACP RG59, M1390, Roll 9, 867N.01/7–2447.

[46] Eliahu Epstein to Acting Secretary of State, New York (August 22, 1947), NACP RG59, M1390, Roll 9, 867N.01/7–2447.

the US Embassy in London, acknowledged that American support for British policy risked making the United States a partner in what public opinion in Europe and the United States viewed as callous and brutal treatment of survivors of the Holocaust. If Britain transferred the Jewish refugees who had been on the *Exodus* to Germany, there "will be sharp deterioration of British popularity and position in this country." He suggested that the British bring them to another British-controlled territory, such as Gibraltar or Malta – but not Palestine.[47]

Upon returning to New York in September, Bernard Marks, the captain of the *Exodus*, held a press conference at the headquarters of Americans for Haganah. He said that the ship had been rammed fifteen or twenty times by a British destroyer on July 18, 25 miles west of Gaza, and that 3 people on board had been killed and 200 injured in the course of three-and-a-half hours of fighting with boarding parties of British sailors.[48] On September 13 Robert Macatee, the American consul general in Jerusalem, sent a detailed ten-page dispatch to the secretary of state describing the role of American crew members of the *Exodus* and their possible prosecution by British authorities in Palestine.[49] On August 8 the State Department reminded the Jerusalem Consulate of President Truman's June 5 statement that Americans should refrain from "any activities which tend further to inflame the passions of the inhabitants of Palestine, to undermine law and order in Palestine, or to promote violence in that country." The Department sought information on "Americans citizens who were actively engaged in promoting illegal immigration."[50] Macatee replied that "it was of course clear" that Marks and the other Americans "were engaged in such activity." However, Macatee urged the British not to prosecute Marks and other Americans involved,[51] and, partly due to Macatee's efforts, the British dropped charges against the Americans on the *Exodus*. While the ship's crew received favorable coverage in the press on their return to the United States, the FBI placed them under investigation for possible violation of

[47] Robert Lovett, Acting Sec State to AMEMBASSY, LONDON, FOR AMB, Washington (August 26, 1947), NACP RG 59, M1390, Roll 9, 867N.01/8–2447.
[48] "Exodus Captain Here, Charges British Strafing: Marks, 25, Says Destroyer Rammed Ship 15 Times and Use Machine Guns"; also "Exodus Crew Tells Its Story," NACP RG 60, Department of Justice (hereafter DOJ), Division of Communications and Records, 71–012–5, Section 2, 11–5–40, Entry A1-ENC 71, Container 18.
[49] Robert H. Macatee to Secretary of State, Jerusalem (September 13, 1947), "Transmitting Information Relevant to the Arrival of the Illegal Immigrant Ship, Exodus 1947 in Palestine, and Protection Accorded to Americans Thereon," NACP RG 60, DOJ, Criminal Division, Entry A1-ENC 71: Class 71 (Neutrality) Enclosures 1924; Division of Communications and Records, 71–012–5, Section 2, 11–5–40, Entry A1-ENC 71, Container 18.
[50] Ibid., 2.   [51] Ibid., 6.

US neutrality legislation.[52] Though the Department of Justice (DOJ) did not bring charges, the FBI, in regular contact with the State Department, continued to investigate Zionist organizations for possible violations of neutrality legislation.

Britain's urgent requests to the State Department to prevent Americans from assisting "illegal Jewish immigration" to Palestine continued after the *Exodus* affair. On October 2 Bromley informed NEA officials that another ship, the SS *Colonel Frederick C. Johnson*, had been "refitted with the intention of being used to carry illegal immigrants to Palestine."[53] On October 23, 1947 Ernest Gross, the State Department's legal advisor, informed Lovett of another "British complaint regarding support in the United States of illegal Jewish immigration to Palestine."[54] Inverchapel had asked Marshall to prevent the departure of the *Colonel Frederick C. Johnson* from the USA and complained about the "regrettable situation" concerning the inadequate efforts of the US government "to prevent the use of our territory as a base for the purchase, equipment, manning and financing of the operations of ships engaged in the illegal smuggling of Jews into Palestine."[55]

Gross's memo also conveyed the frustration in the State Department that the DOJ under attorney general Thomas Clark (1899–1977), a Truman appointee, had not prosecuted Americans involved in those activities. Already in April 1947, in response to British complaints lodged over the previous year-and-a-half about activities in the USA in support of "illegal immigration" to Palestine, the State Department's Legal Office had sent a review of the evidence to the DOJ's Criminal Law Section. Though the DOJ promised prompt consideration about proceeding with prosecution, and despite "numerous telephone calls" from State to Justice, "no decision was transmitted to this Department." A note from Bevin to Marshall led the latter to contact Attorney General Clark directly on August 7 "requesting that the matter be given prompt consideration and that appropriate action should be taken if our laws were violated."[56] Gross noted advertisements soliciting funds on behalf "of numerous

---

[52] Thomas J. McShane, File No. 62–9135 DJ, New York (October 7, 1947), "Palestine Situation, Exodus 1947: Special Inquiry, Neutrality Act Matter"; and William J. Berwanger, No. 2–10, Cincinnati, Ohio (September 24, 1947), "Palestine Situation, Exodus 1947, Neutrality Act Matter," NACP RG 60, DOJ, Division of Communications and Records, 71–012–5, Section 2, 11–5–40, Container 18.

[53] "Memorandum of Conversation: Subject: S.S. Colonel Frederick C. Johnson," Washington (October 2, 1947), NACP RG 59, M1390, Roll 9, 867N.01/10–247.

[54] Ernest Gross to Robert Lovett, Washington (October 23, 1947), "British complaints regarding support in the United States of illegal Jewish immigration into Palestine," NACP RG 59, M1390, Roll 9, 867N.01.

[55] Ibid.   [56] Ibid.

Jewish organizations" which had claimed tax-exempt status because the US Treasury Department had held that they were used for charitable purposes. Yet the evidence offered by the British indicated that "these funds were in fact used to finance operations of two militant organizations in Palestine, namely, the Fighters for the Freedom of Israel or Stern Gang and the Irgun Zvai Leumi." The Legal Office wrote to Treasury Department officials on June 17, 1947 to urge a reexamination of the tax-exempt status of the following organizations: United Zionist Revisionists of America, Inc.; American League for a Free Palestine; National Jewish Council; Brith Trumpeldor of America, Inc.; American Sea and Air Volunteers for Hebrew Repatriation; Israel Zion Fund, Inc.; Palestine Emergency Fund, Inc.; League for Jewish National Labor in Palestine, Inc.; National Jewish Youth Council; and the Nordau Circle.[57] Yet despite assurances from Treasury that it would expedite such a study, Gross told Lovett that, as of October 23, it appeared to be stalled.[58]

Gross's memo made clear that the relevant officials at both the DOJ and Treasury (the latter directed by Truman appointee John Snyder) were not pursuing the Zionist groups with the vigor that both the British government and the State Department desired. To strengthen his case, Gross cited President Truman's statement of June 5, 1947 regarding the consequences of the United Nations decision to investigate the Palestine question, which was sent to all US embassies and consulates two months later: "Activities calculated further to inflame the problem of the inhabitants of Palestine, to undermine law and order in Palestine, or to promote violence in that country are certain to create an atmosphere prejudicial to an early settlement of the Palestine problem and to render still more difficult the task which the United Nations has before it." Truman thus urged "every citizen and resident of the United States, in the interests of this country, of world peace, and of humanity, meticulously to refrain, while the United Nations is considering the problem of Palestine, from engaging in, or facilitating, any activities which tend further to inflame the passions of the inhabitants of Palestine, to undermine law and order in Palestine or to promote violence in that country."[59]

Despite that admonition, Gross continued, "the unfortunate *Exodus* expedition was carried forward with its tragic results." Gross recommended that Truman ask the attorney general "to see that pending investigations are completed promptly, and [that] prompt criminal proceedings are taken to assure that our laws relating to these alien smuggling operations are fully enforced." He further requested that the secretary of the treasury take steps to prevent the departure of the SS *Colonel Frederick*

[57] Ibid., 3.   [58] Ibid., 2.   [59] Cited in ibid., 3.

C. Johnson, and to expedite the State Department's request that Treasury investigate the tax-exempt status of the ten Jewish organizations the State Department had listed.[60] Gross indicated that the Truman appointees heading the DOJ and the Treasury were refusing to proceed as the British and the State Department wished against pro-Zionist activities. The State Department was interpreting Truman's June 5 statement to mean that the United States should also attempt to restrict Jewish immigration to Palestine.

Jews, Refugees, and Communists: Fall 1947

In fall 1947 American officials in Europe continued to send reports linking the exodus of Jewish refugees to the communist regimes in Eastern Europe. On October 1, 1947 John Horner, the chargé d'affaires of the US Embassy in Sofia, Bulgaria informed Marshall's office and US Embassies in London, Bucharest, and Jerusalem that the USS *Adukah* and another unidentified vessel had departed from Bulgarian Black Sea port of Bourgas the previous day "with between two and three thousand Jews aboard" – refugees who had arrived from Romania by rail. The British were "protesting this violation by Bulgarian Government of its pledge not to assist in illegal immigration into Palestine of Jews." At the same time, Horner reported, two additional refugee ships were approaching Bourgas, leading him to conclude that there was "connivance of Bulgarian and Romanian Governments in this exodus due to [their] wish [to] embarrass [the] British."[61]

The SS *Pan Crescent* and SS *Pan York* were two of the larger ships that had been purchased in the USA by Zionist supporters and refitted to transport Jewish refugees to Palestine. The voyages of those and other vessels received careful attention from the top levels of the State Department in fall and early winter 1947. On November 7 Marshall informed American Jewish leaders privately that "unless effective steps were taken to stop this clandestine activity," that is, the departure of ships from the United States to Europe to transport Jews to Palestine, "he would have no other recourse than to treat the matter publicly."[62] Some of the ships purchased and refitted in the United States departed from Panama for Europe. On November 13, in response to urgings from the

[60] Ibid., 4.

[61] Horner to Secretary of State, Sofia, No. 868 (October 1, 1947), NACP RG 59, M1390, Roll 10, 867N.01/10–147.

[62] "Memorandum of Conversation: Departure of Illegal immigrant ships destined for Palestine, especially SS Colonel Frederick C. Johnson," Washington (November 10, 1947), NACP RG 59, M1390, Roll 9, 867N.01/11–1047.

US Embassy in Panama City, the government of Panama appointed a commission to take action "against alleged illegal traffic of Jews to Palestine aboard Panamanian registered ships" including the *Pan York*, *Pan Crescent*, and *Colonel Frederick C. Johnson*.[63]

The following August, in the aftermath of the *Exodus* affair and the press attention that it brought to participation by Americans, Marshall sought a legal opinion on these activities from Attorney General Clark. On September 26 Clark told Marshall that he had concluded that "while the activities of the subjects involved border closely upon those prohibited by the neutrality laws of the United States, they do not, as far as now appears, actually violate any of those statutes."[64] While registration of a number of the groups involved raised issues under the Foreign Agents Registration Act of 1938, challenging them would not prevent continuation of the activities. Moreover, "initiation of prosecution for failure of compliance ... might well supply an occasion for claimed discrimination and oppression which would operate to the advantage of such groups and of the illegal immigration movement generally."[65] Clark added that the FBI was aware of "recruitment within the United States of personnel to serve the Palestine underground against the British," but "no useful purpose" would be served by discussion of violation of the neutrality statutes "at this time."[66]

Clark then addressed the issue of whether the recruitment of crews for the ships violated laws prohibiting American citizens from serving a foreign power in war against a friendly power. He thought it was

open to considerable question whether sporadic, retaliatory outbreaks such as are occurring in Palestine constitute a "war" within the meaning of the law, and to characterize the ships carrying these hundreds of displaced refugees as vessels of war is to torture the fact ... It is only upon the theory that the recruitment in the United States was an integral step in waging war upon the British in Palestine, accompanied by illegal immigration as an equally integral step, that a neutrality violation can be spelled out of the known facts and, as previously argued, such a theory is highly tenuous and untenable."[67]

Clark rejected that theory of the case. That said, the DOJ and FBI continued to investigate recruitment activities of the Sea and Air Volunteers for Hebrew Repatriation, an affiliate of the American League for a Free Palestine (ALFP), itself a liaison with the Irgun in Palestine, as well as

---

[63] AMEMBASSY, PANAMA to Department of State, Washington, "Operation Memorandum," Panama (November 13, 1947), "Foreign Representation: Panama Establishes Commission to Study Charges Panamanian Flagships Transporting Jews," NACP RG 59 M1390, Roll 11.

[64] Tom Clark, Attorney General to Secretary of State George Marshall, Washington (September 24, 1947), NACP RG 59, M1390, Roll 9, 867N.01/9-2447.

[65] Ibid., 1–2.   [66] Ibid., 7.   [67] Ibid., 8–9.

recruitment of the crew for the SS *Exodus*, "for whose sailing the Haganah assumes full responsibility."[68] The British government had also protested political advertisements in American newspapers denouncing its policies in Palestine, but Clark concluded that "no statute is in existence which would permit prosecution on that basis alone."[69]

Clark also rejected the State Department's contention that there was enough evidence to justify prosecution for "conspiracy to injure the property of a foreign government with which the United States is at peace." He wrote that "it is not an offense to conspire to do that which the law does not prohibit but recognizes may be lawfully done without prejudice or injury to the United States . . . provided the means of accomplishment employed are not in themselves unlawful." Yet if the objective of the conspiracy did not, "as here concluded," constitute a crime, then "no offense was committed, unless the means were unlawful, and there is no indication that they were. Accordingly, I must differ from the result reached by the State Department."[70]

On the other hand, Clark noted, "virtually all Zionist groups in this country" were affiliated with the World Zionist Organization, and this, in his opinion, meant that they were "registerable," since they were "'under the direction' of a foreign principal" and transmitted funds to it. The ALFP had supported "illegal immigration and terroristic activities in Palestine," and it was "registrable" as a foreign agent based on its "admitted collection and transmission of funds to the Repatriation Commissioner of the Hebrew Committee for National Liberation (HCNL) at Basel, Switzerland." Those funds had been used to purchase the SS *Abril*, renamed SS *Ben Hecht*, one of the earliest vessels seized as it attempted to run the British blockade in Palestine.[71] The HCNL was registered as an "agent of the Jewish people general," but the DOJ knew that it was raising funds for the Irgun Zvai Leumi. "Its failure to name Irgun Zvai Leumi as its true principal is under consideration as a basis for prosecution for false registration." The DOJ was investigating a number of other organizations raising funds for the Irgun (including American Friends of Jewish Palestine, Betar, the Palestine Resistance Committee, and the Political Action Committee for Palestine), most of them based in New York State. A recently formed organization, Americans for Haganah, also appeared to be "registerable." Investigations were underway into the possible failure of various organizations to register as agents of a foreign power. Given the department's "close cooperation" with the State Department, Clark promised, it would be notified of any "pertinent developments."[72]

---

[68] Ibid., 9.   [69] Ibid.   [70] Ibid., 10.   [71] Ibid.   [72] Ibid., 12.

On October 5 Under Secretary of State Robert Lovett replied to Clark's decision not to prosecute any of the groups under the Foreign Agents Registration Act, urging that, "in view of the seriousness of the situation," those groups should be required to register "as soon as possible." Lovett informed Clark that investigations were continuing into the ALFP. On November 17, 1947 the ALFP took out newspaper ads in the *New York Post* denouncing Britain, partition, and the Jewish Agency. Under the headline "Get Out!" the ALFP wrote:

The British say they will quit Palestine in August 1948. They will not do it unless they are forced to. Let's make sure they are. Let's give them a push and make it January instead of August for only when the British leave will there be peace in Palestine for all who dwell there – Jews, Moslems, Christians alike ... The Hebrews are a brave and noble nation. They are fighting for life and for the dignity of freedom. They are doing fine. Let's give them the means to finish the job.[73]

The same day Inverchapel told Marshall that "the whole tone of the advertisement appears to me to be an open incitement to violence." Because contributions would be tax exempt, Inverchapel claimed, the terrorists in Palestine," that is, the Irgun, "with aid of funds from United States sources, will be enabled to pursue their campaign of violence with such effect that the British administration may be driven out in the near future by force." Such activities made a difficult situation in Palestine worse and were a "direct violation" of the UN resolution of spring 1947, which urged restraint on all concerned.[74]

On November 20 Loy Henderson informed Lovett that NEA officials "believe the British objections to be well taken."[75] While the principle of a free press prevented the State Department from banning such ads, the fact that one stated that contributions were tax exempt by ruling of the Treasury Department "gives the impression that the United States government condones the activities of the organization." Henderson proposed a press statement that "as a matter of policy we are opposed to any solicitation of funds for, or encouragement to, violence in Palestine."[76] It would call such appeals "reprehensible," contrary to the spirit of UN resolutions and to President Truman's statement of June 5 urging all sides in Palestine to refrain from violence. In response to the advertisement, it

---

[73] American League for a Free Palestine, "Get Out!" (November 17, 1947), NACP RG 59, M1390, Roll 11.
[74] Lord Inverchapel to Secretary of State Marshall, Washington (November 17, 1947), NACP RG 59, M1390, Roll 11.
[75] Loy Henderson to Robert Lovett, Washington (November 20, 1947), "Proposed Press Statement on Advertisement by American League for a Free Palestine," NACP RG 59, M1390, Roll 11.
[76] Ibid.

should say, "the appropriate agencies of this government are now reconsidering the ruling whereby contributions to the American League for a Free Palestine are considered as tax-exempt."[77] The statement should also note that the DOJ and Treasury were continuing their investigations into possible violations of foreign activity registration and neutrality laws. Despite all the tough talk, however, Clark's Department of Justice did not proceed to indictments.

On November 10 Marshall replied to Bevin's concern that the *Pan Crescent* and *Pan York* were transporting "a large number of Jewish illegal immigrants from Black Sea ports" to Palestine, and that *Colonel Frederick C. Johnson* was possibly departing from the USA for similar purposes.[78] The US government was, Marshall informed Bevin, conducting "special investigations" to see if that ship could be legally barred from leaving. "In the meantime, armed cutters of the United States Coast Guard" had the ship "under twenty-four hour surveillance," and "all possible steps are being taken to prevent the sailing of this vessel."[79] Marshall told Bevin that he "concurred" with Bevin's views "as to the undesirability of such activities" when the UN General Assembly was discussing the Palestine issue, and assured him that "every effort is being made to ensure that the applicable laws of the United States which relate to these activities are fully enforced." Further, he informed Bevin that he had warned American Jewish leaders that unless this clandestine activity stopped, he would go public with his criticisms and objections,[80] and that the ALFP's tax-exempt status was "being urgently reexamined by the Treasury Department."[81]

On November 14 Marshall wrote to the US Embassy in Bucharest in response to the military attaché's report of October 17 "that Zionists in Romania were working in close liaison with Soviet officials to send emigrants to Palestine."[82] He told the attaché that the British government had repeatedly drawn attention to the SS *Pan York* and SS *Pan Crescent*, vessels under Panamanian registry, largely manned by American citizens, and apparently "purchased with funds provided by American Jewish organizations." "If in fact Communist agents were being placed aboard PAN CRESCENT and PAN YORK destined for Palestine," he said, "this Govt would regard this development as fraught with even more

---

[77] "Draft Press Statement," Washington (November 20, 1947), NACP RG 59, M1390, Roll 11.

[78] Marshall to Inverchapel, Washington (November 10, 1947), NACP RG 59, M1390, Roll 11, 867N.01/11–1047.

[79] Ibid., 2.   [80] Ibid., 4.   [81] Ibid., 5.

[82] Marshall to AMEMBASSY BUCHAREST, Washington, No. 687 (November 14, 1947), NACP RG 59, M1390, Roll 11, 867N.01/10–1447.

serious consequences. Please report fully on any movements of these two vessels and on steps taken to load them with migrants for Palestine whether bona fide Jewish refugees or persons presumably under Soviet influence."[83]

On November 20 Hans Schoenfeld, a career officer serving in the Bucharest embassy, told Marshall that although his embassy had "no direct knowledge" that Zionists in Romania were working with Soviet officials to send emigrants to Palestine, it seemed "a safe inference" that this was the case in light of the operation being prepared by SS *Pan Crescent* and SS *Pan York* in Constanta, Romania; the communist character of the Romanian government; and the concentration of Soviet forces in that area. Anthony Kendall, the British consul in Bucharest, had told Schoenfeld that "Jewish Marxist Youth" were present on the two ships. There was a "high probability of placement of Soviet agents in this group." Preference for space on the ship was "given [to] young Jewish [men] with military training between ages 18 and 34." Military training had taken place in Romanian camps. The Jews had not been required to have Romanian passports; visas were provided by the Uruguayan consul in Prague. Passage for the Jews was free, while Christians had to pay $10,000 for a pair of tickets.[84] Schoenfeld offered what appeared to be compelling evidence that the Romanian government was supporting leftists among the refugees.[85]

Apparently acting on this evidence, the next day Lovett informed the American Embassy in Montevideo, Uruguay that the *Pan Crescent* and *Pan York*, with "11,000 emigrants including Soviet Agents destined for Palestine," were about to depart from Constanta, Bulgaria. The ships, with Panamanian registry, had an American chief officer and were purchased with American funds. The State Department had learned that the passengers had visas issued by the Uruguayan consul in Prague. Lovett ordered the US ambassador in Montevideo to contact Uruguay's foreign minister "immediately" to "state that this Govt attaches great importance at this critical juncture of Palestine discussion before UN to absolute

---

[83] Ibid.

[84] Schoenfeld to Secretary of State, Bucharest (November 20, 1947), No. 203, NACP RG 59, M1390, Roll 11, 867N.01/11–2047.

[85] On State Department efforts to prevent or delay departure of ships in November and December 1947 from the United States or Central America headed to Europe to transport Jewish refugees to Palestine see "Memorandum of Conversation: Subject: SS Gloria and ATR-84 – Possible use as illegal immigrant ships," Washington (November 20, 1947), NACP RG 59 M1390 Roll 11, 867.01/11–2047; also see "Memorandum of Conversation Telephone: Costa Rican Vessels Allegedly Destined for Use in Illegal Palestine Immigration," Washington (November 20, 1947), NACP RG 59 M1390 Roll 9, 867.01/11–2047; and "Memorandum for the Files," Washington (December 1, 1947), NACP RG 59 M1390 Roll 11, 867.01/11–2647.

cessation [of] illegal migration into Palestine." If it was true that the Uruguayan consul in Prague had issued "visas to these illegal emigrants to Palestine," the Uruguayan government should "scrutinize text" of the UN resolution of May 15 1947, which called on all governments to refrain from action that threatened or used force in Palestine. Lovett sent copies of his memo to the US Embassies in London, Prague, and Bucharest and to the US delegation at the UN,[86] and he followed up on November 25 with a note to the US Embassy in Bucharest to ascertain "by what authority" visas to emigrants on the ships had been issued, and ordered them to approach Uruguay's foreign minister "immediately and state that this Govt attaches highest importance to these vessels not (repeat not) reaching Palestine at this juncture."[87]

On November 25, four days before the UN was to vote on the Partition Plan, Marshall had traveled to London to meet with Foreign Minister Bevin and then sent Lovett a note about his conversation. Bevin told him that the now "unanimous political reaction in Great Britain was against the Jewish influence in Palestine." That unanimity "stemmed directly from the execution of the two British sergeants" by the Irgun, an act "which would never be forgotten ... The anti-Jewish feeling in England was greater than it had been in a hundred years." Bevin said that "the Jewish influence from the United States" was making his efforts to find a solution in Palestine "impossible." He claimed that the Balfour Declaration for a Jewish home was an "unfortunate error" that "did not commit British Government to development of Jewish state ... He stated that British information indicated that Jewish groups moving from the Balkan states to Palestine illegally contained indoctrinated Communists which presented a serious threat to Middle East stability." Marshall told Bevin that he "had sympathy for the British in their difficulties in Palestine and under the pressures of the American Jew." He hoped the UN would find an "agreed settlement" and that Britain "would not render such a conclusion impossible."[88]

Bevin did not distinguish between Jews and Zionists, or Haganah vs. Irgun. According to Marshall, he referred simply to "the Jews" and then associated them with unfortunate political influence in the United States, terrorism in Palestine, and communists seeking to destabilize the Middle

---

[86] Robert Lovett to AMEMBASSY Montevideo, Washington, No. 369 (November 21, 1947), NACP RG 59, M1390, Roll 11, 867N.01/11–2047.

[87] Lovett to AMLEGATION BUCHAREST, Washington, Control 4390 (November 25, 1947), NACP RG 59, M1390, Roll 11, 867N.01/11–2047.

[88] Secretary of State George Marshall from London to Secretary of State, MARTEL 6, London (November 25, 1947), "US Urgent, Eyes Only for Lovett from Marshall: Top Secret," NACP RG 59, M1390, Roll 11, 867.01/11–2547.

East. Marshall's own reply refers to the pressures of "the American Jew" in the singular. The use of the singular to refer to the diverse range of American Jews was a standard term of antisemitic prejudice. Not only did Marshall fail to seize the opportunity to remonstrate with this British colleague or urge him to reconsider his views; he reinforced them with his own language.

On December 17 British officials in Bucharest sent Loy Henderson a report on Jewish "illegal immigrant traffic to Palestine," describing a "steady stream of Jews into Romania from U.S.S.R. during the past two years" – one that included "shipments of illegal immigrants in Palestine."[89] The refugees had identity papers provided by "various Romanian Jewish organizations."[90] Training camps in Romania provided them with "para-military training," while the NKVD was providing them with clearance to travel to Palestine at a time when "clearance for normal passengers was practically impossible to obtain," a policy which the British saw as a "significant" indication "of Soviet participation in this traffic." The priority in granting clearance and visas to Jews arriving from the USSR "has been remarkable." A considerable number of illegal immigrants belonged to "extreme-left wing Jewish organizations in Romania ... Russian military transport has been and is said to be still being used for transport of Jewish illegal immigrants across Romania both coastwards and westwards."[91]

On December 19 Moshe Shertok met with Dean Rusk (1909–94), then director of the Office of the State Department's Special Political Affairs, and Fraser Wilkins (1908–89), an NEA official. The topic was the rumored departure of the two refugee ships from Romania for Palestine. Shertok took issue with the British association between Jewish refugees and Soviet expansion, asserting that "Romanian Jews were refugees from antisemitism and communism." The American officials responded that "no step should be taken which would prejudice successful implementation of recent UN recommendation regarding Palestine."[92] In the view of the State Department "illegal Jewish immigration" did exactly that.

On December 22, in a memo to the US Embassy in Bucharest, Lovett continued his efforts to prevent the departure from Constanta of the *Pan Crescent* and the *Pan York*, with their combined load of 12,000 Jewish

---

[89] Henderson to Lovett, Washington (December 27, 1947), "British Report on Movement of Jews in Romania," NACP RG 59, M1390, Roll 11, 867N.01/12–2747.

[90] "Telegram from Bucharest, 17th December 1947," with Henderson to Lovett (December 27, 1947).

[91] Ibid.

[92] "Memorandum of Conversation," Washington (December 19, 1947), "Immigration into Palestine from Romania," NACP RG 59, M1390, Roll 11, 867N.01/12–1947.

refugees. He wrote that there was no Uruguayan consul in Bucharest able to write collective visas (as the consul in Prague had done for previous groups of refugees). Meanwhile, the Bulgarian government had arrested forty-three persons for "forging Honduran and Venezuelan visas for Jews leaving country illegally."[93] Therefore, since the passengers had "no valid visas for Palestine," the group seeking to immigrate was deemed "uncertified." The State Department "deprecates clandestine emigration to Palestine," particularly since the November 29, 1947 UN resolution "provided for substantial legal immigration to Palestine at an early date."[94] On December 27 Donald Heath (1894–1981), the US ambassador to Bulgaria, informed Marshall's office – and thus Lovett as well – that the Bulgarian government had ignored the State Department's requests to prevent departure. Rather, with its permission, "450 Zionist Jews ages 18 to 35 both sexes" departed on December 24 from Bulgarian and Romanian ports to Palestine. The Jewish Agency had purchased 700 entry visas to Palestine from the Bulgarian government at the cost of $30 a person.[95] The report from Bulgaria reinforced the messages Washington was receiving about support by the communist regimes in Eastern Europe for Jewish immigration to Palestine.

On December 29 Lovett asked the American consul general in Istanbul, Clarence E. Macy, for information on the ships' progress. According to information at Lovett's disposal, the two ships were transporting respectively 2,365 men, 1,914 women, and 1,607, children on the *Pan Crescent*; and 2,352 men, 2,924 women, and 987 children on the *Pan York*.[96] On December 30 Macy sent a sent three-page detailed description of the continuing voyage of the ships as they passed through the Bosporus Strait on their way to Palestine.[97] The ships sailed under a Panamanian flag but were American owned; the crews were American, Greek, and Italian Jews; many passengers were young, healthy, and physically fit. Macy wrote that, according to the British, they had been "selected and trained in camps in Poland or Russia, have certainly been thoroughly indoctrinated in the Communist party ideology, and presumably received some basic military training as well. They supposedly

[93] Lovett to AMLEGATION BUCHAREST, Washington, No. 774, (December 22, 1947), NACP RG 59, M1390, Roll 11, 867N.01/12–1147.
[94] "Suggested Press Statement for the Acting Secretary," Washington (n.d.), NACP RG 59, M1390, Roll 11, 867N.01/12–3047.
[95] Heath to SecState, Sofia, No. 1225 (December 27, 1947), NACP RG 59, M1390, Roll 11, 867N.01/12–2647.
[96] Lovett to AMCONSUL ISTANBUL, TURKEY, No. 416, Washington (December 29, 1947), NACP RG 59, M1390, Roll 11, 867N.01/12–2947.
[97] C. E. Macy to Secretary of State, Istanbul, No. 384 (December 30, 1947), NACP RG 59, M1390, Roll 11, 867N.01/12–3047.

represent the shock troops from central Europe moving to the support of the Jews (Haganah) in Palestine." After describing the difficulty the British Navy would have in stopping these ships once they were within the 3-mile limit off the coast of Palestine, Macy wrote: "I wish particularly to call attention to the fact that since these ships are owned and financed by United States citizens the end result of the expedition is that U.S. capital is being used to assist the infiltration of Communist agents into Palestine."[98]

The memoranda arriving in Washington from American diplomats in Eastern Europe – memos that drew on and shared the concerns of British diplomats and intelligence officials – repeatedly updated the association of Jews with communism to now refer to the association of Zionists with communists. American anticommunism in the early Cold War years was not inherently a form of antisemitism, but too often the US officials working on Palestine issues showed scant understanding of how the association of Zionism with communism evoked a grim tradition of the recent past.

I. F. Stone wrote about the echoes of the past. On November 6, 1947 he published "Exposing the Red Scare on Palestine" in *PM*, a furious response to the State Department's insistence that Jewish migration to Palestine was associated with Soviet foreign policy.[99] He wrote that during World War II and the Holocaust there had been mid-level officials in the State Department who had "managed to delay and sabotage rescue efforts, at the cost of many thousands of lives," and others in the British Foreign Office who "preferred (in the last analysis) to let Jews die in Europe [rather] than be annoyed by their attempts to reach safety in the Holy Land." That "same mentality" and some of the same officials were "doing their best to sabotage" the Truman administration's support for the partition recommendations of the United Nations Special Committee on Palestine (UNSCOP). They were also putting obstacles in the way of efforts of Jews to get to Palestine. During the war they had started false rumors that Jewish refugees perhaps were Nazis. Now, in fall 1947, they were spreading suspicion that "maybe they're Reds?" The wartime rumors had helped the British Foreign Office and certain circles in the State Department bureaucracy to "shut off all means of escape while the gas chambers were being prepared for their victims. The buzz-buzz about 'maybe these Jewish refugees are Reds' may be used to delay a UN decision on Palestine until the Germans can take over again in the Reich – and complete the job of exterminating the Jews as their priority."[100]

---

[98] Ibid.
[99] I. F. Stone, "Exposing the Red Scare on Palestine," *PM*, November 6, 1947, 14.
[100] Ibid.

Stone asserted that the Jewish communists among the DPs had returned to Eastern Europe. "Everyone who is not a political ignoramus or a deliberate liar knows that there is no deeper political cleavage in Europe than between those Jews who look to Palestine and Zionism as their only hope of self-respecting life, and those who look to Communism." Many Jewish DPs were Polish and Romanian Jews who had found refuge in the Soviet Union during the war. They could have stayed there but "left for two reasons: They were not Communists. They wanted to build a national home of their own, i.e., they were Zionists." He recalled that the communists had denounced Zionism as "a national bourgeois movement." The result of communist antagonism to Zionism, according to Stone, was that "there is no community in the world where the Communist Party is less influential than in Jewish Palestine. Its dogmatic and traditional opposition to Jewish nationalism made it a party with no following other than a few doctrinaires who had no roots in the community itself. This was true before the war and it is true today."[101]

The Zionists, Stone explained, aimed to build "grass-roots socialism" for "a deeply individualistic people in a thoroughly democratic community." What he called "the buzz-buzz brigade" at the State Department, which associated the Jewish refugees with the communists, was "dealing in malicious slander and hollow fabrication when it trots out the red scare to add to the troubles of the brave survivors of the gas chambers and the robust pioneers who have helped to make a home for them in Palestine."[102] Stone regarded the association of Jewish refugees with the communists after the war as part of a broader "red scare." In "Exposing the Red Scare on Palestine" and subsequent articles Stone asserted that anti-Zionism was also becoming part of the ideological tool kit of the American and British containment of communism.

Nevertheless, the editors of the *New York Times* found the evidence of Soviet and Soviet-bloc support for the Zionists compelling. On its front page on New Year's Day, 1948 the *Times* ran a story headlined "Red 'Fifth Column' for Palestine Feared as Ships Near Holy Land."[103] According to "an authoritative source" in London, presumably in the British Foreign Office or British intelligence, the SS *Pan Crescent* and SS *Pan York* "are full of potential 'fifth columnists.'" The "12,000 visa-less Jews" were believed to have sailed from Varna, Bulgaria. "They are mostly hand-picked Communists or fellow-travelers, with links to the

---

[101] Ibid.   [102] Ibid.
[103] "Red 'Fifth Column' for Palestine Feared as Ships Near Holy Land," *New York Times*, January 1, 1948, 1.

Stern Gang." They "will ultimately reach Palestine at a most crucial moment and the British fear that will make a big difference in the ideological content of Palestine."[104]

The association of Zionism and communism had become a major story in the paper of record, and it elicited vehement liberal indignation. A New York playwright wrote to the editor, asking why "*The Times* lent itself to the gratuitous cruelty of printing this story of such palpably unverifiable 'facts.'" The British were seeking to justify "immoral" acts by presenting them as an effort to prevent the expansion of communism.[105]

But the State Department persisted in its suspicions, reinforced by statements from certain members of the Yishuv. In a cable of January 26, 1948 Ambassador Caffery in Paris reported that, "in a series of articles in the Paris edition of the Communist Yiddish Daily *Neue Presse*, Moshe Sneh, former Chief of the Haganah Defense Force who recently resigned from the Jewish Agency, makes it clear that the extreme Leftist Palestinians [that is, Jews] will rely solely on Soviet Russia for assistance and encouragement and will at least cooperate closely with Soviet satellite states."[106] Caffery's "reliable Jewish source" in Paris said that the "Soviet trained and dominated Stern group," which he mistakenly described as the military arm of the Palestine Communist Party, had "recently joined the Haganah for purpose of infiltration." Sneh argued that the United States "actually does not favor partition of Palestine in spite of voting yes along with the Soviet Union," and that it was a simplification to say that "America and Russia helped us equally for there is no comparison between half-hearted aid" coming from the United States and "complete assistance" offered by the Soviet Union.[107] Sneh, who did not represent the mainstream of Zionist politics, reinforced American suspicions about Soviet influence in the Yishuv.

On February 1, 1948 the *Times* ran a page-1 story by the foreign correspondent Herbert Matthews under the headline "London Insists Communists Were Bound for Palestine."[108] Matthews' article, based on "British official reports, ambassadorial, ministerial and military," offered readers a synthesis of the refugees' journey before, during, and after the voyages of the *Pan Crescent* and the *Pan York*, from Bulgaria to

---

[104] Ibid.

[105] See Ruth Goetz, "Letter to the Editor," *New York Times*, January 1, 1948, 24, and Ruth Goetz Wikipedia entry: https://en.wikipedia.org/wiki/Ruth_Goetz

[106] Jefferson Caffery to Secretary of State, Paris (January 26, 1948), No. 446, NACP RG 59, M1390, Roll 12, 867N.01/1–2648.

[107] Ibid.

[108] Herbert Matthews, "London Insists Communists Were Bound for Palestine: Officials Say Records Show that Many on Seized Ships Were Active Party Agents – Imply Soviet Inspired the Trip," *New York Times*, February 1, 1948, 1.

their seizure by the British off the coast of Palestine. Matthews led as follows:

The unauthorized Jewish immigrant ships Pan York and Pan Crescent, which sailed from behind the "Iron Curtain" for Palestine at the end of December, were carrying many Communist agents, according to British official sources. One thousand of the 15,000 immigrants aboard spoke Russian, many belonged to militant Communist organizations, some may have been non-Jews, and some had documents showing that they had served in the Soviet forces during World War I, these sources say. The immigrants on these vessels and on a number of others that sailed earlier from the Black Sea were collected and sent toward Palestine with the knowledge and sometimes with active connivance of the Soviet Union and its satellites, according to British officials.[109]

The security precautions taken "by and on behalf of" these immigrants were "so thorough that British officials found it impossible to get direct positive evidence that any Russian-sponsored subversive elements were among the immigrants."[110] Nevertheless, British officials were convinced "that large-scale Jewish immigration, far from being discouraged or prevented by Soviet satellite governments, has been deliberately encouraged" and was due to Soviet policy. In the case of the *Pan York* and *Pan Crescent*, the British believed that the Soviet authorities permitted the departure of the two ships "only if 1,000 Jewish Communists were included among the immigrants."[111]

Matthews' summary of British official reports was as follows: "For at least" the past two years, Jews came to Romania from the Soviet Union. As no one could leave the USSR without government permission, the British "take it for granted that Soviet authorities know of this migration," and on occasion "put military transport at the disposal of Jewish leaders to facilitate this transit." The Soviet authorities offered these Russian Jews "priority over Jews from elsewhere in Europe." Though travel clearances "to ordinary travelers are virtually impossible to get, these immigrants [from Russia and Romania] readily get exit clearances." The immigrants received "paramilitary training" with the permission of the Soviet section of the Allied Control Council. Mathews referred to cooperation between the American Joint Distribution Committee and the "Haganah, Zionist militia." The Romanian secret police were "implicated with the tacit approval of Moscow."[112] Despite orders given to the immigrants on the two ships to "destroy all documents," the British found "membership cards of the Union of Communist Youth in Romania, the Romanian Communist Party, the Lenin United Communist Association, the Union of Female Anti-Fascists and the Universal Democratic Front."

---

[109] Ibid.   [110] Ibid.   [111] Ibid., 17.   [112] Ibid.

The British asserted that "all these bodies ... are militant Communist associations." Matthews ended his story by repeating that "every statement in this dispatch is based on British official reports. None is made on the authority of this correspondent or of *The New York Times.*"[113]

For readers convinced that Matthews' dispatch was accurate, Stone's reporting in *Underground to Palestine* now would appear to be a case of fellow-traveling romanticism for the gullible, and an effort to use Jewish suffering to advance the interests of the Soviet Union. The very next day Stone fired back in *PM* under the headline "Debunking N.Y. 'Times' Smear of Jewish Refugees."[114] He argued that the fact that the Soviet satellite governments were supporting Jewish immigration to Palestine was "a long way from proof that these refugees are 'mostly hand-picked Communists' or that a thousand of them are."[115] Most of the Russian speakers on the *Pan Crescent* and *Pan York* were Romanian Jews who spoke Russian because Russia had taken over Bucovina and Bessarabia at end of World War I. Jewish refugees from areas taken over by the Russians during the war, Jewish partisans, and Jews "lucky enough to flee from German territory into the USSR" had served in the Red Army. "While Arabs who served under Hitler are permitted to organize warfare in Palestine against the Jews, are the gates of Palestine to be barred against Jewish refugees who served in the allied armies against Hitler? The *New York Times* is guilty of unfair journalism, and the British government of malicious slander." The new governments in Eastern Europe and the commanders of the Red Army had "refused to add to the unhappiness of these unhappy refugees seeking a new home promised them by Britain's own Balfour Declaration." If the Soviet Union had tried to prevent their immigration, "London and Washington would be gleefully ready to smear Moscow as 'anti-Semitic' if any such steps were taken."[116]

The truth, according to Stone, appeared in shades of grey. Most, but not all, Jewish communists stayed in Europe. Some came to Palestine, as British and American diplomats were reporting, and there made up the membership of the small and unsuccessful Communist Party (Maki) and the larger, left-leaning Mapam Party. It was, however, "malicious slander and hollow fabrication" to suggest that the Jewish exodus was predominantly communist in orientation or that its primary motivation lay in Soviet

---

[113] Ibid. The association of Jews with communism was a feature of Congressional debates about the Displaced Persons Act of 1948, legislation which severely limited Jewish immigration to the United States in favor of non-Jews. See David Nasaw, *The Last Million: Europe's Displaced Persons from World War to Cold War* (New York: Penguin Press, 2020), 424–434.

[114] I. F. Stone, "Debunking N.Y. 'Times' Smear of Jewish Refugees," *PM*, February 2, 1948, 7–8.

[115] Ibid.   [116] Ibid., 8.

foreign policy rather than in Zionist aspirations. Nevertheless, as we will see, the suspicion lingered in official circles in Washington and London that the Mossad Le'Aliyah Bet's efforts to foster clandestine immigration to Palestine was part of a Soviet effort to expand influence in the Middle East.

Anglo-American Intelligence Assessments on Soviet Intentions for the Joint Chiefs of Staff

The guilty association of Zionism with communism existed equally if not more so among American military leaders. It appeared in decision memoranda of the US Joint Chiefs of Staff (JCS) from December 1947 to March 1948. In memos on "The Problem of Palestine" the Joint Chiefs recommended against sending US troops to Palestine and warned against Soviet efforts to place its own troops in the Middle East.[117] On February 25, 1948 the secretary of the British Joint Intelligence Committee sent the secretary of the US Joint Intelligence Committee a report on the "Short Term Intentions of the Soviet Union in Palestine" with the request that it be shown to the US Chiefs of Staff. Two days later the report was transmitted to Admiral William Leahy, chairman of JCS, Air Force General Carl Spaatz, Admiral Louis Denfeld, chief of naval operations, and General Omar Bradley, the chief of staff of the Army.[118] As subsequent JCS documents indicated, the interpretation in "Short Term Intentions of the Soviet Union in Palestine" was repeated in American assessments as well. It offered the same perspective that British officials had conveyed to Herbert Matthews for his reporting in the *New York Times*.

"Short Term Intentions" concluded that Russian policy in Palestine was aimed at "preventing the creation of a Middle East anti-Soviet bloc." The Soviet Union would seek to "foment political disorder throughout the Middle East" and cause a "maximum of embarrassment to British and American interests." Its intention was "to promote the creation of a new State in Palestine, open to penetration and exploitation as a centre of Communist activity." After the establishment of a Jewish state "the Soviet Union would probably try to increase her influence in it" by "penetration

---

[117] Joint Chiefs of Staff, Washington (February 26, 1948), "Top Secret, Decision of J.C.S 1684/9, 26 February 1948"; and "List of Papers," in NACP RG 319 (Army Staff), Plans and Operations Division, Decimal File, 1946–1948, 091.Palestine, Box 24.

[118] Secretary Dalor to Admiral Leahy, General Spaatz, Admiral Denfeld, General Bradley, Washington (February 27, 1948), "British Estimate of Short Term Intentions of the Soviet Union in Palestine," NACP RG 319 (Army Staff), Plans and Operations Division, Decimal File, 1946–1948, 091.Palestine, Box 24.

of the Jewish Civil and Military Administration with a view to future exploitation ... immigration, illegal if necessary, of agents, propagandists and guerrilla leaders ... [and circulation of] propaganda, particularly for Jewish industrial workers." When it came to the Arabs, the Soviet Union would probably exploit their nationalism and "emphasize the sympathy of the Soviet Union with the Arab masses in their conflicts with the Arab ruling classes."[119]

The British warned that Soviet policy toward Palestine was central to its effort to deny and eliminate British and American influence, especially military influence, in the region.

Palestine provides an excellent opportunity for the rapid infiltration of Soviet influence. Its strategic importance is such, furthermore, that if the Soviet Union were to gain even a measure of influence in the country the whole balance of power in the Middle East would be altered. The decision to support the Partition Plan represents a crystallization of Soviet policy with respect to Palestine. It can only have been reached after close analysis of the probable advantages compared to certain undoubted disadvantages.[120]

The memorandum went on to enumerate the disadvantages for the Soviets, most importantly that the communist parties in the Middle East had been "thrown into complete confusion," as they were all "bitterly opposed to partition." There was also the "serious danger ... that the new Jewish state will serve as a centre of American interest and influence in the Middle East." Yet, the British report concluded, for the Soviet Union, the drawbacks of supporting the establishment of a Jewish state in Palestine were outweighed by the advantage of the "creation of a new and unstable state in the Middle East with a Mediterranean coastline." Further, the Partition Plan created "new and better opportunities for creating disturbances," for stoking differences between the UK and the United States, and for using the United Nations to send Soviet troops to the region "under the cover of international law."[121]

"Short Term Intentions" explained why a Jewish state offered more advantages to the Soviet Union than the Arab states did.

Many of the immigrants to Palestine come from the European proletariat and, even when not Communists themselves, have at least the experience of the social issues with which Communism deals. A politically conscious proletariat is almost wholly absent from the Arab world, and the Arab leaders, as they themselves realize, are of a type for whom there is no place in a Sovietized world. Moreover, any pro-Arab display by the Soviet Union to date has been a matter, not of

---

[119] "Enclosure: Short Term Intentions of the Soviet Union in Palestine," in "British Estimate of Short-Term Intentions of the Soviet Union in Palestine."
[120] Ibid., 2.   [121] Ibid.

sentiment, but of calculated advantage. Palestine Jewry, especially when at war with the Arabs, is a much better breeding ground for Communism in the near future than an Arab world ruled by King ibn Saud, King Abdullah, the Mufti and their like. The good will of Jewry is an international asset, though probably of limited duration.[122]

As had the State Department reports from Eastern Europe, "Short Term Intentions" turned the familiar coupling of Jews and communism into a triad of Jews, Zionism, and communism that could produce the "breeding ground" of communism in the Middle East in the form of a Jewish state in Palestine.

According to the British authors of "Short Term Intentions," the establishment of a Jewish state in Palestine would enhance the enduring Soviet aim in the Middle East of preventing the growth of "strong anti-Russian power or group of powers there." In the past the Soviet Union had supported Arab nationalists who opposed and weakened the Ottoman Empire, but two developments had changed its calculus. First, the emergence of a strong Jewish claim to statehood "backed by an army about 80,000 strong, many of whom had fighting experience in the late war, and by terrorist organizations"; and second, "the beginnings of reconstitution of an anti-Russian bloc in the Middle East under the auspices of British policy and the disappearance of the old animosities between Turkey and the Arab world."[123] According to the British, the Russians would do all they could to prevent a Jewish state in Palestine from becoming part of that "anti-Russian bloc." The UN debate on partition in 1947 was "the occasion for, but not the cause of," an "overhaul" of Soviet policy. The Soviets wanted "to drive a wedge into the emergent Middle Eastern bloc against her. The chance of a Jewish State under the surveillance of the Security Council gave her the immediate opportunity of driving such a wedge, and she has tried to drive it home hard." The Soviet Union's "main interest" in the Jewish state would be "to try to insure either that it is won for Communism or that the Communist element has complete freedom of action there."[124]

The British report acknowledged that there were very few communists in Palestine in 1947/8 and that the Jewish Agency had shown alarm at Russian influence. As a result, "the most obvious means of increasing such support is for the Soviet Union to infiltrate Communists among illegal immigrants." It was possible that the Soviet Union would "take a more active interest than hitherto in illegal immigration" and engage in propaganda, "especially among Jewish industrial workers, designed to prove that the 'imperialists' are pro-Arab for strategic and economic

[122] Ibid., 3.   [123] Ibid.   [124] Ibid., 4.

reasons."[125] Hence supporting increased Jewish emigration to Palestine also meant support for advancing Soviet efforts to infiltrate communist agents into the region. Objectively, therefore, urgent appeals to aid persecuted Jewry in liberal and leftist opinion in the United States and Europe served the interests of the Soviet Union and the expansion of communist influence in the Middle East.

The leadership of the Pentagon had expressed sentiments similar to those of the British in a series of drafts beginning in December and continuing into spring 1948. In version 9 of their memo "The Problem of Palestine," adopted on February 26, the Joint Chiefs firmly opposed use of American forces to enforce the Partition Plan. Doing so would "materially reduce the ability of our armed forces to support United States policy in other areas, notably Greece," and would require a partial mobilization at home. But the primary source of opposition was that using US forces to "enforce Partition would result in the implacable hatred of the Arab world. In consequence, access by the United States to the strategic base area in the Middle East and to the oil of Iran, Iraq and Saudi Arabia would, in all probability, be possible only by force."[126] The Joint Chiefs believed that "enforcing the UN Partition plan by force would undermine the following US security objectives in the Middle East": avoid introducing US troops into the area; prevent the "legalized intrusion of Soviet or Soviet satellite forces into the area"; and preserve "continued access to the oil resources of the Near and Middle East." This was an issue "of grave concern to the Joint Chiefs of Staff since a great part of the military strength of the United States is based on oil." Maintaining friendly relations with the Arabs was essential to facilitate access to "strategic base areas and lines of communication in the Middle East in the event of war with the USSR."[127] Thus the UN Partition Plan and the establishment of a Jewish state in Palestine would be to the detriment of American national security interests.

In the cacophony of American voices in the debate about Palestine policy, the previously mentioned American Zionist Emergency Council (AZEC), led by Stephen Wise and Abba Silver, challenged the likelihood of an Arab threat to break with the West. In a full-page statement published in *PM* on October 12, 1947, AZEC leaders noted that the Arab League threatened to wage "Holy War against the Jews," make a

[125] Ibid., 5.
[126] "Joint Chiefs of Staff, Decision on J.C.S 1684/9, A Report by the Joint Strategic Survey Committee on The Problem of Palestine," Washington (February 26, 1948), 48, NACP RG 319 (Army Staff), Plans and Operations Division, Decimal File, 1946–1948, 091. Palestine, Box, 24.
[127] Ibid., 50.

"complete break with the West," and impose sanctions against British and American oil interests in the region as its response to the partition recommendations of the majority of UNSCOP. But AZEC did not believe there was any "substance to these threats," which amounted to an "attempt to blackmail" the UN into submitting to the "demands of the Arab rulers."[128]

In AZEC's view the threat of an Arab revolt against the West was exaggerated. The Arab states at the UN owed their "official standing and prestige" to the West, in particular to Britain and the United States. These Western powers had saved them from Axis occupation in World War II, recognized their independence, admitted them as sovereign states into the United Nations, supplied them with arms and military training, and helped them to develop and exploit their oil resources.[129] Their dependency on Western political and military protection and economic support meant that their withdrawal "would spell complete ruin for their leaders." Loss of oil royalties would mean that Iraq and Saudi Arabia "would lose most of their income." Great Britain had created a "Frankenstein monster" that had "no strength of its own." Thus "all Arab threats to break with the West are mere bluff." That dependency applied to oil as well. The United States was not dependent on Middle East oil, but the Arab states were "*totally dependent on* [emphasis in original] the Western powers to develop and market their oil in peacetime and protect it in wartime." The threat to turn to the Soviet Union was also empty. The "feudal Arab world" and its "Arab potentates would be the very last to invite Soviet influence in their lands and over their peoples." Moreover, given Gromyko's stated support for a partition plan at the UN in May 14, 1947, it appeared that "the Soviet Union is not prepared to go along with Arab plans for the destruction of the Jewish National Home."[130] Thus, AZEC concluded, the Arabs were not rushing into Russian arms. The Arab threat to turn to the Soviet Union was another bluff.

The AZEC statement also cast a skeptical eye on Arab military capabilities and threats of war. Military experts cited by the Anglo-American Committee believed that the Haganah would defeat potential Arab opposition.[131] Yet, even if "the threats of Arab politicians could be taken at their face-value," the UN must

withstand such intimidation. If the spirit of appeasement is to rule at Lake Success [the location of UN meetings near New York that fall], then there is no hope for the world. If the former pro-Nazi agent, Jamal el-Husseini, can browbeat the

[128] American Zionist Emergency Council, "Shall We Submit to Blackmail Diplomacy," *PM*, October 12, 1947, 7.
[129] Ibid.   [130] Ibid.   [131] Ibid.

United Nations with as much success as Hitler enjoyed at Munich, then we may as well liquidate the United Nations and prepare for a new anarchy in the world, for more wars and total destruction ... Organized mankind cannot and must not tolerate blackmail diplomacy even when such threats are based on actual power. But when the threats are empty and baseless, they can only be met with the condemnation they deserve.[132]

Submission to "blackmail diplomacy" would repeat the blunders of appeasement at Munich. The memory of and lessons learned from World War II and the capitulation to the Nazis that had preceded it remained an important theme for American liberals and Zionists.

As became clear during the Pentagon Talks in September and October 1947, high-ranking military and diplomatic officials in the United States and Britain were not as worried that the Arabs would turn against the West as the AZEC authors thought. They, too, viewed the Arab societies as deeply conservative and profoundly anti-communist. In these early days of the Cold War the primary focus of American and British officials was on Soviet policy in Europe, and they feared that a Jewish state in Palestine would become an instrument of Soviet influence. That formidable triad – the association of Jews, Zionism, and communism – remained prominent in the thinking of American as well British diplomatic and military leaders. Truman's challenge was to begin the Cold War against the communists without simultaneously fanning a new wave of American- and British-supported antisemitism fueled in part by the anti-Zionism of the Anglo-American diplomatic and military leadership.

During the *Exodus* affair of summer 1947 parts of the French government and French public opinion revealed a non-communist left that, like Truman, Wagner, Celler, and the AZEC authors, rallied to the Zionists' cause.

[132] Ibid.

7 The French Government, Jewish Immigration to Palestine, and the *Exodus* Affair

> By tolerating the continuation of the British effort off the coasts of France, the French government, despite itself, allows itself to be drawn into de facto complicity in this cruel game.
>
> Édouard Depreux, French minister of the interior, to foreign minister Georges Bidault, August 4, 1947

In the crucial years in which the state of Israel was established, the government of France was divided between a Foreign Ministry focused on sustaining France's position in the Arab world in North Africa and the Middle East and socialist pro-Zionists directing the Ministries of Interior and Transport. Though France's coalition government in the Fourth Republic voted in favor of the UN Partition Resolution of November 29, 1947, it did so only after voting to abstain on several previous resolutions related to partition. French foreign minister Robert Schuman, who saw France's core interests lying more in Europe than in its empire, concluded that when the United States indicated its support for partition, France's effort to deter Soviet influence in Europe called for agreement with the Americans on this issue.[1] The opposition to the Zionist project in the French Foreign Ministry persisted, based on the view that France must align closely with British policy in the face of the Soviet threat in Europe, retain favor in the Arab states, and protect the Christian holy sites in Palestine, three issues that remained enduring themes affecting French foreign policy. These ambivalences postponed France's full, that is, de jure, recognition of the state of Israel until May 11, 1949, almost a year after it was established.[2]

[1] See Frédérique Schillo, "Stratégie politique ou attentisme? Réflexions sur l'attitude de la France," in *La France et la création de l'état d'Israël, 18 février 1947–11 mai 1949* (Paris: Éditions Artcom, 1997), 98–104.

[2] On the French government and the establishment of the state of Israel see Schillo, *La France et la création de l'état d'Israël*; and her "France and the Partition Plan: 1947–1948," *Israel Affairs* 14, no. 3 (2008): 486–498; Alan Swarc, "The Early French Connection to Israel," *Jewish Historical Studies* 43 (2011): 159–187; and his "Illegal Immigration to Palestine, 1945–1948: The French Connection," Ph.D. dissertation, University College London, 2005, Proquest LLC 2013, University of Michigan, Dissertation Publishing, Microform. On the discussion in the French press and politics see David Lazar, *Opinion française et la naissance de l'état d'Israël, 1945–1949* (Paris: Calmann-Levy, 1972).

France's geographical location, both its borders and proximity to Central and Eastern Europe, as well as the ports on its southern coast, meant that the decisions of its Ministries of the Interior and of Transport assumed central importance for the success or failure of the efforts of Mossad Le'Aliyah Bet to bring Jewish survivors of the Holocaust to Palestine. These two ministries controlled France's police, her borders and ports, and issued visas and immigration regulations. In July and August 1947, during the *Exodus* affair, the Jewish Agency in Palestine won one of its most significant and famous political victories against Britain's efforts to prevent large-scale immigration to Palestine. To the great irritation of the British Foreign Office, the French Ministries of the Interior and of Transport played a decisive and, outside of France, less well-known role in support of Jewish "illegal" immigration to Palestine and thus of the foundation of the Jewish state.[3]

As noted in the previous chapter, the SS *President Warfield*, renamed *Exodus*, had departed from Marseille in an unsuccessful effort to bring its 4,500 passengers to Haifa. After a violent confrontation with British sailors off the shores of Palestine the passengers were taken to three British ships, which then sailed offshore of Port-de-Bouc on France's Mediterranean coast. The British asked the French government to compel the passengers to disembark there, by force if necessary. The passengers refused. The British refused to allow the refugees to return to Palestine. A three-week stand-off followed that captured world media attention.

The two members of the cabinet of the Fourth Republic with jurisdiction in the matter, Édouard Depreux (1898–1981), minister of interior (the counterpart to the American Department of Justice), and Jules Moch (1893–1985), minister of transport, rejected Britain's requests (see Figures 7.1 and 7.2). Both were members of the Socialist Party who, like former Socialist prime minister Léon Blum, supported Zionist aspirations. Depreux served as minister of interior from June 24, 1946 to November 24, 1947, while Moch was minister of transport from 1945 to 1947, when he succeeded Depreux at Interior, serving until February 7, 1950. Their policies and decisions infuriated the British government, frustrated their own Foreign Ministry, and made a significant contribution to the success of the Zionist campaign to bring Jewish survivors of the Holocaust to Palestine under the British Mandate and then to the new

---

[3] On the anger of the British government at French policy toward Jewish refugees see Arieh Kochavi, *Post-Holocaust Politics: Britain, the United States and Jewish Refugees, 1945–1948* (Chapel Hill: University of North Carolina Press, 2001).

Figure 7.1 Édouard Depreux, minister of interior, speaking at the former headquarters of the Gestapo at rue des Saussaies in Paris, March 1947, during the inauguration of a commemorative plaque to the memory of those deported during the Nazi occupation. The plaque reads "1940–1944, the National Federation of Resistance Deportees and Interned, To the memory of the heroes tortured by the Gestapo in this building." Source: Keystone-France/Gamma-Keystone/Getty Images.

state of Israel in 1948. This non- and anticommunist left in France demonstrated its sympathies for the Zionist project in words and deeds.

In May 1947 – before the *Exodus* affair unfolded – dramatic political events had taken place in France. A harsh winter had destroyed the grain harvest while prices continued to increase. Strikes that began in the Renault factories expanded on May Day to nationwide demonstrations. On May 4 the French Communist Party refused to support a vote of confidence in the National Assembly of the economic policy of the government led by Socialist prime minister Paul Ramadier. The next day Ramadier expelled the Communists from the governing coalition, one that included Depreux and Moch. The expulsion of the Communists was one of the key events in the early years of the Cold War in France.

Figure 7.2 French interior minister (public works) Jules Moch (left) and French foreign minister Georges Bidault during the *Exodus* affair of 1947, photographed leaving the Élysée Palace in Paris in January 1957. Source: Keystone/Hulton Archive/Getty Images.

Significantly, Depreux and Moch managed to combine opposition to the Communists with support for the Zionists, in contrast to the Anglo-American diplomatic and military leadership.

Support for Zionism in France encompassed a broad span of the political spectrum including Communists, Socialists, Gaullists, Radicals, and various veterans of the French Resistance. While some parts of the French Resistance were more focused on the fate of the Jews during the Holocaust than others, veterans of the Resistance, especially Jewish veterans, were important contributors to the wave of support for the Jews in Palestine, both in public opinion and in government policy after liberation in 1944.[4] It was understandable that, after the war, the Jewish Agency and the Mossad Le'Aliyah Bet made Paris the European headquarters of its efforts to organize clandestine immigration to Palestine.[5] While American supporters of the Zionist cause could raise money and urge the United States to support the Jewish Agency at the United Nations in 1947 and 1948, French supporters, due to the country's location, could exert a direct impact on the immigration issue. Where Truman could do no more than to urge America's British ally to allow Jews to immigrate, Depreux and Moch had the power to make it happen.[6] They did just that.

The Ministry of the Interior was shaped by its founder, Adrien Tixier (1893–1946), a Socialist who served from 1944 until January 1946 (he died shortly afterwards from a botched operation). Tixier, who had been active in the labor movement, was appointed by de Gaulle as representative of the Free French in Washington, where he served from 1941 to 1943. In 1946 he investigated and then banned three French organizations judged to be antisemitic.[7] Under his leadership the Interior Ministry conducted investigations for war crimes and firings of former Vichy officials and fought against efforts to revive fascist politics. The Tixier ministry and the intelligence services associated with it also developed connections to the Mossad Le'Aliya Bet and were well informed about its "clandestine" efforts to foster Jewish immigration to Palestine. If the French ministers of the interior, Tixier, Depreux, and Moch, had wished to prevent the use of French territory to aid Jewish immigration to Palestine from 1945 to 1948 they could have done so. Instead, through both active and discreet means, they offered it vital support.

[4] On the French Resistance and the Jews see Renée Poznanski, *Propagandes et persecutions: La Résistance et le "problem juif" 1940–1944* (Paris: Fayard, 2008).

[5] On the importance of Paris for the Zionists see Tsilla Hershco, "Le Mouvement Sioniste et la France, 1945–1946," in *Entre Paris et Jérusalem: La France, le sionisme et la création de l'état d'Israël, 1945–1949* (Paris: Honoré Champion Éditeur, 2003), 55–74. The resulting connections and friendships were one source of the origins of Israel's tacit alliance with France, its most important in the years from 1949 to 1967. On the subsequent "tacit alliance" see Sylvia K. Crosbie, *A Tacit Alliance: France and Israel from Suez to the Six Day War* (Princeton: Princeton University Press, 1974); and Robert Isaacson, "From 'Brave Little Israel' to 'an Elite and Domineering People': The Image of Israel in France, 1944–1974," Ph.D. dissertation, George Washington University, 2017: https://scholarspace.li brary.gwu.edu/concern/gw_etds/6q182k25k.

[6] See Édouard Depreux, *Souvenirs d'un militant: Cinqante ans de lutte, de la social-démocratie au socialism, 1918–1968* (Paris: Fayard, 1972).

[7] A. [Adrien] Tixier, Le Ministère de l'Intérieur, Décret du prononçant la dissolution des Groupements, "La Renaissance de Foyer Français," "La Fédération des Locataires de Bonne Foi," "l'Union des Commerçants, Industriels et Artisans français," Paris (June 1, 1945), Archives Nationales Pierrefitte-sur-Seine (hereafter ANP), Ministère de l'Intérieur, La Propagande et la Manifestions antisemites," ANP, Ministère de l'Intérieur, F1a 3349.

Ministry officials were aware of the importance the Jewish Agency attached to Jewish immigration to Palestine. French translations of Ben-Gurion's speeches when he was in Paris in 1946 demonstrate the attention they devoted to his efforts. He regularly spoke to audiences of several thousand on evenings that concluded with singing of "La Marseillaise" and "Hatikvah," the song that became the Israeli national anthem. The milieu of those in Paris who attended Ben-Gurion's speeches was a French version of the pro-Zionist liberal and left-liberal milieu in New York at the same time. At the Maison de Mutualité on July 4 Ben-Gurion praised France as "the country of liberty, of the Revolution of 1789, and of General de Gaulle, symbol of the resistance," and criticized Britain's White Paper and the Mufti's return to the Middle East.[8] In an address on October 16 he rejected British accusations that the Jews in Palestine were practicing terror. On the contrary, he pointed out, Palestine was "the only country in the world where the [Nazi-era] Nuremberg [race] laws are in place, where the law is aimed against the Jews, and where the Jews cannot live where they wish to." The reason the British accused the Jewish Agency of terrorism was that they "wished to get into the good graces of the Mufti, a man who should now be [on trial for war crimes] in Nuremberg."[9] On December 10 Ben-Gurion told an audience of the World Jewish Congress in Paris that a Jewish state was "the only means of saving" the survivors of persecution in Europe, guaranteeing immigration without obstacles, and "assuring a free and appropriate life for the Jews not only in the land of Israel but also in the diaspora."[10]

The Quai d'Orsay vs. the Ministry of the Interior

By contrast to the Ministry of the Interior, and like their counterparts in the British Foreign Office and the US State Department, the officials of the French Foreign Ministry (Quai d'Orsay) focused on the Soviet threat and sustaining French influence in the Arab and Muslim world, and thus opposed Zionist aspirations and Zionists' efforts to bring Jews from

---

[8] Direction Générale de la Sûreté Nationale Direction des Renseignement Généraux, Activité Politique (July 11, 1946), Paris, "La Propagande Anti-Britainnique dans le Milieux Juifs de Paris," ANP, Ministère de l'Intérieur, F1a 3369 Sionisme et questions juives (novembre 1946).

[9] "Traduction du discours prononcé par BEN GOURION David, au langue Yiddish, au Palais de la Mutualité, le 10 Octobre courant: sujet traité: Dans la lutte pour l'état Juif," Paris (October 13, 1946), ANP, Ministère de l'Intérieur, F1a 3369 Sionisme et questions juives (novembre 1946).

[10] "Traduction du discours prononcé par BEN GOURION David, Président du Comité Exécutif de l'Agence Juive au Congrès de Exile" (December 16, 1946), ANP, Ministère de l'Intérieur, F1a 3369, Sionisme et questions juives (novembre 1946).

Europe to Palestine. On January 28, 1946 the French ambassador in Vienna sent French foreign minister Georges Bidault a report on "Soviet propaganda in Palestine."[11] It was essentially identical to the report from British intelligence sent to the State Department three months earlier.[12] It too stated that the Soviet Union had begun to send Israeli agents recruited by Polish security services to Italy, Vienna, and the British and American zones of occupation in Austria. After arriving in Italy "these agents present themselves as former detainees in German concentration camps and declare that they do not wish to return to Poland due to fear of antisemitism there. It is for that reason that they want to go to Palestine. In this way they are trying to convince Allied authorities to direct them to their destination."[13] Now Bidault could read that the mission of these agents was fourfold: foster hatred among the Jews of Palestine of the British, who had imposed the White Paper limits; spread the rumor that the British leaned unjustly toward the Arabs, to the detriment of the Jews; incite the Jews against the British authorities and against the Arabs; and stress to the Jews that it is the USSR that supports the Jews' cause in Palestine.[14]

Depreux and Moch had participated in the political battles that led to the expulsion of the Communists from the France's coalition government in May 1947. They understood that although there were communists among the Jewish refugees seeking to go to Palestine, most of those from Eastern and Central Europe still faced antisemitism in in that region after the war and thus they desired to go to Palestine to survive and build a Jewish state, not to spread communist revolution and Soviet influence. Following Tixier's death in February 1946 Depreux assumed leadership of the Ministry of Interior, and from that position he was able to determine France's policy toward the groups of Jews who were crossing into France with the intention of going on to Palestine. In June 1946 the ministry received requests from the American Joint Distribution

---

[11] Le Ministre Plenipotentiare Representant Politique de la République française en Autriche à son Excellence Monsieur Bidault, Ministre des Affaires Étrangères s/c de Monsieur Mayer Commissaire du Gouvernment aux Affaires Allemande & Autriches (January 28, 1946), "a/s Propagande sovietique en Palestine," Archives Diplomatique, Courneuve, 214QO, Département Afrique-Levant, Généralités Proche-Orient 1944–1952, Palestine/URSS.

[12] C. R. Tuff, "Soviet Agents in Palestine" (November 4, 1945), NACP RG 84, Foreign Service Posts of the Department of State, Records of the U.S. Political Adviser to the Supreme Allied Commander, Mediterranean, "Top Secret" File, 1944–47, 711.9–711.10, Box 2.

[13] Le Ministre Plénipotentiaire ... Française en Autriche à ... Bidault ... (January 28, 1946), "a/s Propagande sovietique en Palestine?" (Translations from the French are my own.)

[14] Ibid.

Committee, the World Jewish Congress, and the Hebrew Immigrant Aid Society (HIAS) to assist the immigration of Polish Jews to Palestine.[15] In July there were additional requests to the Interior Ministry from those organizations for visas for Jews claiming persecution in Poland.[16]

The Foreign Ministry, fearful that the migrants would instead stay in France, was reluctant to become involved. But Marcel Pages, the head of the office of the Interior Ministry that dealt with immigration and passports, argued that France was involved not only because of its fortuitous geographical location on the Jews' route to Palestine but because France was "the country of tolerance and the right of asylum" for communities of Jews "decimated by war." "International morality" required that France should allow Jewish emigrants to spend time in France for "the time necessary to obtain immigration visas."[17] In July Pages met with André Blumel (1893–1973), president of the Federation of Jewish Organizations in France (Fédération des Sociétés Juives de France) to discuss the Federation's request to the government to assist Jewish refugees.[18] The previous month Bidault had been elected president of the provisional government, a coalition which included Socialists, Communists, and his Christian Democratic Mouvement Républicain Populaire (MRP). On July 27 Depreux wrote to Bidault in support of offering temporary transit visas to Jews coming to France.[19] Doing so, he said, would conform to "France's traditions of tolerance and assistance," given that the country's location placed it on "the path of exile of Jewish emigrants."[20]

[15] [Marcel] Pages, la Directeur des Direction des Étrangers et des Passeportes, Direction des Étrangers et des Passeports, 1er Bureau au le Ministre de l'Intérieur et Monsieur le Ministre des Affaires Étrangères, Direction des Conventions Administrative, Paris (June 11, 1946), "Transit avec arrêt par la France des ressortissants israélites desirant immigrer Outre-Atlantique," ANP, Ministère de l'Intérieur, F/7/16088, Transit d'Israélites en provenance d'Allemagne et d'Europe centrale.

[16] F. Blanchaud, Direction des Étrangers et des Passeports pour Monsieur le Ministre de l'Intérieur, Paris (July 10, 1946), "Problem du passage an transit en France, d'Israélites en provenance d'Allemagne et de pays d'Europe centrale," ANP, Ministère de l'Intérieur, F/7/16088, Transit d'Israélites en provenance d'Allemagne et d'Europe centrale.

[17] Ibid. I have translated the French term "Israélites" as "Jews."

[18] Marcel Pages to Édouard Depreux, Direction de la Réglementation et des Étrangères, 3ième Bureau, Paris (July 26, 1946), 2373, "Note pour Monsieur le Ministr de l'Intérieur," ANP, Ministère de l'Intérieur, F/7/16088, Transit d'Israélites en provenance d'Allemagne et d'Europe centrale.

[19] Depreux to Bidault, Le Ministre de l'Intérieur au Président du Gouvernement Provinçale de la République Française, Ministre des Affaires Étrangères, Paris (July 27, 1946), 2405, "Problème du passage en transit, en France, d'Israélites en provenance d'Allemagne et des pays d'Europe centrale," ANP, Ministère de l'Intérieur, F/7/16088, Transit d'Israélites en provenance d'Allemagne et d'Europe centrale.

[20] Ibid.

As a result of Depreux's initiative, in July and August 1946 Bidault, who was also the French foreign minister, agreed to institutionalize the cooperation between the French government and Jewish organizations in France for the purpose of assisting Jewish immigration into and out of the country. While ensuring that the immigrants' stay in France would only be temporary, they guaranteed to provide them with food and lodging while they were in the country. The number of Jews admitted originally was set at 5,000.[21] On August 7, 1946 a broad range of Jewish organizations in France and the United States agreed that the Fédération des Sociétés Juives de France led by Blumel would represent them in discussions with the Ministry of Foreign Affairs and the Ministry of Interior concerning the entry and departure of Jews into France from Central and Eastern Europe.[22] By summer 1946 the French government had entered into an agreement to work with the French and American Jewish organizations in cooperation with the Jewish Agency, and thus the Zionist leaders in Palestine, in order to make France a country of transit for Jewish refugees and displaced persons coming from Eastern and Central Europe and from Allied occupation zones in Germany who were trying to emigrate to Palestine.[23]

In 1945 and 1946 American military authorities in their zone of occupation in Germany were allowing Jewish refugees without visas to take trains to France. French officials did not examine whether the refugees had visas or if the visas they had were valid. Several ships bound for Palestine left French ports with Jewish refugees lacking visas. French, British, and American officials met in Paris in August 1946 to address the immigration issue. The French agreed to accept 8,000 Jewish immigrants from Poland, Romania, and Czechoslovakia who had arrived without entry visas or visas for a country of destination. They were permitted to remain in France "for a period needed to obtain entry visas" for other countries. Informed of this "special regime," British officials urged the

---

[21] Ibid., 4.

[22] Depreux to Bidault (à l'attention de M. Bousquet), Paris (August 8, 1946), ANP, Ministère de l'Intérieur, F/7/16088, Transit d'Israélites en provenance d'Allemagne et d'Europe centrale. The other organizations involved included: Agudath Israel; the American Joint Distribution Committee; the Association of Polish Jews (Association des Juifs Polonaise en France); Comité Juif d'Action Sociale et de Reconstruction (COJASOR); Foyer Ouvrier Juif; Oeuvre de Secours aux Enfants (OSE); Organisation-Reconstruction-Travail (ORT); Union des Juifs pour la Resistance et Lentraide (UJR); the Hebrew Immigrant Aid Society (HIAS), and the American Jewish Committee. The Paris branch of the Jewish Agency was involved as well.

[23] Direction de la Réglementation et des Étrangères à Ministre de l'Intérieur, "Transit à travers la France des Israélites en provenance d'Europe Centrale et Orientale," Paris (August 7, 1946), ANP, Ministère de l'Intérieur, F/7/16088, Transit d'Israélites en provenance d'Allemagne et d'Europe centrale.

French to "frustrate" the efforts of "clandestine emigres attempting to reach the territory of Mandate Palestine."[24]

On August 26 the French president, Félix Gouin (1884–1977), also a member of the Socialist Party, as well as Prime Minister Bidault, approved the "temporary stay" in France of 8,000 Polish Jews. While in France they would be the charge of the Jewish Federation's office of assistance to deportees and refugees. The Federation would also assist their further emigration to North or South America or "to Palestine" if they obtained visas for the country of destination. With the inauguration of this cooperation between the French government and the Federation of Jewish Organizations, the French government was supporting the same Jewish immigration to Palestine that Britain was doing all it could to prevent.[25]

On August 8 Depreux informed Bidault that he had decided to issue visas for temporary admission to France of Jewish refugees arriving in groups of up to 7,000 persons. With the agreement of the French government working with the Fédération des Sociétés Juives de France they would be transported in truck convoys or special trains accompanied by representatives of the United Nations Relief and Rehabilitation Administration (UNRRA).[26] In addition, and very importantly, French consulates in Warsaw and Cracow would issue "collective visas" (des visas collectifs) to these groups of Jewish refugees. These travel documents were valid for three months from the date of arrival in France.[27]

On September 18 Pierre Boursicot (1899–1986), head of the passport office in the Interior Ministry, wrote to Bidault to express concerns about trains coming to France with Jews who "had visas of all sorts which in our view were not valid."[28] One French official working in Germany and Austria expressed "the fear that we are now assisting a massive arrival in France of foreigners that does not rest on any rational recruitment basis."

[24] Ministère des Affaires Étrangères, Direction Générale des Affaires Administratives et Sociales, Paris (January 28, 1947), "Note: Séjour en France en admission temporaire d'un contingent d'Israélites venant d'Allemagne ou des pays de l'est de l'Europe," Georges Bidault, 457AP/124, Bidault Archive, Palestine I, 1945–1947, Palestine, janvier-octobre 1947, Émigration Juive aux France et rapport franco-anglais: affaire Exodus, 1119–1/C.

[25] Ibid.

[26] Depreux to Bidault (à l'attention de M. Bousquet), Paris (August 8, 1946), ANP, Ministère de l'Intérieur, F/7/16088, Transit d'Israélites en provenance d'Allemagne et d'Europe centrale.

[27] Ibid., 5.

[28] P. Boursicot, Direction des Étrangers et des Passeports, Le Ministre de L'Intérieur au Président de Gouvernement Provisoire, Ministère des Affaires Étrangères, Paris (September 18, 1946), "A/s du transit en France d'immigrants israélites," ANP, Ministère de l'Intérieur, F/7/16088, Transit d'Israélites en provenance d'Allemagne et d'Europe centrale.

Further, it represented "the danger that these foreigners are using clandestine channels and that Poles hostile to the government in Warsaw who are seeking to go to Italy are slipping in among them."[29] As France did not have the capacity to enforce surveillance of its border with Germany, Boursicot sought agreement in the government on a plan for "systematic deportation to the French [occupation zone in Germany] of the clandestines apprehended" at the French-German border.[30]

That same day an official in the Ministry of Labor and Social Security expressed the fear that the Polish Jews admitted to France would not leave but would remain and compete for scarce jobs. Therefore, he urged that "these foreigners be admitted to transit through our territory only after having obtained a visa to enter the country of refuge."[31] By late December 1946 the issue of Jewish immigration into France was on the radar of France's National Security Agency (Direction Générale de la Sûreté Nationale). On December 22 it reported that four days earlier 430 Jews had arrived in Lyons after a journey that began in Prague and continued from displaced persons camps in the American occupation zone in Germany. There, they were under the care of the Fédération des Sociétés Juives "until their departure for the United States or South America." On December 19,500 Jews arrived in the area of Marseille.[32]

Mixed French Responses to British Complaints

In a memo of December 31 Depreux opposed suggestions that the Jewish refugees be deported back to the Allied occupation zones in Germany.[33] He rejected the argument being made by both the Foreign Ministry and the British Foreign Office that no Jewish emigrants should be allowed to depart from French ports before they possessed visas approved by the

[29] Ibid.   [30] Ibid.

[31] Le Ministre du Travail et de la Sécurité sociale à Monsieur le Ministre des Affaires Étrangères, Paris (September 18, 1946), "Admissionen séjour temporaire en France de Polonais israélites en provenance de Pologne," ANP, Ministère de l'Intérieur, F/7/ 16088, Transit d'Israélites en provenance d'Allemagne et d'Europe centrale. On October 18 the Ministry of the Interior discussed the issue of deportation of refugees lacking visas of destination with the above-mentioned Jewish organizations: Direction de la Règlementation et des Étrangères, Paris (October 18, 1946), "Refoulement des Clandestines Israélites," ANP, Ministère de l'Intérieur, F/7/16088, Transit d'Israélites en provenance d'Allemagne et d'Europe centrale.

[32] Direction Générale de la Sûreté Nationale Direction des Renseignement Généraux, "Question des Étrangères, E.G. Marseille, 22.12.46, Arrive de Convois d'Israélites en provenance d'Europe Centrale," ANP, Ministère de l'Intérieur, F/7/16088, Transit d'Israélites en provenance d'Allemagne et d'Europe centrale.

[33] "Extrait d'une Lettre addressée par le Ministre de l'Intérieur au Ministre des Affaires Étrangères, en date de 31 décembre 1946," ANP, Georges Bidault, 457AP/124, Bidault Archive, Palestine I, 1945–1947.

French Ministry of Interior as well as from ambassadors and legations of the foreign destination countries. He reminded Bidault that French policy was to give exit visas to those wishing to leave France even if they did not have entry visas for a country of destination; requiring entry visas in an effort to prevent Jewish immigration to Palestine would only add to the Jewish refugees' burden.[34] Depreux told Bidault, "Just as I think that we cannot give preferential treatment to Jews, so I believe that we cannot reasonably subject them to a very rigorous and heavy procedure."[35] Depreux pointed out that in reality French police were only issuing exit visas to Jewish emigrants "on collective lists" if they had entry visas in a country of destination. That requirement departed from the legal norm and would lead to a "risk that foreigners who have been granted the right to transit through our territory could be detained in our country." That is, Jews who wished to transit via France to other countries might remain stuck there due to bureaucratic delays receiving visas. "The situation created would present certain dangers which you see as I do." Rather than argue directly for the right of the Jewish emigrants to go to Palestine, which he knew was the majority's desired destination, Depreux advised against requiring entry visas from destination countries since doing so would delay the refugees' departure from France. He concluded that the procedure requested by the British was "too cumbersome and complicated to be effective and could only be damaging to our interests." The British request for such visas "would only damage our own interests."[36]

Alfred Duff Cooper (1890–1954), the British ambassador in Paris, expressed the exasperation of his Foreign Office with the Ministry of Interior's visa policies. French cooperation in stopping the clandestine immigration to Palestine was "indispensable" for British support for French policies in Germany. British foreign minister Ernest Bevin had told René Massigli, the French ambassador in London, that the British believed that "Jewish terrorists" were entering France in the clandestine refugee stream and then traveling to Palestine. The French Foreign Ministry shared the exasperation. On October 19, 1946 the British had informed the Quai d'Orsay that the SS *San Dimitro* had left La Ciotat with 1,200 Jewish immigrants either lacking any visas or with the false visa destination of Ethiopia. On January 18, 1947 the SS *Merkiak* left the port of Sète for Palestine with 640 Jewish immigrants either without visas or with visas giving Cuba as a destination. In both cases it was obvious that the ships intended to sail to Palestine.[37] Ten days later Bidault noted that

---

[34] Ibid.   [35] Ibid., 2.   [36] Ibid., 2–3.

[37] Ministère des Affaires Étrangères, Direction Général des Affaires Administratives et Sociales, Paris (January 28, 1947), "Note: Séjour en France en admission temporaire d'un contingent d'Israélites venant d'Allemagne ou des pays de l'est de l'Europe."

"despite numerous requests by the Ministry of Foreign Affairs to the Ministry of the Interior, no surveillance has been exercised on the departure of these [boats carrying Jewish refugees] and on the validity of the visas of the persons on board."[38]

In his memo Bidault called on the Ministry of Interior to refuse exit visas to Jewish immigrants arriving on collective lists organized by Jewish organizations until Ministry officials inquired in foreign embassies whether the visas were valid.[39] That same month Bidault wrote to Jules Moch, then minister of transport, with jurisdiction over French ports, that it was important to show the British "proof of our good will" by exercising control over the departure from French ports on the Mediterranean of boats "transporting clandestine Jews whose destination was Palestine."[40] Moch claimed that it was not possible to interfere with the free circulation of navigation as long as the ships met international merchant marine standards. Keeping in mind British complaints about French tolerance for "Israelite terrorists" (*terroristes Israélites*) who were arriving via clandestine channels in Palestine, Bidault suggested that Moch did, in fact, have means of effective control.[41] He could prevent ship departures without a French harbor pilot, and they, in turn, could inquire into the actual destination of departing ships, thereby putting an end to the charade of false passports and false destinations.

On March 17, 1947 Ambassador Massigli in London conveyed the British government's ongoing concerns about French assistance to "illegal immigration" to Palestine and offered further evidence that the British were closely monitoring ship departures.[42] They knew that in the previous week three ships that left France had arrived in Palestine: the SS *Merion* from Sète with 650 "illegal passengers"; SS *Miguel*, from Sète, with 807 passengers; and the SS *Abril*, departing on March 9 from Port-de-Bouc, with 600 "Jewish passengers." The Foreign Office believed that the operation had been "carefully organized" by the Zionists to force Britain's hand and increase the Jewish population in Palestine. They intended to move 15,000 people in spring 1947, and Marseille continued

---

[38] Ibid.   [39] Ibid., 4–5.

[40] Le Ministr des Affaires Étrangères à Monsieur Le Ministre des Travaux Publics et des Transports, Paris (February 22, 1947), "Immigration israélite clandestine," ANP, Georges Bidault, 457AP/124, Bidault Archive, Palestine I, 1945–1947, Palestine, Janvier–October 1947, Émigration Juive aux France et rapport franco-anglais: affaire Exodus, 1119–1/C.

[41] Ibid., 1–2.

[42] Ambassade de France en Grande-Bretagne à Ministre des Affaires Étrangères, London (March 17, 1947), No. 635, "Diplomatie Paris," ANP, Georges Bidault, AP457/124, Bidault Archive, Palestine I, 1945–1947, Palestine, Janvier-Octobre 1947, Émigration Juive aux France et rapport franco-anglais: affaire Exodus, 1119–1/C.

to be the center of these operations.[43] Massigli wrote that "these operations currently benefit from the indirect support of our services. By
authorizing the entry and stay in France of a quota of 8,000 Jews without
visas for their subsequent destination, the French government is making it
possible for these emigrants to emigrate illegally to Palestine." The British
had asked the French government to eliminate the quota, but "we refused
to do so, for humanitarian reasons, which the British government appreciates, but today it is asking us to re-examine the problem."[44]

Sir Harold Orme Sargent, general secretary of the British Foreign
Office, urged France to cancel the quota of 8,000 visas for the refugees.
He sought French cooperation in putting an end to the clandestine
immigration traffic and to the "delivery of fictional visas by certain
Consulates and Legations to Jewish emigres who are trying to reach
Palestine."[45] Massigli told Bidault that the French could not remain
"deaf" to British requests in view of "the responsibilities" that France
"incurs in tolerating more or less voluntarily the clandestine émigré
traffic." It was in "the general interest," that is, of Anglo-French relations,
that France did not aggravate those relations by continuing to facilitate
Jewish emigration to Palestine.[46] On March 21 Duff Cooper reinforced
Sargent's plea with a similar message to Bidault.[47]

If the term "clandestine" implied that the British or French governments were unaware of the details of the emigration of Jewish refugees, it
was a convenient fiction. The British knew that the French Ministries of
Interior and Transport were actively facilitating efforts by Jewish refugees
to reach Palestine. Both governments were well informed about the
details of the Mossad Le'Aliyah Bet's operation. At a meeting of foreign
ministers in Moscow on April 7, 1947 Foreign Minister Bevin told
Bidault that the British government regarded "illegal Jewish immigration
into Palestine" to be a matter "of gravest concern." He observed further
that a "considerable number of such immigrants have been coming from
France."[48] Bevin reminded Bidault that Duff Cooper had made "very
strong representations to the French Government asking them to take all
possible steps to prevent illegal immigrants leaving France," and to put an
end to the refugee stream to Palestine departing from France. He had

---

[43] Ibid.   [44] Ibid.   [45] Ibid., 2.   [46] Ibid., 2–3.
[47] Ambassade de Grande-Bretagne, Paris (March 21, 1947), Duff Cooper to Georges
    Bidault, ANP, Georges Bidault, 457AP/124, Bidault Archive, Palestine I, 1945–1947,
    Palestine I, 1945–1947, Palestine, Janvier-Octobre 1947, Émigration Juive aux France et
    rapport franco-anglais: affaire Exodus, 1119–1/C.
[48] Georges Bidault to M. Chauvel, Moscow (April 7, 1947), No. 1239/40, Ministère des
    Affaires Étrangères, CADC, Cabinet du Ministre, Cabinet G. Bidault, 1944–1948, No.
    30, G3 A, Afrique Levant, 1947–1948, G.3 Palestine.

requested that Bidault inform the French cabinet of "the extreme importance we attach to the prevention of illegal immigration."[49]

The following day Jean Chauvel, the secretary general of the French
Ministry of Foreign Affairs, wrote to Bidault and astutely summarized the
objections from the Quai d'Orsay to the "shameful Zionism" (*sionisme
honteux*) of policies put in place by Depreux's Ministry of the Interior.[50]

The tolerance that benefits this illegal immigration on the part of the French
authorities is a kind of shameful Zionism. It is shameful, it does not want any
recognition from Jews in general and American Jews in particular. To the extent
that it is Zionist, it fosters hostile reactions from the British and Arab governments. One cannot underestimate the inconveniences, especially for the situation
in North Africa, of a poor understanding between France on the one hand, and
England and the Arab countries on the other, concerning the Palestine affair.[51]

Chauvel's note left ambiguity as to whether he regarded Zionism itself as
shameful or described French policy as amounting to a Zionism that was
ashamed of declaring itself as such frankly and in public. There was, in his
view, "no doubt" that by "the simple fact of facilitating clandestine
emigration of the Jews to Palestine," France was making the problem
there more acute. France, or at least the Ministry of Interior led by
Depreux and the Ministry of Transport, were helping the Mossad
Le'Aliyah Bet's plans and undermining British policy while refusing to
acknowledge doing so as a public policy.

The position of the Foreign Ministry was, first, that French officials
should not give exit visas to "Jewish emigrants on collective lists or to
persons with individual passports" unless they were assured by diplomatic
representatives of destination countries in Paris that "the visas of entry in
the countries of welcome were valid."[52] Second, the captains of all ships
entering French Mediterranean ports should report to the Ministry of
Transport, which should then send the information to the Foreign
Ministry. Massigli reported that the arrival and departure of ships in
French ports was being reported in the British press.[53] Both the British
government and the French Foreign Ministry were aware that Jewish
immigrants were seeking to get to Palestine via the Mossad Le'Aliyah
Bet's clandestine route and receiving visas with false destinations – usually

[49] Ibid.
[50] [Jean Chauvel,] Ministère des Affaires Étrangères, Secrétaire Général to Georges
Bidault, Paris (April 8, 1947), "Pour le Ministre," CADC, MAE, Cabinet du Ministre,
Cabinet G. Bidault, 1944–1948, No. 30, G3 A, Afrique Levant, 1947–1948, G.3
Palestine.
[51] Ibid.   [52] Ibid.
[53] Massigli à Affaires Étrangères, London (April 15, 1947), No. 814, Ministère des Affaires
Étrangères, CADC, Cabinet du Ministre, Cabinet G. Bidault, 1944–1948, No. 30, G3
A, Afrique Levant, 1947–1948, G.3 Palestine.

for countries in Latin America. They also knew that the high-ranking officials in the Ministry of Interior and Ministry of Transport must have been aware of this de facto pro-Zionist policy which refused to declare itself as such in public in order to avoid causing friction in relations with Britain and the Arab states.

On April 16, 1947 Bidault wrote a ten-page memo on "clandestine Jewish emigration to Palestine departing from French ports" to be discussed at the Council of Ministers meeting on April 21.[54] He recommended deportation (*refoulement*) to the French occupation zone in Germany "of all Jewish immigrants in France without a valid passport and valid visa for entry into France." The international convention of 1929 and the French law of May 31, 1933 concerning the seaworthiness and safety of vessels needed to be applied to ships departing from French ports on the Mediterranean including Marseille, La Ciotat, Sète, and Port-de-Bouc. More than twelve ships with Honduran and Panamanian flags had left those ports in recent weeks without being examined to meet standards of navigability. That failure was due to inspectors in Moch's Ministry of Transport who were not carrying out the verifications required by international and French law.[55] Bidault noted that the continuation of this situation was harming relations with Britain. France's responsibility regarding clandestine Jewish immigration to Palestine was shifting from passivity and failure to carry out inspections to active "complicity." This was particularly so because the boarding of ships in Marseille and the other ports took place in public, that is, with the full knowledge of the Ministry of Transport.[56]

Bidault's memo proposed specific measures to stop French participation or complicity in "the illegal transport of emigrants in Palestine" that was being carried out "in disgraceful conditions for the human person under the aegis of international 'gangs.'"[57] The Jewish organizations in France should participate only in "normal" emigration and should find a country, preferably in South America, that would receive Jewish refugees. Hence the refugees would avoid the journey in dangerous vessels that inevitably would lead to capture by the British Navy and internment in British camps in Cyprus. But these humanitarian concerns, Bidault warned, though important, were secondary to the foreign policy concerns. Continued French toleration of clandestine Jewish emigration to Palestine

---

[54] "Communication du Vice-Président du Conseil, Ministère des Affaires Étrangères, per Interim au Conseil restraint des Ministre du 21 Avril 1947: Émigration israélites clandestine vers la Palestine à partir des ports français," ANP, Georges Bidault, 457AP/124, Palestine I 1945–1947, Palestine. Emigration Juive aux France et rapport franco-anglais: affaire Exodus 1110–1/C, 2.
[55] Ibid., 3.   [56] Ibid., 5.   [57] Ibid., 6.

had "grave consequences" for relations with Britain, undermined France's position in North Africa, and fanned Muslim nationalism.[58]

The foreign minister proposed revising the agreements the French government had established with Jewish organizations in August 1946 to offer collective visas and three-month transit visas with the following four measures: First, France should ensure that entry visas to countries of destination were valid before the police granted visas of departure; second, Jewish emigrants who entered France illegally should be deported to the Allied occupation zones in Germany and Austria; third, the international convention of May 31, 1933 and the French law of June 16, 1933 on the navigability of ships should be applied to all ships departing France's Mediterranean ports; and fourth, the preceding measure should be applied to the SS *President Warfield*, now in Marseille and awaiting departure with immigrants. If implemented, these four measures would end the Mossad Le'Aliyah Bet's ability to use French territory and ports for its efforts to bring Jews to Palestine.

The issue was joined on April 21 at the meeting of officials from the Ministries of Interior, Transport and Public Works, Foreign Affairs, and the Council of Ministers. The ministers of interior and transport succeeded in preventing the Foreign Ministry's effort to halt French support for Jewish emigration to Palestine. The French government would continue to offer a "collective visa" of transit to Jewish refugees in transit in France, but only after the Office of National Security in the Interior Ministry could confirm that the visas were valid and that the refugees had a country of destination.[59] However, Pages, from the Ministry of Interior, reaffirmed the government's agreement to cooperate with Jewish organizations that had been authorized to aid Jews in transit. In addition, he firmly opposed deporting Jews who entered France; such a "veritable hunt" for Jewish refugees would risk "extremely regrettable incidents" and could "revive in our country diverse movements dealing with the

---

[58] Ibid., 10.

[59] "Note pour M. la Ministère de l'Intérieur, Conference interministerielle qui doit se tenir à l'Hôtel Matignon, Lundi, 21 Avril 1947, à 16 heures," ANP, Ministère de l'Intérieur, Direction Général de la Sûreté Nationale, F1 A, 4710, F7 16089, Exodus, (April 22, 1947). Those in attendance were: M. Felix Gouin, Président du Conseil du Plan; M. Yvon Delbos, Ministre d'État; M. Marcel Roclore, Ministre d'État; M. Jules Moch, Ministre des Travaux Publiques et des Transports; M. Bousquet, Directeur Générale des Conventions Administratives au Ministère des Affaires Étrangères; de haut functionnaires du Ministère des Travaux Publics; M. Marcel Pages, Directeur de la Réglementation et des Étrangères au Ministère de l'Intérieur. On collective visas and the *Exodus* affair see "Note pour M. le Ministère de 'Intérieur, Contrôle de la validité des visas collectifs d'entrée déliverées aux étrangers," ANP, Ministère de l'Intérieur, Depart de President Warfield, F1 A, 4710, 23/745 au 13/9/45, F7, 16089, Exodus.

Jewish question," that is, antisemitic movements.[60] Moch also pushed back at Bidault's requests for closer examination of the refugee ships. He found it "extremely regrettable" that France would, "under the pretext that the ship was not seaworthy," try to prevent immigrants with exit and entry visas from departing. An effort to do so would provoke movements in France that were both "philosemitic and antisemitic." Moch rejected both measures on the grounds that they would increase the number of Jewish refugees remaining in France, and that, he thought, would only serve to foster the growth of "antisemitic movements."[61]

Moch and Pages, representing Depreux, defended the collective visa as a practical method of facilitating the departure of Jewish refugees from France. They raised political and moral objections to sending them back to displaced-persons camps in the Allied occupation zones in Germany and Austria. Checking the visa of each individual would cause an administrative logjam that would keep the refugees in France well beyond the terms of their three-month transit visas and thus possibly foster antisemitism in a France that had not yet recovered economically from World War II. The officials in attendance were fully aware that Palestine – not Colombia or Honduras, as many visas indicated – was the desired destination of most of the refugees. Depreux, Moch, and Pages understood that they were adopting policies that would cause problems for Britain while aiding the Zionists' "second exodus." They waged a political battle using the tools of government bureaucracy and arcane visa regulations. As a result of their efforts, the collective visa remained intact. With the assistance of many winks and nods by high-ranking officials in Paris and sympathetic local police officials in France's Mediterranean ports, so did Mossad Le'Aliyah Bet's "clandestine" immigration activities to, within, and from France. In April, May, and June 1947 ships with Jewish refugee passengers continued to depart from French ports. Depreux and Moch refused to implement the measures demanded by Britain and suggested by the Foreign Office. The lack of implementation was the result of policy, not incompetence. What Chauvel called "sionisme honteux" was for Depreux and Moch a matter of moral and political principle. For them it was a source of pride and not shame, while for the Attlee–Bevin government it was a source of intense irritation.[62] In the *Exodus* affair, the result was British diplomatic humiliation and a major political victory for the Zionist cause.

---

[60] Ibid.   [61] Ibid., 5.

[62] On the British response see Kochavi, *Post-Holocaust Politics*. On British decolonization and the end of the Palestine Mandate see, by William Roger Louis, *The End of British Imperialism: The Scramble for Empire, Suez, and Decolonization: Collected Essays* (New York: I.B. Tauris, 2006); *The British Empire in the Middle East, 1945–1951: Arab*

The *Exodus* Affair

The tensions simmering behind the scenes between the British government and the French Ministries of Interior and Transport exploded into the glare of international publicity during the six-week drama of July and August 1947. All eyes were on the SS *President Warfield*, renamed the *Exodus*, with its 4,500 Jewish refugee passengers[63] As noted above, British sailors seized control of the ship during a violent struggle with passengers and crew, then took the passengers onto three British warships. They returned to the French coast, hoping French authorities would take the passengers off the ships, by force if necessary. The French refused, whereupon Attlee and Bevin decided to transport these survivors of the Holocaust back to Germany. Britain's treatment of the refugees dramatically shifted international opinion against British policy and in favor of the Jews and the Zionist, especially so in France.

On July 11 the *Exodus* left the French port of Sète with 4,500 passengers whom the Mossad Le'Aliyah Bet had brought from displaced-persons camps in Germany.[64] Depreux informed prime minister Paul Ramadier (1888–1961) that these "Jewish immigrants [were] former internees in German [concentration] camps, transited to our territory destined for Colombia." Each person had a safe-conduct paper, a photograph, and an entry visa delivered by the Colombian Consulate in Marseille, as well as a valid exit visa from the Rhône police prefecture. The police and customs officials in Marseille checked the documents and found "absolutely nothing to suspect."[65]

The SS *Warfield/Exodus* carried the largest number of immigrants on one ship in the three-year "clandestine immigration" initiative. Depreux and Moch's bureaucratic maneuvers in Paris had counterparts at the local level in France's Mediterranean ports. In her detailed account of the *Exodus* affair Aviva Halamish notes that Sète had been the point of

---

Nationalism, the United States and Postwar Imperialism (New York and Oxford: Oxford University Press, 1984); and "The Dissolution of the British Empire," in Judith Brown and William Roger Louis, eds., *The Oxford History of the British Empire*, vol. 4: *The Twentieth Century* (New York and Oxford: Oxford University Press, 2001), 329–378. On Winston Churchill on the Balfour Declaration and Zionism see, most recently, Andrew Roberts, *Churchill: Walking with Destiny* (New York: Viking, 2018).

[63] For a detailed account see Aviva Halamish, *The Exodus Affair: Holocaust Survivors and the Struggle for Palestine*, trans. Ora Cummings (London and Syracuse: Vallentine Mitchell/ Syracuse University Press, 1996); and Ze'ev Venia Hadari, *Second Exodus: The Full Story of Jewish Illegal Immigration to Palestine, 1945–1948* (London: Vallentine Mitchell, 1991).

[64] "À propos du depart du Président WARFIELD du port de SETE le 10 Juillet dernier, ANP, F1 A, 4710, 23/745 au 13/9/45, Exodus, F7 16089, Départ de President Warfield.

[65] Depreux le Ministre de l'Intérieur à M. le Président du Conseil, Paris (n.d.), "A/S d'un navire étrangère ayant quitté récemment le port de Sète," ANP, Ministère de l'Intérieur, F1 A, 4710, 23/745 au 13/9/45, F7 16089, Exodus, Depart de President Warfield.

departure for four previous illegal immigrant ships. For the Mossad Le'Aliya Bet, Sète had the advantage of being in the constituency of Jules Moch, whom Halamish describes as "an old friend of the Mossad." Both the Socialist and Communist Parties had strong support in Sète and Marseille; according to Halamish, "clerks at the port, the customs, border control and other authorities were activists in the local branch of the Socialist Party." The party's regional director was "a Jew with left-wing leanings, and a cousin of Jules Moch himself."[66]

The unauthorized departure of the *Exodus* from Sète alarmed officials in the Foreign Ministry.[67] On June 27 Bevin informed Bidault that Britain attached "extreme importance" to preventing "this ship" from leaving French ports. Britain was "extremely upset" that, despite French assurances from the relevant officials, the ship had nevertheless departed with such a large number of "clandestine immigrants."[68] On July 12 Bevin again expressed his exasperation to Bidault. "On numerous occasions" the British government had appealed to France to take "all possible steps to stop the illicit Jewish traffic through France."[69] France had responded that it would check "validity of visas of the immigrants ... before they were allowed to leave France." That included controlling the *President Warfield*, which was "strongly suspected of engaging in this illicit traffic." Bevin was "dismayed" to learn not only that the ship had "escaped from France, but that she had been permitted to embark, according to the reports so far available, with some 4,000 illicit immigrants, in spite of the fact that she possessed a clearance certificate valid only for a journey without passengers and in fine weather."[70]

The departure, which included "by far the largest single shipload that has ever sailed for Palestine ... gravely increases the difficulties of His Majesty's Government," Bevin warned. In view of the Treaty of Dunkirk for mutual defense signed between Britain and France in March 1947, Bevin wrote that the British government "felt entitled to expect the friendly cooperation of the French Government in this matter." How would the French government feel "if His Majesty's Government were

---

[66] Halamish, *The Exodus Affair*, 56.

[67] Direction des Conventions Administratives et Sociales to Georges Bidault, Paris (July 11, 1947), "Note pour le Ministre: A.S. Immigration Clandestine israélite au Palestine. 'Président Warfield,'" Ministère des Affaires Étrangères, CADC, Cabinet du Ministre, Cabinet G. Bidault, 1944–1948, No. 30, G3 A, Afrique Levant, 1947–1948, G.3 Palestine.

[68] Ibid., 2.

[69] Ernest Bevin to Georges Bidault (July 12, 1947), ANP, Georges Bidault, 457AP/124, Bidault Archive, Palestine I, 1945–1947, Palestine, Janvier-Octobre 1947, Émigration Juive à France et rapport franco-anglais: affaire Exodus, 1119–1/C.

[70] Ibid.

to facilitate the arrival in some territory for which the French Government were responsible of a large number of elements calculated to disturb the peace there?" Hence he must "protest most strongly against the facilities which have been accorded to the 'President Warfield,'" and he requested that the French Government "re-admit her to France with all the passengers onboard as soon as arrangements can be made to cause the 'President Warfield' to return."

Bevin further requested "any explanations that can be offered as to how this all came about." He asked why the French government had not denied "the very large quantity of 315 tons of bunkers" [cots for sleeping] which she received." "Why were passengers allowed to board the ship even though it lacked the required navigation certificate? Why had the validity of the passengers' visas not been properly checked?" Further, what "necessary disciplinary measures have been taken as regards those who permitted the departure of the 'President Warfield' in contradiction with the assurance of the French Government?"[71] Bevin's requests and questions amounted to asking Bidault, and French prime minister Paul Ramadier, to take "disciplinary measures" against Depreux – two ministers of the French cabinet – as well as Boursicot, the director of national security, and local police and port officials in Sète and Marseille. In view of the power the senior officials possessed in the coalition government, that was impossible for Bidault to do unless he was willing to break up the coalition on which his own power rested.

Bevin referred to five additional ships then in Marseille – the *Paducah*, *Northlands*, *Bruna*, *Luciano*, and *Archangelos* – that were "particularly suspect." He "most earnestly" hoped that Bidault would "take all necessary steps to prevent these vessels from sailing." The French government should deny them "harbour facilities, materials required for repair, provisions surplus to the requirements of the crew, and, of course, clearance for other ports." Bevin also asked Bidault to "agree to maintain a warship in the vicinity of Marseille with standing orders to stop, while they are still in French territorial waters, any of these vessels which may leave the port. You will realize that only a French warship can take effective action to prevent the clandestine embarkation of illegal immigrants in French territorial waters."[72] In short, he requested that the French government firmly and unequivocally support Britain's efforts to put an end to the Mossad Le'Aliya Bet's efforts to bring Jewish survivors of the Holocaust to Palestine.

Lest Bidault wonder if Bevin was motivated by ill will, the foreign secretary sought to reassure him that the British government had the

---

[71] Ibid., 2.   [72] Ibid., 2–3.

most sincere sympathy for these unfortunate people who have been made the victims of those who seek to acquire a pecuniary profit out of the situation that has arisen. Jews in all parts of Europe are being encouraged to sell their possessions in order to purchase at extravagant rates a passage to Palestine. When it is too late they discover that those who have taken their money have no means of affording them a safe passage and they are obliged, having no resources left, to undertake the voyage not only in conditions of extreme misery but also faced by considerable dangers. It is therefore no less in the interest of the immigrants themselves than in the desire to promote peace in Palestine that His Majesty's Government are using their utmost endeavour to put an end to this infamous traffic.[73]

Bevin's statement, replete with antisemitic stereotypes, lent credence to the very impression he was trying to dispel. He depicted the Jewish Agency and the Mossad Le'Aliya Bet as criminal organizations motivated first and foremost by the desire for financial gain. Bevin depicted the Mossad Le'Aliyah Bet's Brichah, the effort to assist survivors of the Holocaust to immigrate to Palestine, as a large-scale shake-down operation – an "infamous traffic" – that exploited the vulnerability of Jewish refugees for financial gain, and thus was another chapter in a supposed long history of Jewish money-grubbing.

Labour MP Richard Crossman later concluded that "it was the stubborn refusal of the Yishuv to be grateful for [Bevin's] protection and to conform to the plans he had made for them that finally tipped him into overt antisemitism."[74] James G. McDonald, soon to become the first US ambassador to Israel, reached a similar conclusion following a conversation he had with Bevin on August 3, 1946 to discuss the recommendations of the Anglo-American Committee of Inquiry. Following Bevin's angry rejection of Truman's request and the committee's recommendation to admit 100,000 Jews into Palestine – McDonald called it a "diatribe" – he wrote: "His bitterness against Mr. Truman was almost pathological: it found its match only in his blazing hatred for his other scapegoats – the Jews, the Israelis, the Israel government."[75] Whatever Bevin personally thought about Jews and Judaism, his frustration with the failures of British policy in Palestine led him to resort to arguments that repeated antisemitic clichés and stereotypes.

At a meeting of the French cabinet on July 22, officials of the Foreign Ministry correctly observed that some of their fellow officials in the French government had been responsible for allowing the SS *President*

[73] Ibid., 3.
[74] Richard Crossman, *A Nation Reborn* (New York: Atheneum, 1960), 69–70.
[75] James G. McDonald, *My Mission in Israel, 1948–1951* (New York: Simon & Schuster, 1951), 26. On this issue also see Louis, *The British Empire in the Middle East, 1945–1951*, 426–427. On antisemitism in England see Anthony Julius, *Trials of the Diaspora: A History of Antisemitism in England* (New York: Oxford University Press, 2010).

Warfield (the *Exodus*) to depart from Sète, noting that the 4,500 passengers had fake passports given them by Colombia's Consulate General in France.[76] The British ships holding the Jewish immigrants were now sailing back to France in hopes that the French government would, if necessary, force the immigrants to disembark in France. However, Pierre Boursicot, speaking for Depreux, stated that the minister would refuse to send them back to Germany or Austria and would not use force to do so.[77] Tensions between the Foreign Ministry officials and those of the Interior Ministry were evident as the former complained that "despite repeated requests from the Foreign Ministry" the French police under control of the Ministry of Interior had not examined the validity of the collective visas of entry on the passengers' passports.[78] Depreux's policy was that the passengers were welcome to return to France if they wished, but he would not allow the use of force to compel them to disembark.[79]

On July 25 the French cabinet, with Prime Minister Ramadier presiding, decided against the use of force to compel the passengers to disembark.[80] That refusal continued during the three weeks that the three British ships remained off the French coast. Depreux appointed a committee consisting of representatives of the Ministries of Foreign Affairs, Interior, Transport, and Public Works, a public health inspector, a Red Cross representative, and André Blumel, president of France's Federation of Jewish Organizations. Its purpose was to negotiate with a committee of refugees on the ships.[81] Except for the representative from the Foreign Ministry, Depreux's committee was in full sympathy with the passengers. On August 4 Depreux informed Bidault that, contrary to press reports and despite French offers of hospitality, very few passengers wanted to disembark in France. Rather, they wanted to go to Palestine.[82]

[76] Ministère des Affaires Étrangères, Direction Général des Affaires Administratives et Sociales, Paris (July 22, 1947), "Note: A.S. 'President Warfield,'" ANP, Georges Bidault, 457AP/124, Bidault Archive, Palestine I, 1945–1947, Palestine I, 1945–1947, Palestine, Januar–October 1947, Émigration Juive aux France et rapport franco-anglais: affaire Exodus, 1119–1/C.

[77] Ibid., 3. Also see Halamish, *The Exodus Affair*, 102–111.   [78] Ibid., 4.

[79] Depreux, le Ministre d l'Intérieur à M. le Prefet de Rhône, Paris (July 25, 1947), ANP, Ministère de l'Intérieur, F1 A, 4710, 23/745 au 13/9/45, Exodus, F7 16089, Organisation Technique de l'Accueil des Passagères des Navires Britanniques.

[80] Ministre de L'Intérieur, Paris (July 25, 1947), "Compte-Rendu de la reunion tenue à l'Hôtel Matignon le 24 Juillet 1947 à 18 H 30," ANP, Ministère de l'Intérieur, F1 A, 4710, 23/745 au 13/9/45, Exodus, F7 16089, Organisation Technique de l'Accueil des Passagères des Navires Britanniques.

[81] See "We Shall not Land!" in Halamish, *The Exodus Affair*, 112–121.

[82] Depreux, le Ministre de l'Intérieur à Ministre des Affaires Étrangères, à Georges Bidault, Paris (August 4, 1947), "Situation des anciens passagères de l'Exodus 47," ANP, Georges Bidault, 457AP/124, Bidault Archive, Palestine I, 1945–1947, Palestine,

Britain, Depreux continued, was keeping the ships within view of the French coast in hopes that the passengers would decide to disembark, but that was "an inhumane maneuver" that was not achieving its desired results. He elaborated:

This tactic, which seeks to break the moral resistance of the immigrants by straining their physical endurance, is equivalent to pressure [on the French government] to implement disembarkation by force. By tolerating the continuation of the British effort off the coasts of France, the French government, despite itself, allows itself to be drawn into de facto complicity in this cruel game. Hence, it is necessary to end Britain's immoral expectation from British ships off the coasts of France. Allowing the British to continue their maneuver could prove to be dangerous and lead to serious consequences that France should not endorse.[83]

On July 31 the French National Assembly, with the support of Prime Minister Ramadier, unanimously passed a resolution condoning the decisions that Depreux and Moch were taking. "The National Assembly congratulates the French government for its liberal action in the tragic Exodus affair. It asks it to inform the British Government, as a matter of urgent matter of the feelings of emotion which animate the Assembly" and its hope that a humane solution would be found as soon as possible.[84]

The reporting in the French press was overwhelmingly favorable to the refugees. *Le Monde* headlined that the passengers had stated they would choose death before disembarkation. Léon Blum's *Le Populaire* also reported that the passengers said they would not be taken off the ship alive. Albert Camus' *Combat* reported on the hunger strikes of the immigrants. *La Riposte*, the Paris organ of the Irgun, declared that the English were seized by a "Hitlerian demon." The communist daily *Humanité* declared that the *Exodus* had become "a floating Auschwitz."[85] Blum, in an essay on "the drama of the Exodus" in *Le Populaire*, while stressing

---

Januar-Octobre 1947, Émigration Juive au France et rapport franco-anglais: affaire Exodus, 1119–1/C.

[83] Ibid.

[84] "Extrait des Debats Parlementaires de 31 Juillet 1947, Assemblée Nationale, p. 3712, Émigrants de l'Exodus," ANP, F1 A, 4710, 23/745 au 13/9/45, Exodus, F7 16089, Articles de Presse.

[85] Articles de Presse: *La Riposte*, "Deportation a la *Nazie*' de 4,400 Hébreux: Les Anglais Saisis par le dimon hitlérien"; *Combat*, August 18, 1947, front page: "Les immigrants de l'Exodus ont fait hier la grève de la faim pour un jour"; *Humanité*, July 30, 1947: "L'Exodus 47: un Auschwitz flottant: Sans eau, entassés, maltraités, les émigrants juifs, arriveés hier en rade de Port-de-Bouc, ont refusé de débarquer"; *Le Monde*, July 30, 1947: "Nous ne débarqueron que morts répondent les émigrants de 'l'Exodus' au délégué français"; *Le Soir*, July 29, 1947: "Les 4,500 immigrants juifs de l'Exodus 47" refusent de débarquer"; *Le Populaire*, July 30, 1947: "'Nous ne descendron pas vivants!' respondent les passagers grillagées sur les points"; ANP, Ministère de l'Intérieur, F1 A, 4710, 23/745 au 13/9/45, Exodus, F7 16089.

the importance of France's alliance with Britain, wrote that the French authorities had, as requested, authenticated the documents provided to them by Zionist organizations and applied international conventions on maritime safety to ships carrying immigrants in French ports. The French government had followed the letter of its obligations to Britain but did not offer the total cooperation London sought. Had it done so it would have "met resistance from a unanimous public opinion, wounded in its feelings of justice and pity," occasioned by the plight of the Jewish survivors and displaced persons that weighed on a "universal conscience."[86]

Édouard Depreux's decision, supported by Jules Moch, Marcel Pages, and Paul Ramadier, to refuse to use force to drag the Jewish refugees off the three British ships was an important moment in the battle between the Jews in Palestine and Britain. Britain's effort to pressure France to use force had failed. Depreux, Moch, and others had not only infuriated the British government; they contributed to a public-relations disaster for Britain. To be sure, the determination of the passengers on the ships to get to Palestine was the most important factor in the turn of events. Without their insistence on forcing the issue the efforts of Depreux and Moch would not have made a difference. While the Jews' persistence won over French public opinion, the two French ministers had the political power needed to assist the Zionists' cause, and they used it. At a time when Jewish sovereignty was not yet a reality and the Jews were dependent on the help of others, the Socialist ministers of the Ramadier coalition government were responsible for making France, more than any other of the Western democracies, including the United States, the state that was both willing and able to tip the scales in favor of the Jewish Agency and against Britain in the political battle about Jewish immigration to Palestine. Thus, in September, when British sailors used force to drag the Jewish passengers off their ships and return them to detention camps near Hamburg, Germany, Britain's self-inflicted diplomatic disaster became a scandal in newspapers around the world.

The Charade Continues

Despite Britain's continuing objections, France did not reverse its policy after the *Exodus* affair.[87] In August and early September 1947 French

---

[86] Léon Blum, "Toujours le drame de l'Exodus," *Le Populaire* (August 9, 1947), ANP, Ministère de l'Intérieur, F1 A, 4710, 23/745 au 13/9/45, Exodus, F7 16089, Articles de Presse.

[87] Le Ministre des Affaires Étrangères [Bidault] à Monsieur le Ministre de l'Intérieur [Depreux], Paris (August 5, 1947), No. 3724, "Exodus 1947," ANP, Ministère de l'Intérieur, F1 A, 4710, 23/745 au 13/9/45, Exodus, F7 16089, Incidents Divers.

police in Marseille sent detailed reports to the Ministry of the Interior in Paris about the past and future departures of ships from French ports. The ships carried Jewish refugees who had come to France from Berlin and Munich with the intent of breaking the British blockade in order to reach Palestine.[88] In September and October Duff Cooper continued to send reports to the French Ministry of Foreign Affairs (MFA) complaining about ships departing from France with "clandestine immigrants" attempting to go to Palestine.[89] Receptive officials in the Quai d'Orsay observed that since April 21,when the French cabinet decided to intensify examination of visas and the seaworthiness of ships, two promises made had been broken: the *Exodus* had departed from Sète with at least three times as many passengers as the ship's legal capacity, thus violating the 1929 and 1933 laws regulating maritime traffic; and 4,500 false passports and false visas of entry to Colombia had been "given to Jewish immigrants of the *Exodus* by Jewish organizations."[90] Bidault informed Depreux that in October the SS *Pan York* received fuel in Marseille, after which it sailed to Constanza in Romania. There, the Romanian government, "at the instigation of the Soviet government," allowed many immigrants to go to Palestine. It had done so "in order to create political difficulties for Britain."[91]

The Foreign Ministry urged the Ministry of the Interior to prevent a repetition of something like the *Exodus* affair. At the same time, it assured the British Foreign Office that France would carry out careful inspections of the seaworthiness of the ships and examine entry visas on both collective and individual passports supposedly destined for Venezuela, Colombia, and Bolivia. Exit visas would be granted only when the entry visas from those countries were confirmed to be valid.[92] There was no doubt in the relevant ministries in France that the Mossad Le'Aliyah Bet's operations involved the use of phony destinations on travel documents. It was not the genius of the Mossad Le'Aliyah Bet that allowed the system to

---

[88] For example, Ministère de L'Intérieur, Direction Générale de la Sûreté Nationale, Origine: R.G/ MARSEILLE-Insp. TURCHI, Marseille (August 22, 1947), "Depart d'un navire du port de MARSEILLE, ANP, Ministère de l'Intérieur, F1 A, 4710, 23/745 au 13/9/45, Exodus, F7 16089, Incidents Divers.

[89] Le Ministre des Affaires Étrangères à Monsieur le Ministre de l'Intérieur, Direction de la Reglementation et des Étrangères, Paris (October 13, 1947), "A.s Navires suspects," ANP, Ministère de l'Intérieur, F1 A, 4710, 23/745 au 13/9/45, Exodus, F7 16089, Incidents Divers; and Direction des Convention Administratives et sociales, "Note: Immigration israélite clandestine," MAE, CADC, Cabinet du Ministre, Cabinet G. Bidault, 1944–1948, No. 30, G3 A, Afrique Levant, 1947–1948, G.3 Palestine, 222–226.

[90] Direction des Convention Administratives et sociales, "Note: Immigration israélite clandestine," 223.

[91] Ibid., 224.   [92] Ibid., 227.

work. Its subterfuges were obvious and easily revealed. Rather, it was the willingness of the minister of interior and the minister of transport and public affairs, probably that of Prime Minister Ramadier, and of many less well-known or unknown officials in Sète, Port-de-Bouc, and Marseille, that allowed the charade to continue.

From summer 1947 to the spring 1948 the British government sent a weekly "suspect shipping list" entitled "British information concerning clandestine immigrant traffic with the destination of Palestine" to the MFA. The MFA, in turn, sent the lists to the Ministry of Transport and Public Affairs, which had jurisdiction over commercial shipping.[93] The report of September 8, 1947 was typical. Referring to the sailing of the SS *Archangelos* to Marseille, it asked that the French government deny the ship access to repair and harbor facilities, food provisions and clearance to use other French ports, and that it "maintain a warship in the vicinity of Marseilles to shadow the ship should it attempt to leave." In the same weekly report it informed the French that the SS *Pan York* had departed from New York and arrived in Genoa on June 17 and in Marseille on July 4. It provided similar information about the journeys of the *Christian Madre*, *Albertina*, *Archangelos*, and *Northlands*.[94] These reports contained extensive information about the routes the vessels had taken and were likely to take as well as details about their purpose, design, ownership, cargoes, and crews' identities and physical appearance. As such, they revealed the considerable resources that the British Navy and intelligence services were devoting to the effort to stop the immigration traffic.

The reports gave the French government the extensive and up-to-date information necessary to identify and deny access to all the ships being used by the Mossad Le'Aliyah Bet in the "clandestine" campaign. Judging by the continuing ship departures, however, it was clear that the French Ministry of Interior and the Ministry of Transport and Public Works were refusing to do so. Depreux, Moch, and the officials in their ministries did not close the transit centers in the Marseille region, nor did they limit the ability of the Jewish Agency and the Mossad Le'Aliya Bet to function in France. On the contrary, they supported the transit centers near Marseille and, according to Ze'ev Hadari, retained contact with Zionist officials in Paris.[95] Moreover, the files that document the receipt of the British information in Paris offer no evidence of

---

[93] "Question des Carburant, M. Le Directeur de l'Inscription Maritime" (September 8, 1947), "Renseignement britannique concernment traffic clandestin d'émigrants à destination de la Palestine: Marseille Le Havre," ANP, 19790622/51, Marine.
   Procès verbaux des réunions de la commission technique et consultative de la Marine Marchande. 1947–48 1946–49.
[94] Ibid.   [95] Hadari, *Second Exodus*.

cooperation by the French Navy with the British Navy in its anti-immigration campaign.

In short, French government officials were fully aware of the movements of vessels that the Mossad Le'Aliyah Bet was using, but they did not prevent them from sailing or from being fitted out to serve the needs of large numbers of passengers for the voyage from France to Palestine and later to Israel. The Mossad Le'Aliyah Bet and the French government tacitly agreed that there was something "clandestine" or hidden about the immigration campaign when they both knew perfectly well that at any time the leaders of the Fourth Republic could have brought the French chapter of Jewish immigration to Palestine to a halt. Instead, they decided to assist it. It was no surprise that Duff Cooper in Paris and Ernest Bevin in London were exasperated with the policy of their French ally.

All of this was complicated by the fact that it was playing out against the backdrop of the growing Cold War. On December 15, 1947 then-interior minister Jules Moch invited Daniel J. Reagan, an official in the US Embassy in Paris, to his office for a conversation.[96] Moch told Reagan that "as he had already told" US ambassador to France Jefferson Caffery, "while his [France's] Government had won the 'first round' with the Communists," that is, with the expulsion of May 1947 and defeat of strike waves that summer and fall, "victory was not final." He expected "another showdown" in February and March unless the government prevented food shortages, which the Communists would use to fan "another outbreak of discontent."[97] If those supplies arrived, "the Communists would probably find little support" from city workers "to create another incident for the purpose of alienating the support of Americans for the Marshall Plan."[98] Moch then shared with Reagan orders that had gone out from the headquarters of the French Communist Party (PCF) to wage "an all-out attack upon the Socialist Party as being the slave of American imperialism." PCF members could be "assured of further substantial funds from Moscow in this 'crusade' against American 'imperialism' which would have as its ultimate aim either the blocking of the Marshall Plan or rendering it ineffectual."[99]

American diplomats in Paris, whether by following the dramatic public clash between the Socialists and the Communists leading to the latter's expulsion from the government coalition or through confidential

---

[96] Daniel J. Reagan to Office of European Affairs, No. 10080, Paris (December 17, 1947), "Comments of Mr. Jules Moch, Minister of the Interior, on the French food situation and information volunteered by him on activities of the Communist Party"; and "Memorandum of Conversation, Mr. Jules Moch, Minister of the Interior, Mr. Daniel J. Reagan" (December 15, 1947), NACP RG 59 CDF, 1945–49, 851.00, Box 6232.

[97] Ibid.   [98] Ibid.   [99] Ibid., 2.

conversations such as that between Moch and Reagan, were well informed about the important role of the French Socialists in the political battle against the Soviet Union and the PCF. These same Socialists who had expelled the Communists from the government coalition, and whom the Communists were attacking as slaves of American imperialism, were also backing the Zionists' efforts in support of clandestine Jewish immigration to Palestine. For these French Socialists, fighting the political and intellectual Cold War in France was fully compatible with supporting the Zionist project in Palestine. This combination of opposition to communism and support for Zionism, so similar in key ways to the Truman White House, did not lead to a reappraisal of policy in the State Department.

A French Government Retrospective on Jewish Immigration to Palestine

In June 1950 the French Ministry of the Interior commissioned a fifty-page classified report, "Le mouvement de Transmigration des Israélites et la question Israélienne" ("The transmigration of Jews and the Jewish question").[100] Where Depreux and Moch were focused on day-to-day decisions, the unnamed author(s) of this report reflected on the moral and political issues that were at stake in those fateful months. It began with a brief reference to the Holocaust, asserting that the group that was most affected by the war was "the Jewish race"; it had endured an "enormous loss of human life" and possessions. After 1945 the survivors were in a "lamentable situation" and had no desire to return to their former homelands. Zionism had held a political and moral appeal for Jews before the war. Afterwards, however, they felt a "great fear," as "the speeches of Dr. Goebbels had had a terrifying impact on a large part of Europe's population."[101] The great majority of Jews wanted to get out of Europe and go to Palestine.

Great Britain opposed the Zionist option, the report continued, but France, "a country of exile, was on one of the principal routes leading to Palestine." Zionist leaders asked the French government for assistance in "right of passage because they knew, given the political humanitarianism always followed by our country, that it could not refuse their request."[102] The port of Marseille and the social and political climate in France were favorable to those organizing the immigration and who wanted to create a

---

[100] "Le mouvement de Transmigration des Israélites et la question Israélienne," Paris (June 1950), "Transit d'Israélites en provenance d'Allemagne et d'Europe centrale," ANP, Ministère de l'Intérieur, F/7/16088, Transit d'Israélites en provenance d'Allemagne et d'Europe centrale.
[101] Ibid., 4–5.   [102] Ibid., 5–6.

"necessary center of transit."[103] The report recalled the discussions of 1946 that led to cooperation between the Jewish Agency and the French government, allowing 8,000 immigrants to go to Palestine, the United States, South or North America, Australia, and Ethiopia with transit visas – visas of entry and of exit as well as collective visas provided by the Interior Ministry. That system of transit visas continued until the state of Israel was established.

From 1945 to 1947, the report noted, fourteen centers were created in and near Marseille, and the French government placed them under the control of Jewish organizations.[104] From 1945 to 1949 approximately 180,000 Jews transited through France to Palestine/Israel, and of them about 136,000 went through the transit centers in and around Marseille. In 1948, during the first Arab-Israeli war, Jews going to Israel from North Africa also came through Marseille.[105] As of May 1948, when the French government considered visas issued by state of Israel to be valid, voyages to Israel were permitted as part of normal travel. The report acknowledged the contribution of French communist organizations which had supported Jewish immigration and the establishment of the state of Israel.[106] Yet, it noted, the result was not a communist- or Soviet-leaning Israel. "On the contrary, the development in Israel of a socialist policy, resolutely hostile to communism, assures us an ally in the Middle East ... Moreover, the Government of Israel is still counting on the support of France, which it will need to ensure the transit and selection of emigrants to Palestine."[107]

When this report was written, Jules Moch had succeeded Édouard Depreux as the minister of the interior. These left-of-center socialist opponents of communism and veterans of the French Resistance constituted one of the indispensable pillars of the Western alliance in France and Western Europe. They understood Zionist aspirations and the politics of the Yishuv better than did the architects of containment in Washington and far better than Bevin and the British Foreign Office officials both in London and in the Middle East. The French Socialist minister's support for Jewish immigration to Palestine from 1946 to 1948 was, in their view, a continuation of the spirit of anti-Nazism and opposition to racism and antisemitism that stemmed from the legacies of the French Resistance; it also helped to support an ally, Israel, that was "resolutely hostile to communism" in the Middle East. The ministry's

---

[103] Ibid. 6.
[104] Ibid., 7. The names of the centers were: St. Jérôme, Camp du Grand Ahenas, Camp David, Michelet, Eylath, Caillols, Banias, Zeboulon, Bath Galim, Camp Juif de St-Chamas, Hopital Mizra, Hôpital Anglais, Villa Gaby, and Rocquefond la Bedoul.
[105] Ibid., 23 and 32.   [106] Ibid., 46–47.   [107] Ibid.

policy demonstrated that the presence, not absence, of short-term memory of World War II and the Holocaust was compatible with politically effective opposition to Soviet and communist efforts in Israel. In the idioms of French politics, they demonstrated that support for the Zionist project as a matter of politics and government policy had been compatible with non- and at times anticommunist politics.

The insights and policies of the French Ministry of the Interior stood in sharp contrast to the assessments and policies taking shape in the power ministries of war and diplomacy in Washington. We now turn to their discussions of fall 1947, when prominent officials in Washington articulated an Anglo-American consensus opposed to Zionist aspirations.

> The fundamental cornerstone of our thinking is the maintenance of
> Britain's position to the greatest possible extent. The US counts heavily
> upon continued close British-American cooperation in the Middle East.
>> Secretary of State George Marshall to Lewis Douglas, British
>> ambassador to the United States, September 8, 1947

Momentum in favor of the partition of Palestine into separate Jewish and
Arab states received a significant boost on September 1, 1947 when the
United Nations Special Committee on Palestine (UNSCOP) submitted
its report to Trygve Lie, the first secretary general of the UN and a former
Norwegian diplomat. The committee's eleven members plus the African
American diplomat and scholar Ralph Bunche (1904–71), appointed by
Lie as his representative, spent the summer doing interviews, holding
hearings, and traveling to Palestine, the Middle East, and Europe.[1] A
seven-member majority composed of the representatives from Canada,
Czechoslovakia, Guatemala, the Netherlands, Peru, Sweden, and
Uruguay supported the creation of separate Arab and Jewish states in
what had been the British Mandate in Palestine. A minority of three
representatives from India, Iran, and Yugoslavia favored a federal state
composed of Arab and Jewish cantons. Australia abstained. Each state
would become independent after a two-year period during which the UN
would govern the area as a Mandate trusteeship. The two states would be
joined by an economic union. One hundred and fifty thousand Jewish
immigrants would be allowed to come to Palestine. Jerusalem would be
declared an international zone. The Arab and Jewish states would temporarily become UN Mandates with a common capital in Jerusalem. Even
the minority report, as the Arab representatives understood, accepted
that the Jews had some legitimate political place – a homeland, if less

---

[1] On UNSCOP see Michael J. Cohen, *Palestine and the Great Powers, 1945–1948* (Princeton:
Princeton University Press, 1982), chapters 10 and 11; Benny Morris, *Righteous Victims: A
History of the Zionist-Arab Conflict, 1881–2001* (New York: Vintage, 2001), 180–184; and
Allis Radosh and Ronald Radosh, *A Safe Haven: Harry S. Truman and the Founding of
Israel* (New York: HarperCollins, 2009), 207–242.

than an independent state – in Palestine. Acceptance of the majority report by countries in Western Europe, Eastern Europe, and Latin America sent a message of broad geographical support from a range of countries, most of which had no significant Jewish populations. By deepening the involvement of the United Nations in its outcome, the UNSCOP report was an important further step in the internationalization of the Palestine question.

The map suggested by the UNSCOP majority created an Arab area composed of the western Galilee and the hill country of central Palestine, except for the Jerusalem area. It would also include territory on the Mediterranean from the town of Isdud (later named Ashdod) south of Tel Aviv to the Egyptian border, the area later called the Gaza Strip, as well as the coast from north of Haifa to the border of Lebanon. The Jewish territory was composed of a slice of the eastern Galilee, the coast and coastal plain from a point south of the town of Acre to Isdud in the south, as well as the Negev desert. The United Nations was to administer the area of Jerusalem under a permanent trusteeship (see Map 8.1).[2] The recommendations fell far short of Zionist aspirations, but for the first time an international organization had offered a map that included a form of Jewish political power in some part of what was then British Mandate Palestine.

Evidence of growing momentum for ensuring that power appeared on the editorial page of the *New York Times*. On September 1 the editors wrote that they had "long had doubts as to the wisdom of erecting a political state on a basis of a religious faith." Now, however, the question was in the hands of the United Nations. Since the editors believed in "the prestige of that great enterprise," they "would stand ready to accept any favorable UN decision." With the *Exodus* episode fresh in mind, the editors supported the "proposed relaxation of immigration restrictions" and an end to "pitiful shiploads of refugees, carried hopelessly from port to port." They hoped for an end "to bloodshed in Palestine, to lawless killings, to cruel reprisals, to martial law, to the stirring up of hate between those whose common interest it is to work in peace in the same promised land."[3]

Two days later the *Times*'s columnist Arthur Krock reported that US officials in Washington were impressed that both the majority and minority reports "concede great merit to the case for a Jewish

---

[2] "United Nations Special Committee on Palestine: Report to the General Assembly," Official Records of the Second Session of the General Assembly, Supplement No. 11 (Lake Success, New York: United Nations, 1947): www.un.org/unispal/document/auto-insert-179435/; J. C. Hurewitz, *The Struggle for Palestine* (New York: W. W. Norton, 1950; repr. Greenwood Press, 1968), 296.

[3] "The Palestine Report," *New York Times*, September 1, 1947, 18; also Clifton Daniel, "Zionists Pleased by Report: Arabs Firm against Division," *New York Times*, September 1, 1947, 1.

Map 8.1 United Nations Partition Plan of 1947-Map-Question of Palestine. Source: United Nations, Map No. 3067, Rev 1, April 1983; un.org.unispal/documents/auto-insert-208958.

homeland."[4] The Arab states had contended that there was "no good case for a Jewish homeland in Palestine."

[4] Arthur Krock, "For a Jewish Homeland: Officials in Capital Impressed by Accord on Claim in Heterogeneous UN Inquiry," *New York Times*, September 3, 1947, 6.

But now the representatives of ten nations, differing widely in origins and native institutions, have come to the contrary conclusion after careful inquiry, some of it at first hand ... The list [of UNSCOP members] includes several kinds of democracies: former colonial areas that were granted, or forcefully won, their independence from empires; countries within the Soviet sphere of influence; and countries that have resisted efforts to draw them into that sphere. "If this doesn't constitute world opinion, what would?" asked an official today who is among those in Washington who consider this aspect of the reports outstanding.[5]

US officials also told Krock that the UNSCOP report lifted a handicap on Washington's policy regarding this issue, namely the belief voiced in Britain that "local American politics has been the chief animation of the executive and Congress in advocating a Jewish homeland and increased immigration quotas." Now that "the world" had supported the idea of Jewish homeland in Palestine "through spokesmen who cannot be charged with the same motive," Washington's "good faith" in seeking a solution "can no longer be questioned or ought not to be."[6] In other words, the imprimatur of the United Nations meant that the US government would not have to bear the primary responsibility, or blame, for supporting the Zionists in Palestine. If the UNSCOP recommendations for partition into two states received the necessary two-thirds majority in the UN General Assembly, those Arabs who opposed a Jewish state in Palestine would now find themselves in opposition not only to the Jews, the Zionists, or the United States but to a majority of the members of the United Nations.

On September 9 Congressman Emanuel Celler, who continued to be the key figure in the House of Representatives in the effort to marshal support for the Zionists, wrote to President Truman with a copy to Secretary of State Marshall. He contended that UNSCOP's "major recommendations conspicuously vindicate" the position Truman had taken two years earlier concerning the entry of 100,000 Jews into Palestine and accorded with Truman's views on partition and setting up a Jewish and an Arab state in Palestine. It now devolved "on our Government to take the lead in obtaining implementation of the majority report." Doing so would now have the authority of a United Nations committee as well as "the mass support of public opinion in this country."[7] Two weeks later he received a reply from Marshall's office that included excerpts from the secretary's comment on the UNSCOP report expressing agreement with those aspects that received unanimous support. However, Marshall wrote, "the final decision" of the UN

[5] Ibid.   [6] Ibid.
[7] Emanuel Celler to Harry S. Truman, Washington (September 9, 1947), NACP RG 59 CDF, 501.BB Palestine/9–947, Box 2115.

General Assembly would have to "await detailed consideration of the report."[8] That is, in contrast to the Soviet Union in May, Marshall would not commit to supporting the Partition Plan before the meeting of the General Assembly in the fall.

Marshall's noncommittal response reflected the fierce opposition to a Jewish state in Palestine that was finding expression in the US national security establishment, and not only in the State Department's Division of Near Eastern and African Affairs, which had long taken this position. The CIA, led by Rear Admiral Roscoe H. Hillenkoetter (1897–1982), was also quick to voice its concerns. On September 11 Theodore Babbitt, the agency's assistant director for reports and estimates, wrote a memo entitled "Probable Arab Reaction to the Partition of Palestine by the UN."[9] Babbitt argued that the reaction of the Arabs was "the most important factor" in "determining the future stability of the Near East." The Arabs would violently oppose partition and possibly adopt an economic boycott of the USA and UK. They would reorient their foreign policy to the USSR. Fierce opposition would come from Syria, Egypt, Iraq, and Lebanon, and probably Saudi Arabia as well. Therefore, "a pro-Zionist development in Palestine would seriously endanger US strategic and commercial interests." The more unfavorable the settlement was from "the Arab point of view," the more unrest there would be. "Communist activity would increase, and with it, Soviet influence. The influence and prestige of the Western powers would decrease proportionately. The Palestine issue is capable of changing the development of the Arab world from one of evolution in cooperation with the West to one of revolution with the support of the USSR." Western strategic and economic interests would "be seriously endangered and the Zionists would be no better off than they now are in Poland, Romania and the Ukraine."[10]

Conversely, Babbitt concluded, if the solution were favorable to the Arabs, "US prestige and influence in the Arab world will be extremely high and US interests will benefit immediately." A decrease in xenophobia would benefit airline and oil companies "freed from the pressure of local hostility towards what are now considered pro-Zionist Americans." An associated "increase in economic development, and at the same time an advance towards political maturity, would increase immeasurably the value of the Arab World as a bulwark against Soviet expansion." But

[8] Norman Armour to Emanuel Celler, Assistant Secretary, Washington (September 24, 1947), NACP RG 59 CDF, 501.BB Palestine/9–947, Box 2115.

[9] Theodore Babbitt to Charles Bohlen, Washington (September 11, 1947), Central Intelligence Group, NACP RG 59 CDF 501.BB Palestine/9–1147, Box 2115.

[10] Ibid., 3–4.

Arabs would not accept aid "from countries that are committed to a Zionist policy. Consequently, a pro-Zionist US policy will make it all the more difficult to build the Arab states into a bastion against the USSR."[11] Conversely, a US tilt to the Arabs would help to build a bulwark against the expansion of communist influence in the Middle East. In Europe the CIA worked with left-of-center political parties who opposed the communists. Its assessments did not entertain the possibility that a Jewish state in Palestine might be a Middle Eastern counterpart to the strategy it was pursuing with British Labour, French and Italian Socialists, and West German Social Democrats. That is, especially in view of Gromyko's "surprise" of May 1947, the United States could afford to support partition without fear that the Arabs would turn to the Soviet Union, which had done so even more emphatically. The result was a significant intelligence failure regarding the impact of a Jewish state in Palestine on American and Western security interests in the Middle East.

The Eddy Memos

The fiercest opposition came from William Eddy (1896–1962), a former professor of English and president of Dartmouth College from 1936 to 1942 who had recently been appointed special assistant secretary of state by George Marshall. He had served as a Marine intelligence officer during World War II, then as US ambassador to Saudi Arabia from 1944 to 1946, and, just before joining the State Department, as a consultant to the Arab-American Oil Corporation, ARAMCO. His appointment by Marshall symbolized the close connections between the US military and the oil industry (see Figure 8.1). On September 13 he wrote a "Comment on the UNSCOP Report" that presumably went to the secretary.[12]

Eddy's comment addressed two crucial issues: "whether there shall be a theocratic, racial Zionist state"; and "whether there shall be [an] area of self-determination, and an end to outside pressure and artificial economy."[13] Eddy found the Zionist project morally objectionable on both of those grounds. He also claimed that the Zionist state would be "incapable of self-defense. Its indefensible and unprotected frontiers had already been rejected by the Revisionists," that is, the Irgun, a minority in the Zionist

[11] Ibid., 5.

[12] W. A. Eddy, "Comment on the UNSCOP Report," Washington (September 13, 1947), NACP RG 59 CDF 501.BB Palestine/9-1347, Box 2115. Also see William A. Eddy to Charles Bohlen, Washington (September 14, 1947), NACP RG 59 CDF 501.BB Palestine/9-1447, Box 2115. On Eddy see Thomas Lippman, *Arabian Knight: Colonel Bill Eddy USMC and the Rise of American Power in the Middle East* (Vista, CA: Selwa Press, 2008).

[13] Eddy, "Comment on the UNSCOP Report," 1.

Figure 8.1 Portrait of US State Department Middle East experts, November 10, 1945, at the White House after meeting President Truman. All opposed the establishment of a Jewish state in Palestine. Left to right: George Wadsworth, ambassador to Lebanon and Syria; Loy W. Henderson, director of the State Department Division of Middle Eastern and African Affairs; S. Pinckney Tuck, ambassador to Egypt; Lowell C. Pinkerton, consul-general at Jerusalem; and Colonel William A. Eddy, ambassador to Saudi Arabia. Source: Bettman/Getty Images.

movement. According to Eddy, the borders proposed by the UNSCOP report would satisfy neither the Zionists nor those who sought refuge for displaced Jews. "It would solve nothing and would only intensify effort for Zionist expansion." By the same token, Eddy asserted, the proposed Arab state would not be viable, as "a visit to the 'ports' of Acre and Gaza will illustrate." He did not explain why the ports could not be expanded.

Adopting the majority UNSCOP report in favor of partition, according to Eddy, would damage US interests and leadership because it was contrary to the American example of a "non-clerical political democracy, without prejudice to race or creed. It is an endorsement of a theocratic sovereign state characteristic of the Dark Ages."[14] A Jewish state in Palestine would alienate the USA from "the goodwill of the Arab and Moslem world, with repercussions that would reach to Indonesia and Pakistan." Eddy predicted that the Arab League would "promptly ally itself with Russia for survival, as we [the United States] found it expedient to do from 1942–1945." Such would be the "certain effect or our support for the Majority Report."[15]

Eddy may have been the first Western diplomat to equate Zionism with racism, though from a perspective radically different from that of the leftist advocates of the "Zionism is racism" resolution in the United Nations in 1975.[16] But his concerns about theocracy and racism did not extend to the United States. He described his own country, where in the South segregation was intact and the suppression of voting rights for blacks was routine, as a democracy "without prejudice to race or creed." He seemed unaware that antisemitism in American life had increased in the course of World War II.[17] Moreover, he said nothing about hatred of Jews and Judaism in the Arab and Muslim societies or about the openly declared Jew-hatred of the Muslim Brotherhood or the Arab Higher Committee. His description of Zionism as a form of racism that would bring the Middle East back to the Dark Ages illustrated his lack of knowledge of the Zionist movement's origins in reactions against the antisemitism of Europe's "dark ages." Eddy, however, was not a fringe voice howling in the wilderness. His title as "special assistant" to Secretary of State Marshall (indeed, appointed by him) meant that the secretary heard and presumably paid attention to his views, as did the Division of Near Eastern and African Affairs and the Policy Planning Staff. As we shall see, his memos and some of his language surfaced in their policy documents and memoranda in the following months.

On September 14 Eddy sent his comments to the legal office of the State Department. He included a twelve-page criticism with the imprimatur of the Research and Intelligence Office in the State Department that expressed his views of the majority report.[18] Though Zionist

---

[14] Ibid., 1–2.   [15] Ibid., 2.

[16] On the debate over and passage of the Zionism is racism resolution in the UN General Assembly in 1975 see Jeffrey Herf, "The United Nations 'Zionism is Racism' Resolution of November 10, 1975," in *Undeclared Wars with Israel: East Germany and the West German Far Left, 1967–1989* (New York: Cambridge University Press, 2016), 288–316.

[17] According to public opinion polls, antisemitism reached its highpoint spring 1944 as American forces stormed the beaches in Normandy. See Charles Stember, *Jews in the Mind of America* (New York: Basic Books, 1966).

[18] William A. Eddy to Mr. Cleland, Washington (September 12, 1947), "Comments on the UNSCOP Report," in Charles Bohlen, Washington (September 14, 1947), NACP RG 59 CDF 501.BB Palestine/9–1447, Box 2115.

organizations had publicly asserted that a Jewish state would extend rights to all citizens, Jews and non-Jews, Eddy described the Partition Plan as one that would create two "theocratic states." It was thus a "political retrogression." Creating such states "would hardly be consistent with certain basic principles of the [UN] Charter." To prevent an Arab majority in a Jewish state, it would be necessary "to bring in large numbers of immigrants," thus causing a "thorny problem vis-à-vis the Arabs." "A single secular state for all Palestine, where there will be no legalized and privileged majorities and where the individual person does not find himself, by the accident of birth perhaps, an unwilling member of a fixed sect, is more in line with American thinking and United Nations plans and the democratic concept recommended in the [UNSCOP] report itself."[19] Eddy ignored Zionist assertions to the contrary which found expression in Israel's Declaration of Independence of May 14, 1948. According to this document, the Jewish state would "uphold the full social and political equality of all its citizens, without distinction of race, creed, or sex; will guarantee full freedom of conscience, worship, education, and culture; will safeguard the sanctity and inviolability of the shrines and Holy Places of all religions; and will dedicate itself to the principles of the Charter of the United Nations."[20] Eddy, however, ignored the modernizing, anti-racist, and democratic themes of the Zionist movement.

As a practical matter, Eddy argued that Jewish resistance to the minority plan (the one calling for a federation) would "be less menacing to world peace than Arab resistance to the Majority Plan." The argument appeared to rest on arithmetic: there were more Arabs than Jews. They had states, the Jews did not, and oil had been discovered in Arab states. Eddy hammered away at what he saw as the un-American nature of Zionism. The aspiration for a Jewish state in Palestine undermined American "cultural, commercial, industrial, and strategic interests." Jewish "extremists" would oppose it, but there was "good reason to believe that many Jews in the US, as well as in the Near East, would view the minority plan with favor." If the UN General Assembly would make a "firm decision in favor of the Federal [that is, neither Jewish nor Arab] State, it was likely that such Jewish support would be forthcoming and the Jewish Agency would accept rather than lose any chance for self-government." The same, however, could not "be said for the Arabs of Palestine or the Arab world regarding the majority (partition) plan."[21]

---

[19] Ibid., 5.
[20] Provisional Government of Israel, "The Declaration of Independence of the State of Israel" (May 14, 1948): www.knesset.gov.il/docs/eng/megilat_eng.htm.
[21] Eddy to Mr. Cleland, Washington (September 12, 1947), "Comments on the UNSCOP Report," 11–12.

The Jews, in other words, having less political clout, would accept defeat more readily than the Arabs. Realism thus called for favoring the apparently more powerful side – the Arabs – and their rejection of the partition compromise. As we will see, the Eddy memo helped to shape a broad consensus in the State Department and the Pentagon that the establishment of a Jewish state in Palestine undermined US political-military goals as well as its fundamental economic interests in the Middle East.

Soon after the release of the UNSCOP report the State Department received multiple messages from the Arab states denouncing the committee's majority recommendations. Iraq's foreign minister told US officials that if the UN General Assembly adopted partition, it would "mean the end of the UN for all Arab States."[22] *Al-Wahda*, a paper controlled by Haj Amin al-Husseini in Palestine, said the population "will never agree to partition in whatever form" and did "not care what UNSCOP reports or recommends." An anti-Mufti journal, *Palastin*, wrote that "the future of Palestine cannot be decided by UNSCOP or by the UN which delegated it."[23] On September 10 Husseini was quoted in *The Times* as saying that he had expected the report to be unjust as the committee failed to recognize independence as the aim of the inquiry, and it "failed to divorce the Refugee questions from the problem of Palestine." The spring Special Session of the UN had "failed utterly to live up to the ideals of its own charter." Yet he "never expected the recommendations . . . to be so unjust or so ridiculous."[24] The Arab state representatives at the UN indicated that rejection of any partition plan that included a Jewish state in Palestine was a consensus position that extended well beyond the Mufti.

In an address to the UN on September 17 Marshall hedged his bets. He said that the United States gave "great weight" to those of the UNSCOP committee recommendations "which have been approved by a majority of that Committee."[25] The representatives from Egypt, Iraq, Lebanon, Saudi Arabia, and Syria mistakenly interpreted Marshall's statement "as meaning full U.S. support" for the majority plan, and that the USA had moved from having been "neutral until today but that even the State

[22] Lewis Douglas to Secretary of State, London (September 3, 1947), NACP RG 59 CDF 501.BB Palestine/9–347, Box 2115.

[23] Reported in Robert Macatee, American Consulate General, to Secretary of State, Jerusalem (September 4, 1947), NACP RG 59 CDF 501.BB Palestine/9–1747, Box 2115.

[24] Reported in Pinckney Tuck to Secretary of State, Cairo (September 10, 1947), NACP RG 59 CDF 501.BB Palestine/9–1047, Box 2115.

[25] Robert Lovett to Certain American Diplomatic and Consular Officials, Washington (September 17, 1947), NACP RG 59 CDF 501.BB Palestine/9–1747, Box 2115. The memo went to US Embassies in Baghdad, Beirut, Cairo, to US Legations in Jeddah and Damascus, and to the American consul general in Jerusalem.

Department was now following a pro-Zionist policy."[26] They did not understand the extent of opposition in the State Department to the Zionist project and the extent to which the secretary of state shared those reservations.

Loy Henderson's Objections

The opposition persisted. On September 22 Loy Henderson (1892–1996), director of the Division of Near Eastern and African Affairs (NEA) and a leading opponent of the establishment of a Jewish state in Palestine, sent a five-page, single-spaced memo to Marshall in response to the UNSCOP report. In his cover letter he emphasized "that the views expressed in this memorandum with regard to the partitioning of Palestine and the setting up of a Jewish State are shared by practically every member of the Foreign Service and of the Department who has been engaged in work intimately connected with the Near and Middle East." To strengthen his case he included the Eddy memo described above.[27] Henderson's background in the Middle East and his position as director of NEA lent his views added weight. His memo expressed core themes of State Department opposition: American policy about "the Palestine problem" could have "far-reaching effects" on relations with the Near East and "with Moslems everywhere." It would influence American ability "to promote world stability and to prevent further Soviet penetration into important areas" still free of Soviet domination. He regarded it as his "duty" to explain why "the overwhelming majority of non-Jewish Americans who are intimately acquainted with the situation in the Near East . . . believe that it would not be in the national interests of the United States for it to advocate any kind of a plan at this time for the partitioning of Palestine or for the setting up of a Jewish State in Palestine."[28] Support for a partition of Palestine or the establishment of a Jewish state there "would be certain to undermine our relations with the Arab, and to a lesser extent with the Moslem, world at a time when the Western world needs the friendship and cooperation of the Arabs and other Moslems."[29]

Henderson added detail to this last assertion. Arab cooperation was needed for British efforts to find and retain military bases in the region, and for the French to retain their position in Tunisia, Algeria, and

---

[26] Henderson to Lovett, New York (September 18, 1947), NACP RG 59 CDF 501.BB Palestine/9–1847, Box 2115.
[27] Henderson to Secretary of State George Marshall, Washington (September 22, 1947), NACP RG 59 CDF 501.BB Palestine/9–447, Box 2115.
[28] Ibid.   [29] Ibid.

Morocco. Resources in the Arab countries were important in "the international economic field." In "the last two years" there had been a growing Arab suspicion toward the United States. A Jewish state in Palestine could push the Arabs into the Soviet camp and strengthen the hands of the "extremists."

Although the Arabs have in general no use for Communism, they feel so emotional with regard to the problem of Palestine that if an attempt should actually be made to set up a Jewish State in Palestine in pursuance of decisions supported by us, they may consider the United States as their foremost enemy and enter into at least temporary cooperation with the Soviet Union against us just as we cooperated with the Russians during the war against our common enemies. If we press for a Jewish state, we shall undoubtedly weaken the position of the moderate Arabs who are friends of the Western world and strengthen that of the fanatical extremists. Just last week, for instance, one of the moderate Arab leaders was slain in Palestine by followers of the fanatical Mufti.[30]

Further, though the Jews in Palestine had not asked for American or UN forces to be sent there, Henderson assumed that there would be expectations, perhaps from their supporters in the United States, that the United States should send forces to implement the Partition Plan. He thought the plans for economic union envisaged between the two states were unrealistic. The Partition Plan ignored principles of "self-determination and majority rule," even though it included a plan for an independent Arab state.

Henderson also repeated the unfounded arguments Eddy had put forth: the proposals "recognize the principle of a theocratic racial state and even go so far in several instances as to discriminate on the grounds of religion and race against persons outside of Palestine." They conflicted with American principles of dealing with citizens "regardless of race or religion" with a "uniform treatment." Yet the "stress on whether persons are Jews or non-Jews is certain to strengthen feelings among both Jews and Gentiles in the United States and elsewhere that Jewish citizens are not the same as other citizens." The United States was "under no obligation to the Jews to set up a Jewish state," as the Balfour Declaration and the Mandate "provided not for a Jewish state, but for a Jewish national home." Neither the USA nor the UK "has ever interpreted the term 'Jewish national home' to be a Jewish national state."[31] Henderson did not cite any Zionist documents that conflicted with the "American principles" of non-discrimination, nor did he refer to Jamal Husseini's defense of "homogeneity in race" speech the previous January in London. He said nothing about the Holocaust.

[30] Ibid., 2.   [31] Ibid., 5.

Henderson then laid out tactics for the United States to pursue at the upcoming fall UN General Assembly session. A solution required "long and protracted discussions during the course of which the moderate Jews and moderate Arabs would find common ground." That moderate outcome would be undermined if the United States took a position for either side at the outset. The United States should not take "an active role" in the General Assembly debates but hope that "moderates in both camps" would support "[the] setting up of a trusteeship for a period of years which would be instructed to function in such a neutral manner as not to favor either partition or a single state." At some unspecified point in the future, probably following admission of at least 100,000 "persons," there could be plebiscite on the question of partition.[32] Moderation in this context came to mean support for an international trusteeship or a binational state.

The tactical implications of Henderson's memorandum were evident in Under Secretary of State Robert Lovett's memo to the US UN delegation the following day.[33] Though the State Department gave great weight to the majority proposal, Lovett ordered the US delegates to the UN Ad Hoc Committee on Palestine, which began meeting in September, to support those recommendations of the UNSCOP minority report that gave the port of Jaffa to an Arab, not a Jewish, state. He added that the majority recommendation that "the southern portion of the Negev [desert] be given to the Jewish State should be carefully reviewed." As there was "little likelihood that sufficient water can be brought to this area to support cultivation ... it would seem, therefore, that Arab herdsmen rather than Jewish colonists could best make use of it."[34] The State Department approached the UN General Assembly session in fall 1947 with public ambiguity and cool reserve that kept the depth and extent of opposition to partition from public view.

Jamal Husseini Defends "Homogeneity in Race" in Speaking to the United Nations in New York

In view of Eddy and Henderson's association of Zionism with racism and their refusal to address the issue of racism and antisemitism in Arab societies, the twenty-six-page, single-spaced statement by Jamal Husseini on September 29 to the UN's Ad Hoc Committee on Palestine is of particular

---

[32] Ibid., 6.
[33] Lovett to US Delegation, New York, Washington (September 13, 1947), NACP RG 59 CDF 501.BB Palestine/9–1747, Box 2115.
[34] Ibid., 5.

Figure 8.2 Jamal Husseini (left), head of the Arab Higher Committee, greets Amir Faisal Al Saud, chairman of the Saudi Arabian delegation, before the opening meeting of the second regular session of the United Nations General Assembly, September 16, 1947. Source: UN7671882, New York. UN Photo/Kari Berggrav

interest – and historical importance.[35] Now, speaking for the Arab Higher Committee to a committee of the United Nations, he repeated word for word the same racist arguments he had delivered the previous January in London (see Figure 8.2). The same arguments, repeated on those two public occasions, constitute one of the more important but least examined documents of the entire international discussion of "the Palestine problem" in the immediate postwar years.

At the UN, Husseini once again described the Zionist project as an "invasion that aims, by force, at securing and dominating a country that is not theirs [the Jews'] by birthright." The Arabs were simply responding to Jewish "aggression" with "self-defense." The "struggle against the Zionist

---

[35] Jamal Husseini statement to the UN Ad Hoc Committee on Palestine cited in Warren Austin to Secretary of State, New York (September 30, 1947), NACP RG 59 CDF 501. BB Palestine/9–2947, Box 2115. The statement was sent as well to Lovett and twenty other officers in the State Department.

invasion" had "nothing to do with anti-Semitism," which was a strictly Western bigotry. "In their history, excluding those years of Zionist invasion, the Jews have never had a more humane benefactor and understanding neighbor than the Arab." However, the "atmosphere of neighborliness" was "poisoned" by the Balfour Declaration and by "the aggressive spirit it created in the Jewish community which became, since then, the pampered child of the British government. The Balfour Declaration was the germ that Great Britain injected in the body of the Holy Land and made it the victim of an ever-heightening fever." The Zionist claims to Palestine had "no legal or moral basis."[36]

Jamal Husseini drew some conclusions from the Zionists' rejection of the Soviet proposal for a Jewish homeland in the Soviet Union, based in the town of Birobidzhan. The Zionists did not want Palestine "for the permanent solution of the Jewish problem or the relief of Jews in distress. They [the Zionists] are after power, and they are after the central and strategic position of Palestine that neither Uganda nor Birobidzhan possess." Further, "the Zionist organizations and press have exploited and utilized the existence of anti-Semitism in very few countries to reap harvests of political and financial support for the Zionist cause."[37] That was all he had to say about the murder of six million Jews during World War II in Europe. The connection he made between the Jews and power, and what he viewed as their cynical exploitation of the existence of antisemitism "in very few countries" repeated standard antisemitic tropes. Yet neither the State Department leadership nor the US delegation criticized his repetition of this hateful repertoire.

Husseini then repeated, word for word, the implicitly racist argument he had expressed in London and which formed an emotional and political core of his rejection of a Jewish state in Palestine:

This brings us to another consideration which is of fundamental importance to us, not only as Palestinian Arabs, but as Arabs of the very core of the Arab world. The Arab world is a racial homogeneity that extends over the southern and parts of the eastern [sea]board [sic] of the Mediterranean Sea from the north of Africa throughout Egypt to the Persian Gulf and from the Turkish borders to the Indian Ocean.

The people of that vast territory speak one language and have the same history, traditions, and aspirations. Their unity in all those matters is a basis for mutual understanding and a solid foundation for peace in one of the most central and sensitive areas of the world. With these characteristics, the Arab world affords a conspicuous contrast to the nations that occupy the northern [sea]board of the Mediterranean. From the Iberian Peninsula to Turkey the different nationalities and non-homogenous communities have clashed in a diversity of interests,

[36] Ibid., 3.   [37] Ibid., 22.

mentalities, and national aims. This condition created always an atmosphere of antagonism that culminated in a calamitous war.

Moreover, one of the greatest political achievements in the world that served as a bulwark of peace and stability was the fusion of several nations into one homogeneous entity. The United States of America, the United Kingdom and the USSR are all created homogeneities that proved of great service in the maintenance of regional and world peace.

It is illogical, therefore, that the United Nations, the peace-making machinery of the world, should associate itself or lend a helping hand to weaken or to break up an existing natural old homogeneity [such] as that of the Arab world by the introduction in its midst of an alien body as is now being contemplated by the sponsors of the Jewish state in Palestine. If such a political monstrosity is carried out, no sane person could expect peace to prevail in that part of the world. Its existence, no matter how and by whom it is being supported and protected, is bound to become a running sore, a new Balkans in that part of the world.[38]

Jamal Husseini's alternative to the Zionist project was "an Arab state in the whole of Palestine" which would promise to protect the "legitimate rights and interests of all minorities." This was "the only" option that was "compatible with the principles of modern civilization." He would not deign to comment on the UNSCOP report because the United Nations had no power to determine the "patrimony of our people." The Arabs of Palestine, whom he was claiming to represent, would oppose "with all means at their disposal" any partition of the country or delivery of it to a minority. Knowing that "big powers" could crush opposition by force would "not deter us from drenching the soil of our beloved country with the last drop of our blood in the lawful defense of all and every inch of it."[39]

Husseini's statement to the UN Ad Hoc Committee on Palestine, now on the desks of Eddy, Henderson, and other even higher-ranking officials in the State Department, was a ringing defense of racial homogeneity, that is, of racism, and an equally emphatic rejection of a diverse and multi-ethnic, multireligious Middle East. His description of the multi-ethnic United States and Soviet Union as having created "homogeneities" was absurd. His statement offered clear evidence that an Arab state governed by the Arab Higher Committee would view "non-homogeneous communities," in this case, one that included Jews, as a threat to the racial, cultural, and religious homogeneity he valued so highly. This text was striking not only because he delivered it to a United Nations committee only two years after the Holocaust, and Nazi Germany's efforts to create a Europe based on racial homogeneity, had been defeated by the Allies, but also because this expression of his racialized thinking was so frank, open,

---

[38] Ibid., 23–24.   [39] Ibid., 25–26.

and unapologetic. Perhaps because the discourse about homogeneity and heterogeneity, uniformity and diversity, racism and antiracism was not ubiquitous then, as it would become in subsequent decades, this remarkable statement did not receive the attention that it warranted. It made clear, however, that, as the journalists at *The Nation* and *PM* and liberal politicians such as Robert Wagner and Emanuel Celler had claimed, the rejection of the Zionist project by the Arab Higher Committee, the ex-Grand Mufti of Jerusalem, and Jamal Husseini rested on the rejection of religious and racial diversity.

Husseini made no secret of his support for racial homogeneity. Perhaps he was unaware of the racist nature of the arguments he was making. In any case, he presented his beliefs as principles to defend, not hatreds that were a source of shame or scorn. Despite his denials, the antisemitic nature of his argument was equally obvious. His speech revealed a wish for an Arab world that was self-enclosed, xenophobic, and intolerant of difference and thus, in a fundamental sense, antimodern and illiberal. His was a reactionary form of nationalism, one that, like its European predecessors, was inseparable from racism. Jamal Husseini, like other advocates of racial homogeneity before him, argued that it was Europe's cultural and "racial" diversity and heterogeneity that had caused World War II. It was, to use more modern terms, an unvarnished attack on difference – in this case, the Jews as the intolerable other.

Jamal Husseini's views on race were not only a form of hatred. As his explanation of the causes of war in Europe made apparent, it was also part of the ideological framework with which he interpreted events.[40] The ideas about the causes of World War II that Jamal Husseini repeated in New York in September 1947 had been commonplace in government offices in Nazi Berlin. Only from this perspective was it thus "illogical" for the United Nations, an organization formed by the victors of World War II, to foster diversity and seek to break up the alleged racial homogeneity of the Arab world with "alien" peoples. In the eyes of Jamal Husseini, the Zionist project, by making the Middle East more diverse, would foster war and disorder just as, in his view, diversity and racial heterogeneity had done in Europe. While the United States, or at least part of it, proclaimed itself a nation of immigrants proud of ethnic diversity, Jamal Husseini praised it for what he saw as its racial homogeneity. In view of subsequent Palestinian arguments that Zionism was a form of racism, there is a

---

[40] On antisemitism as an interpretive framework see Jeffrey Herf, *The Jewish Enemy: Nazi Propaganda during World War II and the Holocaust* (Cambridge, MA: Harvard University Press, 2006).

particular irony to Jamal Husseini's arguments of fall 1947 in praise of racial homogeneity.

Yet the members of the American delegation which had voted to allow the Arab Higher Committee to represent the Palestine Arabs did not rise to denounce Jamal Husseini's racial justification for rejection of any Jewish state in Palestine. The State Department leaders, not only those such as Eddy and Henderson who repeated falsehoods about equal treatment of people of color in the United States, but also Marshall, the former chairman of the Joint Chiefs of Staff in World War II, passed up the opportunity to make a public statement about the moral significance of the war against Nazi Germany that they had helped to win. Jamal Husseini's statement was not about what he, Haj Amin al-Husseini, and other leaders of the Arab Higher Committee had done during World War II. Rather, it was a blunt defense of racial homogeneity, what would more commonly be called racism, and an expression of antisemitic arguments delivered to an organization founded on the rejection of those hatreds. It is true that the American reckoning with the legacies of white racism was still in its infancy, yet the official silence in the face of Husseini's text only two years after the Holocaust was, in that sense, not surprising. That said, it represented a failure of moral judgment and of cultural understanding and interpretation, all of which reinforced the strategic blunder that the State Department was in the process of implementing.

The Pentagon Talks

What became known as the Pentagon talks were a crucial event in the gathering Anglo-American political and diplomatic counteroffensive against Zionist goals. At a meeting in the last two weeks in October 1947 in Washington, American and British military and diplomatic officials discussed the implications of the developing Cold War with the Soviet Union for security policy in the Mediterranean and the Middle East. Reports about Soviet influence in Greece, Turkey, and Iran, Soviet efforts to infiltrate agents into the Jewish immigration to Palestine, Britain's public diplomacy fiasco in the *Exodus* affair, and growing political momentum around the world in favor of partition in Palestine formed the context for this important effort to clarify Anglo-American policy and strategy. The purpose of the talks was to discuss the strategic implications of the policy of the containment of communism for American and British interests in the Mediterranean and the Middle East. One of the organizers and leading participants in the Pentagon talks was George Kennan. On January 24, 1947, three days after Truman appointed him secretary of state, George Marshall had appointed Kennan to be the first director of the Policy Planning Staff, a new unit within the State Department for review and planning of national security policy and strategy. Marshall had read Kennan's "Long Telegram" of February 1946 and heard praise for him from US ambassador Walter Bedell Smith (1895–1961) in Moscow, as well as from Secretary of the Navy James Forrestal.[41]

On September 9 Bevin had met in London with Loy Henderson and the American ambassador to Great Britain, Lewis Douglas (1894–1974). The foreign secretary expressed his frustration with the support the Zionists had been receiving in American politics and in the Truman White House.[42] Truman's statements in favor of admitting 100,000 Jews into Palestine had "a destructive effect on our negotiations," that is, Bevin's failing effort to convince Arabs and Jews to accept a binational state in Palestine with a continued British presence. Bevin told the Americans that it was "no secret that the terrorists in Palestine have received the bulk of their financial and moral support from the United States," that "most of the ships" used to "smuggle illegal immigrants into Palestine have been purchased, outfitted and financed in the United States." Organizations based in the United States had "carried on extensive publicity campaigns with the purpose of encouraging the Palestinian terrorists and the smugglers of illegal immigrants and of discrediting the attempts to maintain law and order. The American government has to an extent emboldened these activities by exempting from income tax donations to organizations so engaged." For nearly two years Britain had tried "without success . . . to prevail upon the American government to take steps to prevent American encouragement of terrorists and illegal activities in Palestine."[43]

Bevin's term "Palestinian terrorists" was a reference to the Jews. He made no distinction between the Haganah, which rejected terrorism, and the Irgun, which employed it. Rather than express empathy for survivors of the Holocaust, he referred to them only as "illegal immigrants." He registered his great irritation both with support for Zionist activities in American politics and with the US government for not doing enough to stop Jewish immigration to Palestine and for giving tax exemptions to American organizations that supported Zionist activities in Palestine. American public and White House support for the Zionist cause had become a source of friction within the Anglo-American alliance.

[41] On Marshall's decision see John Lewis Gaddis, *George F. Kennan: An American Life* (New York: Penguin, 2012), 252–253.

[42] Loy Henderson, "Annex 12: Memorandum of Conversation: British Policies and Principles in the Near East" (September 9, 1947), NACP RG 59, General Records of the Department of State, Policy Planning Staff/Council, Area Files, 1947–1962, From 1947–53 Europe, East To: 1947–53 Near and Middle East, Box 7 (hereafter RG 59 PPS Staff/Council, Area Files 1947–1962).

[43] Ibid.

However, Britain's arguments found a more sympathetic reception in the State Department and the Pentagon than they did in the White House.

The Pentagon talks were crucial for that warm reception. On October 9 the Pentagon talks planning group, which included Kennan and Henderson, concluded that previous US decisions to "resist overt Soviet aggression against Turkey should apply with equal force to the Eastern Mediterranean, including Italy, Greece, and Iran as well as Turkey."[44] Past refusal to offer military assistance to Egypt "might be replaced by an indication of a more cooperative attitude on our part as a means of reinforcing our diplomatic representations to the Egyptians, with a view to inducing them to become more receptive to a mutual assistance pact with the British."[45] More attention should be given to "the sheikdoms, sultanates, etc. in Southeastern Arabia, south of the Persian Gulf, where oil development might be tied up with the installation of 'ghost' airfields, which would provide defense in depth and at the same time be accessible by sea." The "effective use of Trans-Jordan as a base will be vitally affected by its accessibility to the Mediterranean littoral via Palestine. This, in turn, makes of particular importance such final decisions as may be made regarding the allocations of territory to the Arabs and Jews under the proposed partition plan." Finally, "any plan for Palestine which might give the Russians a foot in the door in that area would be dangerous and should be avoided."[46] Transjordan, linked as it was to Britain, should have access to the Mediterranean coast, and "the Russians" should be kept out of any plan for the future of Palestine.

An impressive list of British and American diplomats and military leaders joined Kennan and Henderson, including Robert A. Lovett (1895–1986), deputy secretary of state, and Lord Inverchapel (1882–1951), the British ambassador to Washington, both of whom were present at the opening and closing meetings (see Figure 8.3).[47] The participants prepared and

---

[44] "Memorandum of Conversation: Discussion prior to talks with the British on the Eastern Mediterranean and Middle East" (October 9, 1947), NACP RG 59 PPS Staff/Council, Area Files 1947–1962, Box 7. For a summary of American-British preparations for joint talks that came to be known as "the Pentagon talks," see "Memorandum Prepared in the Department of State," Washington (n.d.), NEA Files: Lot 55-D36, *Foreign Relations of the United States* (hereafter *FRUS*), 1947, *The Near East and Africa*, vol. 5.

[45] "Memorandum of Conversation: Discussion prior to talks with the British on the Eastern Mediterranean and Middle East" (October 9, 1947), 2.

[46] Ibid., 3.

[47] "General Statement by the American Group, Top Secret," Washington (n.d.), NEA Files: Lot 55-D36, *FRUS*, 1947, vol. 5, 582–583. The participants were: Loy W. Henderson, director, Division of Near Eastern and African Affairs; John D. Hickerson, director, Office of European Affairs; George F. Kennan, director, Policy Planning Staff; Raymond A. Hare, chief, Division of South Asian Affairs; Edward T. Wailes, chief, Division of British Commonwealth Affairs; Vice-Admiral Forrest Sherman, deputy

Figure 8.3 Under Secretary of State Robert A. Lovett (left) and the director of the US State Department Policy Planning Staff George F. Kennan in conversation, September 6, 1947, in the weeks before the Pentagon talks. Source: Thomas D. Mcavoy/The LIFE Picture Collection/Getty Images.

discussed twenty-five position papers on the nature and coordination of British and American policy regarding Greece, Palestine, Egypt, Cyrenaica (Libya), Transjordan, Iraq, Iran, Kuwait, Cyprus, Saudi Arabia, Turkey, Ethiopia, Afghanistan, French North Africa, Bahrain, Oman, Qatar, and Yemen; and American and British economic, political, and military interests in those countries. The central issue of the talks concerned how Britain and the United States should coordinate their efforts to deter, contain, or push back against communist and Soviet influence in the Mediterranean and the Middle East.

chief of naval operations; Lieutenant General Lauris Norstad, director of plans and operations, General Staff, US Army; and Major General A. M. Gruenther, United States Army. The British participants included John Balfour, British minister, British Embassy, Washington; M. R. Wright, assistant under-secretary of state, Foreign Office, London; Mr. W. D. Allen, British Embassy, Washington; Mr. T. E. Bromley, first secretary, British Embassy, Washington; Admiral Sir Henry Moore; Air Chief Marshal Sir Guy Garrod; General Sir William Morgan; members of the British Joint Staff Mission, Washington; Lieutenant General Sir Leslie Hollis, chief of staff to the minister of defence; and Air Vice-Marshall R. M. Foster, assistant chief of the Air Staff (Policy).

Figure 8.4 US secretary of state George Marshall (left), and British foreign secretary Ernest Bevin (center), at the United Nations conference at the Palais de Chaillot, Paris, October 16, 1948. Source: Bert Hardy/Picture Post/Hulton Archive/Getty Images.

Toward that end, the Americans reported that the US Joint Chiefs of Staff had expressed alarm that Britain's decision to withdraw troops from Greece "would surely result, in their opinion, in a marked deterioration of the Anglo-American overall strategic position in the Mediterranean and might will provoke a critical situation in Greece itself ... At present the US and Great Britain stand together in Greece on a common front against Communist aggression. Should the British Govt withdraw from this position, the mere act of withdrawal would create a distinct atmosphere of disruption and heightened crisis."[48] Marshall shared their concern. On September 8 he had told Douglas in London to assure Bevin that the "fundamental cornerstone of our thinking is the maintenance of Britain's position to the greatest possible extent" in the Middle East (see Figure 8.4).[49] Four days later, in another memo to Douglas, Marshall added that British withdrawal from Greece would break "the common front" of the

---

[48] Ibid., 2.

[49] Secretary of State George Marshall to American Ambassador [Lewis] Douglas, "Material for Use in Talks with British Concerning Eastern Mediterranean, and Near and Middle East, Annex 11 (September 8, 1947) For the Ambassador from the Secretary," NACP RG 59 PPS Staff/Council, Area Files 1947–1962, Box 7.

US and British stand "against communist aggression," and cause "public resentment" in the United States which, in turn, "could prejudice this nation's support for continued aid to Britain and Europe under the Marshall Plan."[50]

In a position paper prepared for the Pentagon talks the American participants had expressed concern that a broader British withdrawal would create a power vacuum into which the Soviet Union and communist organizations would move. The main US objective was to prevent "great power ambitions and local discontents and jealousies from developing into open conflict which might eventually lead to a third world war."[51] One of those "local discontents and jealousies" was "the Palestine problem."

The essential fact is that because of clear Soviet aspirations in the Middle East which, if fulfilled, would have a disastrous effect not only on American interests in the area but on our general position vis-à-vis the Soviet Union, it is essential that Soviet expansion in that area be contained. Given our heavy commitments elsewhere and Britain's already established position in the area, it is our strong feeling that the British should continue to maintain primary responsibility for military security in that area ... We have already given them [the British] assurance that the cornerstone of our thinking is to maintain the British position in the Middle East as a whole, taking into account popular sentiment in the countries of the area and external pressures and influences which might be brought to bear upon them.[52]

Yet, as the Zionists wanted to replace the British presence in Palestine with an independent Jewish state, they threatened what Marshall called "the cornerstone" of American thinking regarding the Middle East. In view of the Soviet threat and the limits of British capabilities, according to the paper's authors, it was necessary to expand American activity in the region beyond the past protection of American philanthropic and missionary activities in order to take "full cognizance of the tremendous value of this area as a highway by sea, land and air between the East and West," of its "great mineral wealth," and the "serious consequences" that would develop "if the rising nationalism of the peoples of the Middle East should

---

[50] Marshall to Douglas, "Annex 13: No. 3970, For the Ambassador" (September 12, 1947), "Material for Use in Talks with British Concerning Eastern Mediterranean, and Near and Middle East, Annex 11 (September 8, 1947) For the Ambassador from the Secretary," NACP RG 59 PPS Staff/Council, Area Files 1947–1962, Box 7.

[51] "Part 2: The British and American Positions, Material for Use in Talks with British Concerning Eastern Mediterranean, and Near and Middle East," Annex 11 (September 8, 1947), For the Ambassador from the Secretary," NACP RG 59 PPS Staff/Council, Area Files 1947–1962, Box 7, 6. Also in *FRUS*, 1947, vol. 5, 513–514.

[52] "Memorandum Prepared in the Department of State, Top Secret, The American Position," Washington (n.d.), NEA Files: Lot 55-D36, *FRUS*, 1947, vol. 5, 7.

harden in a mold of hostility to the West." The United States should promote political and economic development of the Middle East and the principles of the United Nations. "In the implementation of such policy the implications of recently and clearly demonstrated Soviet expansionist aspirations in the Middle East obviously need no elaboration."[53] Soviet interest in Palestine, along with its activities in Greece, Turkey, and Iran, were evidence of Soviet "expansionist" policy.

The American discussants at the Pentagon talks implicitly affirmed the concerns raised in this paper, concluding that "the security of the Eastern Mediterranean and of the Middle East is vital to the security of the United States." The security of that area "would be jeopardized if the Soviet Union should succeed in its efforts to obtain control of any of the following countries: Italy, Greece, Turkey, or Iran." To prevent that from happening, the United States "should be prepared to make full use of its political, economic, and, if necessary, military power in such manner as may be found most effective."[54] Further, such an expansion of American engagement in the region would be "unrealistic" unless Britain retained its current "strong strategic, political and economic position in the Middle East and Eastern Mediterranean, and unless they and ourselves follow parallel policies in that area." Last, "one of the greatest dangers to world peace" could be "the failure of the Soviet Union to understand the extent to which the United States is prepared to go in order to maintain the security of the Eastern Mediterranean and the Middle East," so the US government should make that determination evident "in a firm but nonprovocative manner."[55] The clear policy implication of pursuing "parallel" policies with Britain to counter Soviet efforts in the region was to support Britain's opposition to the Zionist project in Palestine.

Raymond Hare (1901–94), chief of the State Department's South Asia Division, offered the following apocalyptic assessment to the Pentagon talks of how vital it was for American national security to counter Soviet influence in the Eastern Mediterranean and the Middle East. If the Eastern Mediterranean and the Middle East fell "under Soviet domination, a process of deterioration would thereby be initiated" which, "if not successfully resisted, would constitute a disastrous blow to the preservation of world peace." Indeed, for the United States that "would mean a retreat to the Western Hemisphere" and "the prospect of war of attrition that would spell the end of the American way of life." Britain would be

---

[53] Ibid.

[54] "Memorandum Prepared in the Department of State, Top Secret, The American Paper," (Washington) (n.d.), *FRUS*, 1947, vol. 5, 575–576.

[55] Ibid., 576.

isolated and "subjected to the full impact of a Soviet attack directed from Europe ... Soviet domination of the Eastern Mediterranean and the Middle East would certainly spell the end of the United Nations in anything approaching its present form and concept."[56]

In a separate memo on "The Special Role of the British," Hare added that they "should continue to maintain primary responsibility for the defense of the Eastern Mediterranean and the Middle East as part of an overall concept of resistance to Soviet aggression." To do so, the British "should have bases from which to operate in time of emergency" and thus good relations "of a long-term nature with countries in the area." While the United States should not "blindly follow British policy ... the basic nature of our relationship should be recognition of the common problem of maintaining security" in the region, given Britain's "special responsibility in meeting that problem; and a parallel effort to work together" in the interests of the USA, the UK, and the countries in the area.[57] Following Hare's logic, Zionist efforts to end the British Mandate in Palestine and create a Jewish state there could lead to the "end of the American way of life" and a Britain yet again isolated and fighting a Europe dominated by a hostile power.

The logical implication of "the cornerstone" of American policy of support for the British position in the Middle East was to share Britain's anti-Zionist stance. Although Western policy in Western Europe encompassed left-of-center but anticommunist political parties in Britain, France, Italy, Belgium, the Netherlands, and West Germany, the participants in the Pentagon talks did not envision a similar role for the left-of-center Zionists who led the Jewish Agency in Palestine. It was a peculiar neglect in view of the opportunity created by Soviet support voiced at the UN in May for the Partition Plan, and thus separate Jewish and Arab states.

In a memo to Secretary Marshall on November 14, Bedell Smith in Moscow added his understanding of Soviet policy to buttress the link between the Palestine matter and the Soviet and communist issue. He interpreted Soviet support for partition expressed at the UN in May as "deliberately calculated to ensure unsettlement rather than settlement, and to create maximum difficulties for British and Americans in Near East."[58] The Kremlin, he wrote, had reached two conclusions. First,

---

[56] Raymond A. Hare, "Memorandum by the Chief of the Division of South Asian Affairs (Hare) Vital Character of Security of the Eastern Mediterranean and the Middle East to the Security of the United States," *FRUS*, 1947, vol. 5, 576–577.

[57] Ibid., 579.

[58] "The Ambassador in the Soviet Union (Smith) to the Secretary of State," Moscow (November 14, 1947), *FRUS*, 1947, vol. 5: https://history.state.gov/historicaldocuments/frus1947v05/d871.

Europe and colonial areas were more critical and considerably "'softer' for Soviet exploitation than the 'harder' Arab East." The latter had not been politically or economically shaken by World War II. It was shielded by the United States's "firm US stand in Greece, Turkey and Iran," and was associated with "strong US and British interests and commitments." Further, the Arab states were "controlled by [a] feudal anti-Communist ruling class" that was "unlikely to open doors to Soviet penetration." Second, "in view [of the] weakness [of] indigenous Communist movements, Jews and other minority groups provide [the] Kremlin's only immediately useful tool to 'soften up' [the] area for eventual straight Communist cultivation."[59]

Bedell Smith, who went on to become director of the Central Intelligence Agency in 1950, told Marshall that if the UN accepted the majority recommendations of the UNSCOP report, the Soviet Union would be able to secure "appropriate" implementation measures to ensure adoption of the Partition Plan. That in turn would secure Britain's withdrawal and "their replacement by other great-power influence." The result would be launching an "unsettling and disruptive Jewish-Arab conflict which could be kept going indefinitely by covert Soviet aid and incitement to both sides through local Communist parties who will be heavily reinforced by Communist indoctrinated emigrants from Eastern Europe," thereby "threatening and damaging major US and British interests in an area where USSR has nothing to lose."[60] In a remarkably prescient observation, Bedell Smith added that, "given shortness of man's memory and flexibility of Soviet tactics, [the] Kremlin could quickly recapture Arab good will by a sudden reversal position if and when its interests should so dictate."[61] The memo echoed the consensus that had emerged in the aftermath of the Pentagon talks. The Arab world, governed as it was by a "feudal anti-communist ruling class," was less vulnerable to Soviet penetration than were Europe and Asia. Yet "Jews and other minority groups" – if they were to form a Jewish state in Palestine – would help to "soften up" the region as "Communist indoctrinated emigrants from Eastern Europe" helped to undermine US and British interests in the Middle East.

On November 18, 1947 Marshall sent the results of the Pentagon talks to Admiral Sidney Souers, executive secretary of the National Security Council (NSC), along with his recommendation that the NSC approve its proposals. Its key conclusions were that the security of the Eastern Mediterranean and the Middle East was "vital to the security of the United States," and that the region's security "would be jeopardized if

[59] Ibid.   [60] Ibid.   [61] Ibid.

the Soviet Union should succeed in its efforts to obtain control" of "Italy, Greece, Turkey, or Iran." Hence the United States should "assist in maintaining the territorial integrity and independence" of those countries with recourse to its political, economic, "and if necessary, military power," but only after exhausting diplomatic avenues, including the United Nations. Yet "it would be unrealistic" for the United States to "carry out such a policy unless the British maintain their strong strategic, political and economic position in the Middle East and Eastern Mediterranean, and unless they and ourselves follow parallel policies in that area."[62] Marshall endorsed a policy of mutually reinforcing and parallel tracks of American and British interests in the Middle East that both opposed Soviet advances and maintained British presence to the extent possible. Following the logic of "the cornerstone" of American policy that had emerged from the Pentagon talks, by calling for an end to British rule in Palestine, those working for a Jewish state in Palestine posed a threat to the national security interests of the United States as well. This fundamental strategic perspective was to shape the views of the Departments of State and Defense and the CIA throughout the key period of events in the United States, Europe, and Palestine/Israel in 1947–8. On November 24, 1947 Under Secretary of State Lovett sent the Pentagon talks recommendations to President Truman. By December 4, 1947 Truman had informed Marshall that he approved as well.[63] His decision followed logically from the fact that there was much in the Pentagon talks' recommendations of fall 1947 that echoed the themes of the Truman Doctrine he had articulated the previous March.

The American and British participants in the Pentagon talks added a discussion of "Subversive Activities in the Middle East."[64] They had communists, not ex-Nazis, in mind. The sources of possible support for communism included social and economic conditions aggravated by World War II; "reactionary regimes" in the Arab countries; tension over Palestine; "Arab respect for Soviet power"; and a Muslim minority in the Soviet Union. "On the other hand, Communism was not widespread in

---

[62] Sec. State George Marshall to Admiral Sidney Souers (November 18, 1947), "Enclosure A: Documents Resulting from Conversations with the British in regard to the Eastern Mediterranean and the Middle East" (November 18, 1947), NACP RG 59 PPS Staff/ Council, Area Files 1947–1962, Box 7.

[63] Ibid.

[64] "'Statement by the United States and the United Kingdom Groups: The Problem, Subversive Activities in the Middle East: The Pentagon Talks of 1947' Between the United States and the United Kingdom Concerning the Middle East and the Eastern Mediterranean," FRUS, 1947, vol. 5, 610–611: http://digicoll.library.wisc.edu/cgi-bin/ FRUS/FRUS-idx?type=goto&id=FRUS.FRUS1947v05&isize=M&submit=Go+to +page&page=610.

the Middle East and the Moslem religion was not favorable to it." It was a factor in Lebanon, Egypt, and Iran, but not in Transjordan, Saudi Arabia, or Yemen. The participants agreed that "all possible efforts should be made to combat Communism in the Middle East by measures directed towards the improvement of the social and economic conditions of the peoples of the area."[65] As the Arab societies appeared resistant to communist influence, the focus of concern on "subversive activities" in the region logically turned to the possible Jewish state in Palestine and its potential negative impact on Western-Arab relations. Again, the paper associated the Zionist project with Soviet and communist expansion in the Middle East.

In the weeks preceding the vote on the Partition Resolution at the UN, additional conversations took place between members of the Planning Staff and the British Foreign Office regarding policy in the Middle East. As noted, Loy Henderson, a key participant in the Pentagon talks, was a leading opponent of the establishment of a Jewish state in Palestine. Kennan told Lovett that "everyone concerned, on our side and on the British side, was deeply impressed with Henderson's mastery of the subjects under discussion."[66] On November 24 Lovett sent President Truman a memo "resulting from conversations with the British in regard to the Eastern Mediterranean and the Middle East," and approved by the NSC. "American and British military advisers," he said, had concluded that "the security of the Eastern Mediterranean and of the Middle East is vital to the security of the United States" and that it "would be jeopardized if the Soviet Union should succeed in its efforts to obtain control of any one of the following countries: Italy, Greece, Turkey, or Iran." The United States should, therefore, "be prepared to make full use of its political, economic, and if necessary, military power in such a manner as may be found most effective." Any resort to force should be consonant with the UN Charter and undertaken "in cooperation with like-minded members of the United Nations." [67]

Henderson echoed the core point regarding the continuing British presence in the Middle East. "It would be unrealistic" for the United States to pursue such a policy (containment) "unless the British maintain their strong strategic, political and economic position in the Middle East and Eastern Mediterranean, and unless they and ourselves follow parallel policies in that area." Moreover, "one of the greatest dangers to world

---

[65] Ibid.

[66] George Kennan to Under Secretary of State Robert Lovett (November 11, 1947), NACP RG 59 PPS Staff/Council, Area Files 1947–1962, Box 6.

[67] Robert A. Lovett to President Harry S. Truman (November 24, 1947), NACP RG 59 PPS Staff/Council, Area Files 1947–1962), Box 6.

peace may be the failure of the Soviet Union to understand the extent to which the United States is prepared to go to maintain the security of the Eastern Mediterranean and the Middle East."[68] Close alignment with British policy, and thus opposition to a plan to partition Palestine into an Arab and a Jewish state, animated by concern about Soviet intervention in the region, were foremost on the minds of the Planning Staff. The Pentagon talks had made clear that the architects of the policy of the containment of communism believed that policy was incompatible with the establishment of a Jewish state in Palestine. This anti-Zionist consensus was to persist in the power ministries of the United States throughout the diplomatic maneuvering and war in 1947–9 in Palestine and then Israel.

The United Nations General Assembly Session of Fall 1947

The question of whether the United Nations General Assembly would vote in favor of the partition of Palestine, following the end of the British Mandate, into a Jewish and an Arab state dominated the UN agenda and loomed large as an issue in American politics throughout the fall of 1947. Multiple factors contributed to momentum in favor of partition. It had been recommended by Britain's Peel Commission in 1937, and in September 1947 by the UN Special Committee on Palestine majority report.[69] Since 1944 both major American political parties were on record in support of the establishment of a Jewish state in Palestine, a position that continued to enjoy bipartisan advocacy in the US Congress. Support also came from American Jewish organizations as well as non-Jewish groups and important voices in the press. Truman's earlier support for Jewish immigration to Palestine also appeared to lead logically to support for partition and a Jewish state. Especially in the wake of the *Exodus* affair, the Zionists' "clandestine" immigration campaign from Europe to Palestine had generated international support. The UNSCOP report recommendations added momentum to public support in the United States for the Zionists.

As we have seen, however, Marshall's State Department struck a very different tone. On November 25, as the UN approached the crucial vote on the Partition Plan and when the Soviet Union had publicly declared its support for it, the secretary of state sent instructions to the US delegation to the UN that stopped well short of following suit. The delegation should

---

[68] "Memorandum Resulting from Conversations with the British" (November 24, 1947), NACP RG 59 PPS Staff/Council, Area Files 1947–1962, Box 6.
[69] On the Peel Commission recommendations see Morris, *Righteous Victims*, 138–144.

be guided "by methods best calculated to safeguard the strategic, economic, and political interests of the United States in the Near East." It should ensure that any recommendation about "the Palestine problem" be a "*United Nations*" one (emphasis in original) "in such a way that the final recommendation of the General Assembly cannot be regarded as an 'American plan.'" The delegation "must make no commitment for the use of United States troops in Palestine except as part of a United Nations action," and should make clear that the USA did not "wish in any sense to replace the British in Palestine," nor would it "accept unilateral responsibility."[70]

The State Department was at odds with the White House and public opinion.[71] On November 22 Herschel Johnson (1894–1966), the acting US ambassador to the UN in 1946 and 1947, said to the General Assembly that "we should grasp the nettle and go ahead," that is, support the report of the UN Ad Hoc Committee which had voted overwhelmingly in favor of the UNSCOP majority recommendations to proceed with the Partition Plan. Three days later Marshall cautioned the delegation that Johnson's statement "by no means implied that the United States would necessarily send troops to Palestine."[72] However, if the United States, as a result of a decision by President Truman, voted for the Partition Plan, Marshall thought it was crucial that it not be identified as an American plan, presumably to avoid having Arab antagonism aimed primarily at the United States rather than at the United Nations as a whole. However, the clear meaning of a vote in favor of the Partition Resolution was that it committed the United Nations and the United States to favor the establishment of separate Arab and Jewish states in Palestine. Though the representatives of the Jewish Agency had not requested UN or US troops to enforce a partition plan, Marshall, reflecting the views of the military leadership of the Joint Chiefs of Staff, added that the USA would not send them for that purpose.

On November 26, 1947 Johnson told the General Assembly that the United States supported the report of the Ad Hoc Committee on Palestine to end the British Mandate and partition Palestine into independent Jewish and Arab states. It "offers the best practical present opportunity and possibility of obtaining, in a future foreseeable to us now, a peaceful settlement in Palestine" and had emerged from the

---

[70] "Memorandum by the Deputy Director of the Office of Special Political Affairs (Thompson) to the Under Secretary of State (Lovett)," Washington (November 25, 1947): https://history.state.gov/historicaldocuments/frus1947v05/d889.

[71] On Truman and public opinion in favor of the Zionist project see Radosh and Radosh, *A Safe Haven*.

[72] Ibid., 2.

work of the United Nations.[73] While it would be desirable to have a plan that met with agreement of the principal protagonists, he said,

no plan has ever been presented, either to the Assembly or to the mandatory Government during the long years of tenure, or in any other place, which would command the acceptance of both the Arabs and the Jews. No such plan has ever been presented, and I do not believe that any such plan will ever be presented. If we are to effect through the United Nations a solution to this problem, it cannot be done without the use of the knife. Neither the Jews nor the Arabs will ever be completely satisfied with anything we do, and it is just as well to bear that in mind.[74]

On November 29, 1947 the United States voted in favor of Partition Resolution 181 and contributed to the two-thirds majority in the General Assembly in favor.[75] It did so aware that the Arab Higher Committee and the Arab states opposed it and threatened to resort to force to prevent its realization. The American "yes" of November 29 was not dependent on Arab state agreement. Johnson asserted, in effect, that if the UN were going to implement partition, then force, on the part of either the UN or of the Zionists, would be necessary if the Arabs made good on their threats to go to war to stop it. Johnson's brief statement was, however, the last time that an official of the United States Department of State asserted such clear support for partition even in the face of threats of force by the Arabs to prevent its realization.

At the United Nations in November 1947 the most emphatic support for a partition of Palestine, and thus for a Jewish state in part of it, came from the Soviet Union and the communist regimes of Eastern Europe, Poland most of all. On November 26, 1947 Oskar Lange (1904–65), Poland's UN ambassador, delivered a long and passionate statement backing the Ad Hoc Committee report in support of the Partition Resolution. He said that Poland's interest in the matter was threefold. First, three-and-a-half million Jews had lived in Poland, a major proportion of Jews throughout the world came from Poland, and "we have followed with pride the constructive work of the Jewish community in Palestine," most of whom came from Poland.[76] Second, the "mass extermination of millions of Jews in our country established a community of suffering between the Jews and the Polish nation," one that "turned into a

[73] Herschel Johnson (United States of America), New York (November 26, 1947), 124th Plenary Meeting, UNGA, 1325: https://documents-dds-ny.un.org/doc/UNDOC/GEN/NL4/718/34/pdf/NL471834.pdf?OpenElement.

[74] Ibid., 1326.

[75] On the passage of Resolution 181 see, among much else, chapter 11 in Cohen, *Palestine and the Great Powers, 1945–1948*; and chapter 10 in Radosh and Radosh, *A Safe Haven*.

[76] Oskar Lange, New York (November 26, 1947), 125th Plenary Meeting, UNGA, 1332: https://documents-dds-y.un.org/doc/UNDOC/GEN/NL4/718/34/pdf/NL471834.pdf?OpenElement.

community of resistance and struggle against the forces of the German occupation, a struggle which is known throughout the world through the dramatic and heroic uprising of the Jews of the Warsaw ghetto and of other cities of Poland, an uprising which, for us, was part of the great struggle the Polish nation waged against the German occupation forces." Third, in view of "our own close historical association with the Jewish people, we cannot help sympathizing" with their aspirations to "consider Palestine as their national home."[77] Therefore, Poland would vote in favor of the Committee report calling for partition and the establishment of two independent states, one Arab and one Jewish.

In the same General Assembly session, Andrei Gromyko, the Soviet ambassador to the UN, also supported the Ad Hoc Committee report. Soviet support for partition was not "directed against the Arabs."[78] He was aware that the representatives of the Arab states had claimed that the Partition Plan "would be a historic injustice." He found that view to be "unacceptable, if only because, after all, the Jewish people have been closely linked with Palestine for a considerable period in history." Further, one must "not overlook the position in which the Jewish people found themselves as a result of the recent world war." Gromyko reminded the General Assembly that, "as a result of the war unleashed by Hitlerite Germany, the Jews, as a people, have suffered more than any other people. You know that there was not a single country in Western Europe which succeeded in adequately protecting the interests of the Jewish people against the arbitrary acts and violence of the Hitlerites."[79] And, Gromyko no doubt took a certain pleasure in pointing out, Britain, one of those powers, was opposing the Zionist project.

Gromyko was convinced that "the basic and permanent interests of the Arab people" would lead them to look "towards Moscow" in the expectation of help "in their efforts to cast off the last vestiges of foreign dependence." Contrary to the claims made by the Arab representatives, the decision to partition Palestine was "in keeping with the high principles and aims of the United Nations" and "the principle of the national self-determination of peoples" applicable to both Jews and Arabs. Gromyko described the Soviet Union as a "single united family" that demonstrated its unity in the "fight against the most powerful and most dangerous enemy that a peace-loving people has ever met," that is, in its war against Nazi Germany.[80] The Partition Plan was of "profound historical significance

[77] Ibid.

[78] Andrei Gromyko, New York (November 26, 1947), 125th Plenary Meeting, UNGA, Assembly, 1359: https://documents-dds-ny.un.org/doc/UNDOC/GEN/NL4/718/34/pd f/NL471834.pdf?OpenElement.

[79] Ibid., 1360.   [80] Ibid., 1360–1361.

because this decision will meet the legitimate demands of the Jewish people, hundreds of thousands of whom, as you know, are still without a country, without homes, having found temporary shelter only in special camps in some western countries."[81] Gromyko's reference to the Jews as "a people," with rights of national self-determination and a historical link to the territory of Palestine, went much further than the US delegation did in support of Zionist goals.

Gromyko observed that Alexander Cadogan, Britain's ambassador to the UN, had said that the UK was prepared to implement the General Assembly's decision provided that the Jews and Arabs came to an agreement. Yet, he noted, the discussion at the current session showed that such an agreement was impossible and there was no prospect of one being reached. The UK showed "no real desire, even now, to co-operate fully with the United Nations in solving this problem." As the Arab states had rejected partition but the Jews had accepted it, the British policy amounted giving the Arabs a veto over the UN decision. Conversely, Gromyko said that the USSR, "unlike some other delegations, has from the outset taken a clear-cut, definite and unequivocal stand in this matter. It is consistently maintaining this stand. It has no intention of maneuvering and manipulating votes as unfortunately is done at the Assembly, especially in connection with the consideration of the Palestinian question."[82] The record of the UN meetings from spring to fall 1947 documents a contrast between Soviet support and American ambiguity about a partition of Palestine. There was a clarity and sympathy in the Soviet stance that, except for Johnson's statement of November 26, was absent in the American interventions.

Amir Adel Arslan, Syria's ambassador to the UN, along with the other Arab state representatives, rejected the Partition Plan resolution. In doing so, Arslan raised the communist issue. He responded to Lange's statement in support of the Partition Plan by asserting that the Poles were "silent" about the "violation" of the UN Charter that he argued was evident in the Partition Resolution "because that violation is aimed at founding a Jewish state in Palestine which would allow Poland to get rid of its own Jews."[83] Arslan saw a contradiction between America's opposition to communism and its support for the Partition Plan. His reasoning may have caused some discomfort in the State Department and the Pentagon:

The United States Government is fighting communism not only in its own country but everywhere; it is attacking communists from Hollywood to the

---

[81] Ibid., 1361.   [82] Ibid., 1363.
[83] Amir Arslan (November 26, 1947), 125th Plenary Meeting, UNGA, 1339: https://docu ments-dds-ny.un.org/doc/UNDOC/GEN/NL4/718/35/pdf/NL471835.pdf? OpenElement.

frontiers of Manchuria; it is deporting communists even if they are recommended by very highly placed persons; it is granting all sorts of loans to fight communism in Europe. But if the Black Sea ports could pour half a million communists into Palestine today, the delegation of the United States of America would be all the happier so long as Palestine was swarming with Jews. They are not satisfied with the one hundred and fifty thousand communists who are already in Palestine.[84]

Arslan's arithmetic about the number of communists pouring into Palestine was, of course, a gross exaggeration. His view that "the whole affair" of establishing a Jewish state in Palestine was "only a conspiracy" was no less absurd. He compounded these absurdities by repeating a standard line of Nazi and then Islamist propaganda during World War II, namely that "Zionists and their friends" intended to make "the territory of the Jewish State extend to the Red Sea, that is a threat to the Suez," and thus subject thirty million people in the Arab states to "illegal decisions contrary to the Charter and their vital interest."[85] Yet the association of the Zionist project with the Soviet Union and communism, albeit in more qualified and nuanced form, was, as we have seen, one that had struck many nerves in the halls of power in London and Washington. Arslan was either unaware of or chose not to mention American and British efforts to prevent those very same Jewish communists from migrating to Palestine. He too was willing to play the anticommunist card in ways that refuted State Department fears that the Arab countries, or at least his Syrian government, would become sympathetic to the Soviet Union and the communists.

On November 28 Alexandre Parodi (1901–79), France's UN ambassador, expressed his country's ambivalence in trying to balance the memory of the Holocaust with its interests in the Arab world. Parodi, a veteran of the French Resistance, underestimated the importance of antisemitism in modern French history when he said: "In France, anti-Semitism has never been anything but an ideological adventure on the part of certain intellectuals whose errors of thinking have indeed led them considerably farther: as far as collaboration and fascism."[86] Yet he thought "with horror of the prolonged torture of the Jewish people, of the methods of extermination to which they have been subjected and which have led to the deaths of millions of human beings. At the same time, my country has for more than a century been associated with the life of the Arab world. Moslem deputies sit in the

---

[84] Ibid., 1339–1340.   [85] Ibid., 1340.

[86] Alexandre Parodi (November 28, 1947), 127th Plenary Meeting, UNGA, A/PV.127: https://unispal.un.org/UNISPAL.NSF/0/5C011CD280FD64CA85256CF40052CC22. Antisemitism, as well as collaboration with the Nazis during World War II, went well beyond "an ideological adventure of certain intellectuals." See Robert O. Paxton, *Vichy France: Old Guard and New Order, 1940–1944* (New York: Columbia University Press, 1975; rev. ed. 2001); and Michael R. Marrus and Robert O. Paxton, *Vichy France and the Jews* (New York: Basic Books, 1981).

French parliament. We know the Arabs and we like them." The plan for partition should be a "stage in the development of a situation which, sooner or later, in one form or another, must produce an express or tacit agreement on a *modus vivendi* between Jews and Arabs." Yet, on November 28, France was not willing to take a position in support of the majority report of the Special Committee on Palestine because "the problem was so difficult to us that we had not yet been able to form an opinion."[87] He requested a twenty-four-hour postponement of the vote on the Partition Resolution in the hope of reaching a last-minute agreement.

Poland's Lange opposed Parodi's proposal for a postponement. The UN General Assembly had discussed the issue for half a year in search of compromise, he said, yet the "position of the Arab delegations was so intransigent and so much a repudiation of any possible compromise that we saw no alternative other than to support the majority position" of the UNSCOP report.[88] The next day Herschel Johnson, after recalling the numerous commissions, committees, reports, and debates on the issue, said that there had been "no mention of any conciliation attempt having been made on the part of the Arab Higher Committee representing the people of Palestine, or on the part of the Jewish Agency," and called for an immediate vote.[89] Gromyko was even more dismissive: The USSR delegation "saw no sense in this French proposal. Nothing changed in the last twenty-four hours about an issue that has been debated for 25 years." He urged the General Assembly to vote immediately on the recommendation – one that the USSR would support.[90]

The day before the UN vote the Central Intelligence Agency, in coordination with the departments of the US Army, Navy and Air Force, issued a seventeen-page report on "The Consequences of the Partition of Palestine."[91] Its core conclusion was the following:

The US, by supporting partition, has already lost much of its prestige in the Near East. In the event that partition is imposed on Palestine, the resulting conflict will seriously disturb the social, economic, and political stability of the Arab world,

---

[87] Ibid.

[88] Oskar Lange (November 28, 1947), 128th Plenary Meeting, UNGA, 1407–08: https://documents-dds-ny.un.org/doc/UNDOC/GEN/NL4/718/37/pdf/NL471837.pdf? OpenElement.

[89] Herschel Johnson (November 29, 1947), 128th Plenary Meeting, UNGA, 1416–17: https://documents-dds-ny.un.org/doc/UNDOC/GEN/NL4/717/10/pdf/NL471710.pdf? OpenElement.

[90] Andrei Gromyko (November 29, 1947), 128th Plenary Meeting, UNGA, 1416–17: https://documents-dds-ny.un.org/doc/UNDOC/GEN/NL4/717/10/pdf/NL471710.pdf? OpenElement.

[91] "The Consequences of the Partition of Palestine," Washington (November 28, 1947), CIA CREST system (Release date: May 20, 2013): www.cia.gov/library/readingroom/docs/CIA-RDP78-01617A003000180001-8.pdf.

and US commercial and strategic interests will be dangerously jeopardized. While irresponsible tribesmen and fanatic Moslems are haphazardly blowing up parts of the oil pipelines and attacking occasional Americans, it is possible that the responsible governments will refuse to sign pipeline conventions, oil concessions, civil air agreements, and trade pacts. The various projects which are necessary to raise the standard of living cannot be carried out without US assistance and guidance. With the US committed to partition, such developments will be shelved indefinitely. The poverty, unrest, and hopelessness upon which Communist propaganda thrives will increase throughout the Arab world, and Soviet agents (some of whom have already been smuggled into Palestine as Jewish DP's) will scatter into the other Arab states and there attempt to organize so-called "democratic movements" such as the one existing today in Greece.[92]

If the UN recommended partition, it would be "morally bound" to enforce it "with the major powers acting as the instruments of enforcement" resulting in "dangerous potentialities" for "US-Arab and US-USSR relations [which] need no emphasis." The authors of the report viewed Arab nationalism as "the strongest political force in the Arab world." Its "ultimate aim" was to "preserve and enrich the Arab heritage" and gain the political independence of all Arab lands. Arab nationalists "regard Palestine as the chief stumbling block to the achievement of their political aims."[93] The Arab governments, though, were "probably as greatly influenced by religion as they are by nationalist pressures." They were "capable of a religious fanaticism" which, when joined to politics, was "an extremely powerful force." The Ikhwan al Muslimin (Muslim Brotherhood) "regards Westernization as a dangerous threat to Islam and would oppose any political encroachment of Zionism on Palestine with religious fanaticism." It would be the spearhead of a jihad or holy war. "The Grand Mufti, as head of the Moslem Supreme Council, can count on the unanimous support of all members of the Ikhwan, who are assured entrance into Paradise if they die on the field of battle."[94]

In its discussion of Arab attitudes toward the USA and the UK, the CIA authors recalled the Balfour Declaration, the dissolution of the Arab Higher Committee by Britain in 1937, and the fact that "the arrest of Arab political leaders, and the escape of the Mufti and others across the border" had convinced the Arabs that Britain "was crushing all hopes of Arab political independence."[95] The report did not refer to "some Arabs" or "the Mufti's supporters," but simply to "the Arabs." The authors wrote nothing about the role of Husseini and other members of the Arab Higher Committee in Nazi Germany or Jamal Husseini's recently articulated racist arguments for rejecting an "alien" Jewish presence that destroyed the racial homogeneity of the Arab region. Rather, the report

---

[92] Ibid., 1–2.   [93] Ibid., 4.   [94] Ibid., 4–5.   [95] Ibid., 6.

stated that US prestige among the Arabs had "steadily declined with each new indication that the US supports the Zionists." The good will produced by the meeting between President Franklin Roosevelt and Saudi Arabia's King Ibn Saud of February 14, 1945 and US backing of Lebanese and Syrian claims to independence (from France) was "short lived as result of President Truman's support of Jewish immigration to Palestine and the Anglo-American Committee report."[96]

The CIA described the Soviet Union's three primary aims in the Middle East as: ending the British Mandate and causing the removal of British troops from the area; keeping the situation unsettled; and taking an "active part in 'maintaining order'" in the region. It had already accomplished the first two aims. "Accomplishment of the third aim would give the USSR a base in the heart of the Near East from which to disseminate propaganda, carry on subversive activities, and attempt to organize 'democratic movements' in the Arab states." The Soviet Union had "been actively but secretly assisting the Jews." In addition to aiding "Jewish underground agents in Europe, large ships filled with illegal immigrants have been leaving the Romanian port of Constanza."[97]

From the perspective of the CIA, Jewish migration to Palestine was an effective cover for communist infiltration and subversion in the Middle East. It noted that there was "already in existence a well-organized system for transporting Jewish DP's from Eastern Europe southward, particularly through the Balkans, to Palestine. In the event of an Arab-Jewish conflict, this system would be employed to furnish manpower to the Jewish forces in Palestine." The report accurately described Jewish immigration from Poland, the Soviet Zone in Germany, Hungary, and the Balkans to gathering locations in Austria, Italy, and Germany, as well as transport by ships from Romanian and Bulgarian Black Sea ports which attempted to break the British blockade of Palestine. It depicted this exodus as a threat to American interests. In the event of war, the Jews would likely get arms from Czechoslovakia, as well as sources in France and Belgium.[98]

"The Consequences" asserted that if the UN adopted the Partition Plan, the social and economic stability of the region would be disturbed and US commercial and strategic interests in the region would be "jeopardized." When war came, "inevitably the extremists, the chauvinists, will increase their influence at the expense of those statesmen in the Arab world" who thought the development of their countries called for close ties to the USA and UK. Faced with violence by "fanatic Moslems," the "responsible governments" would refuse to sign "pipeline conventions,

[96] Ibid.   [97] Ibid.   [98] Ibid., 15–16.

oil concessions, civil air agreements and trade pacts." Poverty and hopelessness, "upon which Communist propaganda thrives," would "increase throughout the Arab world, and Soviet agents (already being smuggled into Palestine as DP's) will scatter into other Arab states and there attempt to organize so-called 'democratic movements' such as the one existing today in Greece." Meanwhile in Palestine, the war would increase in intensity. In a war of attrition, the Jews would "gradually be defeated. Unless they are able to obtain significant outside aid in terms of manpower and material, the Jews will be able to hold out no longer than two years." The UN, including the major powers, might then have to intervene with force, thus damaging relations with the Arabs and risking conflict with the Soviet Union.[99] This grim scenario followed logically from the basic assumptions shared by the State Department and the Pentagon.

The Partition Vote and Its Aftermath

On November 29, 1947, with both the United States and the Soviet Union voting in favor, Resolution 181, "The Future Government of Palestine," received a two-thirds majority in the General Assembly. It was a long, detailed plan to establish both an Arab and a Jewish state in what was then the territory of British Mandate Palestine. The boundaries were those recommended by the UNSCOP report. The new state of Israel would receive most of the Negev desert and the coastal plain from north of the Gaza Strip to just north of the city of Haifa. The Arab state would be located on what is now called the West Bank and the East Bank of the Jordan River and would have access to the Mediterranean via the Gaza Strip, the Jaffa enclave next to Tel Aviv, and the coast from the town of Acre north to the Lebanese border. The General Assembly vote was thirty-three votes in favor of the resolution, thirteen opposed, and ten abstentions. Not surprisingly, Britain was among those deciding to abstain.[100] The countries and their votes were as follows:

In favour: Australia, Belgium, Bolivia, Brazil, Byelorussian Soviet Socialist Republic, Canada, Costa Rica, Czechoslovakia, Denmark, Dominican Republic, Ecuador, France, Guatemala, Haiti, Iceland, Liberia, Luxembourg, Netherlands, New Zealand, Nicaragua, Norway, Panama, Paraguay, Peru, Philippines, Poland, Sweden, Ukrainian Soviet Socialist Republic, Union of

---

[99] Ibid.
[100] "Resolution 181: The Future of Palestine" (November 29, 1947), UNGA, A/Res/181 (II): https://unispal.un.org/DPA/DPR/unispal.nsf/0/7F0AF2BD897689B785256 C330061D253.

South Africa, Union of Soviet Socialist Republics, United States of America, Uruguay, Venezuela.

Against: Afghanistan, Cuba, Egypt, Greece, India, Iran, Iraq, Lebanon, Pakistan, Saudi Arabia, Syria, Turkey, Yemen.

Abstained: Argentina, Chile, Colombia, El Salvador, Ethiopia, Honduras, Mexico, United Kingdom, Yugoslavia.[101]

Despite objections to aspects of the plan, the Zionists in Palestine, and their supporters in around the world, greeted the UN vote with jubilation. The Arab Higher Committee and the Arab states rejected it completely. On November 30, 1947 the Arab Higher Committee made good on its threats to respond to the UN Partition Resolution with force by attacking the Jews in Palestine, thus launching the first, civil-war phase of the Arab-Israeli war of 1947–9.[102]

The following day Marshall met with Bevin in London.[103] Bevin said that he hoped the United States would "continue and intensify the measures which they have recently begun to take to restrain those involved in organizing" Jewish immigration to Palestine and "recommend forbearance and moderation to such Jewish representatives with whom they are in contact in the same way as his Majesty's Government have made similar recommendations to Arab representatives."[104] In the months to come the State Department under Marshall's leadership did what it could to assist Britain along those lines. Yet as it did so, it found itself at odds with both the Truman White House and an increasing section of American public opinion. On December 1, for example, the editors of the *New York Times* wrote that "many of us have long had doubts ... concerning the wisdom of erecting a political state on the basis of religious faith. But these doubts must now yield to the fact of a decision made by the necessary two-thirds majority of the voting nations, after a thorough investigation and a full and fair debate."[105]

State Department and CIA warnings that a Jewish state in Palestine would enhance Soviet interests and be a blow to American access to Arab oil had failed to convince President Truman to reject partition. Truman opted in favor of the Partition Resolution fully aware that the Arab states and the Arab Higher Committee were threatening to oppose it, by force if necessary. He did so because he thought it was a moral imperative to do so

---

[101] Ibid. On the French decision to vote in favor see Frédérique Schillo, *La France et la création de l'état d'Israël: 18 février 1947–11 mai 1949* (Paris: Éditions Artcom, 1997).

[102] From the extensive scholarship on the war see Benny Morris, *1948: A History of the First Arab-Israeli War* (New Haven: Yale University Press, 2008).

[103] "The Secretary of State [Marshall] to the Acting Secretary of State [Robert Lovett]," London (December 5, 1947), *FRUS*, 1947, vol. 5: https://history.state.gov/historicaldo cuments/frus1947v05/d904.

[104] Ibid.   [105] "The Partition of Palestine," *New York Times*, December 1, 1947, 20.

after the Holocaust. He believed that the Jews were going to build a democratic state oriented to the West, that the Arabs needed Europe and the United States as markets for their oil, and that the warnings about Zionism and communism were erroneous. Yet, as we have seen, he did so in the face of intense opposition from the CIA, Pentagon, and, as was becoming clear, the State Department as well.

The clear and overwhelming policy implication of the CIA's intelligence assessment and the Pentagon talks and NSC recommendations that fall was to overturn the UN Partition Resolution as a typical example of foreign policy driven by sentimentalism in public opinion rather than by sober assessment of the demands of US national security. In the coming months, through the vehicle of the Policy Planning Staff, the State Department gave clarity to its opposition to partition, an opposition which had become a consensus of the entire American national security establishment.

The US State Department Policy Planning
Staff Memos Oppose the UN Partition
Resolution: January–February 1948

Our vital interests in those areas will continue to be adversely affected to
the extent that we continue to support partition.
> George Kennan, "Report by the Policy Planning Staff on Position of
> the United States with Respect to Palestine," January 19, 1948

The State Dept. pulled the rug out from under me today.
> President Harry S. Truman, diary, March 19, 1948

This surrender to brazen Arab threats is the most humiliating and shocking
political event since the democracies betrayed Czechoslovakia in 1938.
> Thomas Mann, "Gespenster von 1938" [Ghosts of 1938],
> *Aufbau*, March 20, 1948

By fall 1947 it was clear that American policy toward the Arab-Zionist
conflict was proceeding on what we might call two tracks. Track one,
determined by President Truman's decisions, led to American support
for the UN Partition Resolution of November 29, 1947. Track two,
determined by the Marshall-era State Department in cooperation with
the Pentagon and the Central Intelligence Agency, sought to undermine
that resolution, and strip it of the enforcement powers needed to implement it in the hope, thereby, of preventing the establishment of a Jewish
state in Palestine. Track two took the form of classified position papers
circulating among high-ranking officials in those branches of government,
and the resulting efforts to convince Truman of the error of his ways. It
included several elements: imposition of an arms embargo that fell dis-
proportionately on the Jewish Agency, a non-state actor faced with the
hostility of the Arab states; instructions to American diplomats in Europe
to urge governments there to prevent Jewish immigration to Palestine;
and requests to the FBI and Department of the Treasury to stop
American supporters of Israel from assisting clandestine Jewish immigration. At the United Nations track two entailed a determined effort to
replace the Partition Resolution with proposals for "Trusteeship" in
Palestine that would preclude a Jewish state. As the State Department
presented a public face of ambiguity, the extent of behind-the-scenes

opposition was not fully apparent, even to the president of the United States.

In a series of memoranda prepared early in 1948, George Kennan, the director of the Policy Planning Staff in the State Department, made the case that the Zionist project was irreconcilable with the policy of containment of communism. He did so with the same eloquence and analytical clarity that had earlier brought him renown. Since writing the "Long Telegram" of February 22, 1946 Kennan had emerged as the intellectual architect of American global strategy in the emerging confrontation with the Soviet Union and communism. That, plus his association with Secretary of State Marshall, and his leadership of the Policy Planning Staff, meant that his views both mirrored and shaped a consensus that influenced the US national security establishment as a whole.[1] Kennan and his staff did not invent that consensus; his accomplishment was to extend it beyond the anti-Zionists among the Arab specialists in the State Department, the CIA, and the military and connect it to the core strategic policy of the United States in Europe and around the globe in the first years of the Cold War.

On December 1, 1947 President Truman approved a National Security Council recommendation for a review by the Policy Planning Staff (PPS) of "the entire United States position with regard to Palestine."[2] Kennan's staff requested input from William A. Eddy, who by then had left the State Department to work at the Arab-American Oil Corporation (ARAMCO).[3] On January 5, 1948, writing on the ARAMCO letterhead, Eddy sent his report to Kennan. His assessments and conclusions found their way into the subsequent PPS memos. Eddy did not mince words.

Overshadowing all other matters is the adverse effect on Aramco and Taplien of The Pro-Zionist Policy of the United States Government. All Arabs resent the actions of the present United States administration as unfriendly to them ... The prestige of the United States Government among Arabs has practically vanished, while that of Britain has greatly increased. Popular Arab resentment against the United States is at present greater than fear or dislike of the U.S.S.R ... The United States Government appears to the Arabs to be an eager and friendly

---

[1] On Kennan's appointment and his leadership of the Policy Planning Staff see John Lewis Gaddis, *George F. Kennan: An American Life* (New York: Penguin, 2012).

[2] Sidney W. Souers, Executive Secretary, National Security Council, "Memorandum for Mr. Kennan: The Problem of Palestine" (December 1, 1947), NACP RG 59, General Records of the Department of State, Policy Planning Staff/Council, Area Files, 1947–1962, From 1947–53 Europe, East To: 1947–53 Near and Middle East, Box 6 (hereafter RG 59 PPS Staff/Council, Area Files 1947–1962).

[3] William A. Eddy to George Kennan, San Francisco (January 5, 1948), RG 59 PPS Staff/Council, Area Files 1947–1962, Box 6. On Eddy see: https://en.wikipedia.org/wiki/William_A._Eddy.

partisan of the Zionists; whereas the U.S.S.R is considered to be equally indifferent to Arab or Zionist survival, and therefore, being wholly opportunist, the U.S.S.R. is currently thought to be more accessible to a deal whereby they might be induced to protect the Arabs of Palestine in exchange for air bases and warm water ports, which could be opened to them by the Arab League. The Arabs have given up hope of any change or improvement in the United States-Palestine policy.[4]

Eddy reported that Prince Faisal of Saudi Arabia and Azzam Pasha, secretary general of the Arab League, had stated that any American effort to "arm the Jewish state" would lead the Arab governments, including Saudi Arabia, to regard the United States government as unfriendly.[5]

Eddy predicted that as soon as "the Zionist state" was declared, and the British troops then in Palestine withdrawn, "the Arab-Jewish war will begin." It might be "a blood bath next May [1948] or it might be a long guerilla war of attrition lasting many years. In any case, the Arabs will never accept a Jewish state in Palestine."[6] In that conflict, if the United States remained neutral or acted only as required as a member of the UN, the Arabs would concentrate their anger on the Zionists and "then American political and commercial interests have a good chance to survive."[7] If, on the other hand, the United States supported "a Zionist state" and financed, armed, and furnished troops for the Zionists against the Arabs, the following consequences could be expected:

(a) American individuals and companies will be considered as enemies and will be attacked.
(b) American schools and universities will be forced to close.
(c) American commercial concessions may be cancelled, and their property expropriated.
(d) The present Jewish Colony in Palestine, numbering 700,000, formerly accepted by the Arabs, will become targets of Arab military action, which would include the objective of driving all Jews from Palestine.
(e) Jews in other countries outside of Palestine, numbering 500,000 hitherto comparatively safe, will be attacked.
(f) American personnel in Arab countries would have to be evacuated.
(g) The United States would be deprived of friendly bases for potential use by our Armed Forces, from the southern frontier of Turkey to Pakistan.[8]

Eddy was "certain" that the Jews would "ultimately . . . lose their foothold in Palestine." And, due to "widespread anti-Zionism," there would be "shedding of much Jewish blood throughout the entire Near East."

According to Eddy, American support for the Zionist project was "jeopardizing the good will of 30,000,000 Arabs and 220,000,000

---

[4] "Excerpt from Report of W.A. Eddy, December 31, 1947," in ibid., 1 (emphasis in original).
[5] Ibid., 2.   [6] Ibid., 3.   [7] Ibid.   [8] Ibid., 3–4.

Muslims," its cultural and educational leadership in the region, millions of dollars in investment, and "the strategic loss of access to air and naval bases throughout the entire Muslim world." Of the four interested parties, the United States, the Arabs, the Zionists, and Russia, "only Russia stands to gain." That was why Russia supported partition and "was glad to see the United States Government committed to the forced establishment of a racial state" into which it was "already pouring Communist immigrants." The Jewish state would serve as a precedent for other "puppet states," such as Armenia and Kurdistan, that were composed of "racial minorities which can be made into Communist puppets of the U.S.S.R." The State Department's best hope was that the "Department of Defense, already deeply concerned over the consequences of military action against the Arab world, will advise successfully against arming the Zionists."[9] In the ensuing weeks this analysis and some of Eddy's exact language in his January 5 memo found their way into memoranda from the PPS.

On January 9, 1948 Samuel K. C. Kopper (1916–57), an official in the State Department's Division of Near Eastern and African Affairs (NEA), offered suggestions to the PPS for a draft paper on US policy toward Palestine.[10] He asserted that it was "becoming more evident each day" that the task of the UN Commission assigned to implement the Partition Plan "will be rendered impossible if the Arab population does not cooperate voluntarily."[11] In the face of Arab opposition, Kopper presented the three options: support partition into a Jewish and an Arab state; adopt a stance of passive neutrality; or reverse the current US policy of support for partition. He argued for a reversal of policy. If the United States was "determined to see the successful establishment of the Jewish State," it would have to provide economic and military assistance, including use of American troops. Offering such assistance but withholding it from the Arabs would, "in Arab eyes ... be a virtual declaration of war by the United States against the Arab world." Moreover, the Jewish state could not "unaided survive over a long period of time in the face of the combined assistance which will be given by the Arab states, and in lesser measure by the Moslem neighbors, to the Arabs in Palestine."[12] Kopper concluded that the USA should recognize that the Partition Plan was

[9] Ibid., 4.
[10] Samuel K. C. Kopper to Mr. Henderson, "Additional Suggestions Relating to the Draft Paper on Palestine Prepared by the Policy Planning Staff," Washington (January 9, 1948), NACP RG 59 PPS Staff/Council, Area Files 1947–1962, Box 6. On Kopper see "Samuel Kopper, FRAMCO Aid Dies," *New York Times*, June 5, 1947, 35: https://timesmachine.nytimes.com/timesmachine/1957/06/05/84746103.html?pageNumber=35
[11] Kopper to Henderson, "Additional Suggestions," 3.   [12] Ibid., 4.

"unworkable" and, since there was "no prospect of Arab-Jewish cooperation ever being attained under the present plan," should "abandon its support of partition." Further, it should oppose both the sending of armed forces by the UN "or any member thereof for the purpose of implementing partition" and the recruitment of volunteers for that purpose. Finally, the State Department should maintain the embargo "on arms to Palestine and neighboring countries," which it had announced in December.[13] Eddy and Kopper were right to observe that the Arabs were threatening war in response to partition and a Jewish state. They rejected policies that might have deterred them from making good on the threat, either by sending troops from the United States or the United Nations or by lifting the arms embargo on weapons going to the Jews.

The Kennan Memos of 1948

On January 20, 1948 George Kennan sent a Policy Planning Staff memorandum to Secretary of State Marshall regarding Palestine policy along with a report completed on January 19. The report had been prepared "in close collaboration with" Loy Henderson, and had "his general approval."[14] Henderson, of course, was director of the NEA and long known as a leading opponent of Zionism in the department. Receiving Kennan's imprimatur, given the latter's position as director of the Policy Planning Staff and association with Marshall, helped extend the views of the Arab area specialists into a consensus of the State Department, one closely associated with the policy of containment.

In the January 19 "Report by the Policy Planning Staff on Position of the United States with Respect to Palestine" Kennan and the PPS assessed the geostrategic significance of Palestine, and placed access to oil and the danger of Soviet pressure at the center of his concerns.[15] Palestine's location was of great "geostrategic significance to the U.S." Important for control of the eastern end of the Mediterranean and the Suez Canal, it served as an "outlet for the oil of the Middle East" that was

---

[13] Ibid., 7–8.

[14] George F. Kennan, "Memorandum by the Director of the Policy Planning Staff (Kennan) to the Secretary of State" (Washington, DC: January 20, 1948), in *Foreign Relations of the United States* (hereafter*FRUS*), *The Near East, South Asia, and Africa*, 1948, vol. 5, part 2: https://history.state.gov/historicaldocuments/frus1948v05p2/d10. Also see Kennan's diary entry on the subject in George F. Kennan, *The Kennan Diaries*, ed. Frank Costigliola (New York: W. W. Norton: 2014), 2010–2011. Though the report was the product of the Planning Staff, I will list Kennan as the author as he was its primary author and approved the final text.

[15] "Report by the Policy Planning Staff on Position of the United States with Respect to Palestine" (Washington, DC: January 19, 1948), *FRUS*, 1948, vol. 5, part 2: https://history.state.gov/historicaldocuments/frus1948v05p2/d10.

significant for US security. "Particularly in view of the Soviet pressure against the periphery of that area, and Soviet infiltration into the area, it is important that political, economic, and social stability be maintained there." The "present irreconcilable differences between Arabs and Jews in Palestine," the report warned, meant that the area could "become the source of serious unrest and instability which could be readily exploited by the USSR unless a workable solution can be developed."[16]

Kennan observed that the United States and the Soviet Union had played leading roles in bringing about the UN vote in favor of partition; "without US leadership" the necessary two-thirds majority in the UN "could not have been obtained." Hence, understandably, there was a belief in Washington that the United States had "a responsibility for seeing that partition works." Further, what he called "various unauthorized U.S. nationals and organizations, including members of Congress, notably in the closing days of the [UN] Assembly, brought pressure to bear on various foreign delegates and their respective home governments to induce them to support the U.S. attitude on the Palestine question."[17] He was referring to letters from United States senators and members of the House of Representatives urging foreign governments to vote in favor of the Partition Plan.

Moreover, the UN's vote had consequences in the region: "strong nationalistic and religious feelings were aroused throughout the Arab world as a result of the UN recommendation on Palestine." In Palestine, armed clashes between Arabs and Jews were taking place, and "in certain of the Arab states, there have been attacks on Jewish quarters and demonstrations directed primarily against the U.S." Such "manifestations of popular feeling" had not developed into "organized Arab resistance to partition, although a 'jihad' (holy war) against the Jews of Palestine has been proclaimed by Moslem leaders in most of the Arab states and has been joined by Christian leaders in Syria."[18] As British forces were withdrawn from Palestine, "organized large scale opposition by the Arabs is to be expected ... Irregular military units" were being organized in Iraq, Syria, Egypt, Transjordan, and Saudi Arabia to fight in Palestine. At least some of them would move "into the Arab portion of Palestine as defined by the UN" and would "come into violent conflict with the Haganah or other Jewish military bodies operating from the Jewish state."[19]

In Saudi Arabia, "less moderate" elements urged King Ibn Saud to sever links with the United States. Important US oil concessions and air base rights would be at stake "in the event that an actively hostile

16 Ibid., 1.   17 Ibid.   18 Ibid., 3.   19 Ibid.

Government should come to power in Saudi Arabia."[20] As the Arabs were determined to "resist partition with all means at their disposal," it was likely that if the UN attempted to implement partition, with or without US support, moderates in the Arab states, among whom Kennan included Azzam Pasha of the Arab League, "will be swept out of power by irresponsible elements" and "displaced by extremists such as the Grand Mufti of Jerusalem. Hatred of the Zionists or of those identified with Zionism might be extended to include all westerners in direct proportion to the latter's support of Zionist armies in general and of partition, in particular."[21]

Considering this assessment, Kennan echoed the grim predictions of the Eddy memo of late December 1947:

Any assistance the U.S. might give to the enforcement of partition would result in deep-seated antagonism for the U.S. in many sections of the Moslem world over a period of many years and would lay us open to one or more of the following consequences:

(a) Suspension or cancellation of valuable U.S. air base rights and commercial concessions, cessation of U.S. oil pipeline construction, and drastic curtailment of U.S. trade with that area.

(b) Loss of our present access to the air, military and naval facilities enjoyed by the British in the area, with attendant repercussions on our overall strategic position in the Middle East and Mediterranean.

(c) Closing or boycotting of U.S. educational, religious and philanthropic institutions in the Near East, such as the American University at Beirut established in 1866 and the American University at Cairo.

(d) Possible deaths, injuries and damages arising from acts of violence against individual U.S. citizens and interests established in the area. Official assurances of the Arab Governments to afford protection to U.S. interests could not be relied on because of the intensity of popular feeling.

(e) A serious threat to the success of the Marshall Plan. The present oil production of the Middle East fields is approximately 800,000 barrels a day. To meet Marshall Plan requirements, production must be raised to about 2,000,000 barrels a day, since no oil for Europe for this purpose could be provided from the U.S., from Venezuela, or from the Far East. Before the current disturbances, U.S. oil companies had made plans for the required development in the Middle East, with which it will be impossible to proceed if the present situation continues.[22]

In short, US support for the Partition Plan and thus for establishment of a Jewish – and an Arab – state in Palestine would do terrible damage to vital American national security interests in the Middle East. In other words, Kennan asserted that fulfillment of Zionist aspirations clashed directly with American national interests. To make matters worse, the

[20] Ibid., 4.   [21] Ibid.   [22] Ibid.

establishment of a Jewish state in Palestine was also a boon to the Soviet Union's prospects in the Middle East. Kennan wrote:

The USSR stands to gain by the Partition Plan if it should be implemented by force because of the opportunity thus afforded to the Russians to assist in "maintaining order" in Palestine. If Soviet forces should be introduced into Palestine for the purpose of implementing partition, Communist agents would have an excellent base from which to extend their subversive activities, to disseminate propaganda, and to attempt to replace the present Arab governments by "democratic peoples' governments." The presence of Soviet forces in Palestine would constitute an outflanking of our positions in Greece, Turkey and Iran, and a potential threat to the stability of the entire Eastern Mediterranean area.[23]

Rather than send troops, Kennan continued, evidence was accumulating that the Soviet Union either "covertly or indirectly" was supplying arms "not only to the Jews but to the Arabs, thus aggravating friction in the Near East." Whether or not the Soviets sent troops, the UN decision for partition was "favorable to Soviet objectives of sowing dissension and discord in non-communist countries" or even encouraging "partition of areas in Iraq, Iran, Turkey and Greece." Moreover, "so numerous would be the ramifications of mounting Arab ill will, of opening the door to Soviet political and military penetration, and of generally chaotic conditions in Palestine and neighboring countries, that the whole structure of peace and security in the Near East and Mediterranean would be directly or indirectly affected with results impossible to predict at this stage but certainly injurious to U.S. interests."[24] Hence for these reasons as well, partition and the establishment of a Jewish state in Palestine would be "certainly injurious to U.S. interest."[25]

Kennan concluded that the task now was to limit the damage that had already been caused by US support for the Partition Plan. It had caused "U.S. prestige in the Moslem world" to suffer "a severe blow." US strategic interests in the Mediterranean and Near East had "been seriously prejudiced. Our vital interests in those areas will continue to be adversely affected to the extent that we continue to support partition."[26] American support for partition, he argued, was premised on the assumption that "*there was cooperation between the parties concerned*" (emphasis in original). However, "events" had "demonstrated that the Arab inhabitants of Palestine" would "not cooperate even to endeavor to make the Partition Plan work. Therefore, one of the major premises on which we originally supported partition has proved invalid."

While Arab governments had "partially succeeded in restraining demonstrations against the Jews within their borders, in the case of open

---

[23] Ibid.   [24] Ibid., 5.   [25] Ibid.   [26] Ibid.

conflict major massacres of Jews in Moslem countries would seem to be inevitable, despite efforts of the governments of those countries to control popular feeling."[27] Moreover, implementation of the Partition Plan would intensify antisemitism both abroad and in the United States. It would provide a basis

for anti-Jewish agitation in other parts of the world. The process of assimilation or integration of the individual Jew in the life of the country of which he is a citizen, which has been strongly advocated by World Jewry in the past, would be made more difficult and he would be singled out for attack as an alien political factor. In the U.S., the position of Jews would be gravely undermined as it becomes evident to the public that in supporting a Jewish state in Palestine we were in fact supporting the extreme objectives of political Zionism, to the detriment of overall U.S. security interests.[28]

Kennan's prediction about the dire consequences for Jews "in other parts of the world" was disconcerting. At best, his choice of words suggested that the Zionist project constituted a danger to Jews around the world because it appeared to justify "anti-Jewish," not only anti-Zionist, agitation. It would reverse assimilation of "the individual Jew," who "would be viewed as an alien political factor" thereby reversing the goals of an entity called "World Jewry." Kennan's reference to "the individual Jew," to a political subject called "World Jewry," and suggestions that "the individual Jew ... would be viewed as an alien factor" repeated the clichés that in the past had accompanied antisemitic skepticism about the Jews' loyalty to their native lands. It read less as an expression of empathy than a suggestion that such accusations might have some basis and more as a patrician's fear of popular hatreds than a determination to fight against them.

Kennan's report combined prediction and threat. It asserted that the Zionist project constituted a threat to the recently accomplished assimilation and integration of Jews into American society. Jews in the United States who did not want to place their recent gains at risk or face accusations of dual loyalty and being "singled out as an alien factor" would be well advised to distance themselves from the effort to establish a Jewish state in Palestine. Only three years after the end of the Allies' defeat of Nazism and Fascism, the memo suggested that Zionism, which had initially emerged in reaction to European antisemitism, was instead the cause of yet another chapter in its long history. In effect, the Kennan memo of January 19, 1948 concluded that appeasement of Arab rejectionists rather than confrontation with antisemitism served American foreign policy.

[27] Ibid.   [28] Ibid., 5.

But the Partition Plan was not only harmful to Jews. By conflating it with "the extreme objectives of political Zionism" Kennan was also implying that its acceptance would be detrimental to overall US security interests. If the USA sent troops to enforce the Partition Plan, the Soviet Union would do likewise, thereby creating "further opportunities ... for the exercise of Russian influence in the whole Near Eastern Area."[29] American military assistance "given to the Jewish state, but withheld from the Arabs and the Arab States, would in Arab eyes be a virtual declaration of war by the U.S. against the Arab world." Kennan shared the view – expressed by the recent CIA assessment in November – that the proposed Jewish state could not "survive over any considerable period of time" in the face of resistance from Arabs in Palestine, the Arab states, and, to a lesser extent, from Muslim-majority states.[30]

As a result of all these considerations, Kennan concluded that the United States "should take no further initiative in implementing or aiding partition." It should not send troops and should oppose recruitment of volunteers. It should maintain the embargo on arms to Palestine and neighboring countries and attempt to "divest ourselves of the imputation of international leadership in the search for a solution to this problem." Then, "when and if the march of events has conclusively demonstrated" that the UN Partition Plan could not be implemented "without the use of outside armed force," the United States should take the position that "it is impracticable and undesirable for the international community to attempt to enforce any form of partition in the absence of agreement between the parties, and that the matter should go back to the UN General Assembly." Once there, the US position would be to encourage a peaceful settlement between "Palestine Arabs and Palestine Jews" and investigate the possibility of "a federal state or trusteeship, which would not require outside armed force for implementation."[31] Kennan's position in January 1948 aiming at a version of a binational state was essentially identical to that which Bevin and the British Foreign Office had been trying and failing to accomplish since 1945. In both instances the policy gave veto power to Arab rejectionism.

A Plausible Alternative

The Policy Planning Staff considered a narrow range of policy options and assessments, one that did not include those we have examined by American liberals and Zionist supporters. An alternative policy would have been to wage a public campaign against the racism and antisemitism that was

---

[29] Ibid., 3.   [30] Ibid., 6.   [31] Ibid., 6.

fueling Arab rejection of the UN Partition Resolution. Such a campaign could have drawn on the US government's diplomatic, military, and intelligence files on the Grand Mufti's support for the Nazis before 1939 and his active collaboration during the war, all of which was documented in the State Department's own extensive verbatim transcripts of Arabic-language radio broadcasts to the Middle East in World War II.[32] It could have shone a spotlight on the racist arguments made by Jamal Husseini in September at the United Nations. As the public statements of Emanuel Celler, Freda Kirchwey, I. F. Stone, Robert Wagner, and the confidential briefings by the American Zionist Emergency Council demonstrated, there was a continuity between the Mufti's support for the war against the "United Nations" fighting the Axis powers in World War II and the armed rejection of the United Nations Partition Plan Resolution of November 29, 1947. Rather than examine the continuity of Husseini's antisemitism before and after 1945, Kennan focused on Zionism as the cause of Arab anger. To make the case for that alternative policy, there was an abundance of relevant evidence in the files of the CIA, US military intelligence, the State Department, and captured German records available to the US staff working on the Nuremberg war crimes trials. Such an alternative foreign policy was a live option in American politics and public life, but it was not being discussed in the halls of power. Instead, there existed an unfortunate absence of institutional memory of what the State Department and intelligence agencies had learned about the Middle East during World War II and the Holocaust.

Especially in view of support for partition by Truman, the leader who was translating the strategy of containment into American policy, Kennan and his colleagues could have argued that neighboring Jewish and Arab states could serve as the anchor of a series of democracies in the region that would encourage support for American and Western democratic values and interests. The American diplomats might have made the argument that those Arabs who had fought with the Allies against the Nazis would contribute to a compromise with the Zionists, in contrast to the extremists around the Mufti and Muslim Brotherhood who had expressed sympathy for the Nazis and now rejected partition.[33]

---

[32] See the examination of World War II files from the State Department reports from the US Embassy in Cairo, and from the OSS and US military intelligence in Jeffrey Herf, *Nazi Propaganda for the Arab World* (New Haven: Yale University Press, 2009).

[33] On Arabs who fought with, not against, the Allies see Israel Gershoni, ed., *Arab Reponses to Fascism: Attraction and Repulsion* (Austin: University of Texas Press, 2014); and David Motadel, *Islam and Nazi Germany's War* (Cambridge, MA: Harvard University Press, 2014), 114. On Nazi Germany's expectations of Arab collaboration see Klaus-Michael Mallmann and Martin Cüppers, *Nazi Palestine: The Plans for the Extermination of the Jews of Palestine* (New York: Enigma Books, 2010). On Allied views of Arab responses to Nazi propaganda see Herf, *Nazi Propaganda for the Arab World*.

Although, as we have seen, these ideas were part of American public discussion, they did not play a role in Kennan's assessments.

On January 26, 1948 Dean Rusk (1909–94), recently appointed director of the State Department's Office of United Nations Affairs, sent his criticisms of the Kennan PPS memo to Under Secretary of State Robert Lovett.[34] Marshall had assigned to Lovett responsibility for overseeing the State Department's policy on Palestine. Rusk opposed reversing policy and asked what "new situation" had emerged that was not evident when the Partition Resolution was passed in November. Rusk wrote that "it is doubtful that events have indicated as yet any 'new situation' of the character which would itself justify a basic reconsideration of the Assembly resolution."[35]

Rather than acquiesce to Arab objections, Rusk wrote that "armed interference in Palestine by the Arab States to prevent the implementation of the Assembly's resolution would clearly be aggression contrary to the obligations of those states under the [UN] Charter." Were that to occur, the United States could not "avoid its responsibility as a permanent member of the Security Council to act within the limits of the Charter to prevent this type of aggression from outside Palestine." If Arab resistance was more than the new state could handle, "the Security Council might have to intervene to maintain the peace in the Middle East," that is, to possibly counter Arab "aggression from outside Palestine."[36] Where Kennan and Henderson saw the establishment of the Jewish state as the cause of problems, Rusk focused on Arab rejectionism and even potential "aggression." Where Kennan and the PPS, following the consensus at the Pentagon talks, stressed the commonalities of American and British interests, Rusk referred to "the present irresponsible attitude of the United Kingdom toward the Palestine question." He pointed out that after Britain placed the Palestine question before the UN General Assembly, it "offered no suggestions whatever" for a solution but flatly discouraged the adoption of the UNSCOP majority recommendations favoring a partition plan. In other words, "British non-cooperation" amounted to "a rejection of the Assembly resolution."[37]

As the USA had supported the Partition Plan in the UN in November, the State Department had an obligation to support its implementation. It could hold bilateral talks with Britain, and multilateral talks with "moderate Muslim governments such as Turkey and Pakistan" in hopes of exerting diplomatic pressures on the Arab states "to persuade the Arabs

---

[34] "Memorandum by Mr. Dean Rusk to the Under Secretary of State (Lovett)" (January 26, 1948), *FRUS*, 1948, vol. 5, part 2: https://history.state.gov/historicaldocuments/frus1948v05p2/d13.
[35] Ibid., 2.   [36] Ibid.   [37] Ibid., 2–3.

not to use their influence to frustrate the Assembly resolution." In the event of Arab armed resistance to the Assembly resolution, the USA could call on the UN Security Council to use its power "to bring such aggression to a close." Rather than refer, as Kennan had, to "Arab eyes," as if there was a unitary Arab view, Rusk wrote that "Arabs are not of a single mind about the right line of action on Palestine," that "important differences" existed among "several Arab governments," and therefore that "greater attention might be given to the possibilities of turning Arab differences into a 'hands-off' attitude on their part toward Palestine."[38]

Ultimately, however, Rusk took a guarded position. Though he challenged some core elements of the PPS paper, he also retreated from partition. Instead, he proposed the establishment of a "United Nations trusteeship for the whole of Palestine, with the United States taking its fair share of fiscal and security responsibility for the trust territory," in effect replacing Britain in the process.[39] That also precluded the establishment of a Jewish state in Palestine.

More Resistance to Partition

On January 27 the NEA's Kopper wrote another memo to express his opposition to the Partition Plan.[40] The "ominous signs" that "portended the total unworkability of the plan unless it was implemented by force" included the Arab League's decision of December 17, 1947 to "support the Palestine Arabs in the form of arms, ammunition, funds and volunteers, i.e., everything short of actual participation by the states themselves." The United States should treat the General Assembly Partition Resolution of November 29 as only a "recommendation" and ask the UN Security Council to "explore other avenues of a peaceful settlement of the problem." The United States should not "be drawn into any attack on the British position on this matter." It should "now consider abandoning partition as being unworkable" and look into a "transitional trusteeship" or a "Federal State with liberal immigration provisions." Despite the Arab League announcement, to which he referred, the USA should not lift the arms embargo or send its own armed forces.[41]

Rather than invite comment from the advocates of partition in American politics, Kopper urged that those Americans "associated with the Jewish Agency's activities must be given complete and frank

---

[38] Ibid., 3.   [39] Ibid., 4.
[40] "Memorandum by Mr. Samuel K. C. Kopper of the Office of Near Eastern and African Affairs," Washington (January 27, 1948), *FRUS*, 1948, vol. 5, part 2: https://history.sta te.gov/historicaldocuments/frus1948v05p2/d15.
[41] Ibid.

information on how our vital interests are being and will be adversely affected by support of partition." They should be told that the United States would make efforts to deal "more realistically" with the "displaced persons problem," but that it "cannot afford at this juncture in history to let chaos develop in the Near East or to have a hostile Moslem World confronting us. Accordingly, major concessions must be made by the Jewish Agency."[42] What else could that mean if not to urge advocates of establishing a Jewish state in Palestine to abandon the idea in order not to harm American "vital interests"?

Two days later Kennan commented on the Rusk memorandum in a memo to Lovett.[43] Rusk had sought to "gain for us some relief from the difficulties of our present position." However, Kennan argued that he was doing so "at the expense of our relations with the British and the Arabs" and at the cost of deeper involvements to enforce the Palestine decision. Relations with the British were not expendable. Enforcing the UN Partition Plan would mean "the indefinite maintenance by armed force of a status quo in Palestine fiercely resented by the bulk of the Arab world."[44] In view of "violent resistance of the Arab elements in Palestine to the proposed partition," it was "becoming increasingly obvious" that partition could neither be implemented nor maintained "without the use of outside armed force," a reality that, Kennan wrote, "has now become demonstrable fact."[45]

Kennan also rejected Rusk's argument that Arab armed opposition to the UN Partition Plan should be described as "aggression" or that the UN Security Council would have a responsibility to prevent it. Doing so "would cut at right angles across our entire policy with regard to the Middle East, and our world-wide military-political strategy as well."[46] It would also undermine "understanding and cooperation between ourselves and the British" and cause "embarrassment" for them which, in turn, "would be gravely prejudicial to our national interest." Furthermore, the USA should not "put further pressure on the British" to stop arms shipments to Arab countries. On the contrary:

The remaining British strategic positions in the Middle East are among the few real assets which we still have in that area. The British position there is in large part

---

[42] Ibid., 2.

[43] "Memorandum by the Director of the Policy Planning Staff (Kennan) to the Under Secretary of State (Lovett)," Washington (January 29, 1948), *FRUS*, 1948, vol. 5, part 2: https://history.state.gov/historicaldocuments/frus1948v05p2/d18; also in "Policy Planning Staff, Personal Comments by Mr. Kennan on Mr. Rusk's Memorandum of January 26, 1948" (January 28, 1948), NACP RG 59 PPS Staff/Council, Area Files 1947–1962, Box 6.

[44] "Memorandum by the Director."   [45] Ibid., 2.   [46] Ibid., 4.

our position and must be protected as such. It is in the interests of this country that *both* the U.S. and U.K. should not find themselves simultaneously in that position of extreme unpopularity with the Arab world which we occupy today.[47]

With that argument, Kennan supported British arms shipments to the Arabs but opposed American arms shipments to the Jewish Agency. Forced to choose, the United States had to give priority to its relations with Britain, and with the Arab states over that of the not-yet-existing Jewish state. That also meant rejecting support for partition.

Despite the fact that President Truman had supported, and the United States was on record as having voted for, the Partition Plan, Kennan wrote that he did "not know of any specific obligation resting on the Department of State or on this government individually to take measures to increase the chances for successful implementation of the General Assembly resolution."[48] As for Rusk's request that efforts be made to seek out views of Arabs who might support partition, Kennan remarked that doing so "would sacrifice our over-all relations with the Arab world to the requirements of the Palestine situation." It "might achieve a cheap and momentary success," but in the long run he doubted that "the mass of the Arabs would ever forgive us for resorting to it."[49] Although the Arab Higher Committee began the Arab-Zionist civil war in on November 30, 1947, Kennan asserted that "the main responsibility" for the "state of violence" in Palestine "will have to continue to rest with the Jewish leaders and organizations who have pushed so persistently for the pursuit of objectives which could scarcely fail to lead to violent results."[50]

He reiterated that the United States had "no choice but to extricate ourselves from the existing commitments," that is, support for the UN Partition Plan, "as rapidly as possible" and to refuse to add any new ones. The USA "should not attempt to be our brother's keeper or to offer moral advice to other powers when we are unable to bear our own full share of the responsibility for the consequences." While doing so could involve "loss of prestige both for us and the United Nations," it would be "worth it if we can thereby regain the full independence and dignity of our position in this confused and tragic question."[51]

To write that the United States should not be "our brother's keeper" only three years after the murder of six million Jews in Europe was, at best, a poor choice of words. To assert that support for partition had eroded both the "independence and dignity" of American policy suggested, first, that it was beneath the dignity of the United States to support the establishment of a Jewish state, and, second, that doing so would entail

---

[47] Ibid. (emphasis in original).   [48] Ibid., 5.   [49] Ibid., 5.   [50] Ibid., 6.   [51] Ibid.

an inexplicable loss of independence in foreign policy formulation. The implication of that choice of words was that the Zionists and their supporters had gained undue influence over the decisions of the United States. In view of bipartisan support for partition in Congress, that assertion was factually inaccurate; moreover, it implicitly suggested that Truman had also lost his independent judgment. It recalled familiar antisemitic clichés about the alleged excessive power and influence of the Jews. But using the clarity and eloquence that had made him famous, Kennan papered over these fallacies and persisted in arguing that there was an irreconcilable conflict between American national security interests and the establishment of a Jewish state in Palestine.

On February 11, 1948 Kennan and the PPS sent yet another memo on "The Problem of Palestine" to Lovett.[52] This one restated the basic arguments of the January 19 position paper and the reply to Rusk of January 29. This time, however, Kennan acknowledged that public opinion in the United States "was stirred by mistreatment of Jews in Europe and by the intense desire of surviving Jews to go to Palestine."[53] A master of American English, he used the euphemism "mistreatment" to refer to the mass murder of European Jewry. The memo again advocated that the USA "seek another solution to the problem." Drawing on William Eddy's phrase, which had been repeated by Henderson and Kopper, he wrote that if the USA sent aid to the Jewish state but not to the Arabs, that policy "would be construed by the Arabs as a virtual declaration of War against the Arab world," one that would in turn result in "further deterioration of our position in the Middle East and in deep-seated antagonism for the U.S. in many sections of the Moslem world over a period of many years."[54]

"The Problem of Palestine" reiterated the litany of disasters for American interests in the region that would ensue because of partition. These were the same ones Eddy had predicted in December: suspension of air base rights, commercial concessions, and oil pipeline construction; drastic reduction of US trade in the area; loss of access to British air, military, and naval facilities in the area; closing of US Near East educational, religious, and philanthropic institutions; possible deaths, injuries, and damages resulting from acts of violence against US citizens and interests; and "a serious impediment to the success of the European

---

[52] Policy Planning Staff, "The Problem of Palestine," Washington (February 11, 1948), NACP RG 59, General Records of the Department of State, Policy Planning Staff/Council, Area Files, 1947–1962, From 1947–53 Europe, East To: 1947–53 Near and Middle East, Box 6, Entry A1-558CB; also in *FRUS*, 1948, vol. 5, part 2, "Annex: Memorandum of the Policy Planning Staff" (February 11, 1948): https://history.state.gov/historicaldocuments/frus1948v05p2/d37.

[53] Ibid., 1.   [54] Ibid., 5.

Recovery Program, which is dependent on increased production of Middle Eastern oil."[55]

To avoid these disasters, a more emphatic policy reversal was crucial, one that essentially took the side of the Arabs against the Zionists. Support for partition needed to be abandoned "as impracticable and unworkable in view of the demonstrated inability of the people of Palestine to assume the responsibilities of self-government." The UN Security Council and a new session of the UN General Assembly should "consider a new solution in the form of 1) an international trusteeship or 2) a federal state."[56] Such a trusteeship could be exercised by the USA, the UK, and France, or by a general UN Trusteeship Council. A "trusteeship" would involve some kind of continued foreign rule over the peoples of Palestine and was compatible with the continued presence of the British Empire. Kennan and the PPS memos argued that American national interests were compatible with the continued presence of the British Empire in some form in Palestine but were incompatible with the Zionist project.

This course of action "would encounter strong opposition from the Zionists" but have "the support of the Arab states and of world opinion in general." American prestige in the Middle East "would immediately rise and we would regain in large measure our strategically important position in the area" – one that had been lost presumably due to past support for the establishment of a Jewish state in Palestine. "Our national interests would thus be served, and our national security strengthened, notwithstanding the disfavor with which such a procedure would be viewed by Zionist elements."[57]

The leaders of the Jewish Agency responded to reports of the State Department's opposition to the Partition Resolution. On February 22 Moshe Shertok, the head of the Jewish Agency's political department responsible for its foreign policy, replied to Lovett's query about peace moves made by the Jewish Agency.[58] He wrote that the Jews in Palestine had previously and would continue to make approaches "to those Arab personalities and circles whom there is any hope of inducing to accept the internationally decreed settlement. Self-evidently, the Arab Higher Committee does not come into that category. It is not merely that the

---

[55] Ibid., 6–7.   [56] Ibid., 9–10.   [57] Ibid., 10.

[58] "Mr. Moshe Shertok to the Under Secretary of State (Lovett), *FRUS*, 1948, vol. 5, part 2: https://history.state.gov/historicaldocuments/frus1948v05p2/d53. After the establishment of the state of Israel Shertok Hebraicized his name to Sharett: see Gabriel Sheffer, *Moshe Sharett: Biography of a Political Moderate* (Oxford and New York: Clarendon Press/Oxford University Press, 1996). Since all the documents discussed here refer to "Shertok," I have decided to retain that name.

hands of its President [Haj Amin al-Husseini, JH] are drenched in the blood of millions of Jews." The Zionists were convinced that the Arab Higher Committee would only be satisfied with "the conversion of the whole of Palestine into an independent Arab state with the Jews as a crystallized minority at its mercy." Concessions to it now were "bound to strengthen its belief that it can achieve this object."[59] Shertok expressed "greatest alarm" about what turned out to be accurate "rumors now afloat," namely that a move was to be made "for the 'freezing' of the Palestinian situation so that a new effort of conciliation might be undertaken" and that the UN resolution "does not necessarily stand." Such a move would "come as a reward for the campaign of violence now being conducted against the Resolution and encourage the forces of defiance to redouble their efforts once the peace move had failed, as it must." Far from serving the interests of peace, "it would only prolong and intensify the present strife."[60] It was, in other words, a form of appeasement that, as in the past, made war more, not less, likely.

Lovett sent Shertok's note to Loy Henderson and probably to the Planning Staff as well. In a February 24 "Review of Current Trends in U.S. Foreign Policy" Kennan repeated a now-familiar theme: any policy that would tend to "strain British relations with the Arab world" or "whittle down" the British position there was "only a policy directed against ourselves and against the immediate strategic interests of our country."[61] He reiterated complaints about unspecified "pressures to which this government is now subjected" to support the "maintenance, and even the expansion of a Jewish state in Palestine. To the extent that we move in this direction, we will be operating directly counter to our majority security interests in that area." Hence the USA should "avoid being impelled along this path." Without a "fairly radical reversal of the trend of our policy to date," the United States would be militarily responsible "for the protection of the Jewish population of Palestine against the declared hostility of the Arab world, or of sharing that responsibility with the Russians and thus assisting at their installation as one of the military powers in the area. In either case, the clarity and efficiency of a sound national policy for that area will be shattered."[62]

That same day, in an address to the UN Security Council, US UN ambassador Warren Austin offered the first public indication that the State Department was going to abandon support for partition. The Security Council had authority to use force to "remove a threat to

[59] "Shertok to Under Secretary of State," 1.   [60] Ibid., 1–2.
[61] "Report by the Policy Planning Staff," Washington (February 24, 1948), *FRUS*, 1948, vol. 5, part 2: https://history.state.gov/historicaldocuments/frus1948v05p2/d59.
[62] Ibid., 2.

international peace," but the UN Charter did not give it the power "to enforce a political settlement advocated either by the Security Council or the General Assembly." Austin made a distinction between "keeping the peace" and "enforcing partition." Preserving the former thus appeared to require abandoning the latter.[63]

As the civil war in Palestine escalated, the State Department, rather than assign clear blame to the Arab Higher Committee for starting the war, adopted a tone of neutrality. On March 5 Marshall told Austin that there was "clear evidence that the Jews and Arabs of Palestine and the Mandatory Power are not prepared to implement the General Assembly plan of partition by peaceful means."[64] The Partition Plan was an "integral" one that could not succeed "unless each of its parts were carried out." Austin should request that the UN secretary general "convoke immediately" a special session of the General Assembly to "consider further the question of Palestine." Britain should be asked to "reconsider its decision to terminate the mandate on May 15, 1948."[65] Also on March 5, Marshall wrote to Truman that, since it seemed certain that efforts at conciliation between Arabs and Jews Palestine would "prove fruitless ... the future trend seems to be that the [Security] Council will find itself unable to proceed with partition and that it will refer the Palestine problem to an immediate special session of the General Assembly for fresh consideration."[66]

Abandoning Partition: Austin's March 19 Speech at the UN and Clark Clifford's Retort

On March 19 the State Department's reassessment of partition burst into public view when Austin informed the Security Council that the USA had changed its policy and now opposed enforcement of the Partition Resolution.[67] It was clear that partition could not be achieved by peaceful

[63] "Statement Made by the United States Representative at the United Nations [Warren] (Austin) Before the Security Council on February [24] 1948," *FRUS*, 1948, vol. 5, part 2: https://history.state.gov/historicaldocuments/frus1948v05p2/d57.

[64] "The Secretary of State to the United States Representative to the United Nations (Austin)," (March 5, 1948), *FRUS*, 1948 vol. 5, part 2: https://history.state.gov/historicaldocuments/frus1948v05p2/d74.

[65] Ibid., 2.

[66] "Memorandum by the Secretary of State to President Truman and to the Cabinet," (March 5, 1948), *FRUS*, 1948, vol. 5, part 2: https://history.state.gov/historicaldocuments/frus1948v05p2/d73.

[67] "Statement Made by the United States Representative at the United Nations (Austin) Before the Security Council on March 19, 1948," *FRUS*, 1948, vol. 5, part 2: https://history.state.gov/historicaldocuments/frus1948v05p2/d105; also see "U.S. Abandons Palestine Partition; Asks a Special Assembly Session, U.N. Trusteeship Till Final

means. If the British Mandate ended on May 15, 1948, "chaos, heavy fighting and much loss of life" would take place in Palestine. The USA now believed that "a temporary trusteeship for Palestine should be established under the Trusteeship Council of the United Nations to maintain peace." It would allow Jews and Arabs "further opportunity to reach agreement regarding the future government of that country." An immediate session of the General Assembly was needed to consider the proposal. The Security Council "should instruct the Palestine Commission [at work in Palestine] to suspend its efforts to implement the proposal partition plan."[68]

Austin's speech landed like a bombshell at the White House as much as at the UN. The *New York Times* reported that his announcement was received with "shock" and "gloom" at the UN. "Zionist leaders seemed stunned; some seemed near tears" amid fears that Zionist forces "were not strong enough to hold up under the combined weight of Arab attacks and the possibility that that the United States might drop partition formally."[69] In Jerusalem David Ben-Gurion said the USA had surrendered "to the threats of Arab bands armed by the British Foreign Office and brought to Palestine with its support." He rejected a UN trusteeship "even for the shortest time." In Jerusalem the Arab Higher Committee welcomed the decision as a "step in the direction of justice." In view of "widespread speculation" that the change in US policy would "force Zionists into an alliance with the Soviet Union," a Jewish official told the *Times* that Jews in Palestine would remain oriented to the West and their "natural alliance" with the United States, though "some sections of the Jewish community would turn to the Soviet Union."[70]

Austin's speech was not well received in the press. *PM* called the day "Black Friday." T. O. Thackrey in the *New York Post* deemed the speech a "dishonorable and hypocritical betrayal of Palestine."[71] The *New York Times* editors had moved from their lukewarm endorsement of the Partition Plan to anger at the State Department's effort to reverse it. In "The Switch on Palestine," the lead editorial of March 20, they called

---

Solution," *New York Times*, March 20, 1948, 1; and "Declaration by Austin on Palestine Situation," *New York Times*, March 20, 1948, 2.

[68] "Statement Made by the United States Representative."

[69] "Zionists Here Pledge Fight; Arabs Hold Partition Dead, Bewilderment Follows Austin's Palestine Bombshell – US Said to Have Notified Mid-East Spokesmen in Advance," *New York Times*, March 20, 1948, 1.

[70] "Ben-Gurion Spurns a UN Trusteeship; Seeks Arab Treaty," *New York Times*, March 21, 1948, 1.

[71] On Truman's reaction to Austin's trusteeship proposal see Allis Radosh and Ronald Radosh, *A Safe Haven: Harry S. Truman and the Founding of Israel* (New York: HarperCollins, 2009), 301–307.

Austin's statement the "climax to a series of moves which has seldom been matched for ineptness, in the handling of an international issue by an American administration."[72] It was "a plain and unmistakable surrender to the threat of force." There had been no circumstances that were not foreseen when the USA voted in favor of the Partition Resolution that it was now seeking to reverse. Unaware of the almost daily contact and close consultation between Austin and the State Department leadership in Washington, the editors wrote that "there has been a shocking lack of liaison and of common purposes between the American State Department and the American delegation to the United Nations."[73] According to the *Times* editors, it was "obviously and admittedly Arab intransigence that has forced the American government to change its policy and to bow to Arab threats, and to propose that the whole United Nations retreat with us in the face of Arab scorn and fury." In so doing, "we," that is, the United States, "have played a shabby trick on the Jewish community in Palestine, which put its faith in our promises."[74] On March 24, facing an absence of support for calling a second Special Session of the General Assembly, the United States allowed the Security Council to adjourn without considering Austin's proposal to do so.[75]

In 1947 and 1948 Truman had received a steady stream of advice from the State Department and the Pentagon that presented Zionist aspirations as contrary to American strategic interests at the dawn of the Cold War. But on March 6 and 8, 1948 he received strategic arguments from a high-ranking official in his own administration that made the opposite case, namely that implementation of the Partition Plan and the establishment of a Jewish state in Palestine would enhance American interests. These came in from Clark Clifford (1902–98), then a special assistant to the president (see Figure 9.1).[76] In his memo of March 6 Clifford reversed the argument regarding enforcement of partition and the preservation of peace. To preserve peace in Palestine after the end of the British Mandate the USA must support the UN Partition Resolution. It had urged that position upon the UN "in the first place and it is unthinkable that it should fail to back up that decision in every possible way."[77] The United States "should exert every pressure it can bring to

---

[72] "The Switch on Palestine," editorial, *New York Times*, March 20, 1948, E8.   [73] Ibid.

[74] Ibid.

[75] Thomas J. Hamilton, "Opposition to Our Trustee Plan for Holy Land Will Be Studied," *New York Times*, March 25, 1948, 1.

[76] On Clifford's intervention see Radosh and Radosh, *A Safe Haven*, 292–295.

[77] "Memorandum by the President's Special Counsel (Clifford)," Washington (March 6, 1948), *FRUS*, 1948, vol. 5, part 2: https://history.state.gov/historicaldocuments/frus1948v05p2/d78.

Figure 9.1 Clark M. Clifford, special counsel for Harry S. Truman, Washington, November 1, 1948. Source: Thomas D. McAvoy/The LIFE Picture Collection/Getty Images.

bear upon the Arab States to accept partition." Strong pressures "may already have been applied, but it does not look that way to the American people. Rather there have been numerous examples of what appear to be acts of appeasement toward the Arabs." It was "inconceivable to most Americans" and other countries that the USA, "if we really wish to do so," could not apply "effective pressure both on the Arabs and on the British."[78]

Further, Clifford said, the USA should require Britain to comply with the General Assembly resolution and refrain from "any action to prevent, obstruct or delay the implementation" of its recommendations. The United States "should immediately lift its unilateral embargo on arms to the Middle East." Doing so would "give the Jewish militia and Haganah, which are striving to implement the UN decision, equal opportunity with the Arabs to arm for self-defense." Further, the United States should cease "recalling the passports of all Americans serving in Arab or Jewish militia created by the UN."[79] The USA should assist in the formation of an international security force recruited from volunteers to

[78] Ibid.   [79] Ibid.

assist the UN Palestine Commission, but those forces should not include troops from the United States, Russia, or Great Britain. If the Soviet Union insisted on being allowed to send forces, Clifford stipulated that the total from the five Great Powers (the USA, UK, USSR, France, and China) should not exceed half the total and the numbers from any one power should not exceed a fifth of the total. "That would mean ... that Russian volunteers would not be more than 1/10 of the total authorized international security force."[80]

In a second memo on March 8 Clifford reminded Truman that support for the establishment of a Jewish state in Palestine had been "settled policy of the United States" since President Woodrow Wilson approved the Balfour Declaration in 1917.[81] The substance of the Declaration had been restated by Presidents Harding, Coolidge, Hoover, Franklin D. Roosevelt, and Truman. In 1944 both the Democratic and Republican national conventions had adopted resolutions in favor of the establishment of "a free and democratic Jewish commonwealth." Similar sentiments were expressed by a majority of both Houses of Congress in a letter to the president of July 2, 1945 and signed by governors of the forty-eight states. On December 19, 1945 Congress adopted a concurrent resolution stating that the United States should use its good offices to achieve that goal. Truman's "active support of partition was in complete harmony with the policy of the United States ... Had you failed to support partition, you would have been departing from an established American policy and justifiably subject to criticism."[82]

Directly addressing the issue of the Cold War, Clifford argued that partition was the "only course of action with respect to Palestine that will strengthen our position vis-a-vis Russia."[83] At a time when Marshall and others were focused on containing communism in Western Europe, Clifford argued that this focus on Europe was reinforced, not undermined, by support for partition. Support for partition also meant support for the UN. Its rejection would contribute to "the disintegration of the United Nations."[84] The UN was an organization that could consolidate "anti-Soviet forces of the world." Having "crossed the Rubicon" as result of Truman's decision to support partition, "a retreat now" would be a "body blow" to the UN and to US alliances in South America and Western Europe. Russian intervention in the Middle East would be more, not less, likely if war developed between Jews and Arabs and the

---

[80] Ibid.
[81] "Memorandum by the President's Special Counsel (Clifford) to President Truman," Washington (March 8, 1948) *FRUS*, 1948, vol. 5, part 2: https://history.state.gov/histor icaldocuments/frus1948v05p2/d79.
[82] Ibid. [83] Ibid. [84] Ibid.

Russians could step in as "the defenders of world peace and champion of the United Nations." Clear US support for partition would deter the Arab states from launching a war. Clifford also addressed concerns about access to Arab oil. "The Arab states must have oil or go broke." The United States was a major customer. The Arabs' "social and economic order would be irreparably harmed by adopting a Soviet orientation, and it would be suicide for their ruling classes to come within the Soviet sphere of influence."[85]

Clifford noted that the prediction that partition would never work came "from those who never wanted partition to succeed and who have been determined to sabotage it." In a memorable paragraph he invoked for the president the anger at Britain and the State Department that had been percolating in the Congress and in liberal opinion:

If anything has been omitted that could help kill partition, I do not know what that would be. First, Britain, the Mandatory Power, not only publicly declared she would have no part of it, but she has done everything possible to prevent effective action by the Palestine Commission. Next, we have placed an embargo on arms to Palestine, while Britain fulfills her "contractual obligations" to supply arms to the Arabs. Thirdly, our State Department has made no attempt to conceal their dislike for partition. Fourthly, the United States appears in the ridiculous role of trembling before threats of a few nomadic desert tribes. This has done irreparable damage. Why should Russia or Yugoslavia, or any other nation treat us with anything but contempt in light of our shilly-shallying appeasement of the Arabs? After all, the only successful opposition to the Russian advance has been in Greece and Turkey. You proclaimed a bold policy and stood your ground. The Truman Doctrine, has been the one outstanding success in a disintegrating situation.[86]

Clifford pointed out that – contrary to the reports Truman was receiving from the CIA and the British government – "Jewish Palestine" was "strongly oriented to the United States, and away from Russia" and would "remain so unless a military vacuum in Palestine caused by the collapse of UN authority brings Russian unilateral intervention into Palestine." Reversal of the partition decision taken by the UN "at the insistence of the United States" would cause a "serious loss of American prestige and moral leadership all over the world." The Arab League's opposition signaled both defiance of the UN and "deliberate and insolent defiance of the United States which vigorously espoused partition."

Clifford concluded with the following clear alternative to the advice Truman was receiving from the State Department and the Pentagon:

American self-interest, American military security, American interests in Middle East oil, and American prestige in international affairs all demand effective

[85] Ibid., "Proposed United States Policy."   [86] Ibid.

implementation of the UN Palestine decision. The most effective way to prevent Russian penetration into the Middle East and to protect vital American oil interests there is for the United States to take the immediate initiative in the Security Council to implement the General Assembly's Palestine resolution.[87]

Clifford's memoranda of March 6 and 8 sought to convince Truman that the arguments he was hearing from the State Department were fundamentally wrong when they claimed that the presence of a Jewish state in Palestine would undermine American national interests in the Middle East and around the world. Just the opposite was the case. A "Jewish Palestine" would reinforce, not undermine, the global policy of containment and "the Truman doctrine." Clifford gave Truman the argument that support for the partition and a Jewish state in Palestine was not only or even primarily a matter of empathy for Jewish victims of the Holocaust. Turning the State Department's assertions on their heads, he argued that a Jewish state in Palestine would become an important element supporting Truman's own policy of containment of communism.

Clifford's arguments found no echo in the top ranks of the State Department, the Pentagon, or the CIA. The Kennan PPS memos of January and February 1948 articulated a consensus that persisted in the emerging Cold War national security establishment for the duration of the Arab-Zionist war of 1947–9 – and for many years thereafter. According to that consensus, the United States had to choose between an alliance with Britain, access to oil, and containing communism and support for the Zionists and then Israel at the expense of vital US security interests. Kennan's memos of January and February 1948 connected the views of the area specialists in the NEA to global American diplomatic strategy at the top decision-making levels within the State Department. Kennan had not created this anti-Zionist consensus, but he fashioned what had been the provincial preoccupation of the Department's Arabists into a consensus linked to the emerging global strategy of the containment of communism in the first years of the Cold War.

The most important reaction to Austin's speech was that of President Truman. He was embarrassed and angered by the State Department's reversal of policy. In his diary he wrote:

The State Dept. pulled the rug out from under me today. I didn't expect that would happen. In Key West or enroute there from St. Croix, I approved the speech and statement of policy by Senator Austin to UN meeting. This morning I find that the State Dept. has reversed my Palestine policy. The first I know about it is what I see in the papers! I am now in the position of a liar and double-crosser. I've never felt so in my life. There are people on the third and fourth

[87] Ibid.

levels of the State Dept who have always wanted to cut my throat. They've succeeded in doing it.[88]

Marshall and Lovett insisted that in overturning partition they were following Truman's instructions. As Allis and Ronald Radosh write, Clifford later insisted that Truman had authorized Marshall and Austin to propose a UN trusteeship "only *after* three qualifications were met: the Security Council had to exhaust all conciliatory measures: the Council would then recommend alternatives to partition; and finally, the Council would have voted to reject partition entirely. These conclusions had not been met when Austin gave his speech."[89] After a meeting on March 24 with Marshall, Henderson, Dean Rusk, and Clifford, among others, Truman issued a statement that as partition could not be carried out now without the use of force, he would accept the need for a trusteeship, but he insisted that doing so was not a substitute for partition. He stopped short of openly repudiating Austin's speech and the policy that had been developed in the State Department.[90] Yet Truman understood that the public perception was that he had reversed his support for a Jewish state in Palestine.

On April 9 Chaim Weizmann, whom Truman greatly respected, wrote to the president to urge him to express confidence that he would keep his word, and to explain why his original view was the correct one (see Figure 9.2). The clash between "promising Jewish independence in November" – in supporting the UN Partition Resolution – "and attempting to cancel it in March" – with Austin's trusteeship speech – was too obvious to ignore.[91] "I cannot for a moment believe that you would be a party to the further disappointment of pathetic hopes, which you yourself have raised so high." The reversal was making Arab aggression and war more likely because Arab leaders believed their pressure had led to a reversal of partition. The Jews' only choice, he concluded "is between Statehood and extermination. History and providence have placed this issue in your hands, and I am confident that you will yet decide it in the spirit of the moral law."[92]

Truman's decisions of April and May indicated that he was determined to stand by his original support of Jewish statehood, rein in the State

[88] Entry on Truman's calendar, March 19, 1948, in Margaret Truman, *Harry S. Truman*, 424–425, cited in Radosh and Radosh, *A Safe Haven*, 302–303.

[89] See Radosh and Radosh, *A Safe Haven*, 303–304.

[90] On Truman's reaction see ibid., 305–309.

[91] Chaim Weizmann to Harry Truman, April 9, 1948, Letter 138, in *The Letters and Papers of Chaim Weizmann*, Series A, August 1947–1952, 99–101, cited in Radosh and Radosh, *A Safe Haven*, 308–309.

[92] In Radosh and Radosh, *A Safe Haven*, 309.

Figure 9.2 Chaim Weizmann and Eleanor Roosevelt, November 14, 1947, Lake Success, NY, United Nations. Source: Bettmann/Getty Images.

Department, and bring the direction of Palestine policy into the White House. Yet, as we will see, the State Department – and the Pentagon and the CIA – despite Truman's public support for partition and thus a Jewish state in Palestine, continued to pursue policies that worked in the opposite direction.

Kennan against the Nuremberg War Crimes Trials

In the same months in which the Policy Planning Staff was dealing with the Palestine issue, it issued a regular a "review of current trends" around the world. The future of Germany was at the center of its concerns. On February 24, 1948 Kennan expressed opposition to US occupation policy in Germany, especially the programs of denazification and the Nuremberg war crimes trials.[93] In the same weeks during which Kennan called for an

[93] Policy Planning Staff, "Review of Current Trends U.S. Foreign Policy," Washington (February 24, 1948), NACP RG 59, General Records of the Department of State, Policy Planning Staff/Council, Area Files, 1947–1949, From Index/PPS-1 To: PPS-33, Box 1.

end to the Nuremberg trials of Nazi officials, he opposed the establishment of a state by the Jews who had survived the Holocaust.

Kennan was skeptical about Germany and the Germans. They were in "a state of mind which can only be described as sullen, bitter, unregenerate, and pathologically attuned to the old chimera of German unity." Yet "our moral and political influence over them has not made headway since surrender." They were not impressed "by our precepts nor by our example." They would not look to the USA for leadership, and would likely proceed to political polarization "into extreme right and extreme left," both of which "will be from our standpoint, unfriendly, ugly to deal with, and contemptuous of the things we value."[94]

In this grim situation, Kennan's staff wrote, the best to be hoped for would be to bring Germany "into a European federation" but to do so in a way that would not "permit her to dominate" it or endanger the security of others. In doing so, "we cannot rely on the German people to exercise any self-restraint of their own volition, to feel any adequate sense of responsibility vis-à-vis the other western nations, or to concern themselves for the preservation of western values in their own country and elsewhere in Europe."[95] There must, therefore, be "mechanical and automatic safeguards against any unscrupulous exploitation of Germany's preeminence in population and in military-industrial potential." One such safeguard would be "international ownership or control of the Ruhr industries." The Germans must also somehow connect with the wider world. What they needed was not "to be thrust violently upon themselves, which only heightens their congenital irrealism and self-pity and defiant nationalism, but to be led out of their collective egocentrism and encouraged to see things in larger terms." The Germans needed "to learn to think of themselves as world citizens and not just as Germans."[96]

One might think that in light of this bleak view of the Germans, Kennan and his staff would look favorably upon the judicial reckoning with the crimes of the Nazi regime that was taking place in Nuremberg. To the contrary, they wrote: "We must recognize the bankruptcy of our moral influence on the Germans, and we must make plans for the earliest possible termination of those actions and policies on our part which have been psychologically unfortunate." That meant, first, termination of "our establishment in Germany" (the occupation), for "the presence of a victor nation in a devastated conquered area is never helpful." Second, "we must terminate as rapidly as possible those forms of activity (denazification, re-education, and above all the Nuremberg Trials) which tend to set [us] up as mentors and judges over internal problems."[97]

[94] Ibid.   [95] Ibid., 8.   [96] Ibid., 9.   [97] Ibid., pp. 9–10.

On the one hand, Kennan's views of postwar Germany indicated that he had no illusions that a new Germany had emerged from the ashes of defeat. Yet, in opposing continuation of the Nuremberg war crimes trials, Kennan offered views that overlapped with those of the German nationalists he disdained – people whose every impulse was to avoid an Allied reckoning with the crimes of the Nazi regime.[98] It is difficult to understand how Kennan foresaw a better Germany emerging if the process of judicial reckoning was prematurely ended. His plea to end the Nuremberg trials in 1948 implicitly associated the anticommunism of containment with an end to judicial reckoning for the crimes of Nazism. Though Kennan did not make the connection explicit, his views suggested that the mentalities of the emerging Cold War in the West were at odds with a policy of judicial reckoning on Nazi crimes of the past in Germany as well as with the Zionists' hopes for a Jewish state in Palestine.[99]

In the war of 1947 and 1948 the Jews in Palestine needed arms and people. From the beginning to the end of the war the State Department and the Pentagon, with Truman's approval, imposed an embargo on arms shipment to both the Jews in Palestine and the Arab states. The State Department did what it could to slow the emigration of Jews from Europe to Palestine. The opposition to the Zionist project in the State Department and the Pentagon now made itself felt in tangible ways during the war in 1948.

---

[98] On the *Schlussstrichmentalität*, the urge to "draw a line under the past," in West Germany see Norbert Frei, *Adenauer's Germany and the Nazi Past: The Politics of Amnesty and Integration* (New York: Columbia University Press, 2002); and Jeffrey Herf, *Divided Memory: The Nazi Past in the Two Germanys* (Cambridge, MA: Harvard University Press, 1997).

[99] In the same month the Kennan-directed Policy Planning Staff produced "The Utilization of Refugees from the Soviet Union in the U.S. National Interest," a project that sought to use displaced persons from Eastern Europe, including the Baltics, to support the Western Cold War policies against the Soviet bloc. Together with the displaced persons legislation being passed in Congress, such efforts brought former Nazi collaborators to the United States. On this see David Nasaw, *The Last Million: Europe's Displaced Persons from World War to Cold War* (New York: Penguin Press, 2020), 468–478.

10 The US and UN Arms Embargo: November 1947–May 1948

> The only matter that causes us anxiety is our people's deficiency in the equipment necessary for our defense. The Arabs obviously suffer no such lack.
>
> Chaim Weizmann, leader of the World Zionist Movement, to President Harry Truman, December 9, 1947

> The embargo on arms to the Middle East may seem equitable at first glance, but I do believe that if its end result will be that of sufficient arming of the Arabs and none for the Jews, such embargo would be most reprehensible.
>
> Congressman Emanuel Celler to Secretary of Defense James V. Forrestal, December 10, 1947

> One day the historian, with access to State Dept. records, will link the wartime appeasement of the Arabs with the policy which is now unfolding.
>
> Victor Bernstein, *PM*, March 22, 1948

One of the most important consequences of the State Department's policy conclusions of fall 1947 and winter 1948 was the imposition of an embargo on arms both to the Arab states and to the Jews in Palestine. It began as an American initiative in November 1947 and lasted throughout the course of the Arab-Israeli war, until spring 1949. The United States upheld the embargo when the Jewish Agency was at war, first with the forces of Arab Higher Committee led by Haj Amin al-Husseini, then, after May 15, 1948, when Egypt, Iraq, Lebanon, Syria, and Transjordan invaded to destroy the newly declared state of Israel. The State Department also sought to prevent "military-age" Jews, especially Jewish men, from leaving Europe for Palestine and then Israel.

The embargo's advocates claimed that it affected the Arabs as much as the Jews and was done simply to encourage peace in the Middle East. But its supporters in the State Department were determined anti-Zionists, and in reality it reflected the policies articulated in the Pentagon talks of fall 1947 and the State Department Policy Planning Staff papers of

January and February 1948. The US government upheld the embargo even when its military leaders understood that numbers of soldiers and delivery of arms from outside Palestine/Israel would make the difference for the Jews between victory and defeat. If Jews in Palestine had had no other source than the United States for people and weapons, they would have lacked both. Hence the Yishuv would have either been defeated in the war, with incalculable consequences or, at best, forced to accept a settlement short of establishing a Jewish state, presumably in the form of a trusteeship with continued British, and perhaps American, oversight or an Arab-dominated state that would have had the Jews at its mercy. The State Department succeeded in preventing the delivery of arms from the United States during the crucial months of Israel's war for independence in 1948, but it failed to prevent the establishment of the state of Israel because the arms the Jews needed came partly from their own factories, but crucially arrived from communist Czechoslovakia.

In 1979 Shlomo Slonim, then chair of the Department of American Studies at the Hebrew University of Jerusalem, published a carefully documented history of the American embargo and its negative impact on the Jewish Agency and on the state of Israel.[1] Slonim underscored the importance of Truman's support for the Partition Resolution at the UN and then his recognition of the new state of Israel in May 1948. Yet, he concluded, "in what was perhaps the most critical issue of all," that is, the supply of arms to the Jews in Palestine and then to Israel after May 14, 1948, when "the issue in which Israel's security and existence hung most in the balance – the approach of the State Department would seem to have prevailed. During the entire course of Israel's struggle for independence the [arms] embargo was rigorously maintained."[2]

By the time Slonim's important article was published, in an academic journal, the issue of the American arms embargo had faded from public consciousness as well as scholarly inquiry. The prevailing view in the 1970s was shaped by communist and leftist accusations that Israel was a "tool of US imperialism." The emergence of increasing American military assistance to Israel after the 1967 war obscured the realities of the American arms embargo during the war of 1947 and 1948. Slonim's pioneering work offered a starting point for further probing into the files of the State Department and the Pentagon concerning the American response to the Arab-Israeli war of 1947–8.

[1] Shlomo Slonim, "The 1948 American Embargo on Arms to Palestine," *Political Science Quarterly* 94, no. 3 (1979): 495–514.
[2] Ibid., 495–496.

The Embargo's Anti-Zionist Origins: Henderson's Initiative of November 10, 1947

The embargo began with an initiative from Loy Henderson, the State Department's leading opponent of establishing a Jewish state in Palestine. On November 10, 1947 he recommended to Secretary of State George Marshall that "effective immediately we suspend authorization for the export from the United States of arms, ammunition and other war material intended for use in Palestine or in neighboring countries, until the situation in that area has become somewhat more clarified."[3] From then until the end of the war, American officials argued that the arms embargo imposed equal restraints on both the Jews and the Arabs and thus reduced the prospects for an escalation of war. American supporters of the Jewish Agency and then Israel pointed out that an arms embargo on a not-yet-existing state, the Jewish Agency, and on the state of Israel – faced with invasion by five other states – was likely to disadvantage the Jews and Israel far more than the Arabs. They suspected that the unbalanced impact was the embargo's intended, not unintended, consequence.

On November 14, 1947 the Policy Committee on Arms and Armaments (PCAA), an interdepartmental body that brought together officials from the State Department and the military, adopted Henderson's proposal and agreed that, "effective immediately, the United States should suspend authorization for any newly-submitted applications for export from the United States of arms, ammunition, and implements of war intended for use in Palestine or in neighboring countries until the situation in that area has become somewhat more clarified."[4] The committee held weekly meetings to examine assorted arms sales.

Secretary Marshall and Under Secretary Robert Lovett both supported Henderson's proposal. On December 5, 1947 the State Department made it public. The next day Lovett wrote to Marshall that "if and when" the Jewish Agency requested military supplies from the United States, the USA should suggest that it send requests instead to "the British authorities in Palestine" or to the UN.[5] As the British at

---

[3] Loy Henderson to the Secretary [of State], Washington (November 10, 1947), "Suspension of Export of Arms and Ammunition to Arab States and Palestine," NACP RG 59, National Archives Microfilm Publications, M1390, Records of the Department of State Relating to the Internal Affairs of Palestine, 1945–1949, Roll 11, 867N.01/11–1047.

[4] Policy Committee on Arms and Armaments, "Minutes, November 14, 1947," Washington (November 14, 1947), NACP RG 353, Records of the Interdepartmental and Intradepartmental Committees Records of the Policy Committee on Arms and Armaments, 1947–1949 (Lot SSD303), General Records, Minutes-D-2, Box 1.

[5] "The Acting Secretary of State [Lovett] to the Secretary of State [Marshall] at London" (December 6, 1947), 501.BB Palestine/12–647, *Foreign Relations of the United States*

the time were engaged in disarming Haganah forces in Palestine who were defending Jewish communities from Arab attacks, it was bizarre that Lovett could have actually believed that these same British authorities would reverse policy and help to arm the Jews. Moreover, the British Foreign Office had made clear to the State Department that it had "treaty obligations to supply certain Middle Eastern states," Transjordan in particular, to deliver "war materials," and did not intend to cancel those obligations.[6] According to Slonim, it was "clear that the American policy makers, no less than their British counterparts, realized from the outset that while the arms embargo would profoundly affect the defense capabilities of the Jewish community, it would, at most, only marginally affect the Arab states. The latter would continue to receive British supplies in fulfillment of earlier commitments."[7]

The 1947–8 war began on November 30, 1947 with Arab ambushes on Jewish buses and sniping into Tel Aviv from Jaffa. Attacks on December 4 on buses traveling between Tel Aviv and Jerusalem followed a three-day general strike called by the Arab Higher Committee.[8] On December 9 Chaim Weizmann, leader of the World Zionist Organization, wrote to President Truman that "the only matter that causes us anxiety is our people's deficiency in the equipment necessary for our defense. The Arabs obviously suffer no such lack." The Jews, "the only people in the Near East threatened by aggression, are the only people who have not been able to provide freely for their own defense." To "correct this dangerous situation we shall have cause to rely on the good will of your administration."[9] In January Jewish Agency representatives Eliahu Epstein and Abba Eban met with Henderson and Dean Rusk at the State Department to request military assistance. Later that month Moshe Shertok, then foreign policy representative of the Yishuv, spoke of "the most urgent need" of arms assistance in talks with the US delegation at the UN. On January 23 Golda Meyerson (1898–1978; later Golda Meir), then head of the political department of the Jewish Agency, arrived in New York to urge the United States to lift the arms embargo.[10]

(hereafter *FRUS*), *The Near East and Africa*, 1947, vol. 5: https://history.state.gov/historicaldocuments/frus1947v05/d906

[6] Ibid.   [7] Slonim, "The 1948 American Embargo," 499.

[8] "Arabs Make Roads New Battlefields; Rake Bus Convoys," *New York Times*, December 4, 1947, 1. On the beginning of the war see Benny Morris, *1948: The First Arab-Israeli War* (New Haven: Yale University Press, 2009) and his *Righteous Victims: A History of the Arab-Zionist Conflict, 1881–2001* (New York: Vintage, 2001).

[9] Cited in Slonim, "The 1948 American Arms Embargo," 499.   [10] Ibid., 500.

Opposition to the Embargo in US Politics and the Press

On December 10, 1947 Congressman Emanuel Celler (D-New York) made the same case in a letter to the secretary of defense, James Forrestal. Offering military assistance to the Jews in Palestine would be in the United States's strategic interests because their proposed state "will definitely be oriented toward the Western democratic ideology."[11] The United States should "give it our help in encouraging and preserving that orientation. Contrary to some stories that have no foundation in fact, Palestinian Jews have no desire to embrace communist totalitarianism." Moreover, Celler continued, a Jewish state in Palestine offered a "unique opportunity for the United States to serve itself, and its interests in the Middle East, in keeping with our present foreign policy of containment of Russia."[12] Though the threat of "Arab aggression" had been exaggerated, "there is a troublesome element led by the former mufti." As the danger was real, the United States had a "moral as well as self-serving interest" in assuring that the Jewish Agency had "sufficient arms for defense before it becomes a state and has all the legal facilities for acquiring arms and equipment."[13]

Celler stressed the disparate impact of an embargo on the existing Arab states and on the Jews in Palestine.

The embargo on arms to the Middle East may seem equitable at first glance, but I do believe that if its end result will be that of sufficient arming of the Arabs and none for the Jews, such embargo would be most reprehensible. The Arabs already have lend-lease arms and Arab sovereignties can purchase arms from other countries. The Jews cannot do this as a sovereignty. Therefore, such an embargo only encourages aggression on the part of the Arabs for guerrilla tactics and so-called Holy Wars and punishes the Jews who seek arms only for self-defense.[14]

Celler proposed sending American arms to the Jewish Agency as the beginning of an unobtrusive alliance with the Jews in Palestine. To avoid the need to send US troops to enforce the Partition Plan, the "far wiser course" was "to send the necessary equipment" to the Haganah, the defense force of the Jewish Agency in Palestine. It needed small tanks, bazookas, anti-tank weapons, armored cars, light artillery, and aircraft for reconnaissance.

Celler adroitly sidestepped the controversial issue of sending US troops. He said that he had it on "trusted authority that the Haganah would welcome United States personnel for training and technical purposes. This I consider an excellent idea since such personnel could more than any other one factor assure United States influence and self-interest

---

[11] Emanuel Celler to James V. Forrestal, Washington (December 10, 1947), Library of Congress, Emanuel Celler Papers, Box 23.
[12] Ibid., 1.   [13] Ibid., 2.   [14] Ibid.

in the Middle East." The Haganah preferred "American military personnel to any other." Celler asked, "Might it not be possible to send some well-qualified retired army officers to advise and counsel the Jewish community in its transitory period toward statehood? Certainly, our political and economic interests in the Middle East would be best serve by establishing this link. In this manner, we enter and solidify influence unobtrusively and without political fanfare."[15]

Celler's argument that US military assistance would reinforce Israel's ties to the West and the United States stood completely outside the consensus in the State Department and at the Pentagon, which, as we have seen, firmly held that the Zionist project was a threat and liability to American interests. Despite his adroitness on the troops issue, the files of those agencies offer no evidence that any of the key policy makers considered Celler's suggestions as a serious option.

I. F. Stone, in the pages of *PM*, denounced the embargo's pretentions of even-handedness. On January 12, 1948 he called it "neutrality Spanish Civil War-style, an encouragement to the forces of lawlessness and disorder."[16] It had a very "serious loophole." While it was "imposing an embargo on the attacking Arabs and the attacked Jews, the U.S. is supplying arms to Turkey and Iran," and to Pakistan. "Yet all three of these Moslem countries voted against the Palestine decision of the UN, and there is nothing to stop them from passing American arms onto the Arabs." Further, for the State Department to impose an embargo "without a similar embargo order from London ... was to leave open the main Arab source of arms supply while shutting off the only source from which the Jews could hope to obtain arms." The British had renewed their military alliances with Iraq and "have shown no readiness to stop supplying arms to Iraq, Trans-Jordan, Syria or Egypt. Attacks on Palestine are being organized from all four."[17] Stone concluded that American "neutrality" was comparable to Western neutrality during the Spanish Civil War, when the Western embargo worked against the Republic "while Franco with Axis help beat it into submission." The current American embargo was "shutting off supplies to Jewish Palestine while the Arabs, with the aid of Britain and perhaps American arms obtained indirectly through Turkey, Iran or Pakistan, can go on with their attack on the Jews and on the UN decision. Is this perhaps, the State Dept.'s purpose: Does the White House realize what is going on? Does it approve?"[18] Stone's criticism indicated, as it had in his journalism since 1945, how the passions of leftist anti-fascism of the 1930s and 1940s influenced his view of the conflict in Palestine.

---

[15] Ibid. [16] I. F. Stone, "Jokers in the Palestine Arms Embargo," *PM*, January 12, 1948.
[17] Ibid. [18] Ibid.

Members of the Senate then took up the campaign against the embargo. On January 17, 1948 Senator Robert Wagner (D-New York) and Dean Alfange, chairman of the Committee to Arm the Jewish State, sent Marshall the following observations of the first weeks of the war between Jews and Arabs in Palestine: "The Arab attack upon the Jewish people inspired by the ex-Mufti of Jerusalem and former collaborator of Adolph Hitler is also an attack upon the authority of the United Nations and the prestige of the United States."[19] If the UN decision to partition Palestine "be nullified by deliberate sabotage on the part of the Arab states, which profess adherence to the United Nations Charter, the usefulness of that [Charter] should [sic] be irreparably impaired and its future jeopardized." Wagner and Alfange called on Marshall "to take immediate action to modify the arms embargo to the Middle East so as to permit lend-lease and shipment of military equipment to those states that support the United Nations decision to partition Palestine." As the United States had supported the Partition Resolution at the UN,

[It] must now take the leadership with[in] the framework of the United Nations to implement that decision. It is indefensible to exert our initiative to create a Jewish state on paper, and then simultaneously declare an arms embargo, the only effect of which is to enable Arabs to massacre defenseless Jews and prevent the fulfillment of the objective we so ardently sought. We would do simple justice to the Jewish people, while serving the cause of peace, to assist them in their heroic effort to resist aggression perpetrated in violation of international law.[20]

On January 23 Gordon Merriam of the Division of Near Eastern and African Affairs replied to Wagner and Alfange, informing them that "no change is now contemplated" in the arms embargo policy, and that the US government hoped "that the peoples of Palestine will cooperate in the peaceful implementation of the General Assembly [partition] resolution."[21]

On January 16 Senator Warren Magnuson (D-Washington), the lead sponsor of the 1943 Chinese Exclusion Repeal Act (also known as the Magnuson Act), wrote to Marshall in response to the casualties "occurring daily in Palestine." The evidence that the "fighting was premeditated to prevent the realization of Hebrew Palestine – even in its minimum form – is a matter of public record."[22] Inclusion of Palestine in the embargo "was most unfortunate in light of the actual situation." The United States had

---

[19] Senator Robert F. Wagner and Dean Alfange to Secretary of State George C. Marshall, Washington, DC (January 17, 1947), NACP RG 59, M1390, Roll 13, 867N.01/1–1648.

[20] Ibid.

[21] Gordon Merriam to Committee to Arm the Jewish State, Washington (January 23, 1947), NACP RG 59, M1390, Roll 13, 867N.01/1–1748.

[22] Senator Warren G. Magnuson to Secretary of State George C. Marshall, Washington (January 16, 1947), NACP RG 59, M1390, Roll 13, 867N.01/1–1648.

"transferred over $37,000,000 worth of surplus United States property to Arab League States, prior to the December 5 embargo." Britain announced it would continue to send arms worth an estimated $25 million dollars to Egypt, Iraq, and Transjordan, states "capable of aggression against Palestine."[23] Magnuson thought "it would appear self-evident that the present embargo is unilateral in effect, since it leaves the potential victims unarmed and helpless against any [one] carefully prepared and fully armed." It implied that the United States would "remain inert in the face of intensified attacks against the defenseless men, women and children of Palestine. Such a stand will only serve to spur the aggressors in their incendiary course."[24]

Magnuson added that the American public "favors the Hebrew cause in Palestine not only for reasons of sympathy and humanity," but also because of the "importance to the world" of this first test of a UN decision. He was aware that "certain well-intentioned Americans" had sought to "assist the embattled Hebrews by supplying munitions covertly." Such efforts would continue unless the US government changed its policies "because American citizens are drawn by tradition to every struggle for freedom and justice." The "Hebrews of Palestine" were not asking for US troops or foreign volunteers. They were "quite capable of defending themselves if they are permitted the most elementary rights of self-defense and are not cut off from all sources of supply in the face of full-scale military encirclement."[25] Magnuson viewed the Department's current policy as "a serious departure" from one of support for the UN. It was "improper for us to continue to enforce a cruel and arbitrary embargo on those who are in grave peril as a direct consequence of a United Nations decision [i.e. the November 29, 1947 Partition Resolution] which our government approved." He urged the State Department to lift the arms embargo and ensure that such arms include only those "commensurate with defense purposes."[26]

On January 19 the American Christian Palestine Committee (ACPC), whose leaders included Senators Owen Brewster (R-Maine), Edwin C. Johnson (D-Colorado), James E. Murray (D-Montana), Charles W. Tobey (R-New Hampshire), and Robert F. Wagner (D-New York), as well as Bartley Crum from the Anglo-American Committee of Inquiry on Palestine, published a full-page statement in *PM* about "the shameful and deeply disquieting situation" that had arisen in Palestine.[27] "Openly defying the United Nations, the governments of the Arab States,

---

[23] Ibid., 1–2.   [24] Ibid., 2.   [25] Ibid.   [26] Ibid.
[27] Senator Robert F. Wagner et al., "To the United States and the United Nations," *PM*, January 19, 1948.

themselves members of the UN, are deliberately encouraging aggression against the Jews of Palestine." They were using Syria, Lebanon, Egypt, and Iraq as bases, and had launched attacks from Syria and Lebanon "against Palestinian Jews." The result in Palestine was "unbridled violence by armed Arab bands organized by Haj Amin el Husseini, the same Arab leader who during the war [World War II] immeasurably aided Hitler in broadcasts from Berlin urging the Moslems of the Middle East to revolt against the Allies. This campaign of violence has no moral justification."[28]

Arab aggression "aimed to undo a decision of the United Nations" that was "a compromise that granted national states in Palestine to both Jews and Arabs." The current "campaign of violence" was "not a spontaneous uprising by most [of] Palestine's Arabs," for they "wish to live in peace with their Jewish neighbors. But they are terrorized by the ex-Mufti's bands assisted by his confederates in Cairo, Baghdad, Beirut and Damascus." The resulting "campaign of Arab aggression by a group of former Nazi allies and their accomplices across the frontiers" was directed not only at the Jews or the "peaceful majority of Palestine's Arabs but against the authority of the United Nations itself." It was "a bold attempt to blackmail the United Nations into submission ... an attempt by violence to render impotent" the UN's "first great decision." If the UN could not "make its Palestine decision stick, if a handful of willful men can prevent a UN decision from being carried out because they do not like that decision, then no future action of the UN will have more worth than the paper upon which it is written."[29]

Clearly, the ACPC placed responsibility for this state of affairs on "the ex-Mufti and his cohorts" as well as Britain's unwillingness or inability to sustain law and order in Palestine. In the face of Arab attacks on Jewish settlements and traffic on the highway, "British officials and forces have repeatedly interfered with Jewish defense and counterattack, repeatedly arrested and disarmed the defenders, and repeatedly confiscated their armaments." Yet the UN had not yet acted against these Arab members, nor did it react "to the fact that the ex-Mufti's bands and the attitude of the British administration" were "a clear challenge and threat to the UN's authority." Peace and stability demanded containment of this "Arab aggression" waged against both the Jews and the UN.[30]

The ACPC statement called for the United States to implement four measures: issue a "stern warning to the Arab States" to end their "sabotage of the UN decision"; issue a "clear declaration to Great Britain that as long as she remains in Palestine, her armed forces can be neither

[28] Ibid.   [29] Ibid.   [30] Ibid.

neutral nor quasi-neutral but must act in defense of public law and UN decision[s]"; have the "proper UN agencies ... provide international military protection for Palestine Jewry and make immediately available the necessary military force to implement the United Nations decision on Palestine"; and immediately send equipment to the Haganah under UN auspices to enable a "Jewish constabulary defense force to carry out police powers within Jewish territory in Palestine."[31] The signing of this statement by six United States senators, including some of the most prominent, was another challenge to the idea that the Zionist project was a cover for Soviet expansion – unless, of course, it was assumed that support for the Zionists would be seen as de facto evidence of precisely that. As with Celler's letter, the ad's strategic perspective and policy recommendations were worlds removed from the anti-Zionist consensus now embedded in the US national security establishment.

The journalists at *PM* continued their attacks on American policy toward Palestine. On January 28, in an editorial entitled "The Big Swap – Jewish Blood for Arabian Oil," I. F. Stone wrote that the State and War Departments had "made alarming headway in their campaign to win the President [Truman] over to a Pontius Pilate policy on Palestine." Both departments were "largely in sympathy with British plans to aid the Arabs against the Jewish community in the Holy Land, and want the White House to wash its hands of the whole affair and look the other way when the real shooting begins."[32] The United States was cooperating with the British blockade, which shut off supplies to the Jews in Palestine, "while British arms are being shipped to neighboring Arab countries in preparation for large-scale war this spring." British tactics were reflected in an editorial of "the bitterly anti-Zionist *Economist* of London," which envisioned a possible Anglo-American rapprochement in 1948, based on a common interest "to prevent Palestine from becoming 'another battleground between American money and Russian ideas.'"[33] Efforts to win Republicans over to a "bi-partisan" policy amounted to "a conspiracy of silence while a new war of extermination, this time against Palestinian Jewry, is being waged," Stone wrote. "This might be termed the bipartisan policy of the pogrom." According to Stone, both departments had been "engaged in a behind-the-scenes whispering campaign designed to smear Jewish refugees and the Palestinian Jewish community and to spread the view that American needs for oil 'unfortunately' require

---

[31] Ibid.
[32] I. F. Stone, "The Big Swap – Jewish Blood for Arabian Oil," *PM*, January 28, 1948, 4.
[33] Ibid.

betrayal of U.S. obligations to the UN." That, to Stone, boiled down to "a cynical policy of swapping Jewish blood for Arab oil."[34]

On February 5 an "Arms for Jewish Palestine Mass Meeting" took place in New York City. Speakers included Mayor William O'Dwyer, Dr. Abba Hillel Silver of the Jewish Agency, US senator Charles W. Tobey, Moshe Shertok, Dr. Emanuel Neumann of the Zionist Organization of America, and Dr. Israel Goldstein, chairman of the American Zionist Emergency Council. The event announcement in the pages of *PM* asked, "Why does the United States refuse to help the Jews of Palestine arm themselves to defend and perpetuate a United Nations decision? Why is our Government silent about an international force to aid the United Nations Palestine Commission implement a decision of the General Assembly of the United Nations?"[35] The advertisement for the rally illustrated the close links between AZEC and *PM*.

In "Oil and Anti-Zionism," published in *PM* on February 10, Stone expressed anger and even disdain for American Palestine policy and its decision makers.[36] "Ignorance, ill-will and political illiteracy" had combined to create "a state of mind in official circles impervious to rational argument. The brass hats have decided that Jewish refugees are Reds and that a Jewish state in Palestine would be a Soviet base. This is current indoctrination at the War Department." Contrasting American policy in Germany and Palestine, he wrote that former bankers such as James Forrestal and William Draper, both now in government, seemed "to be as intent on destroying the Yishuv as they are on rebuilding the Reich."[37] Stone noted ironically the simultaneity of American support for economic recovery in West Germany with the State Department's suggestion that Nazism's victims were part of a plan for Soviet expansion in the Middle East as well as its decision to impose an embargo on arms to the Yishuv.

In view of the war in Palestine begun by the Arab Higher Committee two months earlier, Stone concluded that implementation of the Partition Plan would require the use of force. He argued that if the goal was to prevent the Arabs from turning to the Soviet Union, then Moscow should be associated with, not excluded from, any action taken to enforce the Partition Resolution. Exclusion would, in the eyes of the Arabs, absolve the Soviets "from responsibility" for and association with the establishment of a Jewish state in Palestine, permitting the communists later to "capitalize on Arab disenchantment."[38] Their inclusion in a UN determination to implement partition even in the face of Arab threats would

---

[34] Ibid.
[35] "Arms for Jewish Palestine Mass Meeting Tomorrow," *PM*, February 4, 1948.
[36] I. F. Stone, "Oil and Anti-Semitism," *PM*, February 10, 1948, 7.   [37] Ibid.   [38] Ibid.

expose them to Arab anger. Stone's insight was not shared by the official architects of US policy toward Israel – Marshall, Lovett, Henderson, Kennan, Forrestal, and the Joint Chiefs of Staff, as well as the CIA's director, Roscoe Hillenkoetter.

Stone also criticized Britain for using the UN debates "to prove that Britain was the only true friend of the Arabs." Iraq's postwar uprising against the British presence and British military bases, along with a "chill" in negotiations for British bases elsewhere, was "the fruit of that oil imperialism perfumed for Arab nostrils with anti-Zionism, which London is urging Washington to imitate."[39] "Oil imperialism" was fanning the flames of anti-Zionism in the interest of seeking and retaining the good will of the Arab regimes. What Stone depicted as the imperialist political coordinates of "anti-Zionism" were miles removed from where they would be in later years of the Cold War when the slogans of anti-imperialism on the global left became part of the anti-Zionist rhetorical arsenal.

Congressional opposition to the arms embargo was not a monopoly of liberals in the Democratic Party. On February 11 thirty Republican members of Congress addressed critical questions to Marshall. The signers included future secretary of state Christian Herter, and future senators Kenneth Keating (R-New York), Jacob Javits (R-New York), and Margaret Chase Smith (R-Maine).[40] Their letter noted reports of "extensive sales of arms" by Britain to the Arabs and expressed fear that there was a "grave danger that if the United Nations Palestine decision is rendered inoperative ... the United Nations itself may be made ineffective." They asked if it was true that Britain was "permitting arms to continue to be shipped to the Arab nations, and if so, does that interfere with carrying out of the United Nations decisions on Palestine?" Did the support of the Arab Higher Committee and the Arab League by the Arab nations "in their announced violent resistance to the UN decision on Palestine endanger the maintenance of international peace and security in the terms of the UN Charter?" What instructions would Marshall send to the US UN delegation "regarding the means for making effective the General Assembly's decision on Palestine?" Last, what was the United States prepared to do "to help in the implementation of the UN decisions on Palestine?"[41]

The thrust of the four questions was clear: these Republican members of Congress supported the November 29 Partition Resolution. They

---

[39] Ibid.
[40] "GOP Congressmen Call on Marshall to Clarify U.S. Policy on Palestine," *PM*, February 11, 1948, 6.
[41] Ibid.

wanted the United States to do so as well. They had read reports that
Britain was violating the arms embargo by shipping weapons to the Arab
states, and they held the Arab Higher Committee and Arab League
responsible for the war in Palestine. They wanted reassurance from
Marshall that the State Department was committed to implementation
of the Partition Resolution. When Republican senators asked Marshall
what the USA would do regarding "the means" for effectively implementing the UN Partition Resolution, they put the State Department on notice
that efforts to associate the Zionists with communists had run into opposition from *both* major political parties.

The drumbeat from *PM* continued. On February 22 Victor H. Bernstein
wrote that the refusal of the USA to support a UN army to enforce the
Partition Resolution had badly damaged the UN's prestige. The "conquest
of the UN by a handful of militant Arab leaders, most of them tainted with
Nazism, would be a final blow."[42] The absence of a UN army meant
"death to partition, death to peace." The result would be war and "the
chaos which would permit Russia, against whom the anti-Zionists are so
resolute [in] shutting the front door, to enter in its own way, and in its own
time, by the back." Bernstein referred to "the lovely . . . pattern for a sell-out
on Palestine" and asked with bitterness about its results: "What matters if
blood flows, so long as the oil flows, too? Ibn Saud [the Saudi king] will get
his billions – for a while. Standard Oil of New Jersey, California (Socony)
and Texas will get their billions – for a while. But the UN will have gotten a
mortal blow, and with the UN will go the world: And on whose hands the
blood?" Bernstein wrote that he hoped Truman and Marshall would
"choose UN morality and peace in preference to 10 Downing St, Beirut
and Standard Oil."[43]

The following week Bernstein continued his criticism in "Pipeline (Oil)
to the White House."[44] ARAMCO officials such as William Eddy
opposed the UN Partition Plan as it "might force abandonment of the
company's projected half-billion dollar pipeline and oil development plan
for Saudi Arabia and the Middle East." He called Eddy the "unofficial
American Secretary of State" who had been appointed to a position in the
State Department "to convince Washington that a half-billion dollar
investment is worth more than the UN, worth more than five million
dead Jews, worth more than any number of live ones." Eddy had a
pipeline of influence and access that crossed Saudi Arabia, to the
Mediterranean and then the Atlantic "directly into the White House."[45]

---

[42] Victor H. Bernstein, "Pattern for Sell-Out in Palestine," *PM*, February 22, 1948, 16.
[43] Ibid.
[44] Victor H. Bernstein, "Pipeline (Oil) to the White House," *PM*, February 27, 1948, 10.
[45] Ibid.

Criticism also emerged from the pages of *The New Republic*. In its February 16 issue, editor and former vice-president Henry Wallace denounced British policy.[46] Since November 29 "the British government, without American opposition," had "done all in its power to obstruct implementation of the partition plan ... waged undeclared war on the Jews, confiscating their weapons while they were under Arab attack ... permitted Arab troops commanded by the ex-Mufti of Jerusalem from his 'exile' in Egypt, to lay siege to the Old City of Jerusalem, to erect road-blocks on Palestine highways, to snipe at Jewish food-supply convoys."[47] Wallace rejected Bevin's claims to "speak, as he has so often done, in the name of 'Western civilization.'" Britain and the Arabs were "waging civil war against the United Nations."[48]

Yet, Wallace claimed, the USA was "undercutting the whole peace-making power of the UN." Having supported partition, it needed to stand behind that position and "insist that the British stop furnishing arms to the Arabs anywhere in the Middle East." Wallace condemned "a system that prevents shipments to Jews and encourages shipments to Arabs." The Arabs and oil resources "must not be pawns in a cold or hot Anglo-American war against Russia." Wallace had "listened to and read a lot of propaganda, much of it no doubt British inspired, to the effect that the Jews in Palestine are Communists, or that recent immigration has been largely communistic." He was "convinced that this is another false 'Red Menace' manufactured with the hope of justifying murder. The Jews of Palestine are not Communists." Many had come from Eastern Europe precisely because they "did not want to live in Communist lands ... The attempt to use the Red paintbrush to smear the Palestine picture is nothing short of criminal."[49]

Wallace urged the United States to order "the establishment of a Jewish defense militia" responsible to the UN. The Security Council should "halt the shipment of arms to the Arab League states which are waging war against the United Nations." The USA had the power to "stop violent deaths in the Holy Land. We must use it."[50] The architects of the Cold War had asserted that they were defending Western civilization. Wallace argued that doing so meant coming to the defense of the Jews in Palestine and supporting the decisions of the United Nations. Known by then for his dissent from Truman's hard line against the communists, Wallace's essay illustrated how the issue of the future of Palestine had become intertwined with debates about communism and anticommunism.

[46] Henry Wallace, "Palestine: Civilization on Trial," *The New Republic*, February 16, 1948, 9–10.
[47] Ibid.   [48] Ibid.   [49] Ibid., 10.   [50] Ibid.

Those, such as Wallace, who criticized Truman's hard line on the communists had a soft spot for Zionism.

Though the journalists at *The Nation* and *PM* made the case for the Jews and denounced the link between "oil and anti-Zionism," they did not directly challenge the State Department's contention, expressed in the Policy Planning Staff memos of January 1948, that a Jewish state would undermine American national interests in the Middle East. On March 6, 1948 two leaders of the United Zionist Revisionists of America, executive director Benzion Netanyahu (future historian of the Spanish Inquisition and father of a future Israeli prime minister) and the historian Joseph Schechtman, chair of its political committee, did just that in a letter to Charles Bohlen, the State Department counselor, following their meeting in March at the department.[51] US policy, they wrote, "must be based predominantly on the interests of this country as a champion of Western ideals, way of life and economic structure." They urged active US support for the establishment of a Jewish state in Palestine because doing so was "in the well-understood interests of the United States: a Jewish state, if established in cooperation with the U.S., will necessarily become a bastion of the Western world in the Middle East, a natural ally of the United States bound to it by ties of gratitude and common interest."[52]

American support did not necessarily lead to armed American intervention in Palestine. However, "a firm, unconditional, uncompromising stand on the part of the United States in favor of a Jewish State, leaving no doubt whatever as to this country's determination not to yield to Arab opposition, threats, sabotage and attacks, will undoubtedly convince the Arab League of the futility of their aggressive policy, which is obviously calculated to impress and intimidate the United States." If the Jewish forces were "adequately supplied with modern arms, and if voluntary enlistment in the Palestine Jewish defense forces is permitted – or at least not opposed – in the United States," the Jews would be able to defend themselves and deter Arab attacks, "for there is not the slightest

---

[51] Dr. B. [Benzion] Netanyahu and Dr. J. [Joseph] Schechtman to Charles E. Bohlen, New York (March 6, 1948), NACP RG 59, M1390, Roll 13, 867N.01/3-248. Their subsequent works as historians include: Benzion Netanyahu, *The Marranos of Spain from the Late 14th to the Early 15th Century According to Contemporary Hebrew Sources* (Ithaca: Cornell University Press, 1999) and *The Origins of the Inquisition in Fifteenth-Century Spain* (New York: New York Review of Books Press, 2001); and Joseph Schechtman, *The Arab Refugee Problem* (Philadelphia: University of Pennsylvania Press, 1952); *The Mufti and the Führer: The Rise and Fall of Haj Amin el-Husseini* (New York: T. Yoseloff, 1965); and *The United States and the Jewish State Movement: The Crucial Decade, 1939–1949* (New York: Herzl Press/T. Yoseloff, 1966).

[52] Netanyahu and Schechtman to Bohlen (March 6, 1948).

doubt that several tens of thousands of American War Veterans would volunteer, thus providing well-trained and enthusiastic manpower for the defense of Palestine."[53]

What is needed is the full realization on the part of this country's statesmen that the establishment of the Jewish State in Palestine is of vital interest to the United States, and the consistent and courageous implementation of this policy by all political, financial and technical means, short of direct military intervention. Such a firm line of conduct will offer the Jews all over the world the long overdue and only convincing proof that the United States is a friendly power and a reliable ally; this and only this, will stop the dangerously growing pro-Soviet trend, provoked and fed by sheer despair, and will secure the enthusiastic allegiance of world Jewry and of the Jewish State to the cause of the Western Allies.[54]

Netanyahu and Schechtman's letter presented the core elements of a policy alternative to that advocated by Henderson and Kennan and pursued by Marshall's State Department. Like Shertok, Wagner and Celler, Kirchwey, Stone, and Clark Clifford – and, by early 1948, some Republican members of Congress as well – they argued that it was the absence, not the presence, of firm and unambiguous support for Zionist aspirations that gave the Arab League the impression that violent rejection of the UN Partition Plan could succeed in bringing about a change in US policy. This uncertainty had made Arab aggression more, not less, likely. The US embargo on arms to the Jews and efforts to prevent American volunteers from fighting in Palestine also sent the message that US policy could be changed through Arab threats and acts of violence.

While the journalists at *PM* spoke of smears, red scares, and malicious slander, Netanyahu and Schechtman expressed concern about what they saw as "the dangerously growing pro-Soviet trend" among supporters of Zionist aspirations. They attributed that trend in part to the very policies the State Department was pursuing under the mantle of the containment of communism. They argued that clear evidence that the USA was "a friendly power and reliable ally" would secure "the allegiance of world Jewry and of the Jewish state to the cause of the Western Allies."[55] Hence, contrary to the consensus in the State Department, they argued that the best way to counter Soviet influence in the Middle East was for the USA to reverse policy, embrace the cause of the Jewish state, and make clear to the Arabs that resort to force was doomed to fail. Their advice fell on deaf ears. It was just a few weeks later, on March 19, that UN ambassador Warren Austin made public US rejection of the Partition Plan and

[53] Ibid.   [54] Ibid.   [55] Ibid., 2.

adoption of a trusteeship proposal that Henderson, Kennan, and the Policy Planning Staff had recommended in January.

Congressional Mobilization

Emanuel Celler remained the crucial driving force and spark plug for Congressional criticism of the State Department/Pentagon opposition to the Zionist project. On March 10 he and Senator James E. Murray,[56] along with forty-one other Democrats, including five US senators and thirty-six members of the House of Representatives, sent a letter to Secretary Marshall. Five of the forty-one, John Blatnik, Emanuel Celler, Sol Bloom, Abraham Multer, and Adolph Sabath, were Jewish.[57] The letter asked Marshall to "allay the rising fears that that the United Nations decision on Palestine is being sabotaged." The "violent opposition of the ex-Mufti of Jerusalem and his adherents is most deplorable, but this was only to be expected. More serious is the attitude of the Arab states, most of them members of the United Nations, who openly engage in acts of aggression against the neighboring country of Palestine." It was also "most regrettable" that Britain was both "refusing to facilitate the execution" of the UN partition resolution and was "using its power of control in a manner hardly calculated to decrease Arab violence" in Palestine.[58] Celler and his colleagues were "perplexed" that "our Government has prohibited the export of arms to the Middle East, irrespective of whether such arms are to be used to defy the United Nations decision, or, on the

---

[56] On Murray see the Congressional biography here: https://bioguideretro.congress.gov/Home/MemberDetails?memIndex=m001108; and the more detailed Wikipedia entry here: https://en.wikipedia.org/wiki/James_E._Murray.

[57] Emanuel Celler to Secretary of State George C. Marshall, Washington (March 10, 1948), NACP RG 59, M1390, Roll 13 867N.01/3–1048. The signatories were as follows: Senate: Carl Hayden (Arizona); Edwin C. Johnson (Colorado); James E. Murray (Montana); Francis J. Myers (Pennsylvania); and Glen H. Taylor (Idaho); House of Representatives: Joe B. Bates (Kentucky); John A. Blatnik (Minnesota); Sol Bloom (New York); William T. Byrne (New York); Joseph R. Bryson (South Carolina); Frank Buchanan (Pennsylvania); Charles A. Buckley (New York); John J. Delaney (New York); John D. Dingell (Michigan); Antonio M. Fernandez (New Mexico); Aime J. Forand (Rhode Island); Martin Gorski (Illinois); Thomas S. Gordon (Illinois); Edward J. Hart (New Jersey); Franck R. Havenner (California); James J. Heffernan (New York); Chet Holifield (California); Walter B. Huber (Ohio); Augustine B. Kelley (Pennsylvania); Eugene J. Keogh (New York); Thomas J. Lane (Massachusetts); Walter A. Lynch (New York); John W. McCormack (Massachusetts); Ray J. Madden (Indiana); Hugh A. Meade (Maryland); Thomas E. Morgan (Pennsylvania); Abraham J. Multer (New York); Donald L. O'Toole (New York); Joseph L. Pfeifer (New York); Philip J. Philbin (Massachusetts); Adam Clayton Powell (New York); John J. Rooney (New York); Adolph J. Sabath (Illinois); Georges G. Sadowski (Michigan); and Emanuel Celler (New York).

[58] Ibid., 1–2.

contrary, to uphold it." Rather than discouraging "armed conflict in Palestine" it was "a matter of common knowledge that Arab bands, supported by neighboring Arab states, are supplied out of stocks made available by our own government in the past, and by the British Government at present. To refuse export licenses to the Jewish defense forces in Palestine could obviously have no other result than to increase the odds against the Jewish defenders of the United Nations decision." The members of Congress were "surprised that such a policy could have been inaugurated by the American Government on its own initiative, and that it is still being maintained."[59]

Further, the members of Congress had received reports that the US government was urging other governments to slow down Jewish immigration to Palestine and had disapproved of the decisions of individual American citizens who had volunteered to join the Jewish defense force, the Haganah. "We do not recall that similar action was taken in either 1914 or 1940 when thousands of American citizens volunteered to defend what they believed to be the righteous cause of maintaining the freedom of Great Britain, France, Finland and other countries." The signatories did not see how such policies could be interpreted by Britain or the Arab governments "as anything but an indication that American support for the United Nations plan is far from genuine, thus encouraging them to undertake further attempts to overthrow the United Nations decision."[60] Celler's jointly signed letter added that "we would be less than frank, however, if we did not express to you our profound misgivings lest the attitude taken by our Government in the specific cases noted above, rather than facilitate the implementation of that decision, would render this implementation more difficult."[61]

On March 25 Lovett, writing for Marshall, replied.[62] Lovett referred to the statement by Austin at the UN on March 19 that it had become apparent that the Partition Plan could not be implemented by peaceful means.[63] That was Austin's way of referring to the Arab Higher Committee's resort to force in order to reject the Partition Plan. Lovett cited Austin's announcement that day abandoning the Partition Resolution in favor of a temporary trusteeship under the auspices of the UN. Lovett told Celler that the arms embargo was "imposed with a view to reducing conflict in the area." The evidence indicated that "arms in the area are being used by both sides for the furtherance of terrorism, murder and intimidation. Until the peoples of Palestine can demonstrate their

---

[59] Ibid.   [60] Ibid., 2.   [61] Ibid.
[62] Robert Lovett to James E. Murray, Washington (March 25, 1948), NACP RG 59, M1390, Roll 13, 867N.01/3–1048.
[63] Warren Austin, cited in ibid., 3.

ability for self-control and self-government, there is every reason to believe that an increase in the supply of arms to either side would but further promote violence in Palestine."[64] Lovett's reply captured the mood in the State Department very well. First, it was one of moral and political equivalence, asserting that the Jews who accepted the Partition Plan were equally to blame for the outbreak of war with the Arabs who resorted to arms to defeat it. Second, it condescended to both Jews and Arabs, as if the outbreak of the war was due of a lack of self-control and self-government. Third, he did not engage with or dispute the alternative account of the events that the senators and members of the House had offered.

Celler replied on April 10. He had read Lovett's letter "with no little amazement."[65] He cited Austin's statement on March 2 that the UN Security Council was entitled to "prevent aggression against Palestine from outside." Authoritative sources had indicated "that 7,500 armed troops have invaded Palestine, particularly from Syria, Lebanon and Iraq. Is this not aggression against Palestine from outside?" There was "overwhelming evidence" that Syria and Egypt were "financing expeditions into Palestine," while the Lebanese government had "openly voted appropriations for arms and men to invade Palestine. Has the United States at Lake Success [near New York City, where the UN was meeting] made any mention of such aggression or even made a gesture of protest?"[66] Celler reminded Lovett of Herschel Johnson's statement at the UN in November that the solution to the Palestine problem "cannot be done without the use of the knife" – that is, the United States understood then that force might be needed to implement the UN Partition Plan should the Arabs take up arms to defeat it.

Celler then turned to Lovett's defense of the arms embargo as one intended to reduce conflict. If that was its intent, it had "obviously failed, giving rise only to the inequitable condition whereby Arabs from within and without Palestine are adequately armed and the Jews of Palestine, fighting a defensive battle, are deprived of the arms they sorely need." In reply to Lovett's comment about a deficiency of self-control and capacity for self-government, Celler asked why Lovett spoke "only of the ability for self-control of the peoples of Palestine," referring to the Jews. In view of the evidence presented in debates of the UN General Assembly, the issue of "self-control and non-interference with

[64] Austin Warren, cited in ibid., 3–4.
[65] Emanuel Celler to Robert Lovett, Washington (April 10, 1948), NACP RG 59, M1390, Roll 14, 867.01N/4–1048.
[66] Ibid.

the affairs of the peoples of Palestine," instead "should be directed to the surrounding Arab states." Celler continued:

You equalize the blame in view of the evidence that it is the Jews who have been placed in the position of self-defense and who have at the same time amply demonstrated their ability for self-government. Why is that distinction not made by the Department of State when that distinction is clearly set forth by the report of the Palestine Commission to the Security Council? Whose purpose is the arms embargo really serving? Is it not a fact that Great Britain and France are sending arms to aggressive Arab states under the cover of "contractual obligations"? France recently shipped seven million dollars' worth of arms to Syria. The British have maintained a strong blockade around the coast to prevent any shipment of arms to Palestine Jews while carrying out their "contractual obligations" to the Arabs. How is self-control among the Arabs strengthened when it is common knowledge that the arms embargo has encouraged them in their intransigency?[67]

Finally, Celler asked "why the possibility of using force in the imposition of a trusteeship is being given consideration while the use of force in imposing partition has been ruled out by our delegation at the United Nations. Can this be satisfactorily explained?"[68] In Celler, the leaders of the State Department, including Marshall, Lovett, and Kennan, had clearly met their match.

Replying on April 20, Lovett cited the language of a UN Security Council resolution of April 17 that called on both the Arab Higher Committee and the Jewish Agency "to cease all activities of a military nature" and "refrain from importing armed groups and individuals, and weapons into Palestine." Lifting the arms embargo would make it possible for "both sides" to obtain arms from the United States and would also conflict with the language of that Security Council resolution. The Security Council had supported the British decision not to make a port available to the Jews "for the importation of arms and men." While it rejected the use of force "to impose a political solution," Lovett said he thought a UN trusteeship would maintain law and order and facilitate an eventual solution.[69] He did not address the substance of the criticism in the Celler–Murray letter.

Eleanor Roosevelt was a member of the US UN delegation. She opposed the State Department's policy on Palestine. On March 22, 1948 she wrote to Marshall in the aftermath of Austin's announcement of the trusteeship proposal. With that in mind, she argued that "if we try to set up a Mandate giving it to several nations and leaving the USSR out, we will offend the USSR deeply and create more tensions between us."[70] She found

---

[67] Ibid., 2.   [68] Ibid., 2–3.
[69] Lovett to Celler, Washington (April 20, 1948), NACP RG59, M1390, 867N.01/4–1048.
[70] Eleanor Roosevelt to George Marshall, Hyde Park (March 22, 1948), NACP RG59, M1390, 867N.01/3–2248.

"ridiculous" secretary of defense James Forrestal's worries that if the Soviet Union sent forces, "we would never get the USSR out of Palestine" and would have to mobilize American armed forces, and said that they had to "face the fact that joint forces, sometimes of equal strength, were the ultimate objective of the United Nations."[71] Currently, the United States was "in every possible way ... acting to hurt the United Nations." It looked as though "the USSR were the only government that was upholding the United Nations Assembly decision," that is, the Partition Resolution of November 29, 1947. She believed that the United States had "a moral obligation due to our acceptance of the Balfour Declaration" and "tacit agreement in the forming of a Jewish homeland" in Palestine. Yet, due to the reversal of policy on partition, "I feel at the present time that we have more or less buried the UN." She offered to resign from the US delegation as it must be "extremely difficult" to have "someone serve under you who criticizes the attitude of the Administration."[72]

Marshall, aware of the damage her resignation could cause, replied two days later. He defended the trusteeship proposal as "the sole remaining resource available to us under the Charter to avoid a period of bloodshed after May 15th," the day when the British Mandate ended. Marshall referred obliquely to "a rather clever propaganda which has twisted the purpose [by] implication of most of our efforts until there is nationwide misunderstanding." He was "most unwilling" to accept her resignation from the UN Human Rights Commission.[73] Eleanor Roosevelt remained on the UN delegation.

In fact, there was no "misunderstanding." Marshall's critics understood, and disagreed with, the State Department's turn against partition. The writers at *PM*, for example, denounced the State Department's maneuvers in the UN. On March 22 Victor Bernstein wrote that "the American policy shifts of the last 72 hours" were not only betrayals of the Jews but of the United Nations as well.[74] Regarding Palestine and the Jews, "the betrayal was in the making for a long, long time. One day the historian, with access to State Dept. records, will link the wartime appeasement of the Arabs with the policy which is now unfolding." Yet, even at the time, journalists could see that there were doubts about how sincerely the United States "threw its weight behind partition."[75] The "betrayal" of Palestine and the Jews began when policy was "handed over for execution to experts who disagree with

[71] Ibid.   [72] Ibid., 2.

[73] George Marshall to Eleanor Roosevelt, Washington (March 24, 1948), NACP RG 59, M1390, 867N.01/3-2248.

[74] Victor H. Bernstein, "Palestine, Trieste and Betrayal of UN," *PM*, March 22, 1948, 10.

[75] Ibid. On this see Jeffrey Herf, *Nazi Propaganda for the Arab World* (New Haven: Yale University Press, 2009).

it." Bernstein thought back on "the pressure which the U.S. delegation consistently brought to bear upon the delegates of the Jewish Agency to yield land in the proposed Jewish state," including the Galilee, Jerusalem, and "hundreds of square miles in the Negev. 'That's the only way to get partition,' the U.S. delegates said. The Jews listened – and gave up the land. To what purpose?" The "betrayal was finally unmasked in the 48 hours which culminated in the trusteeship plan" that Austin had proposed. With his speech, "the sell-out is complete." It made war more, not less, likely, but the oil was flowing and pipelines for ARAMCO would be built "now that partition is dead."[76]

I. F. Stone, in a March 29 *PM* column, "Warning on Zion Embargo Maneuver," called for lifting the embargo on arms to the Jews but continuing to impose it on the Arabs.[77] "The embargo ought to be modified," he wrote, "to allow the Jews to buy arms here for defense but to bar arms to Arab nations defying a UN decision. And the British ought to be ordered by the UN to lift the blockade" because that was the obstacle to delivery of arms that had been purchased in Europe or Latin America. Since the United States on November 29 had supported partition, it was obligated to support the means to bring it about.

Stone's anger about the public shift in American policy led him, for the first time, to name antisemitism as one of the motivating causes of State Department policy. He said he thought it was not clear what the Truman White House would do "from one hour to the next. But what the people in the Washington oil lobby and the anti-Jewish brigade in State Dept. have in mind is something quite different."[78] If the State Department lifted the arms embargo the Arab states would continue to "buy arms here," but "of course" the USA would "not permit the purchase nor the British navy the delivery of arms designed to enable the Jews to defend their new state" against a US, British, and French trusteeship. The Yishuv would be placed in the untenable legal position of "fighting an international trusteeship legalized – if the U.S.A. can muster the vote at Lake Success – by a UN Assembly vote reversing partition."[79] Stone reasoned that since Marshall, Lovett, Kennan, and Henderson were all sophisticated practitioners of international politics, they must understand that objectively their policies were disadvantageous and even dangerous to the Jews in Palestine. Yet, knowing that, they pursued them anyway. The policies did not need to be antisemitic in their inspiration in order to be anti-Jewish and certainly anti-Zionist in their consequences. He

---

[76] Bernstein, "Palestine, Trieste and Betrayal of UN."
[77] I. F. Stone, "Warning on Zion Embargo Maneuver," *PM*, March 29, 1948, 4.
[78] Ibid.   [79] Ibid.

reached those conclusions without knowledge of the classified memoranda examined in previous chapters – memos that, as we have seen, made apparent the depth of official anti-Zionism.

While these public debates were taking place the Jewish Agency's Moshe Shertok and Eliahu Epstein, at Marshall's invitation, met with him and Lovett at the State Department on March 26.[80] Shertok stated that the Jewish Agency would not agree to a truce while "foreign troops were in Palestine and infiltration of reinforcement continued." He estimated that about 6,000 well-armed Arab troops from Syria, Lebanon, Transjordan, and Iraq were then in Palestine. The British had "done little or nothing to oppose them or eject them." Asked if the Jewish Agency would accept a truce if one of the terms included withdrawal of such armed bands from Palestine, Shertok replied that would not be enough as "the period of the truce would be used by the Arabs to build up their forces through infiltration, to run in additional arms, and otherwise to improve their position, since the truce would assure them of a period of time during which they would not be attacked by the Haganah." Failure to "require the withdrawal of the armed bands and prevent future border violation by infiltration or otherwise would be regarded by the Jewish communities in Palestine as a 'complete capitulation to the Arabs.'"[81]

Epstein and Shertok told Marshall and Lovett that the Jewish Agency would only agree to a truce if it included four conditions: hostilities by each party should cease completely; all identifiable groups of armed men should be withdrawn from Palestinian territory; strict border patrols should be instituted as protection against any further infiltration; and the rights of the Jewish Agency should be "reserved" and its position not "prejudiced" by the truce. In response to Marshall's question about the ability of "the Palestine settlement," that is, the Jews in Palestine, to defend themselves, Shertok said that while they were "in desperate need of arms, including artillery, tanks and armored vehicles," they would fight, and do so successfully. If foreign assistance was needed, Shertok felt there would be Jewish volunteers from "all over the world" and "assistance from certain powers." Shertok and Epstein expressed skepticism about the US trusteeship proposal, with Shertok adding that it would be "intolerable" to have the British remain as a trustee.[82]

Despite Truman's anger at the State Department's attempt to reverse US support for the Partition Plan, he did not lift the arms embargo and did not overrule Marshall's rejection of Shertok's request for military assistance. In

[80] "Memorandum of Conversation, by the Under Secretary of State (Lovett)," Washington (March 26, 1948), 867N.01/3–2648, *FRUS*, 1948, vol. 5, part 2: https://history.state.gov/historicaldocuments/frus1948v05p2/d122.
[81] Ibid.   [82] Ibid.

April 1948, at the United Nations, the United States supported truce resolutions that did not call for withdrawal of the Arab state forces in Palestine but did include both maintaining the arms embargo and the possibility of continuing the British Mandate under a trusteeship. On April 2 a remarkably detailed fourteen-page, single-spaced State Department memorandum reflected the time and effort that the Department had devoted to plans for a "trusteeship system" under the UN. Its forty-seven clauses about the future governing structure offered a clear alternative to partition and the establishment of a Jewish and an Arab state in Palestine.[83] American policy toward Palestine continued to run on two tracks, one of rhetorical support for Zionist aspirations associated with the Truman White House, and a second track, conducted by the State Department and Pentagon, that opposed those aspirations in practical, consequential ways. The gap between the two tracks remained in place throughout the course of the war from November 1947 to early 1949.

The UN Security Council Truce Resolutions of Spring 1948

Marshall and Lovett proved skillful at using the UN Security Council to lend support to US policy, as was evident in the shaping of UN truce resolutions regarding the first civil war phase of the war in Palestine. In the Security Council on April 15, 1948 the Colombian delegation introduced a draft of a truce resolution supported by the United States and Canada that echoed the language of political neutrality characteristic of the discourse of the State Department.[84] It included four paragraphs calling on "all persons and organizations in Palestine and especially the Arab Higher Committee and the Jewish Agency" to:

a) cease all activities of a military or a para-military nature, as well as acts of violence, terrorism and sabotage; b) refrain from bringing into Palestine armed bands or individuals, whatever their origin, armed or capable of bearing arms, and from assisting or encouraging the entry into Palestine of such armed bands and individuals; c) refrain from importing or acquiring or assisting or encouraging the importation or acquisition of weapons and war materials; d) refrain, pending further consideration of the future government of Palestine by the General Assembly, from any political activity which might prejudice the rights, claims, or positions of either community.[85]

---

[83] "Memorandum Prepared in the Department of State," Washington (April 2, 1948), "Draft Trusteeship Agreement for Palestine with the United Nations as the Administering Authority," 501.BB Palestine/4–848, *FRUS*, 1948, vol. 5, part 2: https://history.state.gov/historicaldocuments/frus1948v05p2/d133.

[84] United Nations Security Council, S/722, "Draft Resolution Submitted by the Representative of Columbia) at the 282nd Meeting, 15 April 1948": https://documents-dds-ny.un.org/doc/UNDOC/GEN/NL4/829/00/pdf/NL482900.pdf?OpenElement.

[85] Ibid.

In his response to the Security Council Shertok pointed out that the resolution did not mention that one of the essential preconditions for a truce was that "the armed units which had been brought into Palestine from outside should be withdrawn." He rejected the implication in the draft that the Mandatory Power, Britain, had hitherto discharged its responsibilities to maintain peace and order, as that was "not the case."[86] He wanted to delete the stipulation that "all activities of a political and military nature" should cease, since it was far too wide to be practicable and might be interpreted as applying to "all normal defence arrangements." He also objected to the clause opposing the introduction into Palestine of "individuals capable of bearing arms," as doing so would affect – that is, hinder – Jewish immigration. Further, refraining "from importing or acquiring or assisting or encouraging the importation or acquisition of weapons and war materials" during the truce "might be interpreted as imposing, during the truce period, a world embargo on the acquisition of arms for future defence, while leaving the Arab states free to accumulate arms for future fighting in Palestine." Shertok suggested that "[all reference to] acquisition should be deleted," as well as the paragraph calling for refraining from "any political activity which might prejudice the rights, claims, or positions of either community."

But the larger issue for Shertok was that the proposed truce resolution appeared to be part of a strategy to set aside the Partition Plan "for an entirely different solution of the Palestine problem which the Jewish agency found utterly unacceptable."[87] The proposal, "from its very inception, appeared to load the dice very heavily against Jewish interests." By referring only to a truce between the Jewish and Arab communities in Palestine it "ignored the major aspect of the present disturbed conditions of the country, which is the invasion of the country from the outside, organized by the governments of the neighboring Arab states, members of the United Nations and, in the case of Syria, a member of the Security Council itself, and tolerated by the mandatory power [United Kingdom]."[88]

The Jewish Agency was willing to enter a truce only if it was effective, not a "sham cover and protection for the preparation of further aggression," and would not "jeopardize legitimate, long-term Jewish interests."

---

[86] *Yearbook of the United Nations 1947–48* (New York: United Nations, 1948), "Report of the President on Negotiations for a Truce and Consideration of the Columbian Draft Resolution," 412.

[87] Mr. [Moshe] Shertok (Jewish Agency for Palestine), Lake Success, New York (April 15, 1948), United Nations Security Council (hereafter UNSC), S/P.V.292, 25.

[88] Ibid., 26.

If the aggression against the Jews had been confined to the Arabs of Palestine, we would have been ready for a truce unconditionally . . . But the military situation in Palestine has been completely transformed by the invasion of the country from outside. The very presence on the soil of Palestine of foreign armed forces is a permanent act of aggression against the Jews. Unless these forces are removed and further armed aggression prevented, the truce would be a godsend to the aggressor, for under its cover and without the fear of any interference on the part of the Jews, the Arab Command would be able to bring up further reinforcements to occupy points of vantage, to perfect its military organization and to be ready for renewed assault under much more advantageous conditions. Therefore, we here put forward as the essential conditions of the truce . . . that the armed units which have been brought into Palestine from outside should be withdrawn and that no further incursions should be tolerated.[89]

The resolution's demand to "cease all activities of a military or paramilitary nature" was equally unacceptable as it might be interpreted to mean ending measures needed for self-defense. While it welcomed the injunction against bringing armed bands and individuals into Palestine, the Jewish Agency would not accept banning "individuals capable of bearing arms." The Jewish Agency disagreed that Jewish immigrants into Palestine should "whatever their age or physical condition . . . be put on the same footing with those elements that are now being sent into Palestine in violation of its land frontier with the deliberate purpose of upsetting the peace of the country and committing acts of aggression against the Jews and against the authority of the United Nations." The latter had no legal or political right to be in Palestine, while the "Jewish immigrants came to Palestine by virtue of an internationally recognized right. Palestine is their home in which they came to live. The equation of these two categories is untenable."[90] Shertok also rejected the draft resolution's ban on importation or acquisition of weapons and war materials as it could be "interpreted as imposing, during the truce period, a world embargo on the acquisition of arms for future Jewish defense, while leaving it free to the Arab states to accumulate any quantity of arms they may be able to purchase, even during the truce period, for future fighting in Palestine."[91]

Shertok emphasized that "the foreign invasion is the crux of the whole difficulty" and contended that Britain had "allowed it to proceed unchecked." Yet the Security Council had not yet placed responsibility on the Arab states and the United Kingdom "for the present intolerable situation which has been created by this continued process of invasion." Instead, "no doubt encouraged by such inaction of the Security Council," the Arab states were "reliably reported to be preparing plans for the

[89] Ibid., 31–32.   [90] Ibid., 34.   [91] Ibid., 35.

occupation of whole areas of Palestine by their armies which would cross its frontiers from north, east and south immediately after the termination of the United Kingdom mandate. To face this issue squarely is, I submit, the most urgent duty of the Security Council."[92] In short, Shertok argued that the proposed Security Council resolution, one supported by the United States and Great Britain, would damage the Jewish Agency's capacity for self-defense against Arab efforts to undo the UN's own Partition Resolution. The continuation of the arms embargo within the truce proposal was central to that damaging impact. Shertok understood that the United States and United Kingdom, through the seemingly arcane wording of its resolutions, had learned how to use the Security Council to serve purposes similar to those Britain had pursued before handing the issue over to the UN in spring 1947.

As had been the case in May and November 1947, the USSR's Andrei Gromyko again supported Shertok's arguments.[93] In response to the Security Council's call for "all persons and organizations" to "cease all activities of a military or para-military nature, as well as acts of violence, terrorism and sabotage," Gromyko referred to the objections voiced by "the representative of the Jewish Agency," who had said that it was "directed against the interests of one party and is in favor of the interests of the other party." He agreed with Shertok that adoption of this paragraph "would not provide the necessary conditions for the practical establishment of a truce."[94] He also commented on the resolution's paragraph that called for refraining from "bringing into Palestine armed bands or individuals, whatever their origin, armed or capable of bearing arms, and from assisting or encouraging the entry into Palestine of such armed bands and individuals." Gromyko again referred to Shertok's objection that "the paragraph raises a question of immigration and, in particular, of perfectly legal and lawful Jewish immigration into Palestine."[95]

It is the opinion of the delegation of the USSR that the statement made by the representative of the Jewish Agency upon this matter deserves the most serious attention. The paragraph as it now stands, does not take account of the lawful rights of the Jews; it is directed against the protection of the lawful interests of the Jews in particular in connection with this matter of immigration ... The delegation of the USSR cannot accept paragraph 1(b).[96]

---

[92] Ibid., 35.

[93] *United Nations Yearbook 1947–48*, "Report of the President on Negotiations for a Truce and Consideration of the Columbian Draft Resolution," 413.

[94] Mr. [Andrei] Gromyko (USSR), Lake Success, New York (April 16, 1948), UNSC, Verbatim Record of 283rd Meeting, S/P.V. 283, 6–7.

[95] Ibid., 8–10.   [96] Ibid.

Gromyko asserted instead that there was "no proper direct relation between immigration and the problem of the truce, although some delegations," that is, the United States, "have attempted artificially to establish such a connection between lawful Jewish immigration and the establishment of a truce in Palestine" – between stopping such immigration as a precondition for a truce.[97]

Gromyko drew attention to another section of the draft, which called for refraining from "importing or acquiring or assisting or encouraging the importation or acquisition of weapons and war materials." This "very serious question," he said, had been "wrongly" put; it worked "against one party and hardly touches the other." It was acceptable to the USSR delegation "only if the question is also put of the necessity for the withdrawal of armed groups which have entered Palestine from outside in order to take part in the struggle." The region, that is, the Arab states, from which such armed groups came, was "well-known to the Security Council." It was "absolutely essential the matter raised in this paragraph should be linked with the prohibition of further incursions of armed bands from outside Palestine." He proposed a new paragraph in which the Security Council "calls for the immediate withdrawal of all armed bands which have invaded Palestine, and for the prevention into the future of the invasion of Palestine by such groups." That would make the paragraph "more equitable."[98] Gromyko's arguments mirrored Shertok's.

Gromyko also rejected the demand to end all political activity in Palestine; doing so would invalidate the General Assembly Partition Resolution. It exaggerated the immediate political aspect of the problem and underemphasized the military dimension – which was odd, given that the point was to seek a truce in a war.[99] He turned to the draft's summons to "all governments and particularly those of the countries neighboring Palestine" to assist in efforts to prevent "entry into Palestine of armed bands, individuals armed or capable of bearing arms and weapons and war materials." The "defect" of this clause was that it conflated the issue of persons bearing arms in "connection with Jewish immigrants which is perfectly legal. Like the whole of this resolution, this paragraph is directed against the interests of one party and against the legal rights of that party"[100] – that is, against the interests of the Jews in Palestine. Here again, Gromyko echoed the positions taken by Shertok.

Gromyko's concluding judgment of the American-supported resolution was withering. The draft resolution as it stood was "inequitable and unjust. It favors one party and is to the detriment of the legal rights of the other. It corresponds to the interests, narrowly conceived of one party

[97] Ibid.   [98] Ibid., 11.   [99] Ibid., 13.   [100] Ibid.

and is opposed to the interests of the other."[101] Despite the references to "both parties" and the appearance of even-handedness, the resolution "objectively" served the interests of the Arabs and the British, and worked against the interests of the Jews. Gromyko was right on the substance, clear and cogent in his argument, and unabashed in his partisanship for the positions that Shertok had presented.

The Security Council rejected these Soviet amendments to the resolution by a vote of six to two, with the United States and the UK among the no votes, the USSR and Ukrainian SSR voting yes. The original resolution therefore remained fundamentally intact and was adopted by a vote of nine to two. The no votes came from the Soviet Union and the Ukrainian SSR. The contrast between American and Soviet and communist positions in spring 1948 was clear: the former opposed the arguments of the Jewish Agency; the latter supported them.

The next day, April 16, the Security Council adopted an identical truce resolution that remained the key text for all subsequent UN truce proposals until the end of the Arab-Israeli war. It called on the Arab Higher Committee and the Jewish Agency to immediately

(a) Cease all activities of a military or para-military nature, as well as acts of violence, terrorism and sabotage.
(b) Refrain from bringing and from assisting and encouraging the entry into Palestine of armed bands and fighting personnel, groups and individuals, whatever their origin.
(c) Refrain from importing or acquiring or assisting or encouraging the importation or acquisition of weapons and war materials
(d) Refrain, pending further consideration of the future government of Palestine from the General Assembly from any political activity which might prejudice the rights, claims or position of either community[102]

The resolution reflected the policy first elaborated in the Division of Near Eastern and African Affairs (NEA) of the State Department and then adopted by Lovett and Marshall. As we have just seen, in the Security Council discussions preceding its adoption the Soviet Union supported the Zionists' positions, just as it had done in the first Special Session of the General Assembly in May 1947 and in the General Assembly meeting in fall 1947. Whereas in the previous UN meetings the USA had kept a low profile or, as in fall 1947, even lent support to the Zionists, by spring 1948, despite growing criticism in Congress, the State Department's opposition to the Zionists was now

---

[101] Ibid., 14–15.
[102] "Resolution Adopted 17 April 1948 Concerning a Truce in Palestine at the Two Hundred and Eighty-Third Meeting of the Security Council, 16–17, April 1948," UNSC, Security Council, S/723.

clearly visible in truce resolutions – resolutions whose violation could place the Jews in Palestine in danger of finding themselves in opposition to both the Security Council and the United States. The American diplomatic maneuvering in the Security Council in April 1948 was another result of the Anglo-American consensus established during the Pentagon talks and articulated in the position papers of the Policy Planning Staff in in fall 1947 and early winter 1948. In the language of neutrality about "both sides," the UN truce resolutions would continue, as Shertok and Gromyko pointed out, to place the Jews at a disadvantage and obscure the realities of aggression and defense in the coming months. The United States and the United Kingdom had learned how to use the UN Security Council to add international legitimacy to an embargo on arms that originated in the pursuit of their respective national interests.

The Impact of the Resolution from David Ben-Gurion's Perspective

Once the Arabs had begun the war in December 1947, the Jewish leadership in Palestine was determined that the outcome of that war, not UN Security Council resolutions, would determine the "solution" of the conflict in Palestine. In his diary and speeches of these months David Ben-Gurion (1886–1973), the leader of the Jewish Agency and of its armed forces, assessed events abroad from the standpoint of how they affected the course of the war and the fate of the Jews in Palestine. Fully expecting an Arab invasion after the Jews declared statehood, Ben-Gurion was convinced that the question of statehood was also one of whether the Jews in Palestine could survive or not. A year earlier, in remarks to the Zionist Congress in Tel Aviv, he had said that the major problem facing the Yishuv was self-defense. It was used to defending itself against the Palestinian Arabs who occasionally attacked Jewish settlements. "But now we are facing a totally new situation. Israel is surrounded by independent Arab states ... which have the right and capacity to acquire arms ... While the attack of the Palestinian Arabs does not endanger the Jewish community; we are now facing the prospect of the Arab states sending their armies to attack us ... We are thus facing mortal danger."[103] In the face of this grim prospect the Jews' need for arms was dire, especially as the British controlled possession of arms in

---

[103] Cited in Uri Bialer, "The Czech-Israeli Arms Deal Revisited," *Journal of Strategic Studies* 8, no. 3 (1985), 307–315. Original in David Ben-Gurion, *Bama'aracha* 5 (1958): 135–137 (in Hebrew).

Palestine and were offering financial and military support to Transjordan and Egypt.[104]

On April 6, 1948 Ben-Gurion assessed the first four months of the war in an address to the Zionist Action Committee in Tel Aviv.[105] Since November 30, 1947, "the beginning of the attack against us," 900 Jews had been killed, and the Jews of Jerusalem were under siege and in danger of famine. Agricultural settlements in the Galilee, the Jordan Valley, and the Negev had come under assault. "Thousands" of soldiers from Syria, Iraq, Transjordan, and Egypt had entered Palestine, at least some of whom had arms supplied by the British government. "The government of the country," that is, the British Mandate administration, "is hostile toward us." It did what it could in departing to "prevent and interfere with all possibility of defending the Yishuv."[106] Britain, contrary to UN decisions, refused to give the Jews control over a port, patrolled the coast night and day, and had subjected the Yishuv to a "maritime siege directed against the Jews at the same time that the continental frontiers to the east, north and south are open to the Arabs, to their armed bands and their armies." The British confiscate arms from Jews and Arabs, but they "distribute weapons only to Arabs, in towns and villages." Their "constant and clear policy in matters of security is to bind the hands of the Yishuv that is defending itself, and give all possibility to those attacking us, both Arabs in this country and those from foreign countries."[107]

The odds against the Yishuv were daunting. According to Ben-Gurion, "the reserves of the enemy are practically unlimited." Without counting the Arabs of North Africa, the Arab governments of the Middle East had a forty-to-one advantage in numbers of citizens. The invading Arabs had states. Six were members of the UN and a seventh, Transjordan, was an ally of Britain. Conversely:

The Jewish people who have been attacked do not have a state, a government or international recognition. The Yishuv does not exist as a state. It cannot buy weapons because one sells weapons only to recognized governments. Seven independent Arab states, Lebanon, Syria, Transjordan, Iraq, Egypt, Saudi Arabia and Yemen, are arrayed against it. They have more or less well-trained armies, and some have an air force. Egypt also has a navy. This state of affairs confronts us again with an existential question the likes of which we have not faced

---

[104] Ibid., 307.

[105] David Ben-Gurion, "Discours de Ben-Gurion à la Réunion du Comité d'Action Sioniste, Le 6 Avril 1948," in Tuvia Friling and Denis Peschanski, eds., *David Ben Gourion journal 1947–1948: Les secrets de la création de l'état d'Israël* (Paris: Éditions de la Martinière, 2012), 218–231.

[106] Ibid., 218–219.   [107] Ibid., 220.

in 1,800 years. The question is not whether to protect ourselves or surrender. We do not have a choice.[108]

The "tragedy of the Jews in past generations and in our epoch as well," Ben-Gurion pointed out, concerned the right to defend themselves. It was a "question of life and death. We have no other choice but to fight with force, with all of our force until we have established the right to defend ourselves." The current war required victory "that will assure the existence of our people";[109] it demanded a "supreme effort." The Arabs were not fighting against a Jewish army "but against the whole of the Yishuv," with no distinction between the front and the home front. As the Jews had such difficulty acquiring arms from the outside and faced the British maritime blockade, a "general mobilization" of the economy, science, and the press was essential.[110] After May 15, 1948 the British Navy would still control the waters around Israel and would still continue – under the mantle of the United Nations – to prevent the arrival of arms to the new state of Israel.[111] Ben-Gurion left his listeners in no doubt as to which side in the war was benefiting from the American-supported arms embargo, one that after April carried the additional legitimacy of a UN truce resolution.

On April 16 Ben-Gurion commented on the UN ceasefire resolutions in a letter to Shertok.[112] He found two points of the UN's most recent ceasefire resolution to be "most dangerous." He was particularly concerned about the intention to "supervise the good behavior of both sides and the latent interdiction of the immigration of adults." The Jews' fate depended on received weapons and immigrants. By placing an embargo on the first and supporting Britain's efforts to prevent the second, the Security Council truce resolution benefited the Arabs and disadvantaged the Jews. Israeli victories had convinced the Mufti that he could not defeat the Jews only with the forces of the Arab Higher Committee. Ben-Gurion expected he would then turn to the Arab states for assistance. If and when the conflict moved from the first phase of a civil war to a second phase, a war with the regular armies of the Arab states, the Yishuv's need for tanks, planes, and artillery would be even more urgent.[113] Ben-Gurion's diary entries and speeches of these months convey the haunting memory of the

---

[108] Ibid., 220–221. On the efforts of the Yishuv to save Jews in Europe see Tuvia Friling, *Arrows in the Dark: David Ben-Gurion, the Yishuv Leadership, and Rescue Attempts during the Holocaust* (Madison: University of Wisconsin Press, 2005).

[109] Ben-Gurion, "Discours de Ben-Gurion," 221.   [110] Ibid., 222–223.   [111] Ibid.

[112] "Lettre de Ben Gurion à Moshe Sharett à New York, Tel-Aviv, le 16 avril, 1948," in Friling and Peschanski, eds., *David Ben Gourion journal 1947–1948*, 246–247.

[113] Ibid., 247. On the two phases of the 1948 war, those of civil war and war between states, see Morris, *1948*.

recent extermination of Europe's Jews together with his focus on the need to prevent a similar fate being inflicted on the Jews in Israel. His urgent sense of an existential threat stood in sharp contrast to the language of neutrality used in the UN truce resolutions.[114]

Arms and Czechoslovakia in 1948

Unable to acquire the weapons it needed from the United States or any other Western democracy, the Jews turned to communist Czechoslovakia. In February 1948 the Czech communists seized power as part of the imposition of Stalinist regimes in Eastern Europe. The Czech coup, as it came to be called, was one of the defining events of the early Cold War, one that convinced many doubters in the West that a hard line against the communists in Europe was essential. On April 30 Laurence Steinhardt, the US ambassador to Czechoslovakia, reported to Washington on the first wave of arrests of "reactionaries"; the communists were consolidating their position. "No party is giving the Communists any opposition and it seems probable that all non-Communist parties will either soon be dissolved or united with the Communists. Czechoslovakia has become a full-fledged puppet state."[115] Yet it was this same communist dictatorship that was the only government willing and able to provide the new Jewish state with the arms it needed for self-defense.

In sending arms to Israel, the Czech communists were violating the above-described terms of the UN Security Council truce terms of spring and summer 1948, and they did so presumably with permission from the Soviet Union. In the process they were, of course, also deepening the belief of many in the State Department and the Pentagon that there was indeed a connection between the Soviet bloc and the Zionist project. The State Department received a continuous flow of reports on the Czech connection. On March 18, 1948, for example, US military intelligence officials in Europe reported that Czechoslovakia was exporting armaments to "Palestine or Yugo."[116] And there were more to come.

[114] On Ben-Gurion's response to the Holocaust see Friling, *Arrows in the Dark*. On the Zionist resort to force and the determination of the Yishuv to avoid the fate of Europe's Jews see Anita Shapira, *Land and Power: The Zionist Resort to Force, 1881–1948* (Stanford: Stanford University Press, 1999), 277–352.

[115] Laurence Steinhardt to Secretary of State, No. 309, "Analysis of Recent Czechoslovak Crisis" (April 30, 1948), NACP RG 59, General Records of the Department of State, Central Decimal File, 1945–1949, 860F.00/4–148 to 860F.00/12–3148, Box 6573.

[116] "M-Czechoslovakia, Military-Weapons-Small Arms, 1948, 18 Mar 48," NACP RG 319, Records of the Army Staff, Assistant Chief of Staff, G-2, Geographical Index to Numerical Series of Intelligence Documents (ID File) 1944–51, Czechoslovakia, 0401.000m Intelligence, Incoming and Outgoing Messages, 1948, Czechoslovakia, Box 13.

American officials kept a close watch on the movements of Jews headed to Palestine. On March 18 James Minarck, an American military intelligence official in Europe, reported that "during the first week in February, approximately 400–500 young male Jews of military age, and with records of service in the Soviet Army, or the Soviet sponsored Polish Army were shipped from PRAGUE to MARSEILLE, FRANCE for eventual shipment to PALESTINE. Their visas were signed by the French Consulate in PRAGUE and were dated valid for three months."[117] Since the route went through the American zone in Germany, the Jews received clearances from a US officer in Prague. "Provisions for the trip were furnished by the AJDC [American Joint Distribution Committee] but the Czech government provided the train and cars." American intelligence officials told Minarck that "to their knowledge no screening was made of these individuals" when officials in the French Consulate in Prague and American officials in Prague and Berlin approved further travel. He concluded that "a similar shipment of ex-Soviet military personnel is expected sometime in April."[118]

Minarck's report raised suspicions about collaboration between the AJDC and American and French diplomats in Prague and Berlin who were at best careless and at worst were cooperating with the communist regime in Czechoslovakia. It appeared that all were facilitating the immigration to Palestine of "young male Jews of military age" and "ex-Soviet military personnel." The report transformed an accident of geography, namely that these Jewish survivors of the Holocaust came from East European countries that were now part of the Soviet bloc, into a causal analysis that fitted into Washington's fears about the expansion of communism and the need to contain it. It reinforced the prevailing consensus in the national security leadership of the USA that there was some sort of affinity between the Zionists and the communists.

On March 26, 1948 the US government Policy Committee on Arms and Armaments (PCAA) circulated an FBI report on "illegal shipments of arms to Near Eastern countries" and agreed that the Near Eastern Division (NEA) should send the FBI report on to the secretary of state. At the same meeting the committee expressed concern about "reported shipments of arms to Palestine from Latin American countries."[119] On

---

[117] Joseph Minarck, Chief IB Info Sect. (March 18, 1948), NACP RG 59, M1390, Roll 9, 867N.01/4–147–7–3147.

[118] Ibid.

[119] Policy Committee on Arms and Armaments (PCAA), "Minutes, March 26, 1948, Measures to Discourage Illegal Arms Shipments to Near Eastern Countries," Washington (March 26, 1948), NACP RG 353, Records of the Interdepartmental and Intradepartmental Committees Records of the Policy Committee on Arms and

April 2 the committee members rejected a request for armor-plating for ambulances serving the Hadassah Hospital in Jerusalem on the premise that doing so might "provide a loop-hole" in the arms embargo "through which exporters might seek to send material to the Near East." The committee's discussion at that moment reflected a certain remoteness from realities in the war. One member suggested that the existing laws of war would protect ambulances "more effectively than armor plate," as arming them "might draw fire from the Arabs."[120] In direct contradiction to this assertion, on April 13 Arab militiamen attacked a ten-vehicle Haganah convoy carrying mostly unarmed Jewish lecturers, students, nurses, and doctors on their way to Hadassah Hospital on the Mount Scopus campus of the Hebrew University of Jerusalem. British forces refused to intervene in timely fashion, and seventy-eight of the passengers – all civilians except for a few Haganah men – were killed.[121] An initial report of the massacre appeared on of the front page of the *New York Times* on April 15.[122] However, at its meeting the next day the PCAA, following the recommendations of the NEA, rejected "the proposed export of armor for Hadassah Hospital installation in Palestine."[123]

That same month the Belgian government announced that it was proposing to sell surplus military equipment to the Jewish Agency. On April 30 the PCAA informed the US Embassies in Brussels and Paris that it objected to the sale and hoped that "the Belgium Government would closely parallel that of the United States on this sensitive question."[124] And on May 21, 1948 it rejected a shipment of radar to the Hebrew Institute of Technology in Haifa.[125] On May 28, 1948, just two weeks after the state of Israel had been established, the PCAA again refused to approve shipment of armor plates to "Palestine" for Hadassah Hospital.[126]

Armaments, 1947–1949 (Lot SSD303), General Records, Minutes-D-2 (hereafter IICR of PCAA, 1947–1949), Box 1.

[120] PCAA, "Minutes, April 2, 1948, Shipment of Arms to Palestine," Washington (April 2, 1948), NACP RG 353, IICR of PCAA, 1947–1949, Box 1.

[121] On this event see Benny Morris, *1948*, 128–129.

[122] Thomas J. Hamilton, "Soviet Backs U.S. on Palestine Edict," *New York Times*, July 15, 1948, 1 and 15.

[123] PCAA, "Minutes, April 16, 1948, Shipment of Armor Plate to Palestine," Washington (November 14, 1947), NACP RG 353, IICR of PCAA, 1947–1949, Box 1.

[124] PCAA, "Minutes, May 7, 1948, Sale of Surplus Material to the Jewish Agency in Palestine," Washington (May 7, 1948), NACP RG 353, IICR of PCAA, 1947–1949, Box 1, 6.

[125] PCAA, "Minutes, May 21, 1948, Export of One Radar Set Model S)-9 to Haifa, Palestine," Washington (May 21, 1948), NACP RG 353, IICR of PCAA, 1947–1949, Box 1.

[126] PCAA, "Minutes, May 28, 1948, Shipment of Armor Plate to Palestine," Washington (May 28, 1948), NACP RG 353, IICR of PCAA, 1947–1949, Box 1, 6.

In July the committee devoted two meetings to efforts to stop the shipment of arms from Czechoslovakia to Israel and to prevent American volunteers from participating in the deliveries. On July 2 it discussed "certain export violations related to Palestine" involving some commercial airlines "acting in contravention of UN Security Council restrictions in Middle East." There were "reports of arms being shipped from Czechoslovakia to the warring elements of the Palestine areas."[127] On July 9 Trevor Swett, the deputy chairman of the committee, read a letter from Secretary of Defense Louis Johnson to Secretary of State Marshall urging the State Department "to do everything possible to stop the clandestine transport of munitions by air and delivery of aircraft into foreign areas of extreme political sensitivity."[128] The committee learned that the State Department's Munitions Division would recommend to the Civil Aeronautics Board that "letters of registration and passports will be withdrawn from Americans who are operating planes for illicit purposes, particularly with reference to the Palestine-Arab States arms traffic," and that export licenses would not be approved "unless positive proof is presented that the proposed destination and end-use are properly and clearly stated." Swett reported that the Air Force was "fully cooperating" in implementing this policy, and that the Army and Navy were also "fully advised as to control measures."[129]

The US Consulate in Marseille Reports on Jewish Immigration to Palestine

As war raged in Palestine in winter and spring 1948 the Mossad Le'Aliyah Bet continued its efforts to bring Jewish survivors of the Holocaust to Palestine. Marseille continued to be a hub of that endeavor. As discussed in Chapter 7, on November 24, 1947 Jules Moch succeeded Édouard Depreux as the French minister of the interior. In that capacity Moch continued to exercise control over immigration and police functions regarding the arrival and departure of ships in the port. The efforts of the US State Department to enforce the arms embargo and examine possible Soviet involvement in the refugee stream were evident in the extensive cable traffic between the office of Secretary of State Marshall and Under Secretary of State Lovett in Washington with Jefferson Caffery, the US ambassador to France in Paris, and with officials in the

---

[127] PCAA, "Minutes, July 2, 1948, Certain Export Violations Relating to the Palestine Area," Washington (July 2, 1948), NACP RG 353, IICR of PCAA, 1947–1949, Box 1.

[128] PCAA, "Minutes, July 9, 1948, Illicit Traffic in Arms to Sensitive Areas," Washington (July 9, 1948), NACP RG 353, IICR of PCAA, 1947–1949, Box 1.

[129] Ibid., 4.

US Consulate in Marseille, including Cecil W. Gray, the consul general, and his successor, Marcel Malige.

In January 1948 Gray sent detailed reports on the arrival and departures of the ships the Mossad Le'Aliyah Bet was using to transport Jews to Palestine, and on American citizens serving as crew members.[130] On January 14 Secretary Marshall asked Gray to "telegraph names and any other information available [on] alleged Irgun Haganah agents and engineers" mentioned in a cable of December 20, 1947.[131] The following day Gray sent Washington the names of twelve "alleged Irgun Haganah agents"; he made no distinction between the Haganah and the Irgun.[132] On February 11 Gray reported that the SS *Altalena* had arrived in Marseille from Genoa and that he had asked the local police to detain it. He urged the State Department to investigate the ship, as the captain and several crew members were American citizens. He included a list of twenty-five names of passengers, their ages, and cities of origins.[133]

On February 24 Gray reported that an "unsolicited informant of unknown reliability provided original information [about] former American citizens" who were "crew members [on] Jewish refugee ship[,] had visited USSR[,] were being used by Soviets[,] and were due [to] return [to] Marseille." The circumstances surrounding their passport applications were "suspicious" and led local French police to open an investigation into Soviet or "satellite" agents. The next day Gray wrote to Marshall with "Information Regarding SS ALTALENA, a Panamanian vessel of Uncertain Antecedents and Purposes Now in Marseille." He included a list of the thirty-nine crew members with their names, birthdates, ages, and place of birth.[134]

---

[130] Gray to Washington, Marseille (January 2, 1948), No. 1, NACP RG 84 Records of the Foreign Service Posts of the Department of State, France, U.S. Consulate, Marseille, Classified General Records, 1936–1952, 1948–1949: [1948] (hereafter NACP RG 84, U.S. Consulate, Marseille Records, 1936–1952, 1948–1949), Box 7.

[131] George C. Marshall, Washington (January 13, 1948), No. 11, True Reading, NACP RG 84, U.S. Consulate, Marseille Records, 1936–1952, 1948–1949, Box 7. In citing diplomatic cables written in telegraphic style, I have left them in the original but added prepositions or other terms in brackets when needed to clarify meaning.

[132] C. W. Gray to Washington, Marseille (January 15, 1948), No. 10, NACP RG 84, U.S. Consulate, Marseille Records, 1936–1952, 1948–1949, Box 7.

[133] C. W. Gray to Secretary of State, Marseille (February 15, 1948), NACP RG 84, U.S. Consulate, Marseille Records, 1936–1952, 1948–1949, Box 7.

[134] C. W. Gray to Secretary of State, Marseille (February 25, 1948), "Subject: Transmitting Information Regarding SS ALTALENA, a Panamanian Vessel of Uncertain Antecedents and Purposes Now in Marseille" and "List of Crew Members of the Panamanian Steamship ALTALENA and Data taken from Ship's Articles regarding each," Marseille (February 25, 1948), NACP RG 84, U.S. Consulate, Marseille Records, 1936–1952, 1948–1949, Box 7.

Despite hysteria about communists coming from the American right in 1948, the Communist Party in the USA was not a serious political electoral presence in American politics. In France, however, it was. American diplomats in Marseille were observing increasing communist militancy as well as Jewish immigration to Palestine. On March 5 Gray told the US Embassy in Paris that a reliable informant had reported that the communists were planning to "create maximum disruption [of] French economic life accompanied [by] acts [of] criminal sabotage" with the intent to "weaken government . . . Strategic points to be defended at all costs Marseille especially."[135] On March 9 Gray informed the US Consulate in Genoa that an "important shipment Jews and arms [is] due" in the "next few days on coast between Savona and Toulon."[136] On March 13 Gray informed both the US Embassy in Paris and the State Department in Washington that an official in the Marseille police had told him of a "very grave situation" developing "transcending local or regional level." The Soviet Union was taking "direct control [of] Communist operations [in] southern France through recently arrived agents and are preparing direct action through groups armed [and] trained foreigners with probable outside assistance through Italy." Communist action in southern France was designed to "coordinate with possible Soviet war plans." Gray's source in the Marseille police thought "strong American action" was "necessary [to] stiffen French will [to] resist and deter Soviets [from] precipitating [an] explosion."[137] Gray's memos suggested that a causal link could explain the temporal simultaneity and geographical proximity between the Zionists' efforts to bring Jews to Palestine and a Soviet political, perhaps even military, offensive in France.

On March 25 Marshall asked the Marseille Consulate for comments on a report from the military attaché in the US Embassy in Bucharest that two ships then in Marseille, with 15,000 to 20,000 "Jewish emigrants for Palestine" on board, would leave "from Black Sea ports."[138] On April 5 the Marseille Consulate replied that the only ships then in Marseille "identifiable with Palestine immigrant traffic" were the *Archangelos* and the *Altalena*; the American League for a Free Palestine was a co-owner of both ships.[139] On May 3 Marshall cabled the US Embassy in Paris and

[135] Gray to Paris and Washington, Marseille (March 5, 1948), NACP RG 84, U.S. Consulate, Marseille Records, 1936–1952, 1948–1949, Box 7.

[136] Gray to Genoa, Marseilles (March 9, 1948), NACP RG 84, U.S. Consulate, Marseille Records, 1936–1952, 1948–1949, Box 7.

[137] Gray to Paris, Marseille (March 13, 1948), No. 2, NACP RG 84, U.S. Consulate, Marseille Records, 1936–1952, 1948–1949, Box 7.

[138] George Marshall, Washington (March 24, 1948), No. 50, NACP RG 84, U.S. Consulate, Marseille Records, 1936–1952, 1948–1949, Box 7.

[139] Hart to Washington, Marseille (April 5, 1948), No. 67, NACP RG 84, U.S. Consulate, Marseille Records, 1936–1952, 1948–1949, Box 7.

Consulates in Marseille, Trieste, and Bordeaux that "300 Jews secretly departed Sofia at 0400 hours 17 April via Yugoslavia. Group traveling mostly in sport clothes under guise of students." Their place of departure to Palestine was "rumored to be Bordeaux or Marseilles via Paris. Some Jews canceled their going due to anxiety over conditions now in Palestine and their places taken by Communist agents. Number of agents in group report to be from twenty to thirty." As French visas were difficult to obtain for Bulgarians, he expected the group would depart from Yugoslavia.[140] An hour later Marshall sent another cable to the Embassy in Paris and the Consulate in Marseille in a series now called "True Reading." The US military attaché in Bucharest had informed the State Department that "two ships in Marmvillies [*sic*; typo for Marseille] being refitted to haul Jews from Balkans to Palestine." They were expected to arrive in the Black Sea in about three weeks. "Outgoing passengers will consist primarily young men with arms and ammo ... Jewish representatives from Palestine in addition to arranging for above shipment have also been making contacts for procurement arms and ammo from Bulgaria, Rumania and Poland."[141]

On May 7, 1948, in two cables to the US Embassy in Paris and to the office of the secretary of state in Washington on Jewish immigration to Palestine through Marseille, Gray translated and summarized a report by the Marseille police on the subject.[142] The Fédération des Sociétés Juives de France (Federation of Jewish Organizations in France) operated four-teen Jewish refugee camps in the area where the Rhône River flowed into the Mediterranean, between Marseille and the port of Sète. Between April 11 and 16 some 970 "Palestine bound Jews" received "legal entry into France" at Strasbourg and Neuf-Brisach. Of them, 398 had received three-month visas from the French consul in Munich. The fourteen camps were staging centers to facilitate emigration to Palestine. In April 1948 alone six ships sailed from Marseille with 1,302 passengers from these camps; 397 came from Central Europe, 811 from the British occupation zone in Germany, 44 from France, and 49 were of "unstated" origins. While 1,200 stated Palestine as their destination, the destination of 101 was unknown. The legal status of the Fédération des Sociétés

---

[140] George Marshall, Washington (May 3, 1948), No. 71, NACP RG 84, U.S. Consulate, Marseille Records, 1936–1952, 1948–1949, Box 7.
[141] George Marshall, Washington (May 3, 1948), No. 72, NACP RG 84, U.S. Consulate, Marseille Records, 1936–1952, 1948–1949, Box 7.
[142] Gray to Washington, Marseille, (May 7, 1948), No. 91, NACP RG 84, U.S. Consulate, Marseille Records, 1936–1952, 1948–1949, Box 7; and C. W. Gray, American Consulate, Marseille to Hugh Fullerton, American Consul General, Paris, Marseille (May 7, 1948), NACP RG 84, U.S. Consulate, Marseille Records, 1936–1952, 1948–1949, Box, 7.

Juives protected it "from any police control and [Marseille] prefect frankly admits [that the] Federation [is] conducting large scale emigration [and] immigration activities in France without effective control of either camps or inmates."[143] The camps at the mouth of the Rhône area were "easily adequate in size and scope to swallow them [Jewish immigrants] up if they enter France legally or illegally." It was also "commonly known" that there was a "steady stream [of] clandestine immigration" crossing the Italian-French border but a group from Sofia might use another route.[144] The French police memo reported that the following ships had departed from Marseille for Haifa or another port in "Palestine" with "Israelites" on the following dates: April 8, SS *Andeavour* [sic: *Endeavor*] to Haifa with 193 passengers from the British zone of occupation; April 10, SS *Cyrenia* with 33 persons with individual passports; April 12, SS *Kedmah* with 402 passengers, of whom 238 were children from Germany and 168 adults from Central Europe; April 17, SS *Providence* with 68 passengers from Central Europe, SS *Tete* with 44 passengers from France, and SS *Kedmah* with 396 from the British zone of occupation in Germany.[145]

As Gray's memo of May 7 indicated, the French police, and thus the French Ministry of the Interior, were well informed about an effort that remained "clandestine" in name only. They continued to allow it to proceed. The French police knew who the immigrants were, where they came from, and how they entered France. They knew that the intention of the overwhelming majority was to get onto ships taking them to Palestine. The State Department knew that, from Jules Moch's office in the Ministry of the Interior in Paris to the police in Marseille, French officials were allowing the refugee stream to continue without the close surveillance that the British government had been urging the French government to implement for the previous two years. It knew as well that with plausible deniability and public discretion, the French Interior Ministry and police officials in France's Mediterranean ports continued to assist the Mossad Le'Aliyah Bet and to undermine Britain's efforts to prevent such immigration.

In winter and spring 1948 it was obvious to American officials that French government officials in charge of borders and immigration did not agree with the US and UK position on the need for careful screening of "military age men" capable of bearing arms. The French Interior Ministry and its intelligence agencies, led as they were by officials

---

[143] Gray to Washington, Marseille (May 7, 1948), No. 91, NACP RG 84, U.S. Consulate, Marseille Records, 1936–1952, 1948–1949, Box 7.

[144] Ibid.   [145] Gray to Fullerton (May 7, 1948).

sympathetic to the Zionists, were undermining British and American efforts to use UN Security Council truce resolutions to prevent the passage of Jewish males of military age to Palestine. The French government did not send weapons – certainly not in significant quantities – to the Yishuv, but the French Ministries of Interior and Transport were working with the Mossad Le'Aliyah Bet to facilitate what the British called "illegal" immigration of thousands of Jewish refugees to Palestine during the war of 1947–8.

Ambassador Caffery informed Marshall and Lovett that first Édouard Depreux and then Jules Moch had used the power of the French Interior Ministry to defeat communist strike waves and protests in 1947 and 1948. In so doing, they, like Ernest Bevin in Britain and other left-of-center politicians in Western Europe, offered indispensable political support for the Western policy of containment. Marshall and Lovett learned that the same French Socialist politicians who were supporting the Zionists and facilitating immigration to Palestine were leading figures in fighting communist efforts to destabilize France. In so doing, Moch and Depreux's support for Jewish immigration to Palestine in 1947 and 1948 defied the worldview of the State Department's Division of Near Eastern and African Affairs and Policy Planning Staff, which readily conflated Zionist activities with Soviet policy in the Middle East. These anticommunist, pro-Zionist, center-left French government officials had their counterparts among American liberals in the United States Congress such as Emanuel Celler and Robert Wagner, some liberal Republicans, and Clark Clifford in the Truman White House. Marshall, Lovett, and George Kennan all understood the importance of the European leaders of the center left, such as Moch and Depreux, for expanding support for the policy of containment beyond that of conservative anticommunists. But the specific combination of opposition to the communists and emphatic support for the Zionists did not find advocates among Washington decision makers dealing with the problem of Palestine.

As war raged in Palestine in spring 1948, the State Department and the Pentagon resisted calls to lift the arms embargo. In April and May Marshall and his colleagues had proved skillful at using the machinery of the UN Security Council to continue the arms embargo. They continued to sustain that embargo, even after Egypt, Iraq, Lebanon, Syria, and Transjordan invaded the newly declared state of Israel on May 15, 1948.

11   Responses in Washington, the United Nations, and in Europe to the Establishment of the State of Israel: May and June 1948

If the tide did turn adversely and they [the Zionists, the Jewish Agency, and the Jews] came running to us for help they should be placed clearly on notice that there was no warrant to expect help from the United States, which had warned them of the grave risk they were facing.

> Secretary of State George Marshall, memo of conversation with
> Moshe Shertok, director, political department of the Jewish
> Agency, May 12, 1948

The Jews of Palestine have won the world's respect by their willingness to fight their own battles, and to win them.

> *PM*, May 16, 1948

By using all of our influence to prevent the birth of an independent Jewish Commonwealth in Palestine we have been, however, preventing the creation of the one Near Eastern state that would prove to be a true democracy ... a democracy that ... would unquestionably be an unswerving supporter of the Western cause.

> Sumner Welles, former US under secretary of state, June 1948

On May 12, 1948 the tensions between supporters of the Zionist project in the White House and its opponents in the State Department came to a head in what Truman's special assistant Clark Clifford called "The Showdown in the Oval Office." The meeting's purpose was to present the president with arguments for and against recognizing the new state of Israel, whose independence would be declared two days later. The participants from the State Department included Secretary of State Marshall, Under Secretary of State Lovett, Fraser Wilkins of the Near East and African Affairs Division, and Robert McClintock from the US delegation to the United Nations. Clark Clifford, along with Truman's advisors David Niles and Matthew Connelly, also took part. Clifford made the case for recognition.[1] The accounts by Clifford and Marshall agree on what transpired. The May 12 meeting captured the tensions and

---

[1] See the account in Allis Radosh and Ronald Radosh, *A Safe Haven: Harry S. Truman and the Founding of Israel* (New York: HarperCollins, 2009), 324–337; and Clifford's account in his *Counsel to the President: A Memoir* (New York: Random House, 1991).

disagreements that had smoldered over the previous two years between Israel's supporters in the White House, Congress, and the public, on the one hand, and the leadership in the State Department and the Pentagon, on the other.

Marshall reported that on May 8 he had told Israel's Moshe Shertok that "it was extremely dangerous to base long-range policy on temporary military successes," which the "Jewish army" had attained in the previous months in Palestine.[2] There was "no assurance whatever that in the long-range the tide might not turn against them." He also told Shertok that by declaring a state on May 14 the Jewish Agency was "taking a gamble. If the tide did turn adversely and they [the Zionists, the Jewish Agency, and the Jews] came running to us for help they should be placed clearly on notice that there was no warrant to expect help from the United States, which had warned them of the grave risk they were facing."[3] The United States had no obligation to prevent a potential catastrophe which he (Marshall), in effect, blamed on the Jews' own rash decisions.

Marshall's comment about Jews coming "running to us for help" was an unfortunate choice of words; he seemed to be unaware of how such a reference evoked traditional antisemitic stereotypes of Jewish fecklessness and cowardice. Moreover, he appeared to have forgotten the refusal of the US military to intervene in 1944 and 1945 to stop the last phases of the Holocaust (when he was the chief of staff). He also seemed dismissive about the threat the Arab Higher Committee and Arab League posed to the existence of the Jews in Palestine, and uninformed about the Zionists' focus on self-reliance and lack of desire for direct intervention by US armed forces.

According to his own notes, Marshall then responded to a press report that he had sent a "personal message" to Ben-Gurion about the intention of the Jewish Agency to establish a sovereign state on May 14. "In actual fact, no message had been sent to Mr. Ben Gurion, and I did not even know that such a person existed."[4] It was, at the least, an odd comment. In May 1948 David Ben-Gurion was one of the most famous people in world politics. He had been the leading figure of the Yishuv since the 1930s. It is difficult to imagine that the secretary of state did not know who he was, but that is what Marshall's own record of the meeting asserts. If, however, on May 12, 1948, Secretary of State Marshall was claiming

---

[2] "Memorandum of Conversation, by Secretary of State," Washington (May 12, 1948), NACP RG 59, General Records of the Department of State, Central Decimal File, 1945–1949, 501.BB Palestine/5–1248, Box 2118, *Foreign Relations of the United States* (hereafter *FRUS*), *The Near East, South Asia, and Africa*, 1948, vol. 5, part 2: https://history.state.gov/historicaldocuments/frus1948v05p2/d252.
[3] Ibid., 2.   [4] Ibid.

that he did not know who David Ben-Gurion was, then the question arises as to what else he did not know or understand about Zionism, and the Jews.

On the other side, Clark Clifford was urging the president to give prompt recognition to the Jewish state after termination of the British Mandate, and to do so before the Soviet Union did. Taking that step "would have distinct value in restoring the President's position for support of the partition of Palestine." Clifford offered the following language for a public statement by the president:

I look with favor on the creation of a Jewish State in accordance with the provisions laid down in the Resolution of November 29, and I assume that, when a Jewish State is set up, the provisions for democratic government outlined in that Resolution will be complied with. When the Jewish State is set up in accordance with those provisions, I favor the recognition of that State by the United States Government. I have asked the Secretary of State to have representatives of the United States in the United Nations take up this subject in the United Nations with a view toward obtaining early recognition of a Jewish State by the other members of the United Nations.[5]

Marshall dismissed this idea by calling it "premature recognition." Lovett said that recognition before Israel came into existence "would be highly injurious to the United Nations." It would also "be injurious to the prestige of the President." It "was a very transparent attempt to win the Jewish vote ... [The election was then about six months away.] Finally, to recognize the Jewish State prematurely would be buying a pig in a poke. How did we know what kind of Jewish State would be set up?" Lovett then read excerpts from a file of intelligence telegrams and reports "regarding Soviet activity in sending Jews and Communist agents from Black Sea areas to Palestine."[6] Marshall, echoing Lovett, told the president that he thought Clifford's suggestions were wrong, that they were a "transparent dodge to win a few votes that would not in fact achieve this purpose. The great dignity of the office of the President would be seriously diminished." Clifford's suggestions were based on "domestic political considerations," while the problem confronting the United States was international. According to Marshall, "I said bluntly that if the President were to follow Mr. Clifford's advice and if in the elections I were to vote, would vote against the President."[7]

In the end, President Truman did not recognize the new state before it was established, even though he had an opportunity to do so at a press

[5] "Statement Presented by the President's Special Counsel (Clifford) at the White House Meeting of May 12, 1948," Washington (May 12, 1948), *FRUS*, 1948, vol. 5, part 2, Elsey Papers: https://history.state.gov/historicaldocuments/frus1948v05p2/d254.
[6] Ibid., 3–4.   [7] Ibid., 4.

conference held on May 13. But he did take that step just minutes after Ben-Gurion announced that Israel existed on May 14, making the United States the first state to do so when it offered de facto but not full de jure recognition. Four days later Lovett wrote that "my protests against the precipitate action and warnings as to consequences with the Arab world appear to have been outweighed by considerations unknown to me, but I can only conclude that the President's political advisers, having failed last Wednesday afternoon [at the press conference] to make the President a father of the new state, have determined at least to make him the midwife."[8] Marshall and Lovett's emphatic opposition to recognizing the state of Israel was the logical culmination of the policies articulated in the Pentagon talks in September and October 1947, the arms embargo decision of November 1947, the Policy Planning Staff papers of January 1948, the failed trusteeship proposal of March 1948, the Joint Chiefs of Staff position papers on the "Problem of Palestine," and CIA analyses of 1947 and 1948.

Truman's recognition of Israel, which has rightly received much attention from historians, did not, however, constitute a complete break with the policies supported by the State Department and the Pentagon. The establishment of the new state did not assure its survival in the face of the Arab League invasion by Egypt, Syria, Iraq, Jordan, and Lebanon, and American recognition did not bring with it the military assistance the fledgling state might have expected from the United States. From May 1948 until the end of the war in a truce in March 1949 the United States continued to transform the fundamental strategic opposition to the Zionist project described in previous chapters into UN truce resolutions that disadvantaged more than aided Israel's efforts. Israel needed weapons and military-aged people; the United States sought and gained Security Council legitimization to continue the embargo on both. In addition, it worked to whittle down Israel's gains won at great cost on the battlefield in the failed hope that doing so would encourage the Arab states and the Arab Higher Committee to accept the two-state compromise proposed in the UN Partition Plan of November 29, 1947, or at least diminish Arab anger at the United States. With the Arab invasion things did take an adverse turn, but, contrary to Marshall's snide predictions, the Israelis did not "come running" to the United States for help. Instead, they fought on, relying on themselves as well as weapons from the government of Czechoslovakia and from arms dealers in Western Europe,

---

[8] Ibid., 2–3. Lovett did not explain the gendered language, and why Truman's advisers would prefer the president to be a midwife (feminine) rather than a father (masculine) of the new state.

and thousands of volunteers arriving from Europe as well as former, mostly Jewish, members of the US armed forces in World War II.

Clark Clifford had not been alone in supporting recognition; members of Congress also took that position. On May 12, 1948 Senator James Murray, a Democrat from Montana, and Congressman Emanuel Celler had sent Marshall a memo to that effect: "After two thousand years of diaspora, the wandering of the Jews is now ended."[9] The Jews had "shown their true mettle. While you and your colleagues at the State Department were urging that partition could not be implemented" and some had "clung to the plan of federalization with a Jewish Ghetto in Palestine," the Jews had won a series of military victories in Palestine. "While the United States floundered about in a sea of words, the Jews proceeded with arrangements for departments of civic and governmental functions." They had been "developing all the attributes of statehood." After declaring their own state on May 14 the Jews "will have the right to ask that the nations of the world recognize [it] as a sovereign unit. It is time to end all the unreal discussions on trusteeship and federalization."[10]

Recognition, according to Murray and Celler, was not only a matter of facing the reality that, against the expectations of many, the Jews in Palestine had defeated the Arab Higher Committee's effort to undermine the Partition Plan. Poland and Guatemala had already indicated they would recognize the new state of Israel, and the other states of Eastern Europe were likely to do so as well. It would be "a blunder of the highest magnitude" for the United States not to do so, the two legislators warned Marshall. The new state would need financial assistance in the form of loans. The arms embargo should be lifted, "since its continuance is, in effect, an unfriendly gesture toward the newly created State." The British and French governments would continue to

send and sell arms to the Arab countries. The Jews of Palestine, who by themselves have succeeded in implementing the United Nations resolution of November 29th, must not be placed at so grave a disadvantage. The need to defend themselves will continue, possibly on a greater scale. Their fate cannot be permitted to be a matter of indifference to us. If the arms embargo continues, there is not equalization of opportunity between the Arabs and the Jews in obtaining arms. Courage and determination and wit in military planning are now on the side of the Jews, as they have demonstrated, but numbers and military equipment are not.[11]

[9] James E. Murray and Emanuel Celler to George Marshall, Washington (May 12, 1948), NACP RG 59, National Archives Microfilm Publications, M1390, Records of the Department of State Relating to the Internal Affairs of Palestine, 1945–1949, Roll 14, 867N.01/5–1248.
[10] Ibid.   [11] Ibid.

But the secretary of state was not persuaded. On May 21 Charles Bohlen (1904–74), then an advisor to Marshall and a future ambassador to the Soviet Union, replied to Celler and Murray on Marshall's behalf. He noted that Truman had recognized Israel on May 14, that the issue of "suspension of licensing of arms shipments to the Near East [is] under continuous study," and that Israel had not yet made a request for loans.[12] Bohlen did not address the substance of Celler and Murray's concern, namely that the arms embargo was primarily harming Israel and aiding the Arabs.

That concern coincided with a mood of celebration that greeted Israel's birth. *PM* reported that the Jewish population of New York "rejoiced at the proclamation of the national Jewish state in Palestine."[13] Ceremonies took place at the midtown office of the Jewish Agency and in the Bronx and Brooklyn. Chaim Shertok's wife Zipporah and their fourteen-year-old son Chaim raised the blue-and-white flag of Israel at the midtown office. Mayor William O'Dwyer joined Jewish leaders in sending congratulations to Ben-Gurion. Speakers at rallies included Albert Einstein, Bartley Crum (then the publisher of *PM*), Senator Robert A. Taft, Stephen Wise, former New York governor Herbert Lehman, Eleanor Roosevelt, and Mayor O'Dwyer.[14]

On May 16 *PM*'s editorial was entitled "To Israel: Welcome."[15] This passionate expression of leftist opinion bears quoting:

[The founding of Israel was] an historic day for the Jews of Palestine and of the entire world. It spelled victory for the hopes of generations of brave and determined men and women. The partition which they had won by their own struggle had already been an accomplished fact, but yesterday it was recorded for history in [a] world which it will be impossible now to erase from men's minds ... The Jews of Palestine have won the world's respect by their willingness to fight their own battles, and to win them.[16]

The editors of *PM* found many reasons to celebrate the new state (see Figure 11.1). For one, it meant that a "window has been opened in the Middle East" through which "new ideas and new skills" would pour in, raising the standard of living "for millions of people whose poverty and illiteracy have been a curse to themselves and a danger to the world." Israel would be a modernizing, liberal, progressive force in a region of semi-feudal autocracies.

[12] Charles E. Bohlen to Emanuel Celler, Washington (May 21, 1948), NACP RG 59, M1390, Roll 14 867N.01/5–1248, 2.
[13] Gene de Poris, "New Yorkers Dance in the Street, Cheer New Flag of Israel," *PM*, May 16, 1948, 5.
[14] Ibid.   [15] "To Israel: Welcome," editorial, *PM*, May 16, 1948, 13.   [16] Ibid.

Figure 11.1 "May 16, Salute the Jewish State, Mass Demonstration, Madison Square Garden," American Zionist Emergency Council announcement of meeting in the newspaper *PM*. Speakers: Henry Morgenthau, Mayor William O'Dwyer, Mrs. Eleanor Roosevelt, Dr. Abba Hillel Silver, Senator Robert A. Taft, Dr. Chaim Weizmann; chairman: Dr. Emanuel Neumann. Source: *PM,* May 13, 1948, digital photo by author.

The editors saw international benefits to the founding as well. President Truman had received "divided counsel on the diplomatic problems involved" but won "high credit for the promptness with which he recognized the sentiments of the overwhelming majority of the American people." Now there was a chance to strengthen the United Nations, for though it had "fumbled the ball, it never dropped it, and the boundaries of the new state, like partition itself, rest firmly on United Nation acts." *PM* also found "a thread of hope in our tangled relations with the Soviet Union." Insofar as "the Russians have backed partition and independence from the start" the founding reflected the unusual agreement between the Soviet Union and the American president who launched the Cold War. They viewed the establishment of the state of Israel as a significant victory for the global left in May 1948 (see Map 11.1).

The response of the *New York Times* was more guarded. On May 17, in "The War in Palestine," its editors stopped short of the enthusiasm in the streets of New York and the pages of *PM* about the new state of Israel, noting simply that it now existed and had been given de facto recognition by the United States.[17] But they still saw trouble ahead: the conflict was "insoluble by reason alone." Yet, if a settlement of the tragic conflict was to be possible, the editors – remarkably – called "for an immediate repeal of the American embargo on arms to enable Israel to defend itself," and stated: "It is to be hoped that President Truman will see his way clear to take quick action before it is too late."[18] The same paper that five months earlier had prominently featured reports of communist influence among the Jewish refugees trying to get to Palestine was now joining the growing chorus to send arms to Israel.

Sumner Welles: *We Need Not Fail*

On June 1, 1948 Houghton-Mifflin published Sumner Welles's *We Need Not Fail*, a searing, book-length attack on the "abandonment" of the Partition Plan by the State Department that spring.[19] Welles, under secretary of state in the Roosevelt administration from 1936 to 1943 and a contributor to the text of the UN Charter, offered three main criticisms of State Department policy (see Figure 11.2). First, by refusing to allow the

---

[17] "The War in Palestine," editorial, *New York Times*, May 17, 1948, 18.   [18] Ibid.
[19] Sumner Welles, *We Need Not Fail* (Boston: Houghton-Mifflin, 1948). Also see the discussion of Welles in William Roger Louis, "Postmortem Appraisal of the United Nations Game: Sumner Welles and the Zionists," in *The British Empire in the Middle East, 1945–1951: Arab Nationalism, the United States, and Postwar Imperialism* (New York and Oxford: Oxford University Press, 1984), 487–493.

Map. 11.1 "A Jewish State is Born," map of Israel published in *PM*, May 16, 1948. Source: digital photo by author.

Figure 11.2 Former US under secretary of state Sumner Welles, author
of *We Need Not Fail*, delivering a talk on "Palestine's Rightful Destiny"
to the American Christian Palestine Committee in Baltimore, May 14,
1946. Source: Robert F. Wagner Papers: Palestine Files, Georgetown
University, Booth Family Center for Special Collections, digital photo
by author.

UN Security Council to use force if necessary to implement the Partition
Plan, it was repeating the errors of the League of Nations in the 1930s when
it failed to stop aggression by the Axis powers. Second, it was failing
morally by not supporting the just cause of persecuted Jewry and its need
for a state in Palestine. Third, it had committed a major strategic blunder
with its vain efforts to appease the Arabs while failing to support the Zionist
project, because a Jewish state would be the most reliable ally of the West
and a bulwark against Soviet expansion in the Middle East. As these
criticisms came from a senior figure in the Roosevelt administration, they
carried weight in the political establishment.[20]

Welles argued that the State Department's policy was also undermining the United Nations. The Arab states, having observed that the UN

---

[20] See reviews by the historian Crane Brinton, "Sumner Welles on Palestine: Consider the
Basic Human Dilemma," He Suggests a Common Sense Solution, *New York Times Book
Review*, June 13, 1948, 1; and Richard Crossman, "Mr. Welles on Palestine," *The Nation*,
June 6, 1948, 721–722.

"could be defied with impunity," had "resorted to armed aggression. They have invaded Palestine." The United States, faced with that reality, had "declared itself unwilling" to have the UN Security Council "enforce the will of the General Assembly" and had instead "proposed that the United Nations should abandon the decision it had reached" on November 29, 1947. With these actions it was not only repeating the blunders of the 1930s but also revealing that it was "unwilling to abide by its own commitments."[21]

We Need Not Fail recalled the role of Arab collaboration with the Axis powers in World War II.[22] While the Egyptian government declared its neutrality, "Axis agents infested Cairo and Alexandria. The Court and the Departments of the Government were filled with Axis sympathizers." Had it not been for Britain's military strength in Egypt, "the outcome might well have been far different ... When the victorious Rommel was advancing toward Alexandria, and had not yet been halted at El Alamein, a popular uprising in Cairo in support of the Axis was only averted by the narrowest of margins."[23] Welles reminded his readers of Haj Amin al-Husseini's role in winning over "a considerable number of young Arab nationalists to the Axis side" who, "throughout the war, operated as an active Fifth Column in Palestine" and sought to help the Axis armies to "gain control of the Near East."[24] He recalled the Iraqi coup of 1941 and its importance when the war hung in the balance. Had the British not been able to crush the revolt, the "outcome of the war might have been altogether different."[25] In those same "dark years when the fate of the Western countries hung in the balance, the one element in all of the Near East that remained unalterably loyal to the cause of democracy was the Jewish community in Palestine."[26] He described and denounced Britain's policies of opposition to Jewish immigration to Palestine "as Hitler's mass liquidation of the Jews increased in scale and in horror."[27] Jewish leaders understandably focused on Palestine "as the only solution for the problems resulting from the catastrophe which has overwhelmed their people." Welles cited Roosevelt's pro-Zionist statement of March 16, 1944: "when future decisions are reached full justice will be done to those who seek a Jewish National Home, for which our Government and the American people have always had the deepest sympathy, and today more than ever in view of the tragic plight of hundreds of thousands of homeless Jewish refugees."[28]

---

[21] Welles, *We Need Not Fail*, xiii.

[22] "Palestine during the Second World War," in ibid., 20.

[23] Ibid., 20. For a reconstruction of the propaganda and context of summer 1942 see Jeffrey Herf, *Nazi Propaganda for the Arab World* (New Haven: Yale University Press, 2009).

[24] Welles, *We Need Not Fail*, 20–21.   [25] Ibid., 21.   [26] Ibid.   [27] Ibid., 22–23.

[28] Franklin Delano Roosevelt, cited by Welles, ibid., 26.

Welles discussed the strategic value of Palestine as "the key" to Britain's position in the Eastern Mediterranean and "as a base which affords air and naval supremacy in the areas adjacent to the Suez Canal and in the Red Sea." It was "by far the safest and cheapest outlet for the Arabian oil fields" and was "the only possible alternative bastion for Great Britain's naval and military forces when these had to be withdrawn from Egypt." He wrote that if "the Soviet Union should seek to dominate the Dardanelles, the Balkan Peninsula, and the Eastern Mediterranean, the retention of Palestine in British hands could prove to be of determining, strategic importance." As a result, the Labour government had reversed its position on Palestine and "seemed to be precisely the same as that developed under the Cabinet of Neville Chamberlain."[29]

Welles summarized the history of commissions and plans about Palestine of the previous three years and Britain's decision to send the matter to the United Nations.[30] He described the opponents of Zionism as "the Arab propagandists" of the Arab Higher Committee and representatives of the Arab League; those who believed that "British hegemony in the Arab world" was "essential if the British Empire is to be preserved, and that any solution which antagonized the Arabs would be counter to British interests"; British and American oil companies active in the Arab countries; antisemites in Western Europe and the United States; and Americans who feared that a UN enforcement of the Partition Resolution would involve the USA in war.[31]

The book recalled the facts about the Holocaust and the desperate situation of the survivors faced with postwar antisemitism. Three years after the war they were still "confined like criminals in concentration camps." All the Western nations, to a greater or lesser degree, had to share in the responsibility for the failures that had permitted the rise of Hitlerism and the mass murders of the Jews of which it was guilty. "Are they now willing to fail in accomplishing such atonement as is now still possible – that is, to secure through the United Nations a final settlement of the Palestine problem that will provide moral and physical rehabilitation for the hundreds of thousands of refugees who can find it no other way?" If the UN failed to support the Partition Resolution, its "commitment to human rights and the dignity and worth of every human person would be undermined."[32] The issue of antisemitism was central to the problem of Palestine. Too many in the United States ignored the issue or blinded themselves "to the shameful truth that it exists in our own midst." The establishment of a Jewish state would not eliminate that hatred, but it would give the Jews a home and would foster achievement of the "four

---

[29] Ibid., 27.   [30] Ibid., 41–42.   [31] Ibid., 44–45.   [32] Ibid., 49–50.

freedoms" of speech and worship and from want and fear for which the Allies had fought World War II.[33]

Welles took direct aim at the policy of the State Department toward the UN Partition Resolution of November 29. The resolution's "cardinal defect" was a failure to provide a method of enforcement in view of the anticipated armed opposition. The Arabs might have offered a compromise if they knew that the UN would be prepared to resort to force to enforce it. Absent that, "the Arab leaders were naturally soon convinced that they could embark upon a campaign of aggression with entire impunity."[34] While the Arabs were receiving arms, the American embargo on arms as well as British refusal to permit arms imports from other sources put the Jews at a disadvantage. As Arab aggression mounted, "the Security Council continued to remain silent."[35] And, of course, Welles denounced the reversal of American support for partition announced by Warren Austin on March 19, 1948.[36]

Welles pointed to three influences that shaped Palestine policy in Washington: US military leadership, the oil lobby, and the State Department. The military leadership viewed Palestine as "nothing more than a problem of strategy. They saw the Near East as a probable base for future military operations against the Soviet Union, and as an area which contained perhaps as much as forty per cent of the oil resources of the world ... Any policy that might induce the Arab Governments to refuse their cooperation to the United States or to hinder American access to this oil seemed to them criminally stupid." The establishment of a Jewish state in Palestine and fulfillment of the UN Partition Resolution was, in their view, "wholly mistaken so long as it might result in Arab disfavor and endanger American control of the oil fields." The oil lobby gave "enthusiastic support to the military standpoint."[37]

Welles criticized the State Department for "permitting the Arabs to block any Palestine settlement which does not meet their approval."[38] In spring 1947 the American reluctance to clearly support partition stood "in sharp contrast to the unequivocal declaration of the Soviet delegate that the Soviet Government envisaged partition as presumably the only feasible solution" in view of the unlikelihood of agreement between the Jews and Arabs. In late 1947 and early 1948 Soviet-American relations deteriorated in the face of "the Soviet program for aggressive expansion" evident in efforts to "sabotage the European Recovery Program," support disruptive campaigns by the French and Italian communists and "rebellion against the constitutional government of Greece," and carry out "the

---

[33] Ibid., 54.   [34] Ibid., 66.   [35] Ibid., 68.   [36] Ibid., 70–71.   [37] Ibid., 74–75.
[38] Ibid., 75–76.

seizure of Czechoslovakia."[39] Suggestions for collective security in Palestine in the form of a UN force that included British, American, and Russian troops collided with these deepening tensions between the West and the Soviet Union, especially in Europe. For Welles, however, tensions with the Soviet Union made the territory of Palestine especially important "as a base for the air and ground forces of the Western powers."[40]

Welles viewed the American turn against partition as both an abandonment of moral leadership and a strategic blunder. On March 26, 1948 the German refugee novelist Thomas Mann denounced the American reversal of support for partition in a short essay entitled "Ghosts of 1938" that ran in the German-language New York newspaper *Aufbau*.[41] Welles quoted Mann: "This surrender to brazen Arab threats is the most humiliating and shocking political event since the democracies betrayed Czechoslovakia in 1938." It degraded "the ideals of democracy, truth, liberty and justice." It was a "deplorable decision" that had dealt a "blow" to "the authority of the United Nations and its ability to maintain world peace."[42] That month, Mann observed, the United States was failing to counter "Arab aggression" carried out by leaders who had supported the Nazis a decade earlier. In quoting Mann, Welles underscored the connection between the anti-Nazi passions of World War II and support for the Zionist project in its aftermath.

In *We Need Not Fail* Welles denounced the American embargo on arms to the Jews as it "deprived them of any chance to obtain the arms and ammunition that they desperately needed from the United States" as long as Britain prevented imports from other sources. The Arabs were "getting all of the military equipment they needed" from neighboring Arab states which had purchased much of it from Britain.[43] The arms embargo represented "an act of flagrant injustice for which there can be no extenuation."

In Welles's view the State Department was making a serious strategic blunder. The American abandonment of partition rested on the mistaken hope that doing so would win support for it from the Arab world. Yet Great Britain had "catered to Arab ambitions and to Arab prejudices" for

---

[39] Ibid., 81.   [40] Ibid., 81–82.

[41] Cited by Welles in ibid., 89. See Thomas Mann, "Gespenster von 1938," in *Thomas Mann, Meine Zeit, Essays 1945–1955* (Frankfurt am Main: Fischer Verlag, 1977), 96–97. On Thomas Mann in the United States see Hans Rudolf Vogel, *Thomas Mann, der Amerikaner: Leben und Werk im amerikanischen Exil, 1938–1952* (Frankfurt am Main: Fischer Verlag, 2011).

[42] Welles, *We Need Not Fail*, 89. In the full essay Mann contrasted the "feudalism of the Arab oil magnates" with the democracy that the Jews were building in Palestine.

[43] Welles, *We Need Not Fail*, 96.

"many generations" without success. Again, Welles recalled the Iraqi revolt of 1941, the Mufti's collaboration with the Axis, the popularity he enjoyed in the region, and the other Nazi collaborators leading the Arab Higher Committee.[44] In turning against partition, the United States was now failing to look at those realities clearly.

Further, by "using all of our influence to prevent the birth of an independent Jewish Commonwealth in Palestine," the USA was blocking "the creation of the one Near Eastern state that would prove to be a true democracy" and which would "unquestionably be an unswerving supporter of the Western cause."[45] He rejected assertions that "a Jewish state would be overwhelmingly Communist in its sympathies and a willing tool of the Kremlin," that groups of refugees were "packed with Soviet agents," and that "the Jewish resistance forces are led by Soviet officers." Certainly, there were "Soviet agents in Palestine," just as there were in the United States. But the economic structures that the Jews had established in Palestine were "wholly anticommunist in nature." The cooperatives were "fiercely democratic," and industry was privately owned. The "overwhelming majority of the Palestine Jews are vehemently anti-communist in their political beliefs and would resist as intolerable any attempt by the Soviet Union upon their individual liberties."[46] The leadership of the Jewish Agency was composed of a coalition of left-of-center and conservative labor groups. By weakening the prospects "for the construction of a Near Eastern bulwark of Western democracy" the United States had "thereby lessened the likelihood that many of the strategic advantages that it hoped to secure by abandoning partition can now be won."[47] The reversal of support for partition in spring 1948 weakened "the structure of collective security" and thus undermined the USA's "capacity to build a new world order" based on freedom and security.[48]

We Need Not Fail summarized the American liberal critique of the policies adopted by the Marshall-era State Department and the Department of Defense. As the preceding chapters indicate, the arguments were by then voiced by a range of persons and organizations. *We Need Not Fail* had a particular impact both because it brought all of those arguments together in a single volume combining an argument about morality with one about collective security and power politics, and because its author wrote with the authority of a former under secretary of state. Published only two weeks after Truman recognized the state of Israel, it illustrated the strength of resistance to that decision within the

[44] Ibid., 124–125.　[45] Ibid., 125.　[46] Ibid., 125–126.　[47] Ibid., 126.
[48] Ibid., 133–135.

State Department and thus accounted for the gap between rhetorical support and the absence of material support that persisted for the remainder of the Arab-Israeli war. It remains a singularly important document that expressed the hopes for collective security via the United Nations and the Zionist project in the first months of the Cold War.

12 International Responses to the Arab-Israeli War I: May–June 1948

But the enemy has, without a doubt, succeeded in the political battle.

David Ben-Gurion commenting on UN resolutions,
Tel Aviv, May 4, 1948

It thereby threatens not only to place in jeopardy some of our most vital interests in the Middle East and the Mediterranean but also to disrupt the unity of the Western world and to undermine our entire policy toward the Soviet Union.

George Kennan, State Department Policy Planning Staff memo,
May 21, 1948, on the impact of Truman's decision to
recognize the state of Israel

Above all, speed in the provision of such arms is urgently necessary.

Israeli president Chaim Weizmann to US president
Harry Truman, May 25, 1948

The Security Council requested the arms embargo several months ago and that we complied with it to prevent bloodshed, and that request still stands.

Harry Truman, May 27, 1948

David Ben-Gurion declared Israel's independence on May 14, 1948 (see Figure 12.1). The United States was the first state to offer it de facto recognition, on the same day. The second phase of the Arab-Israeli war, which transformed it from a civil war between Arabs and Jews within Palestine into one between Arab states and the state of Israel, began the following day when the armies of Egypt, Iraq, Lebanon, Syria, and Transjordan, with some participation of forces from Saudi Arabia and Yemen, invaded Israel. Egypt invaded from the south, Transjordan from the east, and Syria, Iraq, and Lebanon from the north and east. Four weeks of battle ended in an Israeli victory and the First Truce on June 11. The Israelis both held on to the territory allotted to them in the UN Partition Resolution and added to it in Jaffa, the western Galilee, and the Jerusalem Corridor. As Benny Morris has written, "the strategic initiative had passed from Arab into Israeli hands and was to remain there for the duration of the war. And politically, the Israelis enjoyed hesitant international support

Figure 12.1 David Ben-Gurion reads Israel's Declaration of Independence, Tel Aviv, May 14, 1948, during ceremony founding the state of Israel. Source: Zoltan Kluger/GPO/Hulton Archive/Getty Images.

whereas the Arabs were commonly seen as the aggressors."[1] Yet, even in the face of the Arab invasion, the reservations that had shaped American policy before Israel's establishment persisted.

The First Truce negotiated by the UN mediator Folke Bernadotte lasted until July 8, when Egypt launched an offensive and Israel responded with offensives of its own on all three fronts. These "Ten Days," as the Israelis called them, ended on July 18 when the UN Security Council imposed the Second Truce. In those ten days the Israelis consolidated their gains, but their victory was not decisive enough to force the Arab states to enter peace negotiations.[2] After the Second Truce the Egyptian army was on the outskirts of Jerusalem, and occupied

---

[1] Benny Morris, *1948: The First Arab-Israeli War* (New Haven: Yale University Press, 2008), 261.

[2] The Arab decision to wage war rather than accept the partition compromise turned into a catastrophe for the Palestine Arabs, 400,000 of whom became displaced persons and refugees. A discussion of the Palestinian refugee issue is beyond the scope of this work. See Morris, *1948*; and Benny Morris, *The Birth of the Palestinian Refugee Problem Revisited* (New York and Cambridge: Cambridge University Press, 2004).

significant parts of the Negev desert that had been earmarked for Israel in the Partition Resolution. If a truce were to freeze the boundaries in place as of mid-July, a Jewish state would exist, but without most of the Negev.

The outcome of the clash of arms, not debates at the UN, was going to be the decisive factor determining whether a Jewish state would be established in Palestine. The truce resolutions, debated in the often arcane and abstract language for which the UN became famous, had an important impact on the war. By July 11 Israel had defeated the first Arab efforts to destroy it, but the battlefronts left Arab – especially Egyptian – forces ensconced in territory that had been earmarked for the Jews in the UN Partition Resolution. The Israelis feared that UN truces that precluded further military action could prevent them from driving the Arab armed forces out of what the UN had declared to be the state of Israel. Debates in the UN Security Council about truces in summer and fall 1948 were about finding international legitimacy for each side's desired outcome of the war.

United Nations Security Council resolutions of spring and summer 1948 offered language of neutrality, but in David Ben-Gurion's view their clear impact was to the disadvantage of the Jews. On May 4, 1948 he expressed skepticism about the UN's role up to that point to his colleagues in Tel Aviv: "We cannot count only on resolutions and on the conscience of humanity" for their well-being. "Above all we must rely on our own strength."[3] Since November 30 the Jews had prevailed on the field of battle. "But the enemy has, without a doubt succeeded in the political battle."[4] In his view the Arabs were winning at the United Nations. For Ben-Gurion, the truce resolutions supported by the United States in the UN Security Council rested on "fallacious and illusory" assumptions that the cause of the war was to be equally shared by both sides and that therefore a UN commission should oversee negotiations between the Jews and the Arabs. "We did not begin this war and it is not to us that one should address the need for a cease-fire." Rather, "as soon as the Arabs cease combat in all of the country, we will also cease fire."

Articulating a theme that the Israelis would repeat in the coming months, Ben-Gurion said that the ceasefire proposals in the Security Council would result in "freezing the creation of its state, just as it seeks to freeze the state of affairs in another very serious direction, by putting a brake on immigration."[5] The Jewish Agency would "reject any and all

---

[3] Tuvia Friling and Denis Peschanski, eds., *David Ben-Gurion journal 1947–1948: Les secrets de la création de l'état d'Israël* (Paris: Éditions de la Martinière, 2012), 304.
[4] Ibid., 306–307. [5] Ibid., 307–308.

conditions of an armistice that implies a paralysis of action for independence or a limitation on Jewish immigration. We will not accept an armistice disguised to limit Jewish security forces and that would permit neighboring countries to dispatch armed forces to occasionally attack us." The Jews would not be driven from "this country which is ours." They would no longer be strangers and dispersed. They were ready for peace but would respond to force with force.[6] At the United Nations, Israel's diplomats fought a political battle to lend international legitimacy to the justice of their cause and the validity of Israel's actions on the battlefield. As before at the UN, it was the Soviet Union and Soviet bloc, not the United States and the Western European democracies, that continued to offer Israel the most emphatic and consistent support, even if, as Ben-Gurion put it, it was losing that battle in New York.

On May 14, 1948, at its second Special Session, again devoted to the "Problem of Palestine," the UN General Assembly had appointed a "mediator" to be chosen by a committee consisting of China, France, the USSR, the UK, and the USA. Its purpose was to "promote a peaceful adjustment of the future situation in Palestine" and send regular progress reports to the Security Council and the secretary general. The Swedish diplomat Count Folke Bernadotte (1895–1948) was appointed to the position.[7] That evening, in Tel Aviv, Ben-Gurion declared the independence of the state of Israel. The following day the seven Arab states invaded the new state of Israel with the intention of destroying it and undoing the UN Partition Plan. In so doing, they initiated the second phase of the hostilities, one that changed it from a civil war within Palestine to a war between the new state of Israel and the Arab states.

The record of debates in the UN Security Council throughout the entire history of the war of 1948 indicate that the United States and the Soviet Union maintained the positions they had held since May 1947. The Soviet Union was emphatic and clear in its support for the Israelis while the United States' stance was one of cool reserve expressed in the language of political and moral equivalence. Typical was US ambassador Austin's statement on May 17 that "the situation with respect to Palestine constitutes a threat to peace."[8] It was not, of course, "the situation" that was a threat to peace, but the invasion of Israel by seven Arab states.

---

[6] Ibid., 309–310.

[7] "Resolution 186 (S-s) Adopted by the General Assembly on May 14, 1948," *Foreign Relations of the United States* (hereafter *FRUS*), *The Near East, South Asia, and Africa*, 1948, vol. 5, part 2 (May 17, 1948): https://history.state.gov/historicaldocuments/frus1948v05 p2/d272.

[8] "Statement Made by Ambassador Austin before the Security Council on May 17, 1948," *FRUS*, vol. 5, part 2 (May 17, 1948): https://history.state.gov/historicaldocuments/fru s1948v05p2/d285.

On May 18 the UN Security Council sent lists of questions to the Jewish Agency and to the Arab Higher Committee. Four days later, Israel's acting representative, (Aubrey) Abba Eban, pointed out that, after May 14, the term Jewish Agency or "Jewish Authorities" had been supplanted by the "Provisional State Council and the Provisional Government of the State of Israel."[9] Asked whether that entity was conducting armed operations in areas where Arabs were a majority or outside Palestine, and if so with what justification, Eban replied that Israel was doing so "in order to repel aggression, and as part of our essentially defensive plan, to prevent these areas being used as bases for attacks against the State of Israel." Asked if Israel had "arranged for the entry into Palestine in the near future of men of military age from outside Palestine" and if so, how many and from where, Eban replied that "arrangements have been and are being made for the entry into Palestine of Jewish immigrants of all ages and both sexes from various countries in accordance with the avowed objective of the State of Israel to open its gates for large-scale immigration. The State of Israel regards immigration as a matter within its domestic jurisdiction."

The Security Council asked whether the Jewish Authorities would enter negotiations for a truce or a political settlement, and Eban replied that, following the November 29 (1947) resolution, the Arab League had been informed that the Jews were ready to negotiate for "peaceful collaboration" on its basis. The Arab League did not reply. King Abdullah of Jordan rejected offers of peace, insisting that "the whole of Palestine come under his rule" and that the Jews accept Arab nationality. Eban asserted that Israel was willing to enter into truce negotiations even as Arab forces had penetrated its territory in the northern Negev and Jordan Valley; planes of the Egyptian and Iraqi Air Forces were bombing Tel Aviv, Jewish settlements in the south, and the northern Jordan Valley; and Syrian and Lebanese armies were shelling settlements in the upper Galilee from across the frontier.[10]

The Security Council sent a similar set of questions to the Arab Higher Committee (AHC). On May 24 Jamal Husseini replied, acknowledging that the AHC had requested assistance from governments outside Palestine.[11] "The Arab majority, in their effort to preserve their rights

---

[9] Aubrey S. Eban, Office of the Acting Representative at the United Nations, to Secretary General, United Nations, New York (May 22, 1948), "Reply State of Israel," United Nations Security Council, S/766, (hereafter UNSC), 4–5: https://documents-dds-ny.un.org/doc/UNDOC/GEN/NL4/807/66/pdf/NL480766.pdf?OpenElement.

[10] Ibid., 4–5.

[11] Jamal Husseini to Office of the Acting Representative at the United Nations, to Secretary General, United Nations, New York (May 24, 1948), "Reply State of Israel," UNSC, S/766, 4–5: https://documents-dds-ny.un.org/doc/UNDOC/GEN/NL4/807/75/pdf/NL480775.pdf?OpenElement.

and defend themselves in their own country, had no course to follow other than to seek outside help in order to resist this Jewish aggressive invasion of their country."[12] To whom else should they turn "if not to the Arab State Members of the Arab League, who are linked to them all by ties of nationality" and were "only segregated from them by the imperialistic ambitions of foreign powers?" Faced with "a Jewish minority intent upon the actual seizure of their country by force of arms, the Arabs of Palestine naturally resorted to the Arab League for assistance at the dawn of their independence."[13] Thus it requested assistance from Egypt, Saudi Arabia, Yemen, Iraq, Lebanon, Syria, and Transjordan for the purpose of "pacification, not invasion." The AHC claimed "authority over all the area of Palestine as being the political representative of the overwhelming majority of the population." Palestine was "one unit"; any force that opposed this Arab majority "wherever they may be are regarded as unlawful."[14] Hence, as the AHC regarded the Zionist project as illegitimate, there was no point in negotiations with it. He rejected acceptance of the Partition Resolution and any kind of Jewish state in Palestine.

The Jews had accepted the UN Partition Resolution; the AHC and seven Arab states rejected it. However, blunt talk about Arab aggression and firm support of the Partition Resolution contradicted the strategic consensus that had evolved in the US national security leadership over the previous year. Carrying out the resolution would deepen tensions with Britain, which the State Department knew was sending military assistance to Transjordan and other Arab states. On May 20 Marshall, acknowledging that Britain was aiding the Arabs militarily, asked British officials in London if they intended to "to continue assistance to Abdullah and other Arab States pending action by the UN which would make such continuance of assistance contrary to UK obligations under the Charter."[15] On May 21 Sir John Balfour at the British Embassy in Washington informed Robert Lovett, Loy Henderson, and Dean Rusk that Foreign Minister Ernest Bevin did not intend to recognize the Jewish state and would not support it becoming a member of the UN.[16]

Bevin further requested that, although the USA had recognized the Jewish state "de facto" on May 14, it refrained from recognition of its boundaries, as they might differ from those recommended in the General Assembly's Partition Plan. Bevin also urged the USA to maintain its arms

---

[12] Ibid., 5.   [13] Ibid.   [14] Ibid., 5–6.

[15] George Marshall to AMEMBASSY LONDON, Washington (May 20, 1948), 1836, NACP RG 59 CDF 1945–1949, 501. BB Palestine/5–2048, 2, Box 2118.

[16] "Memorandum of Conversation, by the Under Secretary of State (Lovett)," Washington (May 21, 1948), FRUS, 1948, vol. 5, part 2: https://history.state.gov/historicaldocuments/frus1948vo5p2/d295.

embargo. That is, he did not want to recognize boundaries that could result from Israel's response to the Arab invasions of May 15. If Britain reversed course and allowed arms shipments to Israel, Britain "would almost certainly be obliged" to raise its "own embargo on the export of arms to certain Arab states," thus leading to "the unfortunate position" in which "one side [was] being largely armed by the Americans and the other by the British." Specifically, Britain's treaty with Transjordan would oblige the UK to come to Transjordan's assistance, "should the Jews obtain military successes and pursue retreating Arab forces over the frontier" into that country.[17] Bevin said that Truman's recognition of Israel had "placed a heavy strain on Anglo-American cooperation in the Middle East." It had "aroused bitter Arab resentment against the United States in an area which the British and American Governments regard as of high strategic and political importance to both of them." Unless the Arab countries could be "induced to retain some confidence in the friendly understanding and fairness of both the United States Government and HMG [His Majesty's Government] on the Palestine issue, they may turn away from Western countries altogether."[18] Bevin ignored past British assessments about Arab opposition to Soviet influence and communism as well as the very public fact that the Soviet Union and Soviet bloc were supporting the new state of Israel.

On May 21 George Kennan sent a memo to Marshall expressing the Policy Planning Staff's "deep apprehension over the trend of U.S. policy" on "the Palestine matter" following Truman's recognition of Israel.[19] He recalled the staff papers of January 19 and January 29, which recommended that the United States "should not take any action which would (a) lead us to the assumption of major responsibility for the maintenance and security of a Jewish state in Palestine; or (b) bring us into a conflict with the British over the Palestine issue." Those documents had "specifically warned ... against our acceptance of the thesis that armed interference in Palestine by the Arab states would constitute aggression, which this Government would be bound, as a member of the United Nations, in opposing." American policy following Truman's recognition of Israel and at the UN was leading the United States "in the direction of all of these situations. It thereby threatens not only to place in jeopardy some of our most vital interests in the Middle East and the Mediterranean but also to disrupt the unity of the Western world and to undermine our entire policy toward the Soviet Union." It might also "initiate a process of disintegration

[17] Ibid., 1–2.   [18] Ibid., 2.

[19] George F. Kennan, "Memorandum by the Director of the Policy Planning Staff (Kennan) to the Secretary of State," Washington (May 21, 1948), *FRUS*, vol. 5, part 2: https://history.state.gov/historicaldocuments/frus1948v05p2/d296

of the United Nations itself."[20] Kennan was fighting a straw man; the Israelis had only requested that the USA support the Partition Resolution it had voted for on November 29, 1947, not that it assume military responsibility for Israel's security. Most importantly for Kennan – and Marshall: clear support for the new state of Israel might shatter Western, that is, Anglo-American, unity and thus, in their view, undermine the core of Western policy: containment of communism in Europe.

The following day Marshall received a similar message from US ambassador Douglas in London. Douglas thought a "crevasse" was "widening between US and Britain" that could not be confined to Palestine or the Middle East. It was "already seriously jeopardizing [the] foundation-stone of US policy in Europe – partnership with a friendly and well-disposed Britain." The "worst shock" so far was American recognition of the Jewish state "without prior notice of our intentions to British Government."[21] The "worst prospect" Douglas could see on the "horizon of American-British relations" would be a US decision to "raise [the] embargo on Middle East arm shipments to favor Jews." In that event, it would be "only a short step" until the British government, "impelled by what it conceives to be its vital interests in the Middle East extending as far as Pakistan," might "lift embargo" on supplying arms to the Arabs. "When this happens, the two great democratic partners will indirectly be ranged on opposite sides of a battle line scarcely three years after May 8, 1945."[22]

At the UN, however, the USA and Britain remained in fundamental agreement concerning Security Council resolutions related to the war. For example, Security Council Resolution 49 of May 22 called "upon all Governments and authorities, without prejudice to the rights, claims or positions of the parties concerned, to abstain from any hostile military action in Palestine" and to order a ceasefire to their military and paramilitary forces within thirty-six hours.[23] Faced with the Arab invasion, the resolution deployed a discourse of moral equivalence and impartiality.

On May 25 Henderson wrote to Marshall that it was important to uphold the principles of the UN Charter and not weaken the UN "by the creation of new antagonistic blocks, as for instance, a bloc of Asiatic countries or a bloc of peoples of non-European origin who feel that the

[20] Ibid.

[21] "The Ambassador in the United Kingdom (Douglas) to the Secretary of State," London (May 22, 1948), *FRUS*, vol. 5, part 2: https://history.state.gov/historicaldocuments/frus1948v05p2/d306.

[22] Ibid.

[23] "Resolution 49 (1948) Adopted by the Security Council on May 22, 1948," *FRUS*, vol. 5, part 2 (May 22, 1948): https://history.state.gov/historicaldocuments/frus1948 v05p2/d302 .

principles of the Charter are being applied differently to them than to peoples of European origin."[24] He thought "that the majority of the thinking peoples of Asia are convinced that the Zionists, with the aid of certain western countries, have for years been engaged in a slow process of aggression against the Arabs of Palestine and that this process is now reaching the stage of armed aggression. Furthermore, many of them are convinced that the Zionist ambitions extend beyond the confines of what the Zionists now call their state." As long as that feeling existed, the UN needed to exercise "great circumspection" and "proceed with caution in enforcing decisions which so many peoples believe to be based upon considerations other than a determination to uphold the principles of the Charter."[25] In short, American policy toward the Zionist project should be influenced by the views of unspecified "thinking peoples of Asia," that is, not only by the Arabs of the Middle East, and who also viewed the Zionist project as a form of aggression that violated the UN Charter. Henderson did not propose to tell these people that Zionism was not a form of aggression, that there were many "non-European" Jews in North Africa and the Arab states who supported the Zionists, or that antisemitism constituted another form of attack on the principles of the UN Charter.

Chaim Weizmann, Now as Israel's President, Requests Arms from Truman

After the establishment of Israel on May 14 Chaim Weizmann (1874–1952), leader of the World Zionist Organization, became its first president. On May 25 Weizmann wrote to Truman again, this time to request military assistance. The new state faced "two basic problems: first, national survival in the face of Arab aggression supported by the British; second, the resettlement and rehabilitation of the homeless DP's."[26] There was "little hope" that the Arabs would accept a ceasefire "without crippling limitations." The British felt they could "divide American opinion and render American policy irresolute" while the Arabs continued to rely on "guidance and assistance by the British." Bringing peace to the Middle East required "modification of the arms embargo established by the United States."[27]

---

[24] Loy Henderson to George Marshall, Washington (May 25, 1948), NACP RG 59 CDF, 1945–1949, 501.BB Palestine/5-2548, 2, Box 2118.

[25] Ibid., 2.

[26] "Memorandum by the President of the Provisional Government of Israel (Weizmann) to President Truman," Washington (May 25, 1948), FRUS, 1948, vol. 5, part 2: https://history.state.gov/historicaldocuments/frus1948v05p2/d317.

[27] Ibid.

That was an action that would be "most effective" in changing British and Arab policy. Weizmann told Truman that Israel needed "anti-tank weapons; anti-aircraft weapons; planes; and heavy artillery" in amounts that were small by American standards, "but in the context of the current activity in Israel they may well be decisive. Above all, speed in the provision of such arms is urgently necessary. Would it be possible to make limited quantities of these weapons available from depots or other store places in the Middle East?"[28]

Truman, despite his admiration for Weizmann, was not persuaded. The following day he gave the State Department approval to maintain the arms embargo as long as the UN ceasefire order was followed by "governments and authorities participating in hostilities in Palestine."[29] At a press conference on May 27 Truman said that the "security council requested the arms embargo several months ago and that we complied with it to prevent bloodshed, and that request still stands."[30] The Security Council's "request," Truman noted, was itself the result of the initiative of the State Department. Preventing bloodshed was a laudable goal but an odd one to stress in the weeks after the Arab states invaded the new state of Israel. In view of the opposition in the Pentagon and State Department, it is certain that if Truman had decided to lift the embargo on arms to the new state of Israel, he would have faced at least fierce opposition from Marshall and Forrestal, perhaps even to the point of resignations and a crisis in his administration. The key point is that the American embargo on arms to Israel and the Arab states remained in place for the remainder of the 1948 war.

That same day, in keeping with Truman's directive, Marshall instructed UN ambassador Warren Austin to support action by the Security Council "to order all governments to refrain from the shipment of weapons and war materials, and the rendering of other military assistance, to governments and authorities now participating in hostilities in Palestine." An arms embargo had to be pursued "with vigor and singleness of purpose," Marshall explained. If not, the Security Council would "be demoralized and our attitude toward lifting the arms embargo itself

---

[28] Ibid. Weizmann also asked Truman for his support for Israel's application for a loan from the Export-Import Bank Second, to support the costs of bringing Jewish displaced persons in Europe and Cyprus to Israel at the rate of 15,000 persons per month.

[29] "Memorandum by the Department of State to President Truman," Washington (May 22, 1948), *FRUS*, vol. 5, part 2: https://history.state.gov/historicaldocuments/frus1948v05p2/d301.

[30] Robert Lovett to US Embassy London, Washington (May 28, 1948), NACP RG 59 CDF 1945–1949, National Archives Microfilm Publications, M1390, Records of the Department of State Relating to the Internal Affairs of Palestine, 1945–1949, Roll 15, 867N.01/5–2848.

might become the cause of even greater bloodshed in Palestine."[31] The following day, just a week after the Arab invasion, Marshall told Austin that the United States did "not wish at this time to charge either party as being an aggressor."[32] No one in the top ranks of the State Department made the case that firm and clear support for the new state of Israel would have deterred the Arab League from launching the expanded war in the first place or pushed it to cease operations once the war began. Especially in view of Soviet support for Israel, such an American policy would have angered the British Foreign Office but carried little risk of driving the Arabs into the arms of the Soviet Union.

The conviction that opposition to communism was compatible with support for the new state of Israel was shared by President Truman, Congressman Emanuel Celler and Senator Robert Wagner and other members of the US Congress, Clark Clifford, former Under Secretary of State Sumner Welles, the Socialist ministers of interior in France, the leaders of AZEC, and Ben-Gurion and Moshe Shertok, but not by the leadership in the US State Department, Pentagon, and CIA, and certainly not by the British foreign secretary, Bevin, and Britain's Foreign Office.

The Arab states indicated very clearly how they would react if the USA lifted the embargo on arms to Israel. On May 27 the State Department's Division of Near Eastern and African Affairs received a synthesis of messages from US ambassadors and military observers in Cairo, Beirut, Damascus, and Jerusalem written in the past few days regarding the effect of a possible "repeal of the arms embargo to permit aid to Israel."[33] Based on conversations with Arab leaders, the diplomats wrote that throughout the Near East, doing so would be considered a virtual American alliance with the Jewish war effort and an American declaration of war against the Arab states. It would immediately evoke hostile and violent mob reactions against the United States and irreparably damage American-Arab relations. It would result in the destruction of American tactical and strategic security throughout the entire Near East and would lead ultimately to the loss of the American stake in this area.[34]

Echoing the predictions of the Policy Planning Staff papers of January 1948 and the Eddy memorandum of December 31, 1947, the

---

[31] George Marshall to UN NEW YORK, Washington (May 26, 1948), 327, NACP RG 59 CDF, 1945–1949, 501.BB Palestine/5–2648, Box 2118.

[32] "The Acting Secretary of State to the United States Representative at the United Nations (Austin), Washington (May 27, 1948), 331, *FRUS*, vol. 5, part 2: https://history .state.gov/historicaldocuments/frus1948v05p2/d333.

[33] "Memorandum Prepared, in the Division of Near Eastern Affairs," Washington (n.d.), *FRUS*, 1948, vol. 5, part 2: https://history.state.gov/historicaldocuments/frus1948v05 p2/d331.

[34] Ibid.

diplomats again predicted that lifting the arms embargo would: endanger the security of American citizens and officials in the Arab states and Arab-occupied parts of Palestine; lead to destruction or seizure of American educational institutions, oil installations and other property in the same areas and to attacks on Jews and possibly foreigners in Arab States, especially in the event of Arab military reverses; intensify popular hatred against the United States, and the West; and prolong hostilities and "increase the possibility of anti-foreign, anti-Jewish, and anti-Christian violence throughout the Moslem world."[35]

The US consul general in Jerusalem, Thomas Wasson, saw things differently. On May 19, four days before he was killed, either intentionally or in a crossfire in the war, he wrote to the secretary of state about the entry into Palestine of troops from Egypt, Transjordan, Iraq, Syria, and Lebanon. Though intelligence reports suggested that the Arab armies would not risk any major battles, Wasson told Marshall that, "should Arab troops be successful in a major operation with Jews this would probably give Arabs desired impetus to drive forward and attempt annihilation of Jewish state" (emphasis in original). Wasson thought Jews would be able to retain a coastal area, but without "generous and immediate assistance from abroad particularly the United States" the Jewish state "would be unable to survive long surrounded by hostile Arab states." Truman's de facto recognition and rumors of an "early repeal of arms embargo will undoubtedly give Jews great courage to face world." That, along with economic assistance "from American and South African Jewry plus reasonable policy of Jewish leaders toward" Transjordan's Abdullah might create a "favorable atmosphere."[36] Wasson's views remained the exception among the State Department diplomats working on the Middle East.

On May 19, at the 296th meeting of the Security Council, the United States introduced a draft resolution ordering "all Governments and authorities to cease and desist from any hostile military action" and issue a "cease-fire and stand-fast order" to their "military forces and paramilitary forces," to become effective in thirty-six hours. The resolution came four days after the Arab invasion, so it was absurd to request that the Israelis issue a ceasefire order while under attack. The language of equivalence obscured the reality of Arab aggression.[37] The resolution would

---

[35] Ibid., 1–2.

[36] Thomas Wasson to Secretary of State, Jerusalem (May 19, 1948), No. 650, NACP RG 59 CDF 1945–1949, M1390, Roll 15, 867N.01/5–1948.

[37] "Draft Resolution on the Palestinian Question Submitted by the Representative of the United States at the Two Hundred and Ninety-Third Meeting of the Security Council, 17 May 1948," United Nations Security Council, S/749: https://documents-dds-ny.un.org /doc/UNDOC/GEN/NL4/807/49/pdf/NL480749.pdf?OpenElement. Also see *Yearbook of*

apply equally to Israel and the invading Arab states. Vasyl Tarasenko, the representative of the Ukrainian SSR, which was then on the Security Council, said that documents submitted by Egypt and Transjordan "clearly stated that their troops had entered Palestine" with a "very definite military and political objective."[38] Stressing that the existence of Israel was an "established fact," and that the new state was "determined to defend its territory," he rejected the equivalence implicit in the US draft. On May 21 Andrei Gromyko in the Security Council reiterated his support for the partition of Palestine into two independent states that should be implemented "through joint efforts of all members of the United Nations."[39] He criticized the UK for supporting the actions of Transjordan and preventing the Security Council "from taking effective action to suppress the existing threat to and breach of the peace in Palestine," that is, implicitly, the Arab League invasion. The American-sponsored resolution would have the effect of leaving the Arab armies inside the new state of Israel. It was apparent that Soviet and Soviet-bloc partisanship for Israel conflicted with the American rhetorical and diplomatic stance of moral and political equivalence.

In any event, on May 22, with Syria, then one of the non-permanent members of the Security Council – the others were Argentina, Belgium, Canada, Colombia, and Ukrainian SSR – (for the reversed reasons), the Ukrainian SSR and the USSR abstaining, the Security Council adopted a resolution that followed the language of the May 19 American draft. It called "upon all Governments and authorities, without prejudice to the rights, claims or position of the parties concerned, to abstain from any hostile military action in Palestine" and to issue a ceasefire order to become effective within thirty-six hours.[40] A week later Tarasenko said that the Ukrainian SSR had abstained because the resolution had not been clear enough about the cause of the absence of peace. The cessation of hostilities was being delayed "in accordance with the imperialistic interests of the United Kingdom, which was in fact participating in the hostilities by supplying arms and personnel to the Arab forces."[41] On May 28 Britain's UN ambassador Alexander Cadogan proposed a resolution stipulating a four-week ceasefire during which "both parties" would "not introduce fighting personnel or men of military age into

the United Nations 1947–48 (New York: United Nations Department of Public Information, 1949), 419.

[38] Yearbook of the United Nations 1947–48, 420.   [39] Ibid., 420–421.

[40] "Resolution on the Palestine Question Adopted by the Security Council at the Three Hundred and Second Meeting, May 22, 1948, UNSC, S/773: https://documents-dds-ny.un.org/doc/UNDOC/GEN/NL4/807/73/pdf/NL480773.pdf?OpenElement.

[41] Yearbook of the United Nations 1947–48, 422.

Palestine," and calling upon "both parties and all Governments to refrain from importing war material into Palestine" during the truce.[42]

Tarasenko responded that the UK draft resolution

was designed to stifle the State of Israel. At the end of the four-week period, the Jews would find their resources depleted while the Arabs would be prepared for a renewed onslaught. The invaders would be permitted to retain their forces in Palestine and use it as a base for larger operations. All the large arsenals of the United Kingdom would be at the disposal of the Arabs, and a virtual blockade would be established around Israel. Jewish emigration was an internal matter for Israel. The provision for enforcement action by the Security Council against any party which rejected the resolution was clearly designed to obtain sanctions against the Jews. The whole draft resolution was biased and unacceptable.[43]

Tarasenko had punctured the language of apparent neutrality in the US-supported truce resolution. In effect, he argued that the Security Council's language of neutrality avoided the reality of Arab aggression and disadvantaged the Israelis.

On May 29, at the 309th meeting of the Security Council, Gromyko proposed a resolution that clearly placed the blame for the hostilities on the Arabs and described Israel as a victim of aggression. As the Security Council's resolution of May 22 on cessation of hostilities "has not been carried out, in view of the refusal of the Arab states to comply with this decision," the text would read, the Security Council "orders the Governments of the States involved in the present conflict in Palestine to secure cessation of military operations" within thirty-six hours.[44] At the same meeting Gromyko said that the UK proposals were "illegal and were contrary to the interests of both Jews and Arabs and to the General Assembly's resolution of November 29, 1947." Their adoption by the Security Council "would be equivalent to imposing sanctions on the Jewish State, the victim of aggression." The British resolution was "an expression of the imperialistic policy of the United Kingdom, designed to prolong the conflict in Palestine by inciting Arabs to fight Jews, to make it impossible for the Jewish State to maintain its independence, or for a new

[42] "Revised Draft Resolution on the Palestinian Question Submitted by the Representative of the United Kingdom at the Three Hundred and Tenth Meeting of the Security Council, 29 May 1948," UNSC, S/795/Rev.2: https://documents-dds-ny.un.org/doc/U NDOC/GEN/NL4/811/69/pdf/NL481169.pdf?OpenElement; also see *Yearbook of the United Nations 1947–48*, 423–424.

[43] Vasyl Tarasenko, cited in *Yearbook of the United Nations 1947–48*, 424.

[44] "Revised Draft Proposal of the Palestinian Question Submitted by the Representative of the Soviet Socialist Republics at the Three Hundred and Ninth Meeting of the Security Council, 29 May 1948," UNSC, S.794/Rev.2: https://documents-dds-ny.un.org/doc/U NDOC/GEN/NL4/811/68/pdf/NL481168.pdf?OpenElement; also see *Yearbook of the United Nations 1947–48*, 423.

and independent Arab State to emerge in the Arab part of Palestine."[45] Gromyko reminded the Security Council that its resolutions were now also undermining the prospect for an Arab state on parts of what had been British Mandate Palestine. The United States had refused to support a resolution that clearly placed the blame for the expanded war on the seven Arab states that had supported the invasion of the new state of Israel. The Soviet denunciation of Arab aggression was deleted from the draft resolution by the Security Council majority led by the United States and Britain.[46]

Later that same day the Security Council adopted Security Council Resolution 801, a slightly revised version of the draft truce resolution introduced by the British. It called for a ceasefire of four weeks' duration.[47] The language became important in the coming weeks. The Security Council called upon

both parties and all governments and authorities concerned [not to] introduce fighting personnel into Palestine, Egypt, Iraq, Lebanon, Saudi Arabia, Syria, Transjordan, and Yemen during the cease fire ... Should men of military age be introduced into countries or territories under their control, to undertake not to mobilize or submit them to military training during the cease-fire ... and to refrain from importing or exporting war material into or to Palestine, Egypt, Iraq, Lebanon, Saudi Arabia, Syria, Transjordan and Yemen during the cease fire.[48]

The resolution called on the UN mediator to "supervise the observance" of these provisions and report to the Security Council. The Soviet Union, Colombia, Syria, and the Ukrainian SSR abstained, but the resolution passed with nine "yes" votes including the United States, Britain, and France. The adoption of the resolution was clearly a victory for the British Foreign Office and the US State Department. The Americans and the British, with support from the French Foreign Ministry, defeated the Soviet Union's effort to place primary responsibility on the Arabs for the expansion of the civil war of December 1947 to May 1948 into a war between states following the Arab invasion of May 15.[49] That same day Under Secretary Lovett sent the text of S/801 to US diplomats in Moscow, London, Jerusalem, Baghdad, Damascus, Beirut, Jeddah, and Cairo.[50]

---

[45] *Yearbook of the United Nations 1947–48*, 425.   [46] Ibid., 426.

[47] "Resolution on the Palestinian Question Adopted at the Three Hundred and Tenth Meeting of the Security Council, 29 May 1948," UNSC, S/801: https://documents-dds-ny.un.org/doc/UNDOC/GEN/NL4/808/01/pdf/NL480801.pdf?OpenElement.

[48] Ibid.

[49] On France at the United Nations, see Frédérique Schillo, *La France et la création de l'état d'Israel: 18 fevrier 1947–11 mai 1949* (Paris: Éditions Artcom, 1997). On the members of the French delegation to the UN see 248–250.

[50] Robert Lovett to Certain American Diplomatic and Consular Offices, NACP RG 59 CDF 1945–1949, 501.BB Palestine/5–2948, Box 2118. Also see "Resolution 50 (1948)

Communist Czechoslovakia Breaks the Embargo on Arms to Israel

The truce resolution of May 29 offered the imprimatur of the UN Security Council to the US (and UK) arms embargo on both the Arab states and Israel. Its ambiguous and vague reference to "all governments and authorities" and "both parties and upon all governments" avoided the reality of the Arab states' invasion of May 15. It equated Israel's efforts at self-defense with the Arab invasion and fostered the fiction that an arms embargo on Israel, surrounded by hostile neighbors, would have a comparable impact on the Arab states, which had multiple sources for acquiring arms and already had standing armies and air forces. It put Israel in the position of defying this UN Security Council resolution as it sought arms to defend itself, a right it had under the UN Charter. Thus objectively, in terms of its consequences, the resolution served the interests of the Arab states. It formed the basis for the instructions given to the UN mediator, Folke Bernadotte, as he attempted to establish UN truce resolutions in the coming months.

As Tarasenko had pointed out, the impact of the resolution in the following months was to block Israel's efforts to obtain military assistance. Moreover, beyond occasional verbal criticisms, it did not stop British aid flowing to the Arabs. As Celler had pointed out, the Arab states had the advantages of sovereignty, such as ports, airports, trade relations, and alliances with one another, advantages which Israel was only beginning to enjoy. If Israel was going to receive any military assistance during the war, it would have to come from a country or countries willing to flout not just the United States but the United Nations Security Council resolutions of spring 1948 as well. None of the Western democracies dared to do so; Communist Czechoslovakia, presumably with the agreement of the Soviet Union, did.

Ben-Gurion and Shertok sent warm expressions of thanks to Truman following his decision to recognize the new state of Israel on May 14. American diplomats informed Washington about the notes of thanks the Israelis sent to other countries as well, particularly those in the Soviet bloc. On May 14 Shertok wrote the following fulsome expression of gratitude to the Czech foreign minister, Vladimír Clementis. He expressed

the profound gratitude of the Palestinian Jewish nation which is shared by Jewry all over the world for the sincere and active sympathies expressed by Czechoslovakia for the recognition of the Jewish nation in Palestine, and for the

Adopted by the Security Council on May 29, 1948," *FRUS*, vol. 5, part 2: https://history .state.gov/historicaldocuments/frus1948v05p2/d347.

cause of a Jewish State and for the valuable support given to these aims by the late President Liberator T.G. Masaryk and by President [Edward] Benes, to whom I beg you to convey my deep admiration."[51]

Shertok recalled "with gratitude" the Czech delegates' drafting of a proposal on the United Nations Special Committee on Palestine (UNSCOP) to set up a Jewish state, and "the determined defense of this proposal by the Czechoslovak delegation at regular and extraordinary sessions of UN."[52]

A week later Czechoslovakia offered full – that is, de jure – diplomatic recognition to Israel.[53] Clementis wrote that the Czech government

appreciates the effort which the Jewish nation has made for the cause of peace and social progress, and is convinced that the establishment of an independent Jewish state will be a real contribution to the maintenance of peace and will help to strengthen security in the Middle East, and that the new State will always be one of the exponents of cultural and social progress all over the world.[54]

Clementis played a key role in Operation Balak, the clandestine delivery of military assistance from Europe to Israel in 1948. It is important to recall that when the Czechs sent arms to the Israelis, they were doing so in accordance with Soviet policy. Like the German Communist Paul Merker, the Polish UN ambassador Alfred Fiderkiewicz or, most famously, like Andrei Gromyko, the Czech leaders were following, not departing from, Soviet foreign policy at the time.[55] A hero to the Israelis, he enjoyed no such recognition from his own government once Stalinism prevailed in the Soviet bloc. In 1952 he was arrested and accused of being a member of a "Titoist-Trotskyist-Zionist conspiracy" in the "Slansky trial" in Prague. His role in the assistance to Israel in 1948 was an important piece of evidence that led to his execution by hanging along with ten others.[56]

[51] (Laurence) Steinhardt to Secretary of State, No. 366, Prague (May 21, 1948), "Enclosure No. 1 to Dispatch No. 366," Mr. Moshe Shertok to Dr. Clementis, NACP RG 59 CDF 1945–1949, M1390, Roll 15, 867N.01/5–2148.

[52] Ibid.

[53] Laurence Steinhardt to Secretary of State, Prague (May 21, 1948), No. 366, "Subject: Czechoslovakia recognizes State of Israel and its Provisional Government de jure," NACP RG 59 CDF 1945–1949, M1390, Roll 15, 867N.01/5–2148.

[54] Ibid., 366. On the Czech support for the Yishuv and for Israel in 1948 see Arnold Krammer, *The Forgotten Friendship: Israel and the Soviet Bloc, 1947–53* (Urbana: University of Illinois Press, 1974).

[55] On Paul Merker's support for Zionist aspirations, and then his arrest and secret trial in the wake of the Slansky trial see Jeffrey Herf, *Divided Memory: The Nazi Past in the Two Germanys* (Cambridge, MA: Harvard University Press, 1997), 69–161.

[56] On the Slansky trial see, for example, Karel Kaplan, *Report on the Murder of the General Secretary* (Columbus: Ohio State University Press, 1990); and Meir Kotic, *The Prague Trial: The First Anti-Zionist Show Trial in the Communist Bloc* (New York: Herzl Press, 1987).

On May 18, 1948 Elbridge Durbrow (1903–97), the US ambassador in Moscow, informed the secretary of state that the news agency Tass had published Shertok's long and warm telegram to Soviet foreign minister Vyacheslav Molotov, expressing his

profound gratitude and thankfulness of Jewish people of Palestine, shared by Jews throughout the world, for firm position taken by Soviet delegation to UN, aimed at establishment of sovereign and independent Jewish state in Palestine, and for its stubborn defence of this position despite all difficulties, for sincere expression of sympathy with suffering Jewish people in Europe beneath the Fascist butchers, and for support of principle that Jews of Palestine are a nation with right to sovereignty and independence.[57]

The next day, in his country's announcement of its recognition of the state of Israel, the Polish foreign minister, Zygmunt Modzelewski (1900–54), stated that "the Polish Government has consistently maintained an attitude of sympathy and friendly feeling for the Jewish nation, fighting for freedom and for its own sake, in the international forum, especially in the United Nations." He hoped that "the basis for further cooperation will grow and that the ties of friendship between our two nations" and governments "will be constantly strengthened."[58] Such expressions of warm thanks were likely to reinforce the suspicions of those in the State Department and the Pentagon who associated Zionism and Israel with the Soviet Union.

In France, a gap comparable to that in the United States existed between a pro-Zionist public opinion and the Foreign Ministry's determination to avoid antagonizing the Arabs. The French government did not recognize the state of Israel until January 12, 1949. From Paris on May 18, 1948 Ambassador Jefferson Caffery quoted *Le Monde* on "the apparently most incoherent attitude" of the United States "which, up to yesterday, proposed a dozen contrary solutions, only finally to reach a sensational decision which surprised the Jews themselves: the recognition 'de facto' of the new state."[59] Caffery reported that, not surprisingly, the French Foreign Office was "very unhappy about question of recognizing Jewish state and fear it may be used by Arab nationalist elements in French North Africa as pretext for causing trouble." French "public and

---

[57] Message from Moshe Shertok to Soviet Foreign Minister Vyacheslav Molotov, cited in [Elbridge] Durbrow to Secretary of State, Moscow (May 18, 1948), NACP RG 59 CDF 1945–1949, M1390, Roll 15, 867N.01/5–1848.

[58] American Embassy, Warsaw to Secretary of State, Warsaw, Poland (May 20, 1948), "Enclosure No. 2 to Despatch 315, "Note of the Polish Government to the Provisional Government of Israel" (May 18, 1948), NACP RG 59 CDF 1945–1949, M1390, Roll 15, 867N.01/5–2048.

[59] Jefferson Caffery to Secretary of State, Paris (May 18, 1948), NACP RG 59 CDF 1945–1949, M1390, Roll 15, 867N.01/5–1848.

parliamentary opinion" was in favor of recognizing Israel, but France did not want to be among the first nations to do so.[60] As in the United States, popular opinion did not agree with the diplomats. On May 21 the French National Assembly passed a motion of "sympathy" and "fraternal greetings" to the new Jewish state. Although this fell short of recognition, some deputies were concerned to "avoid hasty decisions" in view of France's Muslim population in North Africa. However, "with the Communists and Socialists strongly supporting the motion, it was finally voted without difficulty."[61]

On May 20 in the French National Assembly, Florimond Bonté (1890–1977), a member of the Central Committee of the French Communist Party, again in accord with Soviet bloc policy of the time, said the following in support of France's immediate recognition of the state of Israel:[62]

We cannot forget that on the territory of Europe dominated by Hitlerism, half of the Jewish population has been exterminated and that, for three years, millions of human beings have been reduced to scraps of emaciated skin to ask for help which could not be granted to them. We must pay tribute to those who fought alongside us during the war for the liberation of all peoples from the racial danger stemming from the barbaric philosophy of Hitlerism. It was from their attitude that the possibility of the creation of the Jewish state was born. On the other hand, if Palestine were not located at a strategic crossroads, a focal point of considerable oil wealth, we would certainly not be seeing antagonism manifested between the Muslim and Jewish populations. The facts show, in fact, that the Arabs and the Jews can get along and collaborate when the regime of kings due to oil does not come to disturb their efforts to do so. [Loud applause from the far left.][63]

Bonté reflected widespread sentiment on the French left. On May 26 Cecil Gray, the consul general in the US Consulate in Marseille, informed Marshall that the local newspapers were "without exception sympathetic and friendly to the new State of Israel."[64] On June 23 the American consul in Lyon told him that Jewish veterans of the French Resistance, together with Socialists and Communists, had organized a meeting in Lyon to voice criticism of the French government for not

[60] Ibid.
[61] Jefferson Caffery to Secretary of State, Paris (May 21, 1948), No. 2704, NACP RG 59 CDF 1945–1949, M1390, Roll 15, 867N.01/5–2148.
[62] Florimond Bonté in *Journal Officiel de la République Française, Débats Parlementaires, Assemblée Nationale*, Paris (May 20, 1949), 2784 Among Bonté's published books was *Six million de crimes* (Paris: Éditions Sociales, 1964).
[63] Bonté in *Journal Officiel de la République Française*, 2784.
[64] C. W. Gray to Secretary of State, Marseilles, France (May 26, 1948), "Marseilles Editorials on the Situation in Israel," NACP RG 59 CDF 1945–1949, M1390, Roll 15, 867N.01/5–2648.

yet having recognized the state of Israel, and urged it to do so.[65] American diplomats in France kept the State Department well informed about the popular support, in particular from liberals, Socialists, and Communists, first for the Zionists and then for the state they founded.

US Joint Chiefs of Staff on "The Problem of Palestine" in June 1948

In Washington, the US Joint Chiefs of Staff (JCS) updated their assessment of the strategic consequences of the establishment of the state of Israel. On June 15 they agreed on the content of "Revision of Project 'Intelligence Estimate-Palestine,'" another in their extensive reports in the "The Problem of Palestine" series.[66] Circulated to the leaders of the Army, Air Force, and Navy on June 21, the report expressed the persistent Cold War consensus in the US military leadership.[67] The authors wrote that the United States "was primarily responsible" for the UN General Assembly's partition recommendation of November 29, but the USSR was "endeavoring by various means to bring about chaotic conditions in the area and to establish its own influence, particularly in the new Jewish state."[68]

The Army "Intelligence Estimate" of June 15 offered the following historical perspective: Palestine had been inhabited by "Arabs and by a small number of Jewish colonists" who sought refuge from oppression in Russia and in Europe. They were accepted by the Arabs. Zionism became a significant "political factor only when the wealthy Jews of Western Europe and the United States, moved by humanitarian motives, subsidized and organized migration from the U.S.S.R and Eastern Europe." Between the two World Wars, "a fierce struggle developed within Jewry" between an "old social Zionism" and a "new political or nationalist Zionism. The latter won and Jewish leaders admit that they will not be content until all Arabs have been removed from Palestine, Transjordan, south Syria, and south Lebanon."[69] In fact, Zionist leaders had made no plans for the removal of Arabs from Palestine, not to

---

[65] Horatio Mooers, American Consul to Secretary of State, Lyon (June 23, 1948), "Jewish Volunteers and Veterans of French Army Hold Rally to Support French Recognition of Israel," NACP RG 59 CDF 1945–1949, M1390, Roll 15, 867N.01/6–2348.

[66] "List of Papers, 091 Palestine," NACP RG 319 (Army Staff) Plans and Operations Division, Decimal File, 1946–1948, 091. Palestine, Box 24. The series of papers had the number "JCH 1684."

[67] Plans and Operations Division, GSUSA, Washington (June 21, 1948), "Revision of Project 'Intelligence Estimate-Palestine,' (JICM 120)" NACP RG 319 (Army Staff) Plans and Operations Division, Decimal File, 1946–1948, 091. Palestine, Box 24.

[68] Ibid., 1.   [69] Ibid.

mention the bordering Arab states. Not only was the report making unsubstantiated charges of Israeli aggressiveness, it also carried tinges of antisemitism with its reference to "wealthy Jews"; moreover, given Zionism's core of support among less affluent Jews in Eastern Europe, it was simply inaccurate.[70]

Equally telling were the historical review's silences. It said nothing about Nazi Germany, antisemitism, and the mass murder of European Jewry or the impact of those events on the course of Zionism and events in Palestine. It failed to examine the legitimacy of claims to consider Palestine as a place for the Jewish homeland. Rather, the authors wrote that "the Arabs have lived in Palestine and have constituted the overwhelming majority of the population for over 1,200 years." They ruled it for "900 years" and had a population of over 1.3 million compared to only 654,000 Jews. Arab hostility to Zionism had become "progressively stronger as Arab nationalism developed." Open warfare "broke out" on November 30, 1947 only after the passage of the UN Partition Resolution. Arab feeling was "intense and involves all classes from the wealthy landowners to the peasant farmer and the desert nomad." This feeling was expressed by the Arab League representing seven Arab states. The report made no mention the Nazi collaborationist past of members of the Arab Higher Committee.[71]

The Army Intelligence Estimate offered the following assessment of Soviet activities:

For the Soviet Union, Palestine presents the best wedge for penetration into the Near East. For the past two years the U.S.S.R. and its satellite states have been facilitating the passage of Jewish immigrants to Palestine through their territories. Significant numbers of Soviet agents have already been introduced into Palestine as Jewish refugees. One leftist Jewish terrorist organization is now receiving Soviet financial aid. Soviet-directed Communist influence is believed to be rapidly increasing in the Jewish Agency and among Jewish political parties. If United States support in the UN for partition is unsatisfactory to the Jews, further Zionist-Soviet rapprochement will result, but in any case, close Zionist-Soviet relationships are to be expected. Any Jewish state created in Palestine is expected to become more and more pro-Soviet and eventually to be oriented entirely toward the U.S.S.R.[72]

Furthermore, and without evidence, the authors added that there was "substantial opposition to excessive zeal of the Zionists among American Jewry. Many Jews in the United States are already aware of the potential development of anti-Semitism which might occur as the result of the

---

[70] On this see Joseph Bendersky, The "Jewish Threat": Anti-Semitic Politics of the U.S. Army (New York: Basic Books, 2000).
[71] Plans and Operations Division, "Intelligence Estimate-Palestine," 3–4.   [72] Ibid., 4.

overzealous efforts on the par of those favoring the creation of a Jewish state."[73] It sounded like a threat cloaked in the guise of a prediction.

"Intelligence Estimate" concluded that if the fighting continued "through a war of attrition, it is estimated that the Arabs would be able to force the Jews to accept Arab terms by the end of two years." That estimate assumed that the Jews would "receive no significant outside aid." The Jews, however, were "vigorously enlisting assistance from whatever source is available, including the U.S.S.R." If the Jews received that aid, it would "overbalance the Arab effort" unless the Arabs also received outside aid. "Such a situation has serious implications as possibly leading to a third World War." The Soviets might hesitate to use Soviet troops

because of the opprobrium it would bring them from the Arabs. On the other hand, they appear to be planning to aid the Jews in order to use Palestine as a base for covert penetration of the Near East. The Soviets are encouraging carefully screened and ideologically indoctrinated and trained Jewish recruits for Jewish armed organizations to emigrate from Soviet-controlled Europe to Palestine. Unless a firm UN sea blockade is established and effectively maintained, large-scale immigration of these Jewish recruits may be expected this summer.[74]

The US Army Plans and Operations Staff "Intelligence Estimate" exemplified the thinking of the early years of the Cold War. It recycled and somewhat updated the consensus in the US military leadership that, as we have observed, was articulated clearly in the Pentagon talks of fall 1947. As had been the case in American military intelligence memoranda in these years, it made no mention of the Holocaust, Arab collaboration with the Nazis, antisemitism in postwar Europe and in the Arab countries, or of Arab responsibility for beginning the war in 1947 and escalating it in May 1948. It displayed no understanding of the fact that the vast majority of Jewish survivors of the Holocaust in Europe who wanted to go to Palestine did so for reasons of survival that had nothing to do with communism or Soviet policy. The association of the Jews with the Soviet Union, and thus of Jews with communism, in such reports also indicated that the authors had devoted scant reflection to the importance that coupling had been for Nazi Germany and the key role it had played in modern antisemitism. The place of "the Jewish question" and the realities of the war on the Eastern Front in Europe in World War II had not sunk into the consciousness of these senior American military officers, all of whom had been officers in that war. Far from welcoming the establishment of

[73] Ibid., 5.   [74] Ibid.

the state of Israel, the report saw it as a vulnerability that the Soviet Union was exploiting. The policy implication was clear: support Britain's efforts, now cloaked in the halo of UN truce resolutions, to prevent the Jewish state from receiving supplies and persons that could aid it in the war with the Arab states.

13 International Responses to the Arab-Israeli War II: July–August 1948

[The Bernadotte Plan] would be tantamount to the liquidation of Israel and, of course, could never be accepted.

> Vasyl Tarasenko, representative of the Ukrainian SSR to the UN Security Council, July 15, 1948

The struggle of the Jewish people on the territory of Palestine is connected to the struggle that is unfolding in other parts of the world. The Greek partisan, the soldier in the Chinese popular army, the Spanish combatant, the democrats in Vietnam, the Indonesian patriots, the Hindu resistant are all comrades [*compagnons*] of the battle waged by the soldiers of the Haganah.

> Florimond Bonté, member of the Central Committee of the French Communist Party, speaking in the French National Assembly, July 20, 1948

As a friend of Israel, we deem it of paramount importance that this new republic not place itself before the bar of world public opinion and the United Nations in the role of an aggressor.

> Secretary of State George Marshall, "Memorandum for the President," August 16, 1948

From May to July 1948, as war raged between Israel and the Arab states, the policy guidelines that connected the Cold War to the Middle East continued to influence the dispatches that came back to Washington from American diplomats and intelligence officers in Europe. In accord with Marshall and Lovett's instructions, they continued to send reports of the Mossad Le'Aliyah Bet's efforts to bring people and weapons from Europe to Israel. On May 20, for example, Rudolph Schoenfeld of the US Legation in Bucharest wrote that ships had arrived in Constanta, Bulgaria from Marseille and were waiting to "take arms and munitions through Soviet channels here and to pick up group of immigrants for Palestine." He reported that the Soviet military attaché had been negotiating with Jewish representatives.[1]

---

[1] Schoenfeld to Secretary of State, Bucharest (May 20, 1948), No. 555, NACP RG 59 CDF 1945–1949, National Archives Microfilm Publications, M1390, Records of the Department of State Relating to the Internal Affairs of Palestine, 1945–1949, Roll 15, 867N.01/5–1948.

Russell Brooks, the American consul general in Bordeaux, told a different story, one that varied somewhat from the others but still adhered to the US government's basic assumptions about what was going on. On May 21 he reported that Jewish immigrants were passing through Bordeaux to Palestine. It was difficult for vessels to engage in the arms trade in Bordeaux as the port was in the middle of the city, and "concealment would not be possible." His investigations had revealed "no instance of shipments of arms or passengers from Bordeaux for Palestine."[2] On June 15 Cecil Gray sent a more concerning cable about the situation in Marseille, where he had witnessed the departure of the SS *Altalena*, with 700 passengers and 600 tons of arms that had been loaded by passengers.[3] Two days later he reported that the SS *Endeavor*, flying a Panamanian flag, had left for "Palestine" with 300 young displaced Jews of Central European origin.[4] That same day Robert Murphy (1894–1978), the political advisor in Berlin to General Lucius Clay, the high commissioner in charge of the United States Military Government in Germany, telegraphed Marshall to say that, in view of "various reports Communist indoctrination [of] Palestinian Jews from Iron Curtain countries does Department approve according transit via US Zone Germany? Should any distinction be made on basis military age?" He added that a considerable number of transit applications were being received in West Berlin by Jews coming from Warsaw.[5]

The United States Enforces the Embargo

On May 27, twelve days after the Arab invasion of Israel, Marshall sent a circular to multiple embassies and consulates regarding "Soviet merchant vessels." Officials should "report by air gram arrivals, departures, cargo, destination, and last port of call of any Soviet vessel entering your Consular district (the port at the capital city in the case of missions), including any pertinent or unusual activities in connection therewith. Always give name and type of ship."[6] Marshall also sent a regular stream

---

[2] Russell Brooks, American Consul General to Secretary of State, Bordeaux (May 21, 1948), "Subject: Telegram Naval Attaché, Sofie, regarding possible passage of Bulgarian Jews through Bordeaux," NACP RG 59 CDF 1945–1949, M1390, Roll 15, 867N.01/5–2148.

[3] C. W. Gray, American Consul, Marseilles to Secretary of State, Marseilles (June 15, 1948), NACP RG 59 CDF 1945–1949, M1390, Roll 15, 867N.01/6–1548.

[4] C. W. Gray to Secretary of State, Marseilles (June 17, 1948), NACP RG 59 CDF 1945–1949, M1390, Roll 15, 867N.01/6–1748.

[5] Robert Murphy to Secretary of State, Berlin (June 17, 1948), NACP RG 59 CDF 1945–1949, M1390, Roll 15, 867N.01/6–1548.

[6] George Marshall to Certain American Diplomatic and Consular Offices, Washington (July 27, 1948), "Soviet Merchant Vessels," NACP RG 59, Department of State, Decimal File, 1945–1949, 851.00/1–147–851.00/12–3147, Box 6232.

of instructions to American diplomats in Europe to see that the embargo terms of the UN resolution of May 29 were enforced. On June 18 he asked officials in the US Embassy in Rome to inform Italy's Foreign Ministry that the airline Lineas Aéreas de Panama "may be engaged in smuggling of arms, munitions and implements of war into Palestine, particularly from various European countries and that Rome is the Eastern terminus of this company."[7]

Four days later Marshall instructed Philip Jessup (1897–1986), deputy chief of the US delegation to the UN, to inform the UN secretary general, Trygve Lie, as well as the president of the UN Security Council, Syria's Faris al-Khoury, that the United States had taken four steps to cooperate with and support the UN mediator.[8] First, it had sent instructions to "appropriate authorities to take necessary steps to prevent departure of fighting personnel from the US" to Israel or the Arab states at war. Second, it had sent similar instructions to the "Chairman of the US Maritime Commission" drawing attention to the statement concerning "men of military age" in Count Bernadotte's truce proposals. Third, since November 14, 1947 it had "applied a rigorous arms embargo covering shipments of all war material from US and its possessions to Palestine and the countries of the Near East." Fourth, it had provided the UN mediator with military observers, aircraft, and communications equipment and was considering sending three naval patrol vessel and ten more military observers. In addition, Marshall noted (as we have seen), the United States had contacted "all its diplomatic missions" calling attention to the clauses of the Security Council resolution of May 29 that required UN members "to take necessary steps to prevent shipments of war material to Palestine and Arab States as of effective date of the truce."[9]

American officials continued to closely follow the deliveries of weapons from Czechoslovakia to Israel. On July 1 James Dunn (1890–1979), the US ambassador to Italy, informed Marshall that on June 23 a Panamanian aircraft departing from Brno, Czechoslovakia made a forced landing in Italy. The five crew members all had US passports. "Cargo of aircraft comprised 5 cases each containing two submachine guns and 35 cases each containing 500 cartridges for them." The real destination was

---

[7] George Marshall to AMEMBASSY, Rome, Washington (June 18, 1948), No. 693, NACP RG 59 CDF 1945–1949, M1390, Roll 15, 867N.01/6–1848.
[8] "The Secretary of State [George Marshall] to the Acting United States Representative at the United Nations [Philip] (Jessup), Washington (June 21, 1948), 501.BB Palestine/6–1648, *Foreign Relations of the United States* (hereafter *FRUS*), *The Near East and Africa*, 1948, vol. 5, part 2: https://history.gov/historicaldocuments/frus1948v05p2/d395.
[9] Ibid.

Palestine. "In conformity with UN Resolution of May 29, Italian authorities arrested aircraft, crew and cargo."[10]

Also on July 1 Marshall sent a telegram cable about enforcement of the UN Security Council resolution of May 29 to the following twenty-five US embassies: Ankara, Athens, Belgrade, Bern, Brussels, Caracas, Ciudad Trujillo, Copenhagen, Dublin, The Hague, Havana, Lisbon, London, Madrid, Mexico City, Oslo, Ottawa, Panama, Paris, Port-au-Prince, Praha (Prague), Reykjavik, Rio de Janeiro, and Rome; and eight legations, in Stockholm, Vienna, Beirut, Baghdad, Cairo, Damascus, Jerusalem, and Jeddah:

Three B-17 Flying Fortresses recently left Miami reported destination Israel. Believed here these planes intend engage in transport munitions or troops to Middle East or as bombers. This is inconsistent with intent UN Security Council Resolution regarding Palestine Truce. Moreover, planes left U.S. in violation export laws and without proper clearance to land in foreign country. Various other cases have also been reported involving illegal export from U.S. of aircraft and use of American planes by American citizens in transporting arms between points outside U.S. Department desires all appropriate measures be taken to prevent such traffic. Accordingly, you instructed request appropriate foreign authorities, unless deem inadvisable, that any information concerning such clandestine activities be reported to this government. Particular attention should be given to activities of non-certified irregular air carriers (tramp airlines) operating on non-scheduled basis, as some of these are known to be engaged in gun running. Advise Department promptly of reaction foreign government as well as any information obtained.[11]

In accord with Marshall's telegram, on July 2 the US chargé d'affaires in Caracas informed the Venezuelan Foreign Office that various "military planes have clandestinely left the United States of America which may be destined for the new State of Israel, for use in the movement of arms and ammunition or troops or for other war-like purposes."[12] Such activity violated the UN truce resolution as well as American laws. Since the US government "desires to make every appropriate effort to prevent this clandestine traffic in munitions and military aircraft," the Embassy would appreciate any information from Venezuelan government, in particular about "tramp airlines."[13] On

---

[10] (James) Dunn to Secretary of State, Rome (July 1, 1948), 2834 NACP RG 59 CDF 1945–1949, 501.BB Palestine/7-148, Box 2119.

[11] George Marshall to Certain American Diplomatic Officers, Washington (July 1, 1948), 290, NACP RG 59 CDF 1945–1949, 501.BB Palestine/7-148, Box 2119.

[12] Chargé d'Affaires to Jacinto Fombona Pachano, Caracas (July 1, 1948), "Transmittal of Embassy Note to Venezuelan Foreign Office Concerning Clandestine Traffic in Munitions and Military Aircraft," NACP RG 59 CDF 1945–1949, 501.BB Palestine/7-748, Box 2119.

[13] Ibid.

July 10, the US Embassy in Athens reported that the Greek Foreign Office had offered assurances that instructions had been given to "halt any suspicious planes for investigation" and would keep the Embassy informed about "three B-17s and any other planes possibly destined Palestine or Arab states."[14]

The UN truce resolutions were about people as well as weapons. American officials in the US occupation zone in Germany were on alert for possible violations of the UN truce resolution regarding "military-age" men going to Israel. On July 1 C. Offie, an official in the Office of the US Political Adviser for Germany, forwarded a report by Lieutenant Colonel William M. Slayden of the US Counter-Intelligence Corps (CIC) to the secretary of state about "Jewish Military Training in the United States Zone of Germany."[15] "Attempts to give military training to Haganah recruits" were "widespread throughout the United States Zone of Germany." It was "carried out in many Jewish Displaced Persons Camps." Training lasted ten to twelve days and consisted "for the most part of close order drill, physical training and classroom tactics instructions." A few of the camps had "from two to ten rifles for instruction purposes, but searches and raids" had "failed to confirm the reported use of weapons in the alleged training areas." Shortly after the training was completed, "the recruits allegedly are shipped to Palestine."[16] The CIC report included descriptions of training in camps near eleven towns: Ulm, Kassel, Heidenheim, Lagerstein Camp, Geretsried, Wolfratshausen, Lepheim, Feldafing, Stuttgart, Landsberg, and Zeckendorf Farm.[17]

The significant amount of time and effort by US counterintelligence officials to monitor Jewish military training was evident in the following level of detail in Slayden's report: "On 4 June 1948, an estimated thirty-five to forty Jews between the ages of seventeen and thirty-five paraded before the Café Weiss, headquarters of the Jewish Committee in Walden. The military manner, snap and precision with which the group responded to the commands of the leader indicated that they were well trained in

---

[14] Rankin to Secretary of State, Athens (July 10, 1948), No. 1292, NACP M1390, Roll 16, 867N.01/7–948.

[15] C. Offie, Political Adviser, United States Political Adviser for Germany (POLAD Germany) to Secretary of State, Heidelberg (July 1, 1948), No. 439, "Subject: Jewish Military Training in United States Zone of Germany," NACP M1390, Roll 16, 867N.01/7–148.

[16] Ibid.

[17] Wm. M. Slayden, Lt. Colonel, GSC, Chief, R&A Branch, "Enclosure in Despatch No. 439, Subject: Jewish Military Training in U.S. Zone, Germany," NACP M1390, Roll 16, 867N.01/7–148. On Feldafing and other DP camps see Atina Grossmann, *Jews, Germans and Allies: Close Encounters in Occupied Germany* (Princeton: Princeton University Press, 2009).

close order drill."[18] Through the prism of Marshall's efforts to enforce the UN truce resolution, Slayden's report presented that demonstration of Jewish self-respect and revival after the Holocaust as instead an unwelcome effort to violate the UN resolution banning the entry of military aged Jewish men to Israel.

American officials kept a close watch on the ships involved in the clandestine effort that were leaving from Italian ports and from Yugoslavia. On July 11 the American Consulate in Naples reported that it had "good reason to believe following Italian ships leaving Naples for Palestine carrying men, probably arms: Caserta, Borea, Avionia, Resurrection."[19] On July 12 the US Embassy in Belgrade reported that a source in the Joint Distribution Committee said that the government of Yugoslavia had assured the Jewish community that "exit visas for Israel would be granted all desiring to go," but then modified that policy so that "only military age desired." Though it was not known if the recruits were destined for the Irgun or the Haganah, "Israeli agents made all travel arrangements and provided transportation."[20] The Yugoslav government official had approved a Jewish community drive to collect funds and recruit volunteers and "conveyed oral approval for passports and exist visas [for] those Jews who 'desire participate in fighting.'" "Registration forms for volunteer fighters" were to be circulated by the Federation, after which the Yugoslav government would negotiate with Israel's representative on "exit and transport arrangements and would issue group passport and exit visa." The Jewish Agency was "prepared to bear all expenses, arrange transport to Yugoslav coast and supply ships." Of the "3,000 possible volunteers there may be perhaps 1,000 Communists."[21] On July 22 the US Consulate in Marseille reported that the SS *Kedmah* had departed from Marseille for "Tel Aviv with six hundred reported Jewish combat troops."[22]

The files demonstrate that US State Department and US intelligence officials devoted a great deal of time and effort to examining the connection between Jews trying to get to Palestine and then Israel,

[18] Wm. M. Slayden, Lt. Colonel, GSC, Chief, R&A Branch, "Enclosure in Despatch No. 439."

[19] Brandt to Secretary of State, Naples (July 11, 1948), 185, NACP M1390, Roll 16, 867N.01/7-1048.

[20] [Robert] Reams to Secretary of State, Belgrade (July 12, 1948), No. 889, NACP M1390, Roll 16, 867N.01/7-1248.

[21] Ibid.

[22] [William] Christianson to Secretary of State (July 22, 1948), NACP RG 84, Records of the Foreign Service Posts of the Department of State, France, U.S. Consulate, Marseille, Classified General Records, 1936–1952, 1948–1949: [1948] 13- to 1948–1949 [1949] 690, Box 7.

and the communists and the Soviet bloc, and to urging other governments to uphold UN resolutions blocking those efforts. If the State Department and intelligence agencies were also paying attention to Nazis seeking to escape from Europe to the Middle East, references to those efforts are few and far between in the massive Palestine files of 1945–9. Rather, in American government eyes it was now Jews, especially men of military age, migrating to Israel who had become a "threat."

On June 22, following the embarrassment of Austin's March 19 UN speech, the near-disastrous confrontation with Marshall in the Oval Office, and aware of the need for a representative in Israel sympathetic to the Israeli leaders, Truman appointed James McDonald (1886–1964) to be his special representative to Israel. Unusually, he gave McDonald the authority to communicate directly with the president and the secretary of state. As we shall see, during the 1948 war McDonald offered Truman and Marshall a dissenting and important voice regarding developments in Israel and the Middle East.[23]

Florimond Bonté and the French Communists on Israel and Anticolonialism in 1948

In France, the most important source of support for the Zionist project remained members of the Socialist Party and other veterans of the French wartime resistance to the Nazis, including Gaullists, Radicals, and Communists. However, given the sharpening of Cold War tensions in Berlin and Prague, and communist strikes and demonstrations in Italy and France, the American Embassy in Paris paid attention to what the French Communists had to say about Israel. Jefferson Caffery paid particular attention to a speech in the National Assembly delivered by Florimond Bonté, the member of the Central Committee of the French Communist Party (PCF) who had warmly greeted Israel's establishment in May. The importance that the PCF attached to his speech, "Sur le territoire de la Palestine, carrefour stratégique du monde" (On the territory of Palestine, strategic crossroads of the world) was apparent when the text was published in the July issue of PCF's monthly theoretical journal,

---

[23] Robert Lovett, "Appointment of James Grover McDonald as Special Representative in Palestine" (June 22, 1948), NACP RG 59, M1390, Roll 15, 867N.01/6–2448. On McDonald see James G. McDonald, *My Mission in Israel, 1948–1951* (New York: Simon & Schuster, 1951); and Norman J. W. Goda, Barbara McDonald Stewart, Severin Hochberg, and Richard Breitman, eds., *To the Gates of Jerusalem: The Diaries and Papers of James G. McDonald, 1945–1947* (Bloomington: Indiana University Press/ United States Holocaust Memorial Museum, 2015).

Cahiers du Communisme.[24] Caffery also thought the speech was of suffi-
cient importance that on July 20 he sent an exposition of the text to
Marshall.[25] In it, Marshall could read that a member of the PCF's
Central Committee denounced Arab aggression, oil imperialism, and
British and American policy – and welcomed the new state of Israel.

Bonté wrote that "the French Communist Party" sent the new state of
Israel "good wishes for a long life, prosperity, and well-being in a peace
that is democratic, solid, and durable."[26] He recalled the "physical
destruction" and misery of the Jews in Europe, who had been left "without means of existence and without a country." None of the Western
European countries had defended them. Now, hundreds of thousands
wanted to live in Palestine in a "free, democratic, and independent state
in which their destiny and security is no longer dependent on the charity
or good will of this or that other state." The recent events had moved the
idea of a Jewish state from abstraction to "practical realization."[27] Bonté's
text included Israel's declaration of independence and much of the UN
Partition Resolution of November 29, 1947. He recalled the Soviet
Union's support for the Partition Plan, Britain's efforts to "systematically
sabotage" it, and the "impressive about-face" by the United States in
renouncing its initial support and working to "torpedo its execution."
Unfortunately, Bonté said, French diplomacy had aligned with
Washington. Yet the United States had offered "de facto" recognition
to the new state. By contrast, the Soviet Union had offered Israel full de
jure recognition. Bonté wrote that the Arab states that had invaded Israel
on May 15 were "under Britain's control," received arms from Britain,
and had British officers. Their invasion was "a flagrant violation" of
decisions by the United Nations.[28]

Palestine, he contended, was a "strategic crossroads of the world,"
close to enormous oil reserves and to the pipelines that carried the oil of
Iran and Iraq to Mediterranean ports. It was at a crossroads of maritime
traffic between Europe, Asia, and Africa, and on routes that connected
Britain to India and other Asian outposts of the British Empire. It was
close to the Suez Canal and British military bases on the Arabian
Peninsula and the Persian Gulf that were important for defending the
oil supplies. "Large capitalist companies such as [the] Anglo Iranian Oil
Company, Gulf Oil Company, Standard Oil Company, Texas Oil

---

[24] Florimond Bonté, "Sur le territoire de la Palestine, carrefour stratégique du monde,"
   Cahiers du Communisme 9 (July 1948), 703–721.
[25] Jefferson Caffery to Secretary of State, Paris (July 20, 1948), No. 3785, NACP RG 319,
   Records of the Army Staff, Assistant Chief of Staff, G-2 (Intelligence), Incoming and
   Outgoing Messages. 1948, France, Box 16.
[26] Bonté, "Sur le territoire," 703.   [27] Ibid., 703–704.   [28] Ibid., 705–710.

Company, [and] Arabian American Oil Company" had interests in the region. Despite "imperialist rivalries" between the United States and Britain, they found a "common interest in not leaving Palestine, not abandoning their position, and defending it tenaciously against all danger." It was this common imperialist interest that had led to their efforts to torpedo the UN Partition Resolution that would have led to both Jewish and Arab states and thereby enable both peoples to become "masters of their destiny and possessors of the riches of the soil and those below ground."

Bonté blamed the British and Americans for fostering racial hatred and nationalist passions between Arabs and Jews in Palestine. Such discord facilitated their goal of remaining in Palestine.[29] While Britain greeted the establishment of the state of Israel by aiding the Arab states, the United States responded with a "brusque recognition" (*la reconnaissance brusque*) that did not express "solicitude to the Jews. It was a matter of oil and dollars." At the United Nations the "two imperialisms" tried to buy time with "new resolutions to prevent the UN from characterizing the Arabs as aggressors" in order to consolidate a "regime which would leave the Jewish and Arab population the right to obey the orders of the potentates of oil."[30]

The Soviet Union, on the other hand, was, according to Bonté, "the enemy of national and racial oppression and colonial exploitation in all its forms." It favored cooperation and peace between Jews and Arabs. The PCF and the Soviet Union viewed the war between Israel and the Arab states as "the result of intrigues, maneuvers, machinations, and the politically reactionary tactic of 'divide and conquer' by the Anglo-American imperialists in order to defend their economic privileges and justify their military presence." Israel was fighting "a just war in the course of which the Jewish people were defending their right to existence as a nation developing in the territory of Palestine" against an Arab "war of aggression."[31]

The Arab League, on the other hand, linked as it was to British imperialism, was not a force of Arab national liberation. Far from expressing popular sentiments, Bonté said, it made common cause with "reactionary and fascist organizations of all sorts: the Muslim Brotherhood, Phalangists," and the Misr al-Fatat organization in Cairo. Progressive Arab forces denounced the Arab League's links to "imperialists in London and Washington." The Arab League was working to form "an Oriental anti-Soviet bloc for the common struggle with the Western bloc against the USSR, the new democracies [in Eastern Europe], and

[29] Ibid., 712–713.   [30] Ibid., 714.   [31] Ibid., 715 and 717.

democratic movements." Hence its "orientation was imperialist, anti-democratic, and anti-popular." It was part of a common front against communism. "That is why our condemnation of the aggression on order of the Anglo-Saxon imperialists against the new state of Israel is a contribution to the emancipation of the Arab peoples and defense of their inherent rights."[32]

Having defined imperialism and anti-imperialism in this manner, Bonté then connected the Jews' struggle in Palestine to those of other battles for national liberation around the world.

The struggle of the Jewish people on the territory of Palestine is connected to the struggle that is unfolding in other parts of the world. The Greek partisan, the soldier in the Chinese popular army, the Spanish combatant, the democrats in Vietnam, the Indonesian patriots, the Hindu resistant are all comrades [*compagnons*] of the battle waged by the soldiers of the Haganah. In France, the French Communist Party is the only party to adopt a politically consequential stance against colonial oppression which subjects the Arabs in North Africa. In Asia, Africa, and Europe the struggle of oppressed people for liberation from the colonialist yoke is an integral part of the struggle for peace, for liberty, democracy, and independence. This is why the French Communist Party, in order to support the just struggle of the Jewish people, never ceases to denounce the imperialists' intrigues and interventions, to call for the strict implementation of UN decisions, and to demand that the French government officially recognize the new state of Israel.[33]

Bonté assumed that there was indeed something called "the Jewish people" and that the war in 1948 was their struggle for national liberation, one of the many anti-imperialist, anticolonial revolts taking place elsewhere in former colonial areas. Unfortunately, the French government – or at least the French Foreign Ministry – had taken the side of the British and American imperialists in sustaining a colonial regime in the Orient and seeking to sustain and enhance a strategic base to protect access to oil in the Arab states. Bonté expressed confidence that the forces of anti-imperialism and democracy, in which he included the new state of Israel, would "in common action" achieve "liberty, democracy, independence, and peace."[34]

"Sur la territoire de la Palestine" is a canonical text that defined the meanings of "left" and "right" regarding Israel in 1948 for French Communists. Caffery's summary for Marshall, though shorter than the one just provided, was full enough to offer the secretary of state the essence of the PCF's support for "the fighting companions of the Haganah." It was also sufficient to confirm suspicions in the State Department that the

[32] Ibid., 719.   [33] Ibid., 720–721.   [34] Ibid., 721.

establishment of the Jewish state in Palestine was indeed part of the Soviet effort to both undermine an anticommunist bloc in the Middle East and expand its influence in the region, just as participants at the Pentagon talks and members of the Policy Planning Staff had long feared was the case.

On July 24 Caffery wrote again to the secretary of state to convey the palpable fear in France of Soviet policy in Europe. The "major foreign policy preoccupation in France today is cold war against Soviet expansion and more specifically [the] German problem," that is, the danger that Germany would be unified under Soviet control. "French people," he continued, were "acutely conscious of fact that they are on the front lines and their reactions are largely based on fear of being overrun and concern over amount and timeliness of assistance to be expected from US."[35] Caffery described a coming Soviet propaganda offensive against American "imperialism" in colonies designed to establish "offensive" military bases directed at the Soviet Union, in the hopes of "arousing colonial peoples against US and promoting Communist movements in Indonesia, North Africa, et. Cetera."[36] In summer 1948, coming soon after the communist assumption of total power in Prague in February 1948, the sequence of Caffery's exposition of Bonté's speech and French concerns about Soviet expansion reinforced the view in Washington that the establishment of the new state of Israel was part of a global Soviet-inspired and -supported anticolonial revolt aimed at undermining American and Western interests, just as Kennan had foreseen in his Policy Planning Staff memos in January. It was true that communists were arriving in Palestine, but they remained a small minority within the Jewish population in Palestine and did not represent the dominant current of opinion in the political parties that were now governing the new state of Israel. Nevertheless, in London as well as Washington, suspicion about the Zionists and the communists lingered.

Over the summer Marshall continued to instruct American diplomats abroad to keep a close watch on foreign efforts to aid the state of Israel. On August 12 he sent a circular cable about "clandestine air operations of American planes by American citizens between points outside US." It went to the following American Embassies and Consulates "for action": Ankara, Athens, Belgrade, Bern, Brussels, Caracas, Ciudad Trujillo, Copenhagen, Dublin, The Hague, Havana, Lisbon, London, Madrid, Mexico City, Oslo, Ottawa, Panama, Paris, Port-au-Prince, Prague, Reykjavik, Rio de Janeiro, Rome, Stockholm, and Vienna; and "for

---

[35] Jefferson Caffery to Secretary of State, Paris (July 24, 1948), No. 3867, NACP RG 319, Records of the Army Staff, Assistant Chief of Staff, G-2 (Intelligence), Incoming and Outgoing Messages. 1948, France, Box 16.
[36] Ibid., 4–5.

information" to Beirut, Baghdad, Cairo, Damascus, Jerusalem, Jeddah, and the US UN delegation in New York, "to be transmitted to the UN Mediator."[37] Since the United States did not have statutory authority over US "irregular air carriers" operating abroad, it could "exercise only indirect control by representations to foreign governments whose air space or airports are used." That said, in order to prevent such carriers from flying in "sensitive areas," the USA had "asked and is asking foreign governments" to "exercise close vigilance and as effective control as possible over all US non-certified and irregular air carriers operations if inspection or other forms of surveillance by authorities [of] such governments indicate cargo or personnel carried contravenes United Nations Security Council Resolution of July 15, 1948," a resolution that repeated the ban on the introduction of war material or men of military age into Palestine or the Arab states.[38] Marshall's directive led to further reports from Europe and Central America about shipments of persons or cargo to Israel, and about suspicious associations of persons involved with Jewish immigration to Palestine with Soviet and communist efforts to infiltrate agents into Israel.

Typical was the cable of August 30 by William Christianson at the Marseille Consulate. The *Yucatan*, having sailed from Vera Cruz, Mexico, was now being repaired in "berth no. 6" in the Marseille harbor. His informant reported that the ship would be carrying refugees "for the Palestine trade" and that it would perhaps be used "as a gun runner because [of] its great speed." As it was a converted coast guard cutter, it was "an ideal ship for such purposes."[39] Reports with details about the ownership, identity of the crew, and intentions to take Jewish immigrants to Palestine continued into fall 1948.[40] Christianson's reference to "the Palestine trade" and the ship as a "gun runner" captured the mood of suspicion and irritation about the Mossad Le'Aliyah Bet's effort to undermine the UN Security Council truce resolutions. The State Department remained well informed about the efforts to transport Jews to Israel from Marseille and other southern ports in France but, in

[37] George Marshall, Washington (August 12, 1948), Circular, NACP RG 84, France, U.S. Consulate, Marseille, Classified General Records, 1936–1952, 1948–1949: [1948] 13- to 1948–1949 [1949] 690, Box 7.

[38] Ibid., 1–2.

[39] William H. Christianson to Walter Linthicum, American Consul Paris, Marseille (August 30, 1948), "Confidential," NACP RG 84, France, U.S. Consulate, Marseille, Classified General Records, 1936–1952, 1948–1949: [1948] 13- to 1948–1949 [1949] 690, Box 7.

[40] See Nutler to Secretary of State, Havana (November 15, 1948), NACP RG 84, France, U.S. Consulate, Marseille, Classified General Records, 1936–1952, 1948–1949: [1948] 13- to 1948–1949 [1949] 690, Box 7.

view of the previously examined efforts of the French ministers of the interior, was unable to stop it.

An Astute Analysis of the Arab-Israeli War for the Joint Chiefs of Staff

Secretary of Defense James Forrestal was also interested in the question of how outside assistance was affecting the outcome of the Arab-Israeli war. On July 16, 1948 his special assistant, John H. Ohly, asked CIA director Roscoe Hillenkoetter to prepare an assessment for the Joint Chiefs of Staff on the UN truce proposals. In particular, and again, the Joint Chiefs were interested in "the present intentions and activities of the U.S.S.R."[41] Two days later Carter Clarke, the deputy director of intelligence of the Army General Staff, sent a most interesting assessment to the Army chief of staff.[42] Clarke wrote that in mid-July Israel had the military initiative. However, "in the absence of substantial aid to either side from abroad or of foreign intervention ... after two years or so the Arabs will gain the upper hand."[43] The Jewish leadership had prepared for war with the Arabs. It had given military training both in Palestine and in Europe before immigration. It had developed organizations for "the clandestine transfer of military personnel and material from Europe and the United States into Palestine." The Jewish forces in Palestine "must be considered superior to those of the Arabs in strength, training, discipline, leadership, combat experience and in serves of arms and munitions. For the moment, the Arabs have a superiority in artillery, aircraft and possibly in armor."[44]

With the lifting of the British naval blockade and in the absence of any international controls, the new government of Israel will be able to bring from Europe thousands of trained officers and men and quantities of arms and munitions. Although Jewish officials flatly deny the presence in Palestine of any Soviet-trained military personnel, the evidence indicates that significant numbers of officers, including trained staff officers, of Soviet origin have been moving in the Jewish underground toward Palestine since 1946. Various Jewish factions, including the Haganah, have been reliably reported to have had dealings with Soviet officials. Informally, Jewish officials admit that pilots, planes, arms, and other

---

[41] John H. Ohly, Special Asst., Secretary of Defense to Admiral Hillenkoetter, Washington (July 16, 1948), "Memorandum for the Joint Chiefs: Subject: Intelligence Division Special Briefing," NACP RG 319, Army-Intelligence Project Decimal File 1946–1948, Palestine, Box 260.

[42] Carter Clarke, Colonel G.S.C, Deputy Director of Intelligence, Washington (July 18, 1948), "Memorandum for the Chief of Staff: Subject: Intelligence Division Special Briefing, The Palestine Situation," NACP RG 319, Army-Intelligence Project Decimal File 1946–1948, Palestine, Box 260.

[43] Ibid., 1.   [44] Ibid.

munitions are already collected and ready for shipment. These accessions of men and material cannot fail to increase the capabilities of the Jewish forces in Palestine.[45]

Clarke's reference to the Soviet dimension was conventional wisdom in the Pentagon. Less so was his willingness to offer an "estimate of ultimate Jewish defeat." That was based less on the immediate military factors of July 1948 "than on those basic economic and political factors that in the long run determine military potential." The Jews faced considerable disadvantages. First, they had to import "half their food when local Arab produce is available." Under wartime conditions even that would not be available and Jewish food production would decline as well. An increase in the population due to immigration would "add to the food deficit." Second, Jewish civilian and military transport, industry, and agriculture were "almost entirely dependent on imported fuels and lubricants," but the Arabs would cut Israel off from oil. Third, the financial situation of the new state was precarious. The mobilization for war made loans essential, compelling the Jews to become "dependent upon subsidization either by a foreign state or by the Jewish world community." The Arabs, on the other hand, were "self-sufficient in all civilian essentials." Guerilla warfare against Israel required "the minimum of military equipment and supplies." They would be far "less dependent" on foreign assistance "than will the Jews."[46] The course of the war of 1948, therefore, would "depend primarily upon the reaction to the struggle in the international sphere" and on the "actions of those powers which control the routes by which men, armaments and supplies can reach the belligerents. Great power relationships and possibly UN action will determine the fate of Palestine."[47] Clarke's clear-eyed assessment was one with which Ben-Gurion would have agreed.

Clarke's analysis effectively integrated military factors with political and economic realities. It challenged the arguments of Henderson and then Marshall that the UN truce resolution and related arms embargo affected Israel and the Arab states equally. Instead he observed that an embargo would contribute to "ultimate Jewish defeat" unless countered by supplies of weapons and persons from other sources. Arab state self-sufficiency in vital economic resources and the minimal military requirements of guerilla war gave them the advantage over the long term. For all these reasons, the potential leverage of the United States over Israel was enormous. Clarke's assessment made clear to the Joint Chiefs of Staff that American strategy and policy of an embargo on arms would, if not compensated by the actions of other powers, contribute to "ultimate

[45] Ibid., 2.   [46] Ibid.   [47] Ibid.

Jewish defeat." His analysis for the Joint Chiefs confirmed the arguments made by Moshe Shertok, Vasyl Tarasenko, and Andrei Gromyko in the UN Security Council in May that the embargo's primary victim was Israel. It also challenged the State Department's public position that the embargo contributed to peace and affected both sides of the war equally.[48]

Dissent from US policy also emerged from within the American delegation to the UN. On July 10 Philip Jessup, deputy chair of the US UN delegation, sent Marshall a memo expressing his views and those of others on the US delegation (probably Eleanor Roosevelt) that sharply diverged from the tone and substance of the statements coming from Marshall and Warren Austin since 1947.[49] Jessup rejected assigning equal blame to Israel and the Arabs. The evidence, he wrote, was "incontrovertible" that the Arab League had "created a threat to peace" when in early July it refused Bernadotte's request to extend the truce he had negotiated in June. "The circumstantial evidence" was "equally clear that military action by Egypt at least, probably also by Iraq and Syria," constituted "a breach of the peace and an act of aggression." Israel had accepted extension of the truce "unconditionally on terms proposed by Mediator [Bernadotte]." Military action by Israel in response to the Arab invasion could "not possibly be considered a breach of the peace or act of aggression." Rather, it "must be considered defensive action" as defined by the UN Charter." The Arabs had "no excuse" and "no reason for delay" in accepting a truce.[50]

Jessup continued that "we," that is, the United States government, "must obviously oppose Arab argument that they are still acting to defend Palestine against 'Zionist invaders.'"[51] The Arabs were "living in a dream world where the political fact of existence of Israel (supported by USSR and US – in the US strongly by both political parties) is denied and where

---

[48] UN mediator, Folke Bernadotte, however, did believe that preventing war materials from reaching either side contributed to peace. He insisted that doing so was crucial to preserving the truce he had negotiated between Israel and the Arabs in June to early July. See Thomas J. Hamilton, "Bernadotte Suggests Firm Security Council Order for Palestine Peace," *New York Times*, July 13, 1948, 1 and 17; and Count Folke Bernadotte, "Mediator's Conclusions," *New York Times*, July 13, 1948, 17.

[49] "The Acting United States Representative at the United Nations [Philip] (Jessup) to the Secretary of State [George Marshall]," New York (July 10, 1948), 501.BB Palestine/7–1048, *FRUS*, 1948, vol. 5, part 2, Document 452: https://history.state.gov/historicaldocuments/frus1948v05p2/d452. Jessup went on to teach at Columbia University and serve as a justice on the International Court of Justice in The Hague. See Eric Pace, "Philip Jessup Dies, Helped End Berlin Blockade," *New York Times*, February 1, 1986, 13.

[50] "The Acting United States Representative at the United Nations to the Secretary of State" (July 10, 1948), ibid., 1206.

[51] Ibid.

it is imagined that even the ghost of this fact may be laid by resort to arms." While the USA must try "as far as possible to maintain maximum possible friendly relations with the Arab states, we cannot ignore our relations with Israel ... Delay, weakness or equivocation in our policy" would "unquestionably" give the "Russians strong propaganda advantage not only in SC [Security Council] and in Israel but also among world Jewry."[52] The Soviet Union was benefiting from American unwillingness to emphatically declare the Arabs the aggressor.

Jessup then drew the following policy implications: The United States had followed a policy of "strict neutrality and impartiality between the parties" in the month since the truce was declared on May 29. If, however, the Arabs were to repudiate the truce and resume fighting, it should consider itself obligated "to maintain measures designed to prevent military aid reaching Arab states which were illegally waging war in violation [of the UN] charter."[53] Jessup did not go so far as to call for lifting the American embargo on arms to Israel, but he did present a basis for abandoning the policy of "strict neutrality and impartiality between the parties." The United States, together with Britain, should make clear in the "strongest terms and without equivocation to all Arab capitals" that the USA had made the judgment that "the sovereign state of Israel is here to stay, that no amount of fighting or other action by Arabs can possibly alter this situation in either [the] short or long run, and that simple fact of political life must be taken as basis for continued truce and efforts to work out peaceful adjustment of future situation." The Arabs must be disabused of the idea that US support for Israel was inspired by domestic political considerations. Such a notion is "specious," as "both major political parties [are] emphatically taking same position; no change in this bipartisan position is conceivable."[54]

Jessup acknowledged that there was a risk of Arab reaction regarding oil resources and air base facilities, but "in view of strong bipartisan support of Israel in this country," that reaction would "have to be faced up to sooner or later." "We," that is Jessup and other dissenting members of the US UN delegation, believed that "strong UN pressure" would encourage the Arabs to come to terms with the existence of the state of Israel, and accept a peace based on the compromise offered in the UN Partition Plan.[55] When the leaders of the Arab states were convinced that they could not undermine American support for the new state and that war was pointless when faced with firm opposition from both the Soviet Union and the United States, they would leave their "dream world" and accept the reality of the Jewish state in their midst. The arguments

[52] Ibid., 1208.   [53] Ibid., 1207–1208.   [54] Ibid.   [55] Ibid., 1208.

made for months by Wagner, Celler, Kirchwey, Stone, and Welles among others, now, at last, were voiced by a member of the American delegation to the United Nations.

Marshall was not convinced. He wrote to Jessup on the same day that the United States sought continued "concerted action with the UK to maximum extent possible consistent with US policy." He saw "no special advantage" in going beyond the unspecific "concept of a threat to peace" or "drawing sharp distinctions" among governments, that is, labeling the Arab League invading states as aggressors and abandoning the rhetorical stance of neutrality and impartiality in favor of a position of unequivocal support for Israel as the best way of bringing about an end to the war.[56] He held fast to "the cornerstone of our policy" in the Middle East, support for the continuing British presence. In August 1948 that meant continuing the embargo on arms to Israel as it fought to drive the Arab armies out of Palestine.

On July 13 Bernadotte had sent a report to the UN Security Council presenting the first version of what came to be called the Bernadotte Plan. The state of Israel existed. It was created with support of the UN Partition Resolution of November 29, 1947. The Arab states had resorted to war to destroy it and undo the UN resolution.[57] Yet, having stated the obvious, Bernadotte refrained from labeling the Arabs the aggressor. Instead, he offered a generalized denunciation of the resort to "armed force as a means of settlement of the Palestine issue … Ending the use of force in Palestine will in fact make possible an eventual peaceful settlement."[58] Yet ending the use of force and the Jews' need for self-defense were incompatible. "If the employment of armed force is not forbidden, the issue of the Jewish state in Palestine will be settled on the field of battle."[59]

Rather than suggest UN sanctions or threats against the Arab states for attacking Israel as a violation of a UN resolution, he offered the Arabs a reward for their invasion: by amending the map of partition of November 29 to make the port of Haifa and Lydda Airport free of Israeli or Arab sovereignty. Further, he called for replacing the Partition Plan for two separate states with a federal regime that assigned the Arab area to Transjordan. The whole of Jerusalem would be part of the Arab state,

---

[56] "The Secretary of State [Marshall] to the Acting United States Representative at the United Nations [Jessup], at New York" (July 10, 1948), 501.BB Palestine 7/1048, *FRUS*, 1948, vol. 5, part 2, 1210: https://history.state.gov/historicaldocuments/frus1948v05p2/d453.

[57] Bernadotte, "Mediator's Conclusions," 17. Also see Benny Morris, *1948: The First Arab-Israeli War* (New Haven: Yale University Press, 2008), 269–270; and Simon A. Waldman, *Anglo-American Diplomacy and the Palestinian Refugee Problem, 1948–1951* (New York: Palgrave Macmillan, 2015).

[58] Bernadotte, "Mediator's Conclusions," 17.   [59] Ibid.

with the Jewish areas enjoying municipal autonomy. The crux of the plan reduced the size of the Jewish state by transferring the Negev to Transjordan and giving Israel the western Galilee. In so doing it established territorial continuity between British bases in Iraq and Egypt via Transjordan.[60] In the original Partition Resolution most of the Negev had been made part of the proposed Jewish state. Bernadotte's plan deprived Israel of the Negev and of control of Haifa, its most important port, in the hope that doing so would foster Arab willingness to make peace. That it did so in a language of neutrality and even-handedness could not obscure the reality that it was offering the Jews less and the Arabs more than they had received in the UN Partition Resolution. In effect, it handed the Arabs a bonus for the invasion of May 15.

The clear alternative, as Shertok and Gromyko were suggesting, was for the United Nations Security Council, in agreement with the Soviet Union, to declare that the Arab states had launched a war of aggression against the state of Israel in defiance of the UN Partition Plan and that, therefore, the United Nations should offer military and economic assistance to the new state of Israel to ensure its security and deter further attacks. With the advantage of support from the Soviet bloc, the United States now had the opportunity to form a united front against Arab aggression, freed from the danger that the Arabs would turn to the Soviets. The United States could have declared that the Arab states were waging a war of aggression based on racial and religious hatred and intolerance, that the Arab League and the Arab Higher Committee were attacking a decision of the United Nations and deserved to be labeled "aggressors" under the terms of the UN Charter. As Philip Jessup had pointed out, only when the Arab states and the Palestine Arabs clearly understood that continued defiance of the Partition Plan was senseless would they abandon visions of destruction of the state of Israel and turn to a state of peaceful coexistence. The Arabs had an opportunity to form yet another Arab state in significant parts of Palestine, including significant access to the Mediterranean coast both south and north of the Israel, and in the process end the Palestinian refugee tragedy. All the elements of this alternative policy were evident either in American political debates or in the debates in the UN Security Council that summer.

In the Security Council debates of July 13–15, however, the United States opposed, while Israel and the Soviet Union supported, that alternative policy. Abba Eban, speaking for Israel, told the Security Council that since the Arabs, following the First Truce, had resumed their attack

[60] Morris, *1948*, 269–270.

on Israel, they had committed an act of aggression as defined by Chapter VII of the UN Charter.[61] The Arabs had rejected all appeals by the Security Council and the UN mediator to prolong the truce. Thus, according to the UN Charter, the responsibility of the Security Council was "quite clear." As its previous efforts at a pacific settlement had failed, it now had to "take action by other means to end the fighting," that is, send armed forces to stop the Arab aggression.[62] Though the United States agreed that the Arab states were to blame for renewal of the war, it introduced a resolution that again ordered unnamed "governments and authorities" to adopt a ceasefire "not later than three days from the date of the adoption of this resolution." It declared that their failure to do so would be regarded as a breach of the peace.[63] Eban argued that the language of the American resolution also suggested the possibility, again, of trying to revise the Partition Resolution of November 29, 1947.[64]

In the July 14 Security Council session Eban said that while the US resolution recognized the fact of Arab responsibility for continuation of the war, it "did not draw any conclusions from this record" for Security Council policy. Eban regretted that the neutral reference to a "threat to peace" obscured what was actually "an act of aggression of one side," that is, the Arab invasion of May 15. The resolution, he said, led to a "false equilibrium between attack and defence and an implication that preparation for attack and defence should be equally controlled and impeded." While Israel welcomed the ceasefire orders in the UN's resolution, it regretted that it was accompanied by "appeals to renew arrangements which had been outstripped by events," especially by "the fact of Arab aggression."[65]

Gromyko also objected to the US resolution for similar reasons. Those "who had started the hostilities in Palestine," that is, the Arabs, he said, "had in fact been preparing for the renewal of the fighting." Gromyko criticized Bernadotte for "advancing some suggestions which ignored previous decisions of the General Assembly," that is, the Partition Resolution, and "by reopening the question, had helped aggravate the

[61] Abba Eban cited in *Yearbook of the United Nations, 1947–48* (New York: United Nations, 1948), 436. On the definition of aggression in Chapter VII of the UN Charter see www .un.org/en/sections/un-charter/chapter-vii/index.html.

[62] Ibid., 436.

[63] Ibid., 436; and United Nations Security Council, S/890 (July 13, 1948): https://docu ments-dds-ny.un.org/doc/UNDOC/GEN/NL4/808/90/pdf/NL480890.pdf?OpenEleme nt; also reprinted as "Resolution 54 (1948) Adopted by the Security Council on July 15, 1948," *FRUS*, vol. 5, part 2, 1225: https://history.state.gov/historicaldocuments/fru s1948v05p2/d468.

[64] *Yearbook of the United Nations, 1947–48*, 436.   [65] Ibid., 438.

situation."[66] In doing so he was lending encouragement to the Arabs' belief that resorting to force might lead the UN General Assembly to reverse the decision of November 29, 1947. Gromyko pointed out that the American resolution "hinted at the possibility of the General Assembly adopting another resolution regarding Palestine." Doing so would pave the way for the "reconsideration of the whole Palestine question" at the next General Assembly session. He stressed that it was the Security Council's responsibility in July 1948 "to implement the decisions which had been adopted in the past," that is, the Partition Resolution of November 29, 1947.[67] He correctly saw the US resolution as an effort by the State Department to undermine the UN Partition Plan and revive the trusteeship proposal that had been defeated in the General Assembly in April. Warren Austin confirmed that the USA believed that "it was clear that the Security Council and the General Assembly might, if circumstances required it, adopt some new resolutions on the Palestine question."[68] In July 1948 the State Department was not giving up on its efforts to end UN legitimization for the state of Israel embedded in the UN Partition Resolution.

Ukraine's Vasyl Tarasenko, speaking to the Security Council on July 15, denounced Bernadotte's "actions and suggestions" as "responsible to a large extent for the renewal of hostilities. They were in contradiction to the Assembly's resolution of November 29, 1947 and jeopardized the legitimate interests of one party." Bernadotte had suggested holding a plebiscite to resolve the future of Palestine. That, he said, "would be tantamount to the liquidation of Israel and, of course, could never be accepted."[69] Despite these criticisms, from Israel, the Soviet Union, and the Ukrainian SSR, the US resolution emerged unscathed and was adopted by the Security Council by a vote of seven in favor, one opposed (Syria), and three abstentions (Argentina, Ukrainian SSR, and the Soviet Union.)[70]

The parliamentary maneuvers in the UN Security Council debates in mid-July 1948 demonstrated yet again that the Soviet Union and the Ukrainian SSR displayed the same unequivocal support for Israel that the Soviet Union, Poland, and Czechoslovakia had shown for the Jewish Agency in 1947 and in the General Assembly in 1948. They denounced Bernadotte's suggestions which, in their view, rewarded the Arabs with territorial concessions and implied rejection of the Partition Plan. The communist delegates made arguments in favor of Israel that were identical to those being made in the United States by non- and anticommunist

---

[66] Andrei Gromyko, in ibid., 439.   [67] Ibid.   [68] Jessup/Austin, in ibid., 440.
[69] Vasyl Tarasenko, in ibid., 440.   [70] Ibid., 441.

liberal and left liberals in the press and in both houses of Congress, and even by some Republican senators. Conversely, the arguments of the State Department's UN delegation in favor of Bernadotte's truce proposals in July 1948 reflected the persistent irritation of US State Department toward the emergence of the Jewish state in Palestine. The American stance of apparent neutrality was, in reality, one of pressure on Israel to abandon successes won on the field of battle in the hope of currying good will among the Arab states. For Wagner and Celler, such a policy was in accord with a policy of appeasement of the Arabs they had been criticizing all along. Yet for those in the Pentagon and State Department who saw the Arab-Israeli war through the lens of the Cold War, the more that Soviet and Israeli positions in the UN Security Council aligned, the more evidence they seemed to offer for those who viewed the Zionist project as associated in one way or another with Soviet policy.

During these same weeks American diplomats in Europe continued to send reports to the Office of the Secretary of State in Washington about the efforts of Jews to immigrate to Israel and related violations of the UN truce resolutions. A report from Berlin stated that another 400 emigrants were departing from Marseille, including "military age personnel."[71] On July 22 the SS *Ledma* left Marseille for Tel Aviv, reportedly "with 600 Jewish combat troops,"[72] On July 23 Alexander Kirk, the American ambassador to Belgium and former US ambassador in wartime Cairo, sent Marshall a translation of an extensive report by the Belgian intelligence services on the migration of Jews to Palestine.[73] That document concluded that "the Soviet Government perceives that the mass emigration to Palestine of leftist elements may result in the formation of a Communist majority in that country."[74] On July 27 the Embassy in Rome reported that the SS *Sorol* had left Los Angeles on May 14 "loaded with large quantity of war material listed on manifest as foodstuffs." Then it left Genoa on July 15 or 16 for Naples and Messina, "where it will depart with considerable number of well-armed Jews." The Italian Foreign Office alerted police to "prevent embarkation of armed persons,

[71] [James] Riddleberger to Secretary of State, Berlin (July 23, 1948), NACP RG 59 CDF 1945–1949, 501.BB Palestine/7-2348, Box 2119.

[72] Christianson to Secretary of State, Marseille (July 22, 1948), NACP M1390, Roll 16, 867N.01/7–2248.

[73] Alexander Kirk to Secretary of State, Brussels (July 23, 1948), No. 478, "Subject: The Migration of Jews to Palestine,"), NACP M1390, Roll 16, 867N.01/7–2348. On Kirk's very important reports to Washington on Nazi Arabic broadcasts to the Middle East in World War II see Jeffrey Herf, *Nazi Propaganda for the Arab World* (New Haven: Yale University Press, 2009).

[74] Kirk to Secretary of State, Brussels (July 23, 1948).

but not known what has transpired."[75] On August 9 Marshall wrote to the Rome Embassy with details of the contents on the *Sorol*. The US Customs authorities had "erroneously permitted airport parts to be exported without a license."[76] That same day officials in the US Embassy in Prague reported the belief "that Communist trained Jews are passing through France en route to Israel is probably correct."[77]

By mid-August the Israelis had thwarted the initial Arab invasions. Yet rather than view their success as an opportunity for American policy to pressure the Arabs into accepting the original partition plan consisting of separate Jewish and Arab states, Marshall expressed irritation with the Israelis. On August 16 he informed President Truman that a "wide variety of sources" caused the State Department to have "increasing concern" about the tendency of Israel "to assume a more aggressive attitude in Palestine."[78] It was evident in the hostility of Israelis to UN military observers, the "inflammatory speeches" of Israeli foreign minister Shertok with "regard to alleged 'rights' of Israel in Jerusalem," military occupation of much of the Jerusalem area, "systematic violations of the UN truce by Israeli forces, sniping and firing on Arab positions," and "conclusive evidence of arms shipments to Palestine from France, Italy and Czechoslovakia."[79]

Marshall told Truman that Bevin had again warned that the USSR would "take advantage of this situation." The British foreign secretary thought that "the Palestine situation was as serious as Berlin," that is, as serious as the blockade of the city of Berlin begun by the Soviet Union on July 24. The State Department thought it would be wise to tell Eliahu Epstein, Israel's representative in Washington, that, "as he undoubtedly knows, the United States is the best friend of Israel," evident in the fact of diplomatic recognition. It had a "desire to see that it continue in existence and prosper as a peaceful member of the community of nations."[80]

---

[75] Byington to Secretary of State, Rome (July 27, 1948), No. 3174, NACP M1390, Roll 16, 867N.01/7–2748.

[76] George Marshall to AMEMBASSY ROME, Washington (August 9, 1948), NACP M1390, Roll 16, 867N.01/7–2748.

[77] Kekick to Secretary of State, Prague (August 9, 1948) 1283, NACP M1390, Roll 16, 867N.01/8–948.

[78] "Memorandum by the Secretary of State to President Truman," Washington (August 16, 1948), *FRUS*, 1948, vol. 5, part 2: https://history.state.gov/historicaldocuments/frus1948v05p2/d531; and G. C. Marshall, "Memorandum for the President: Subject: Proposed Representation to Provisional Government of Israel Regarding Maintenance of Peace in Palestine," Washington (August 16, 1948), NACP RG 59, 501.BB Palestine/8–1648, Box 2117; also in NACP RG 218, Records of the U.S. Joint Chiefs of Staff, Chairman's File, Admiral Leahy, 1942–1946, Box 10.

[79] Ibid.   [80] Ibid.

On the other hand, Marshall continued, there were three issues pending for a discussion with Epstein: the possibility of moving from de facto to de jure recognition of Israel; the question of Israel's membership in the UN; and the prospect of a loan from the Export-Import Bank. Marshall wrote that it would be "extraordinarily difficult ... to advocate a loan to Israel if that country is likely to resume hostilities. Similar difficulties would arise concerning membership in the United Nations."[81] After suggesting using these three issues as leverage in discussions with Israel, Marshall offered an additional threat: "As a friend of Israel, we deem it of paramount importance that this new republic not place itself before the bar of world public opinion and the United Nations in the role of an aggressor. We should like to tell Mr. Epstein for the information of his government that we shall be not less zealous in the Security Council to oppose aggression from the Israeli side as we were when the attack was launched by the Arab side."[82] If Israel opened hostilities against Transjordan, Britain would "honor its commitments under an existing treaty" to support the latter, leading to an "outcry in the United States for the lifting of our arms embargo in favor of Israel with the result that the two great Anglo-Saxon partners would be supplying and aiding two little states on the opposite sides of a serious war, from which only the Soviet Union could profit."[83] A change in British policy was one way to avoid such an American-British clash, but Marshall did not suggest it. Instead, he was proposing that the president use the levers of de jure recognition, UN membership, and financial assistance to pressure Israel into accepting the Bernadotte Plan.

In the UN Security Council, the State Department led the opposition to Soviet suggestions and Israeli requests to place clear blame for continuing the war on the Arabs. Contrary to Marshall's assertion, the United States had not been "zealous" in denouncing Arab aggression. In fact, it had successfully fought to adopt language that sustained the arms embargo and placed blame equally on "both parties." The reality was that in spring and summer 1948 Israel's "best friend" at the United Nations was the Soviet Union, not the United States. Israel's "best friends" in Europe were the Socialist ministers in the French government who supported immigration of persons to Israel and the communist government in Czechoslovakia which sent the weapons Israel needed for success in the war. When its outcome hung in the balance, the US secretary of state and former five-star general George Marshall must have understood very well that preventing aid from reaching Israel was, as Carter Clarke had pointed out to the Joint Chiefs of Staff and the

[81] Ibid., 1–2.   [82] Ibid.   [83] Ibid., 2–3.

secretary of defense, James Forrestal, a means to help bring about Israel's "ultimate defeat." It was not a policy one would expect from what Marshall described as "Israel's best friend."

The Zionists had not asked for the intervention of outside forces; they wanted assistance so they could defend themselves. One way to defeat a policy suggestion is to mischaracterize it as something that has not actually been proposed. Secretary of Defense Forrestal adopted this approach. On August 19 he summarized the views of the Joint Chiefs of Staff in a memo to the National Security Council.[84] Ignoring the actual intent of the Israeli request, Forrestal instead focused on a possible UN effort to use force to implement the Partition Plan in the event of violations of the UN truce resolutions which would likely include the entry of Soviet forces into Israel.

The entry of Soviet forces into Palestine would have the most far-reaching strategic implications in that the Soviets would then be entitled to land or sea line communications, either of which would entail the very serious consequences of Soviet entry into other Near and Middle East areas, and in that there would be no limitation on the number of Soviet forces that might enter Palestine with or without justification by the developing situation. The way would thus be open for Soviet domination of the Near and Middle East, which would exert tremendously harmful influence on and even jeopardize our global strategy and resources in the event of war with our most probable enemy. The foregoing would also apply eventually to the entry of any Soviet satellite forces into Palestine in view of their close relationship with and control by the Soviets.[85]

Forrestal and the Joint Chiefs took the view that sending US forces to Israel "would be incompatible with the security interests of the United States to have either United States or Soviet or Soviet satellite forces introduced into Palestine." Therefore the USA should "neither endorse nor permit a decision by the United Nations to employ military enforcement measures in Palestine."[86] Forrestal's memo was effective bureaucratic politics in rejecting a policy – US or UN troops to defend Israel – that the Israelis were not in fact requesting. They had called for lifting the arms embargo but had not requested that the UN send troops. Forrestal's lack of understanding of the Zionist leadership's opposition to communism and its equally emphatic support for liberal democracy continued to be an intelligence failure that was shaping US policy toward the Arab-Israeli war.

---

[84] "Memorandum by the Secretary of Defense (Forrestal) to the National Security Council," Washington (August 19, 1948), S/S-NSC Files, Lot 63, D351, 1322–1324, *FRUS*, 1948, vol. 5, part 2: https://history.state.gov/historicaldocuments/frus1948v05 p2/d541.

[85] Ibid., 1322.   [86] Ibid., 1323–1324.

On August 24 James McDonald wrote directly to Truman to express his alarm at the pressure Marshall was proposing to exert on Israel; he sent a copy to Marshall. "If not handled wisely both in Washington and Israel," there was a danger that Israel would be faced with "the tragic alternative of accepting the dangerous humiliation from the US and the UN or of defying both US and UN."[87] Washington's focus on truces and Arab refugees missed the key issue of how to bring about peace. The Israelis regarded the UN truce resolutions "as merely a thinly disguised continuation of the war." Israel wanted peace negotiations with the Arabs, while the USA focused on the important but secondary issues of the demilitarization of Jerusalem and refugees. The large number of Arab refugees was a result of the war; it was an issue that could only be resolved at a peace conference. Washington suffered from the "illusion" that sanctions could force Israel to change policy, but Shertok and Ben-Gurion would not yield to threats of sanctions. They had told him that "what we have won on the battlefield we will not sacrifice at the conference table."[88] McDonald concluded that, "rather than submit to what would be regarded as infringement of independence or weakening of security, they would fight both the US and the UN." Aware that that some in the State Department were tempted to impose sanctions and label Israel as the aggressor, he sent an "urgent plea" to Truman and Marshall, asking that the United States government not let its "good intentions and love of peace betray it into supporting a UN policy which would mean armed conflict with Israel," one that could potentially bring the United States armed forces into combat against the state of Israel.

Surprisingly, in view of McDonald's stunning presentation of a possible clash of arms between the United States and Israel, Truman approved a reply that Marshall had written to be sent to McDonald in Tel Aviv.[89] It was "essential that US and UK policy be coordinated" with that of the UN mediator before the "question of Palestine" came before the United Nations. "We do not, as member of UN, intend to see solution of Palestine problem by force of arms ... The leaders of Israel would make a grave miscalculation if they thought callous treatment of this tragic issue," that is, the issue of Palestinian refugees, "could pass unnoticed by world opinion." He did "not concur in your conclusion that 'Jewish emphasis on peace negotiations now is sounder than present US and UN

[87] James McDonald to Secretary of State, Tel Aviv (August 24, 1948), NACP RG 59 CDF 1945–1949 501.BB Palestine/8–2448, Box 2117.

[88] Ibid., 2.

[89] George C. Marshall, "Memorandum for the President," Washington (August 31, 1948), NACP RG 59 CDF 1945–1949 501.BB Palestine/8–2448, Box 2117.

emphasis on truce and demilitarization and refugees.'"[90] Marshall had won a temporary victory in the ongoing battle over policy toward Israel. The embargo and the pressure on Israel continued.

Marshall wrote to Truman as if the decision by the Arab states to invade Israel had not altered the realities. He urged the Israelis to accept what would soon become known as the Bernadotte Plan, that is, more territory in the Galilee "in return for relinquishing a large portion of the Negev to Transjordan." He warned that the USA "will be zealous in advocating that Council apply measures, if necessary, under Chapter VII of Charter, to restrain resort to arms, whether by Arabs or by Israel." Israel's leaders should see that non-military sanctions approved by the Security Council, "for example, a ban on any financial transactions with aggressive state or modification of an arms embargo, would have immediate consequences in such a state as Israel." That is, if Israel did not accept the Bernadotte Plan, Marshall was threatening to introduce a Security Council resolution that would declare Israel the aggressor, one that might compel the USA to cut off access to loans or perhaps even send arms to the Arabs. Marshall hoped that the leaders of Israel will "perceive that a new state cannot exist except by acceptance of international community and that PGI [the provisional government of Israel], of all the new govts, should be most responsive to this fact."[91] Marshall's threat to urge the "international community" to withdraw "acceptance" was now explicit.

With the Israelis calling for a peace conference and the Arabs refusing to negotiate, Marshall could have aimed his hopes for peace and his pressure tactics instead at the Arab Higher Committee and the seven invading Arab states, the parties that had started and then escalated the war. Instead, his pressure campaign was aimed at Israel. In accord with Marshall at the end of August 1948, Truman agreed to the primacy of the alliance with Britain and to Marshall's efforts to pressure the Israelis to accept truce terms that would roll back their battlefield victories. In these years of the massive preponderance of American power on the world stage, it was odd that even Truman was reluctant to insist that the British government change its policies or challenge the Arab states. Yet the president was up against a formidable set of adversaries at home in the form of the national security establishment in Washington, DC. It is crucial to keep in mind the key areas of fundamental agreement between Truman and the State Department, the Pentagon, and the CIA regarding overriding concern with containing communism. That perspective, which he had articulated in the Truman Doctrine, was his basic foreign policy priority. In the unanimous opinion of the leadership of the State

[90] Ibid., 3.   [91] Ibid., 4–5.

Department, Pentagon, and the CIA, sending weapons to Israel would undermine the policy of containment that Truman himself had set in motion.

As the outcome of the war hung in the balance, the role of outside powers had a profound impact on the clash of arms between Israel and the Arab states. Israel needed arms and people. As the United States continued its embargo on arms to Israel, Israel had to seek arms where it could get them. The Soviet bloc and communist Czechoslovakia did what the United States refused to do. The Czech government, with approval from the Soviet Union, sent the weapons and, along with France, aided the Mossad Le'Aliyah Bet's efforts to bring people as well that Israel needed to defend itself and win the war for its independence. The United States continued to use its majority on the UN Security Council to support the Bernadotte Plan in a persistent effort to undermine the Partition Resolution of November 29, 1947, and prevent Israel from holding or gaining the territory that had been allocated to it.

14 The USA and Britain Again in Opposition: From the Bernadotte Plan to the End of the 1948 War

> ... the rear-guard action fought by the [British] Foreign Office and the State Department against partition.
>
> I. F. Stone, on the Bernadotte Plan, "Secretary Marshall's Blunder," *The New Republic*, October 18, 1948

> Time and again, Foreign Minister Moshe Shertok has stated that Israel wants the equal friendship of both the East and West. But if only the East will give her help, then she must turn to the East for survival.
>
> Lawrence Lader, "From Junk Heap to Air Might," *The New Republic*, November 8, 1948

In early July the UN mediator, Count Folke Bernadotte, negotiated a second truce in the war. It went into effect on July 15. No major battles took place in the war until October 15, allowing Israel to import light weaponry during July and August. Yet, as Benny Morris writes, "in heavy weapons, such as tanks, combat aircraft, and antitank guns, the IDF [Israel Defense Force] remained abysmally deficient."[1] On the other hand, the arrival of foreign volunteers and foreign conscripts "accounted for about twenty thousand of Israel's eighty-five thousand-strong army in October and November 1948; almost all arrived after 15 May."[2] Some of those volunteers were Americans. Most came along the routes described in previous chapters beginning in Eastern Europe, and continuing through Black Sea ports, and ports in France and Italy.

Emanuel Celler on the State Department's "Weapons of Attrition" against Israel

In addition to continuing the arms embargo, the US State Department withheld de jure recognition of the state of Israel and continued attempting to prevent military-age Jewish refugees in Europe and American volunteers from reaching the Jewish state. On September 5

---

[1] Benny Morris, *1948: The First Arab-Israeli War* (New Haven: Yale University Press, 2008), 298.
[2] Ibid.

Congressman Emanuel Celler sent an article entitled "The Department of State Divorces Performance from Promise in Policy toward the State of Israel" to Isaac Rosengarten, the editor of the monthly journal *The Jewish Forum*.[3] Celler used it to decry "inconsistencies between declared policy," that is, between Truman's stated policies and the "attitude of our Department of State." Although the United States, especially following Truman's recognition decision on May 14, "had removed itself from neutrality," the State Department was "playing havoc with a stated policy" by "behaving as if our policy called for strictest neutrality between the Arabs and the Jews." Were that so, the United States "should have abstained" from even voting, much less voting in the affirmative, for the Partition Resolution in the "face of violent Arab opposition."[4] Celler, yet again, drew attention to the gap between Truman's policy of support for Israel and the State Department's refusal to provide the means needed to achieve the ends publicly supported by the president.

Celler specifically criticized a decision by Under Secretary Lovett to withhold an Export-Import Bank loan to Israel, a loan that was to be used to transport Jewish displaced persons in Europe to Israel and to feed, clothe, and house them once there. The decision was "one of the weapons of attrition to wear down Jewish resistance which could not be upset militarily." Celler also denounced the policy of withholding full recognition to Israel. Granting it, he said, "would immediately notify the Arab world that the United States meant what it said in the United Nations in November of 1947." In response to the Department's excuse that the Israeli government was only a provisional one, Celler recalled that the United States had recognized provisional governments before, such as the Kerensky government of Russia in 1917 and the Provisional French Government following the French Revolution of 1789. There was no uncertainty as to where authority rested in Israel. In "matters military and civil" the state of Israel "exists and does so with the support of its people," but the State Department "has forsaken all acts of independence with reference to Israel so that Anglo-American relations could be of a piece."[5] Celler correctly understood the priority given to close relations with Britain by the US national security establishment.

He then turned to the State Department's decision to refuse all exit permits "of Jewish refugees of 'military age' en route to Palestine from DP

---

[3] Emanuel Celler, "The Department of State Divorces Performance from Promise in Policy toward the State of Israel," Library of Congress, Manuscript Division, Emanuel Celler Papers, Box 23.
[4] Ibid., 2.   [5] Ibid., 4.

centers." The UN truce terms had called for denying entry of "fighting personnel," not to men of military age. Celler wrote:

The fact that a [person's] body is between 15 and 45 years of age does not automatically classify him as fighting personnel. Many of the displaced Jews after years of denial and deprivation are anything but fighting personnel. These are the men to whom getting to Israel has become the difference between living and dying, but these are the very same ones who are denied entrance. Such an order follows closely the action of the British authorities who detain all Jews on the Island of Cyprus of "military age." Again, I do not hesitate to call it another act of attrition.[6]

Celler expanded the demographic balance from Palestine to the Arab world. There were "some thirty million Arabs. What is this fear of upsetting a balance by adding a few additional thousands [of Jews] now?" If all the DPS and "all the Jews all over the world" were permitted to enter Israel, "it could not come even near to equaling the numbers of men of military age residing in the Arab countries. We view a population of 800,000 against some 30,000,000." It was thus "nonsense" to prevent Jews of military age from entering Israel. The State Department was "substituting the will of the British Foreign Office for the will of the people of the United States."[7]

Celler was not the only figure in Washington, DC to grasp what was going on; the leadership in the State Department, the Pentagon, and the CIA also understood that the arms embargo and efforts to cut Israel off from supplies from the outside was neither neutral nor evenhanded in its effect. The embargo, along with the effort to prevent Jews of military age from getting to Israel, disadvantaged Israel and benefited the Arabs. In addition, those three agencies, joining with their close ally Britain, managed to use the UN to lend international legitimacy to their own ongoing efforts to reverse the Partition Resolution or, failing that, to whittle down the state of Israel to as small a size as possible in hopes of appeasing Arab anger in the face of the failure the war of aggression that the Arab League states launched on May 15, 1948. Over the following summer American pressure on Israel to give up territory it had gained in the first months of the war of defense took the form of a United Nations scheme called the Bernadotte Plan, named after the UN mediator who was its author.

The Bernadotte Report

In August and the first half of September 1948 the State Department and the British Foreign Office continued trying to replace the boundaries set by the Partition Plan of November 29, 1947. They sought to give the

---

[6] Ibid., 5.   [7] Ibid.

Negev desert to Transjordan and place Jerusalem under an international, rather than Israeli, authority. The vehicle for doing so was the Bernadotte Plan, formally submitted to the UN in September.[8] Following Bernadotte's murder, Ralph Bunche assumed the position of UN mediator. His work in that role led to the Nobel Peace Prize in 1950.[9] He drafted and completed Bernadotte's report and submitted to the Secretary General on September 16. The next day, however, Bernadotte was assassinated by four gunmen from Lehi, an extremist Zionist paramilitary outfit.[10] His murder outraged members of the United Nations and was both a surprise and an enormous embarrassment for the Israeli government. Lehi was a fringe organization, yet the mood in Israel that summer had turned against Bernadotte and the UN as the Israeli government was angered by what it viewed as insufficient UN responses to repeated and unpunished Arab violations of the UN truce, and to the mediator's efforts to restrict the flow of men and weapons to Israel. The Israeli government and public had concluded that the UN truce served Arab interests and blocked an Israeli victory, and thus a more rapid end to the war.[11]

Following the assassination the Israeli government launched a massive crackdown on Lehi that was so severe that the organization ceased to exist. Nevertheless, the murder of Bernadotte weakened Israel's position at the UN, gave further credence to the expression "Jewish terrorists," and, temporarily at least, improved the prospects for adoption of a second version of the plan that now bore Bernadotte's name. Yet, as damaging as the Bernadotte Plan was to Israel, it at least acknowledged Israel as an established fact, albeit one with less territory than foreseen by the Partition Resolution of November 29, 1947. For that reason alone the Arabs, although they could have seized the moment to use the UN to create a smaller, more vulnerable Israel, rejected the Bernadotte Plan as a

---

[8] Folke Bernadotte, "Progress Report of the United Nations Mediator on Palestine Submitted to The Secretary-General for Transmission to the Members of the United Nations," Paris (September 1948), United Nations, General Assembly Official Records: Third Session Supplement No. 11 (A/648): https://unispal.un.org/UNISPAL.NSF/9a7 98adbf322aff38525617b006d88d7/ab14d4aafc4e1bb985256204004f55fa?OpenDocument. Though Ralph Bunche edited the final draft, the text was commonly referred to simply as the Bernadotte Plan or Bernadotte Report. I have used that designation.

[9] On Bunche's opposition to the establishment of the state of Israel see Elad Ben-Dror, "Ralph Bunche and the Establishment of the State of Israel," *Israel Affairs* 14, no. 3 (2008): 519–537; and his *Ralph Bunche and the Arab-Israeli Conflict: Mediation and the UN 1947–1949* (London: Routledge, 2015).

[10] Lehi, or Lohamei Herut Israel (Fighters for the Freedom of Israel), also called the Stern Gang, was a Zionist paramilitary organization founded by Avraham ("Yair") Stern in Mandatory Palestine.

[11] Morris, *1948*, 311–312.

whole. Its fatal flaw in their eyes was that it assumed that Israel, however diminished, should continue to exist.

The Bernadotte Report referred obliquely to "the chain of unfortunate events which began in Palestine almost immediately after the adoption of the resolution of 29 November." That oblique language referred to the decisions of the Arab Higher Committee (AHC) and the Arab League to wage war against the Jewish Agency and the state of Israel. The report did acknowledge that "the necessary Arab willingness to co-operate was lacking" and that "a dangerous antagonism existed which was provoking virtual civil war even before the termination of the Mandate on 15 May 1948." Despite the fact that the Jewish Agency had accepted the Partition Plan and the AHC and Arab states had rejected it, Bernadotte observed that "in these ten months since the adoption of the partition resolution it has become increasingly clear that any plan based on the essential assumption of immediate co-operation between Arabs and Jews in Palestine must ignore the harsh facts of existing relationships there."[12] The Israelis faulted the report for a language of equivalence that avoided placing primary responsibility on Arab rejectionism and resort to force.

The report did acknowledge that "the most significant development in the Palestine scene since last November is the fact that the Jewish State is a living, solidly entrenched and vigorous reality." It had received de jure or de facto recognition from an increasing number of states, and it exercised "all the attributes of full sovereignty." Israel's establishment "constitutes the only implementation which has been given to the resolution [of November 29, 1947], and even this was accomplished by a procedure quite contrary to that envisaged for the purpose in the resolution." The text quoted from Bernadotte's previous report to the Security Council of July 12, 1948: "The Jewish State is 'a small State, precariously perched on a coastal shelf with its back to the sea and defiantly facing on three sides a hostile Arab world. Its future may be assessed as uncertain, and if it survives this war its security will be likely to present a serious problem for a good time to come.'" Arab determination to eliminate it could be realized only by armed force in sufficient strength to overwhelm it. In any case, resort to armed force as a means of settling the problem has been prohibited by the Security Council.[13] That statement implied that the Security Council had both the will and the means to prohibit such an effort. Due to American pressure, however, it exercised neither.

The Bernadotte Report simultaneously criticized Arab rejectionism and expressed some understanding for it. The Palestinian Arabs and

---

[12] Bernadotte, "The Basic Factors of the Palestine Situation," in "Progress Report," 5–6.
[13] Ibid., 6.

invading Arab states found it "extremely difficult to accept even the fact of a Jewish State in Palestine" and "bitterly reject Jewish nationalistic aspirations for a separate State. That the Arab States made a tragic mistake in employing force in Palestine cannot be questioned. But the very fact that they resorted to this extreme action and were willing to run the risk of thus offending the international community is in itself a measure of the intensity of their feeling on the question."[14] The Arabs' "dilemma" was that the UN had determined "that the war could not go on and that the Palestine dispute must be settled by peaceful means." As "the Jewish State" – only once did Bernadotte and Bunche refer to "Israel" – had been "established under the cloak of United Nations authority," it could "be eliminated only by force." The UN had "decreed that force must not be employed. Therefore, the Arab States must resign themselves to the presence of the Jewish State or pursue the reckless course of defying the United Nations and thereby incurring liabilities the full burden and danger of which cannot be calculated in advance."[15]

But when the Arabs ignored the UN decree that "force must not be deployed" to undermine its Partition Resolution, the UN, primarily in response to American policy, had refused either to use its own forces or to allow military assistance to the Jews to sustain partition. For the Israelis, promises and warnings from the UN Security Council without the credible threat of force were no substitute for armed self-defense and, as was the case for all other states, self-reliance. By supporting an embargo on arms and military-age men, the UN truce resolution of May 29 made it difficult for Israel to defend itself.

While the second Bernadotte Report did not condone "the armed intervention of the Arab States," it stated that "it would be helpful to the solution of the problem if both the international community and the Jews of Israel were to be more understanding of the Arab viewpoint." The Arabs "[looked] upon the nationalistic Jews of Palestine as interlopers and aggressors." It was "at least understandable that, in their fervor, they not only [reject] the historical claims of the Jews but even the legal basis for their presence in Palestine which the terms of the Mandate provided."[16] The Arabs were pursuing a "reckless course of defying the United Nations," yet theirs was a recklessness that received Bernadotte's understanding.

The Arabs feared that that the Jewish state "would not stay within its defined boundaries" and, due to an increase in population resulting from "unlimited immigration, encouragement and support from world Jewry, and burgeoning nationalism," it would pose a threat "not only to

---

[14] Ibid., 7.   [15] Ibid.   [16] Ibid.

Palestine but to the entire Arab Near East." The report could "appreciate the Arab views and fears, although on appraisal they may in large measure be found extravagant and unfounded." But since they existed, "no settlement can be on solid foundations unless every reasonable reassurance possible is afforded them, not only by the Jewish State but by the United Nations."[17]

If, as the report acknowledged, the Arabs' views of Israeli expansion to "the entire Middle East" were "unfounded and extravagant," then those views deserved sharp criticism, not "understanding." The idea that a Jewish state in Palestine would pose a threat to the "entire Arab Near East" had been a staple of Nazi Germany's anti-Zionist propaganda in World War II, but the Bernadotte Report did not mention that as one of the origins of that assertion. It did, however, assert that the Arab proposal for "a unitary Arab State in Palestine, with full rights and guarantees for the Jewish minority, as the acceptable solution of the Palestine problem" was, in light of the existence of the Jewish State, "unrealistic." The report acknowledged that the Arabs' decision to go to war rather than coexist with the Jewish state shattered the belief that the Jews could be safe in a unitary, Arab-majority state.

The Bernadotte Plan concluded with seven "basic premises" followed by "specific conclusions." First, peace must return to Palestine and hostilities should not be resumed. Second, "a Jewish State called Israel exists in Palestine and there are no sound reasons for assuming that it will not continue to do so." Third, "the boundaries of this new State must finally be fixed either by formal agreement between the parties concerned or failing that, by the United Nations." Fourth, boundary arrangements based on "the principle of geographical homogeneity and integration . . . should apply equally to Arab and Jewish territories, whose frontiers should not therefore, be rigidly controlled by the territorial arrangements envisaged in the resolution of 29 November." Fifth, "the right of innocent people, uprooted from their homes by the present terror and ravages of war, to return to their homes, should be affirmed and made effective, with assurance of adequate compensation for the property of those who may choose not to return." Sixth, "the City of Jerusalem, because of its religious and international significance and the complexity of interests involved, should be accorded special and separate treatment." Seventh, "international responsibility should be expressed where desirable and necessary in the form of international guarantees, as a means of allaying existing fears, and particularly with regard to boundaries and human rights."[18]

---

[17] Ibid.   [18] "Conclusions," in ibid., 17–18.

From Israel's viewpoint, Bernadotte's seven premises were problematic. To say that "there were no sound reasons" for assuming that Israel would not continue to exist fell short of asserting that it had a legitimate right to exist. Two "sound reasons" were the report's refusal to focus on the fact of Arab aggression and its efforts to deny the entry of military-age Jewish men to Israel. Rather than acknowledge that the UN Partition Resolution had lent legitimacy to the establishment of the state of Israel, Bernadotte simply acknowledged its existence. The report gave the UN the authority to fix Israel's borders, a power that ignored Israel's sovereignty and the results of the war. The fourth premise, which questioned the continuing relevance of the November 29, 1947 resolution, deepened these concerns. Premise five, dealing with refugees, said nothing about the Arab aggression that had caused the war during which thousands of Palestine Arabs fled. Premise six was another blow to Israeli sovereignty by implying that "separate and special treatment" for Jerusalem meant that the city would be placed under some form of international control.

Bernadotte's "specific conclusions" were also disadvantageous to Israel. They began with an air of unreality, saying that the Security Council had "forbidden further employment of military action in Palestine as a means of settling the dispute." Yet the Security Council demands rang empty, as they lacked credible means of enforcement. The current truce should be superseded by "a formal peace, or at the minimum, armistice which would involve either complete withdrawal and demobilization of armed forces or their wide separation by creation of broad demilitarized zones under United Nations supervision." Israel had requested precisely such a formal peace to be arranged through direct negotiations with the Arab League and Arab states, but the Arabs refused to enter such direct negotiations. The call for Israel to demobilize its armed forces as long as the Arabs refused either to accept its existence or negotiate a peace agreement ignored Israel's elementary requirements for survival.

The most prominent feature of the report was its recommended territorial boundaries. In exchange for granting more of the Galilee to Israel, it allocated the Negev desert to Transjordan. Rather than have the results of war establish boundaries, it recommended that the UN assume the right to do so. The boundaries at the UN on November 29, 1947 should be made "more equitable, workable and consistent with existing realities in Palestine." The Galilee would "be defined as Jewish territory." The Negev desert, which had been part of Israel in the November 29 Partition Plan, would "be defined as Arab territory," thereby depriving Israel of 60 percent of the territory it had been offered in November

1947.[19] For the Israelis the Bernadotte Report rewarded Egyptian military advances which in the summer months had its army occupying large parts of the Negev.

In another blow to Israel, the report again recommended that "the port of Haifa, including the oil refineries and terminals, and without prejudice to their inclusion in the sovereign territory of the Jewish State or the administration of the city of Haifa, should be declared a free port," that is, one not included in Israel's sovereign territory. Yet Haifa was Israel's most important port, and its control was vital for the new nation's economy and security and for reception of immigrants, economic commerce, and military assistance. Instead, the report advocated "free access for interested Arab countries and an undertaking on their part to place no obstacle in the way of oil deliveries by pipeline to the Haifa refineries whose distribution would continue on the basis of the historical pattern."[20] As the Israelis had already shown their willingness to allow Arab oil to flow to international markets, the problem instead should have been addressed to the Arab League, which was advocating an economic boycott of Israel and thus refused to allow it to have access to Arab oil.[21]

The Bernadotte Report's third blow to Israeli sovereignty was the recommendation that Jerusalem "should be placed under effective United Nations control with maximum feasible local autonomy for its Arab and Jewish communities with full safeguards for the protection of the Holy Places and sites and free access to them and for religious freedom." The Zionists had assumed that Jerusalem would certainly be part of the Jewish state.

The report stressed that the UN should affirm "the right of the Arab refugees to return to their homes in Jewish-controlled territory at the earliest possible date." It did not connect the refugee issue to that of a peace agreement to end the state of war. Moreover, it called for the establishment of a UN commission to supervise and assist refugees' "repatriation, resettlement and economic and social] rehabilitation, and payment of adequate compensation for the property of those choosing not to return." Such a commission would also "supervise the observance of such boundary, road, railroad, free port, free airport, minority rights and other arrangements as may be decided upon by the United Nations" and "report promptly to the United Nations any development in Palestine likely to alter the arrangements approved by the United Nations in the

---

[19] "Specific Conclusions," in ibid., 17.   [20] Ibid.

[21] On the issue of access to oil as a central priority of Israel's foreign policy see Uri Bialer, "A Land of Milk and Honey but No Oil," in his *Israeli Foreign Policy: A People Shall Not Dwell Alone* (Bloomington: Indiana University Press, 2020), 109–135.

Palestine settlement or to threaten the peace of the area."[22] A commission
with those powers would eviscerate Israeli sovereignty.

In sum, except for offering a dispassionate acknowledgment of the fact
that Israel existed and rejecting the use of armed force to destroy it, the
Bernadotte Report of September 1948 tilted heavily toward the Arabs. It
deprived Israel of the Negev and of control over its major seaport, the
definition of its borders, and the city of Jerusalem. It gave priority to the
issue of return of refugees but separated it from negotiations to sign a
peace agreement. It said nothing about the Arab aggression that had
caused the war to begin with. It did not insist on Arab recognition of
Israel and an end to a state of war as preconditions for discussion of the
refugee issue. It proposed all these of things, which were inherently
injurious to Israel's interest, in the language of even-handedness and
neutrality. For the Israelis and their supporters the Bernadotte Report
made "diplomacy" synonymous with illusion.

On October 28 Israel's representative to the UN, Abba (Aubrey) Eban,
submitted Israel's formal response to the Bernadotte Plan.[23] It was
"inconsistent with all fairness." Its changes from the November 29,
1947 Partition Resolution would cause Israel to "lose two-thirds of its
territory and the only territorial reserves available for development; any
prospect of the scientific utilization of the natural resources of the Negeb
would be destroyed and the progress and development of Israel would be
halted for several generations." The mediator was proposing "an entirely
fresh plan of partition" depriving Israel of 9,800 square kilometers of the
Negev, thus reducing Israel's territory from 14,700 square kilometers in
the November 29 Partition Plan to 5,650. At the same time the map
expanded Transjordan to 110,000 square kilometers.[24] The map he
presented clearly illustrated how dramatically the plan would reduce
Israel's size and how much of a regression, from Israel's perspective, it
represented (see Map 14.1).

The American Response

Not surprisingly, on September 21 in Paris, Secretary of State George
Marshall announced that the United States would urge the UN General

---

[22] Bernadotte, "Specific Conclusions," in "Progress Report," 18.

[23] Aubrey S. Eban, "Letter dated 28 October 1948 from representative of Provisional
Government of Israel to Secretary General transmitting a document concerning territorial issues proposed in the Mediator's progress report," Official Records of the [UN]
General Assembly, 3rd Session Part I, 1st Committee, 1948: annexes to the summary
records of meetings, 40–41.

[24] Ibid., 41.

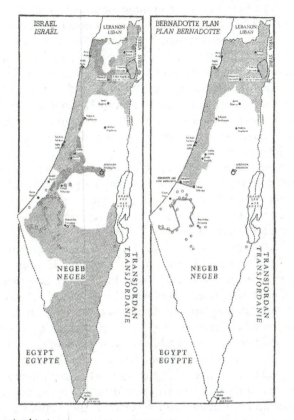

Territory assigned to the State of Israel by the decision of the General Assembly of the United Nations of 29 November 1947.

Territoire attribué à l'Etat d'Israël par la décision de l'Assemblée générale des Nations Unies du 29 novembre 1947.

Territory occupied by Israel in the course of its struggle against the aggression of the Arab States.

Territoire occupé par Israël au cours de sa lutte contre l'agression des Etats arabes.

Territory of the State of Israel occupied by the Arab armies.

Territoire de l'Etat d'Israël occupé par les armées arabes.

Jewish colonies established in the Negeb (the dot at the border of the Dead Sea marks the site of the southern plants of the Palestine Potash Co.).

Colonies juives établies dans le Negeb (le point au bord de la mer Morte marque l'emplacement des usines sud de la Palestine Potash Co.).

Pipe line supplying water to the colonies in the Negeb.

Pipe-line desservant en eau les colonies du Negeb.

Modern City of Jerusalem occupied by Israel.

Ville moderne de Jérusalem occupée par Israël.

Map 14.1 Map of Bernadotte Plan alongside map of territory occupied by Israel, October 28, 1948. Source: Eban's letter of October 28, 1948 to UN secretary general.

Assembly to accept Bernadotte's recommendations in full.[25] Marshall said that the United States considered them "a generally fair basis for settlement of the Palestine question." It viewed them as "sound, and strongly urges the parties and the General Assembly to accept them in their entirety as the best possible basis for bringing peace to a distracted land."[26] That is, Marshall thought it was "sound" and "generally fair" to deprive Israel of the Negev desert; hand it over to Transjordan, which was in a state of war with Israel; deprive Israel of full sovereignty over its major port on the Mediterranean; and deprive the state of Israel of sovereignty over the city of Jerusalem.

The following day Under Secretary of State Robert Lovett sent a cable to all Arab capitals, to US diplomats in Tel Aviv, Jerusalem, London, and Paris, and to the US UN delegation. He instructed them to bring Marshall's statement to the attention of the relevant heads of state, prime ministers, and foreign ministers. They should emphasize that the United States "considers that acceptance of Bernadotte's conclusions would provide Arab and Jewish leaders with statesmanlike opportunity of making major contribution to NE [Near East] peace and thereby to world peace." Conversely, rejection of what Lovett called a "reasonable settlement . . . would prolong present disturbed conditions" in the region and "would undoubtedly have further detrimental effect on [the] well-being" of its peoples and on the "stability and security of the whole NE [Near East]."[27] In other words, should Israel reject Bernadotte's proposals, the United States was, as of September 1948, preparing to accuse it of rejecting a "reasonable settlement," and therefore of bearing responsibility for undermining stability and security in the Middle East and threatening "world peace."

On October 4 James McDonald, Truman's recently appointed special representative, wrote from Tel Aviv to inform Truman and Marshall of the views of "a well-informed and influential Israeli official" about Bernadotte's proposal to give the Negev to Transjordan and why it would not achieve its stated purpose. The state of Israel was "deeply grateful for US support" and was "oriented toward the West politically

---

[25] See "The Acting Secretary of State to Certain Diplomatic and Consular Offices," Washington (September 21, 1948), 1416: https://history.state.gov/historicaldocuments/frus1948v05p2/d610. Also see Sam Pope Brewer, "U.S. Gives Support: Secretary of State for Mediator's Report as a Basis for Peace," *New York Times*, September 22, 1948, 1–2.

[26] "Marshall's Statement," in Brewer, "U.S. Gives Support," 1.

[27] "The Acting Secretary of State [Robert Lovett] to Certain Diplomatic and Consular Offices," Washington (September 22, 1948), in *Foreign Relations of the United States* (hereafter *FRUS*), *The Near East, South Asia, and Africa, 1948*, vol. 5, part 2, 1418: https://history.state.gov/historicaldocuments/frus1948v05p2/d613.

and culturally."[28] The Arab states, by contrast, were "weak, vacillating, and of dubious friendship toward the West and the US, as evidenced in World War II," and they had already been offended by US support of the November 29 Partition Resolution. "What has been done cannot now be undone," McDonald cautioned. US support of the British proposal to give the Negev to Transjordan "would not endear the other Arab states to the US" and "would create a miniature State of Israel, which would inevitably become embittered toward the US. By forcing transfer of the Negev, the US would thus gain no further friends in the Middle East and lose one friend." Further, if the British were able to force the "gift" of the "Negev to Transjordan to secure air bases" in the region for use in the event of an "East-West clash," it would "do so at the cost of creating an embittered and hostile State of Israel directly adjacent. This doesn't make much sense."[29]

According to McDonald, American and British support of the Bernadotte Plan had "virtually destroyed any hope of Transjordan" negotiating with Israel because its ruler, King Abdullah, "will hardly be disposed [to] settle for less than the proposals in the Bernadotte report. The Jews once again see themselves in [the] hopeless position of having their minimum position being considered maximum and being whittled down from minimum." McDonald concluded that while the Bernadotte Plan "might serve British strategic interest," it "sows dangerous seeds of bitterness" in Israel.[30]

On October 13 Lovett replied to McDonald after discussing his note with Marshall and President Truman. "Every thoughtful Israeli" knew the "disadvantages" of not adopting a stand on the side of the Western democracies. The USA had given "ample evidence [of] its support of Israel," but at the same time the "importance to [the] West of friendship of [the] Arabs as majority inhabitants of strategic ME is obvious."[31] Lovett reiterated American support for the Bernadotte conclusions as a "generally fair basis for settlement." They offered a "just common denominator upon which to found mutual accommodation."[32]

I. F. Stone took issue with American support for the Bernadotte Plan. In his piece "Secretary Marshall's Blunder," published in the October 18

[28] "The Special Representative of the United States in Israel [McDonald] to the Secretary of State," Tel Aviv (October 4, 1948), 501.BB Palestine/10–448, *FRUS*, 1948, vol. 5, part 2, 1451: https://history.state.gov/historicaldocuments/frus1948v05p2/d643.

[29] Ibid.   [30] Ibid.

[31] "The Acting Secretary of State [Lovett] to the Special Representative of the United States in Israel [McDonald]," Washington (October 13, 1948), 501.BB Palestine/10–448, *FRUS*, vol. 5, part 2, 1473: https://history.state.gov/historicaldocuments/frus1948 v05p2/d660.

[32] Ibid., 1474.

issue of *The New Republic*,[33] Stone called it part of "the rear-guard action fought by the [British] Foreign Office and the State Department against partition." The mediation proposal "promised a means of revising the partition plan without the necessity of a vote formally revoking the November 29 decision." Marshall and his aides hoped to use the mediation resolution adopted in May by the UN Security Council "to reduce Israel in size and sovereignty." It sidestepped the need to enforce the UN's endorsement of partition. "To mediate between Jews who accepted the November 29 decision and Arabs who were still fighting, it was necessary to seek some way of placating the latter at the expense of the former." In sponsoring the mediation resolution, the United States and Britain were, in effect, rewarding Arab defiance of the United Nations.[34]

Stone argued that the result was an effort to whittle down the Jewish state with proposals "so drastic as to constitute another partition of Palestine." He wrote that Bernadotte's transfer of the Negev to Transjordan would leave Israel with 2,200 square miles while increasing Transjordan to 42,500 square miles. Cannily, Stone pointed out that while the proposals were put forth as an effort to appease Arab anger over partition, the primary beneficiary was Britain. The expansion of Transjordan, "the only Arab state securely under British domination," accomplished that goal. So did the plan to give "the Anglo-American oil companies undisturbed and unregulated use of their huge refineries under a special regime in Haifa," and to detach the Negev from the Jewish state as it was "long wanted by the British as a military base."[35] Separating the Negev from Israel also raised a serious military issue. "The Jews hold the Negev. They will not give it up. The Arabs have shown that they cannot take it from them. Will the State Department, which prevented the mobilization of an international force to implement the November 29 decision against Arab opposition, now propose to raise an army to fight the Jews?"[36]

Stone captured the grim consequences of the State Department's diplomatic maneuvers at the UN. If pursued to their logical endpoint, they would lead to raising a UN army to force Israel to give the Negev to the Arabs after it had been promised to the Jews in the UN Partition Resolution, and after the Israelis had defeated the Arab states' efforts to destroy the state of Israel. Stone's realism, evident in his willingness to think through the consequences of policy, however unfair, was again in evidence. He saw that the logical outcome of American policy could lead to the UN and the United States going to war with Israel, only three years

---

[33] I. F. Stone, "Secretary Marshall's Blunder," *The New Republic*, October 18, 1948, 18–19.
[34] Ibid., 18.   [35] Ibid.   [36] Ibid., 19.

after the end of World War II and the Holocaust. Marshall and Lovett did not appear to understand that, absurd and immoral as it would be, such an American war with Israel was a possible result of the State Department's insistence that Israel accept the recommendations of the Bernadotte Plan.

The Cold War, Again

As noted previously, when Israel could not get the weapons, especially heavy weapons, it needed from the Western democracies, it turned to communist Czechoslovakia for assistance. To those in the State Department, Pentagon, and CIA who had focused on the alleged Zionist-Soviet connection, the Israeli dealings with Czechoslovakia confirmed their views. In a memo of June 14, 1948 to CIA director Roscoe Hillenkoetter, FBI director J. Edgar Hoover wrote that an "informant of unknown reliability" had said that persons returning from Palestine to the USA reported that Israel had asked for military aid "from Russia" and was expecting "20 bombers to be delivered by that country." According to these travelers, "an unspecified number of Russian soldiers are now in Italy, awaiting transportation to Israel. It was [their] consensus ... that Israel must go communist to exist." Although Hoover noted that the information came from someone the informant "considers to be a communist sympathizer," he also forwarded his memo to the directors of intelligence of the Air Force and of the Army General Staff, and to the chief of naval intelligence.[37]

The US government learned about Israel's assistance from Czechoslovakia from diplomatic reporting in Europe as well as through investigations of Zionist supporters in the United States. The records of both the US Army General Staff Intelligence Division and the FBI document investigations into the recruitment of reserve US army officers for service in the Israeli armed forces.[38] On October 22, 1948 FBI agent Francis D. O'Brien of the New York office, in a report covering the period of May 25 to September 30, summarized the results of extensive FBI investigations into efforts to recruit Americans to enter

---

[37] J. Edgar Hoover, Director, Federal Bureau of Investigation to Director, Central Intelligence Agency, Washington (June 14, 1948), "Palestine Situation Internal Security-X," NACP RG 319, Army-Intelligence Project Decimal File 1946–1948, Palestine, Box 260.

[38] Rudolf J. Perkins, 118th CIC Detachment, Washington (April 23, 1948), GSGID 201, "Recruiting of Reserve Officers for Haganah Forces by Unknown Persons in the Department of the Army"; and Leman G. White, Major, GSC, Washington (May 20, 1948), GSGID 918.3 and GSGID 912.3 (May 24, 1948), NACP RG 319, Army-Intelligence Project Decimal File 1946–1948, Palestine, Box 260.

the armed forces of Israel.[39] That investigation led to information about the Czech connection.

On October 29 O'Brien submitted a twelve-page, single-spaced report about Jewish veteran US Air Force pilots who had been flying for the Israeli Air Force since June 1948. They had received flight training in Czechoslovakia "in the new modified ME-109 (Messerschmidt) [a revised German World War II fighter plane] which Palestine government [i.e. Israel] was purchasing from the Czechs at $60,000 per plane." O'Brien's informant, who had returned from flying for the Israeli Air Force, reported that C-46 and C-47 cargo planes were being used to shuttle spare parts, engines, ammunition, bombs, and other war material from Czechoslovakia to Tel Aviv. The informant had flown the Messerschmidt 109 fighters "on numerous missions, some combat, other reconnaissance."

The informant offered the following account of the activities of eleven former US Air Force pilots in Israel in June–July 1948:[40] Three B-17 Flying Fortresses, C-46s, and Halifax heavy bombers were operating from bases at Sofia, Bulgaria and Prague, Czechoslovakia. The heavy bombing missions carried out on Egypt and other Arab countries were "initiated at Sofia and Prague and all servicing on these aircraft is completed at depots located on these bases." The planes were "refueled in Israel and returned to Sofia" to protect them from Arab armed forces. The pilots and crews were "former American Air Force fliers of the Jewish faith." The planes had been delivered "by ferry pilots flying the southern route touching South America and North America, Rome, Italy and Prague." Legal clearances and visas "pursuant to the regulations of the Civil Aeronautics Administration" had been arranged by a "former Army Air Force colonel with the Air Transport Command at Homestead, Florida."[41]

O'Brien's report listed eleven names of the pilots, their home addresses, and home phone numbers.[42] He then added the following:

Confidential Informant T-1 stated that it is his, as well as other Jewish people's considered opinion, that these Americans, fighting for the cause of Israel, are loyal

---

[39] Francis D. O'Brien, Federal Bureau of Investigation, New York (October 22, 1948), "Palestine Situation, Recruiting Program, Registration Act, Neutrality Act," NACP RG 319, Army-Intelligence Project Decimal File 1946–1948, Palestine, Box 260.

[40] Francis D. O'Brien, FBI New York, New York (October 29, 1948), 97–116, "Palestine Situation Recruiting Program, Registration Act, Neutrality Act," 6, NACP RG 319, Army-Intelligence Project Decimal File 1946–1948, Palestine, Box 260.

[41] Ibid.

[42] Ibid., 10–11. The names of eleven pilots were: Colonel Spurling, Eugene Cooper, Robert Fine, Cy Freedland, Arnold Illewite, Harold Livingston, (first name unknown) Firestone, Morris Way, Calvin Berle, Colman Goldstein, and Louis Lamand.

to the United States but feel that they must help their people in the uneven fight against the Arabs. At the time these men joined the Israeli Air Forces in the early summer of 1948, the Arabs were conducting an air war using British Mark 9s Spitfires and bombing Jewish cities at will. The Jewish Air Force consisted of nothing more than light aircraft and fighter planes. In a short time, these men, with the help of fast fighter aircraft and transport aircraft, turned the tide of war and gained control of the skies over Palestine. In the opinion of Informant T-1, at no time would they do anything which could be termed disloyal to the Government of the United States.[43]

The pilots were "former Marine, Army, or Navy pilots of the Jewish faith ... Approximately eighty-five per cent" held the Distinguished Flying Cross and Air Medals. They were "experienced war pilots" and received "no pay for the service they perform." They were "presently operating an airline carrying supplies between Prague and Tel Aviv and also comprise the pursuit squadron of ME 109s operating from Aguar Airport in Israel."[44] O'Brien's report confirmed information arriving at the Pentagon from Air Force and Army intelligence in Europe regarding the Czech weapons deliveries and participation of American veterans in the operation.

In the November 8, 1948 issue of *The New Republic*, Lawrence Lader (1919–2006), a World War II veteran and journalist who later became a leader in the movement for abortion rights and was one of the founders of the National Abortion Rights Action League (NARAL), published "From Junk Heap to Air Might," an extensive report on the Israeli Air Force, "still the most closely guarded secret of the war in Palestine."[45] Israel needed new planes and armaments "to defend itself in the present Negev fighting." They would not come from Britain

nor from the United States, which has refused to lift its embargo. Israel, therefore, will be forced to turn to the East, to Czechoslovakia and Russia. This is not a policy of choice. Time and again, Foreign Minister Moshe Shertok has stated that Israel wants the equal friendship of both the East and West. But if only the East will give her help, then she must turn to the East for survival.[46]

---

[43] Ibid., 11–12. Additional names and details from investigations conducted in July and September 1948 about American Jewish pilots flying for the Israeli Air Force are in FBI reports that arrived in July and September 1948: NACP RG 319, Army-Intelligence Project Decimal File 1946–1948, Palestine, Box 260.

[44] Ibid.

[45] Lawrence Lader, "From Junk Heap to Air Might," *The New Republic*, November 8, 1948, 10–14. On Lader see Douglas Martin, "Lawrence Lader, Champion of Abortion Rights is Dead at 86," *New York Times*, May 6, 2006: www.nytimes.com/2006/05/10/nyregion/10lader.html; and Patricia Sullivan, "Laurence Lader, 86," *Washington Post*, May 11, 2006: www.washingtonpost.com/archive/local/2006/05/11/lawrence-lader-86/54a4cff0-d6b3-4b7c-9d65-5fa3a8477955/

[46] Ibid., 14.

The State Department had demanded that Czechoslovakia close the airfield outside Prague from which Israeli pilots were flying in arms and supplies, but the Czechs refused. "This would have cut off Israel's lifeline. The effect would have been catastrophic" for Israel, Lader wrote. The contrast between Czech support for Israel and American efforts to cut it off "did not win friends for America in her ideological struggle against Eastern Europe."[47] Lader, like Wagner and Celler before, made a liberal's case against the State Department's policy in the Middle East; but it was to no avail. The nuance and complexity encompassed by the center-left in the policy of containment in Western Europe was absent in the Marshall-era's State Department's policy toward Israel.

The amount of weaponry, including heavy weapons, that Israel received from Czechoslovakia was substantial. In his 1974 work *The Forgotten Friendship*, still the standard work on the Soviet bloc and Israel during the war, historian Arnold Krammer concluded that Czechoslovakia's government had supplied the following arms to Israel in 1948:

57,000,000 rounds of 7.92 mm. ammunition
1,500,000 rounds of 9 mm. ammunition
1,000,000 rounds of anti-tank ammunition
24,500 P-19 Mauser rifles
10,000 bayonets for the P-19 rifles
5,015 (light) ZB-34 machineguns
880 (heavy) ZB-37 machine guns
250 9 mm. Zbrojovka pistols
12 16-ton tanks with ammunition
20 9.5-ton tanks with ammunition
25 Avia Messerschmidt 109 (s-199) fighter planes
59 Spitfire IX fighter planes
4,184 2 Kg. bombs
2,988 10 Kg. bombs
146 20 Kg. bombs
2,614 70 Kb. Bombs.[48]

In 2017 Haggai Frank, Zdeněk Klíma, and Yossi Goldstein, drawing on recent scholarship and the Haganah archives, examined the impact of Israel's arms purchases from Czechoslovakia on the war of 1948.[49] Israel purchased $28 million worth of weapons (about $302 million in 2021

---

[47] Ibid.

[48] Arnold Krammer, *The Forgotten Friendship: Israel and the Soviet Bloc, 1947–53* (Urbana: University of Illinois Press, 1974), 105–106.

[49] Haggai Frank, Zdeněk Klíma, and Yossi Goldstein, "The First Weapons Procurement behind the Iron Curtain: The Decisive Impact on the War of Independence," *Israel Studies* 22, no. 3 (Fall 2017): 125–152.

dollars) from Czechoslovakia, thus contributing significantly to that country's much-needed foreign currency reserves. The authors report that in addition to the weapons, Czechoslovakia trained "approximately 80 pilots and approximately 70 ground personnel for the new Israeli Air Force; some 30 tank soldiers, 24 paratroop commandos; and a force of approximately 1,330 soldiers, NCOs and officers for setting up a combined brigade group of local Jews that were meant to be sent to fight in the War of Independence."[50]

In 1968 then-former prime minister Ben-Gurion, in an interview in *Haaretz*, told Ze'ev Schiff, one of Israel's leading military affairs journalists, that the arms deliveries from Czechoslovakia in 1948 "saved the country. I have no doubt about that. The Czech arms deal was the biggest help we had then, it saved us and without it I very much doubt whether we could have survived the first month" of the war of 1948.[51] He made similar remarks at the end of a gathering of the protagonists of the Czech-Israeli arms deal. On Israel's Voice of Israel broadcast, he said: "The Czech weapons truly saved the state of Israel ... Without these weapons, we would not have remained alive."[52]

Robert Lovett on the Mufti's "Reprehensible Wartime Activities"

In October Lovett, in a classified cable to American diplomats in all Arab capitals, London, Paris, and Tel Aviv, acknowledged what the American liberal critics and Zionists in general had been saying publicly since 1945: a Palestine governed by Haj Amin al-Husseini would be a disaster. Lovett did not express regret either for the State Department's refusal to indict Husseini for war crimes in 1945 and 1946 or for the Department's willingness to give the Husseini-led AHC the right to represent the Palestine Arabs at the United Nations. Lovett refrained from mentioning that in December 1947 the United States did not blame Husseini, the Muslim Brotherhood, or the AHC for beginning the war with the Jews in Palestine in 1947, or that in numerous UN meetings in 1947 and 1948 the United States failed to put the AHC on the defensive by publishing its abundant documentation of Husseini's collaboration with the Nazis.

---

[50] Ibid., 146.
[51] Cited in Uri Bialer, "The Czech-Israeli arms deal revisited," *Journal of Strategic Studies* 8, no. 3 (1985): 307–315, at 313. Originally in Ze'ev Schiff, "Stalin ora lesapek neshek le'yisrael," *Haaretz*, May 3, 1968 (Hebrew). Also see Uri Bialer, "The War of Independence," in his *Israeli Foreign Policy*, 56–75.
[52] Frank et al., "The First Weapons Procurement," 146.

Yet now, belatedly, Lovett did acknowledge that establishment of an Arab government led by Husseini and the AHC would be "prejudicial" to a "successful solution" of "the Palestine problem" and to the "best interests" of the Arab states and the "Arab inhabitants of Palestine."[53] Apparently there were plans in place, presumably by the AHC, to set up such a government "without prior consultation [with the] wishes [of] Arab Palestinians." It "also appears [to be] dominated by [the] Mufti, an adventurer, whose reprehensible wartime activities in association with our enemies cannot be forgotten or forgiven by US." By claiming to speak for all Palestinians, a Mufti-led government "affords ready pretext to Jewish revisionists [to] make similar claims for right of PGI [the provisional government of Israel] [to] control all [of] Palestine." If asked about the US attitude on the "future of Arab Palestine, you should recall to questioners that US Govt has announced its support of all Bernadotte conclusions."[54]

The problem with a Husseini-led government was not primarily that it would give a "pretext to Jewish revisionists" to make claims to all of Palestine, as if these revisionists, many of whom had fought with the Allies against the Nazis, were as objectionable as Husseini. It was rather that a Mufti-led government, as the State Department's critics had been pointing out since late 1945, would be led by a former collaborator with the Nazis who had started the war of 1947–8 because he remained inflamed by unreconstructed hatred of Jews, Judaism, and thus Zionism.[55]

Lovett's was the only reference to Husseini's "reprehensible wartime activities" that I have come across from high-ranking officials in the thousands of pages of the State Department's "Palestine File." I have found nothing similar in either the public or classified statements of Secretary of State Marshall, director of the Policy Planning Staff George Kennan, members of the Joint Chiefs of Staff led by Admiral William Leahy, Secretary of Defense James Forrestal, or CIA director Roscoe Hillenkoetter. None of these officials suggested that Husseini's hatreds and the antisemitism fanned by the Muslim Brotherhood and the AHC were a primary cause of Arab rejectionism and the war of 1947–8. The State Department's refusal to listen and learn from its liberal critics in American public life made it possible for this unreconstructed antisemite

---

[53] "The Acting Secretary [Lovett] to Certain Diplomatic Offices," Washington (October 2, 1948), 501.BB Palestine/10–248, *FRUS*, vol. 5, part 2, 1448: https://history.state.gov/historicaldocuments/frus1948v05p2/d640.

[54] Ibid.

[55] See Matthias Küntzel, *Nazis und der Nahe Osten: Wie der Islamische Antisemitismus Entstand* (Berlin and Leipzig: Hentrich & Hentrich, 2019).

and Nazi collaborator to return to political life in Palestine and then lead the Palestine Arabs into a disastrous war against the Jews and against the United Nations Partition Resolution. When Lovett's brief and long over-due recognition of these facts finally arrived, he combined it, reflecting the consensus in the State Department leadership, with support for the Bernadotte Plan, which, as we have seen, sought to use the United Nations to deprive Israel of the territory promised to it by the United Nations in the Partition Resolution. The extent of the strategic blunder of 1945–6, when the United States, Britain, and France – and, for that matter, the Soviet Union as well – refused to put Husseini on trial for war crimes and crimes against humanity, was now painfully apparent.

October Battles in the Negev and Debates at the UN

The UN's Second Truce in the war had left the Egyptian army in the Negev desert, 20 miles (32 kilometers) south of Tel Aviv. Its presence lent weight to the Bernadotte Report's proposal to deprive Israel of the Negev. On October 6 the Israeli cabinet decided to launch Operation Yoav to destroy the Egyptian expeditionary army or drive it out of the Negev. On October 15 the Israeli Defense Forces launched a combined air and ground assault.[56] Ben-Gurion called it "the gravest [that is, most import-ant] since we decided to establish the state."[57] The next day the Security Council called for a ceasefire, but Israel rejected it as it pursued an offensive in the Negev.[58] On October 18 Sydney Gruson, the *New York Times* correspondent in Tel Aviv, reported that Israel had been victorious in battles with the Egyptian army in the Negev, had linked the Negev to the new state, and had cut Egyptian lines in many places. Gruson wrote that "the Israeli forces staged a seventy-two-hour miniature blitzkrieg to open the way to the Negeb ... The battle proved the superiority, at least on this front, of the infant Israel Air Force. Its bombers flew practically unhindered to their targets three nights in succession and its fighters maintained a round-the-clock air patrol that proved impenetrable."[59] On October 21 the Israelis captured the town of Beersheba from the Egyptian army.[60]

---

[56] Morris, *1948*, 320–330.   [57] Ibid., 322.

[58] Sydney Gruson, "Israel Turns Down Cease Fire of U.N.; Raids Negeb Town," *New York Times*, October 16, 1948, 1 and 26.

[59] Sydney Gruson, "Israel Victorious in Negeb Battles, Asks Direct Talks," *New York Times*, October 19, 1948, 1 and 5. In some reporting of the time the Negev is spelled "Negeb." I have left the original spelling when quoting.

[60] Sydney Gruson, "Israelis Capture Beersheba, Sever Egypt Supply Line," *New York Times*, October 22, 1948, 1 and 6.

On October 22, following the Israeli victory in the Negev, Israel agreed to a UN ceasefire with Egypt that ended what Gruson called "the war's biggest campaign."[61] On October 28 Britain and China introduced a resolution to the UN Security Council to impose sanctions against either party in Palestine that continued to defy its orders to return to the positions occupied on October 14 – that is, before Israel's victories over the Egyptians in the Negev. Should either party not agree, the draft called for implementation of the UN Charter's Article 41, which allowed the Security Council to use any measure short of armed force including "complete or partial interruption of economic relations, means of communication, and the severing of diplomatic relations" against an offending party, which in this instance referred to Israel.[62] It was an effort to use UN machinery to deprive Israel of a battlefield victory that had brought the promised Negev under its control.

At this point, events in the American presidential election campaign of 1948 forced the State Department into a retreat from its support for the Bernadotte Plan. On October 23 Governor Thomas Dewey, the Republican candidate for president, criticized the Truman administration, or at least the State Department, for supporting the measure.[63] As had been the case since Robert Taft's early support for the Zionists, the Republicans undermined the argument that the Zionist project was on the "wrong" side of the communist issue in the emerging Cold War. The American electoral competition pushed each party to demonstrate its support for the new state of Israel. The following day, determined not to be outflanked by Dewey, Truman reiterated his support for the Democratic Party's platform, which approved Israel's claims to "the boundaries set forth" in the UN resolution of November 29, 1947, to be revised "only if fully acceptable to the State of Israel." The party supported Israel's admission to the United Nations, called for "the revision of the arms embargo to accord the State of Israel the right of self-defense," and offered de jure recognition when a permanent government was in place in Israel.[64] In other words, Truman rejected the Bernadotte Plan to deprive Israel of the Negev, thus challenging not only Britain's

---

[61] Sydney Gruson, "Cease-Fire in the Negeb Put in Force by Israel and Egypt," *New York Times*, October 23, 1948, 1 and 4.

[62] Sam Pope Brewer (Paris), "Security Council Sanctions Urged if Its Palestine Orders are Defied," *New York Times*, October 29, 1948, 1 and 14.

[63] "The Acting Secretary of State to the Secretary of State, at Paris," Washington (October 23, 1948), 501.BB Palestine/10–2348, *FRUS*, vol. 5, part 2, 1508: https://history.state.gov/historicaldocuments/frusv05p2/d694.

[64] "The Acting Secretary to the Secretary of State in Paris," Washington (October 24, 1948), 501.BB Palestine/10–2448, *FRUS*, vol. 5, part 2, 1513: https://history.state.gov/historicaldocuments/frusv05p2/d694.

position but, yet again, that of his own State Department. Truman's statement was a defeat for State Department efforts to pressure Israel to accept the Bernadotte Plan recommendations.

Marshall, in a memo to Lovett of October 25, made clear that, even in the face of Israel's military victory in the previous ten days, he was not willing to give up on the Bernadotte Plan's proposal to separate the Negev from Israel. He still hoped to determine boundaries as a result of decisions of a UN conciliation commission, not as the outcome of the war itself.[65] If Israel held to an "extreme position" of insisting on the Negev, that would "completely destroy the Bernadotte plan." If the US told the Egyptians that the US favored giving the northern Negev to Israel, that "would cause incalculable harm [to] our relations [with] Egypt and other Arab states" and harden their opposition to the Bernadotte plan.[66]

Marshall also opposed allotting the northern Negev to Israel because doing so would stiffen Israel's intention to "retain positions won during last week's military operations in defiance [of] SC [Security Council] truce and contrary to [the] clear intent [of] SC action" of October 19 that the parties "should withdraw to previous military positions." Allowing Israel to hold on to its battlefield gains in the Negev would strengthen the Arabs' belief that the United States delayed consideration of the Bernadotte Plan "to permit time for Israelis [to] achieve military conquest [of] northern Negev," something that would damage the prestige of the Security Council and the United States.[67] Lovett agreed. The Department had "no desire to break" with Britain over the Palestine issue. It was "keenly aware" that the "principal hope" of "achieving some UN arrangement on Palestine lay [in] U.S. solidarity with Britain. The Bernadotte Plan offered a "broad basis for working out permanent solution."[68] In other words, sustaining Britain's place in the region – what Marshall had called the "cornerstone" of American policy – remained firmly in place.

On October 29 Truman delivered a presidential campaign speech to a crowd of 15,000 at Madison Square Garden in New York City. With the election looming, he reaffirmed the Democrats' election platform plank on Israel and recommended that the boundaries of the state be those in the Partition Plan of November 1947. As Warren Moscow wrote in the

---

[65] "The Secretary of State [Marshall] to the Acting Secretary of State [Lovett]," Paris (October 25, 1948), *FRUS*, vol. 5, part 2, 1515: https://history.state.gov/historicaldocuments/frusv05p2/d701.

[66] Ibid.   [67] Ibid.

[68] "The Acting Secretary of State [Lovett] to the United States Delegation in Paris," Washington (October 27, 1948), 501.BB Palestine/10–2548, *FRUS*, vol. 5, part 2: https://history.state.gov/historicaldocuments/frusv05p2/d706.

lead article on the *New York Times*'s front page, "a split between the President and the Secretary on the Bernadotte plan seemed indicated by the speech last night."[69] Speaking to members of the Liberal Party, Truman extolled Franklin Roosevelt, the New Deal, and American liberalism, and denounced Republican "reaction." It was his "responsibility to see that our policy in Israel fits in with our foreign policy throughout the world." He desired "to help build in Palestine a strong, prosperous, free and independent democratic state. It must be large enough, free enough and strong enough to make its people self-supporting and secure."[70]

The president recalled that in 1945 he had called for "the immediate opening of Palestine to immigration to the extent of at least 100,000 persons ... The United States under my administration led the way in November 1947 and was responsible for the resolution in the United Nations setting up Israel, not only as a homeland, but as a free and independent political state." The United States "was the first to give full and complete recognition to the new state of Israel in April 1948, and recognition to its provisional government." Truman claimed that he had "never changed" his "position on Palestine or Israel," and that he stood by the Democratic Party platform of 1944 and that of 1948, which had gone "a little further." The United States now needed "to help the people of Israel." They had proved themselves to be "hardy pioneers" and had "created out of a barren desert a modern and efficient state with the highest standards of western civilization. They've demonstrated that Israel deserves to take its place in the family of nations. That's our objective." It was

the spirit in which all liberals face the issues of this campaign. We are concerned with justice, and we are deeply concerned with human rights – here in America as well as in the rest of the world. I'm happy to say to you tonight that the spirit of liberalism is going to triumph at the polls on November the second, just as sure as you're sitting in this hall.[71]

The spirit of liberalism was at one with firm support for the new state of Israel. In New York Truman asserted, as he had on May 14, that in effect, he, not the State Department or the Pentagon, was determining American foreign policy toward Israel.

The following day the lead headline in the *New York Times* read: "Truman in Strongest Pleas for Israel Backs Boundaries in First U.N.

---

[69] Warren Moscow, "Truman in Strongest Plea for Israel Backs Boundaries in First U.N. Plan; Crowds in City Welcome him," *New York Times*, October 29, 1948, 1–3. The paper printed the full text of the speech as well. See "The Text of Truman's Address at Madison Square Garden," *New York Times*, October 29, 1948, 4.
[70] "The Text of Truman's Address."   [71] Ibid.

Plan; Crowds in City Welcome Him."[72] Yet a headline on the other side of the front page gave evidence of the overlap between the early years of the Cold War and the establishment of Israel and the last months of the Arab-Israeli war: "Stalin Asserts West Aims at 'Unleashing a New War'; Charges Promptly Denied."[73] For the leaders in the State Department and Pentagon, the *Times* front page captured the essence of the issue: the Soviet Union, the same government that was accusing the West of threatening a new war, had blockaded the city of Berlin, and supported the coup in Prague, was leading the diplomatic fight in the UN in support of Israel, while the communist regime in Czechoslovakia was breaking the UN arms embargo and sending arms to Israel. From the perspective of some of the architects of containment and defense planners in the Pentagon, it appeared as if the state of Israel was, if not subjectively, then objectively, serving the interests of the communist project as well.

The day after his Madison Square Garden stemwinder, Truman ordered the US delegation at the United Nations to withdraw support from a joint UK–Chinese resolution supporting sanctions against either party in Palestine that ignored the Security Council order for restoration of the Negev truce line. The resolution, if passed, would have imposed sanctions on Israel for refusing to give up the territory in the Negev that its armed forces had just acquired as a result of the largest operation of the war. Following Truman's decision, the United States now joined the Soviet Union and France in opposing Britain's efforts to pressure Israel to give up the newly won positions in the Negev.[74] That week Syria had opened a front in the Galilee in the north. On October 31 the Israeli government claimed complete victory there as well.[75]

The Cold War and the Arab-Israeli War at the UN

Truman was reelected on November 2, but the State Department officials at the UN persisted in their efforts to keep the Bernadotte Plan alive. The arguments took place in the UN's First Committee, which dealt with military and security issues when it met from October 15 to 20, and from

---

[72] Moscow, "Truman in Strongest Plea for Israel."

[73] "Stalin Asserts West Aims at 'Unleashing a New War'; Charges Promptly Denied," *New York Times*, October 30, 1948, 1 and 12.

[74] Sam Pope Brewer, "U.S. Switches on Palestine; Won't Consider Sanctions; Change is Laid to Truman," *New York Times*, October 30, 1948, 1 and 2.

[75] Sydney Gruson, "Israel Claims Rout of Arabs in North: Peace Talks Seen," *New York Times*, November 1, 1948, 1 and 2.

November 15 to December 4.[76] The records of these meetings display the by-then familiar pattern of Soviet bloc/communist support for Israel in – at times contentious – exchanges with Britain and the United States. In their arguments and their votes the Soviet Union, Poland, and Czechoslovakia repeatedly supported Israel's factual assertions and policy recommendations while the UK and the USA supported all or part of the Bernadotte Plan.

On November 22 Semyon K. Tsarapkin (1905/6–84), the Soviet representative, reaffirmed support for the Partition Resolution of November 29, 1947 and denounced the British and American resolutions based on the Bernadotte Report as contrary to its letter and spirit. They were pursuing a policy dictated by British strategic interests and American "oil monopolies," he said.[77] Oskar Lange, Poland's UN ambassador, seconded Tsarapkin's resolution. He criticized the United States for its reversals of policy on Palestine and Israel, blaming it for the war in Palestine and for a policy designed to preserve the British Empire and expand a new American empire. He also condemned the Bernadotte Report as contrary to the General Assembly's partition decision.[78]

The *New York Times* reported that "many delegates believe that the British want airfields contiguous to the Suez Canal to make up for their diminished influence in Egypt."[79] Tsarapkin stressed that the Soviet Union had "stood fast" in support of the Partition Plan and that Britain and the United States were supporting the Bernadotte recommendations "as a means of preventing the partition resolution from being carried out."[80] On November 25 he introduced a resolution aimed at the Arab states recommending the "immediate removal from Palestine of all foreign troops and foreign military personnel."[81] The next day Poland submitted a draft resolution affirming the resolution on November 29, 1947, not the Bernadotte Plan, as the basis for a final settlement. The British and Americans attempted to keep the Bernadotte Plan, or a version of it, as the basis for a peace agreement, but Abba Eban, Israel's representative, and Tsarapkin, for the Soviet Union, objected to its continued relevance.[82]

[76] "Discussion in the First Committee: III. Political and Security Questions. A. The Palestine Question," *Yearbook of the United Nations, 1948–49* (New York: United Nations, 1950), 167.

[77] Thomas J. Hamilton (Paris), "Soviet Asks U.N. Set Peace in Palestine on Partition Plan," *New York Times*, November 23, 1948, 1 and 10.

[78] Ibid., 1.

[79] Thomas J. Hamilton, "British Drop Bernadotte Aim, Back Our Palestine Proposals," *New York Times*, December 1, 1948, 1 and 6.

[80] "Discussion in the First Committee," 167.   [81] Ibid., 168.

[82] Hamilton, "British Drop Bernadotte Aim," 6.

Eban did not refrain from criticizing British and US policies. On November 30 he protested that the United States amendments and the British resolution both placed equal emphasis on the Partition Resolution and the Bernadotte Plan. He insisted that the UN Political Committee should make the Partition Resolution "the basis and starting point" of a permanent settlement.[83] For this, he received support from the Soviet Union, along with Poland, the Byelorussian SSR, Czechoslovakia, the Ukrainian SSR, and Yugoslavia. Tsarapkin argued that the Partition Resolution of November 1947 "was the only right and equitable solution" and was "in conformity with the interests of Arabs and Jews alike, both of whom had a right to self-determination."[84] Unfortunately, rather than carrying out that decision, Eban lamented, a majority of the General Assembly "had yielded to pressure from the United States and the United Kingdom and had created the position of Mediator." Bernadotte, rather than limiting himself to enforcing the truce and settlement by peaceful means, had gone beyond his authority to suggest what the final settlement should be. The Bernadotte Plan "would give control of Palestine to the United Kingdom, which dominated Transjordan."[85]

Eban called the UN Partition Resolution "a remarkable achievement" supported by both the USA and the USSR. Its "realism" was confirmed "when the State of Israel was established on territory roughly corresponding to that which had been assigned to it by the resolution." But the UN had been prevented from carrying out the resolution "by the fact that on the very day when the British Mandate in Palestine came to an end, Egypt, Transjordan, Syria and Lebanon had had recourse to armed force in Palestine."[86] According to Eban, the Soviet bloc representatives were correct in blaming the failure to implement the Partition Resolution on the decision of the Arab states to launch the invasion of Israel on May 15. As usual, the United States remained silent on this issue.

The Soviet bloc representatives also opposed substituting the Bernadotte Plan for the November 1947 resolution, extending the territory of Transjordan to include the Arab portion of Palestine (subsequently called the West Bank), and assigning the Negev to Transjordan. The United Nations *Yearbook* summarized the Soviet bloc view of the cause of the current war as follows:

On the question of the withdrawal of foreign troops, they [the USSR, Poland, et al.] asserted that the presence of foreign troops and military personnel which had invaded the country was responsible for the present disorders and sufferings of the population. Moreover, the presence of foreign troops constituted an obstacle to the re-establishment of peace, the objective of the General Assembly.

---

[83] Ibid.   [84] "Discussion in the First Committee," 167.   [85] Ibid.   [86] Ibid., 170–171.

Foreign intervention was clearly manifest on the Arab side, for there was a British general, Glubb Pasha, and British officers commanding Transjordan troops. These troops, as well as those of Egypt, Syria and Lebanon had invaded the territory earmarked for the Arab State of Palestine. This State had not been established, as provided for in the 1947 resolution. On the other hand, the State of Israel had been set up within the territorial limits established by the General Assembly resolution. The withdrawal of troops was a necessary condition for the establishment of peace and for any settlement of the Palestine question in accordance with the 1947 resolution.[87]

This account was essentially the same as that offered by Abba Eban and Moshe Shertok in their public statements in the summer and fall of 1948. Like them, the Soviet bloc placed emphasis on the Arab invasion and the need for the troops of the Arab states to be withdrawn as the first step toward direct negotiations with Israel.

The Soviet bloc position stood in stark contrast to the vague and more neutral language offered by the United States. The Soviet bloc representatives placed the blame for the war unequivocally on the Arab states and connected the establishment of Israel to a decision legitimized by the UN General Assembly. They opposed the British proposal to transfer the Negev "and an area set aside for the Arab state in Palestine to Transjordan, thus reestablishing indirect control for the United Kingdom over a large part of the area of Palestine."[88] Short of a denunciation of the AHC's past collaboration with the Nazis, the Soviet bloc position was about all Israel could have asked for. Nevertheless, on December 4, at its 228th meeting, the First Committee (also called the Political and Security Committee), by a vote of twenty-six to twenty-one, accepted the US-supported resolution establishing a Palestine conciliation commission.[89] The Soviet proposal calling for "withdrawal of all foreign troops and foreign military personnel from Palestine" was defeated by a vote of only seven in favor and thirty-three against, with eight abstentions. It would have applied to both Arab and British forces.[90] The Israelis and their Soviet bloc supporters lost these key votes in the First Committee.

The simultaneity of Soviet support for Israel and Soviet policy in Europe was again evident on the front pages of the *New York Times*. On October 24 it reported that "the Communist-led French coal strike had become an avowed revolt against the government."[91] On November 7

---

[87] Ibid.   [88] Ibid.

[89] Thomas J. Hamilton, "Palestine Conciliation Body is Voted by U.N. Committee," *New York Times*, December 5, 1948, 1 and 4.

[90] Thomas J. Hamilton, "U.N. Council Delays Action on Israel's Membership Bid," *New York Times*, December 2, 1948, 1 and 4.

[91] Lansing Warren, "French Strikers Increase Defiance; Ask Help Abroad," *New York Times*, October 24, 1948, 1 and 8.

General Lucius Clay, the US military governor in Berlin, expressed confidence that the US and British airlift to the Western sectors in Berlin could deliver 4,000 tons of supplies "without difficulty." Clay called the blockade of Berlin "part of a general Russian plan to instill fear in Western Europe and impede the progress of recovery." It had "done more to inculcate democracy in Berlin than anything we have been able to do in the last three and one-half years."[92] On November 8 the *Times* reported on page 1 that "De Gaulle Scores a Major Victory; French Reds Lose."[93] The same Soviet Union that was imposing a blockade on Berlin and supporting strikes in France was supporting the Israelis at the UN while Czechoslovakia was sending it weapons.

Marshall and the State Department did not give up the effort to sustain the Bernadotte Plan and use the UN to deprive Israel of its battlefield gains. On November 4 the United States supported a UN Security Council resolution that called on Egypt and Israel to withdraw troops to positions in the Negev desert held before the fighting broke out there on October 14 – that is, before Israel drove the Egyptian army out of the Negev. The United States had amended the resolution to delete the threat of sanctions, but, as the *Times*'s Sam Pope Brewer wrote, "Israel was the obvious target" of the resolution. An Israeli source told Brewer that the text as amended by the USA was "'a club to hold over us' if Israel did not accept the Bernadotte report."[94] On November 5 the Israelis rejected the resolution. The country's boundaries would be established either in battle or in direct negotiations with the Arabs but not by the UN Security Council. From Tel Aviv, Sydney Gruson reported that the Israelis believed that "the main result of the resolution ... would be to stiffen Arab resistance to direct negotiations."[95]

But Harry Truman's reelection had consequences. On November 8 in Paris the United States withdrew its support of the British–Chinese resolution which was intended, as the *Times* headline put it, "to punish Israel" by imposing sanctions if it refused to give up positions won in the recent fighting in the Negev "in violation of the truce."[96] Four days later Marshall held a press conference in Paris in which he described "recent

---

[92] Drew Middleton, "Clay is Confident on Winter Airlift," *New York Times*, November 7, 1948, 1 and 18.

[93] Lanning Warren, "De Gaulle Scores a Major Victory; French Reds Lose," *New York Times*, November 8, 1948, 1 and 7.

[94] Sam Pope Brewer, "U.N. Orders a Withdrawal in Negeb, Shelves Sanctions," *New York Times*, November 5, 1948, 1 and 10.

[95] Sydney Gruson, "Israeli Rejection of U.N. Order Seen; Egyptians Retreat," *New York Times*, November 6, 1948, 1 and 4.

[96] Sam Pope Brewer, "U.S. Said to Retract Support for Plan to Punish Israel," *New York Times*, November 9, 1948, 1 and 7.

statements by Soviet leaders as constituting a propaganda effort that he felt was very dangerous because everyone sincerely wanted peace."[97] He spoke of the success, especially in France and Italy, of the European Recovery Program (ERP), known by then as the Marshall Plan. At the same time, he said, the "efforts of the Soviet bloc to filibuster against the resolution" in the UN General Assembly's Political Committee, that is, against the British–Chinese resolution to impose sanctions on Israel, "constituted proof that it regarded the resolution as a very undesirable thing to have on the books of the United Nations."[98]

At the United Nations, the same Soviet Union that Marshall said was attempting to undermine the ERP, making false accusations about American threats to start a new war, and seeking to expand its influence in Europe was also opposing the US-supported truce resolution that urged Israel to return to the boundaries it had before its victories in the Negev. By combining his comments on Europe with others about Soviet policy at the United Nations, Marshall suggested in public what was clearly stated at the State Department in private: Soviet support for Israel was part of a new political offensive to expand influence in the postwar era both in Europe and in the Middle East. Correlation in time suggested a common causal connection.

War and Diplomacy in the Last Months of the 1948 War

On November 13 Ralph Bunche, in his capacity as the UN mediator, called on Israel to withdraw its forces in the Negev to positions they had held on October 14, before they had conquered the town of Beersheba. That area would be demilitarized and placed under Arab civilian administration.[99] The Israelis saw Bunche's statement as an effort to use the Bernadette proposals to deprive them of their battlefield victories and, again, of the territory allotted to them in the Partition Resolution.[100] Such proposals asked the Israelis to do what no other country would do, that is, to place its security in the hands of the UN, and of an Arab civilian administration in Beersheba, a town the Israelis had just fought to free from Egyptian control. Bunche's order only made sense if its goal was, as the Israelis believed, to deprive Israel of the Negev desert even after Israeli forces had driven the invading Egyptians out. Yet again, from Bunche,

---

[97] Thomas J. Hamilton (Paris), "Marshall Brands Soviet Peace Drive Propaganda Move," *New York Times*, November 13, 1948, 1 and 6.

[98] Ibid.

[99] Thomas J. Hamilton, "Israel and Egypt Get Bunche Order to Retire in Negeb," *New York Times*, November 14, 1948, 1 and 11.

[100] Ibid., 11.

not Bernadotte, the UN language of apparent impartiality and call for a truce from both sides was at odds with its consequences: reduction of the size of the Jewish state by almost 60 percent. While the Arab states protested that Bunche's order did not go far enough, as their goal was to eliminate the Jewish state entirely, they were fortunate that first Bernadotte and then Bunche, acting with instructions from the UN Security Council, were, in effect, attempting to rescue them from the consequences of the war they had launched with the invasions and offensives of May 15.

On November 16 the UN Security Council, by a vote of eight to one with abstentions by the Soviet Union and the Ukrainian SSR, adopted a resolution ordering an armistice throughout Palestine. In accord with the armistice order, Bunche again called on Israel to withdraw its forces from the Negev to the lines they held on October 14. Moshe Shertok had said Israel would fight rather than give up the Negev. The representatives of Syria, Lebanon, and Egypt at the UN meetings in Paris told the Security Council they were unwilling to negotiate directly with Israel because doing so "would signify the acceptance of Israel as an independent state."[101] Thomas Hamilton concluded his *Times* report by observing that the Security Council armistice order of November 16 made it possible for the UN Political and Security Committee to continue considering the Bernadotte Report, "which would modify the partition resolution of last year and assign all of the Negeb to the Arabs and the Galilee to Israel." He observed that the three Arab representatives, including Ahmad Shukairy of the Arab Higher Committee and later the first leader of the Palestine Liberation Organization, along with the representatives of Syria and Egypt, also rejected the Bernadotte Report because it rested, in part, "on partition and the existence of a Jewish state," both of which "were wholly unacceptable to the Arab world."[102]

On November 17 Sydney Gruson reported from Tel Aviv that peace talks had collapsed "under the impact of the Security Council's resolution ordering the Israeli Army out of the Negeb."[103] The Israeli representatives at the UN believed that the resolution had "again raised Arab hopes that the United Nations will order severe action against Israel if the order should be rejected." Hence the Israeli government in Tel Aviv offered a "chilly reception" to the UN armistice plan which was likely to continue "so long as the Negeb withdrawal is linked to it." Further, there was not

---

[101] Thomas J. Hamilton, "Palestine Armistice Ordered by the Security Council, 8–1," *New York Times*, November 17, 1948, 1 and 5.

[102] Ibid., 5.

[103] Sydney Gruson, "Israeli-Arab Talks on Peace Collapse; U.N. Move Blamed," *New York Times*, November 18, 1948, 1–4.

"any inclination to agree to disarmament during the existence of a state of war." Gruson quoted "the moderate newspaper Haaretz" as reflecting official reaction when it wrote that the "Army of Israel will yield no part of the state to international control or demilitarization ... We cannot forego our army so long as the threat of invasion remains."[104]

By late November the American position at the UN had descended into incoherence. On November 20 in Paris the US delegation announced that it would not seek to change Israel's borders without its consent, yet insisted that whatever gains Israel had made beyond those outlined in the Partition Resolution should be offset by giving up land elsewhere.[105] The incoherence of the US position was evident on November 21 and 23 in Paris as US representative Philip Jessup illogically asserted that the United States supported both the Partition Resolution of November 1947 and the Bernadotte Report as a basis for renewed efforts to reach a peaceful settlement.[106] UN members found the American position puzzling. The confusion was, of course, due to the battle that had been going on within the United States government for two years between the White House and the power ministries of diplomacy and war.

In December 1948 the UN General Assembly debated the Bernadotte Plan for the last time. Again, Israel's strongest support came from the Soviet Union, the Ukrainian SSR, Poland, and Czechoslovakia. One of the more troubling contributions to the debate came from Robert Schuman, the French foreign minister and one of the famous founding figures of the project of West European economic integration. His views departed significantly from the French voices of sympathy for the Jews examined in the previous chapter but echoed those of the French Foreign Ministry. France's position on Israel remained torn between sympathy in the Interior Ministry and distance from the Foreign Ministry as the latter considered both relations with the Arabs and the reservations of the Catholic Church. On December 11 Schuman referred to the "tragic conflict" between "native and immigrant," that is, the Arabs and the Jews in Palestine.

It was unthinkable that the horrors perpetrated during the war against the Jewish population in Europe should be repeated or should be reproduced in respect of the Arab population. Such a situation, which was a disgrace to mankind, must be brought to a close. That was all the more essential since those events were taking place in a land where, twenty centuries ago, a great message of peace and

---

[104] Ibid., 4.

[105] George Barrett, "U.S. Bars Frontier Changes without Israel's Consent; Insists Additions be Offset," *New York Times*, November 21, 1948, 1.

[106] Thomas J. Hamilton, "Jessup Gives Aims: Asks Bernadotte Plan and Partition Stand Be Use by U.N.," *New York Times*, November 23, 1948, 1 and 4.

brotherhood had first been propagated and where for the first time in the history of the world, charity and respect for humanity had been preached. It was essential that that land which had so many memories and which was holy ground not only for Christians, but for Jews and Mohammedans also, should cease to be the scene of strife and hatred.[107]

Schuman's statement, lost in the vast ocean of words produced by UN debates, was stunning on several levels. He was one of the first Western politicians, perhaps the first mainstream postwar political leader, to accuse the Jews of treating the Arabs the way the Nazis had treated the Jews, an accusation that the late historian of antisemitism Robert Wistrich called "Holocaust inversion."[108] One source of his willingness to hurl the accusation at the Jewish state lay in his view that ideas about "peace and brotherhood" and "charity and respect for humanity" were first articulated by Jesus "twenty centuries ago" and thus were presumably absent from the preexisting religion of Judaism. Schuman's assertion fitted very well into a longstanding Christian antagonism to Judaism.[109] That he would repeat these distortions about Judaism three years after the Holocaust revealed a paucity of reflection on Christianity's contribution to antisemitism. Now his indignation was devoted to stopping "the disgrace for mankind" which he alleged, in so many words, that the state of Israel was perpetrating. Schuman's revealing comments captured some cultural roots of the antipathy to the Zionist project.[110]

The communist delegations again rose to defend Israel and denounce efforts to weaken or replace the Partition Resolution of November 29, 1947. The Polish representative and director of the Polish Ministry of Foreign Affairs, Tadeusz Zebrowski, defended the Partition Resolution.[111] Its implementation had been obstructed by the "maneuvers and machinations" of Britain and the United States. Britain opposed the emergence of independent states as that would "lessen its imperialistic hold over the Middle East" and used one "device after another" to "support the faltering structure of the British Empire in the Middle

[107] Robert Schuman (France), Paris (December 11, 1948), 184th Plenary Meeting, UNGA, 3rd Session.
[108] See Robert Wistrich, "Antisemitism and Holocaust Inversion," in Anthony McElligott and Jeffrey Herf, eds., *Antisemitism before and since the Holocaust: Altered Contexts and Recent Perspectives* (London: Palgrave Macmillan, 2017), 37–50.
[109] From the large scholarship on Christian antagonism to and misunderstanding of Judaism see David Nirenberg, *Anti-Judaism: The Western Tradition* (New York: W. W. Norton, 2013).
[110] On Schuman's key role as French prime minister and foreign minister in French decision making see Frédérique Schillo, *La France et la création de l'état d'Israël, 18 février 1947–11 mai 1949* (Paris: Éditions Artcom, 1997).
[111] Tadeusz Zebrowski (Poland), Paris (December 11, 1948), 185th Plenary Meeting, UNGA, 3rd Session, 957–965.

East," while "American imperialistic designs were looking for new opportunities for exploitation." According to this representative, US policy "fluctuated between the aims of its military interests on the one hand, and the necessities of its domestic policies on the other." The UK and the USA were responsible for "undermining the General Assembly's decision and for the war, devastation and misery in Palestine." The Arabs needed to learn the painful lesson of relying on the "Great Powers," while Israel should learn same lesson, to "follow a close alliance with the democratic Powers," that is, with the Soviet bloc.[112]

Zebrowski accurately pointed to American and British efforts to undermine the Partition Resolution. "Twice in the course of the past year" the UK and USA had sought to use the General Assembly to reverse "its previous decisions." In spring 1948 they "tried to replace independence with Trusteeship" and now in fall 1948 were using the current session to "undo what had already been implemented." They attempted to replace the resolution of November 29, 1947 with the recommendations of the Bernadotte Plan, "which in itself was the object of their desires" and was unacceptable to the majority in the UN's First Committee in September and October.[113] The British offered proposals for a permanent international regime for Jerusalem "as though the resolution of 29 November 1947" was "non-existent."[114] Those proposals were also a "cloak" to assume executive powers in the city which would "allow these powers to interfere with November 29, 1947" and "perpetuate a state of chaos in Palestine."[115]

Vladimir Houdek, Czechoslovakia's UN ambassador, offered a particularly vehement defense of Israel's position. The Czech delegation "had always advocated the establishment of a Jewish home in Palestine, and at the same time had manifested its full understanding of the national aspirations of the Arabs."[116] It stood by its support of the UN Partition Resolution. The current conflict was not due to that resolution but to the fact that it "had not been fully implemented." There appeared to be "a systematic effort to undermine" the foundations of the General Assembly approach. The British had been uncooperative. "The radical change in United States policy in the spring of the current year, and its wavering attitude, could not but increase the existing difficulties by offering grounds for unrealistic political speculations." Houdek stated that "the proclamation of the State of Israel had completely changed the situation." It was regrettable that "the Arab State of Palestine" had not also come

---

[112] Ibid., 958.   [113] Ibid., 960.   [114] Ibid., 962.   [115] Ibid.
[116] Vladimir Houdek (Czechoslovakia), Paris (December 11, 1948), 185th Plenary Meeting, UNGA, 3rd Session, 965–970: A/PV.185.

into existence. Israel was a "reality which had not been seriously challenged by the regrettable and the uncompromising attitude of the Arab states." Israel's "actual existence ... must always be taken into consideration." He rejected Bernadotte's plan and British and American efforts to have the General Assembly reconsider it. The plan to transfer the Negev to Transjordan "would signify an infringement on the sovereignty of the State of Israel" and amount to a "flagrant violation" of the UN Charter. Such a transfer and annexation to Transjordan would also "deprive the Arab population of Palestine of the right to establish a state of their own."[117] The British resolution, based as it was on Bernadotte's report, "ignored" the "inescapable reality in Palestine" of the existence of the state of Israel.

Andrey Vyshinsky, the Soviet foreign minister notorious for his role in the purge trials of the 1930s, offered the Soviet Union's criticism of the resolution to establish a UN Commission.[118] He said that the General Assembly was dealing with the issue of Palestine for the fourth time because the UK and the US had used their economic, political, and military resources to realize "their plans for Palestine," something they had been unable to do in the preceding three General Assembly sessions. Vyshinsky rejected the British argument that the November 29, 1947 resolution could only be implemented if both parties agreed to it. This argument was "a screen for its real intentions" toward Palestine. That purpose became evident with the Bernadotte Plan, the purpose of which was "to wreck the Assembly's resolution of 29 November 1947."[119] Britain's attempt to take the two-thirds of the state of Israel consisting of the Negev was an effort to fulfill a wish that "had been expressed by representatives of British military authorities." If the mediator's plans were implemented with the aid of the UK and USA, British "control over the greater part of Palestine would be established through Transjordan." The organization of such a "puppet Arab state" in the part of Palestine that was not part of the state of Israel would be contrary to the UN resolution of November 29, 1947.[120] The US–UK resolution before the General Assembly was "entirely contrary" to the UN Partition Resolution. With the trusteeship proposal in spring 1948 the British and the Americans had tried and failed to undermine partition. Now, the Anglo-American policy was to introduce "a number of new measures

---

[117] Ibid., 967–968.
[118] Ibid., 965–970: On Vyshinsky's role in the purges of the 1930s and at the Nuremberg war crimes trials see Francine Hirsch, *Soviet Judgment at Nuremberg: A New History of the International Military Tribunal after World War II* (New York and Oxford: Oxford University Press, 2020).
[119] Houdek, 185th Plenary Meeting, UNGA, 3rd Session, 982.   [120] Ibid., 985.

which, for all practical purposes, would nullify the original resolution" without using the words "nullify" or "withdraw." The Soviet Union, by contrast, "had been entirely consistent" toward the Palestine issue.[121] It continued to support the Partition Resolution of November 29, 1947. Vyshinsky, whose name was linked to injustice, lies, and arbitrary power in the Stalin era, had offered a broadly accurate summary of American and British policy at the UN.

On December 12 the UN drafted a resolution naming the United States, France, and Turkey to a conciliation commission to attempt to work out a permanent settlement in Palestine.[122] In order to obtain the necessary two-thirds majority needed to pass the resolution the United States and Britain had to eliminate all reference to the Bernadotte Plan. As Thomas Hamilton reported in the *New York Times*, the effect of the resolution was to "increase the probability that a final settlement in Palestine merely would formalize existing battle lines – in other words, that Israel would hold on to territory it now occupies." That included the coastal plain, virtually all of the Negev in the south, and the Galilee in the north.[123] Although none of the Soviet bloc countries served on the Conciliation Commission, communist bloc diplomacy at the UN had defeated the Anglo-American effort to deprive Israel of its wartime gains via the mechanism of the Bernadotte Plan.

In early January, in Operation Horev, Israeli forces encircled the Egyptian army in Gaza, leading the Egyptians to agree to a ceasefire and to sign an armistice. At the same time, under pressure from British threats to assist the Egyptians and the State Department's criticism of Israel's "aggressiveness" and "complete disregard" of the United Nations, the Israelis withdrew their troops from the Sinai. As Benny Morris writes, the Great Powers and UN intervention of late December 1949 "saved the Egyptian army from annihilation."[124] Morris observes that the Western Great Powers, that is, Britain and the United States, refrained from using force to implement the Partition Resolution and failed again to intervene "when the Arabs launched a war of aggression in defiance of the UN resolution, against the Yishuv." Yet "acting through the United Nations and often directly and independently, [they] significantly cramped the IDF's style and curtailed its battlefield successes in a series of cease-fire and truce resolutions."[125] The pattern of UN truce resolutions that prevented clear Israeli victories "and saved the Arabs from ever greater humiliations" left the Israelis "with a permanent resentment toward and

---

[121] Ibid., 986.
[122] Thomas J. Hamilton, "Plan Wins, 35 to 15: Arab and Soviet Groups Vote against Board in the Assembly," *New York Times*, December 13, 1948, 1 and 32.
[123] Ibid.   [124] Morris, *1948*, 367–368 and 404.   [125] Ibid., 405.

suspicion of the United Nations."[126] The record examined in the present work indicates why the Israelis felt that way. Yet while the UN had curtailed Israeli battlefield successes it had not prevented the realization of their consequences, namely the establishment of a Jewish state in former Palestine, as called for in its own Partition Resolution of November 29, 1947.

In late 1948 and early 1949 two defining features of Israel's Moment prevented a victory for the British Foreign Office and the US State Department over Israel at the UN: first, American public opinion and the reelection of Harry Truman; and second, the opposition to Anglo-American policy by the Soviet bloc at the UN. The records of UN debates can become a fog of committee names, resolutions, and rhetoric so "diplomatic" that they obscure the obvious. Through fog, the following conclusions are clear: First, during the war of 1948 when the Jews in Israel faced what their leaders believed were matters of survival, the United States supported an embargo on the arms that Israel needed to defend itself. The embargo affected the new state of Israel more than it did the older Arab states, which already possessed armies, airports, seaports, and, in several instances, deliveries from Great Britain. Second, the United States at the UN conducted what Emanuel Celler aptly described as a diplomatic war of attrition to reduce the size of Israel by 60 percent and deprive it of the fruits of its battlefield victories. Third, the United States pursued these policies using the misleading language of neutrality and even-handedness. The policy of Marshall's State Department was not even-handed. It did not remain "caught in the middle" or torn between supporting Israel or the Arabs. It consistently opposed the aims first of the Jewish Agency in Palestine and then of the state of Israel. Fourth, in every UN debate, in special committees, the General Assembly and the Security Council, the representatives of Soviet Union, Poland, Czechoslovakia, and the Ukrainian SSR took positions in favor of the Jews and then Israel. They, not the United States, were Israel's "best friends" at the UN. The very public records of the United Nations document the simultaneity of Soviet bloc support for Israel in the very same months in which the Cold War was reaching a deep freeze in Europe.

On the other hand, as has been abundantly documented, President Harry Truman supported the Zionist project and then the new state of Israel. He did so in the face of opposition from the entire US foreign policy and national security establishment. Yet there were clear limits to the extent to which he was able or willing to depart from such a formidable

---

[126] Ibid., 404.

consensus of experienced decision makers in the State Department, the Pentagon, and the CIA. Alone among the leading foreign policy decision makers of his administration, Truman made decisions that combined the passions of two eras – the anti-Nazi passions of World War II and the anticommunist passions of the Cold War that he himself had launched. Israel's Moment was that short period in time in which the passions of those two eras coexisted in Truman's convictions and in his decisions, and ironically, they found agreement with his arch adversaries in the Cold War, the Soviet Union and Soviet bloc. His decisions to support Israel, as well as the limits to which he was willing to go in that support, reflect the battle of those two eras and their respective passions and allegiances in his own thinking.

15   Israel's Admission to the UN, and Sharett and Ben-Gurion's Retrospectives

Had the Jews waited on US or UN they would have been exterminated.
Israeli prime minister David Ben-Gurion to US ambassador
James McDonald, May 29, 1949

Israel won its independence in the war of 1948, but at a great cost. It signed armistice agreements with Egypt on February 24, 1949, Lebanon on March 23, Jordan on April 3, and Syria on July 20. The Iraqis refused to enter armistice negotiations.[1] Some 5,700–5,800 Jews and others fighting with them, a quarter of them civilians, died in the fighting. They represented 1 percent of the 628,000 members of the Yishuv in November 1947 and 649,000 in May 1948. In addition, the Yishuv suffered about 12,000 seriously wounded. The Palestinian losses are estimated to have been about 12,000, while the Egyptian government estimated its losses as 1,400 dead and 3,731 permanently invalided.[2] The experience of fighting alone for national survival and the large scale of dead and wounded left deep legacies (see Map 15.1).[3] As much as Israel's leaders admired Harry Truman, they had vivid memories of the assistance they had not received from the United States and the Western democracies when the war hung in the balance.

On March 4, 1949 the UN Security Council voted to admit Israel to the United Nations. The United States, France, and the Soviet Union voted in favor; Britain abstained. Indicative of the reservations in the French Foreign Ministry, France had recognized Israel belatedly on January 12, 1949, long after the United States and the Soviet Union had done so. On May 11, 1949, at its 207th Plenary Session, the UN General Assembly, by a vote of thirty-seven in favor, twelve opposed, and nine abstentions, admitted Israel to UN membership. The United States, the Soviet Union, France, Poland, and Czechoslovakia were among those voting

---

[1] Benny Morris, *1948: A History of the First Arab-Israeli War* (New Haven: Yale University Press, 2008), 375.

[2] Ibid., 406–407.

[3] See Uri Bialer, "The War of Independence," in his *Israeli Foreign Policy: A People Shall Not Dwell Alone* (Bloomington: Indiana University Press, 2020), 56–75.

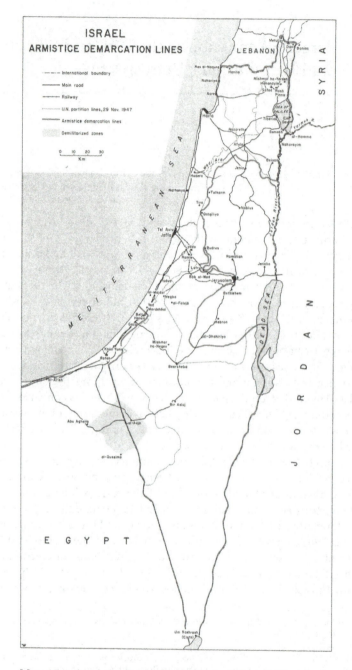

Map 15.1 Armistice lines after 1948 Arab-Israeli War. Source: Israel Ministry of Foreign Affairs, https://mfa.gov.il/MFA/AboutIsrael/Maps/Maps/Armistice-Line-1949-1967.jpg.

in favor; the United Kingdom abstained.[4] By that time Israel had received diplomatic recognition from fifty-four countries, forty-five of them members of the UN.[5]

Jan Drohojowski (1901–78), Poland's ambassador to the United Nations, explained his government's support for the motion.[6] In the spirit of remarks made by some of his predecessors, he recalled that "Poland had actively assisted the Jews in their aspirations not only for a national home but also full statehood." Poles and Jews had been associated with one another "for a thousand years, owed much to each other ... had suffered together." Many Jews "had suffered from the racial hatred encouraged by reactionary elements in Poland's pre-war government circles."[7] The "Jewish people" had developed "certain valuable characteristics in many fields of human endeavor, particularly in the sphere of progressive thought." A "period of sentimental interest in the fate of Israel had come to an end," to be replaced by one of cooperation and mutual interest. "The Jewish people, advancing along peaceful and progressive lines, could rely on the assistance of Poland, the Soviet Republics and the peoples' democracies of Europe. Israel would doubtless remember that those countries had been its true friends at the troubled time of its emergence."[8]

Drohojowski then turned to what he viewed as the very different policies of Britain and the United States. "The British Foreign Office had tried and failed to prevent the creation of Israel." The diplomacy of the UK and the USA "had been ready to betray the new State before its birth." The USA had changed its policy toward Israel "for reasons of political expediency divorced from any sense of justice or faith in Israel's future." Israel's leaders "should remember that the selfish interests of the international reactionary movement would try, and were indeed already trying, to mortgage the political future of the new state. Neither should it be forgotten that Israel was deeply indebted to the working classes."[9] If one eliminates some of the standard communist rhetoric, Drohojowski's description of British and American policy – that is, the actual policy

---

[4] Mr. [Jan] Drohojowski, "Application of Israel for admission to membership in the United Nations: report of the Ad Hoc Political Committee" (A/855), New York (May 11, 1949), 207th Plenary Meeting, UNGA, 307–309: www.un.org/ga/search/view_doc.asp?symbol=A/PV.207&Lang=E.

[5] "Speech to the General Assembly by Israeli Foreign Minister Sharrett, May 11, 1949," Israel Ministry of Foreign Affairs: www.mfa.gov.il/MFA/ForeignPolicy/MFADocuments/Yearbook1/Pages/Speech%20to%20the%20General%20Assembly%20by%20Foreign%20Minister.aspx.

[6] Drohojowski, "Application of Israel." For a biographical sketch see Jan Drohojowksi: https://en.wikipedia.org/wiki/Jan_Drohojowski#cite_note-:1-1.

[7] Drohojowski, "Application of Israel," 308.   [8] Ibid.   [9] Ibid.

being pursued by the Foreign Office and the State Department as opposed to the verbal support offered by Truman – contained a good deal of truth.

In contrast, the statement of US ambassador to the UN Warren Austin avoided any enthusiasm about the existence of the state of Israel. Instead he focused on the importance of a "just solution of questions relating to Palestine, and especially those of Jerusalem and the Arab refugees."[10] He reiterated US support for resolution 194, passed on December 11, 1948, which called for international control of Jerusalem, repatriation of refugees, and the establishment of a conciliation commission that would continue the work of a UN mediator. That resolution did prioritize direct peace talks between Israel and the Arab states. Austin's lukewarm and legalistic expression of support for Israel's admission to the UN was in line with the policies of the State Department he had helped to fashion since 1947.

Speaking for France, René Chauvel stressed the importance of protecting the "Holy Places" in Jerusalem. Rather than refer specifically to the fate of Europe's Jews, he said that "the thoughts of many inevitably turned to those who had suffered persecution throughout the long years under the yoke of totalitarian regimes."[11] He spoke of France's "ancient bonds" to the countries of the Middle East, which made it possible for his country "to understand, perhaps better than others, the great currents of passion, intelligence and faith which had left their trace in that part of the world." Of the war, he said France was pained "to see the recent strife which had threatened to obliterate those irreplaceable vestiges of a glorious past and promises of an equally bright future." Israel was now "offered the opportunity to exercise its responsibilities. Its adventure would not be complete unless, after suffering pain and violence, it demonstrated it could also exercise charity. No human accomplishment was lasting unless it was built on love. No nation was better equipped to show its generosity and sense of justice than the very people which had suffered so long from injustice and hatred."[12]

Chauvel's condescending remarks conveyed the unhappiness of the French Foreign Ministry about the new state of Israel. While he expressed concern about unnamed "irreplaceable vestiges of a glorious past," he did not mention the over 5,000 Jews who had just lost their lives in the war. Rather than calling on the Arab states to recognize and make peace with Israel, he offered maudlin rhetoric about love and charity, thus placing the burden on Israel in future negotiations. His comments about the Jews'

---

[10] Warren Austin, in "Application of Israel," 313.
[11] René Chauvel, in "Application of Israel," 321.   [12] Ibid., 322.

Figure 15.1 Israeli foreign minister Moshe Shertok (center) requests Israel's admission to United Nations, November 29, 1948 to UN Secretary General, Trygve Lie (right). At left Abba Eban, first Israeli ambassador to the UN. Source: AFP Photo/Gaillourdet/Getty Images.

suffering from injustice implied that Israel was being ungenerous and unjust. Chauvel, who was one of the French officials who had facilitated Husseini's return to the Middle East, voted for Israel's admission to the UN only after the French government had decided that it could not adopt a stance that diverged from both the United States and the Soviet Union.[13]

On the same day in May 1949, Moshe Shertok, who had Hebraized his name to Moshe Sharett, delivered his first address to the General Assembly as the foreign minister of the state of Israel (see Figure 15.1).[14] He said that Israel's admission to the UN "was the consummation of a people's transition from political anonymity to clear identity,

---

[13] On France's belated decision to recognize Israel and vote for its admission to the UN see Frédérique Schillo, *La France et la création de l'état d'Israël, 18 février 1947–11 mai 1949* (Paris: Éditions Artcom, 1997).

[14] Mr. Sharett, in "Application of Israel," 313.

from inferiority to equal status, from mere passive protest to active responsibility, from exclusion to membership in the family of nations."[15] Israel, he said, "expressed fervent wishes for the security, dignified existence and equality of rights of Jews everywhere." He "expressed deep gratitude to those nations, which, at a time when the Jews had no voice in world councils," had championed their aspirations for the Jews' "claim to nationhood" both in the League of Nations and in the UN. Further, "he expressed [the] profound and everlasting thankfulness of the Jewish people of all nations" to the nations whose delegations supported the "historic resolution" of November 29, 1947 and later its admission to UN membership. "Two historic trends had converged to bring it [the creation of the Jewish state] about: catastrophe in Europe and achievement in Zion."[16]

Sharett (Shertok) then recalled basic truths about the nature of World War II and the Holocaust, the anti-Nazi coalition, the role of the Jews in it, and the connection between the Allied victory and the establishment of the Jewish state. From 1945 to 1949 no leading official in the State Department or the Pentagon, whether in public statements or in classified government communication, had ever expressed agreement with or understanding of what Sharett told the UN General Assembly:

At no stage in the tribulations of the Jewish people had its basic insecurity been more tragically laid bare than in the Second World War, when three out of every four Jews in Europe, one out of every three Jews in the world, had been put to death. It should not be forgotten that the United Nations in its origin represented an anti-Nazi coalition born in common battle against the darkest forces of evil that had ever menaced the destiny of civilized mankind. It should also be remembered that in that titanic and victorious struggle, the Jews of all the Allied nations had taken a full part and the Jews of Palestine had borne their share as a nation in arms. Allied victory would have missed one of its essential objectives, although perhaps unperceived at the time, and the triumph of the United Nations over the scourge of humanity would have remained incomplete if the Jewish people, as a people, had still remained homeless without a country of their own.[17]

In "their ancestral home," Sharett said, the Jews had demanded "the right of self-determination." The Arab delegates had excoriated the establishment of Israel as an act of aggression and colonialism. On the contrary, "in the emancipated Middle East, where one country after another had achieved sovereign status, the denial of independence to the Jewish people would have been a flagrant anomaly and grievous wrong." The conviction that "their own survival and freedom" as well as "the hopes of countless generations" were at stake was crucial for the

[15] Ibid., 332.   [16] Ibid.   [17] Ibid., 332–333.

Jews' "ability, outnumbered and with inferior arms, to defend themselves and to uphold their independence."[18]

Then, turning to the origins of the Partition Resolution, Sharett again accentuated the historical context of its emergence and, without referring to the United States by name, made clear what the government of Israel thought of American diplomacy at the UN in 1947–8:

Mankind's revulsion against the European tragedy and a deep insight into the realities of Palestine had found joint expression in the historic Resolution of 29 November 1947. It had been an act of faith, of international justice and of creative statesmanship. Having once set that course, the Assembly never swerved. On two notable occasions it had refused to endorse retreats from a policy which would either have annulled the independence of Israel or crippled its territory. By admitting Israel into its fold, it did no more than sanction the final application of its own decree.[19]

Again, neither in its public statements nor in its confidential memos did the State Department led by George Marshall ever publicly state the obvious connection between "the European tragedy" of the Jews and the resolution of November 29, 1947 – this despite the fact that prominent politicians in the US Congress from all over the country and journalists in Washington and New York had repeatedly done so. Sharett's audience in the General Assembly must have understood that the "two notable occasions" to which he referred were the American-sponsored efforts to substitute a trusteeship for the Partition Plan in March–April 1948 and then in summer and fall the efforts to use the Bernadotte Plan and the UN mediator truce mechanism to deprive Israel of the Negev desert. As the evidence of preceding chapters indicates, both the public statements and classified memoranda of the United States government confirm that the United States was attempting to do precisely what Sharett described.

Sharett also placed Israel's desire for peace in a longer historical context. "Scattered as they were in all lands, the Jews had suffered incomparably more than any other people from the last war. None therefore dreaded another war more than Israel." For Sharett, peace was a condition of its existence and future development. Alluding obliquely to the emerging Cold War, he said that he hoped there would be a "significant diminution of tension in Great Power relationships." The admission of Israel into the UN "was a not unhopeful omen," as both the United States and the Soviet Union were among the states "which had joined in welcoming Israel into the world."[20] Sharett offered an olive branch to the Arab states. "Israel was deeply aware of the common destiny uniting it

[18] Ibid., 333.   [19] Ibid.   [20] Ibid., 333–334.

with them forever." He praised the "outstanding role in man's progress in ancient and medieval times" made by the Middle East, and said he looked forward to relationships of friendly cooperation. He hoped that Israel's membership in the UN, "bringing it within a common forum with six Arab states, might facilitate progress toward understanding" and lead to a "future peace settlement."[21]

Sharett then cited Prime Minister Ben-Gurion's statement of five basic principles that would guide Israel's foreign policy: first, loyalty to the UN Charter and "friendship with all peace-loving states, especially the United States of America and the Union of Soviet Socialist Republics"; second, "efforts to achieve an Arab–Jewish alliance based on economic, social, cultural and political co-operation with the neighboring countries" within the framework of the UN; third, support for measures that strengthened peace, guaranteed the rights of men and the equality of nations, and enhanced the authority of the UN; fourth, "the right of all Jews who wish to resettle in their historic homeland to leave the countries of their present abode"; and fifth, "the effective preservation of the complete independence and sovereignty of Israel."[22]

Ben-Gurion's first principle in May 1949, that of friendship with both the United States and the Soviet Union, was going to be a very difficult balancing act as tensions between them hardened into a long Cold War. As Uri Bialer writes in his important history of its formative years, Israel's foreign policy then was one "between East and West."[23] The Israelis acknowledged the contributions both the USA and the USSR had made to Israel's establishment, a message that by fall 1949 was unwelcome in both Washington and Moscow. For the American architects of containment the establishment of the state of Israel was, at best, an irritant to the Anglo-American effort to contain Soviet influence in the Middle East. Conversely, to those in the Soviet Union who divided the world into "two camps," laying the foundations for a decades-long propaganda assault on the Western democracies, Ben-Gurion's first principle suggested that Israel would not be a reliable ally in the Soviet battle against "U.S. imperialism."[24]

Indeed, Israel did not wish to abandon its political and emotional ties to the United States. As the anti-Hitler coalition broke ever further apart

---

[21] Ibid., 334.   [22] Ibid., 335.

[23] Uri Bialer, *Between East and West: Israel's Foreign Policy Orientation, 1948–1956* (New York and Cambridge: Cambridge University Press, 1990). Also see his *Israeli Foreign Policy*.

[24] On the two camps doctrine and the Soviet reinterpretation of World War II which disparaged the contribution of the Western Allies, the classic text is Andrei Zhdanov's "Two Camp Policy," in Gale Stokes, ed., *From Stalinism to Pluralism: A Documentary History of Eastern Europe since 1945* (New York: Oxford University Press, 1996), 38–42.

and, after 1949, definitively gave way to the reversed fronts of the Cold War and then to antisemitic purges in the Soviet bloc, the actual international history of the creation of the state of Israel as well as its continued existence became, for both Washington and Moscow, an embarrassing and discomfiting memory of the policies they had each pursued – American diffidence and Soviet support – in 1947–9. Ben-Gurion's first principle would soon be revised as the Soviet Union turned against Israel. The foundation of the state of Israel was, first and foremost, the result of the sacrifice, skill, and determination of the Jews of the Yishuv, the Jewish community of Mandate Palestine who waged and won the War of Independence of 1947–8. Yet the international factors were indispensable to their victory. In fact, the foundation of the state of Israel was made possible by the last act in world politics of the lingering memories, passions, and beliefs of the anti-Nazi coalition, that is, of the first "United Nations," which had brought the USA and the USSR together to wage war against the Axis powers.

In the same month that Israel was admitted to the UN, negotiations took place in Lausanne, Switzerland between Israel and the Arab states regarding the fate of Arab refugees and a possible peace settlement. Israel rejected Arab demands for the return of refugees unless doing so was part of a peace settlement. But the Arabs refused to make peace or end the state of war. Israel also refused to accept the changes in the November 29, 1947 borders that had resulted from the war and from the Arab states' refusal to recognize Israel or make peace with it.

George Marshall departed the office of secretary of state on January 21, 1949, to be succeeded by Dean Acheson (1893–1971). Policy toward Israel along the lines elaborated in the many memos and decisions examined in the preceding chapters did not fundamentally change. On May 27 Acheson forwarded a memo to the president that attributed "the present instability" in the region to "the new Israeli position," which the Arabs would interpret "as confirming their constant fears of Israeli territorial expansion." Acheson was referring to Israel's stance that discussion of the return of refugees needed to be part of a peace settlement in which the Arabs ended the state of war and accepted the existence of the state of Israel. Acheson's view was that Israel's position would deepen Arab mistrust of Israel and foster charges that the USA was "passive no matter how unreasonable the demands of Israel" were.[25] The State Department drafted a text which Truman agreed to send to Ben-Gurion on May 29,

---

[25] Dean Rusk to Mark Ethridge, Bern (May 24, 1949), "Eyes Alone for Ethridge from Rusk," NACP RG59 CDF 1945–1949, 501.B Palestine/5–2449, Box 2024; Dean Acheson to Certain American Diplomatic and Consular Officers, Washington (May 29, 1949), NACP RG59 CDF 1945–1949, 501.BB Palestine/4–3049, Box 2024.

1949.[26] In it, the Department expressed its irritation that Israel had rejected US proposals that Israel offer the Arabs "territorial compensation" and repatriation of refugees and that Israel was trying to change the US position "through means available to them in the United States." The implication of Acheson's statement was that those means – democratic politics and public opinion – were somehow an inappropriate way to influence American foreign policy.

Acheson's State Department believed that the time had now come "to make a basic decision concerning our attitude toward Israel." In its May 27 memo to Truman it laid out some basic principles. The United States had given generous support to the foundation of the Jewish state, "since we believed in the justice of this aspiration."[27] (Belief in the justice of Zionist aspirations had, in fact, not been an element of American public diplomacy in the previous two years.) As Israel was not adopting a "reasonable attitude," the Department "considers that it is now essential to inform the Israeli Government forcefully that, if it continues to reject the friendly advice with this Government has offered solely in the interests of genuine peace in the Near East, this Government will be forced with regret to revise its attitude toward Israel."[28] The memo concluded that, "in addition to a generally negative attitude in the future toward Israel," measures to convince Israel to change its stance could include refusing Israel's request for US technical advisors and training of Israeli officials in the United States, and withholding approval for $49 million of an as-yet-unallocated $100 million Export-Import Bank loan. Though such a course of action would serve the national interest, it "would arouse strong opposition in American Jewish circles," so the president would wish to ask his advisors to give careful consideration to the implications of these suggestions.[29] Acheson's memo to the president made clear that the State Department was continuing to wage what Celler had called its "war of attrition" of the past two years.

On May 28, 1949 Truman agreed to send a shorter version of the memo to Ben-Gurion, stating that the United States government was "seriously disturbed by the attitude of Israel with respect to a territorial settlement in Palestine and to the question of Palestinian refugees."[30] The USA had "given generous support to the creation of Israel because

[26] James E. Webb, "Memorandum by the Acting Secretary of State to the President," Washington (May 27, 1949), 867N.01/5-2749, in *Foreign Relations of the United States* (hereafter *FRUS*), *The Near East, South Asia, and Africa*, 1949, vol. 6, 1–2 : https://history .state.gov/historicaldocuments/frus1949v06/d697.

[27] Ibid.   [28] Ibid.   [29] Ibid.

[30] [James] Webb, "The Acting Secretary to the Embassy in Israel," Washington (May 28, 1949), 501BB.Palestine/5-2849, *FRUS*, 1949, vol. 6: https://history.state.gov/historical documents/frus1949v06/d705.

they have been convinced of the justice of this aspiration." However, it did not regard the present attitude of the Israeli government "as being consistent with the principles on which US support has been based" and was "gravely concerned lest Israel now endanger the possibility of arriving at a solution of the Palestine problem" that would contribute to friendly relations between Israel and its neighbors. The USA did not support "excessive Israeli claims to further territory within Palestine." It urged Israel to "offer territorial compensation for territory which it expects to acquire beyond the boundaries" of the UN resolution of November 29, 1947. If Israel continued to reject the basic principles set forth by the UN General Assembly resolution of December 11, 1948 and the "friendly advice" offered by the United States "with the sole purpose of facilitating a genuine peace in Palestine, the US Govt will regretfully be forced to the conclusion that a revision of its attitude toward Israel will become unavoidable."[31] Truman had signed off on a memo that expressed the real convictions of the US national security establishment.

On May 29 the memo was sent to Ben-Gurion by cable, with a copy to James McDonald, who was now serving as the first United States ambassador to Israel. That same day McDonald met with Ben-Gurion and Sharett (Shertok) in Tel Aviv. Ben-Gurion acknowledged that the United States had "helped us much before and after" the state of Israel was established. Therefore, it had "a right to have a say" about Israeli policy. But Truman's note of May 29 note ignored "two fundamental facts."[32] McDonald reported Ben-Gurion's objections as follows:

November 29 resolution never carried out by UN, US or Middle East States. It contemplated two states, Israel, and independent Arab Palestine, united by customs and other ties at peace with one another and neighbors. Prime Minister [Ben-Gurion] unable [to] recall any strong action by US or UN [to] enforce November 29 or prevent aggression by Syria, Egypt, Lebanon and Iraq. Instead embargo encouraged aggressors against Israel whose very existence was in danger. Had Jews waited on US or UN they would have been exterminated. Israel was established not on basis [of] November 29 [UN Partition Resolution] but on that of successful war of defence. Hence [Truman's] note's suggestion is today unjust and unrealistic for it ignores war and continued Arab threats which make November 29 boundaries impossible.[33]

Ben-Gurion was willing to discuss the issue of refugees, but only as part of a peace settlement, yet the Arab states refused to make peace. So long as

---

[31] Ibid.
[32] James McDonald to Secretary of State, Tel Aviv (May 29, 1949), No. NIACT 406, NACP RG 59 General Records of the Department of State, CDF 1945–1949, 501.BB Palestine, Box 2124.
[33] Ibid., 1.

their attitude persisted, the "refugees are potential enemies of Israel. If war were renewed could Israel appeal to US to send arms or troops for defence against refugees fighting on the side of the aggressors? Upon whom does US ask Israel to rely?" In what McDonald described as "an impassioned conclusion" that was "off the record," Ben-Gurion said that the "US is powerful and we are weak; we could be destroyed; but we do not intend to commit suicide by accepting November 29 settlement in today's fundamentally changed conditions."[34] The changed conditions referred to the Arab states' continuing hostility and their refusal to enter negotiations aimed at a peace settlement.

In these brief, laconic remarks Ben-Gurion stated the essence of what the many details of the preceding chapters have documented. His blunt question – "upon whom did the United States ask Israel to rely?" – drew on fresh memory of recent events. In the crucial months, when the Jews in Palestine faced attacks launched by the Arab Higher Committee, an organization led by former Nazi collaborators, and then when the Arab League states invaded the new state of Israel, the United States imposed an arms embargo. Ben-Gurion was correct to point out to Truman that if the Jews had depended on the United States or the United Nations, they would have been defeated, and possibly exterminated. It was only because they had circumvented extensive British, then American, and then UN efforts to prevent assistance from arriving that the Jews, first via the Jewish Agency and then new state of Israel, were able to acquire arms and personnel with which to fight and win Israel's War of Independence. The arms and personnel arrived despite decisions made, obviously in the British Foreign Office, but also in the US State Department and the Pentagon. Help arrived because there were some gaps in the embargo in Europe, especially in Czechoslovakia, France, and Italy, and because American supporters of the Zionists offered funds, material, and even their own bodies, in the face of US government efforts to stop them. Israel won the war for its independence despite, not because of, the policy of the United States.

For Israelis, in Uri Bialer's words, the war "was an unprecedented, all-encompassing, existential military confrontation with the Arabs of Palestine and the Arab states" which took "an extremely heavy human and economic toll, which would in themselves carve this event into collective memory."[35] As we have seen, this appreciation for the existential aspect of the war – that it would determine whether or not Israel would survive,

[34] Ibid., 2.

[35] Bialer, *Israeli Foreign Policy*, 56–57. He cites Ben-Gurion's comment to chief of staff Moshe Dayan: "Our downfall is that we cannot lose. They can lose once, twice; we can defeat Egypt ten times – and it means nothing. They can defeat us once – and it's over": ibid., 62.

and that the Arabs could be defeated many times but a single Israeli defeat would end the Zionist enterprise – was not uppermost in the minds of decision makers in the State Department and Pentagon in 1947–8.

A Cold War Postscript

Beginning in 1949, in the "anticosmopolitan" purges infused with anti-semitic conspiracy theories and accusations, the Stalin regime turned vehemently against Israel. In so doing, the Kremlin did all it could to suppress the public memory of the important and short-lived era of Soviet bloc support for Zionist aspirations from April 1947 to March 1949. The memory of the anti-Nazi alliance also became inconvenient in Moscow, as the former Western allies were reinserted into conventional Marxist-Leninist ideology as enemy Western imperialists. In the Soviet Union and Eastern Europe, communists accused of Zionist sympathies were driven from office, arrested, forced to flee. Most infamously, in the 1952 Slansky trial in Prague, they were executed. In the Middle East the Soviet Union presented itself as the supporter of Arab nationalism against Western – especially American – "imperialism," which, it claimed, was associated with and responsible for the establishment of the state of Israel. Over the next four decades its antagonism to Israel reached the level of an undeclared war.[36] The false assertion that Israel was the product of American imperialism was central to that four-decade-long campaign of communist anti-Zionism and to the success of that appeal in many places around the world including, ironically, the United Nations.

In 1953, presumably in an effort to remind Arab leaders of who actually supported and who opposed the establishment of the state of Israel, the analytical division of the CIA wrote a detailed and accurate account of the UN deliberations from the first Special Session of April–May 1947 to the General Assembly Session of September to December 1948. The CIA analysts entitled their report "Communist Bloc Opposition to Arab Aspirations in Palestine."[37] They noted that the UN had considered

---

[36] A full history of the Soviet bloc assault against the state of Israel remains to be written. On the purges in East Germany see Jeffrey Herf, *Divided Memory: The Nazi Past in the Two Germanys* (Cambridge, MA: Harvard University Press, 1997); and Jeffrey Herf, *Undeclared Wars with Israel: East Germany and the West German Far Left, 1967–1989* (New York: Cambridge University Press, 2016). On the shift from antifascism to the Cold War see François Furet, *The Passing of an Illusion: The Idea of Communism in the Twentieth Century* (Chicago: University of Chicago Press, 1999).

[37] Central Intelligence Agency, "Communist Bloc Opposition to Arab Aspirations in Palestine: An Analysis of the Communist Position on the Palestine Question," Washington (June 23, 1953), CREST (Document Release Date, July 8, 1998): CIA-RDP62-0086SR000200180002-1.

three options: an independent and unitary (majority-Arab) state; partition into a Jewish and an Arab state; and temporary trusteeship. The
representatives of the USSR and Poland took the initiative and "assumed
the task of influencing the Assembly to adopt resolutions the Communist
bloc sponsored."

On major issues the Communist position was directly opposite to that of the Arab
States. Whereas the Arab States wanted the Assembly to pass a resolution for
creation of an independent unitary state in Palestine, the Communists championed passage of the Partition Plan; and whereas the Arab States favored study-
ing the trusteeship proposal submitted by the United States during the Second
Special Session [April–May 1948], the Communists raised vehement objections,
allegedly because the proposal would nullify the Partition Plan.
    The records of the United Nations reveal beyond any doubt that the
Communist delegates were responsible for (1) passage of the Partition Plan, (2)
defeat of the various Arab States' proposals on the Palestine question, (3) defeat of
the US proposal to create a temporary trusteeship, (4) survival of the Partition
Plan during the Second Special Section, and (5) present conditions in Palestine
and consequent instability throughout the Arab East.[38]

The CIA did not mention that President Truman had supported the
Partition Plan and countermanded efforts by his State Department to
replace it with a trusteeship proposal, but "Communist Bloc Opposition
to Arab Aspirations in Palestine" made accurate use of the documents to
press its case.
    The US security establishment's antagonism toward Zionism and the
new state of Israel and its association with communism and the Soviet
Union, which had been so apparent in the crucial years of 1947–8, was
fully evident in this CIA analysis of 1953. The report sought to counter a
Soviet disinformation campaign whose purpose was to liberate the Soviet
bloc from guilt by association with Israel, pin the blame for the Jewish
state instead on the Americans, and then present the Soviet Union as a
loyal friend of the Arabs in their battle against "U.S. imperialism." It was
a bold lie but, told often enough, it became an article of faith among
communists and many noncommunist leftists around the world over the
next seven decades.
    In the 1950s both the Soviet Union and powerful elements of the
American national security leadership were continuing to distance themselves from the new state of Israel. At the same time in France, veterans of
the French Resistance from center right to center left, some of them the
same politicians who had supported the Zionists and frustrated the British
in 1947 and 1948, made France into Israel's most important and reliable,

---

[38] Ibid.

if very discreet, ally. It was France that offered Israel crucial scientific expertise in the nuclear field and became its primary weapons supplier, especially for the Israeli Air Force. The Israelis carried out preemptive strikes in the first hours of the Six Day War using French Mirage Jets. From 1948 to 1967 it was France, not the United States, that was Israel's most important military ally among the Western democracies. The origins of that alliance lay in the years of Israel's Moment.[39]

---

[39] The history of the French-Israeli relationship goes beyond the scope of this work. Now that archives of those decades are open, there is further scholarly work to be done. See Sylvia K. Crosbie, *A Tacit Alliance: France and Israel from Suez to the Six-Day War* (Princeton: Princeton University Press, 1974); Robert Isaacson, "The James Bond of Cherbourg: Imagining Israel in Pompidou's France," *French Historical Studies* 40, 4 (October 2017): 675–699; and his "From 'Brave Little Israel' to 'an Elite and Domineering People': The Image of Israel in France, 1944–1974," Ph.D. dissertation, George Washington University, 2017. The "special relationship" between the Federal Republic of Germany (West Germany) and Israel began with the restitution agreement of 1952, that is, after the events examined in this work. On the origins of West German economic assistance to Israel in the 1950s see, from an extensive scholarship, Constantin Göschler, *Schuld und Schulden: Die Politik der Wiedergutmachung für NS Verfolgten seit 1945* (Göttingen: Wallstein Verlag, 2005).

16   Conclusion

Israel's Moment was that brief period, an interregnum, between 1945 and 1949, and especially in 1947–8, when the antifascist passions of World War II had not completely given way to and overlapped with the at times contrary priorities of the Cold War. David Ben-Gurion understood that the window of opportunity created by the agreement of the US president and the Soviet Union on November 29, 1947 would likely be short-lived. The Yishuv leadership seized on a unique and unexpected circumstance that emerged in 1947 when Stalin, for his own reasons – certainly not due to principled support for Zionism – thought that a Jewish state in Palestine would advance Soviet interests and drive the British Empire out of the Middle East, and when liberals and noncommunist leftists in the United States and France recalled the very recent history of Nazism and its crimes against the Jews of Europe.

The internationalization of the "problem of Palestine," when it became a matter to be handled by the United Nations in 1947, was accompanied by a most unexpected surprise, an agreement between the Soviet Union and the anticommunist president of the United States to support a partition of what had been the British Mandate in Palestine into two states, one Jewish and one Arab. The Zionists seized on the opportunity created by that fleeting agreement. Yet, of the two powers, the United States, despite President Harry Truman's Zionist sympathies, proved to be the less supportive. The State Department learned how to use UN Security Council resolutions to advance its view of American national interests. As a result, the same international organization whose resolution of November 29, 1947 gave international legitimacy to establishing a Jewish state in Palestine also facilitated truce resolutions and an arms embargo that hindered that goal. For the Zionists the internationalization of the conflict at the United Nations was a decidedly mixed blessing.

The Zionists were fortunate that in Harry Truman the United States had a most atypical Cold Warrior as president. In contrast to his diplomatic and military leadership, he combined opposition to communism with support for the Zionist cause. In launching the containment of

communism while supporting the Zionist project in Palestine, he advocated policies that leaders at the State Department, Pentagon, and CIA
believed stood in conflict with one another. The state of Israel was established first and foremost because the Holocaust confirmed the basic
Zionist argument that without a state the Jews faced extermination in
a world in which antisemitism had not died with the defeat of Nazi
Germany. That conviction, in turn, fired a determination to establish
a state immediately, as the costs of statelessness were now obvious. Yet
international factors were important as well, notably the verbal support of
the American president, the practical support for immigration by officials
in the government of France, and the delivery of weapons from
Czechoslovakia to establish a Jewish state in Palestine.

During the Cold War the Soviet Union repressed memories of the
realities of the crucial two years of Soviet and Soviet bloc support for
the Jewish state in 1947 and 1948. Indeed, it accused those communists
who had followed Soviet pro-Zionist policy of being hostile agents of
American imperialism and international Zionism. Conversely, the
American alliance with Israel that emerged in full force only after the
Six Day War of 1967 tends to obscure from memory the opposition and
distance of the days of Israel's birth. In fact, in 1947 and 1948, despite the
support of President Truman, the US government was more of
a hindrance than a help to the Yishuv and then to the new state of
Israel. Israel won the war of 1948 primarily because of the skill, commitment, and sacrifice of its own people. It did so despite the obstacles that
Anglo-American diplomatic and military leadership put in its path, and in
part because of the practical support it received from the very communist
governments that subsequently became its enemies, as well as from parts
of the French government.

Contrary to four decades of Soviet, Arab state, Islamist, and Palestinian
nationalist propaganda, Zionism was not a product or tool of British or
American imperialism. For the communists the benefit of that false
accusation was to obscure the memory, especially in the Arab and other
parts of the developing world, of the crucial assistance that the Soviet
Union, Poland, and Czechoslovakia offered to the Zionists and then to
Israel when the outcome of the Arab-Israeli war of 1948 hung in the
balance. From 1945 to 1949 the Zionists had four primary foes: the
Attlee–Bevin Labour government in London; former Nazi collaborators
leading the Arab Higher Committee; the reactionary Arab regimes of the
time and their allies in British, American, and European oil corporations;
and the national security establishment of the United States.

The motivations for their opposition differed, but all four did what they
could to prevent Israel from being created, and surviving once it came

into being. When the president of the United States decided to support Israel's existence, the State Department and Pentagon did not go so far as to seek its destruction. Yet in 1948 the State Department waged a campaign of diplomatic pressure to reduce Israel's military gains and territorial extent. Israel came into existence and survived despite the policy and strategy adopted by the US State Department, Pentagon, and CIA in the crucial months and years of its war for independence. When Soviet propagandists denounced Israel as a tool of US imperialism, they began one of the great lies of the global Cold War, one that unjustly gave the United States credit (or blame, depending on one's perspective) for something that its diplomats and soldiers had actually tried to prevent.

Historians of the war of 1947–8 have been well aware of this absence of consequential American support, and of support from the Soviet bloc and the French Ministry of the Interior. Yet that awareness has not diffused to the broader scholarly and intellectual public. The warm glow surrounding what I have called "track one," Truman's support for the admission of Jewish refugees, and for the November 29, 1947 UN Partition Resolution for recognition of the new state on May 14, 1948, has obscured adequate awareness of the practical consequences of "track two," the anti-Zionist consensus in the State Department led by George Marshall and in the Pentagon by James Forrestal. Admiration for George Kennan's brilliance and insight into the Soviet dictatorship has also deflected attention from his key role in making opposition to the establishment of a Jewish state in Palestine into a component of the global strategy of the containment of the Soviet Union and communism. It is important for historians and the public to recall and emphasize the connection between Cold War anticommunism in 1947–8 and State Department and Pentagon opposition to the establishment of the state of Israel. The absurdity and mendacity of Senator Joseph McCarthy's attack in 1951 on communists in the State Department stands out in even sharper relief when seen against the background of the creation of the anticommunist consensus within the State Department beginning in 1946 and its impact on the debate over the creation of the Jewish state in Palestine.

In fall 1947 participants in the Pentagon talks articulated an Anglo-American consensus that a Jewish state in Palestine would undermine American, British, and Western interest in the Middle East. That consensus persisted throughout the crucial two years of Israel's Moment. It rested on a significant misunderstanding of Zionism's political orientation, which led to a strategic blunder: the failure to take advantage of short-lived Soviet support for the establishment of a Jewish state in Palestine and to support what would become the most effective source of opposition to Soviet expansion in the Middle East. At the time

American critics of US policy argued that a firm pro-Zionist policy that supported the UN Partition Resolution of November 29, 1947 and delivered arms to the Jews and then to Israel might have deterred the Arabs, or at least the Arab states, from launching the war of 1948, and would have fostered Israel's links to the Western powers. They had a point.

The architects of American policy in the Cold War, extolled for their far-sighted wisdom in the recovery of Western Europe, and especially of West Germany and Japan as allies in the Cold War, saw less clearly when it came to questions about the Jews in Palestine and the new state of Israel. Marshall and Kennan focused on the economic recovery of Western Europe and making common cause with those British and Western European political leaders who were committed to containing Soviet influence in Europe. Zionism, with strong roots in Eastern Europe and its obvious focus on the evils of Nazi Germany, struck a discordant note in the halls of power in Washington. American national security officials' mistaken association of Zionism with Soviet policy, along with the commercial benefits of Arab oil, blinded them to the democratic essence of the Zionist project and to the democratic nature of the Jewish state it created. It also led them to minimize the danger posed by the racism and antisemitism of the leaders of the Arab Higher Committee. They misconstrued Zionist willingness to seek assistance where it could be found as support for communism and Soviet goals. The classified memoranda of the US State Department do not support the conclusion that an animus against Jews and Judaism – that is, antisemitism – was a driving force of American foreign policy regarding the future of Palestine. That said, it is clear that, had it been up to the leadership of the State Department, the United States would not have supported the Partition Plan of November 29, 1947, and would have turned against it in spring 1948. In their minds, they did so because they were convinced that a Jewish state in Palestine would undermine American national security interests in the early months of the Cold War.

That said, to associate Zionism so closely with Soviet expansion in 1947 could not help but arouse memories of attacks in recent history on "Judeo-Bolshevism." As Congressional debates about displaced-persons legislation in 1947 and 1948 indicated, raw antisemitism and the association of Jews with communism was heard in the halls of the US Capitol in 1948, leading eventually to attacks on the State Department itself. Yet, it is fair to say that the most emphatic opponents of the Zionist project in the State Department, and even more so in the Pentagon, did not display awareness of the way in which opposition to the Zionist project in 1947 could be motivated by or stimulate the longest hatred. Nor did they seize the opportunity to publicly denounce the antisemitism that clearly was evident in the leadership of the Arab Higher Committee.

It is not the wisdom of hindsight that leads to this criticism of George Marshall, Robert Lovett, George Kennan, and Loy Henderson for refusing to make a public issue of the antisemitism and racism of the Arab Higher Committee, even though World War II and the Holocaust were so recent. The files of the State Department, the Pentagon, the OSS, and then CIA were full of material about the links between the Arab leaders they were dealing with – men such as Haj Amin al-Husseini – and the crimes of the Nazis that had been revealed in Nuremberg in 1945–8. They could read Jamal Husseini's celebration in 1947 in London and New York of the benefits of "homogeneity in race." Or they could read about such matters in the pages of *The Nation*, *PM*, and the *New York Post*, or hear about them from Robert Wagner, Emanuel Celler, or their fellow diplomat Sumner Welles.

Yet the State Department, Pentagon, and CIA files about "the problem of Palestine" offer little evidence of reflection on Nazi Germany's race war on its Eastern Front, the mass murder of Europe's Jews, Nazism's impact on the Middle East, or the nature of antisemitism in an Islamic and Arab context and the consequences of those hatreds. Had American diplomatic and military leaders done so, they might have weakened Arab rejectionism and enhanced the prospects for a compromise two-state solution that the United States voted for in November 1947. Instead, when the Arab states invaded Israel the following May, they continued an arms embargo and offered UN resolutions that obscured the realities of Arab aggression and responsibility for war.

The American official antagonism to the Zionist project examined in the preceding chapters was not only due to the influence of State Department Arabists led by Henderson. It was also understandable in a society that was only beginning to challenge antisemitism and racism against African Americans. The association of Zionism with the Soviet Union and communism that appeared so frequently in US – and British – assessments in these years rested on a cramped and provincial understanding of World War II, as well as on the persistence of old antisemitic stereotypes about Jews and communism. A national security establishment more aware of these issues and better informed about the nature of Zionism would have viewed the presence of communists among Jewish refugees to Palestine as an understandable consequence of the Nazi war on "Jewish Bolshevism," and understood that they were a small minority of the refugee stream, posing no threat to British or American interest in the Middle East. Marshall, Lovett, Kennan, even Henderson were not antisemites; but if they recognized antisemitism where it existed, most importantly in Arab Higher Committee, they did not fight against it or make an issue of it. Perhaps there was a discomfort in having the United States associated with a clearly Jewish enterprise – if so, that would be a sign of a polite antisemitism that kept Jews out of decision-making positions in the State Department.

The preceding chapters have presented the evidence that criticism along these lines is not the product of the historian's hubris and arrogance of hindsight. The criticisms and the outlines of an alternative foreign policy were in the public discussion of 1945–9 in the United States. They came from the revelations about Arab collaboration with the Nazis in the pages of *PM* by Victor Bernstein, I. F. Stone, and Alexander Uhl, and in the *New York Post* by Edgar Mowrer; the analytical journalism of Freda Kirchwey and I. F. Stone in *The Nation*; the memos of AZEC representatives Stephen Wise, Abba Silver, Joseph Schechtman, and Benzion Netanyahu; the speeches and legislative efforts of Senator Robert F. Wagner and Congressman Emanuel Celler; the arguments made by Truman's counsel, Clark Clifford; published work by Sumner Welles, Richard Crossman, Bartley Crum, and the memos of James McDonald; and many others in public life and politics who viewed support for the Zionist project as both morally right and beneficial to American national interests. Again, the argument that the establishment of a Jewish state in Palestine would serve, rather than undermine, American interests in the Middle East was a live option at the time. Celler, Wagner, and Welles made a powerful case, both in public and in private correspondence, that the Jewish state would be a democracy oriented to the West.

From Kennan's "Long Telegram" in 1946 through the debate over Palestine and Israel, American policy makers in the State Department made a stunningly rapid switch from World War II to the Cold War and from the mentalities of wartime antifascism to those of the containment of communism. Truman remained the exception among American foreign policy decision makers; he combined opposition to communism with a budding grasp of the catastrophe of the Holocaust. Unfortunately, those who could combine the passions of World War II and the early Cold War, who could envisage "both-and" rather than "either-or," were not in decision-making positions in the State Department, the Pentagon, or the CIA.

One result of the switch to the Cold War and France's desire to sustain good will in North Africa and the Middle East was the American, British, and French decision not to indict Haj Amin al-Husseini for war crimes when he was in their grasp in French custody. That was both a setback for judicial reckoning and a major strategic blunder. The history of relations between Arabs and Jews in Palestine might have turned out differently had there been a trial which placed the full history of his collaboration with the Nazis before global public opinion. Placing Husseini on trial would have produced a mountain of evidence, and testimony from many witnesses. Such a trial might very well have ended his efforts to revive his political career and thereby perhaps blunt the forces of antisemitism and rejection of compromise in Palestine and the Arab states. The failure to bring him and his associates to trial was perhaps the most important of many examples of a politically convenient forgetting of the crimes of the Nazi past, and of Nazi collaboration that was also one aspect of the early years of the Cold War. It was a Middle Eastern chapter of the "Vichy syndrome" of amnesia, apologia, and myth making that historians have examined in postwar Europe. The Jews and the Zionists brought facts available at the time to the attention of policy makers in Washington and Nuremberg, but judicial reckoning for the most important Arab collaborator with Hitler was not on the agenda of the American, British, and French governments in 1945 and 1946. It was, to repeat, justice delayed and denied, as well as a significant strategic blunder.

Soviet and communist support for the establishment of the state of Israel was one of the great ironies of mid-twentieth-century international politics. Stalin, whose antisemitism emerged most fully in the "antic-osmopolitan" purges of 1949 to 1953, placed an inexpensive bet on the Zionists in hopes that they would drive Britain and the United States out of the Middle East. Other communists supported the Zionists because they believed that doing so was a continuation of the antifascism of World War II and that, as communists, they regarded a Jewish state as a logical consequence of the Holocaust and the Allied victory over Nazism. As the public records of the UN General Assembly, Security Council, and special committees indicate, the delegates from the Soviet Union, Poland, Ukrainian SSR, and Czechoslovakia repeatedly supported the Yishuv's and then Israel's positions far more than did the United States. Gromyko's speech of May 14, 1947 became famous, but the statements by Oskar Lange and Alfred Fiderkiewicz for Poland, and Vasyl Tarasenko of the Ukrainian SSR were equally emphatic in their memories of the Holocaust and embrace of the Zionist project. American diplomats were not wrong in seeing the efforts as part of the USSR's overall strategy in the Cold War, but even the most hardened cynic could not deny the depth of conviction that came from Poland's Fiderkiewicz when he informed the UN General Assembly that, as a survivor of Auschwitz, he supported the Jews' drive for statehood in Palestine. American journalists and commentators in New York took note of the communists' support for the Jewish Agency and then Israel at the UN and its contrast with the ambiguities and circumlocutions of the US ambassador Warren Austin as he followed detailed instructions from Washington.

Many of the communists in the Soviet bloc who supported the Jews and then Israelis in 1947–8 paid for their Zionist sympathies with destroyed careers, jail time, or even their lives during the anticosmopolitan purges. Whatever the mix of ideology and realpolitik, Soviet bloc support in 1947–8 was consequential. Truman offered moral and verbal backing, but the Jews of the Yishuv and then Israel needed weapons and immigrants. Though Truman supported the entry of 100,000 Jews in Europe to Palestine, they arrived there despite the efforts of American diplomatic and military leaders to help Britain prevent what it called "illegal immigration," and also to sustain the ongoing arms embargo which disadvantaged the Jews more than the Arabs.

In the fall of 1949 Stalin reverted to the Marxist-Leninist orthodoxy that had receded somewhat during the 1941–5 alliance with the United States and Britain and continued in the years of Soviet support for the Zionists in 1947–8. As a result, the Soviet Union identified Zionism with Western imperialism, and the Arab states and Palestinian Arabs with anticolonialism. The anti-Zionist turn was also due to Stalin's own antisemitism, the attendant conspiracy theories about Jews' links to the Western democracies, and fears aroused by the enthusiasm of Soviet Jews for the new state of Israel. Perhaps he was also angered by the results of Israel's first election for members of the Knesset in 1949. Maki, the Israeli Communist Party, received only 3.5 percent of the vote and four seats in Israel's parliament. The left-wing, then pro-Soviet, Mapam Party did somewhat better, winning 14.7 percent of the vote and nineteen seats, but Ben-Gurion's Mapai Party captured 35.7 percent of the vote and forty-six seats, allowing him to form Israel's first coalition government with five other parties but *without* Mapam and Maki.[1]

It became clear that while the Zionists had fought against the British Mandate and British rule in Palestine, they were not, in their vast majority, communists or supporters of the Soviet Union. The hopes of the Kremlin and the fears of the State Department and Pentagon of a pro-Soviet Israel were revealed to be a mixture of illusions, paranoia, and intelligence failure. Angered that his bet on the Jews had not paid off, Stalin and his propagandists turned language into a pretzel, gave the terms "imperialism" and "anti-imperialism," "racism" and "anti-racism" meanings that almost no one outside the conservative Arab

---

[1] "1949 Israeli Legislative Election": https://en.wikipedia.org/wiki/1949_Israeli_legislative_election.

governments or the Arab Higher Committee would recognize in 1947–
8. In the Slansky trial of 1952 in Prague that ended with confessions
under torture and then executions, some of the Czech communist
leaders who had sold weapons to the Jews in 1947 and 1948 were
denounced as stooges of an alliance between Zionism and US imperialism. In Prague and Moscow, and across the Soviet bloc, an anti-
Zionism with thinly veiled antisemitic overtones emerged. It remained
in place well into the 1980s.

Zionism gained adherents around the globe in the years during and
after the Holocaust because the murders of Europe's Jews had made it
abundantly clear to Jews and others that without a sovereign state of
their own, Jews were powerless to defend themselves against those
determined to murder them. Antisemitism remained a reality, both in
postwar Europe and in the Middle East. Even though the Yishuv had
created impressive political and economic institutions as well as the
elements of a formidable armed force in the form of the Haganah, the
fundamental political reality for Jewish survivors of the Holocaust and
the Jews of the Yishuv was the absence of state sovereignty and thus
the political power that even a small state can wield. The Holocaust
had made clear that survival required statehood. The Jews had learned
the oldest lesson of power politics. As Thucydides wrote, the strong
do what they will and the weak suffer what they must. The passion for
Zionism in those years rested on the need to never again be among the
weak.

In the United States and Europe, Jewish citizens participated in democratic politics. They peacefully petitioned their governments to support
the Zionist project. In that sense, like other citizens in democracies, they
were not totally powerless. Yet there were clear limits to their political
influence. They were unable to convince the Allied victors to indict
Husseini for war crimes; unable to convince the French government to
block his return to the Middle East; unable to prevent the UN from
granting the Arab Higher Committee the honor of representing the
Palestine Arabs at the UN; unable to convince the US State
Department or the British Foreign Office to publish their extensive files
on Arab collaboration with the Nazis, even though the topic was a matter
of public discussion in the United States, and France in particular; and
unable to prevent the State Department in fall 1948 from undertaking
efforts to deny the new state of Israel the Negev desert and full control of
the port of Haifa.

Israel's supporters in the United States were unable to convince
a president who was sympathetic to their concerns to lift an arms
embargo, even after the Arab states invaded the state of Israel on

May 15, 1948. The Zionists' allies in France did have sympathetic Socialist ministers of the interior who did support Jewish immigration to Palestine and Israel. Yet even Édouard Depreux and Jules Moch could not deliver heavy weapons to the Zionists, nor could they overcome the Foreign Ministry's opposition to recognition of the new state until January 1949. Nor could the Jews convince the Western foreign policy establishment that a Jewish state in Palestine would serve to block, not welcome, Soviet influence.

Harry Truman blunted the anti-Zionist consensus in the State Department and Pentagon but he could not defeat it entirely, based as it was on a broadly shared consensus that establishment of the Jewish state in Palestine was at cross purposes to the Cold War and to American access to Arab oil. When Soviet and Polish representatives at the United Nations and liberal and left-leaning journalists such as Victor Bernstein, Freda Kirchwey, Alexander Uhl, and I. F. Stone in *The Nation* and *PM*, or Henry Wallace at *The New Republic*, or French Communists and Socialists supported Zionist aspirations; when communist officials in Eastern Europe or French Socialists in Paris and Marseille were facilitating Jewish immigration to Palestine, and when the government of Czechoslovakia sold heavy weapons to the Zionists, they all, singly or taken as a whole, confirmed the view in the State Department and Pentagon that the new Jewish state had suspicious connections to the wrong side of new Cold War. Kennan, who saw so clearly into the heart of darkness of Stalin's regime, denounced Zionist policy as a threat to America's national interest in the same weeks that he called for an end to the Nuremberg trials and denazification efforts in occupied Germany. I. F. Stone was right to comment bitterly on the simultaneity of Marshall Plan loans to foster economic recovery in West Germany and the embargo on arms to the Jews in Palestine.

The support for the Zionist project did extend beyond liberalism and the left; it included Republican senators such as Robert Taft, Republican members of the House of Representatives such as Jacob Javits, Kenneth Keating, and Margaret Chase Smith, Gaullist veterans of the French Resistance such as Alfred Coste-Floret in Paris, and the then-out-of-power Winston Churchill. Support for the Zionist project was not an exclusively liberal or leftist cause. Yet the strongest, most persistent, and most consequential support for establishing the Jewish state in Palestine came from liberals and leftists in the United States and France, and, from the communist regimes of the Soviet bloc.

In 1947 and 1948 the meaning of emotionally laden words such as "left," "liberal," and "progressive" in connection with the Zionist project connoted the reverse of what they came to mean after the Soviet bloc "anticosmopolitan" purges of 1949–53, and then after the global radical left echoed that transformed meaning during and after the Six Day War of 1967. A key goal of the preceding pages is to bring the connection between the liberal and leftist spirit of the antifascism of World War II and its associated support for Zionism to the attention of several generations of readers whose political vocabulary dates primarily from the years since 1967. Together, the above-mentioned journalists writing for *The Nation*, *PM*, the *New York Post*, and at times *The New Republic*; Zionist intellectuals such as Joseph Schechtman and Benzion Netanyahu; politicians and political figures such as Robert Wagner and Emanuel Celler, Richard Crossman, Bartley Crum, Sumner Welles, and James McDonald produced a contemporary written record that bears reading today.

The coalitions of France's governments of these years were divided between a Foreign Ministry intent on preserving French power and influence in the Arab world and the liberal and left-leaning currents in the Ministry of the Interior and Ministry of Transport, which offered practical assistance to the Mossad Le'Aliyah Bet's organization of clandestine Jewish immigration to Palestine. From the Socialist ministers of the interior Adrien Tixier, and then Édouard Depreux and Jules Moch, who so frustrated British efforts to prevent ships transporting immigrants to Palestine, to Jean-Paul Sartre's plea for "weapons for the Jews" in February 1948, the very vivid memories of Nazism and its crimes played a crucial role in French support for Zionist aspirations. Conversely, those in the French Foreign Ministry, such as Henri Ponsot, who were intent on preserving France's colonial power in North Africa and the Middle East, opposed the Zionist project because supporting it would put France at odds with the Arab states. He and others facilitated Husseini's return to politics in the Middle East. In Paris and Marseille, on the other hand, support for the Jews and the Zionists by Socialist ministers and local officials was the apparent logical extension of the leftist and liberal passions of the French and European resistance.

The present work has brought these realities of Israel's Moment into view. To the extent to which the antisemitic mind became the anti-Zionist mind, it did so in part because it believed that Israel was a new version of the powerful and evil Jew of the Western and Islamist imagination. The Israeli as "Nazi" or "imperialist" gave this old hatred a secular form. As David Ben-Gurion and Moshe Shertok understood very well, the Jews in Palestine and then the new state of Israel did not have access to the vast powers that were always a figment of the antisemitic imagination. Indeed, they were almost completely on their own. They had few allies in the world, and fewer still who were willing and able to offer the kind of help they urgently needed. Yet in those brief four years after the end of World War II there was enough memory in East and West of the extermination of the Jews of Europe and, equally important, of the passions of antifascism and anti-Nazism, to offer some support to the Jews in their efforts – at that particular historical moment – to replace centuries of statelessness with sovereignty and self-reliance.

Bibliography

Archives

National Archives and Records Administration of the United States, College Park, Maryland (NACP)

Record Group (RG) 59 U.S. Department of State, Central Decimal File

Central Decimal File, 1945–1949: 501.BB Palestine
Central Decimal File, 851.00/1–147 to 12–3147
Central Decimal File, 1945–49, 860 F.001: Czechoslovakia
National Archives Microfilm Publications: M1390: Records of the Department of State Relating to Internal Affairs of Palestine, 1945–1949, 867N.01, Rolls 1–26

Policy Planning Staff/ Council, Area Files, 1947–1962:

——1947–1953, Europe, East to 1947–53 Near and Middle East
——1947–1953, Near and Middle East
——Policy Planning Staff/Council: Numbered Staff Studies, 1947–1949: Index/PPS-1 to PPS-33

Records of the Legal Adviser Relating to War Crimes, Lot File No. 61 D33; Records Relating to German War Crimes, 1942–1942
Records of the Executive Secretariat: Memos for the President (Oct. 1944–Feb. 1949), Lot 53D444

LM 163, Confidential US State Department Central Files: Palestine-Israel, Internal and Foreign Affairs, 1945–1949, Rolls 23–24

RG 60 Department of Justice, Criminal Division

Class 71 (Neutrality) Enclosures 1924–1968, 71–012 thru 71–45–13 Serial 1

RG 84 Records of the Foreign Service Posts of the U.S. Department of State

France, Paris Embassy, General Records, 1946; 1948
France, U.S. Embassy, Paris, Classified General Records, 1944–1963, 1947; 1948

Italy, Caserta, POLAD [Political Adviser] for Supreme Allied Commander, Mediterranean, 1944

France, U.S. Consulate, Marseille, Classified General Records, 1936–1952: 1948–1949

Munich Consulate General: Classified General Records, 1943–51, 1947

Rome Embassy and Consulate, General Records, 1946

Records of the U.S. Political Adviser to the Supreme Allied Commander, Mediterranean, "Top Secret" File, 1944–47

Union of Soviet Socialist Republics, U.S. Embassy, Moscow, Classified General Records, 1941–1963

RG218 Records of the U.S. Joint Chiefs of Staff

Chairman's File. Admiral Leahy, 1942–48

RG 319 Records of the Army Staff

Army-Intelligence Project Decimal File, 1946–1948, Palestine

Army-Intelligence Project Decimal File, 1946–1948, Czechoslovakia

Army-Intelligence Document File

(Army Staff) Plans & Operations Division. Decimal File 1946–1948. 091. Palestine

Assistant Chief of Staff, G-2 Intelligence: Incoming and Outgoing Messages, 1948, France

Assistant Chief of Staff, G-2 Intelligence: Incoming and Outgoing Messages, 1948, Czechoslovakia

Geographical Index to the Numerical Series of Intelligence Documents (ID File). 1944–51: France; Czechoslovakia

RG 341 Records of Headquarters U.S. Air Force (Air Staff)

Staff Message Division: Top Secret Incoming and Outgoing Messages, September 1947–

RG 353 Interdepartmental and Intradepartmental Comm. (State Department)

Policy Committee on Arms and Armaments (Working Committee on Arms Control): Country File, 1945–49

Centre des Archives Diplomatiques de La Courneuve (CADC): Ministère des Affaires Étrangères

Cabinet de Ministre G. Bidault, 1944–1948

————Y international 424, y455, Occupation Zone américains, Juin 1947–mai 1948; Juin 1948–Oct 1948

————Y international 443 Y55 Zone francaise, Nov–Dec 1947; Jan–Avril 1948

Ministres des Affaires Étrangères et Européennes, Direction Afrique-Levant, Généralités Proche-Orient:

Cabinet G. Bidault Afrique-Levant, 1947–1948

Cabinet B. Bidault, G.3.Palestine

214QO/38 Grand Mufti Hadj Amin el Husseini, September 1943–November 1952

214QO/97 Relations diplomatiques, 1944–1952: Palestine/URSS

214QO/38, 1947–1952

214QO/100 Afrique

Questions Militaries Armament, 1946–1951

Relais diplomatique: Palestine/URSS

Ministre des Relations Exterieure

Y international 1944–1949: Directoire des Prisionnaires de Guerre et personne deplacé, Dec 1946–Fevrier 1947, No. 608

372QO O NUOI 1944–1949, 40: Questions Juives

207QO Z Europe 1944–1949: Tchecoslovaque 46, 49

208QOO Z Europe URSS, 1944–1949, 463–34: Églises françaises, Question juive, No. 29–30, 15 oct 1947–Mars 1949

U.R.S.S., No. 46 check, Politique Exterieure, Dossier General, Octobre 1946–Mars 1947

Archives Nationales, Pierrefitte-sur-Seine (ANP)

Ministère de l'Intérieur

Cabinet d'Adrien Tixier, ministre de l'Intérieur (1944–1946): F/1a à F/1a/3380, 1944–1947

Cabinets des ministres de l'Intérieur du GPRF et de la IVe République (1944–1958): F/1A/*/4707-F/1A/*/4753

Cotes F/1a/4707 à 4727 pour les cabinets d'Adrien Tixier, d'Édouard Depreux et Jules Moch (courrier départ et courrier arrivée)

F/1a/3368; F/1a/3369, Sionisme: F/1a/3303, 3345, 3346, 3349

F/1a/3369, Direction Générale de la Sûreté Nationale Direction des Renseignement Généraux, Activité Politique: Sionisme et questions juives (novembre 1946)

19790622/52 Correspondance ministérielle (transports – affaires étrangères et franco-anglaise: immigration et émigration clandestine vers la Palestine. 1946–49

Direction de la Réglementation. Archives du bureau de la sûreté de l'Etat (1947–1990) et du bureau des assignations à résidence (1957–1967): 19920172/1–19920172/11 (1947–1990)

Direction des libertés publiques et des affaires juridiques

19920172/8 Émigration juive Nord-africaine vers Israël, 1947–1961

Direction de la Sûreté nationale (1876–1966): F/7/16029-F/7/16126

"Service des étrangers"

F/7/16088 Transit d'Israélites en provenance d'Allemagne et d'Europe centraleF/7/16089 Affaire de l'Exodus: rapports des Renseignements généraux, coupures de presse, 1947–1948

F/60/859 Palestine, sionisme, Égypte

Fond Georges Bidault (XXe siècle):

Repertoire 457AP/124–126: Palestine

457AP/124, Bidault Archive, Palestine I, 1945–1947, Janvier-Octobre 1947, Emmigration Juive aux France et rapport franco-anglais: affaire Exodus, 1119–1/C

Marine:

19790622/51 Procès verbaux des réunions de la commission technique et consultative de la Marine Marchande. 1947–48 1946–49

Central Intelligence Agency: CREST: A 25 Year Program Archive

"The Consequences of the Partition of Palestine" (November 28, 1947). SYMPHONY VOL. 1, "Symphony Project," 1946

"Possible Developments from the Palestine Truce" (July 27, 1948)

"Probable Effects on Israel and the Arab States of a UN Arms Embargo" (August 5, 1948)

"Communist Bloc Opposition to Arab Aspirations in Palestine: An Analysis of the Communist Position on the Palestine Question" (June 23, 1953)

"The Jewish Question in Soviet and Satellite Propaganda" (February 10, 1953)

United Nations Records

General Assembly, Official Records, UN Official Documents System (ODS) online.

Records of the Security Council. Some sessions available online; others on microfilm at Library of Congress, Washington, D.C.

Library of Congress, Washington, D.C.

Emanuel Celler Papers, Manuscript Division

Benjamin Cohen Papers, Manuscript Division

Robert H. Jackson Papers, Manuscript Division

————Nuremberg War Crimes Trial: Office Files-U.S. Chief of Counsel, Grand Mufti of Jerusalem (Haj Amin Husseini)

Georgetown University, Booth Family Center for Special Collections: Research Center

Robert F. Wagner Papers: Palestine Files

Columbia University School of Law Library, Manuscript Collection
Telford Taylor Papers

Center for Jewish History, New York City
La Riposte, 1946–1948

Franklin Delano Roosevelt Library and Museum
Sumner Welles Papers, Series 10: Speeches and Articles, 1928–1951

Newspapers, Journals
Combat, 1944–1948
Haaretz, 1968
Le Monde, 1945–1948
The Nation, 1945–1948
The New Republic, 1945–1948
New York Post, 1945–1947
New York Times, 1944–1949
PM, 1945–1948
Le Populaire, 1946–1948
Washington Post, 1948

Published Documents and Records

Annuaire diplomatique et consulaire de la République Française (Paris: Imprimerie Nationale, 1947).

Avriel, Ehud, *Open the Gates! A Personal Story of "Illegal" Immigration to Israel* (New York: Atheneum, 1975).

Begin, Menachem, *The Revolt* (New York: Nash Publishing, 1951).

Ben-Dror, Elad, *Ralph Bunche and the Arab-Israeli Conflict: Mediation and the UN 1947–1949* (London: Routledge, 2015).

"Ralph Bunche and the Establishment of the State of Israel," *Israel Affairs* 14, no. 3 (2008): 519–537.

Bernstein, Victor, *Final Judgment: The Story of Nuremberg* (New York: Boni & Gaer, 1947).

Bonté, Florimond, *Six million de crimes* (Paris: Éditions Sociales, 1964).

"Sur le territoire de la Palestine, carrefour stratégique du monde," *Cahiers du Communisme* 9 (July 1948): 703–721.

Bosworth, Patricia, *Anything Your Little Heart Desires: An American Family Story* (New York: Touchstone, 1998).

Celler, Emanuel, *You Never Leave Brooklyn: The Autobiography of Emanuel Celler* (New York: John Day, 1953).

"Punishment of War Criminals: Hearings Before the Committee on Foreign Affairs, House of Representatives, Seventy-Ninth Congress, First Session on

H. J. Res. 93" (March 22, 1945) (Washington, DC: US Government Printing Office, 1945).

Clifford, Clark with Richard Holbrooke, *Counsel to the President: A Memoir* (New York: Random House, 1991).

Crossman, Richard, *A Nation Reborn* (New York: Atheneum, 1960).

Palestine Mission: A Personal Record (New York: Harper, 1947).

Crum, Bartley, *Behind the Silk Curtain: A Personal Account of Anglo-American Diplomacy in Palestine and the Middle East* (New York: Simon & Schuster, 1947).

Depreux, Édouard, *Souvenirs d'un militant: Cinquante ans de lutte, de la social-démocratie au socialism, 1918–1968* (Paris: Fayard, 1972).

Documents on Israeli-Soviet Relations, 1941–1953: Part I: 1941–May 1949 (London: Frank Cass, 2000).

Foreign Relations of the United States (FRUS)

1946, *The Near East and Africa*, vol. 7

1947, *The Near East and Africa*, vol. 5

1948, *The Near East and Africa*, vol. 5, part 2

"'The Pentagon Talks of 1947,' between the United States and the United Kingdom concerning the Middle East and the Eastern Mediterranean."

1949, *The Near East, South Asia, and Africa*, vol. 6

Friling, Tuvia, *Arrows in the Dark: David Ben-Gurion, the Yishuv Leadership, and Rescue Attempts during the Holocaust* (Madison: University of Wisconsin Press, 2005).

Friling, Tuvia and Denis Peschanski, eds., *David Ben Gourion journal 1947–1948: Les secrets de la création de l'état d'Israël* (Paris: Éditions de la Martinière, 2012).

Jarblum, Marc, *La Lutte des Juifs contre les Nazis* (Paris: Éditions Realité, 1944).

Kennan, George F., *Memoirs, 1925–1950* (New York: Pantheon, 1967).

The Kennan Diaries, ed. Frank Costigliola (New York: W. W. Norton, 2014).

Lerner, Max, *America as a Civilization: Life and Thought in the United States Today* (New York: Simon & Schuster, 1957).

Mayer, Daniel, *Les Socialistes dans la Resistance: souvenir et documents* (Paris: Presses Universitaires de France, 1968).

McDonald, James G., *My Mission in Israel, 1948–1951* (New York: Simon & Schuster, 1951).

Moch, Jules, *Une si longue vie*, (Paris: Éditions Robert Laffont, 1976).

Mowrer, Edgar Ansel, "The Rise of Another Mass Murderer – Mufti's Career Rivals Hitler," *New York Post* (June 1, 1946).

The Nation Associates, *The Arab Higher Committee: Its Origins, Personnel, and Purposes, the Documentary Record Submitted to the United Nations, May 1947* (New York: The Nation Associates, 1947).

Sheffer, Gabriel, *Moshe Sharrett: Biography of a Political Moderate* (Oxford and New York: Clarendon Press/Oxford University Press, 1996).

Sartre, Jean-Paul, *Anti-Semite and Jew* (New York: Schocken, 1948), translation of his *Reflexions sur la Question Juive* (Paris: Paul Morihein, 1946).

Stone, I. F., "The Big Swap – Jewish Blood for Arabian Oil," *PM* (January 28, 1948).

"Oil and Anti-Semitism," *PM* (February 10, 1948), 7.

"Secretary Marshall's Blunder," *The New Republic* (October 18, 1948), 18–19.

Underground to Palestine (New York: Pantheon, 1978 [1946]).

"Warning on Zion Embargo Maneuver," *PM* (March 29, 1948), 4.

The War Years, 1939–1945 (Boston: Little, Brown: 1988).

Sulzberger, C. L., "German Preparations for the Middle East," *Foreign Affairs* 20, no. 4 (July 1942): 663–678.

Taylor, Telford, *The Anatomy of the Nuremberg Trials: A Personal Memoir* (New York: Knopf, 1992).

Uhl, Alexander, "France Letting Grand Mufti Slip out Free: Hitler's No. 1 Arab Collaborator May Now Be in Middle East," *PM* (April 10, 1946), 305.

"Plot to Get Grand Mufti to Middle East Reported," *PM* (February 15, 1946), 3.

US House of Representatives, *Committee on International Relations, Selected Executive Session Hearings of the Committee, 1943–50, Volume 2, "Problems of World War II and Its Aftermath, Part 2: The Palestine Question and Problems of Postwar Europe"* (Washington, DC: US Government Printing Office, 1976).

Welles, Sumner, "How the U.S. Bungled Palestine," *Macleans* (July 15, 1948).

Palestine's Rightful Destiny (New York: American Christian Palestine Committee, 1946).

"Palestine and World Peace," *The Nation* (October 23, 1947), 439–441.

We Need Not Fail (Boston: Houghton-Mifflin, 1948).

Yearbook of the United Nations (New York: United Nations, 1947, 1948, 1949, 1950).

Secondary Works

Alpern, Sara, *Freda Kirchwey: A Woman of "The Nation"* (Cambridge, MA: Harvard University Press, 1987).

Applebaum, Anne, *Iron Curtain: The Crushing of Eastern Europe, 1944–1956* (New York: Doubleday, 2012).

Azouvi, François, *Le mythe du grand silence: Auschwitz, les français, la memoire* (Paris: Fayard, 2012).

Bartov, Omer, *The Eastern Front, 1941–45: German Troops and the Barbarization of Warfare* (New York: Oxford University Press, 1985).

Bauer, Yehuda, *Flight and Rescue: Brichah* (New York: Random House, 1970).

Becker, Ulrike, "Die deutsche Militärberatergruppe in Ägypten 1951–1958," in Martin Cüppers, Jürgen Matthäus, and Andrej Angrick, eds., *Naziverbrechen: Täter, Taten, Bewältigungsversuche* (Darmstadt: Wissenschaftliche Buchgesellschaft, 2014), 319–334.

Bendersky, Joseph W., *The "Jewish Threat": Anti-Semitic Politics of the U.S. Army* (New York: Basic Books, 2000).

Bensimon, Doris and Benjamin Pinkus, *Les Juifs de France, le sionisme et l'état d'Israël* (Paris: Publications Langues, 1989).

Bezias, Jean-Rémy, *Georges Bidault et la politique étrangères de la France (Europe, États-Unis, Proche-Orient) 1944–1948* (Paris: L'Harmattan, 2006).

Bialer, Uri, *Between East and West: Israel's Foreign Policy Orientation, 1948–1956* (New York and Cambridge: Cambridge University Press, 1990).

"The Czech-Israeli Arms Deal Revisited," *Journal of Strategic Studies* 8, no. 3 (1985): 307–315.

Israeli Foreign Policy: A People Shall Not Dwell Alone (Bloomington: Indiana University Press, 2020).

Blum, Léon, *L'Oeuvre de Léon Blum, 1947–1950* (Paris: Éditions Albin Michel, 1963).

Blumel, André, *Léon Blum: Juif et Sioniste* (Paris: Éditions de La Terre Retrouvée, 1951).

Boog, Horst, et al., *Germany and the Second World War*, vol. 4: *The Attack on the Soviet Union* (New York and Oxford: Oxford University Press, 1998).

Bradley, Mark, "Decolonization, the Global South and the Cold War, 1919–1962," in Leffler and Westad, eds., *The Cambridge History of the Cold War*, vol. 1: *Origins, 1945–1962*, 464–485.

Breitman, Richard and Norman W. Goda, *Hitler's Shadow: Nazi War Criminals, U.S. Intelligence, and the Cold War* (Washington, DC and College Park, MD.: National Archives and Records Administration, 2010).

Breitman, Richard and Norman J. W. Goda, eds., *U.S. Intelligence and the Nazis* (New York: Cambridge University Press, 2005).

Breitman, Richard and Allan J. Lichtman, *FDR and the Jews* (Cambridge, MA: Harvard University Press, 2013).

Cesarani, David, *Becoming Eichmann: Rethinking the Life of a "Desk Murderer"* (London: De Capo Press, 2004).

Cohen, Gerard Daniel, *In War's Wake: Europe's Displaced Persons in the Postwar Order* (New York: Oxford University Press, 2012).

Cohen, Michael J., *Palestine and the Great Powers, 1945–1948* (Princeton: Princeton University Press, 1982).

Cohen, Stuart A., "Imperial Policy against Illegal Immigration: The Royal Navy and Palestine, 1945–48," *Journal of Imperial and Commonwealth History* 22, no. 2 (May 1994): 275–293.

Crosbie, Sylvia K., *A Tacit Alliance: France and Israel from Suez to the Six Day War* (Princeton: Princeton University Press, 1974).

Cüppers, Martin, *Walther Rauff – in deutschen Diensten: Vom Naziverbrecher zum BND-Spion* (Darmstadt: Wissenschaftliche Buchgesellschaft, 2013).

Deak, Istvan, Jan Gross, and Tony Judt, eds., *The Politics of Retribution in Europe: World War II and Its Aftermath* (Princeton: Princeton University Press, 2000).

Epelbaum, Didier, *Pas un mot, pas un ligne? 1944–1994: Des camps de la mort au genocide rwandais* (Paris: Éditions Stock, 2005).

Evans, Richard, *The Third Reich at War* (New York: Penguin, 2009).

Frank, Haggai, Zdeněk Klíma, and Yossi Goldstein, "The First Israeli Weapons Procurement behind the Iron Curtain: The Decisive Impact on the War of Independence," *Israel Studies* 22, no. 3 (2017): 125–152.

Frei, Norbert, *Adenauer's Germany and the Nazi Past: The Politics of Amnesty and Integration* (New York: Columbia University Press, 2002).

Fulbrook, Mary, *Reckonings: Legacies of Nazi Persecution and the Quest for Justice* (New York: Oxford University Press, 2018).

Furet, Francois, *The Passing of an Illusion: The Idea of Communism in the Twentieth Century* (Chicago: University of Chicago Press, 1999.

Gaddis, John Lewis, *The Cold War: A New History* (New York: Penguin Press, 2005).

George F. Kennan: An American Life (New York: Penguin, 2012).

Gensicke, Klaus, *Der Mufti von Jerusalem und die Nationalsozialisten* (Darmstadt: Wissenschaftliche Buchgesellschaft, 2007).

The Mufti of Jerusalem and the Nazis: The Berlin Years (London: Vallentine, 2014).

Gershoni, Israel, ed., *Arab Reponses to Fascism: Attraction and Repulsion* (Austin: University of Texas Press, 2014).

Ginat, Rami, "Soviet Policy towards the Arab World, 1945–48," *Middle Eastern Studies* 32, no. 4 (October 1996): 321–335.

Goda, Norman J. W., Barbara McDonald Stewart, Severin Hochberg, and Richard Breitman, eds., *To the Gates of Jerusalem: The Diaries and Papers of James G. McDonald, 1945–1947* (Bloomington: Indiana University Press/ United States Holocaust Memorial Museum, 2015).

Goda, Norman J. W., Richard Breitman, Barbara McDonald Stewart, and Severin Hochberg, eds., *James G. McDonald, Envoy to the Promised Land: The Diaries and Papers of James G. McDonald, 1948–1951* (Bloomington: Indiana University Press, 2017).

de la Gorce, Paul-Marie, *Naissance de la France moderne: l'après guerre, 1944–1952* (Paris: Bernard Grasset, 1978).

Göschler, Constantin, *Schuld und Schulden: Die Politik der Wiedergutmachung für NS Verfolgten seit 1945* (Göttingen: Wallstein Verlag, 2005).

Grossmann, Atina, *Jews, Germans and Allies: Close Encounters in Occupied Germany* (Princeton: Princeton University Press, 2009).

Guttenplan, D. D., *American Radical: The Life and Times of I. F. Stone* (New York: Farrar, Strauss & Giroux, 2009).

Hadari, Ze'ev Venia, *Second Exodus: The Full Story of Jewish Illegal Immigration to Palestine, 1945–1948* (London: Vallentine Mitchell, 1991).

Hahn, Peter L., *Caught in the Middle East: U.S. Policy toward the Arab-Israeli Conflict, 1945–1961* (Chapel Hill and London: University of North Carolina Press, 2004).

Halamish, Aviva, *The Exodus Affair: Holocaust Survivors and the Struggle for Palestine*, trans. Ora Cummings (London and Syracuse: Vallentine Mitchell and University of Syracuse Press, 1996).

Hardy, Alexander, *Hitler's Secret Weapon: The "Managed" Press and Propaganda Machine of Nazi Germany* (New York: Vintage, 1967).

Herf, Jeffrey, *Divided Memory: The Nazi Past in the Two Germanys* (Cambridge, MA.: Harvard University Press, 1997).

"Haj Amin al-Husseini, the Nazis and the Holocaust: The Origins, the Nature and the Aftereffects of Collaboration," *Jewish Political Studies Review* 26, nos.

3–4 (Spring 2016): http://jcpa.org/article/haj-amin-al-husseini-the-nazis-and-the-holocaust-the-origins-nature-and-aftereffects-of-collaboration/

The Jewish Enemy: Nazi Propaganda during World War II and the Holocaust (Cambridge, MA: Harvard University Press, 2006).

"The Nazi Extermination Camps and the Ally to the East: Could the Red Army and Air Force Have Stopped or Slowed the Final Solution?" *Kritika: Explorations in Russian and Eurasian History* 4, no. 4 (September 2003): 913–930.

Nazi Propaganda for the Arab World (New Haven: Yale University Press, 2009).

Undeclared Wars with Israel: East Germany and the West German Far Left, 1967–1989 (New York: Cambridge University Press, 2016).

"The US State Department's Opposition to Zionist Aspirations during the Early Cold War: George F. Kennan and George C. Marshall in 1947–1948," *Journal of Cold War Studies* 23, no. 4 (Fall 2021): 1–28.

Hershco, Tsilla, *Entre Paris et Jérusalem: La France, le sionisme et la création de l'état d'Israël, 1945–1949* (Paris: Honoré Champion Éditeur, 2003).

"France and the Partition Plan: 1947–1948," *Israel Affairs* 14, no. 3 (2008): 486–498.

"Histoire d'une évasion: Le grand mufti de Jérusalem en France," *Controverses* 10, no. 2 (2006): 244–273.

Hirsch, Francine, *Soviet Judgment at Nuremberg: A New History of the International Military Tribunal after World War II* (New York and Oxford: Oxford University Press, 2020).

Hitchcock, William I., *The Struggle for Europe: The Turbulent History of a Divided Continent, 1945 to the Present* (New York: Anchor Books, 2004).

Hixson, Walter, *Israel's Armor: The Israel Lobby and the First Generation of the Palestine Conflict* (New York: Cambridge University Press, 2019).

Hoffmann, Bruce, *Anonymous Soldiers: The Struggle for Palestine, 1917–1947* (New York: Vintage, 2015).

Holland, Max, "I. F. Stone's Encounters with Soviet Intelligence," *Journal of Cold War Studies* 11, no. 3 (Summer 2009): 144–205.

Hurewitz, J. C., *The Struggle for Palestine* (New York: W. W. Norton, 1950; repr. Greenwood Press, 1968).

Ilan, Amitzur, *The Origins of the Arab-Israeli Arms Race: Arms, Embargo, Military Power and Decision in the 1948 Palestine War* (New York: New York University Press, 1996).

Isaacson, Robert, "The James Bond of Cherbourg: Imagining Israel in Pompidou's France," *French Historical Studies* 40, no. 4 (October 2017): 675–699.

"From 'Brave Little Israel' to 'an Elite and Domineering People': The Image of Israel in France, 1944–1974," Ph.D. dissertation, George Washington University, 2017: https://scholarspace.library.gwu.edu/concern/gw_etds/6q182k25k

Jockusch, Laura, *Collect and Record! Jewish Holocaust Documentation in Early Postwar Europe* (New York: Oxford University Press, 2015).

Judt, Tony, *Postwar: A History of Europe since 1945* (New York: Penguin, 2006).

Julius, Anthony, *Trials of the Diaspora: A History of Antisemitism in England* (New York: Oxford University Press, 2010).

Kaplan, Karel, *Report on the Murder of the General Secretary* (Columbus: Ohio State University Press, 1990).

Kennedy, Brian, "The Surprising Zionist: Senator Robert A. Taft and the Creation of Israel," *The Historian* 73, no. 4 (Winter 2011): 747–767.

Kimmage, Michael, *The Abandonment of the West: The History of an Idea in American Foreign Policy* (New York: Basic Books, 2020).

Kochavi, Arieh, "Britain and the Illegal Immigration to Palestine from France following World War II," *Holocaust and Genocide Studies* 6, no. 4 (December 1991): 383–396.

  Post-Holocaust Politics: Britain, the United States and Jewish Refugees, 1945–1948 (Chapel Hill: University of North Carolina Press, 2001).

  "The Struggle against Jewish Immigration to Palestine," *Middle Eastern Studies* 34, no. 3 (July 1998): 146–167.

Koselleck, Reinhard, *The Practice of Conceptual History: Timing History, Spacing Concepts* (Stanford: Stanford University Press, 2002).

Kotic, Meir, *The Prague Trial: The First Anti-Zionist Show Trial in the Communist Bloc* (New York: Herzl Press, 1987).

Krammer, Arnold, *The Forgotten Friendship: Israel and the Soviet Bloc, 1947–53* (Urbana: University of Illinois Press, 1974).

  "Soviet Motives in the Partition of Palestine, 1947–48," *Journal of Palestine Studies* 2, no. 2 (Winter 1973): 102–119.

Küntzel, Matthias, *Nazis und der Nahe Osten: Wie der Islamische Antisemitismus Entstand* (Berlin and Leipzig: Hentrich & Hentrich, 2019).

Lagrou, Pieter, *The Legacy of Nazi Occupation: Patriotic Memory and National Recovery in Western Europe, 1945–1965* (Cambridge and New York: Cambridge University Press, 2007).

Lazar, David, *Opinion française et la naissance de l'état d'Israël, 1945–1949* (Paris: Calmann-Levy, 1972).

Leffler, Melvyn P., "The Emergence of American Grand Strategy, 1945–1962," in Leffler and Westad, eds., *The Cambridge History of the Cold War*, vol. 1: *Origins, 1945–1962*, 67–89.

Leffler, Melvyn P. and Odd Arne Westad, eds., *The Cambridge History of the Cold War*, vol. 1: *Origins, 1945–1962* (Cambridge and New York: Cambridge University Press, 2010).

Liebreich, Fritz, *Britain's Naval and Political Reaction to the Illegal Immigration of Jews to Palestine, 1945–1948* (London and New York: Routledge, 2005).

Linfield, Susie, *The Lion's Den: Zionism and the Left from Hannah Arendt to Noam Chomsky* (New Haven: Yale University Press, 2019).

Lippman, Thomas, *Arabian Knight: Colonel Bill Eddy USMC and the Rise of American Power in the Middle East* (Vista, CA: Selwa Press, 2008).

Litvak, Meir and Esther Webman, *From Empathy to Denial: Arab Responses to the Holocaust* (New York and London: Columbia University Press/Hurst, 2009).

Louis, William Roger, *The British Empire in the Middle East, 1945–1951: Arab Nationalism, the United States and Postwar Imperialism* (New York and Oxford: Oxford University Press, 1984).

"The Dissolution of the British Empire," in Judith Brown and William Roger Louis, eds., *The Oxford History of the British Empire*, vol. 4: *The Twentieth Century* (New York and Oxford: Oxford University Press, 2001), 329–378.

The End of British Imperialism: The Scramble for Empire, Suez, and Decolonization: Collected Essays (New York: I. B. Tauris, 2006).

The End of the Palestine Mandate (Austin: University of Texas Press, 1986).

Mallmann, Klaus-Michael and Martin Cüppers, *Nazi Palestine: The Plans for the Extermination of the Jews of Palestine* (New York: Enigma Books, 2010).

Mann, Thomas, "Gespenster von 1938," in *Thomas Mann, Meine Zeit, Essays 1945–1955* (Frankfurt am Main: Fischer Verlag, 1977), 96–97.

Marrus, Michael R. and Robert O. Paxton, *Vichy France and the Jews* (New York: Basic Books, 1981).

McElligott, Anthony and Jeffrey Herf, eds., *Antisemitism before and since the Holocaust: Altered Contexts and Recent Perspectives* (London: Palgrave Macmillan, 2017).

Milkman, Paul, *PM: A New Deal in Journalism, 1940–1948* (New Brunswick, NJ: Rutgers University Press, 1997).

Morin, Gilles and Pascal Plas, *Adrien Tixier, 1893–1946: l'Heritage méconnu d'un reconstructeur de l'état en France* (Le Geneytouse: Lucien Soumy, 2012).

Morina, Christina, *Legacies of Stalingrad* (New York: Cambridge University Press, 2011).

Morris, Benny, *1948: The First Arab-Israeli War* (New Haven: Yale University Press, 2008).

The Birth of the Palestinian Refugee Problem Revisited (New York and Cambridge: Cambridge University Press, 2004).

Righteous Victims: A History of the Zionist-Arab Conflict, 1881–2001 (New York: Vintage, 2001).

One State, Two States: Resolving the Israel/Palestine Conflict (New Haven: Yale University Press, 2009).

Motadel, David, *Islam and Nazi Germany's War* (Cambridge, MA: Harvard University Press, 2014).

Muller, Jan Werner, *Memory and Power in Postwar Europe: Studies in the Presence of the Past* (New York and Cambridge: Cambridge University Press, 2002).

Müller, Rolf Dieter and Gerd R. Ueberschar, *Hitler's War in the East: A Critical Assessment*, trans. Bruce D. Little (New York: Berghahn Books, 2002).

Nachmani, Amikam, *Great Power Discord in Palestine: The Anglo-American Committee of Inquiry into the Problems of European Jewry and Palestine, 1945–1946* (London: Frank Cass, 1987).

Nasaw, David, *The Last Million: Europe's Displaced Persons from World War to Cold War* (New York: Penguin Press, 2020).

Netanyahu, Benzion, *The Marranos of Spain from the Late 14th to the Early 15th Century According to Contemporary Hebrew Sources* (Ithaca: Cornell University Press, 1999).

The Origins of the Inquisition in Fifteenth-Century Spain (New York: New York Review of Books Press, 2001).

Nirenberg, David, *Anti-Judaism: The Western Tradition* (New York: W. W. Norton, 2013).

Nouzille, Vincent, *Histoires secretes: France-Israël 1948–2018* (Paris: Éditions les Liens Qui Libèerent, 2018).

Orbach, Danny and Mark Solonin, "Calculated Indifference: The Soviet Union and Requests to Bomb Auschwitz," *Holocaust and Genocide Studies* 27, no. 1 (Spring 2013): 90–113.

Overy, Richard, *Why the Allies Won* (New York: W. W. Norton, 1995).

Paxton, Robert O., *Vichy France: Old Guard and New Order, 1940–1944* (New York: Columbia University Press, 1975; rev. ed. 2001).

Pinkus, Benjamin, "Change and Continuity in Soviet Policy towards Soviet Jewry and Israel, May–December 1948," *Israel Studies* 10, no. 1 (Spring 2005): 96–123.

Poliakov, Leon, *De l'antisionisme à l'antisémitisme* (Paris: Calmann-Lévy, 1969).

Poznanski, Renée, *Propagandes et persecutions: La Resistance et le "problem juif" 1940–1944* (Paris: Fayard, 2008).

Priemel, Kim Christian, *The Betrayal: The Nuremberg Trials and German Divergence* (Oxford: Oxford University Press, 2016).

Rabinbach, Anson, *Begriffe aus dem Kalten Krieg: Totalitarismus, Antifaschismus, Genozoid* (Göttingen: Wallstein Verlag, 2009).

Radosh, Allis and Ronald Radosh, *A Safe Haven: Harry S. Truman and the Founding of Israel* (New York: HarperCollins, 2009).

Richter, Melvin, *The History of Political and Social Concepts: A Critical Introduction* (New York: Oxford University Press, 1995).

Rioux, Jean Pierre, *The Fourth Republic, 1944–1958* (New York: Cambridge University Press, 1987).

Roberts, Andrew, *Churchill: Walking with Destiny* (New York: Viking, 2018).

Ro'i, Yaacov, *Soviet Decision Making in Practice: The USSR and Israel, 1947–1954* (New Brunswick, NJ, and London: Transaction Books, 1980).

Rousso, Henry, *The Vichy Syndrome: History and Memory in France since 1944* (Cambridge, MA: Harvard University Press, 1991).

Rucker, Laurent, "Moscow's Surprise: The Soviet-Israeli Alliance of 1947–1949," Working Paper #46 (July 15, 2005), Woodrow Wilson International Center for Scholars.

Stalin, Israël et les Juifs (Paris: Presses Universitaires de France, 2001).

Ruffner, Kevin C., "A Rocky Beginning to a Critical Relationship: Project SYMPHONY: US Intelligence and the Jewish *Brichah* in Post-war Austria," *Studies in Intelligence* 51, no. 1 (2014): 33–46.

Safrian, Hans, *Eichmann's Men*, trans. Ute Stargardt (New York: Cambridge University Press, 2010).

Schechtman, Joseph B., *The Arab Refugee Problem* (Philadelphia: University of Pennsylvania Press, 1952).

The Mufti and the Führer: The Rise and Fall of Haj Amin el Husseini (New York: T. Yoseloff, 1965).

The United States and the Jewish State Movement: The Crucial Decade: 1939–1949 (New York: Herzl Press/T. Yoseloff, 1966).

Schillo, Frédérique, *La France et la création de l'état d'Israël, 18 février 1947–11 mai 1949* (Paris: Éditions Artcom, 1997).

"France and the Partition Plan: 1947–1948," *Israel Affairs* 14, no. 3 (2008): 486–498.

La Politique francaise à l'égard d'Israël, 1946–1949 (Paris: André Versaille Éditeur, 2012).

Schoenbaum, David, *The United States and the State of Israel* (New York: Oxford University Press, 1993).

Shapira, Anita, *Land and Power: The Zionist Resort to Force, 1881–1948* (Stanford: Stanford University Press, 1999).

Shapiro, Daniel H., *From Philanthropy to Activism: The Political Transformation of American Zionism in the Holocaust Years, 1933–1945* (New York and Oxford: Pergamon Press, 1994).

Slonim, Shlomo, "The 1948 American Embargo on Arms to Palestine," *Political Science Quarterly* 94, no. 3 (1979): 495–514.

Steinacher, Gerald, *Nazis on the Run: How Hitler's Henchmen Fled Justice*, trans. Shaun Whiteside (New York: Oxford University Press, 2011).

Stember, Charles, *The Jews in the Mind of America* (New York: Basic Books, 1966).

Swarc, Alan, "The Early French Connection to Israel," *Jewish Historical Studies* 43 (2011): 159–187.

"Illegal Immigration to Palestine 1945–1948: The French Connection," Ph.D. dissertation, University College London, 2005.

Szulc, Tad, *The Secret Alliance: The Extraordinary Story of the Rescue of the Jews since World War II* (New York: Farrar, Strauss & Giroux, 1991).

Teveth, Shabtai, *Ben-Gurion: The Burning Ground, 1886–1948* (Boston: Houghton-Mifflin, 1987).

Thomas, Teresa Fava, *American Arabists in the Cold War Middle East, 1946–75: From Orientalism to Professionalism* (New York and London: Anthem Press, 2016).

Valena, Jiri and Leni Friedman Valena, "The Birth of Israel: Prague's Crucial Role," *Middle East Quarterly* 25 (Winter 2019): 1–14.

Vassiliev, Alexander, John Earl Haynes, and Harvey Klehr, *Spies: The Rise and Fall of the KGB in America* (New Haven: Yale University Press, 2009).

Vogel, Hans Rudolf, *Thomas Mann, der Amerikaner: Leben und Werk im amerikanischen Exil, 1938–1952* (Frankfurt am Main: Fischer Verlag, 2011).

Wagner, Steven, "British Intelligence and the 'Fifth' Occupying Power: The Secret Struggle to Prevent Jewish Illegal Immigration to Palestine," *Intelligence and National Security* 29, no. 5 (2014): 698–726.

Waldman, Simon A., *Anglo-American Diplomacy and the Palestinian Refugee Problem, 1948–1951* (New York: Palgrave Macmillan, 2015).

Wasserstein, Bernard, *Britain and the Jews of Europe, 1939–1945*, 2nd ed. (New York: Leicester University Press, 1999).

Wein, Martin, *A History of Czechs and Jews: A Slavic Jerusalem* (London: Routledge, 2015).

Weinberg, Gerhard, *A World at Arms: A Global History of World War II* (New York: Cambridge University Press, 2005).

Welles, Benjamin, *Sumner Welles: FDR's Global Strategist: A Biography* (New York: St. Martin's Press, 1997).

Westad, Odd Arne, "The Cold War and the International History of the Twentieth Century," in Leffler and Westad, eds., *The Cambridge History of the Cold War*, vol. 1: *Origins, 1945–1962*, 1–19.

The Global Cold War: Third World Interventions and the Making of Our Times (Cambridge and New York: Cambridge University Press, 2005).

Wievioraka, Olivier, *The French Resistance* (Cambridge, MA.: Harvard University Press, 2016).

Wistrich, Robert, *A Lethal Obsession: Anti-Semitism from Antiquity to the Global Jihad* (New York: Random House, 2010).

Zamir, Meir, "'Bid' for Altalena: France's Cover Action in the 1948 War in Palestine," *Middle Eastern Studies* 46, no. 1 (2010): 17–58.

Zertal, Idith, *From Catastrophe to Power: Holocaust Survivors and the Emergence of Israel* (Berkeley and Los Angeles: University of California Press, 1998).

Zhdanov, Andrei, "Two Camp Policy," in Gale Stokes, ed., *From Stalinism to Pluralism: A Documentary History of Eastern Europe since 1945* (New York: Oxford University Press, 1996), 38–42.

Index

Acheson, Dean, 148, 445. *See also* United States, State Department
Afghanistan, 38, 146, 147, 243, 261
al-Ahram, 119
AJDC. *See* American Joint Distribution Committee
Akhbar al-Yom, 62, 63
Akzin, Benjamin, 41–42, 55–57. *See also* American Zionist Emergency Council
Algeria, 98, 128, 233
All-India Muslim League, 111
American Christian Committee for Refugees (CCR), 159
American Christian Palestine Committee (ACPC), x, 26, 28, 299, 342
American Friends of Jewish Palestine, 174
American Joint Distribution Committee (AJDC), 159, 162–163, 184, 325
American League for a Free Palestine(ALFP), 155, 171, 173, 176, 329. *See also* Hecht, Ben; Rogers, Will; Bromfield, Louis
American liberals, 19, 33, 79, 86, 122, 191, 272, 332
American occupation zone in Germany, 202
American Sea and Air Volunteers for Hebrew Repatriation, 171
American Zionist Emergency Council (AZEC), ix, x, 12, 42, 56, 76, 120, 189, 273
"Arms for Jewish Palestine Mass Meeting," February 1948, 302
Madison Square Garden rally, June 1946, 51
memos to State Department on Haj Amin al-Husseini, December 1945, 42–46
July 1946, 55–61
"Salute the Jewish State Mass Demonstration," May 1948, 4, 339

"Shall we Submit to Blackmail Diplomacy," October 12, 1947, 189–191
on whitewashing Husseini, 24. *See also* Akzin, Benjamin; Jewish Agency; Silver, Abba; Wise, Stephen
Americans for Haganah, 169, 174
Anglo-American alliance, 79, 81, 165–166
Anglo-American Committee of Inquiry (AACI), 18, 35, 50, 52, 70, 87, 89, 96, 102, 122, 139, 213, 299
anticolonialism, 4, 6, 459
anticommunism, 36, 165, 181, 291, 454
antifascism, 1, 6, 7, 24–26, 68, 84, 297, 458, 463
and postwar support for Zionism, 34
and switch to containment of communism, 457
anti-Hitler coalition, xiii, 5, 28, 31, 41, 444. *See also* United Nations, meaning of
anti-imperialism, xiii, 7, 141, 381, 459
antisemitism, 61, 65, 69, 79, 85, 161, 179, 181, 191, 198, 209, 230, 235, 256, 271, 272, 357, 369, 418, 453, 459, 460
American policy makers and, 455–457
as antiracism, 12
in "Axis Broadcasts in Arabic," 39
Bevin remarks, June 1946, 53, 241
Crossman on Bevin's, 213
examined in *PM*, 71
French Socialists' opposition to, 11, 26, 221
Haj Amin al-Husseini and, 58
Jamal Husseini and, 235, 237
missed opportunities to examine, 458
in postwar Europe, 96, 198
Schuman and "Holocaust inversion," 431
State Department and, 313
Stalinist purges and, 458
Stone in *The Nation* on, 84

479